EAST ANGLIAN ARCHAEOLOGY

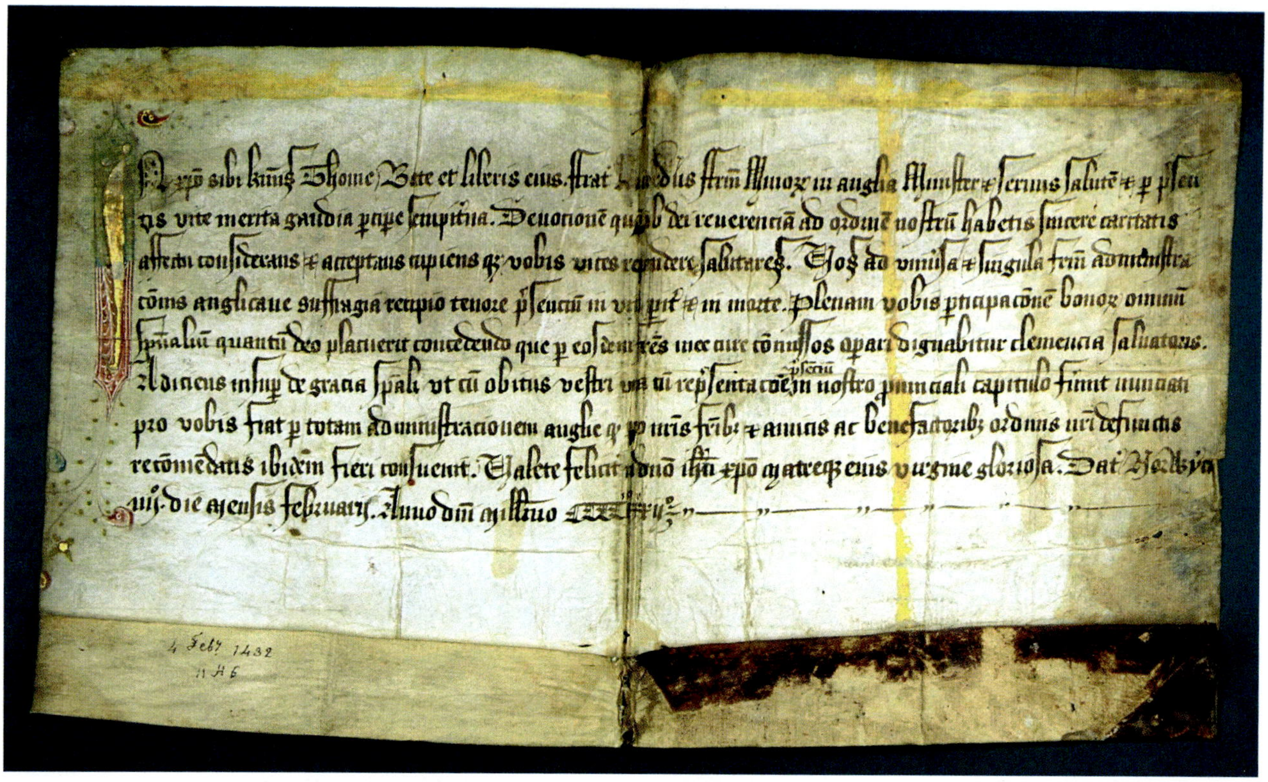

Frontispiece:
Letter of confraternity addressed to Thomas Bate and his children and dated at Norwich in 1433. A translation is given in Appendix 3. NRO Phi 567, 578X8; *reproduced courtesy of Norfolk Record Office; photograph by Jason Dawson*

this book is dedicated to the memory of Kay Harvey (1966–1993)

Norwich Greyfriars: pre-Conquest town and medieval friary

by Phillip A. Emery

with a major contribution by
Elizabeth Rutledge

and contributions from
Martin Allen, Marion M. Archibald, Steven Ashley, Alex Bayliss, Mark Blackburn, Francesca Boghi, David G. Buckley, Paul Cattermole, Jane Cowgill, G.M. Cruise, John A. Davies, Roger Doonan, Paul C. Ensom, Geoff Egan, I.C. Freestone, Val Fryer, Helen Geake, Zena Green, Richenda Goffin, Alison Goodall, Helen Howard, Julia Huddle, Richard Kemp, David King, Irena Lentowicz, Paul Linford, Alice Lyons, Richard Macphail, J.M. Mills, Marta Moreno-García, Peter Murphy, Rebecca A. Nicholson, Mark Noel, Sarah Percival, Ian Riddler, Mark Samuel, John Shepherd, Elizabeth Shepherd Popescu and C.P Stapleton

illustrations by
Steven Ashley, David Dobson and Trevor Ashwin

photographs by
Jason Dawson, Phillip A. Emery, Helen Howard, Sarah Reilly and David Wicks

East Anglian Archaeology
Report No. 120, 2007

Historic Environment
Norfolk Museums and Archaeology Service

EAST ANGLIAN ARCHAEOLOGY
REPORT NO. 120

Published by:
Historic Environment
Norfolk Museums and Archaeology Service
Union House
Gressenhall
Dereham
Norfolk NR20 4DR

in conjunction with:
ALGAO East
www.algao.org.uk/cttees/regions/

Typeset in Times Roman by World Tree using ™ Corel Ventura Publisher
Printed by Henry Ling Limited, The Dorset Press

ISBN 978 0 905594 46 0

For details of *East Anglian Archaeology*, see last page

East Anglian Archaeology was established in 1975 by the Scole Committee for Archaeology in East Anglia. The scope of the series expanded to include all six eastern counties and responsibility for publication was transferred in 2002 to the Association of Local Government Archaeological Officers, East of England (ALGAO East).

Cover illustration
15th century illustration from Valerius Maximus' *Fairs et dits memorables*, showing an Athenian painter perched on a trestle table. MS fr.6185, fol.243v

Contents

List of Plates

List of Figures

List of Tables

Contributors

Where a section of this report is not attributed to a specific named contributor, the author is Phillip A. Emery who, alongside Elizabeth Shepherd Popescu, is also responsible for all sections of introductory and linking text.

Martin Allen
Fitzwilliam Museum, Cambridge
Coins

Marion M. Archibald
British Museum
Late Saxon lead weight

Steven Ashley
Norfolk Landscape Archaeology
Illustrator, armorial copper alloy artefacts, stone coffin lid

Alex Bayliss
Ancient Monuments Laboratory, English Heritage
Co-ordination of radiocarbon and archaeomagnetic dating of bell-casting pit

Mark Blackburn
Fitzwilliam Museum, Cambridge
Viking penny

David G. Buckley
consultant
Lava quernstones

Paul Cattermole
consultant
Bell casting

Jane Cowgill
formerly City of Lincoln Archaeology Unit
Ironworking slags

John A. Davies
Norfolk Museums & Archaeology Service
Numismatic items

Jason Dawson
formerly NAU
Photographer

David Dobson
NAU Archaeology
Illustrator

Roger Doonan
Ancient Monuments Laboratory, English Heritage
Metallurgical debris (non-ferrous)

Phillip A. Emery
Gifford, London
Principal author

Paul C. Ensom
Yorkshire Museum
Geological identifications of worked stone objects

Geoff Egan
Museum of London Specialist Services
Lead/lead alloy artefacts

I.C. Freestone
Dept. of Scientific Research, British Museum
Analysis of white glass vessel

Val Fryer
consultant
Iron artefacts, plant macrofossils, molluscs

Helen Geake
Portable Antiquities Scheme
Middle Saxon and medieval brooches

Zena Green
formerly Dept of Archaeological Sciences, University of Bradford
Mollusca

Richenda Goffin
Suffolk County Council Archaeology Service
Middle Saxon pottery, ceramic lamps, ceramic crucibles

Catherine Hassall
UCL Painting Analysis Ltd, History of Art Dept., University College London
Oyster shell palette (preliminary report)

Helen Howard
Scientific Dept, National Gallery (formerly Courtauld Institute)
Oyster shell palette

Julia Huddle
NAU Archaeology
Copper alloy artefacts, worked antler/bone, shale, spindle whorls, ceramic building material (Areas A, B, CB and C)

the late Richard Kemp
formerly City of Lincoln Archaeology Unit
Ceramic building material (Area D)

David King
consultant
Window glass and lead cames

Irena Lentowicz
consultant
Post-Roman ceramics

Paul Linford
GeoQuest Associates
Archaeomagnetic dating of bell casting pit

Alice Lyons
consultant
Roman ceramics

Richard Macphail
Institute of Archaeology, University College London
Soil micromorphology

J.M. Mills
consultant
Worked stone artefacts, ironworking slags

Marta Moreno-García
Instituto Portugues de Arqueologia, Lisbon
Faunal remains

Peter Murphy
English Heritage
Plant macrofossils, mollusca

Rebecca A. Nicholson
Dept. of Archaeological Sciences, University of Bradford
Avian and fish bone

Mark Noel
GeoQuest Associates
Archaeomagnetic dating of bell casting pit

Sarah Reilly
formerly NAU
Site Assistant (photography)

Ian Riddler
consultant
Identification of bone and antler species (artefacts)

Elizabeth Rutledge
consultant
Documentary research

Mark Samuel
consultant
Architectural worked stone

John Shepherd
consultant
Vessel glass

Elizabeth Shepherd Popescu
CAM ARC, Cambridgeshire County Council
Co-author of various sections; editor

C.P Stapleton
Dept. of Scientific Research, British Museum
Analysis of white glass vessel

David Wicks
Norfolk Landscape Archaeology
Photographer

Personal Communication

The following people provided information by personal communication:

Trevor Ashwin
consultant

Brian Ayers
County Archaeologist, Norfolk Museums & Archaeology Service

Justine Bayley
Ancient Monuments Laboratory, English Heritage

Trevor Jennings
Loughborough Bell Founding Museum

The late Sue Margeson
formerly Archaeology Dept, Norwich Castle Museum

Tim Pestell
Archaeology Dept, Norwich Castle Museum

Judy Read
Hales Hall, Norfolk

Fiona Roe
Stone objects consultant

Keith Wade
Archaeological Service Manager, Suffolk County Council

Acknowledgements

Fieldwork, together with on-site finds and environmental work, was carried out at the former Mann Egerton site by a total of 43 staff, 30 volunteers and four work-experience students. The evaluation and excavation teams comprised: David Adams (Ghost), Jim Ball, Jayne Bown, Phil Emery, Rupert Eris, Steve Every, Kevin Forrest, Tony Frost, Kären Gaffney, Kellie Gorbould, the late Kay Harvey, Steve Hickling, Benjamin Hobbs, Su Leaver, Andy Letch, Katie Lister, Tim Longman, Malcolm McKenzie, Steven Manifold, Richard Moore, Neil Moss, John Percival, Sarah Percival, Tim Pestell, Sam Pittam, Chris Phillips, Sara Reilly, Jenny Roberts, Ewen Rutter, Christine Smith, Martin Smith, Melanie Stone, Lucy Talbot, Danny Voisey, Heather Wallis, Peter Warsop, Lisa Wastling and David (Mavis) Whitmore. Environmental sieving was the responsibility of Richard Owen and finds processing was carried out by Julia Huddle, Alice Lyons and Julie Curl, with Peter Cheer.

Excavation, finds and environmental tasks were also undertaken on a voluntary basis by the following individuals: Diane Badger, Jim Ball, Kirsty Baker, Lee Beech, Bobs Beer, Richard Birkett, Paula Dove, Annabel Durnford, Simon Gee, Rodney Hooper, Thomas Lovekin, Annie Maidstone, Elinor McCline, Leslie McCormack, Shayne Morter, Mary Muir, Dorothy Palmer, Kerry Perdy, Linda Polkowski, Doff Ransome, Peter Robins, Judy Simms, Jim Stabb, Tony Stevens, Dick Taylor, Eilidh Taylor, John Taylor, Lee de Vere, Margaret Wallis and Sandra Walster. In addition, school pupils Vicki Birch, Michelle Hill, Richard Sapey and Jason Slack all participated in the project as part of work experience assignments.

Evaluation of the site in March/April 1990 was supervised by Heather Wallis. Jayne Bown managed the project between 1991 and 1995. The author, who had deputised for Jayne Bown since 1992, inherited overall responsibility during post-excavation. Throughout the fieldwork Jayne's leadership, and her investment in providing mechanisms that enabled staff to gain a range of experience, helped to sustain a rewarding working environment. Site supervisors during 1992–5 were Kären Gaffney, Andy Letch, Kevin Forrest and Neil Moss. Neil also liaised with the contractors during a particularly complex phase of the 1995 fieldwork. During post-excavation, Myk Flitcroft, Niall Donald and David Whitmore provided invaluable assistance in computerising the site records. Julia Huddle is acknowledged for maintaining the Small Finds database and for logistical management of the finds as a whole. David Whitmore and Neil Moss made significant contributions to the stratigraphic analysis of the site.

Metal-detecting during the main excavation (1992–3) was carried out by Tony Frost, while two volunteer metal-detectorists, Rodney Carriage and George Kemp, assisted during the 1995 works.

Most of the illustrations in this volume are the work of Steven Ashley, although many were later amended by David Dobson, who also produced supplementary drawings of certain of the pottery, ironwork and stone items, mounted the pottery drawings and producing the maps presented in Figs 1.1, 2.24 and 3.21, as well as the cross-section of the site in Fig. 3.22. Trevor Ashwin revised many of the figures and prepared all of the artwork for the press. Some of the on-site and finds photography was carried out by David Wicks. Other site photographs were taken by members of the excavation team, in particular Sara Reilly who co-ordinated the photographic record. After the completion of fieldwork, additional finds and a number of maps and documents were photographed by Jason Dawson.

Documentary research, carried out by Elizabeth Rutledge, has provided not only chronological and spatial frameworks for interpretation but also the names of many individuals whose lives and occupations were reflected in the archaeological record. Chris Barringer and the King Street Group are thanked for generously making available to Elizabeth their archive of notes and transcripts relating to the area. Information from the Norfolk county Sites and Monuments Record was provided at various stages by Jan Allen and Edwin Rose (Norfolk Landscape Archaeology Section) and Bill Milligan (Norwich Castle Museum). Guidance concerning historic maps was given by Raymond Frostick and access for photography of maps was provided by Bill Milligan and Mark Hingley (Norfolk Record Office). Susan Maddock (NRO) is thanked for allowing us to reproduce the images for the frontispiece and Plate 4.1. Joyce Gurney-Read is also thanked for making available historic photographs relating to the Mann Egerton works. Translation of various foreign sources was carried out by Niall Donald and Marianne Penn (German) and Tessa Ireland (French). Tim Pestell, Gary Brown and Roberta Gilchrist provided advice and reference material concerning friaries.

The Greyfriars Project benefited immensely from the close involvement of the Conservation Department at Norwich Castle Museum, managed by Cathy Proudlove. In addition to the work carried out on the hundreds of objects of other materials, over 1500 metal items were X-rayed and, in many cases, treated by a succession of archaeological conservators: Mary Davis, Gordon Turner-Walker and Elena Makridou.

Finds and environmental reports were contributed by numerous experts, each of whom is warmly thanked. Several others also deserve acknowledgement for various contributions to the project.

The late Sue Margeson's *Norwich Households* volume (1993) fundamentally influenced the structure of the finds chapter and the author is greatly indebted to Sue for making available so much of her considerable knowledge of medieval artefacts.

Robin Lucas commented on the assemblage of bricks during the fieldwork. Worked flint was catalogued by Peter Robins. Stephen Heywood kindly appraised some items of architectural worked stone during the fieldwork. The late Keith Darby (Fielden and Mawson) and John Houston (Building Research Establishment) are acknowledged for providing information about the source and uses of Purbeck Marble. John Arram kindly appraised the architectural worked stone in terms of potential for petrological analysis.

Access to FTIR facilities at Imperial College, London University, for analysis of the oyster shell painter's palette was generously funded by English Heritage. Charmian Woodfield kindly allowed Helen Howard to draw on the unpublished report on the Coventry palette. Information on the Canterbury, Haverfordwest, London, Merton Priory and Salisbury shells was provided by David Sherlock, Tim Pestell, Geoff Egan, Derek Seeley and Andrew Middleton respectively.

Trevor Jennings (Loughborough Bell Founding Museum) is acknowledged for his expert advice relating to interpretation of the bell-casting evidence. Related radiocarbon dates were provided by Queen's University of Belfast.

Andrew Jones commented on a group of fish bones as part of the environmental assessment and Rosemary Luff worked with Marta Moreno-Garca to produce the assessment of the animal bones. Richard Macphail and G.M. Cruise (Institute of Archaeology, University College London) wish to thank Ian Dormor for thin section manufacturing assistance. Analysis of the relationship between the presence of arable plant material and of thermoactinomyces (hyphal, saprophytic bacteria) on the site was carried out by Anita Jackson (Department of Biology, University of Essex).

Remote investigation of the Friary Great Drain, using an electronic probe and remote-controlled cameras, was carried out by the former City Works Department of Norwich City Council. Michael Clarke provided information about the history of water management in Norwich.

The author is very grateful to many people associated with the project, who have openly shared their ideas and have given encouragement during the production of this report. These include Steven Ashley, Trevor Ashwin, Brian Ayers, Jayne Bown, Jane Cowgill, Geoff Egan, Val Fryer, Helen Geake, Julia Huddle, David King, Neil Moss, Patrick Ottaway, Tim Pestell, Andrew Rogerson, Elizabeth Rutledge, Elizabeth Shepherd Popescu and David Whitmore.

Elizabeth Shepherd Popescu revised and edited this volume during the final stages of preparation and was instrumental in driving it to publication. Her support and advice, offered throughout the project, are particularly appreciated.

Abbreviations

Documentary

AC Arundel Castle Archive
Cal.Lib.Rolls Calendar of Liberate Rolls
Cal. Nch. Deeds Calendar of Norwich Deeds
Cal.Pat.Rolls Calendar of Patent Rolls
CAR Chamberlain's Account Rolls, 1457–8, Norwich City Muniments Norfolk Record Office
EDP Eastern Daily Press
G.A. King Coll. G.A. King Collection, Norfolk and Norwich Archaeological Society Library, Norwich
L and P for. and dom Letters and papers foreign and domestic
NCCR Norwich City Court Rolls, Norwich City Muniments, Norfolk Record Office
NRO Norfolk Record Office
PCC Prerogative Court of Canterbury

General

BMC British Museum Catalogue
BMS British Museum Sylloge (Archibald and Blunt 1986)
BNJ British Numismatic Journal
BS environmental sample (bulk)
cat. catalogue
CTCE *Coinage in Tenth-century England* (Blunt *et. al* 1989)
D diameter
EVE Estimated Vessel Equivalent
Fig. Figure
FTIR Fourier transform infra-red microspectroscopy
g gramme
HC hand collected
ID indicators method
kg kilogramme
L length
M&LA Dept Medieval and Later Antiquities, British Museum
MCT microchemical tests
MNI minimum number of individuals
MWS mandible wear stage
NAU Norfolk Archaeological Unit
NISP number of identified specimens per taxa
no. number
PLM polarised light microscopy
Qty quantity
SCBI Sylloge of Coins of the British Isles (Oxford, British Academy)
SEM/EDX scanning electron microscopy with energy dispersive X-ray analysis
SF Small Find
SFB sunken-featured/sunken-floored building
SMR County Sites and Monuments Record
SRS soil riddled sample
T thickness
taq *terminus ante quem*
tpq *terminus post quem*
W width
Wt weight
XRD X-ray diffraction
XRF X-ray fluorescence

Pottery fabrics

DREW: Dutch Red Earthenware
EMSSW Early Medieval Sparse Shelly ware
EMSW Early Medieval Sandwich ware
EMW Early Medieval ware
EPM Early Post-medieval ware
GRE Glazed Red Earthenware
IGBW Iron Glazed Black ware
LMT Late Medieval and Transitional ware
LMU Local Medieval Unglazed ware
TGE Tin-glazed Earthenware
TTW Thetford-type ware
WNBC West Norfolk Bichrome ware

Summary

by Phillip A. Emery and Elizabeth Shepherd Popescu

Large scale excavations and associated research during 1990–5 have provided new insights into the development of a substantial area within medieval Norwich, to the east of the Castle, at the former Mann Egerton premises on Prince of Wales Road. Archaeological evidence survived for the geography and use of plots dating from the Late Saxon period until the acquisition of this area by the Franciscan Friary in the late 13th century. The remains of at least three small Late Saxon buildings were found. Two of these structures, located at the western and eastern extremities of the site, appeared to have been workshops: that to the west contained a penny of Alfred (AD 887–9), although the building itself was evidently in use during the 11th century. Mapping of various waste materials recovered allowed a range of manufacturing activities to be located. Mutually exclusive distributions of antler-working and metallurgical debris provided striking evidence of specialisation of function within identifiable plots. Metalworking evidence included residues from the melting of copper alloys and silver, silver refining and iron smithing. In addition, a Viking lead weight bearing the name of Alfred, probably struck at Norwich in the earlier 880s, was recovered, its presence alongside evidence for silver-working suggesting possible minting activity.

Archaeological remains from the 12th to 13th centuries include the earliest indications of the development of buildings along the east side of King Street and, in the eastern part of the site, the earliest unequivocal evidence of a north-to-south-road crossing the area, and traces of adjacent plots. The findings include evidence for the cemetery of St John the Evangelist, which had disappeared by the late 13th century, and a number of pieces of evidence which may link to the nearby church of St Vedast. When combined, the new evidence makes important contributions to current understanding of Norwich's developing urban topography (specifically the street pattern) and a wide range of socio-economic issues relating to the Late Saxon, Saxo-Norman and immediately pre-Friary periods.

Each of the four main orders of friars came to Norwich: the Franciscans (Greyfriars or Friars Minor), Dominicans (Blackfriars), Augustinian or Austin Friars and Carmelites (Whitefriars) (each precinct is located in Ayers 1994, fig. 46). The Franciscans, who arrived in 1224, were the most numerous order and had established forty-nine houses in England by 1256. Only two years after their arrival in Britain, they settled in Norwich between the churches of St Vedast and St Cuthbert, the related precinct only later being extended to encompass the excavated area. Substantial enlargement of the Friary at the end of the 13th century, attested by a licence in mortmain of 1292, allowed the church and claustral buildings to be redeveloped on a much larger scale. Archaeologically, this process was demonstrated by the clearance of buildings, infilling of hollows (such as cellars and pits) and, most dramatically, the closure of at least one lane and possibly two.

Archaeological remains of the Friary took the form of earthworks associated with preparation of the site for construction and landscaping, extant flintwork (some upstanding), compacted laminated earthen foundations, floors, drains and wall robber trenches. Although fragmentary, the recorded remains were sufficient to allow some reconstruction of the conventual complex to be attempted. They are interpreted as elements of the west and south ranges of the cloister and include a part of the Suffragan's lodging and guesthouse, buildings on the King Street frontage, a section of the south boundary wall of the precinct (over 60m long) and a dovecote. Reconstruction of the layout of the Friary complex was based on a combination of archaeological and documentary evidence, the latter comprising the survey of William Worcestre (1479) and 16th-century leases. A bell-casting pit, in use between 1490 and 1525, was recorded adjacent to the King Street frontage.

Use of the site between the Dissolution in 1538 and the establishment of the Mann Egerton works (*c.* 1904/1912 below) was interpreted from both archaeological and documentary sources, during which time much of the site functioned as gardens. Archaeological evidence included eleven 16th–18th-century cloth seals, the first such group found in the important worsted-production centre of Norwich during the course of formal excavation.

Résumé

Des fouilles et des recherches importantes menées pendant les années 1990–95 ont apporté des éclaircissements sur le développement d'un grand quartier dans le Norwich médiéval, à l'est du château et sur l'ancien site de l'entreprise Mann Egerton sur Prince of Wales Road. Il subsiste des traces archéologiques de l'emplacement et de l'utilisation de ces lieux depuis la période saxonne tardive jusqu'à l'acquisition de ce quartier par l'ordre franciscain à la fin du treizième siècle. On a ainsi trouvé les vestiges de trois petits bâtiments de la période saxonne tardive. Deux de ces bâtiments au plancher affaissé et situés aux extrémités ouest et est du site ont probablement été des ateliers, celui qui est situé à l'ouest contenait un penny du roi Alfred (887–889 AD), bien que le bâtiment lui-même fût manifestement encore utilisé pendant le onzième siècle. La localisation des différents déchets récupérés permet de dresser la carte d'un ensemble d'activités de fabrication. Le travail des ramures et du métal s'excluant mutuellement, l'emplacement des débris correspondants ont montré avec clarté que des espaces identifiables étaient spécialisés dans des fonctions différentes. On compte parmi les preuves du travail du métal des résidus provenant de la fusion d'alliage de cuivre et d'argent ainsi que de l'affinage de l'argent et de la fusion du fer. On a également retrouvé un poids Viking en plomb portant le nom d'Alfred, qui fut probablement frappé à Norwich au début des années 880; sa présence à côté de traces du travail de l'argent semble indiquer qu'on battait monnaie à cet endroit.

Les vestiges archéologiques du douzième et treizième siècle représentent les indications les plus anciennes de la construction de bâtiments sur le côté est de King Street. Ils contiennent également de façon incontestable les marques les plus anciennes d'une route nord-sud traversant le site, ainsi que des traces des quartiers adjacents. Les fouilles ont permis de mettre à jour la trace du cimetière de St Jean l'Évangéliste, qui disparut vers la fin du treizième siècle, ainsi que d'autres vestiges en rapport avec l'église voisine de St Vedast. Ces nouvelles preuves, une fois rassemblées, constituent une contribution importante à la compréhension actuelle de la topographie urbaine de Norwich au cours de son développement, en particulier pour la disposition des rues. Elles permettent également de mieux comprendre les questions socio-économiques liées aux périodes saxonne tardive et saxo-normande sans oublier les tout débuts de la période pré-monastique

Chacun des quatre principaux ordres monastiques est venu s'installer à Norwich. Les franciscains (les Greyfriars ou frères mineurs), les dominicains (Blackfriars), les augustiniens ou frères augustins et les carmélites (Whitefriars). Pour localiser leurs différents établissements, vous pouvez vous reporter au Ayers 1994, fig. 46. Les franciscains arrivèrent en 1224. Représentant l'ordre qui compta le plus de membres, ils avaient établi quarante neuf maisons en Angleterre dès 1256. Seulement deux ans après leur arrivée en Grande-Bretagne, ils s'installèrent à Norwich entre l'église de St Vedast et celle de St Cuthbert, et c'est seulement plus tard que leurs établissements furent étendus au point d'inclure la zone fouillée. Les vestiges archéologiques des monastères prirent la forme d'ouvrages de terre associés à la préparation du site pour la construction et l'aménagement paysager, de débris de silex (dont certains sont encore en position verticale), de fondations en terre tassée et stratifiée, de planchers, d'égouts et de tranchées creusées par des voleurs de murs. Malgré leur nature fragmentaire, les vestiges inventoriés étaient suffisamment nombreux pour qu'on tente une reconstruction du complexe conventuel. On pense qu'il s'agit d'éléments des côtés ouest et sud du monastère comprenant une partie des logements et de l'hôtellerie de Suffragan, des bâtiments donnant sur King Street, un tronçon du mur qui entourait au sud les établissements des religieux, sans oublier un pigeonnier. La reconstruction du complexe conventuel s'est appuyée pour la configuration générale sur la combinaison de preuves archéologiques et documentaires, ces dernières comprenant le relevé de William Worcestre (1479) ainsi que des baux du seizième siècle. Le monastère prenant une grande importance à la fin du treizième siècle, attestée par un certificat de mainmorte datant de 1292, il fut possible d'agrandir largement l'église et les bâtiments du cloître. La preuve de ce changement est apportée sur le plan archéologique par la destruction de bâtiments, le comblement de trous (tels que des caves ou des fosses), et d'une façon très spectaculaire, par la fermeture d'une voie et peut-être de deux. Une fosse destinée au moulage de cloches, utilisée entre 1490 et 1525, fut également découverte à côté des bâtiments donnant sur King Street.

L'interprétation de sources à la fois archéologiques et documentaires permet de conclure qu'entre la Dissolution de 1538 et l'établissement de l'usine de Mann Egerton (vers les années 1904–1912), une grande partie du site fut transformée en jardins. On compte au nombre des objets découverts onze sceaux en tissu (« cloth seal ») du seizième au dix-huitième siècle, dont le premier groupe a été découvert dans l'important centre de fabrication de laine peignée de Norwich au cours de fouilles officielles.

(Traduction: Didier Don)

Zusammenfassung

Durch umfangreiche Ausgrabungen und damit einhergehende Forschungen konnten zwischen 1990 und 1995 neue Einblicke in die Entwicklung eines ausgedehnten Gebiets im mittelalterlichen Norwich östlich der Burg auf dem ehemaligen Mann-Egerton-Gelände an der Prince of Wales Road gewonnen werden. Die archäologischen Befunde betreffen geografische Merkmale und die Grundstücksnutzung von der spätangelsächsischen Periode bis zum Erwerb des Gebiets durch die Franziskaner im späten 13. Jh. Es wurden Überreste von mindestens drei kleinen spätangelsächsischen Gebäuden ausgemacht. Zwei dieser eingetieften Häuser, die am äußersten Rand im Westen und Osten der Stätte angesiedelt waren, waren allem Anschein nach Werkstätten. Obwohl das Gebäude im Westen offensichtlich im 11. Jh. in Gebrauch war, enthielt es eine Münze mit dem Abbild Alfreds (887–889 n. Chr.). Durch die Kartierung verschiedener Abfälle konnte eine Vielzahl handwerklicher Tätigkeiten festgestellt werden. Klar voneinander abgegrenzte Geweihbearbeitungs- und metallurgische Abfälle lieferten erstaunliche Hinweise auf spezialisierte Funktionen in klar identifizierbaren Bereichen. Als Belege für die Metallverarbeitung dienten Rückstände aus dem Schmelzen von Kupfer- und Silberlegierungen, der Silberabscheidung und dem Schmieden von Eisen. Ein weiterer Fund war ein nordisches Bleigewicht mit dem Namen Alfreds, das vermutlich kurz nach 880 in Norwich gegossen wurde. Gemeinsam mit den Belegen für die Silberverarbeitung deutet dies auf eine mögliche Prägetätigkeit hin.

Zu den archäologischen Überresten aus der Zeit zwischen dem 12. und 13. Jh. zählen erste Anzeichen für die Entstehung von Gebäuden an der Ostseite der King Street und, im östlichen Teil der Stätte, die frühesten eindeutigen Belege für eine in Nord-Süd-Richtung verlaufende Straße durch das Gebiet mit Spuren angrenzender Bebauung. Dazu gehörten Hinweise auf den Friedhof von St. John the Evangelist, der bereits vor dem Ende des 13. Jh. nicht mehr existierte, sowie mehrere Gegenstände, die mit der nicht weit entfernten Kirche St. Vedast in Verbindung stehen könnten. In ihrer Gesamtheit leisten die neuen Befunde einen wichtigen Beitrag zum derzeitigen Verständnis der Stadtentwicklung Norwichs (vor allem zum Straßenmuster) sowie zu zahlreichen sozioökonomischen Gesichtspunkten bezüglich der spätangelsächsischen, der angelsächsisch-normannischen und der unmittelbar vorklösterlichen Zeit.

Alle vier großen Klosterorden fanden sich in Norwich ein: die Franziskaner (die »Greyfriars«, d. h. grauen Mönche oder Minoriten), die Dominikaner (die »Blackfriars« oder schwarzen Mönche), die Augustiner (oder »Austin Friars«) und die Karmeliter (die »Whitefriars« oder weißen Mönche) (ihre Bezirke sind in Ayers 1994 dokumentiert, Abb. 46). Die Franziskaner, die 1224 ankamen, waren der zahlenmäßig größte Orden. 1256 hatten sie in England bereits 49 Häuser eingerichtet. Nur zwei Jahre nach ihrer Ankunft in England bauten sie in Norwich zwischen den Kirchen St. Vedast und St. Cuthbert ein Kloster, das erst später in das Grabungsareal hinein ausgedehnt wurde. Die Überreste des Klosters traten in Form von Erdwerken in Erscheinung, die zur Vorbereitung des Geländes auf die Bebauung und landschaftliche Gestaltung angelegt wurden, sowie in Form erhaltener Flintstrukturen (einige davon aufrecht), Schichten verdichteter irdener Fundamente, Böden sowie Abzugs- und Raubgräben. Trotz ihres fragmentarischen Charakters ließ sich die Klosteranlage aus diesen Resten zum Teil rekonstruieren. Die noch vorhandenen, als Teile der westlichen und südlichen Klosterbereiche interpretierten Reste zeigen einen Teil des Wohnbereichs und der Gästeunterkunft des Suffragans, zur King Street hin ausgerichtete Gebäude, Teile der südlichen Begrenzungsmauer des Geländes (mehr als 60 m lang) und ein Taubenhaus. Der Klostergrundriss wurde mithilfe einer Kombination aus archäologischem und dokumentarischem Material rekonstruiert. Zu den schriftlichen Quellen zählten die Aufzeichnungen von William Worcestre (1479) sowie Pachtverträge aus dem 16. Jh. Bei der erheblichen Vergrößerung des Klosters gegen Ende des 13. Jh., attestiert in einer Überlassungsurkunde an die Kirche von 1292, wurden die kirchlichen und klösterlichen Gebäude stark erweitert. Archäologisch belegt ist dieser Prozess durch Spuren von Gebäudeabrissen, verfüllten Vertiefungen (beispielsweise Kellern und Gruben) und am deutlichsten durch die Schließung von einem oder vielleicht sogar zwei Wegen. Neben der Vorderfront der Gebäude an der King Street wurde eine Glockengussgrube ausgemacht, die zwischen 1490 und 1525 in Gebrauch war.

Die Nutzung des Geländes zwischen der Auflösung der Klöster im Jahr 1538 und der Errichtung des Mann-Egerton-Werks (ca. 1904/1912) wurde anhand von archäologischen und dokumentarischen Quellen rückverfolgt. In dieser Zeit diente ein Großteil des Geländes als Garten. Die archäologischen Funde umfassten elf Tuchplomben aus dem 16. bis 18. Jh. — der erste Fundkomplex seiner Art, der im Verlauf der offiziellen Ausgrabung in der bedeutsamen Kammgarnstadt Norwich zum Vorschein kam.

(Übersetzung: Gerlinde Krug)

1. Introduction

I. PROJECT BACKGROUND

(Figs 1.1 and 1.2)

Excavation at the former Mann Egerton premises in central Norwich (Fig. 1.1; SMR Site 845N), located just over 100m to the south of Tombland (the pre-Conquest market place and focal point of the Late Saxon town), offered a valuable opportunity to study an extensive part of the early settlement. Given the proximity of the site to both the Castle and the Cathedral, the Greyfriars project promised to shed new light on how these Norman developments affected the geography of the town. The imposition of both establishments upon the pre-existing settlement geography had the effect of preserving, below ground, a cumulative record of a sequence of urban development that had been abruptly arrested. This phenomenon had already been demonstrated graphically by major excavations by the Norfolk Archaeological Unit (NAU) in the north-eastern and southern baileys of Norwich castle, which revealed Late Saxon plots, buildings and pits, a church and numerous pre-Conquest cemeteries (Ayers 1985; Shepherd Popescu forthcoming). In a similar manner the Franciscan Friary, which was founded in 1226, absorbed an area of some 10.4 acres (4.2ha) of the area of medieval Norwich in a succession of well-documented enlargements to its precinct. A significant part of the project was concerned with understanding the religious house itself and how it interacted with the lay community. The archaeological excavations undertaken within the Friary precinct (accounting for approximately 85% of the overall excavation site) represented an 8.1% sample of the total area of the precinct in its ultimate form, *i.e.* immediately prior to its dissolution during the reign of Henry VIII.

The redevelopment site was located on the south side of Prince of Wales Road (a major east-to-west route driven through the precinct in the 19th century) and to the east of King Street (Fig. 1.2). The archaeological investigations were necessitated by two planning applications submitted by National Farmers Union Mutual and Avon Group in respect of proposals to redevelop the site for offices. These threatened the comprehensive removal of surviving archaeological deposits over much of the development site. The first planning application, relating to 91% of the area ultimately investigated, was made in 1990. The associated archaeological fieldwork comprised an evaluation and subsequent large-scale excavations. An application to redevelop an adjoining site (11, 11a and 13 Prince of Wales Road) was made in 1995, and this accounted for the remaining 9% of the total excavation site discussed in this volume. Planning consent for the proposed scheme was partly contingent upon the provision by the developer of appropriate measures for the recording of archaeological deposits. The archaeological work was funded by the developer.

The aims of the project were threefold:

1. to increase understanding of the Late Saxon and early medieval town;
2. to investigate the Franciscan Friary;
3. to examine the post-Reformation urban development.

Each of the three research objectives is addressed in this monograph by a dedicated chapter (Chapter 2, 'Pre- Friary Development'; Chapter 3, 'The Franciscan Friary'; Chapter 4, 'The Dissolution and Afterwards') which presents and discusses the relevant archaeological and documentary evidence. Finds are presented by functional category in Chapter 5, with zooarchaeological and environmental remains appearing in Chapter 6. A brief conclusion follows (Chapter 7).

II. EXCAVATIONS 1990–5

(Fig. 1.3, Pls 1.1–1.3)

The initial site evaluation, supervised by Heather Wallis, was carried out by the NAU in March and April 1990. Ten trial trenches were located strategically (Fig. 1.3) to elucidate the changing depth and character of surviving archaeological deposits across the site.

A series of archaeological interventions, co-ordinated to take place between demolition and construction operations, took place between 1992 and 1995. The main phase of large-scale excavation work, undertaken between October 1992 and July 1993, was directed by Jayne Bown. This was supplemented by a watching brief and additional excavation from December 1993 to February 1994. This latter phase of work, which was supervised by the author, was associated with the demolition of the last remaining buildings fronting onto King Street and Prince of Wales Road. Finally, the incorporation of a further three properties (11, 11a and 13 Prince of Wales Road) into the redevelopment necessitated an additional watching brief and excavation. This work was carried out between May and October 1995, also under the direction of the author.

The site was divided into four areas: A, B, CB and C (Fig. 1.3). Excavation of Area A during the 1992–3 phase of work was largely conducted within standing buildings. This was supplemented by investigation in 1994, following demolition (see below). Medieval deposits were encountered immediately below the basement floor in Area A.

Areas B, CB and C were entirely cleared of buildings prior to excavation. Large parts of Area B were formerly occupied by the concrete basement of the Mann Egerton works, the construction of which had caused extensive truncation. The depth of made ground increased towards the east end of the site, the natural ground surface falling away sharply at the boundary between Areas B and CB. Access to the medieval levels within Area C, where the made ground was deepest, could only be gained practically through the machining of a step-sided trench. In Area CB the NAU was restricted from excavating below the formation level of the proposed new buildings.

Demolition of buildings on the frontages of King Street and Prince of Wales Road and the emplacement of continuous piling along the site's perimeter, necessitated a further period of work. The machine-excavation of the pilot trench for the piling (December 1993) was attended by the author. Additionally, two areas were excavated in January and February 1994 (Fig. 1.3): one adjacent to King Street, the other next to 11 Prince of Wales Road.

Incorporation of 11, 11a and 13 Prince of Wales Road into the redevelopment (see above) entailed an additional phase of fieldwork (hereafter referred to as Area D). To allow its accommodation within a complex sequence of demolition and underpinning operations, this archaeological work was organised as a series of separate interventions, the records from which required later integration. For this phase of excavation the fieldwork *Brief* required that an understanding of the full depth of deposits should be sought, irrespective of the formation level of the new development. Therefore, the depth of excavation was in this case only restricted by safety considerations.

In October 1997 the NAU was required to carry out an evaluation comprising three small trenches, for a second client (Norwich School), at a site formerly occupied by Wallace King on St Faith's Lane (Site 373N; Fig. 1.2).

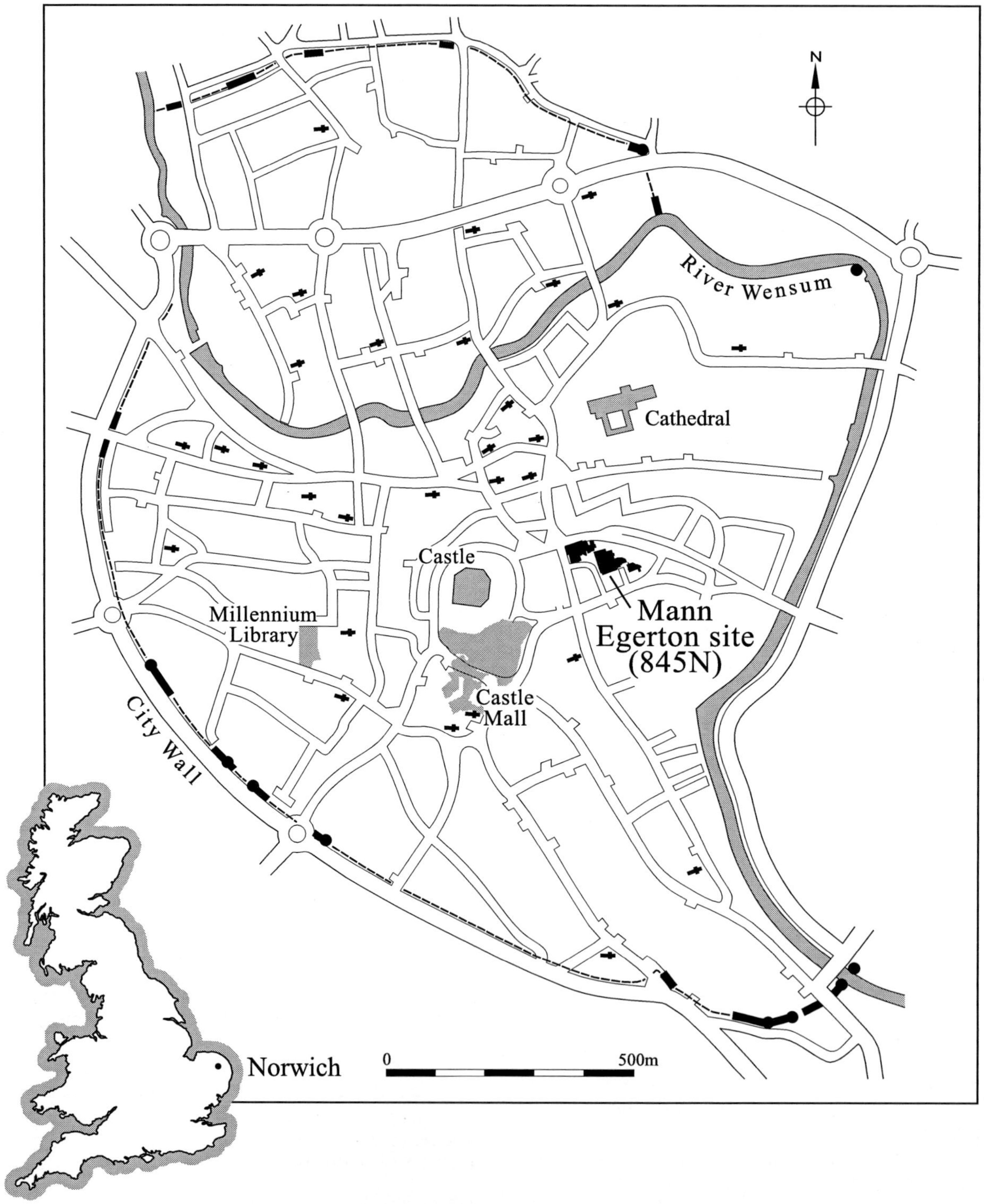

Figure 1.1 Norwich, showing location of Mann Egerton site (845N), Norwich Castle and Cathedral, and recent major excavations at Castle Mall (777N) and Norwich Millennium Library (26437N)

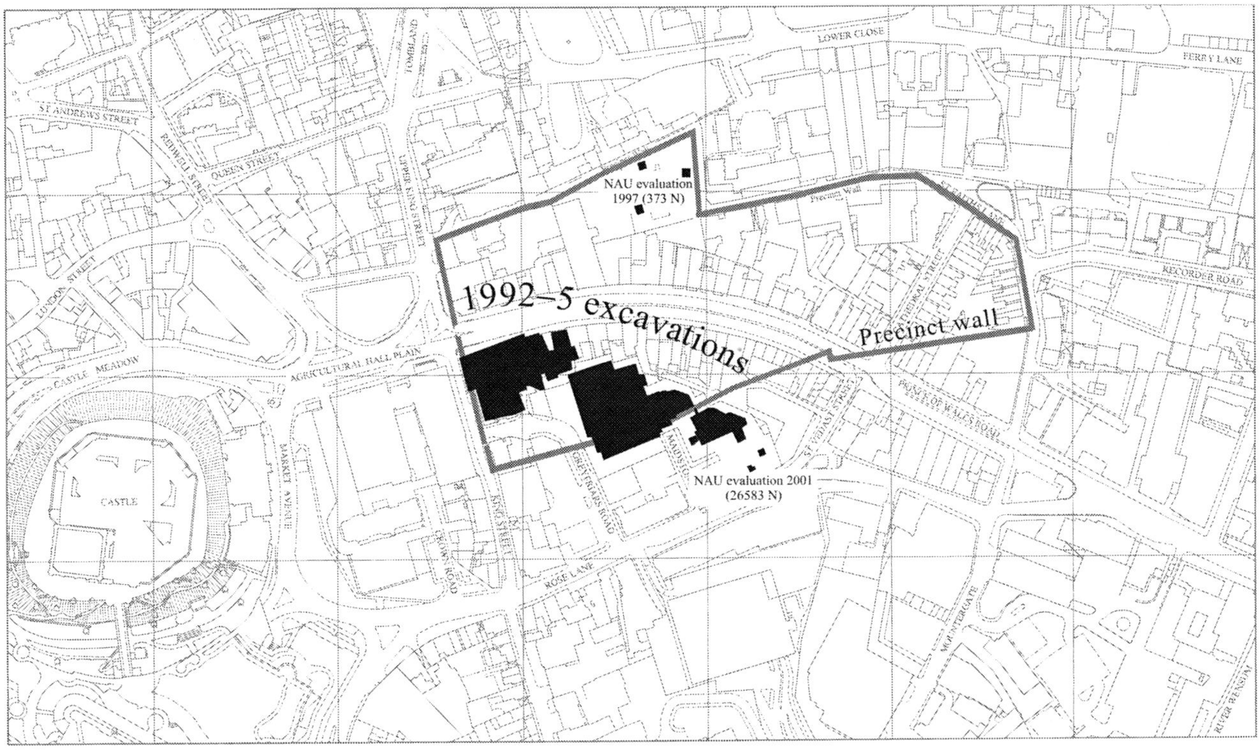

Figure 1.2 Location of Mann Egerton site (845N)

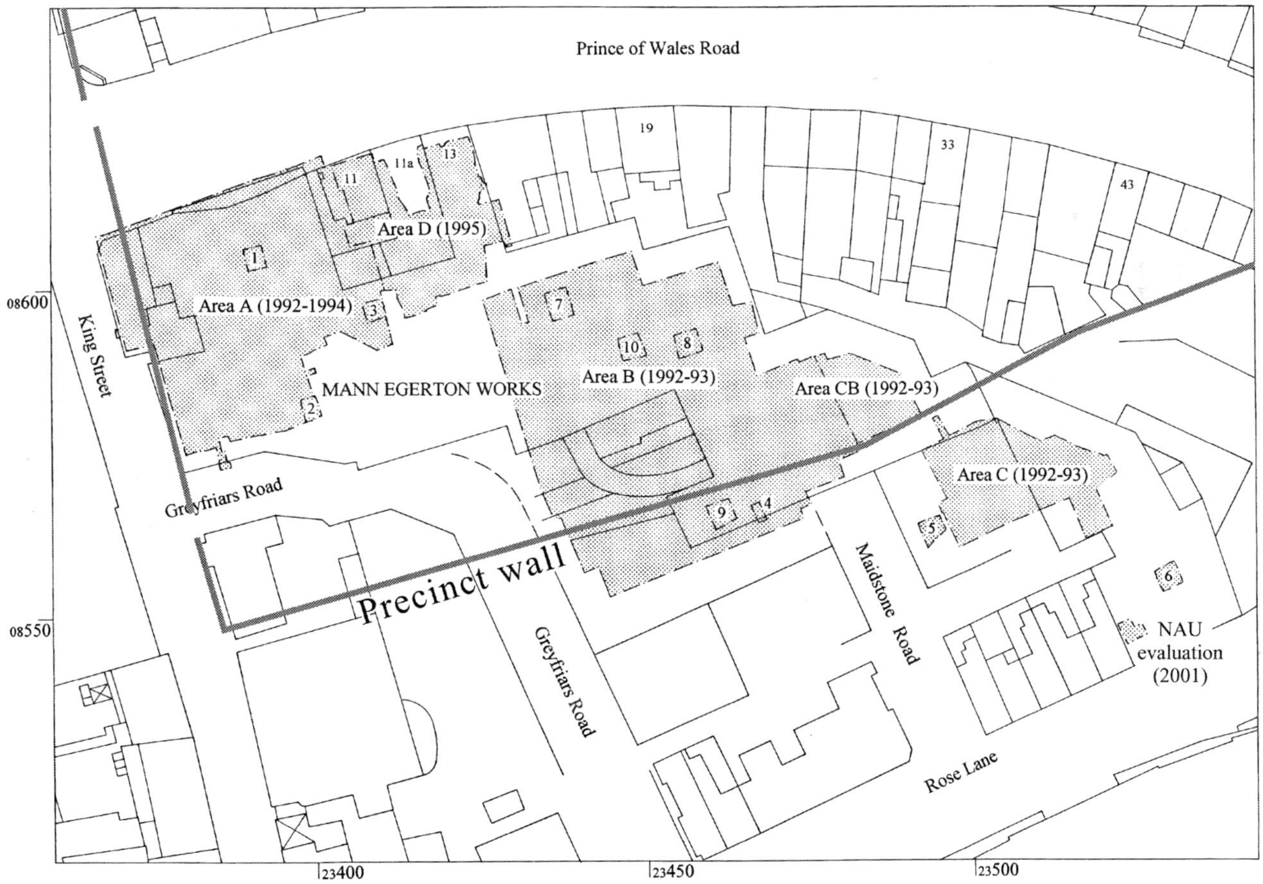

Figure 1.3 Plan of Mann Egerton site (845N) showing location of evaluation trenches

Plate 1.1 Interior of the Mann Egerton garage, *c.* 1910

Plate 1.2 Prince of Wales Road frontage of the Mann Egerton garage

Since this site lay within the precinct of the Franciscan Friary (post-1292), the insights gained by this investigation (specifically, selected artefacts and Friary-related burials) are incorporated into this report in summary form. Subsequent extensive excavation here by Northamptonshire Archaeology will be reported on separately (Soden in prep.). A further evaluation (Site 26582N) was carried out by the NAU in January 2001 for a third client, Twigden Homes Ltd, in connection with a housing development proposal. This took the form of a single trench on the Rose Lane frontage.

The overall depth of archaeological deposits varied considerably across the Greyfriars site. Much of the west and central parts of the excavated area (Areas A, B and D) had been truncated by construction of buildings associated with Prince of Wales Road in the late 19th century and of the Mann Egerton works in *c.* 1905 (Pls 1.1 and 1.2). Somewhat ironically, some of the best survival of deposits was observed at the perimeter of Area A, beyond the 19th-century cellars, during a watching brief (late 1993 to early 1994) associated with the excavation of a pilot trench for the continuous piling. By contrast, the natural horizon lay some 5m below modern ground level at the east end of the site (Area C). In areas which had been occupied by 19th-century cellared buildings, the floors and walls of the Franciscan Friary had suffered very heavily. For this reason, reconstruction of the groundplan of the Friary had to be based on isolated sections of walling and discontinuous remnant floors.

Excavation in both Areas A and D (characterised by the presence of structural remains of the Franciscan Friary: Pl. 1.3) was constrained by the requirement for archaeological work to be carried out within and adjacent to standing buildings. Although in both areas an opportunity was provided to revisit the parts formerly obscured after demolition, this staged method of working had implications for overall efficiency, the coherence of the record and (perhaps most importantly) imposed constraints upon the volume and depth of deposits accessible at any one time.

III. METHODOLOGIES

Excavation, post-excavation and publication

On-site records specific to individual contexts consisted of photographs (colour transparencies and black and white prints), plan, section and elevation drawings, and standard context *pro forma* sheets. Where samples were extracted from a context, a *pro forma* was completed for each sample. Stratigraphic sequence diagrams (matrices) for each discrete area of investigation were maintained during the excavation. Having been integrated with each other where possible, these formed the basis of stratigraphic analysis in the post-excavation phase.

The apparent absence of archaeological deposits in some parts of the site reflects constraints upon excavation, and is therefore potentially misleading. For example, work in the southern half of Area A was restricted to the planning and minimal excavation of Friary and later deposits: given the southward fall in the natural ground surface, deposits pre-dating the Friary hereabouts would have been buried beneath substantial landscaping deposits. Reconstruction of many of the postulated buildings in Area B rests partly upon the configuration of cut features of ambiguous date, this in turn being a function both of limited excavation and of frequent stratigraphic isolation. (The latter problem resulted in an over-dependence upon pottery for dating deposits, bringing with it the inherent problems posed by residuality.)

As no lateral deposits attributed confidently to the pre-Friary period survived within Area A, ground surface levels could only be inferred indirectly. Minimum levels were therefore taken from the top edges of contemporary cut features. In addition, some indication of the pre-Friary ground surface was provided by an examination of the subsequent external yard areas and internal floors of the Friary itself. However, given that Friary-period metalled surfaces directly overlay natural sand in the vicinity of an earlier sunken-floored building, the laying-out of the precinct clearly involved the rationalisation of the ground surface, and some localised truncation.

During stratigraphic analysis, the archaeological sequence was rationalised progressively into a hierarchy of subgroups and groups, which were assigned to subperiods and periods. In defining these periods, account had to be taken not only of the date ranges assigned to context-specific pottery assemblages, but also of the known history of the site. Some chronological overlaps between sub-periods were unavoidable, due both to the nature of the site itself and of the dating evidence. The first two periods (Periods 1 and 2) were in effect defined by pottery date-ranges. Contexts assigned to Period 2.2 were those which were ceramically and stratigraphically dated to the 12th–13th centuries, without any further refinement being possible. The initial period structure reflected an attempt to relate the archaeological sequence to the chronology of the establishment and Dissolution of the Franciscan Friary (Period 3: 1226–1538). As noted above, however, documentary research subsequently revealed that the incorporation of the site area into the Friary was not a simple process. Indeed, it was only after mortmain licences of 1292 and 1299 that most of the area studied by the excavation became part of the precinct. This meant that archaeological evidence dating to the 13th century (Period 2.3) had to be separated from that which could be confidently ascribed to the existence of the Friary on the site (Periods 3.1 and 3.2). (See important note relating to specialist environmental analyses on p. 209.)

Site periods

Period 1: Late Saxon/Norman (10th–11th centuries) (Chapter 2)

Period 2: Pre-Friary (12th–13th centuries) (Chapter 2)
- *Period 2.1:* 12th century
- *Period 2.2:* 12th–13th centuries
- *Period 2.3:* 1200–1290s

Period 3: Friary (1290s–1538) (Chapter 3)
- *Period 3.1:* 1290s–1400
- *Period 3.2:* 1400–1538

Period 4: Dissolution and Afterwards (1538–1800) (Chapter 4)
- *Period 4.1:* Dissolution (1538–66)
- *Period 4.2:* Post-Dissolution (1567–1800)

Period 5: Modern (19th to 20th centuries) (Chapter 4)

Interpretation of the layout and development of the Franciscan Friary has entailed integration of the archaeological and documentary evidence. Reconstruction of the conventual complex and identification of component buildings were regarded as prerequisites of achieving a satisfactory understanding of the archaeological evidence. The conventional layouts adopted by friaries, particularly those of the same order, can be relied on to some extent to offer an idealised/model groundplan, although the layouts of many friaries had to be adapted to the constraints of particular sites, giving rise to considerable variation and thereby necessitating caution in the use of parallels.

Interpretation of the functions of individual elements of the Friary encountered during excavation was hampered by a number of factors, as follows.

1. The extent of robbing following the Dissolution (this being a consequence of the scarcity of available building stone in the area) and construction of basemented buildings that latterly formed part of the Mann Egerton works.
2. The relatively restricted scope of the excavation within a large precinct.
3. Uncertainties surrounding the location of the Friary church and the relative position of the cloister.
4. The limited usefulness of analogy with the more complete groundplans of other Franciscan friaries, given the apparent variability noted above. The groundplan of the Franciscan house in Norwich may well have been idiosyncratic, given the physical constraints that would have been posed by this particular site. These included variations in ground level across the site, necessitating large-scale terracing, and issues raised by the load-bearing capacity of the ground surface, with deep footing trenches infilled with compacted layers of earth being required in areas disturbed by earlier pit-digging.

In order that the pattern of outward development and the evolving internal geography of the Friary could be understood it was essential to ascertain the location of the Friary church from the later 13th century onwards, when the precinct was considerably enlarged. Whilst no part of this later church lay within the excavated area the archaeological remains of other buildings, considered in the light of documentary evidence, allowed a reconstruction of the layout of the redeveloped complex to be proposed (Fig. 3.21). Chapter 3 uses this reconstruction as a basis for interpretation (although alternative interpretations are documented in the site archive).

Deposits relating to the destruction of Friary buildings in the years following the Dissolution of 1538 could be attributed to this historical event on the basis of physical attributes with some confidence. It had to be recognised, however, that demolition and salvage processes took place over some time (Period 4.1). Documentary evidence provides a chronology for the disappearance of most of the Friary structures following the Dissolution.

Archaeological evidence presented in Chapters 2–4 is described broadly from west to east across the site. The project archive is held by Norfolk Museums & Archaeology Service under the site code 845N, with the material from the evaluation at St Faiths Lane held under the site code 373N.

Specialist analyses and catalogue

Methodologies for finds and environmental material are summarised where appropriate in this report, or are available in the project archive. Small Finds (SF) are referenced, illustrated and catalogued using their identifying number (*e.g.* SF1234). A separate system of catalogue numbers has only been used for window glass, to aid identification in cases where numerous fragments from a single context were assigned the same SF number. Catalogue entries are presented in a format similar to that used by Margeson (1993). Contextual information appears in italics and the fields used are: context and origin (*e.g.* 'culvert fill *10778*') and period. Un-illustrated items are not catalogued. Artefacts recovered from the St Faith's Lane (Site 373N) evaluation are denoted using the site's SMR number, *e.g.* 373N/SF6.

Documentary research

by Elizabeth Rutledge

The aim of the documentary research element of the project was not to write another comprehensive history of the Norwich Franciscan Friary although, naturally, the history of the Friary plays an important part. Instead its objective was to examine the documentary evidence for the occupation and use of the excavated site from as early as possible to the present day. With so much already written about the Norwich Greyfriars, the work started with a critical reading of the published material. This left many key questions unanswered. There was little about the nature and possible position of the Friary buildings, and almost nothing on the pre-Friary site or the period after 1650.

At the time that documentary research was begun the Norfolk Record Office was still closed after the destruction of the Norwich Central Library building by fire in August 1994, and was not expected to reopen before its completion. This situation was compounded by the loss of local history material held by the Norwich Central Library and the temporary closure of the Library as a whole. The post-1650 history of the site has therefore been based almost entirely on printed maps and street directories held elsewhere, and no attempt has been made to deal with this period in more detail. The brief history of the Friary given here is also based mainly on secondary material, although original sources have been used to compile Appendices 1 and 2. Further research, however, would have been seriously limited by the fire had it not been for the generosity of Chris Barringer and the King Street Group, who made available their archive of notes and transcripts relating to the area. Of particular use in considering the likely position of the main Friary buildings was the information from the Norwich city lease books supplied by Mary Rogers. These sources were supplemented by visits to the Public Record Office, to the archives of the Duke of Norfolk at Arundel Castle in search of immediate post-Dissolution material, and to Lambeth Palace Library in search of individual friars. Finally, the extension of the excavation into Area D meant that the Norfolk Record Office did re-open before the end of the project, and this made it possible to check documentary references and to follow up leads suggested by the printed accounts.

Two aspects of this research have been unexpected. The first was the existence of no fewer than three sets of dimensions: those for the property acquired *c.* 1292 (Table 4), for the church and cloister in 1479 (William Worcestre) and for the plots leased in 1565–71 (Table 5). The second was the amount of information that could in fact be discovered about the Norwich Greyfriars and its inhabitants with comparatively little trouble, considering that neither buildings nor Friary documents survive.

IV. THE SITE

Location

(Figs 1.1 and 1.2)

The excavation (Site 845N) was situated to the south of Prince of Wales Road, to the north of Rose Lane and to the east of King Street (Fig. 1.2). Fronting both King Street and Prince of Wales Road at its western corner, the site ran eastward behind properties on Prince of Wales Road, ultimately meeting Rose Lane to the east of Maidstone Road. The northern part of the site lies in the early-modern parish of St George Tombland, the southern part being within St Peter Parmentergate. The boundary between the two parishes follows the projected line of the west-to-east portion of Greyfriars Road. During the medieval period the western part of the precinct lay in the parish of St Cuthbert, the north-eastern (probably) in the parish of St

Plate 1.3 General view of the excavation (Site 845N) looking west towards Norwich Castle, showing the Friary precinct wall in the centre of the photograph

Mary in the Marsh and the south-eastern in the parish of St Vedast (Fig. 2.1). The total area of the redevelopment was *c.* 4400m². Those parts of the site investigated archaeologically amounted to *c.* 3985m².

Natural relief and surface geology

(Fig. 3.22)

There is a general fall in the natural ground level across the site from west to east, levels ranging from 9.0m OD at the King Street frontage to 1.2m OD in Area C (see schematic section, Fig. 3.22). This fall of *c.* 7.8m occurs over a horizontal distance of some 160m. A marked break of slope, effectively forming a terrace, occurs *c.* 50m from the south-east extremity of the site. This may represent the western limit of the cumulative erosion of the meandering course of a stream (the Fresflete: Fig. 2.1). An additional depression in the middle of the site corresponded to another, un-named, stream (flowing north-to-south) which appears on the map drawn by Millard and Manning in 1830 (see Chapter 4, Pl. 4.4). The excavated area lies *c.* 300m from the west bank of the River Wensum.

The highest/north-western part of the site (Area A) was characterised by firm weathered chalk with irregular inclusions and bands of sand (Norwich Crag). Around the

SMR Site No.	*Description*
Churchyard of St Cuthbert	
137	Human skeletal remains probably lying within former churchyard of St Cuthbert's found at 1 Upper King Street (1964).
164	East-to-west flint wall — probably south wall of St Cuthbert's church — and fragments of human bone found at rear of 15 Upper King Street (1939).
189	Two human skeletons found at 7 Upper King Street (1952).
398	St Cuthbert's church, Upper King Street. Dedication suggests a pre-Danish foundation. United with St Mary the Less in 1492. Demolished in 1530.
26516	Medieval grave probably lying within former churchyard of St Cuthbert's found at 27–28 Tombland (1999).
Churchyard of St John the Evangelist	
76	Site of St John the Evangelist in Conesford on corner of Rose Lane and King Street. Sherd of Ipswich ware and medieval and post-medieval pottery found (1964). Human skeletal remains, probably derived from St John's churchyard, found (2000).
111	Medieval and post-medieval pottery found at filling station at 6–22 Rose Lane (1967).
788	Medieval pottery found in Greyfriars Road (1990).
Churchyard of St Vedast	
131	Churchyard of St Vedast (see Site 395). Quantities of human skeletal remains and a fragment of medieval architectural stone found during excavation of pile holes (1970 and 1971).
395	Site of St Vedast's church on corner of Rose Lane and St Vedast Street (see Chapter 2.I).
Precinct of Franciscan Friary	
65	Medieval and post-medieval pottery found at angle of Greyfriars Road (1962).
74	Early medieval pottery found within Mann Egerton works at 23–25 King Street (1913). Ivory tweezers and ear pick with concentric decoration and medieval and post-medieval pottery found (1934). Tweezers identified by Jope as Late Saxon/Viking but MacGregor (1985) dates such items to 16th-century or later.
102	Medieval pottery found at 36 Prince of Wales Road (1946).
103	Post-medieval pottery, glass and clay pipes found at 39–41 Prince of Wales Road (1964).
239	Post-medieval pottery (mainly stoneware) found at 45–51 Prince of Wales Road (1974).
241	Late Saxon, medieval and post-medieval pottery found at 90 St Faiths Lane (1973).
270	Late Saxon to medieval pottery found at Wales Square (1974 and 1975).
373	Franciscan Friary (see Chapter 3, this volume). Human bone found during building work at rear of Norfolk Club (1991). Evaluation by NAU on former Wallace King site, St Faith's Lane (1997), located six burials confirming presence of Greyfriars cemetery (Emery 1997b; summarised in Chapter 3, this volume). Subsequent excavation (1998) by Northamptonshire Archaeology recorded 137 burials, including those encountered by evaluation (Soden 2001).
394	Extensions to Wallace King (behind 28–30 Prince of Wales Road) cut through wall of Greyfriars and disturbed numerous skeletons (1950).
845	Trial excavation within Mann Egerton site (1990). Full excavation (1992–5). (See this volume)
26329	Medieval stone bridge beneath St Faiths Lane. ?late 13th-century. Span of 15 feet (Jervoise 1932).
26583	Evaluation trench excavated on Rose Lane, within former Mann Egerton site (2001). Medieval stratified deposits and Late Saxon, medieval and post-medieval pottery and other finds recovered (Whitmore 2001).

Table 1 Previous archaeological observations

northern edge of Area B, this deposit gave way to a consistent buff coloured sand which was seen throughout the eastern part of the excavation.

Previous archaeological observations

Past archaeological observations associated with building work within the former precinct of the Franciscan Friary have contributed greatly to the understanding of the area (Table 1). Particularly useful information has been provided by such records about the extent of former cemeteries, notably those of the churches of St Vedast and St John the Evangelist and of the Franciscan Friary itself.

Additionally, some accounts of observations relating to the Franciscan Friary are not logged in the Norfolk Historic Environment Record. A member of the Norfolk and Norwich Archaeological Society believed he had seen the west end of the Friary church when Greyfriars House was demolished (anon. 1924, 139). Skeletons were found at 13 Prince of Wales Road in 1878 and at 22 Prince of Wales Road in 1867 and 1925 (EDP, 8, 9 and 12 January 1925), while the builder of 13 and 15 Greyfriars Road (Plot L, Fig. 3.6) found a quantity of worked stone, including window mullions, when digging out the cellars; he also used an old flint wall as a foundation (EDP, 9 October 1925).

2. Pre-Friary Development (Late Saxon to *c.* 1290)

I. ARCHAEOLOGICAL AND HISTORICAL BACKGROUND

by Elizabeth Shepherd Popescu and Phillip A. Emery (Figs 2.1 and 2.24)

It has been suggested that Norwich originated as five small hamlets or villages (*Westwick, Coslany, Conesford, Needham* and *Northwic*) founded in the 8th–9th centuries, which had coalesced to form the town of Norwich by the 11th century. These Middle Saxon settlements were largely identified by place-name evidence (summarised by Carter 1978, *passim*), tentatively supported by scattered archaeological finds such as 8th–9th century material from the Cathedral Close. The Greyfriars site lies in or near the putative area of *Conesford* (*Cunegesford*), settlement perhaps being attracted here by the presence of three small streams (Figs 2.1 and 2.24) which rose within the later Friary grounds and ran south-eastwards towards the River Wensum (see below and Chapter 3.II). The etymology is ODan *kunung* (king), OE *ford*, the former element perhaps replacing an earlier OE *cyning* (Sandred and Lindström 1989, 114); the physical location of any ford remains unknown. King Street itself, immediately to the west of the site, was referred to as Conesford or Superior Conesford from the mid-12th until the mid-18th century, the earliest references relating to the leet of Conesford. Mountergate was referred to as Inferior Conesford from at least the 13th century (Sandred and Lindström 1989, 118–19), while Rose Lane was later known as Nether Conesford or St Faith's/St Vedast's Lane (Sandred and Lindström 1989, 132). (Named roads are illustrated in Fig. 1.2.)

By the Late Saxon period (*c.* 850–1066), the southern part of Norwich was effectively bounded on three sides by watercourses: the River Wensum to the north and east, and the Great Cockey stream to the west (Fig. 2.24). To the south there is growing evidence for the presence of a defensive bank and ditch, marking a possible southern 'burh' (Site 777N, Shepherd Popescu forthcoming; Site 26577N King St, former brewery, Penn 1999; Lloyd *et al.* 2002, 8 and section 1). The outer extent of settlement in the Late Saxon period is suggested by the irregular line of Mountergate/St Faith's Lane, this road following the landward edge of the river marsh and possibly reflecting the line of the newly-discovered defences. The Greyfriars site lies well within this defensive boundary, between it and the old market place of Tombland to the north. Previous understanding of the pre-Conquest plan of this area (later to be largely destroyed by insertion first of the Norman Cathedral and then the Greyfriars precinct) was presented by Ayers (1996, 65–8 and fig. 10), which indicates that little was known about its precise layout, other than that the position of churches appeared to indicate some kind of gridded street pattern. The position of a major north-to-south road some 200m to the east of King Street, first postulated in the 1970s, is suggested by various parish and property boundaries and church locations; this route would have connected a crossing in the vicinity of modern Whitefriars bridge and trading area at *Bychil* (Palace Plain) with the bend in Rose Lane, and the crossing and transepts of the Norman Cathedral were eventually imposed upon it (Carter 1978, fig. 7). Millard and Manning's map of 1830 (Pl. 4.4) shows a property boundary following this alignment and curving westwards before meeting Rose Lane. This curved corner, rather like that of a playing card, lies adjacent to the site of St Vedast's church and now appears to have formed the south-eastern limit of a rectilinear street arrangement (see Discussion, below).

Four probable pre-Conquest churches once surrounded the investigation area (Fig. 2.1): St Cuthbert (Site 398N) and St Ethelbert both to the north (Table 1), St John the Evangelist to the south (Table 1) and St Vedast to the east (Site 395N). In addition, the church of St Mary in the Marsh lay some distance to the north-east. The site of the church of St Vedast lay immediately to the east of the excavated area: a pre-Conquest foundation date has been suggested on the basis of its dedication (to SS Vaast and Armand, both Flemish saints), which may indicate the presence of a Flemish community (Campbell 1975, 6; Sandred and Lindström 1989, 54), as was perhaps the case in London (Ayers 2003, 49). Alternatively, its dedication to St Armand, a 6th-century saint, might suggest earlier contact with the Low Countries (Ayers 1994, 25, 34). The earliest direct documentary reference is for 1154–60. Although the church itself was demolished in 1540–1, the churchyard remained in use until at least 1744. A pre-Conquest Viking cross shaft was built into the angle of a local 19th-century house which was demolished in 1896 for road widening. This may have formed part of a monument in the churchyard (Site 131N): it is decorated with animals in an interlace design of the Mammen style and is of 10th-century date (Margeson 1997, fig. 30). The Church of St John the Evangelist disappeared during the 13th century (see below).

The three streams that evidently rose within the later confines of the Friary precinct included the Dallingflete and the Fresflete, with the third being un-named (Fig. 2.1). The Dallingflete (now lost) once fed into the River Wensum to the south of Lovell's Staithe. Its name, first documented in 1296, probably comes from a personal name followed by OE *flęot*, ME *flęte* meaning 'estuary, inlet', or possibly 'watercourse, ditch' (Sandred and Lindström 1989, 5). It may once also have been known as the Kings Flete (*ibid.*). Although it was infilled during the 19th century, a stone bridge across the stream survived to be recorded in 1888 (Chapter 3.I, Pl. 3.3). The Fresflete (also lost) joined the Wensum to the south of Foundry Bridge, the first part of its name originating in OF *freis*, *fresche* ('fresh') (Sandred and Lindström 1989, 6); the earliest known reference dates to 1290. Such minor streams are referred to in Norwich, and in East Anglia generally, as 'cockeys' and were often used as sewers: the etymology is equivocal, although it may have a Scandinavian origin (Sandred and Lindström 1989, 7).

As is indicated in Chapter 1 and Table 1, relatively little archaeological examination of the development area (or, indeed, the entire Greyfriars precinct) had taken place prior to the 1990s excavations. The evidence presented above, however, aroused expectations that pre-Conquest remains survived here.

II. DOCUMENTARY EVIDENCE

by Elizabeth Rutledge
(Figs 2.1–2.3 and 2.24)

Early history of the site

There is little direct documentary evidence for the Greyfriars site before the coming of the Franciscan friars in 1226. As noted above, indirect documentary and archaeological evidence for the pre-1226 period suggests that the site lay well within the Late Saxon town, to the south of the market place at Tombland and surrounded by early churches. Figure 2.1 shows a possible 11th-century street pattern, which considerably supplements existing knowledge. The southern end of the main north-to-south street across the subject area was described as a former highway in 1285 (Fig. 2.2). The minor north-to-south routes are suggested by the late 13th-century property boundaries shown on Fig. 2.3. They also take account of the probable course of two of the little streams or cockeys that ran south and slightly east to the river, the remnants of which are shown on Millard and Manning's map of 1830 (Pl. 4.4). The lanes leading to the church of St Mary in the Marsh are mentioned in early 14th-century deeds (NRO MC 146/52 plan 80). The east-to-west lane leading to the church of St Vedast is documented as running east from the former highway in 1298 (Fig. 2.2), and it was probably a continuation of this way (211ft x 12ft) that the friars closed in 1285 (Cal. Pat. Rolls 1281–92, 155). An intermediate minor lane, shown on Fig. 2.1 to the west of the former highway, follows the late 13th-century property boundaries and might explain why the sequence of properties given on Fig. 2.3 apparently starts again at this point. The east-to-west lane south of the cemetery of St Cuthbert is called Neugate or Bugate in a document written by *c.*

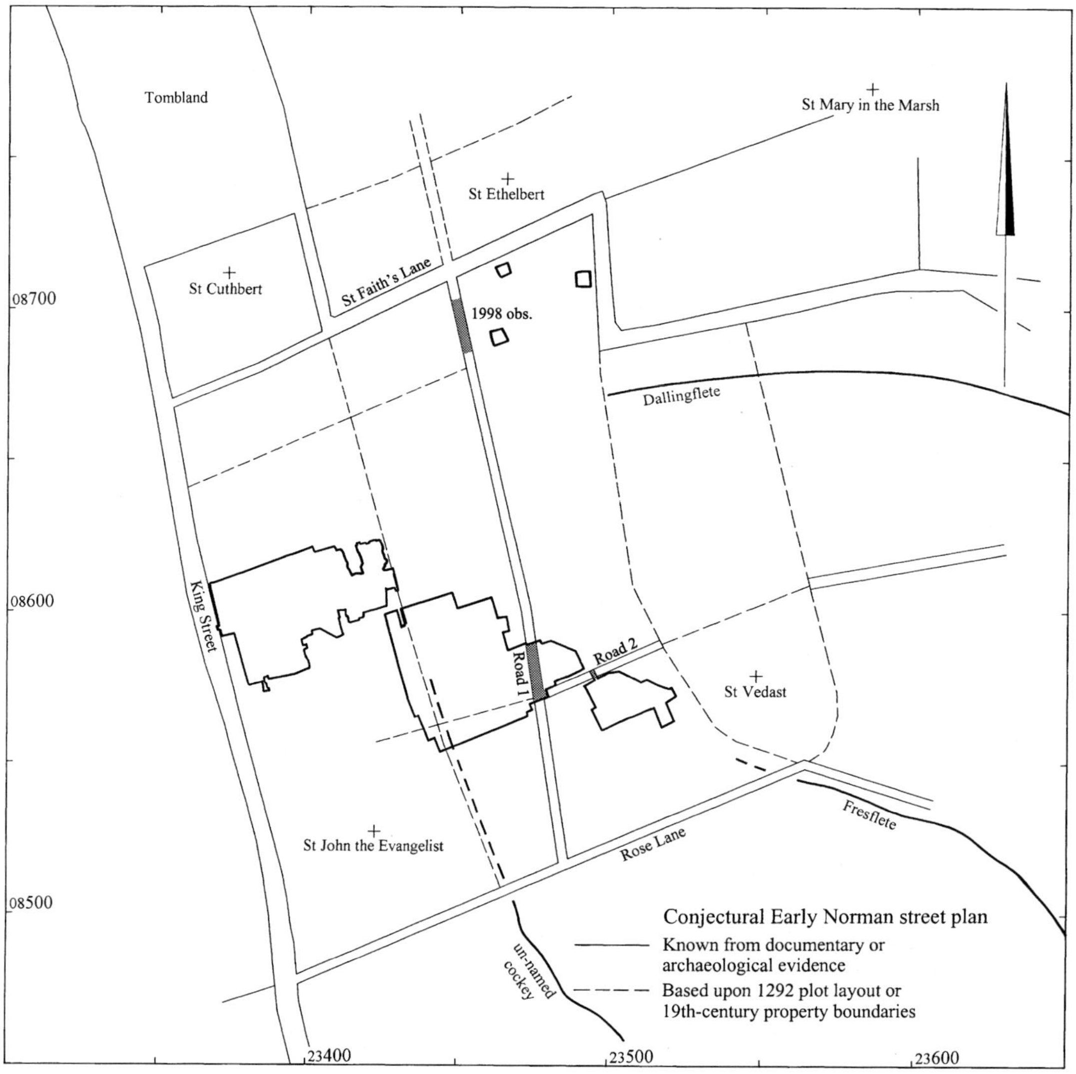

Figure 2.1 Conjectural early Norman Street plan

1400 and described then as previously taken over by the Greyfriars (Hudson and Tingey 1906–10, I, 54–5). The crosses indicating churches in the early Norman period (Fig. 2.1) do not show the precise position of any church, but rather the approximate location of a church and churchyard. The most problematical — the church of St John the Evangelist — was described soon after 1272 as the place 'where is the tavern of William Seysun' (Hudson 1910, 106–7) and can be equated with William de Sessons' property on the corner between King Street and Rose Lane on Fig. 2.2.

The whole area between Rose Lane and Tombland must have been badly affected by the changes of the late 11th and early 12th centuries. The building of the castle to the west, and then the establishment of the cathedral and cathedral priory to the north, not only destroyed a large part of the surrounding Late Saxon town but also cut the site off from the new market centre in the French Borough, to the west of the castle. By the 13th century it would appear to have been considerably depopulated. The former highway had deteriorated into a lane by 1285 (NRO MC 146/52 plan 100) while properties A–J and M–Q on Fig. 2.3 were void by 1292, although they had previously been built up and paid 6d in landgable (a ground rent payable to the city: Kirkpatrick 1845, 110). Even Plot L, built upon and paying landgable in 1292, was described as only a piece of land in 1284 (NRO DCN 45/8/3). Another indication of the state of the area by the 13th century is provided by the disappearance of the church of St John the Evangelist. It is not known when this occurred. Poverty could have led to the church's omission from the Norwich Taxation of 1254 (Hudson 1910, 106–7), and the cemetery still acted as an abuttal in an undated mid-13th-century deed (NRO DCN 45/40/20). On the other hand, since the site was a tavern by *c.* 1272 and the church is not mentioned at all in the late 13th-century deeds for the King Street/Rose Lane corner (NRO MC 146/52 plan 115), it had probably gone by the middle of the century.

Another factor in the early history of this area was that of legal and ecclesiastical jurisdiction. Part at least of the later Friary precinct lay within the parish of St Mary in the Marsh. This parish had been granted to the Cathedral Priory at its foundation and was therefore claimed to be under the jurisdiction of the prior rather than that of the city of Norwich. The area of this parish within the Friary precinct, however, was probably quite small. Known properties on the King Street frontage lay in the parish of St Cuthbert and all the land acquired by the Greyfriars as a result of mortmain licences of 1292 and 1299 (Fig. 3.3) paid, or had paid, landgable to the city and so lay within the city's jurisdiction. The parish of St Mary in the Marsh clearly did not extend beyond the eastern half of the precinct and probably came no further south than the Dallingflete. This interpretation is supported by the early 14th-century deeds of the parish and by two slightly differing descriptions of the land granted to the Cathedral Priory, written about 1400 (NRO MC 146/52 plan 80; Hudson and Tingey 1906–10, I, 55–6). One of these, in a possible reference to the Dallingflete, refers to St Mary in the Marsh as being partly within the precinct of the Friars Minor (*i.e.* the Franciscans) 'and downwards to the water'.

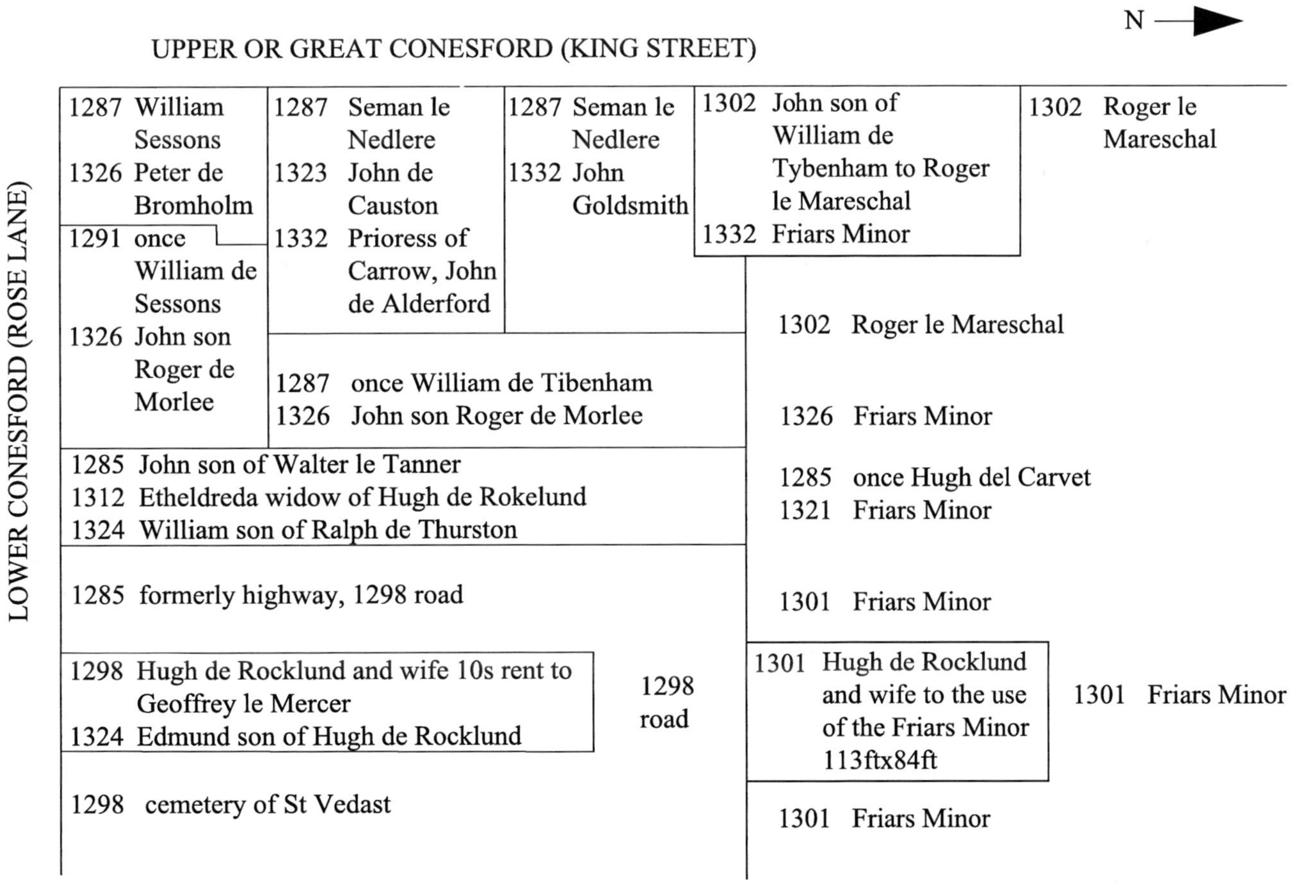

Source: NRO MC 146/52 plans 100, 115. Not to scale.

Figure 2.2 Land holdings on King Street/Rose Lane corner *c.* 1300

The rest of the eastern sector, like the properties to the east of St Vedast churchyard (NRO MC 146/52 plan 100), would have belonged to the parish of St Vedast. The jurisdiction of the prior is unlikely to have been of any practical importance once the north bank of the Dallingflete became part of the Greyfriars' precinct.

Pre-Friary land-use

The site may effectively be divided into two areas: the lower-lying eastern section, including most of the land acquired by the friars between 1226 and 1292 (Fig. 3.3), and the higher ground along the King Street frontage.

There is no direct evidence that commercial activity was displaced by the Greyfriars from the eastern part of their precinct. Mid-13th to early 14th-century deeds, however, note a significant number of tanners and possible tanners holding property east of St Faith's Lane, between the precinct and Rose Lane, and along the southern side of Rose Lane (NRO MC 146/52 plans 99–100). Another mid-13th century deed for a property next to the church of St John has among its witnesses and probable near neighbours two skinners (*pelliparii*, dealers on pelts or furs) and two tanners (*tannatores*) (NRO DCN 45/40/20), while Alexander de la Sarteryn, co-grantor of Plot I on Fig. 2.3, may have been the skinner of that name who bought a property in Norwich market in 1291 (Rye 1903, 37). It seems likely that before the arrival of the Friars Minor the lower eastern area of the precinct was partly occupied by tanners, making use of the water from the Dallingflete. The furriers (the skinners, also known as parmenters) did not need the access to water. They were sufficiently active in the area, however, for the neighbouring church to be known as St Peter Parmentergate by 1254 (Sandred and Lindström 1989, 52, 119–20).

A little more direct evidence is available for the higher ground to the west. Among the plots acquired by the friars in 1292 (Fig. 2.3) Plot L was granted by Giles le Peyntour, identified by an earlier deed as Giles le Flemming, painter (NRO DCN 45/8/3) and who, as Giles le Flemengg of Bruges, sold property in the parish of St Peter Hungate, Norwich, in 1294 (Rye 1903, 49). Plot R was granted by a possible glazier (William le Wyrly/Virly) while further south on the King Street frontage the Greyfriars acquired property owned by carpenters in 1264 (NRO DCN 45/8/1) and by a possible farrier in 1302 (Roger le Mareschal: Fig. 2.2). South of the precinct lay a needle maker (Seman le Nedlere *alias* Seman de Blitheburgh, *acuarius*, fl. 1287–92), whose property was later acquired by a possible goldsmith (John Goldsmith, fl. 1301–32) (Fig. 2.2 and NRO MC 146/52 plan 115). John could have been one of several goldsmiths called John who appear in the Norwich records of this date. In short, the Franciscan Friary may have displaced a series of artisan workshops along the King Street frontage.

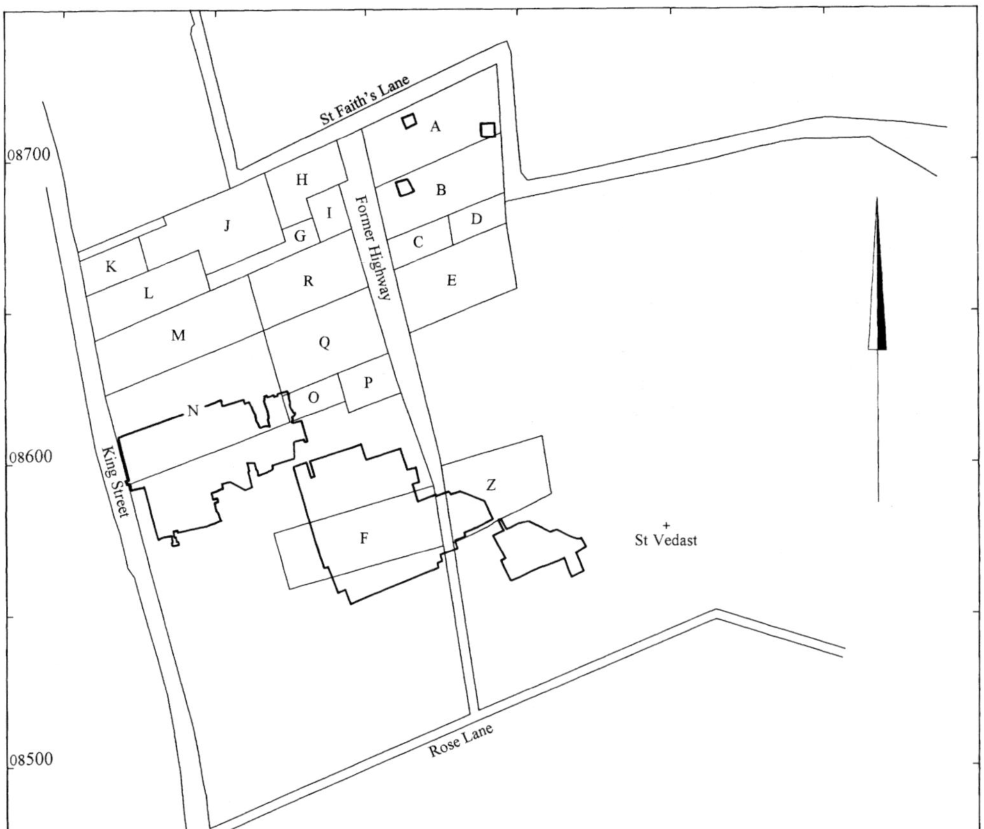

Figure 2.3 Conjectural layout of plots licensed 1292

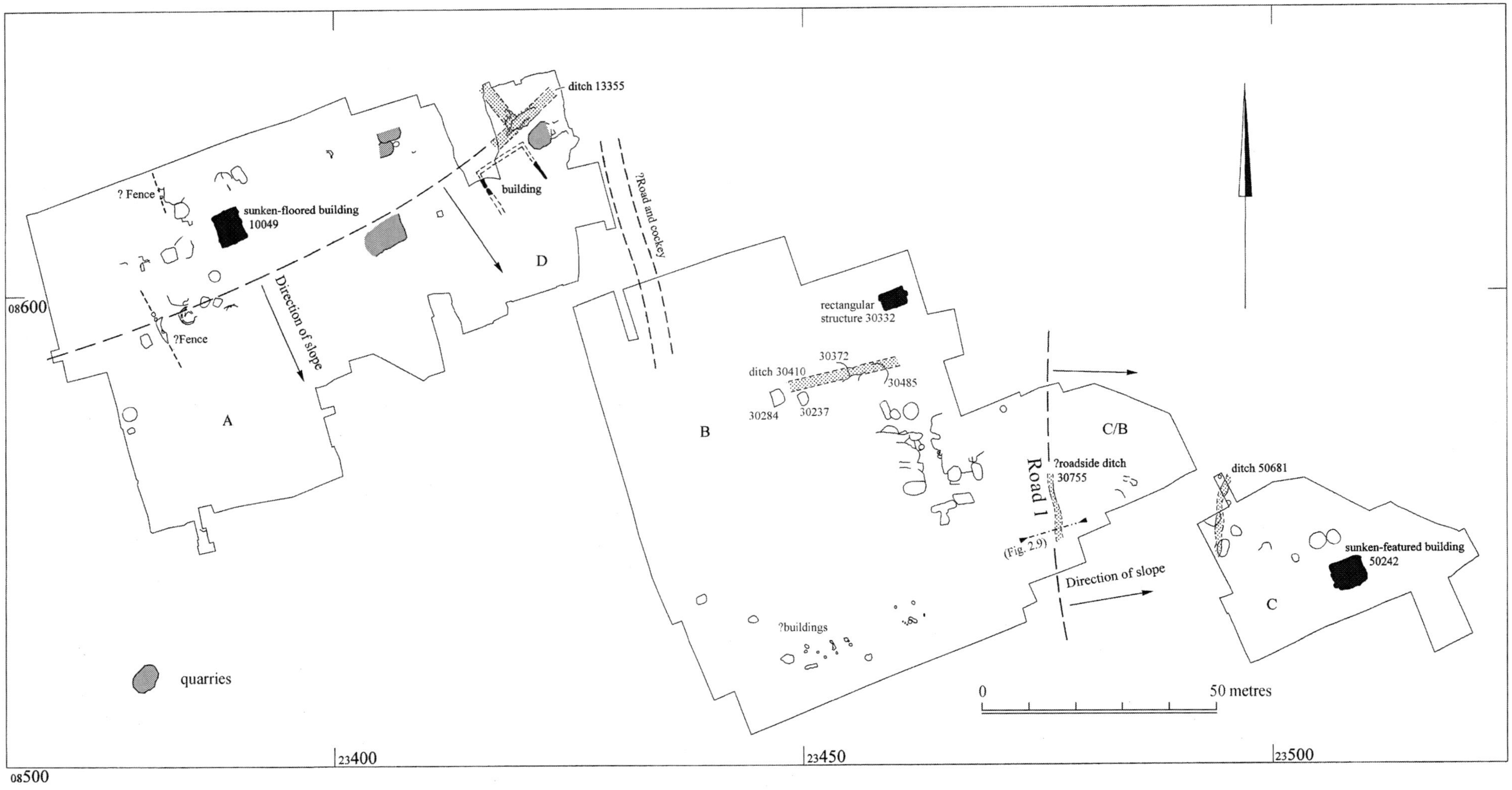

Figure 2.4 Phase plan: Late Saxon/Early Norman (10th–11th centuries

III. ARCHAEOLOGICAL EVIDENCE

Period 1: Late Saxon to Early Norman (10th–11th centuries)

(Fig. 2.4)

Summary

Features ascribed to the 10th and 11th centuries (Period 1) are divided geographically into two parts by a north-to-south boundary represented in this period by a ditch (*30755*) and later by a road (Road 1, Period 2.1). The position of this boundary corresponds with a break of the natural slope across the site. Between it and King Street to the west the ground rises gradually (Fig. 3.22). To its east the natural ground surface falls away relatively sharply and then becomes almost level. To the west, the alignment of a ditch in Area C dating to the 11th century appears to have been determined by the natural topography.

Most features of 10th- and 11th-century date investigated in the western part of the site lay in a 16m-wide strip adjacent to the northern edge of the excavation. The apparent absence of features to the south of this concentration (*i.e.* in the southern half of Area A: Fig 2.4) is misleading: here the natural ground surface falls away, becoming progressively buried by make-up deposits relating to the Friary and later episodes. This circumstance, combined with constraints upon the depth of archaeological excavation, meant that deposits of earlier medieval date were never exposed in the southern part of Area A.

The remains of at least three small buildings were found, along with the fragmentary remains of others. Located away from the frontages of plots, these may have been artisans' workshops. The distribution of production waste materials in relation to these buildings and adjacent ditched plots suggested craft specialisation. A plot adjacent to King Street, represented by a sunken-floored building and associated clusters of pits, was characterised by antlerworking and metalworking waste.

Dating the earliest activity at the site is somewhat problematic. Numismatic items include a penny of the Vikings of the Danelaw type, which was probably lost shortly after 895 (SF756: Blackburn, Chapter 5.II) and was found apparently residually in a sunken-floored building. A small assemblage of Middle Saxon pottery

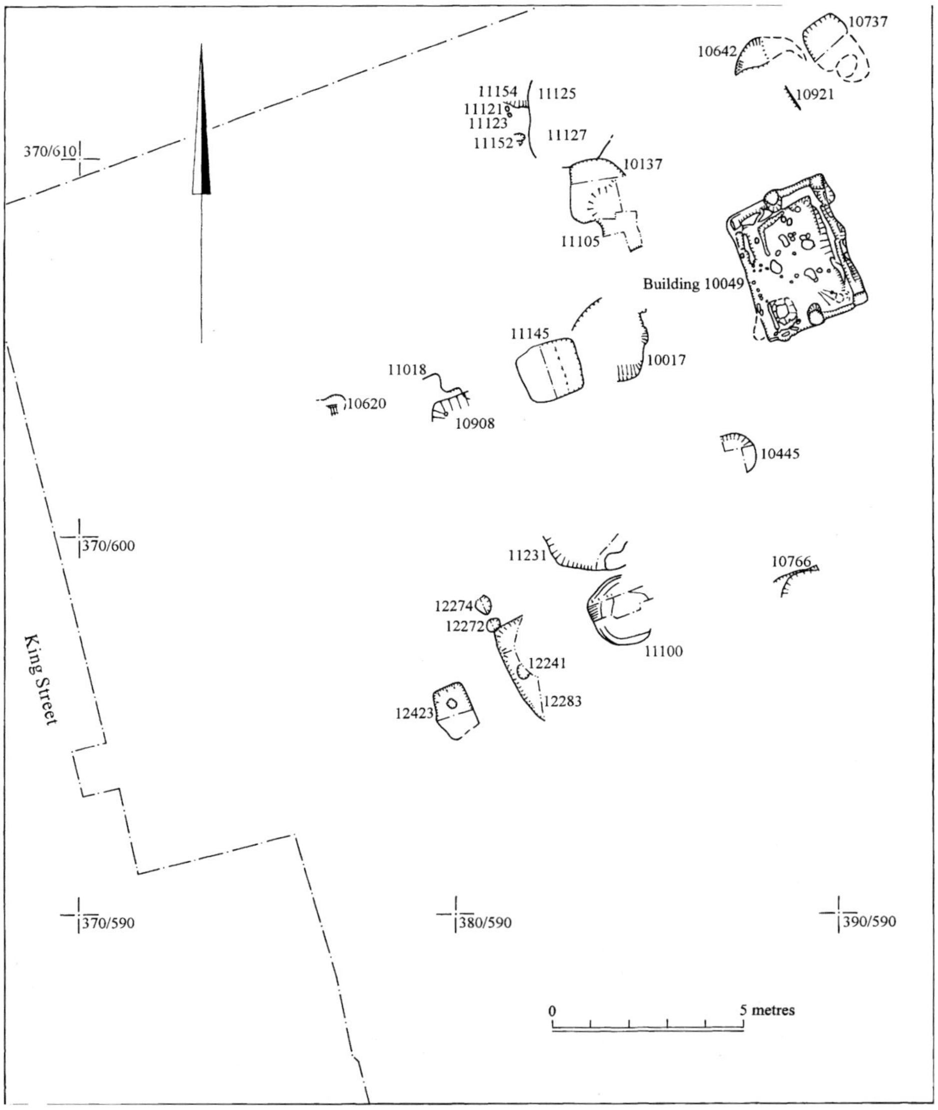

Figure 2.5 Period 1: features adjacent to King Street frontage, Area A (10th–11th centuries)

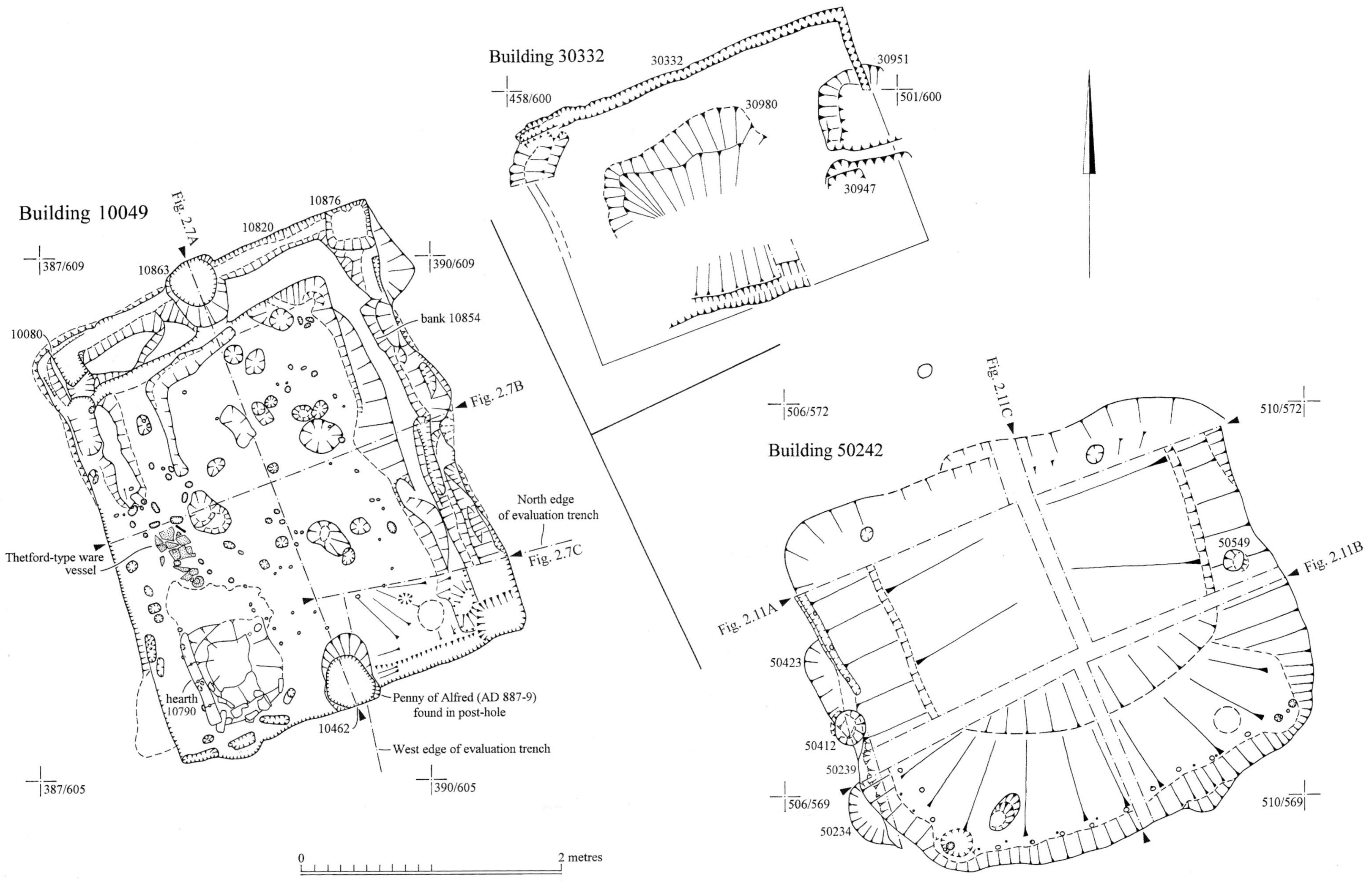

Figure 2.6 Three 10th–11th-century buildings, Areas A, B and C

Category	*Material*	*Description*	Qty	SF no.(s)	Context(s)	Fig. /Plate
Structural	Stone	Fragment	2			
	Iron	Nail	16			
Metal-working	Copper alloy	Fragment	2			
	Lead	Fragment	1			
	Iron	Fragment	1			
	Ceramic	Crucible with silver residue	2		10619, 10725	
Antler-working	Antler	Wedge	1	259	10337	
		Fragment	4			
Textile-working	Antler	Pin	1	379/596	10619	Fig. 5.33
	Bone	Pin	1	269	10337	Fig. 5.33
			2	615	10619	
			1	613	10725	
			1	1210	10827	
			1	616	10856	Fig. 5.33
	Ceramic	Spindle-whorl (bi-conical)	1	594	10619	Fig. 5.35
			2	590, 595	10725	Fig. 5.35
Food processing	Lava	Quernstone	Multiple			
	Stone	Mortar	1	1041	10725	
Trade	Silver	Penny: Alfred (AD 887–9)	1	756	10457	Plate 5.5
Household equipment	Antler	Tube: spacer?	1	760	10725	Fig. 5.79
	Iron	Knife	1	844	10725	
	Lead	Vessel repair plug	1	1593	10479	Fig. 5.74
	Stone	Hone	1	617	10856	
			1	1683	10875	
	Stone	Lamp	1	1041	10725	Fig. 5.48
Dress accessory	Shale	Bracelet	1	422/83/593	10337/10618/10725	Fig. 5.85
	Glass	Bead	1	1439	10726	Fig. 5.82
Unknown function	Iron	Unidentified objects	5			
	Bone	Unidentified object	1			

Table 2 Small Finds recovered from building *10049* (Periods 1 and 2)

Plate 2.1 Sunken-floored building *10049* (Area A)

Plate 2.2 Hearth *10790* in south-west corner of sunken-floored building *10049* (Area A)

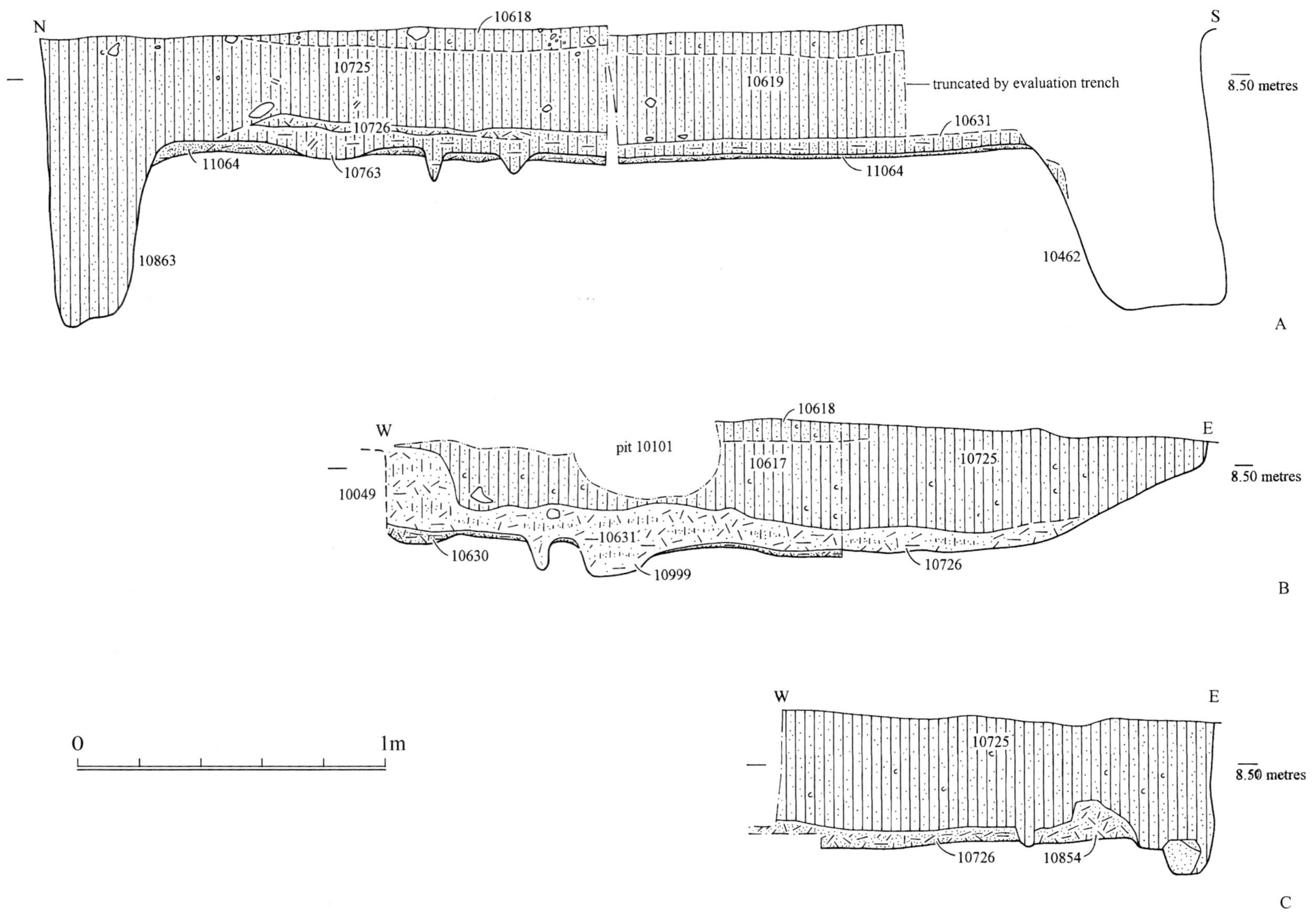

Figure 2.7 Period 1: sections through building *10049*, Area A (10th–11th centuries)

Plate 2.3 Two Thetford-type ware vessels found within building *10049* (Area A)

was recovered from Period 1 deposits (8 sherds, 0.219kg: Goffin, Chapter 5.II and Table 22). Despite the notable presence of these and other categories of finds attributable to the 9th century (see Discussion, below, 40), the ceramics present indicate that occupation became firmly established at the site during the 10th or 11th centuries, with a local *floruit* in the 11th century. Over 28kg of Late Saxon pottery was recovered from features and deposits attributed to this period. This assemblage was dominated by Thetford-type wares (TTW) of 10th- and 11th-century type, supplemented by other Late Saxon and early medieval fabrics: amongst the TTW, forms spanning the 10th and 11th centuries are common at the site, although 11th-century 'high level' forms are more common than 10th-century types (Lentowicz, Chapter 5.III).

Archaeological sequence

Building *10049*

(Figs 2.4, 2.5, 2.6 and 2.7; Pls 2.1–2.3)

The most significant archaeological feature ascribed to this period was a rectangular building (*10049*) which was 3.5m long (north-to-south) by 2.9m wide and was cut into the natural sand. This structure lay some 19m to the east of the King Street frontage. It was further defined by a series of perimeter post-holes and slots, while a succession of hearths and other internal deposits represented its use. Its base occurred at *c.* 8.25m OD and its sides were truncated at a maximum elevation of 8.70m OD. The main structural elements of the building were two single, oval post-holes, each about 350mm in diameter, at the centre of each of the shorter, northern and southern edges; these were supplemented by smaller, square post-holes at the corners (Fig. 2.6, Pl. 2.1). The post-hole in the south-eastern corner had been lost through truncation in the 12th century. The arrangement of post-holes indicates that the more substantial, centrally placed uprights carried a ridge beam. The nature of the walls is debatable. They were represented by a series of slots, some continuous and others discrete, occurring on all four sides of the rectangular cut.

The inner edges of the linear slots that occurred along the eastern and northern sides of the feature were formed by banks of compacted chalky sand. A further bank, about 1m long, lay at the north end of the western side of the building cut. These deposits, which have been attributed to the initial phase of construction of the building, appeared to be the result of material having been embanked against the base of walls, presumably to prevent inward slumping. The shape of the slots would be consistent with their having contained horizontal planks (set on edge). Additionally, the top of these banks was flat and conformed to a uniform level. This gave the impression that they supported a floor, an assertion that is further supported by the evidence, most clearly seen in the northern part of the feature, that the banks were themselves revetted internally. At the base of the cut, the slumped profiles of the interior banks suggested that the revetting had collapsed. A basal hearth was installed in the south-western corner of the structure (see below), apparently following the removal of the collapsed material. Its occurrence directly on the base of the cut certainly indicates that any raised timber floor had either been removed or did not extend into this part of the structure.

Use of the structure, following the putative removal of the supported floor, was represented by a complex sequence of hearth constructions, rake-outs and surfaces, and a series of small, discrete cuts. The hearth manifested itself in three clearly identifiable phases of construction and rebuilding. Its initial extent was some 1.1m north-to-south by 0.7m. The area of the fire was bounded on three sides by a raised edge formed by

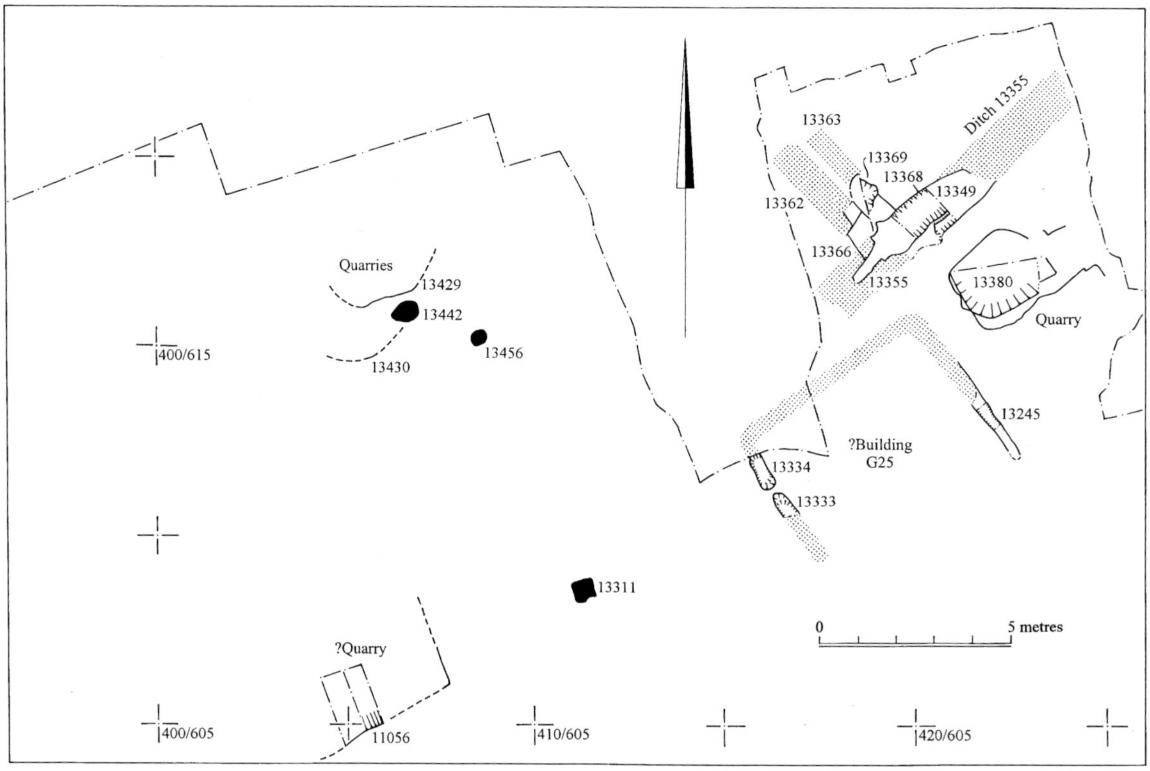

Figure 2.8 Period 1: features, Areas A and D (10th–11th centuries)

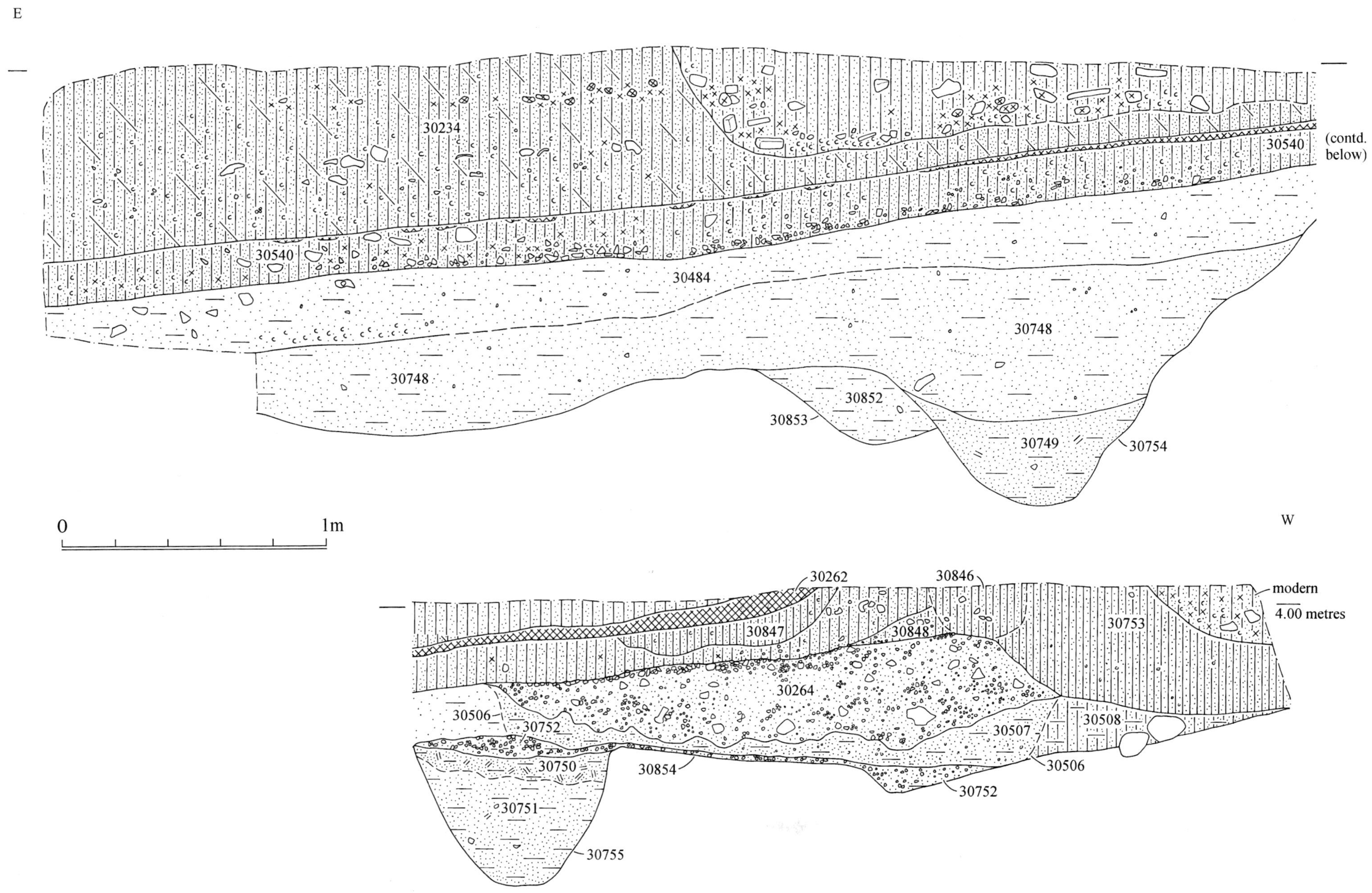

Figure 2.9 North-facing section through road and roadside ditches and landscaping layers associated with the laying out of the Friary precinct, Area B

re-used Roman bonding tiles set in clay (Pl. 2.2). The Roman tile is discussed by Huddle and Kemp (Chapter 5.I, 'Ceramic building material'). This edge was more substantial on the west and south sides, possibly reflecting measures taken to protect the walls of the building from the heat. The remaining north side of the hearth was open and occupied by a succession of ashy layers which represented repeated raking-out. In its later phases, the structure of the hearth was less regular.

The significance of the various holes in the floor of the building is unclear. Although a rectangular grouping of larger cuts, including one that was L-shaped in plan, occupied the northern half of the floor, most of the holes seemed to be randomly distributed. Such a pattern may have resulted cumulatively from the emplacement and repositioning of internal fittings, spits, trestles or even looms.

Underlying disuse deposits (Period 2.1) were two articulated clusters of sherds of Thetford-type ware representing a type AB1 jar and a type AE1/AD1 handled jar or pitcher (Pl. 2.3; Fig. 5.56 f and g). The central post-hole on the south edge (*10462*) contained a silver penny of Alfred the Great which dated to c. AD 880–95 (SF756; see Blackburn, Chapter 5.II), although this appears to have been residual and pottery indicates mid–late 11th-century usage (Lentowicz, Chapter 5.II; Fig. 5.56). Most of the other diagnostic artefacts occurred in fills representing the disuse of the building (Period 2.1). These include bone needles, ceramic spindle whorls, a shale bracelet and antler-working waste, and are generally consistent with domestic activity and craftworking (Table 2). The artefact assemblage from the building is summarised in Table 2, while pottery is illustrated in Fig. 5.56.

Pits associated with building *10049*

(Figs 2.4 and 2.5)

Numerous pits of varying function clustered around building *10049*. Some of the larger examples may in fact have represented further buildings. A cluster of pits to the south-west appeared to have conformed to a common southern boundary. A rectangular, sheer-sided pit (*12283*), aligned roughly parallel to the sunken-floored building, lay some 9.5m to the south-west of the structure and 10.5m from the King Street frontage. At least 2.8m in length, only its western side and part of the northern edge survived; its maximum possible width was *c.* 1.6m, with a maximum recorded depth of 1.25m. Given its elongated shape, the feature probably served as a quarry, although its infilling involved the disposal of both cess and household waste. A number of cross-context joins amongst the pottery finds indicate that infilling was fairly rapid. Two groups of sherds of a Thetford-type ware jar were found in one of the fills (*12275*), together with fragments of chalk. This material seemed to represent a single pot containing chalk or lime, presumably used in association with disposal of cess. Other finds from this pit include three fragments of sawn antler and an iron heckle tooth.

A line of three post-holes (*12241*, *12272* and *12274*) post-dated the infilling of the quarry and lay roughly parallel to its western edge. These may represent a fence delineating a boundary between properties. Its line was broadly parallel to that of another fence represented by four post-holes to the north-east (see below).

Lying 1.2m to the west of the quarry pit, and aligned parallel to it, was a rectangular pit (*12423*) measuring 1.4m by 1m wide and 0.8m deep. An ovate post-hole (*12428*) was recorded in its base to the north of centre. The feature appears to have been a cess-pit, the post-hole possibly representing a vertical timber support for a frame. An antler wedge was recovered from the pit fill.

The northern edge of what may have been a second sunken-floored building (*10766*) lay *c.* 6m due south of building *10049*. Its flat base occurred at 8.06m OD, and the feature had been truncated at 8.66m OD.

Two apparently circular pits (*11231* and *11100*), whose straight south-west edges appeared to be co-aligned, were partially investigated. Their substantial depths (1.6 and 2.5m respectively), established by augering, suggest that they were cess-pits.

A circular pit (*10455*), *c.* 1.2m in diameter, lay about 2.5m to the south-west of building *10049*. A dark stain observed around the pit's edge may indicate a timber lining.

Another line of features lay to the north, immediately to the west of building *10049* and conforming to the alignment of its southern edge in an east-to-west row. The line included two substantial pits (*10620* and *11145*) and a possible structure (*10902*/*10908*/*11018*). The depth of the pits indicates that they, too, were probably cess-pits, perhaps initially dug in order to quarry sand. Pit *11145* lay 4.75m to the west of the building. Its fills contained large quantities of domestic waste including pottery, over 7kg of animal bone and 0.9kg of shell, as well as significant amounts of slag and brick. Its depth (2.3m) suggested that it was originally a cess-pit, which became infilled with domestic refuse on disuse. A suggestion that cut *10908 etc.* represented the base of a building rests upon these features' individual morphologies, their overall arrangement, and their association with a rammed chalk linear feature (*10902*: not illus.).

Closer to building *10049* but continuing the same line, a sub-circular cut 2.2m in diameter (*10017*) was found to have been dug to a depth of over 5m (to below 2.1m OD), which might suggest that it served as a well. (See note below, however, on the probable altered level of water table in relation to building *50242*: below, 22) Occurring 2.65m to the west of the building, and respecting the projected alignment of the southern edge of that structure, the pit appears to have been associated with the sunken-floored building. Its upper fills were probably of 13th-century date (Period 2.3), indicating infilling immediately prior to the construction of Friary-related walls.

Four pits (*10137*, *11105*, *11125* and *11127*) lay *c.* 2.5m to the north-west of building *10049* and appeared to have been bounded to the west by a fence-line (see below). They contained little datable material and are ascribed to this phase on stratigraphic grounds. The latest pit (*10137*) was ovate in plan and was established by augering to be *c.* 3.4m deep. Only this pit contained any finds (pottery, animal bone and slag); it appears to have been a cess-pit in which domestic rubbish was deposited when it became disused.

A north-west to south-east line of three post-holes, with a fourth offset to the east (*11121*, *11123*, *11152* and *11154*), was recorded in a slot trench cut into the floor of the Mann Egerton basement near to the north edge of the excavation. This probably represented a plot boundary marked by a fence, roughly parallel with another line to the south (described above).

Three pits (*10642*, *10737* and *10921*), the last of these almost entirely truncated, were recorded to the north of the sunken-floored building. Pit *10737* contained primary and secondary waste from antlerworking, suggesting that this activity took place in the plot within which the pit was located.

Two features lay isolated to the south-west along the putative 10th–11th century King Street frontage. A small pit (*10659*) was found *c.* 2.5m to the east of the postulated line of the contemporary street, with a broadly contemporary cess-pit (*12000*) containing alternating fills of chalk and dark grey silt lying further to the north.

Features to the north of ditch *13355*

(Figs 2.4 and 2.8)

Two small early ditches in Area D (*13366* and *13368*), both aligned north-west to south-east, had been cut to the south-east by a large boundary ditch (*13355*: see below). Pottery in the fill of the easternmost ditch dated to the 11th century. A pair of post-holes (*13362* and *13363*) just to the north, cutting into and co-aligned with a linear gully-like feature (*13361*/*13369*), may represent the remnants of a timber building standing immediately to the north of the major ditch.

Two quarry pits (*13429* and *13430*) containing 10th–11th century pottery occurred in the north-west corner of Area D. Both had been infilled with domestic refuse. Adjacent to them were two isolated ovate post-holes (*13442* and *13456*) which probably represent structures contemporary with the buildings identified further east.

Boundary ditch *13355*

(Figs 2.4 and 2.8)

A substantial ditch aligned south-west to north-east (*13355*) was recorded over a length of 4.5m. It appeared to follow the brow of the south-facing slope, reflecting the natural contour, although the degree to which the slope had continued to the north prior to surface truncation is unknown. This truncation had begun with the laying out of the Friary, although construction of a 19th-century cellar had in turn removed Friary ground surfaces. The boundary implied by this ditch seemed noticeably at variance with the disposition of pre-Friary pits, ditches and structures lying to the west (*e.g.* building *10049*), perhaps indicating the manner in which plot boundaries respected local variations of the terrain. The westward extent of the ditch is unknown, although it may have continued right through to the King Street frontage. The pottery finds suggest that it became disused in the 11th century.

Building and pits to the south of ditch *13355*

(Figs 2.4 and 2.8)

To the south of ditch *13355* was a building consisting of two parallel beam-slots (*13333*/*13334* and *13245*), *c.* 5.75m apart, whose alignments were perpendicular to that of the ditch. The external width of the building was 6.1m (20ft), although its north-west to south-east dimension is unknown since the beam-slots did not survive to their full extent. The western beam-slot comprised two separate sections, their termini being only *c.* 170mm apart. This narrow gap may represent the location of a doorway, the jambs being set some way along the slots. Pottery from the beam-slot fills dates to the 11th century.

Immediately to the east of the building was a quarry pit (*13380*), measuring 2m by 2m and conforming to the alignment of both the adjacent ditch and building. Domestic refuse dumped into it comprised large quantities of pottery (1.18kg) and animal bone (3.41kg), together with tile and oyster shells. The pottery suggests that it was finally infilled in the early 12th century. An isolated square post-hole (*13311*), measuring 0.59m across, lay to the west.

To the south-west lay a large rectangular pit (*11056*), recorded over an east-to-west distance of 3.35m. It may have been in excess of 5m long, however, suggesting use as a quarry. Its alignment tallied closely with that of contemporary features in the vicinity. Pottery from its fills implies an 11th-century date.

Buildings and pits to the west of ditch *30755*
(Figs 2.4 and 2.6)
A rectangular structure (*30332*, *30947*, *30951* and *30980*) lay *c.* 10m to the west of north-to-south ditch *30755*, which may have lain at the side of the forerunner of the excavated road (Road 1: Period 2.1). The building was 2.8m long by 1.9m wide, and represented by slots for timbers and a post-hole (Fig. 2.6). A shallow cut (*30980*) within the structure contained quantities of antlerworking waste (Huddle, Chapter 5.II, 'Antlerworking'), probably associated with its use. Being too small to have been habitable, the structure was probably a workshop; its position relative to the road suggests that it lay within the back yard of a tenement. The full extent of this yard is suggested by a linear cluster of pits from which crucibles and antler waste were recovered.

Part of an east-to-west aligned linear cut (*30410*), recorded over a 1.3m length, was stratigraphically the earliest feature in a recorded series. This ditch possibly defined the boundary between adjacent tenements. Its truncation by pits indicated that it had become disused when these plots were subsequently amalgamated, or when the boundary between them shifted.

The location of four pits into a narrow east-to-west strip suggests that they lay within a yard associated with building *30332* to the north-east. Two cess-pits (*30237* and *30284*) lay *c.* 5m to the west of the surviving section of ditch *30410*. The former was oval in plan, measured 1.44m by 1.23m east-to-west and was 0.82m deep, and appears to have been used in the mid-11th century. The latter, *c.* 1.5m to the west, was rectangular in plan and 1.6m long (north-to-south). The fills of both pits contained quantities of pottery and animal bone, indicating the deposition of domestic waste.

Two large pits (*30372* and *30485*) had been cut into ditch *30410*. The former was *c.* 2.1m in diameter and 2.25m deep. Its alternating sequence of organic brown and clean sandy fills, together with the degree of subsidence observed and consequent downward distension of filling deposits within it, indicated that this was a cess-pit. Pit *30485* was similar in proportions (measuring 3.2m long) although its fills were significantly different in character and had been subject to burning. This suggests that the pit had been used in an industrial/craft process.

Numerous other pits of 10th–11th century date lay to the south of ditch *30410* (Fig. 2.4). In the south-western part of Area B there were numerous cut features, including post-holes that conceivably represented up to four separate buildings.

Ditch *30755*
(Figs 2.4 and 2.9)
Ditch *30755*, aligned north-to-south, was recorded in Area B/CB both in plan and in section (Fig. 2.9). It represented a property division forming part of the earliest boundary system, dating to the 10th–11th centuries. It had become infilled by the 12th century, when a road was constructed above it on a similar alignment. The limited depth of its profile (0.53m) suggested severe truncation. There was no evidence for the existence of any contemporary road adjacent to it, although this may simply reflect the degree of truncation hereabouts. Indeed, it seems probable that any associated road would have lain immediately to the west of the ditch, the position of which coincided with a change in the slope of the natural ground surface. To the east, the ground fell away relatively steeply before flattening out.

Early pits and post-holes
(Fig. 2.4 and 2.10)
Three pits clustered in the north-west corner of Area C (*50493*, *50448* and *50458*) were dated by pottery to the 11th century. These were the earliest features in this area and represent its use prior to its division by a ditch (*50681 etc.*). No boundaries to the plot within which the cluster of pits lay were identified. To the north of the pit group was a pair of post-holes (*50678* and *50683*).

Four other pits (*50689*, *50691*, *50693* and *50695*) lay to the north-west of a sunken-featured building (*50242*: see below). Some association between the pits and the structure is suggested by their contemporaneity (based upon pottery dating) and their proximity to each other. All four pits had been cut by a later ditch (*50665*).

Ditch *50681*
(Fig. 2.10)
A later 11th-century ditch (*50520*/*50402*/*50681*), aligned broadly north-to-south, cut the series of pits in the north-western corner of Area C. This may have delineated the eastern limit of plots lying between it

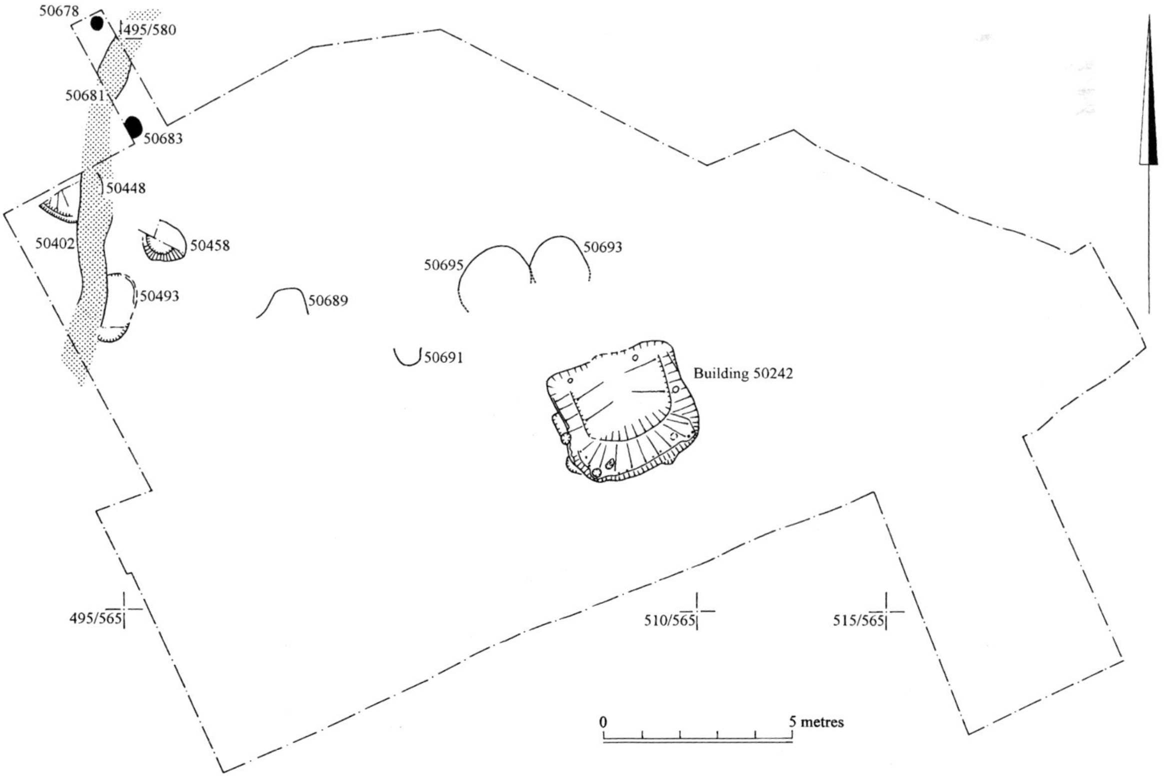

Figure 2.10 Period 1, features, Area C, including building *50242* (10th–11th century)

Category	*Material*	*Description*	*Qty*	*SF no.*	*Context(s)*	*Fig.*
Structural	Iron	Nail	6			
Antler-working	Antler	Fragment	1			
Textile-working	Bone	Pin	2	291, 591	50263	
	Ceramic	Spindle-whorl (spherical)	1	509	50263	Fig. 5.35
	Iron	Heckle tooth	1	480	50263	Fig. 5.31
Food processing	Lava	Quernstone fragments	Multiple			
Furnishing	Iron	Hasp	1	958	50263	Fig. 5.46
Dress accessory	Copper alloy	Dress pin (Middle Saxon)	1	25	50258	Fig. 5.83
Unknown function	Iron	Unidentified objects	28			

Table 3 Small Finds recovered from building *50242* (Period 1)

and ditch *30755* to the west, as well as the western boundary of the plot containing building *50242*.

Building *50242*

(Figs 2.6, 2.10 and 2.11; Pl. 2.4)

A roughly rectangular construction cut (*50242*), 3.6m long, 3m wide and 0.65m deep, was recorded near the eastern end of Area C. The base of the feature was relatively flat, with no discernible traces of a floor surface and the sides were quite steep with a gently curving base of slope. Six main post-holes, arranged in an elongated hexagon, lay within the perimeter of the cut (Fig. 2.6). An additional post-hole, which may represent a remedial support, was found in the south-west corner of the feature. The posts placed centrally along the west and east sides of the cut (*50412* and *50549*) were the largest, and may have supported a ridge beam. An internal bank of hard-packed gravel and sand, 0.6–0.8m wide and *c.* 0.25m high, was preserved on the west and south sides of the feature. It is likely that this bank had been retained by planking, which was subsequently removed. Rows of stake-holes were found along the southern and western edges of the break of slope but none existed to the north or east. Those lying along the western edge of the structure were set within a slot. While the line of stakes lay on the outside of the two posts on the southern edge, it ran inside the location of central post-hole *50412* on the west edge. Three possible structural cuts (*50234*, *50239* and *50423*; *50423* and *50234* on Fig. 2.6) were located along the west edge of the structure. Although these features appeared to be stratigraphically earlier than the building's construction cut, their position strongly suggested an association with it.

One of the earliest features in the easternmost area of the site, this is believed to represent the remains of a building, although it is conceivable that it was a wattle-lined cess-pit similar to examples recorded in both London and Ipswich. Assuming that it was a building, the four post-holes at its corners would have held upright posts that were located within a timber frame at roof level. The two central posts at the east and west ends (the gable ends) would have supported a ridge beam. Stake-holes set inside a narrow slot indicated that the walls were of wattle construction. The location of the entrance is unclear. While a gable end would have offered the advantage of optimum vertical clearance below the roof, the only possible physical trace of an access lay on the north side where the level of the edge of the cut was locally reduced. Alternatively, however, this depression may have been produced by a later pit.

Plate 2.4 Sunken-featured building *50242* (Area C)

Fills within the structure contained significant quantities of dumped rubbish, including animal bone, pottery, burnt daub and slag. Micromorphological samples taken from these deposits indicate trampled surfaces and abandonment processes, the soils containing possible cereal processing waste and other midden materials (*50263*, *50258*; micromorphological samples 6 and 7: Macphail and Cruise, Chapter 6.VIII).

Objects recovered from the disuse fills of the feature (Fig. 2.11) included 27 iron items, a copper-alloy pin, two bone pins, a ceramic spindle whorl, four antler comb fragments (from post-hole *50549*) and seven fragments of lava quern (Table 3). Pottery indicates disuse in the 11th century (Lentowicz, Chapter 5.III and Fig. 5.57).

The edges of the feature were not degraded and the stake-holes were sharply defined, indicating that the wattle walls remained *in situ* after the structure had ceased to be used as a covered building. Similarly there was little evidence that the posts had been removed. The proximity of the water table, however, made recording difficult (Macphail and Cruise, Chapter 6.VIII). As the modern water table lies at almost the same depth as the base of the feature; it can be inferred that historically it was significantly lower.

The purpose of the building is unclear. There are no surviving surfaces or related accumulations within the structure to provide any evidence of function, and material incorporated into its fills was not necessarily locally derived. Additionally, any relationship between finds recovered from nearby, contemporary pits and activities carried out within the structure is equivocal. This building appears to stand alone within the site landscape, although it is unlikely to have been isolated originally and other similar structures may have lain to the south and east beyond the limits of the excavation.

Period 2.1: Norman/early medieval (12th century)

(Fig. 2.12)

Summary

The earliest archaeological evidence for the development of a sequence of buildings fronting King Street (Area A) has been ascribed to this period. The earliest structure in this sequence was a timber building dating to the 12th century. This was superseded by three buildings which, although broadly contemporary, were quite different in character. To the east, Late Saxon building *10049* seems to have continued in use into the early 12th century. Its alignment was respected by another rectangular cut of similar proportions further to the east, also of 12th-century date, which could also have been a building. Surrounding this new building were ditches, constituting the only recorded traces of 12th-century boundaries in the western part of the site. A linear cluster of contemporary pits lay to the south-east, following the contour of the south-facing slope; some of these had probably been dug after the buildings had been removed.

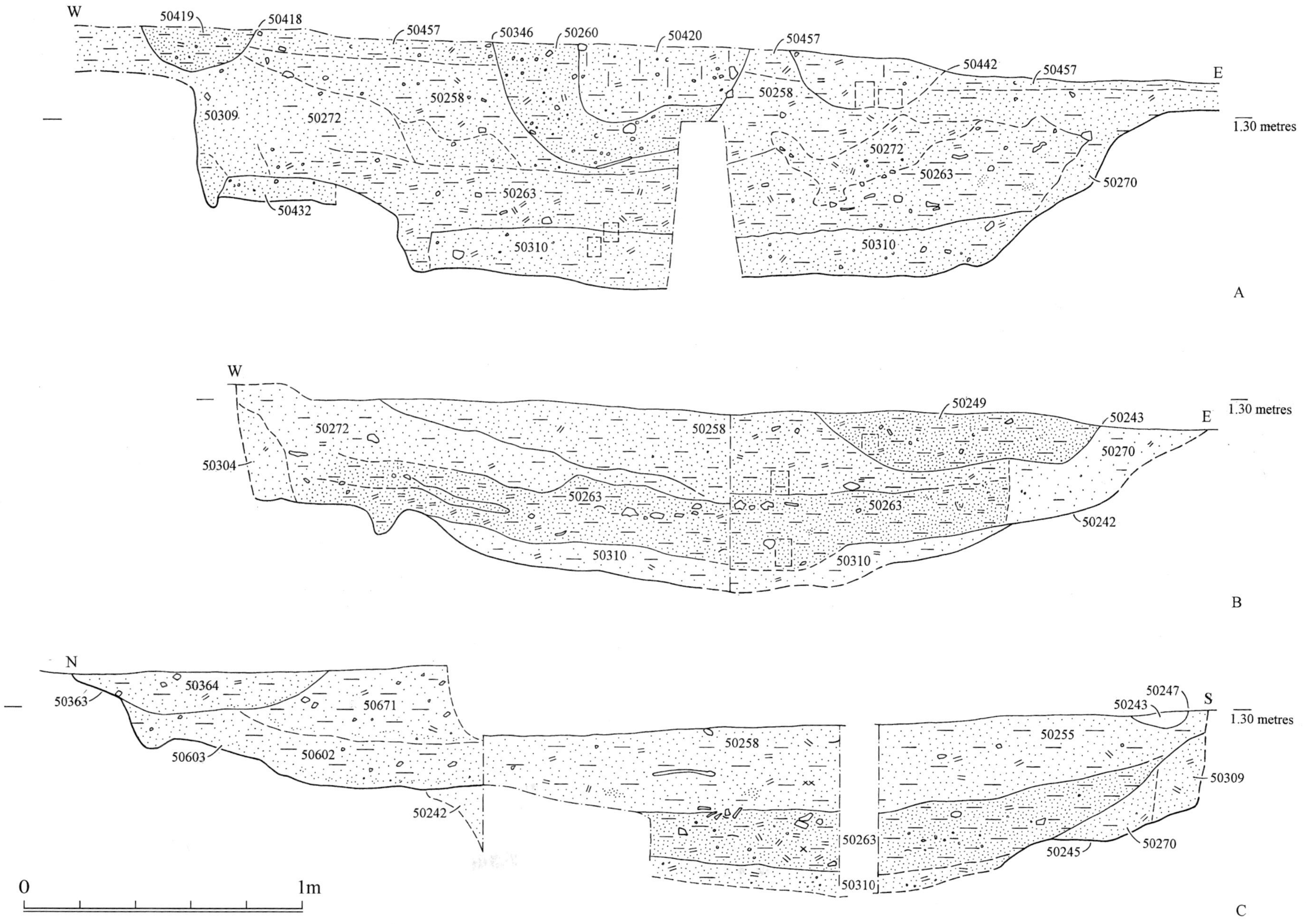

Figure 2.11 Sections through building *50242*, Area C (10th to 11th centuries)

A single grave in the southern part of Area B had been truncated by landscaping associated with construction of the south wall of the Friary precinct. Further to the east (Areas B and CB), the principal feature dating to the 12th century was a north-to-south road (Road 1) which was laid out along the line of an earlier ditch. Adjacent to this to the east was another possible road (Road 2), aligned east-to-west, accompanied by surrounding ditchworks and pits.

The 12th-century pottery assemblage recovered from deposits of this phase (over 18kg) is still dominated by TTW, but includes an increased proportion of early medieval wares with Local Medieval Unglazed ware (LMU) making its first appearance at the site (Lentowicz, Chapter 5.III). Amongst the other diagnostic finds are two coins attributable to Stephen (AD 1135–54: Davies, Chapter 5.II), found in a pit containing crucibles and indicating that metalworking continued into the 12th century.

Archaeological sequence

Timber building and surrounding features
(Fig. 2.13)
An L-shaped beam-slot with a possible westward projection clearly represented the corner of a rectangular timber building on the King Street frontage (Area A: *12454* and *12448*), which survived despite heavy truncation by a later Friary wall and by a quarry. A post-hole (*12326*), integral with the slot, was 0.5m in diameter and 0.2m deep. The beam-slot was 0.21m deep and had a mean width of 0.56m, measuring 0.92m east-to-west. Its southward return was 0.4m long.

A rectangular pit (*12461*) occurred 2.5m from the King Street frontage, just to the north of the building described above. This was 1.6m long (east-to-west) by 1.0m wide and survived to a depth of 1.3m. Some 7.0m to the east of the timber building lay another small pit (*12429*).

Building *10049* and surrounding features
(Figs 2.7 and 2.13)
The Late Saxon sunken-floored structure in the north-western part of the site (building *10049*) appears to have continued in use into the 12th century, but was superseded in the later 12th/early 13th centuries by a post-built structure cutting its disuse fills (see Period 2.2: below). Disuse of the building was represented by a fill of light brown orange sandy loam (*10617/10619/10725*: Fig. 2.7) up to 340mm thick. Finds from these deposits are summarised in Tables 2 and 3. Pottery from these fills spans the late 12th to the 14th centuries, although the stratigraphic evidence suggests that it dates to the late 12th–early 13th centuries.

Immediately adjacent to the western side of the building was a deep pit (*10090*), roughly square in plan and conforming to the alignment of the building. It was infilled with refuse including large quantities of domestic waste, comprising 1.4kg of animal bone and 12.4kg of shells (mostly oyster) in addition to quantities of 12th-century pottery, brick and tile, slag and worked stone. This feature is interpreted as a cess-pit (on the basis of its considerable depth of 4.94m). Another pit (*10814*) lay to the north of the building.

Ditches
(Figs 2.12 and 2.14)
Further evidence for activity during the 12th century was recorded towards the eastern side of Areas A and D. An east-to-west ditch (*12251*) with a V-shaped profile was found close to the north edge of the excavation. Only the southern half of the feature was exposed, but its profile suggested an original width of *c.* 2m. The ditch had clearly lain open for some time as it contained a primary fill of light grey sandy silt, overlain by a dark grey humic silt. It appears to have defined a boundary between plots, running approximately parallel to the earlier course of ditch *13355* *c.* 7m to the south (Period 1: Fig. 2.4). Given its considerable width, the ditch may have represented a major property boundary, although the limited length observed means that its relationship with other boundaries cannot be appreciated. It seems to have become infilled during the 13th century. A north-to-south ditch (*13426*), seemed to form a right-angled junction with ditch *12251*.

Running broadly parallel to ditch *13426*, some distance to its west, were two elements (*10607* and *12602*) of what was probably one single ditch. This linear cut, aligned north-west to south-east and located just over 6m to the north-east of building *10049*, offers an additional insight into plot boundaries during the 12th century.

Rectangular cut (?building)
(Fig. 2.14)
A rectangular cut, measuring 4.4m by 3.5m (*12549/13529*), lay within the angle of the junction formed by ditches *12251* and *13426*, 34m to the east of the King Street frontage. Constraints of access prevented full excavation and the eastern part of the feature had been removed by the construction of No. 11 Prince of Wales Road. Its flat base was exposed at a level of 7.6m OD on its west edge, however. Similarities with sunken-floored building *10049* in terms of size and orientation, together with the observation that the southern edges of both cuts conformed to a common line, suggest that the cut represented a further sunken-floored structure.

Pitting
(Fig. 2.14)
An area of pitting lay to the south-east of (and in some cases stratigraphically above) ditch *13426*. These features included several quarry pits (*13272*, *13410*, *13290* and *13341*). Two of these features (*13272* and *13290*) lay adjacent to each other and shared a distinctive north-west to south-east alignment, which differed only slightly from that of an earlier building, perhaps indicating that earlier plot configurations persisted here.

Eight other pits (*13331*, *13337*, *13462*, *13257*, *13225*, *13240*, *13254* and *13247*) lay further to the north-east. While the pottery from these pits ranges in date from the 10th–11th to the 12th centuries, similarities in the size and shape of these features suggest that they were associated. Two of the pits clearly post-dated a Late Saxon/Early Norman building (*13245 etc.*: Period 1), while two other pits occurred within its perimeter.

?Cemetery of the church of St John the Evangelist
(Fig. 2.12; Pl. 2.5)
An isolated grave cut (*31008*), probably of 12th-century date, was found to the west of a 13th-century boundary ditch (*30155*, Period 2.3) and immediately to the north of the later precinct wall. The grave appeared to have been contemporary with a row of post-holes, which shared its alignment. It had been severely truncated by construction of the Friary precinct wall, represented by a make-up layer (*30943*) forming a raft upon which the flint masonry had been laid. The grave contained the remains of an articulated skeleton (*30702*) of a late adolescent female exhibiting a range of pathologies (Boghi, Chapter 6.I, 'Human bone').

Four metres to the east of the grave, disarticulated elements of two other individuals (a child of 10–15 years and an adult) were recovered from a make-up deposit (*30614*: not illus.) which may have been associated with landscaping prior to construction of the south wall of the Friary precinct.

The presence of human skeletal material from three individuals, separated by a distance of no more than 5m, suggests that grave *31008* was not a lone outlier. Although their relation to the boundary defined by the precinct wall might have suggested that they were burials made within the Friary precinct, their stratigraphic position would imply rather that they were associated with the churchyard of St John the Evangelist. From this, it may be inferred that this churchyard had extended at least 70m from King Street and 59m from Rose Lane prior to the laying-out of the enlarged Friary precinct after 1292. Truncation of surrounding graves occurred either during the laying-out of the enlarged precinct (*c.* 1300) (landscaping and construction of the precinct wall) or as a result of more recent horticulture. Subsequent contraction of the cemetery westwards is indicated by the position of the later ditch (noted above).

Plate 2.5 Grave *31008*, disturbed by south wall of Friary precinct (Area B)

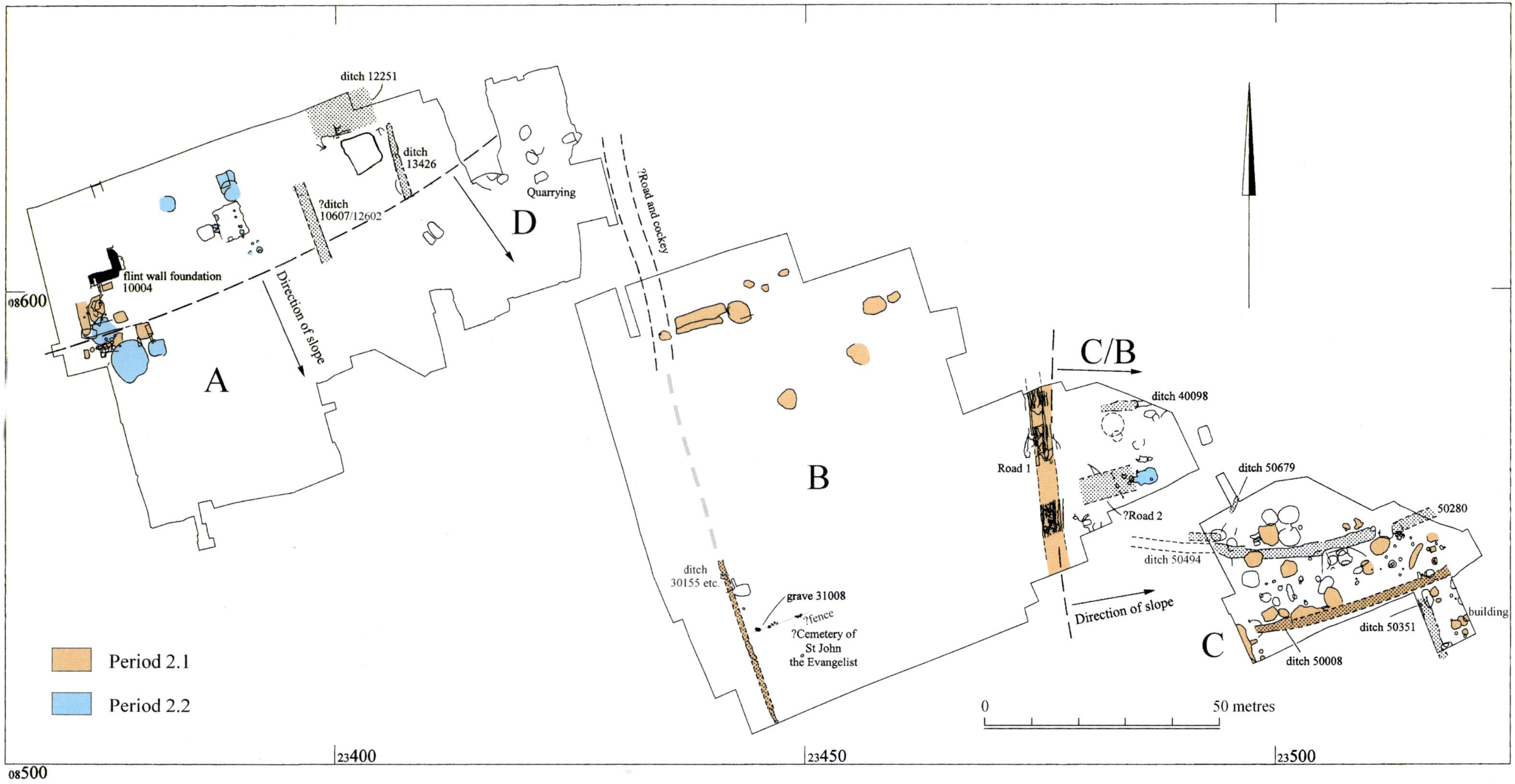

Figure 2.12 Period 2: phase plan, pre-Friary (12th–13th centuries)

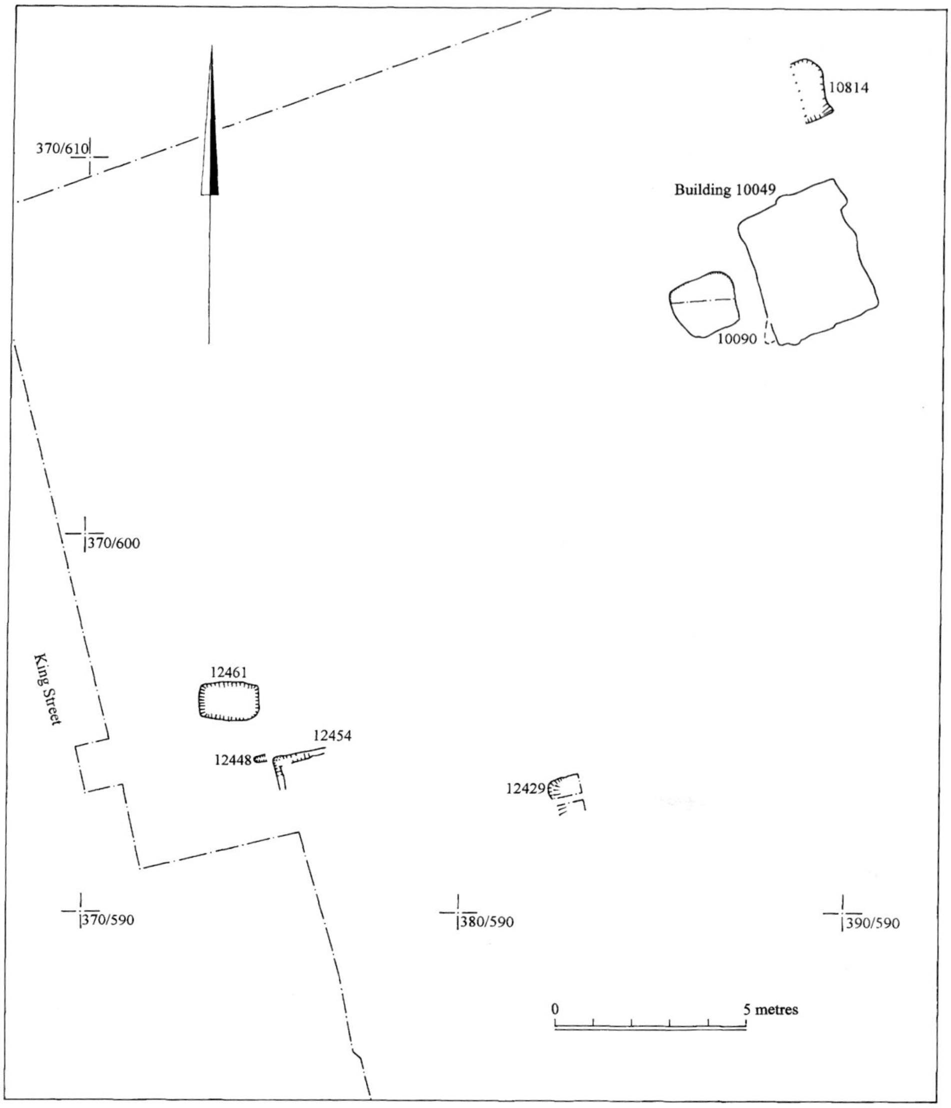

Figure 2.13 Period 2.1: features adjacent to the King Street frontage, Area A (12th century)

Road 1 and roadside ditch

(Figs 2.9, 2.12, 2.15, 2.16 and 2.20)

A north-to-south road, represented by a succession of surfaces, repairs and accumulations *c.* 2.2m wide and some 0.5m thick, spanned the 12th to 13th centuries. A total length of 16m was investigated in Area B, and the feature clearly continued beyond the northern and southern limits of the excavation. The earliest clear evidence for the road was a ditch (*30591/30754/30866/30264*: Fig. 2.9), although an earlier ditch (*30755*: Period 1) may indicate a precursor. The alignment of the roadside drain followed the scarp of the natural ground surface. Ceramics from its fills span the late 11th–late 12th centuries. Road surfaces associated with the ditch lay immediately to its west. The relationship between the road surfaces and the ditch is not certain further to the north (Fig. 2.16), where the metalling seems to have encroached upon the fills of the ditch.

The initial gravelled road surface (*30588*, *30609*, *30610* and *30752*) sealed the earlier ?roadside ditch and other features (Figs 2.9, 2.15 and 2.16). This surface, which appeared as a very compact and rather stained horizon, lay within a cutting (*30854*) into the sloping natural ground. The alignment of the road was exactly parallel to that of the underlying ditch, indicating stability of property boundaries in the vicinity. Again, ceramics present date to the late 11th to 12th centuries.

This road is assumed to be that referred to as a former highway in 1285 (Rutledge, above, 10–13); Figs 2.2 and 2.3).

?Road 2

(Figs 2.9, 2.15 and 2.17)

Pre-Friary ground surfaces and make-up layers (*40012*, *40035* and *40036*) were recorded in section in Area CB. An undulating boundary was apparent above one of them (*40012*: Fig. 2.17). Although at the time of excavation this was believed to have resulted from ploughing, similarities with the adjacent road sequence, together with the manner in which chalk lies within two of the depressions on the north side of the surface, suggests rather that it represents a further road surface that had been rutted by traffic. The surface was over 3.5m wide. Although its precise alignment could not be determined, this putative east-to-west lane would have formed a junction with Road 1, its surface appearing to be flush and contemporaneous with road surface *30752* (Fig. 2.9). The overall profile exhibits a distinct general camber, falling most markedly at its southern edge. This road would appear to equate with that documented as having led to the church of St Vedast (Rutledge, above, 10).

Ditches (east of Road 1)

(Figs 2.10, 2.12, 2.15 and 2.18)

A complex sequence of boundary ditches was established to the east of Road 1 (Fig. 2.12). To the east of this road and north of possible Road 2 an east-to-west aligned ditch (*40098/40150*) was traced for a length of over 5m. Pottery from its fills indicated that the ditch became disused in the 12th century. The ditch was perpendicular to Road 1 and parallel to Road 2, implying that it represented a boundary of an adjoining plot.

Late Saxon/Early Norman (Period 1) ditch *50402* in Area C (see Fig. 2.10) was cut by another ditch (*50492/50403/50679*, Fig. 2.18)

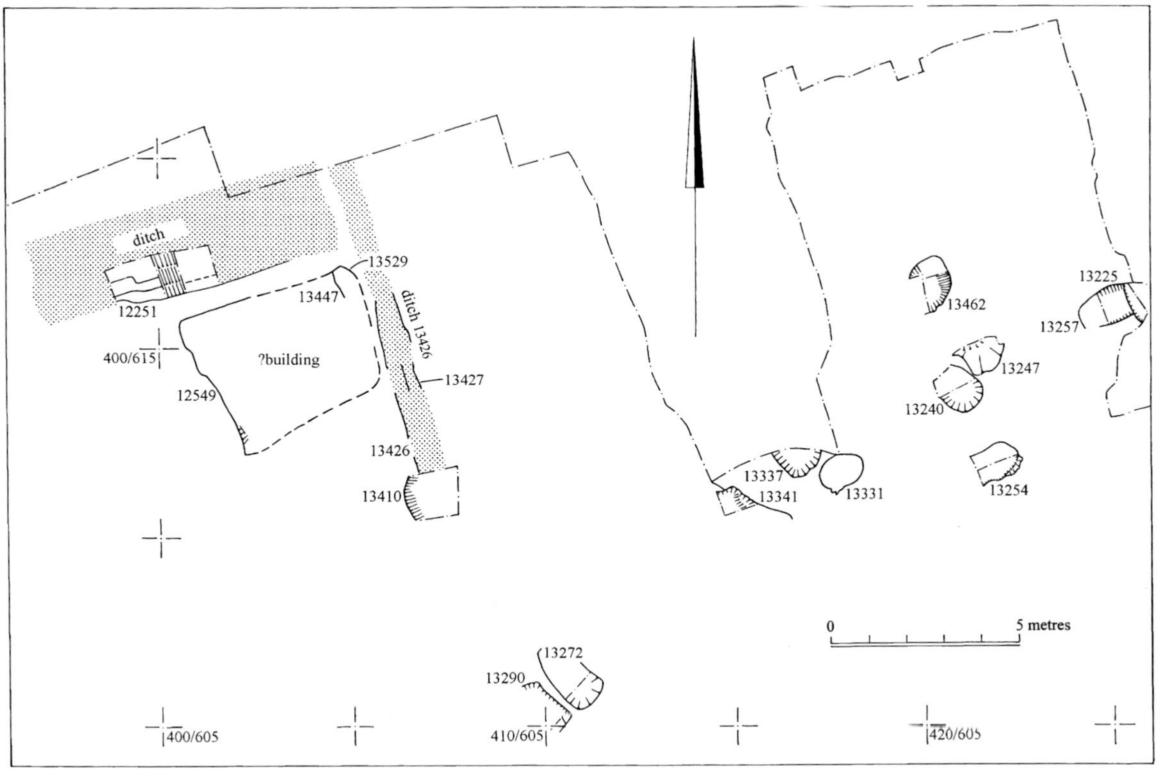

Figure 2.14 Period 2.1: features, Areas A and D (12th century)

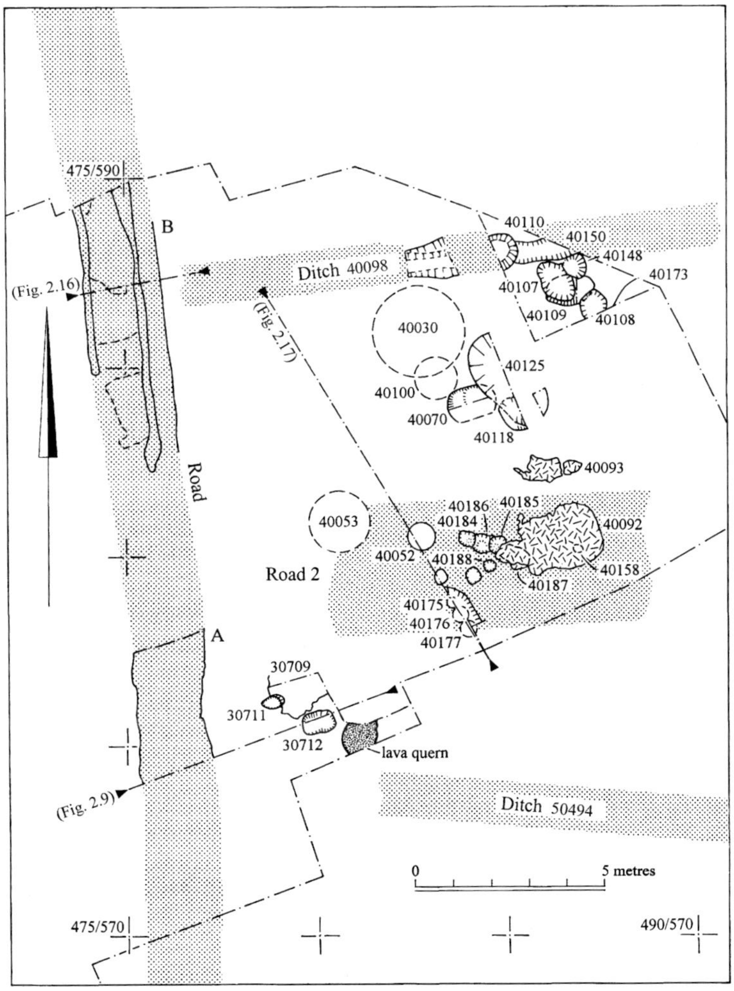

Figure 2.15 Periods 2.1–2.3: Road 1 and features to its east, Areas B and CB

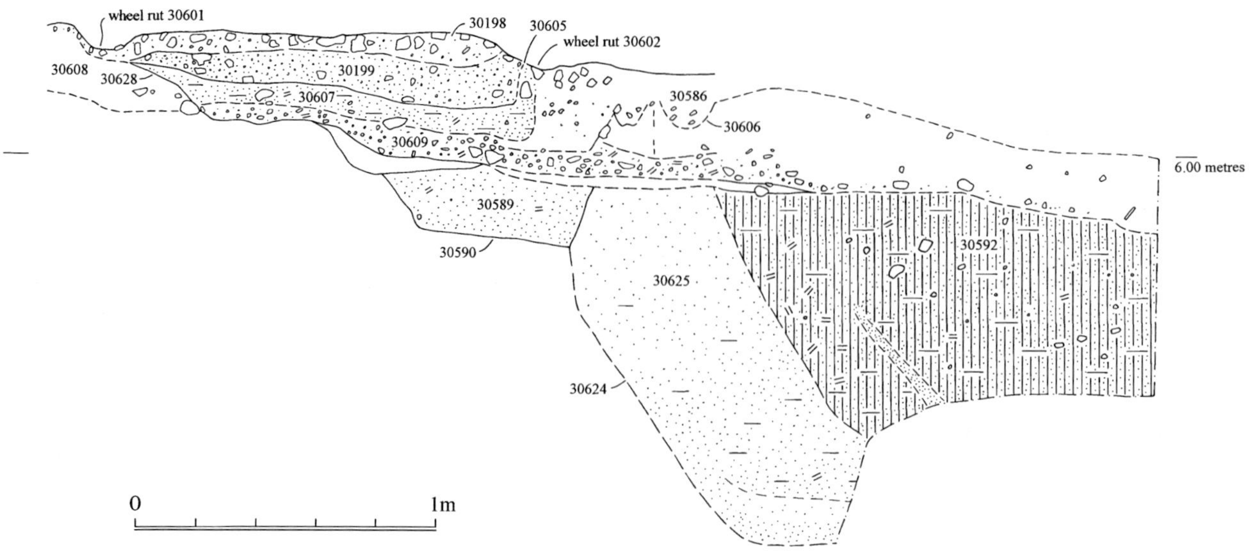

Figure 2.16 South-facing section through Road 1 and sequence of roadside ditches, Areas B and CB

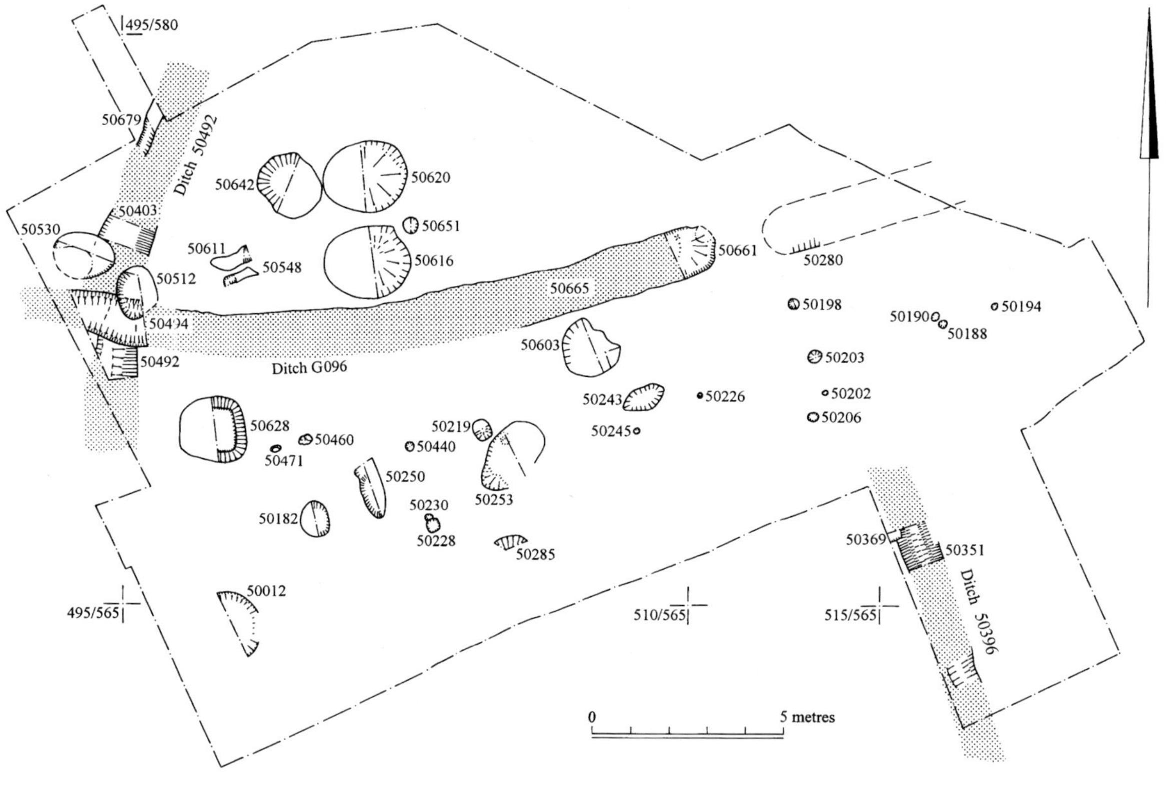

Figure 2.18 Period 2.1: features, Area C (12th century)

immediately to its west. Dating to the 12th century, this probably defined the eastern limit of plots coming off the east side of the road. The boundary shift of up to 1.5m appears to have occurred over a period of about half a century.

This boundary was cut across in turn by a slightly curving ditch (*50494*/*50661*/*50665*), aligned approximately west-to-east and traced for 17m from the western edge of Area C (Fig. 2.18). Its eastern end would have coincided with the line of a north-to-south running ditch (*50351*, see below), which may have been contemporaneous. Some 2m to the east of the east end of ditch *50661* was another cut (*50280*/*50505*) which may have formed a continuation of the same boundary. Ceramics from the feature are of 11th–early 12th century date; some at least are likely to be residual.

The projected line of another ditch to the south-east (*50396*/*50351*) appeared to respect the end of ditch *50665*, to which it ran at a right-angle. The northern terminus of ditch *50351* was not defined (but apparently occurred close to the junction with that of later east-to-west ditch *50008*: see below). The 5.5m-wide gap between the two ditches may reflect a point of access to a field defined by the ditches, or might indicate that there was a routeway immediately to the south of the curving ditch.

The relationship between the ditches and many of the surrounding pits is uncertain. Pottery recovered from ditch *50994* indicates a 12th- or

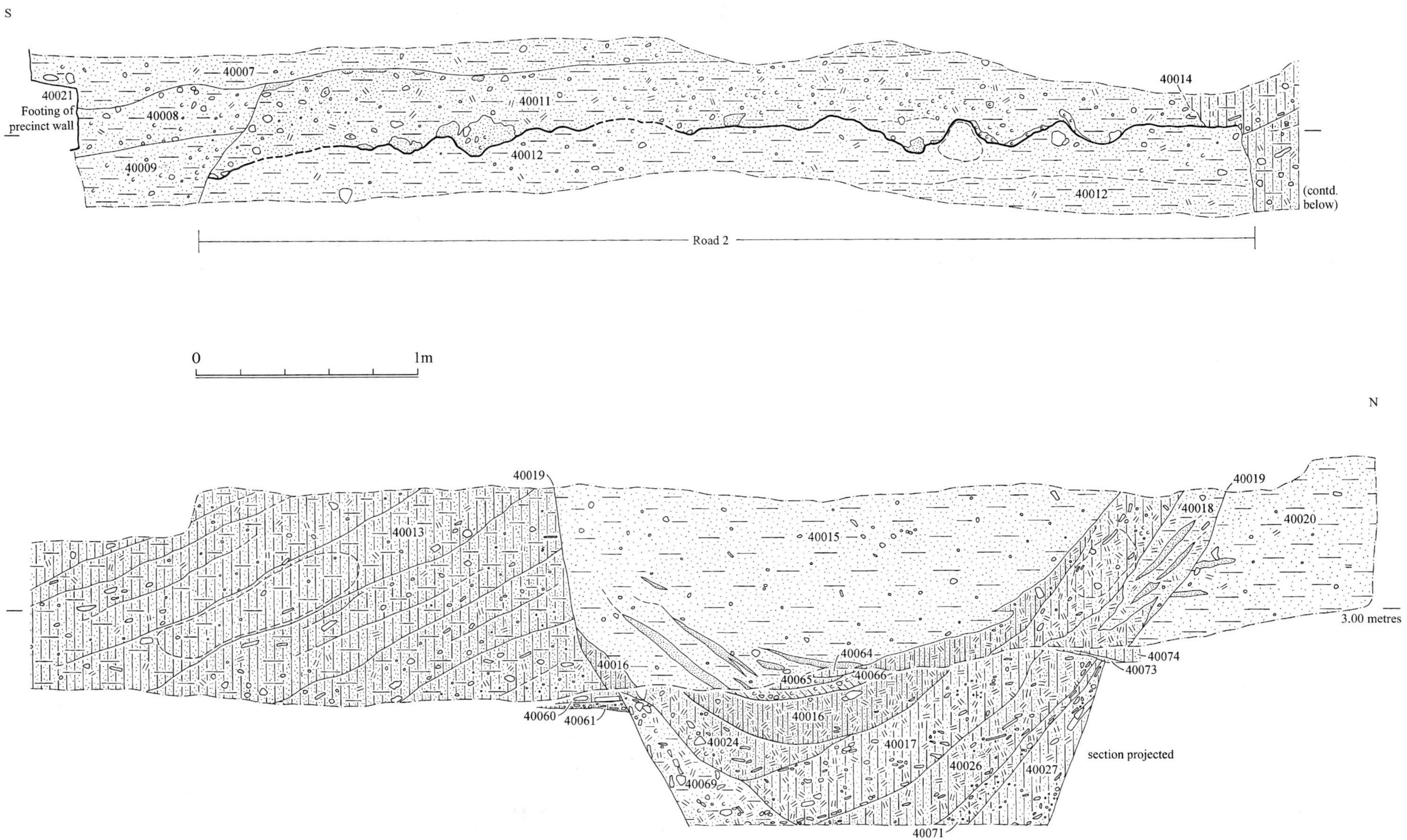

Figure 2.17 East-facing section through Road 2, pre-Friary deposits and late Friary pits, Area CB

even early 13th-century date for the cutting of the feature. The ditches may have defined enclosures. Their construction appears to represent an eastward extension, towards the River Wensum, of activity beyond the limits of the north-to-south ditches evident in Period 1, and gradual colonisation of the river marsh.

Structural features and surfaces (east of Road 1)

(Figs 2.12 and 2.15)
Structural traces to the east of road 1 indicated the presence of buildings. A few post-holes and/or small pits (*40109*, *40110*, *40108* and *40173*), possibly representing a structure of indeterminate extent or layout, were recorded immediately to the south of ditch *40098* in the north-east corner of Area CB. Pottery recovered from the fills suggests that the structure had been removed *c.* 1100.

Another cluster of post-holes (*40158*, *40177*, *40184*, *40185*, *40186*, *40187* and *40188*) of similar date lay *c.* 6.0m further south. These overlay Road 2 described above, indicating that this was now out of use. The T-shape distribution of some of these post-holes indicates that they may represent a building which fell from use in the early 12th century.

Closer to Road 1, and sealing an infilled roadside ditch, was another group of structural features (*30709*, *30710*, *30711* and *30712*) comprising chalk and clay floor surfaces, post-holes and a wall footing (not planned) dating to the late 12th century. Part of the flooring was formed by a near-complete lava quern (*30710*, SF1261).

Later, similar, activity in the area is described in Period 2.3 below.

Pitting (east of Road 1)

(Fig. 2.18)
Three large pits (*50616*, *50620* and *50642*) lay to the north of ditch *50665* in Area C. Although two other nearby pits (*50512* and *50530*) contained no finds, they lay above 11th-century ditches and probably date to the early 12th century. More 12th-century pitting was evident to the south of curving ditch *50665*. This included two large examples (*50012* and *50628*), the latter containing two coins of Stephen (1135–1154) and ceramic crucibles while the former was cut by a ditch of clear 13th-century date. In the same area were three truncated pits (*50243*, *50502* and *50603*), lying above disused sunken-featured building *50242*.

Four other pits (*50182*, *50250*, *50253* and *50285*) lay in the same area. The sides of oval pit *50283* had apparently slumped as a result of erosion, suggesting that it remained open to the elements for some time. The fill contained quantities of slag, possibly indicating that metal-working was carried out nearby at the time of infilling.

Post-holes and gullies (east of Road 1)

(Figs 2.12 and 2.18)
Six post-holes (*50219*, *50228*, *50230*, *50440*, *50460* and *50471*) were recorded to the south of ditch *50665*, their orthogonal arrangement suggesting that they represented a structure. A large number of other post-holes to the east (*50198 etc.*) could neither be allocated to any discernible structure nor definitively dated. A pair of parallel gullies (*50548* and *50611*) recorded to the north of the curving ditch may have been related to the same structure. The alignment of the gullies did not respect that of the ditch, and they may relate to a structure that preceded the ditch and transcended its line. The post-hole lay on the projected alignment of the gullies.

Period 2.2: pre-Friary (12th–13th centuries)

(Fig. 2.12)

Summary

Small-scale quarrying occurred on the King Street frontage, while pre-Conquest building *10049* to the east was eventually superseded by another structure (represented by fifteen post-holes) in the later 12th–early 13th centuries. Activity continued to the east of Road 1, above Road 2. Micromorphological analysis of a soil deposit in this area may indicate the advent of cultivation at the site.

Nearly 15kg of pottery was recovered from deposits ascribed this phase (Lentowicz, Chapter 5.III); while earlier forms are still present, LMU accounts for a much higher proportion of the assemblage. Medieval glazed wares make up a small proportion of the group, indicating a general 12th–13th century date.

Archaeological sequence

Quarrying

(Figs 2.12 and 2.19)
An initial phase of renewed activity on the King Street frontage was indicated by the cutting of three closely grouped quarries (*12470/12463/12476*, *12307* and *12374/12511*), the largest measured over 4m in diameter. The vertical northern edge of a rectangular cut (*12124/12406*), recorded 2m to the north of quarry pit *12307*, might indicate the presence of a fourth quarry.

Timber building

(Fig. 2.19)
Fifteen post-holes (*105*, *107*, *109*, *112*, *126*, *128*, *130*, *10133*, *10336*, *10635*, *10636*, *10652*, *10740* and *10841*), some with recorded traces of post-pipes, may have formed part of a single structure. They lay close to the earlier sunken-floored building (*10049*, Period 1) and may have been of 12th–13th century date.

Pitting

(Fig. 2.19)
To the north of the timber building, and perhaps sharing its alignment, was a rectangular pit (*10521*) measuring 1.4m long by 1.15m wide and 1.0m deep. Significant quantities of household waste (pottery, animal bone and shell), as well as slag, brick and tile, were recovered from its fills. Three other pits (*10135*, *10429* and *10522*) were also recorded in this area.

?Building

(not illustrated)
Towards the eastern end of Area A/D, the south-west corner of a rectangular cut (*12231*) and two associated post-holes (*12222* and *12233*) occurred at the north edge of the excavation. These may be the remnants of a building. A pit (*12500*) immediately to the south-west of the feature may have been associated with it.

Activities east of Road 1

(Figs 2.12 and 2.15)
Lying to the east of Road 1, above earlier structural traces (Period 2.1), was a lateral deposit extending across an area of at least 4m (east-to-west) by 5m (north-to-south). Two spreads of burnt clay (*40088*, *40092*, *40093*, *40111* and *40189*) were in elongated shapes which may reflect the venting of a fire from one side. The absence of metalworking waste or pottery may indicate that the burning was associated with gardening, crop-drying or domestic activity. Three post-holes and a pit (*40095*, *40175*, *40176* and *40087*) had been cut into this layer. Some of the posts to the north (*40107* and *40148*) had been replaced.

Cultivation?

A charcoal-rich deposit, containing bone, mortar, ash and coprolitic material (*50026*; micromorphological sample 9: Macphail and Cruise, Chapter 6.VIII) was also recorded in Area C adjacent to structure *50242*. This had been biologically worked and appeared to represent an anthropogenic accumulation which had been disturbed, possibly by cultivation.

Period 2.3: pre-Friary (13th century)

(Fig. 2.12)

Summary

The northernmost of a series of new buildings on the King Street frontage was a substantial flint structure overlying earlier quarries, immediately to the south of which was a cellared building. A third building, represented by post-holes, lay furthest to the south.

An area of sloping ground in the northern part of Area B appears to have been utilised for sand extraction during the 13th century, prior to the development of the Friary buildings (*c.* 1300 from documentary evidence). Further south, a north-to-south aligned ditch may indicate an early alteration to the boundary of the cemetery of St John the Evangelist, while to its east the earlier road (Road 1) was altered, with new surfacing laid down.

During the 13th century, a new east-to-west ditch appeared in the eastern part of the site (Area C). This may indicate the laying-out or eastward extension of a new, narrow plot immediately to the south of the earlier boundary recorded in this area. Adjacent to these ditches in the far eastern part of the site was a substantial, possibly aisled, timber building.

Over 43kg of pottery was recovered from deposits assigned to this phase (Lentowicz, Chapter 5.III), dominated by LMU but with quantities of Grimston Glazed ware and continental imports. While the pottery indicates 12th–13th, 13th or 13th–14th century dates for particular context groups, stratigraphic evidence indicates a probable 13th century date for this activity.

Archaeological sequence

Buildings fronting King Street

(Figs 2.12 and 2.19)

Infilling of the quarries along the King Street frontage was immediately followed by the construction of buildings adjacent to and aligned with the street. The northernmost structure consisted of a substantial wall foundation with a westward return at its southern end (*10004*/*12594*/*12490*). The foundation was composed entirely of mortared flint and lay 8m behind the street frontage. The flint masonry (up to 1m wide) appears to have been laid within a shallow construction cut (*10615*). The surrounding natural had apparently been cleared of overlying deposits prior to construction. The placement of the wall was followed immediately by the making-up of the ground surface both to its south and north.

A cellared building was subsequently inserted (*12253* and *12396*), the northern edge of which respected and lay parallel to the pre-existing wall. The cellared area consisted of a rectangular cut (*12396*), over 4.5m north-to-south by at least 4m east-to-west, which survived to a depth of 0.45m. The cellar was originally bounded to the west by a wall (presumably masonry) which, although not extant, was represented by a sheer-sided linear robber cut (*12252*). The flat base of the feature consisted of undisturbed natural compact chalky sand, with an oval-shaped burnt patch (*12333*) at the centre of the sunken area perhaps indicating a hearth. However, an extensive surrounding deposit of ash may indicate that the burning was associated with the demolition of the building. A sand and chalk clay footing/?flooring (*12395*/*12397*) for the south edge of the cellar may have supported a timber sill beam. Such a construction presumably keyed into a north-to-south wall represented by robber trench *12252*.

After the cellar had completely infilled a new cut was created (*12375*), with its southern edge *c.* 1m further north from that of its predecessor. Its base lay at the same level as that of the earlier cut and the structure was ultimately infilled in the 14th century.

A broadly east-to-west line of post-holes (*12295*, *12402*, *12404*, *12442*, *12450*, *12458* and *12467*) and two north-to-south gullies (*12465* and *12473*) some 3.7m long, may have formed elements of the north wall of another building to the south of the cellared structure. A remnant patch of clay floor (*12389*) may also have been a remnant of this building.

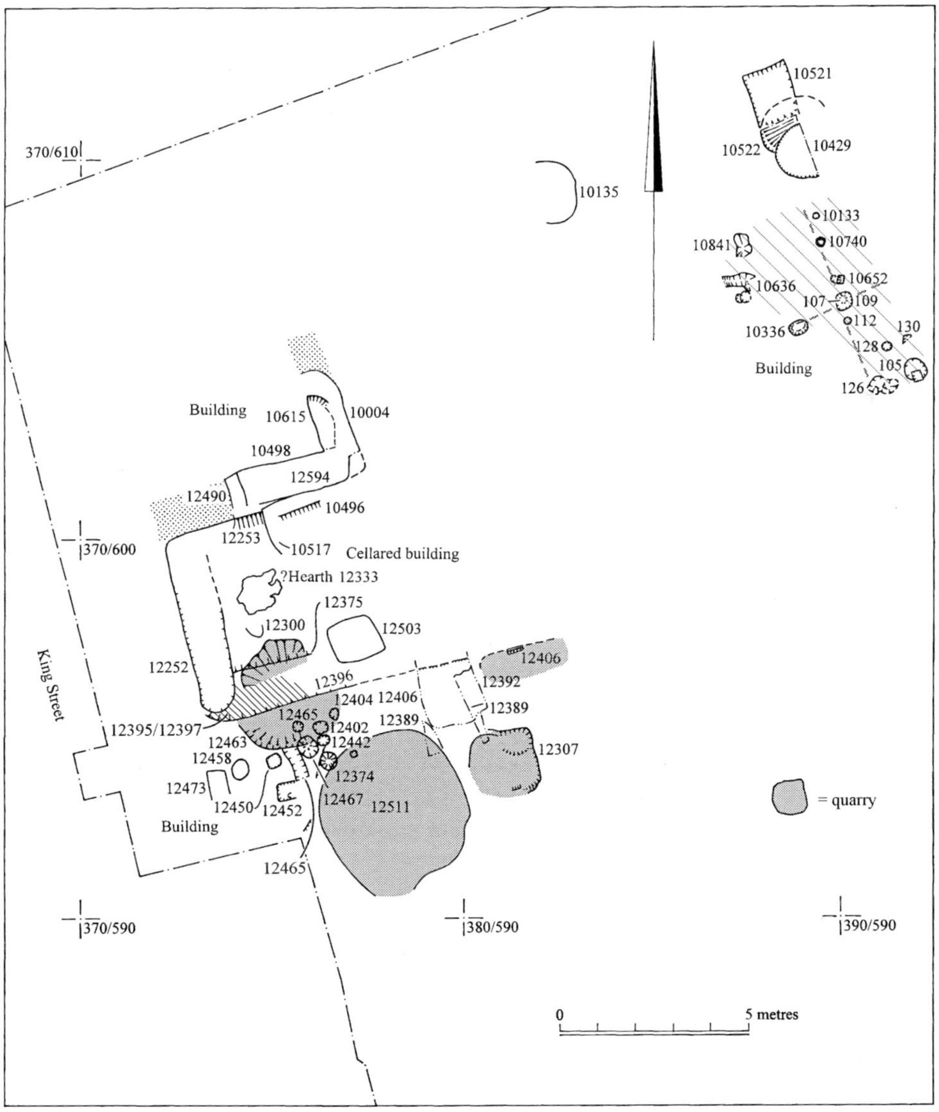

Figure 2.19 Periods 2.1–2.3: features adjacent to King Street frontage, Area A

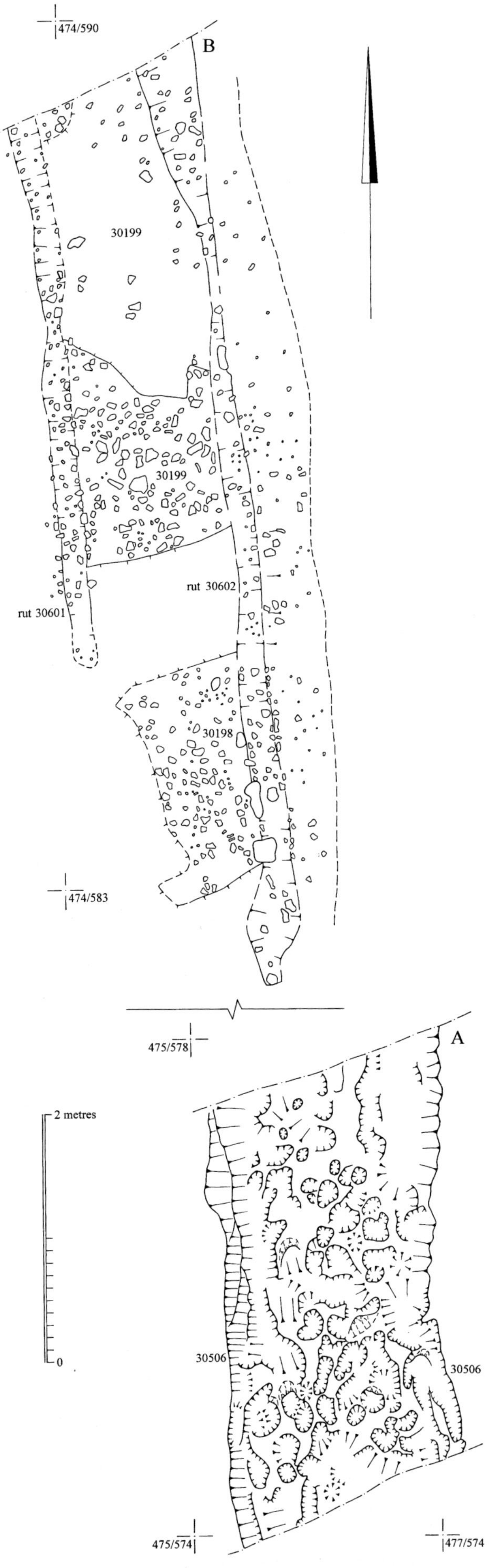

Figure 2.20 Road 1, showing hoof impressions to south and ruts to north

Plate 2.6 Excavation of hoof impressions in Road 1 (Areas B and CB)

Quarrying
(Fig. 2.12)
In the area to the south of a line shown crossing Areas A and D on Fig. 2.12 the natural ground in the western part of the site falls to the south by up to 2.2m over a horizontal distance of 6.5m. An east-to-west linear grouping of deep pits (*30637* (not illus.), *30254*, *30230*, *30290/ 30629*, *30213* and *30249*), about 9.5m long, occurred *c.* 4.5m from the northern edge of Area B. Although these clearly originated in the 13th century, pottery from their fills indicates that infilling continued until the late 14th century. One pit (*30032*) contained cereal grains indicating germination prior to sprouting (Fryer, Chapter 6.V).

Numerous other large pits were recorded in Area B, although excavation of these was limited. Whilst their dating was inconclusive (due to the likelihood of redeposition, and the restricted volume of fills excavated) it is possible that many were associated with the development of the Friary precinct in the 13th century. Pottery from these features is generally uninformative, and was spot-dated to the 12th–14th centuries. The pits have been assigned to Period 2.3 in the absence of any firm evidence for their association with the construction of the Friary. The size of the cuts suggests that they were created by quarrying for sand for use in construction of buildings and surfaces. It was from the upper fills of one such quarry (*13339*: located on Fig. 3.7) that a painter's palette in the form of an oyster shell (SF2621) was recovered: this item was probably associated with the Friary (see Chapter 3.II and Howard and Park, Chapter 5.II, 'Painting').

Pits
A notable group of mollusc shells came from the upper fills of possible well *10017* (Period 1), which had evidently been levelled over in the 13th century (Green, Chapter 6.IV).

?Cemetery of St John the Evangelist: boundary ditch
(Fig. 2.12)
A ditch (*30155/30298/30964*), aligned north-to-south, was recorded at three points in the southern part of Area B. Two of the excavated segments (*30155* and *30298*) lay to the south of the line of the south wall of the Friary precinct, and one (*30964*) to the north. Lying stratigraphically below the construction of the Friary wall, the ditch appears to have delineated a pre-Friary plot boundary. Its alignment corresponds closely to that of a north-to-south lane inferred from late 13th-century property boundaries shown on Fig. 2.3. The ditch may have marked the eastern limit of the churchyard of St John the Evangelist (Fig. 2.1) before its eastward extension, although the location of grave *31008* indicates that the cemetery at some stage extended further to the east.

Landscaping and re-use of Road 1
(Figs 2.9, 2.17 and 2.20; Pls 2.6 and 2.7)
Destruction of buildings to the east of Road 1 was followed by a general levelling of the ground surface, this event being represented by a sequence of layers. An extensive layer up to 0.4m thick sealed earlier surfaces of both Roads 1 and 2. This deposit was a homogeneous mid-grey silty sand with occasional chalk flecks and flint pebbles (*30484*, *30508* – Fig. 2.9; *40011*, *40020* – Fig. 2.17; *40034*, *40146* and *40154*). Clearly a significant change in land-use had occurred. While it

might be suggested that large-scale earth-moving in this area is most likely to have formed part of preparations of the site by the friars for their expanded precinct following the acquisition of numerous plots in the 1290s, the thoroughfare clearly remained in use. Its reinstatement was represented by a cut (*30506*: Fig. 2.20) into the make-up deposit, which was up to 0.25m deep and could be described as a hollow-way. In the base of this cut lay a deposit (*30507*) of darker grey silt with lenses of pale brown sand, which accumulated during continuing use of the road. This in turn was honeycombed by multiple oval and irregular-shaped holes almost certainly produced by equine and bovine hooves (Pl. 2.6). Measuring between 50mm and 150mm deep, these hoof impressions indicate that traffic was hindered by muddy conditions caused by poor drainage following the making-up of the ground around the road. During this phase of use, there is no evidence of the passage of wheeled vehicles.

A layer of gravel dating to the mid–late 13th century (*30199*, *30586*, *30263*, *30198* and *30264*) infilled the hoof impressions and the hollow-way itself. This deposit represented the repair of the road and the provision of a surface that would be more effective for heavy traffic. In effect, the deposition of the gravel represented the reinstatement of a viable road surface once landscaping was completed. Linear depressions, co-aligned with the road and measuring *c.* 0.25m wide, were recorded in the northern part of the excavated length of the gravel road surface (Pl. 2.7). These linear hollows, which were traced for over 7m, were clearly wheel-ruts. The alignment of the metalled surface was at variance with that of its predecessor, indicating that a perceptible bend in its course near the southern end of the excavated stretch was being smoothed out.

Plate 2.7 Metalled road surface with ruts (Road 1, Areas B and CB)

Ditches

(Figs 2.12 and 2.21)

Renewed ditch-digging occurred in Area C. A ditch aligned west-to-east was constructed in the mid–late 13th century (*50356/50446/50283/50008*). It cut several earlier pits and was in turn cut by pits dating from the 13th to 14th centuries. Earlier ditches in the area had been infilled by this time and it would appear that this feature formed the new southern boundary of the activity previously bounded by ditch *50665*.

The terminus of another east-to-west aligned ditch (*50515*) was also recorded within Area C (Fig. 2.21). This ditch was roughly perpendicular to an earlier ditch (*cf.* Fig. 2.18). Although not co-aligned with each other, and differing in depth by at least 0.3m, the two new ditches may have been broadly contemporary. The offset alignments could be explained by the continuing existence of a property boundary on the line

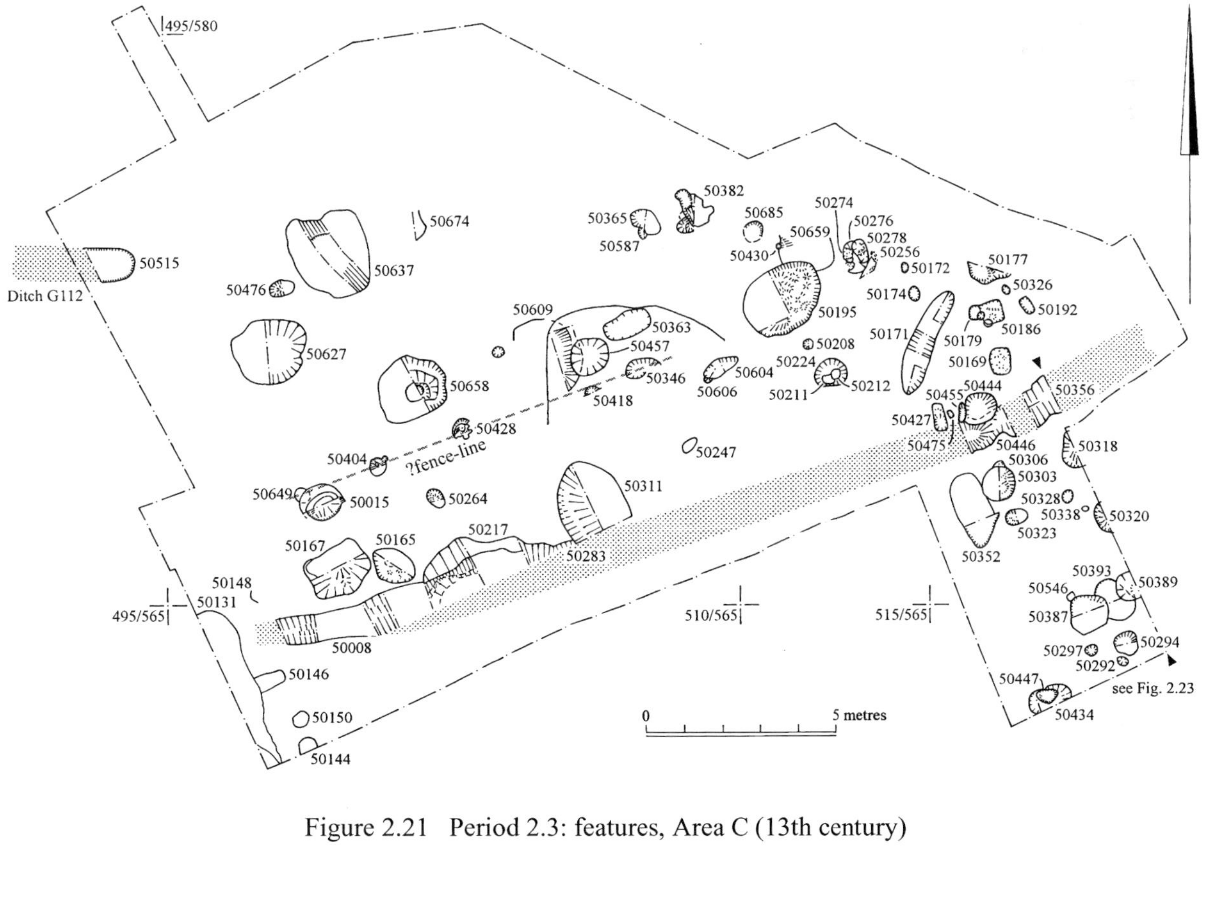

Figure 2.21 Period 2.3: features, Area C (13th century)

of a north-to-south ditch (*50403*/*50492*: Fig. 2.18), the line of which both appeared to respect.

Buildings, structures and pitting
(Figs 2.12, 2.21, 2.22 and 2.23)
Numerous features were recorded adjacent to and encroaching upon the new ditches in Area C. A cluster of substantial post-pits (ranging from 0.9m to 1.20m in diameter) was found in the south-east extension of the area (*50292*, *50294*, *50297*, *50303*, *50306*, *50318*, *50320*, *50323*, *50328*, *50338*, *50387*, *50389*, *50393*, *50434*, *50444* and *50546*). These clearly represent at least one major timber building, given their consistency of size and character, although the exact shape and extent of these structures cannot be determined on account of the restricted area of the excavation trench. The occurrence of a post-pipe in pit *50328* confirmed these features' structural interpretation. Ceramics from the post-pits span the 12th to the 14th centuries, although a date early in the range appears likely. Overall there was an apparent symmetry in this arrangement about a central axis aligned south-west to north-east through post-pit *50320*. The outlying pits could be seen as forming part of outer rows which would imply that the structure had two aisles. With only the post-holes upon which to base an interpretation — no floor levels could be discerned in section — the function of this building remains ambiguous.

A large group of over 30 other post-holes and post-pits identified within Area C was ascribed to the 13th–14th centuries (Figs 2.21 and 2.22). While some pairs of post-holes could be readily defined, grouping post-holes into larger combinations was less easy. Five post-holes (*50346*, *50404*, *50418*, *50428* and *50649*) occurred in a straight south-west to north-east line to the north of ditch *50356* and probably indicate a fence line. Other post-holes in the area may indicate the presence of similar structures or buildings.

Eighteen pits were located largely to the south of the line of ditch *50515*. The similarities in both character and pattern displayed by pits dating from the 12th through to the 14th century lying outside the later Friary precinct suggests continuity in the land-use of this area throughout the medieval period.

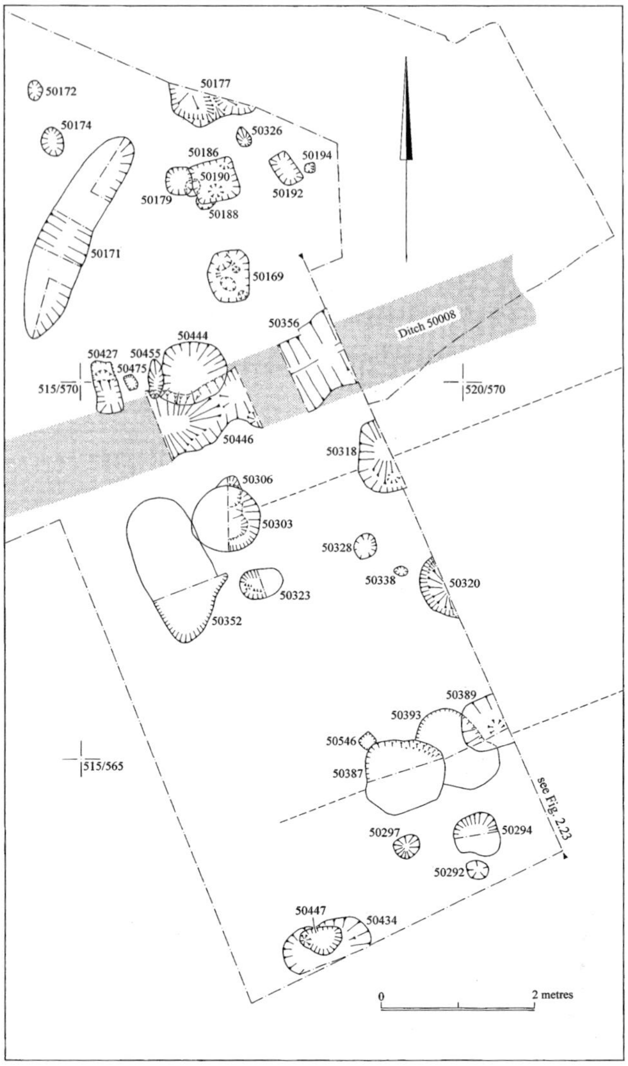

Figure 2.22 Period 2.3: features, Area C extension (13th century)

IV. DISCUSSION: PRE-FRIARY DEVELOPMENT

by Phillip A. Emery and Elizabeth Shepherd Popescu

Prehistoric and Roman

Early populations favoured well-drained locations that also afforded access to natural resources in the valley floor. Traces of Bronze Age settlement, for example, were located on a terrace at an elevation of 3.0m OD during evaluation at Busseys Garage some 400m north of the subject site in 2000 (Emery and Ashwin 2001). Significant palaeoenvironmental evidence has been recorded close to the Wensum at Riverside (Emery 1998; Wiltshire and Emery 2000). Reconstruction of the prehistoric river-edge landscape on the opposite bank of the Wensum, developed from geotechnical borehole data as part of the Riverside project, informed the targeting of subsequent investigation at the Norwich City Football Stadium, Carrow Road, where an important assemblage of Mesolithic worked flint was recovered (Adams 2002). Most of the other prehistoric finds located across modern Norwich, such as a re-used polished flint axe found at King Street (Site 254N), are isolated findspots. A few finds have come from the area of the Castle, to the west of the Greyfriars site, including Mesolithic and Neolithic worked flint and sherds of Beaker/Bronze Age pottery from the Castle Mall excavations (Site 777N, Shepherd Popescu forthcoming), as well as a flint arrowhead of probable Bronze Age date from the north-east bailey (Ayers 1985, 33, fig. 29). Larger quantities of finds, as well as *in situ* features indicating cultivation, were found at the Millennium Library site (now the Forum), on high ground to the west of the Castle (Percival and Hutcheson in prep.). Given the paucity of findspots in the immediate vicinity of the Greyfriars site, the lack of evidence for prehistoric activity is unsurprising. Only three worked flints (a blade and two ?Neolithic scrapers) were found, while the five fragments of prehistoric pottery include Iron Age and Bronze Age sherds (Percival, Chapter 5.III).

Few traces of Roman activity have yet been discovered beneath modern Norwich, although ditches probably dating to the 3rd–4th century have recently been excavated at the Chapelfield site to the west of the Castle and may represent field systems and trackways (Whitmore 2004). To the west of the Greyfriars site, King Street — which runs along the base of the eastern side of a spur of high ground known as the Ber Street ridge — has been postulated as a Roman route. Despite extensive recent excavations by the NAU alongside the southern stretch of the street, however, no Roman features have been recorded and only a limited range of Roman objects and pottery has come from the area. Aside from the present site, fourteen interventions of various kinds have been conducted along King Street by the NAU in recent years, yielding a total of only seven sherds of Roman pottery and

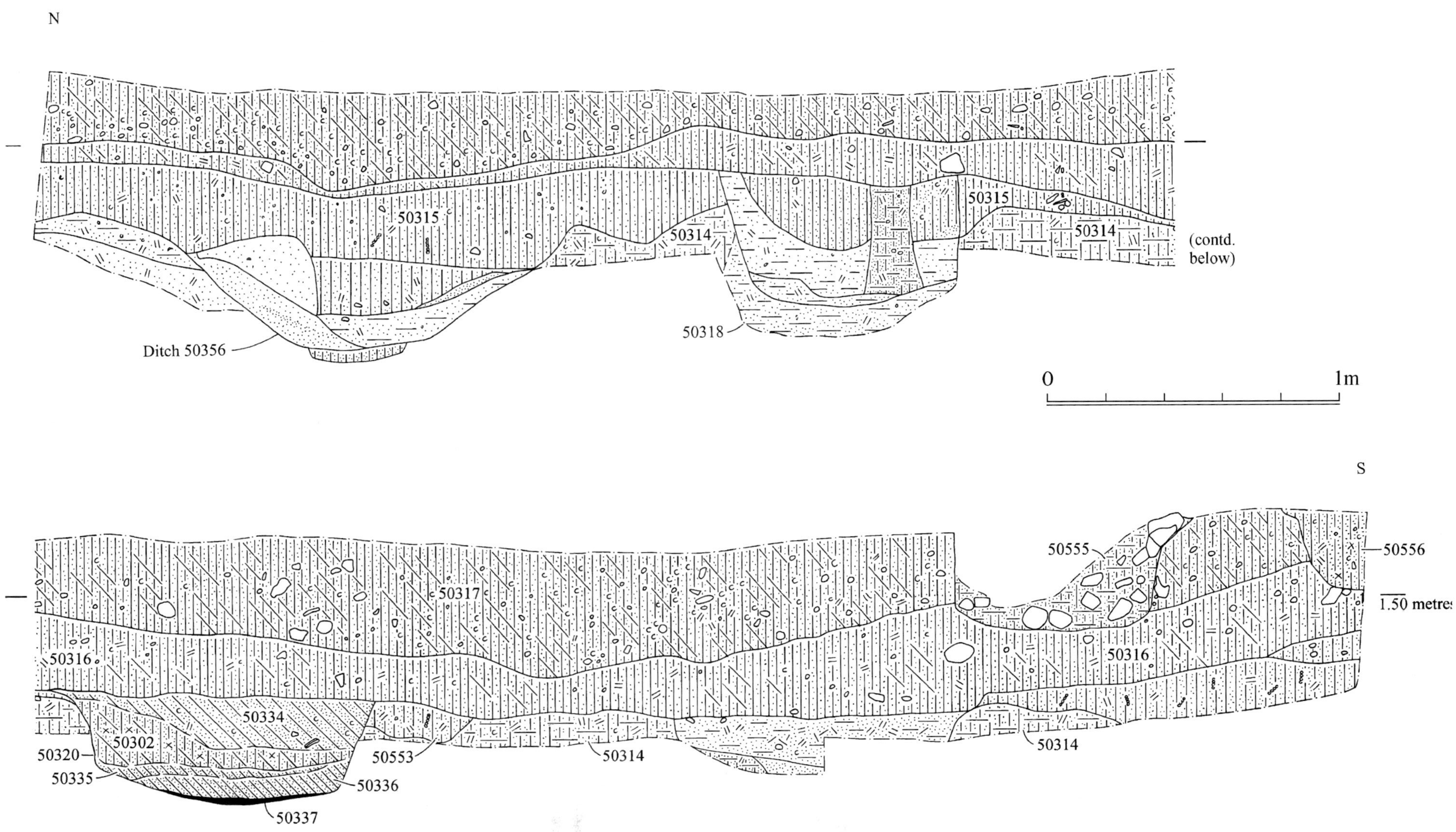

Figure 2.23 Section through post-pits, Area C extension

a spindle whorl. By comparison with other Norwich excavations, therefore, the Greyfriars site produced a relatively large assemblage of Roman pottery (69 sherds: Lyons, Chapter 5.III). The few dateable pieces indicate a mid-Roman assemblage with some later sherds; the high levels of recorded abrasion and absence of contemporary archaeological features imply that these sherds are residual, perhaps originating from as-yet undiscovered Roman activity in this area and/or imported during topsoil movement associated with creation of the Friary or later gardens. One of the late Roman sherds was retrieved from the topsoil in the eastern part of the site (Area C), which also contained a Roman shale bracelet (Huddle, Chapter 5.III, 'Bracelets (shale)').

Roman tile, incorporated into the hearths of pre-Friary buildings at the subject site (see below and Huddle with Kemp, Chapter 5.I, 'Ceramic building material'), may have been salvaged either from *Venta Icenorum* (now Caistor St Edmund, founded in the 1st century AD and lying 5km south of Norwich) or from Roman buildings that are likely to have been scattered in the area of modern Norwich itself.

Early Saxon

Evidence for the Early Saxon period beneath the modern city is limited and includes sherds of pottery found within the Cathedral Close (Sites 45 and 46N, *c.* 350m to the north to the Mann Egerton site), a single fragment of urn from the church of St Michael at Plea (Ayers 1994, 22) and a 5th–6th-century brooch from the Castle Mall excavations *c.* 300m to the south-west (Site 777N: Shepherd Popescu, forthcoming). Several sherds of pottery from Greyfriars appear to date to the very end of the Roman era (late 4th–5th centuries AD) and are perhaps transitional to the Anglo-Saxon period (Lyons, Chapter 5.III). Five other Roman sherds came from the sunken-featured building in the same area (*50242*, Period 1): although recovered from two 'disuse' dumps within the structure, these sherds are significant since they may indicate Late Roman/Early Saxon activity in the vicinity.

Middle Saxon Conesford?

As outlined above (9–10), the Greyfriars excavations lay broadly within (or just to the south of) the area often attributed as *Conesford.* Nearby, Middle Saxon burials recently been identified at the Castle Mall site were possibly related to the settlement of *Needham* (Shepherd Popescu forthcoming).

The concentration of Middle Saxon finds in the south-eastern part of the excavation is notable and may indicate a focus of activity, perhaps consisting of only a few houses, near Rose Lane. (Anglo-Scandinavian finds attributable to the 9th century are considered further below: 39.) A 'Runic' type *sceat* (found in an Area C pit: Davies and Allen, Chapter 5.II, 'Coins') dates to the first half of the 8th century: only two other examples have been found in Norwich. Two ?Middle Saxon dress pins were also recovered (Huddle, Chapter 5.IV, 'Dress pins'), one coming from sunken-featured building *50242*. A 9th-century openwork disc brooch — the first of its kind to be found in the city — was again recovered from Area C (Geake, Chapter 5.IV, 'Disc brooch'). In addition to metalwork, eighteen sherds of Ipswich-type ware (date range *c.* 720–850) were retrieved, most of which (thirteen sherds) came from Area C (Goffin, Chapter 5.III, 'Middle Saxon pottery'). Small quantities of similar Middle Saxon pottery have been recovered from many other sites in Norwich, including several along King Street, with possible concentrations of activity in areas situated close to the River Wensum.

In summary, the findings provide significant new evidence for the origins of this part of Norwich, potentially indicating Roman, Early Saxon and Middle Saxon activity in the vicinity of what may have been *Conesford.* Further comments on the dating of settlement can be found elsewhere in this chapter.

Street pattern

(Figs 2.1 and 2.24)

The excavations provide crucial new evidence about Norwich's early street pattern. While the likely primary elements of the Late Saxon street plan (including King Street and the road connecting Whitefriars Bridge with the bend in Rose Lane) exhibit some regularity in their alignments, it is now clear that the shape of the intermediate, secondary roads was influenced significantly by the local terrain. The proposed revised layout of early Norman roads in the vicinity of the excavation presented in Fig. 2.1 has been reconstructed on the basis of archaeological evidence and of 13th- and 14th-century documents. This pattern is shown in the wider context of the Late Saxon town in Fig. 2.24, this reconstruction working on the assumption that at least some of the proposed roads may have pre-dated the Conquest. The north-to-south road recorded in Area B (Road 1) and possibly located again during excavations in St Faith's Lane in 1998 represents a significant addition to knowledge of the early street system in this part of the town, with implications for its pre-Conquest layout. The road lay approximately midway between King Street and the line of the major road running around this south-western part of the town. It was presumably one of several minor, intermediate roads within the gridded layout of which little trace is visible in post-medieval maps. Projected northwards, the excavated lane would have passed in front of the west end of the Cathedral. It was established by the 12th century, although may have a pre-Conquest origin. It corresponds to the position of a 'former highway' in 1285 (see Rutledge, above, 10), having deteriorated into a lane by that date.

The position of Road 1 reflects the presence of a terrace identified through reconstruction of the profile of the natural ground surface (see below and Fig. 3.22). The falling ground to its east can be attributed to the cumulative erosion of the Fresflete, whose 19th-century course is visible in contemporary maps within the meadows associated with the river. The brow of a localised steep slope on which the road lies formed the western limit of the stream's floodplain. The earliest manifestation of this thoroughfare (dating to the 10th–11th centuries: Period 1) was a north-to-south ditch (Fig. 2.4). Having subsequently been effectively buried by an extensive make-up event, the road was evidently reinstated as a cutting or 'hollow-way' (Period 2.1). This in turn rapidly silted up and the laboriousness of subsequent passage along it by

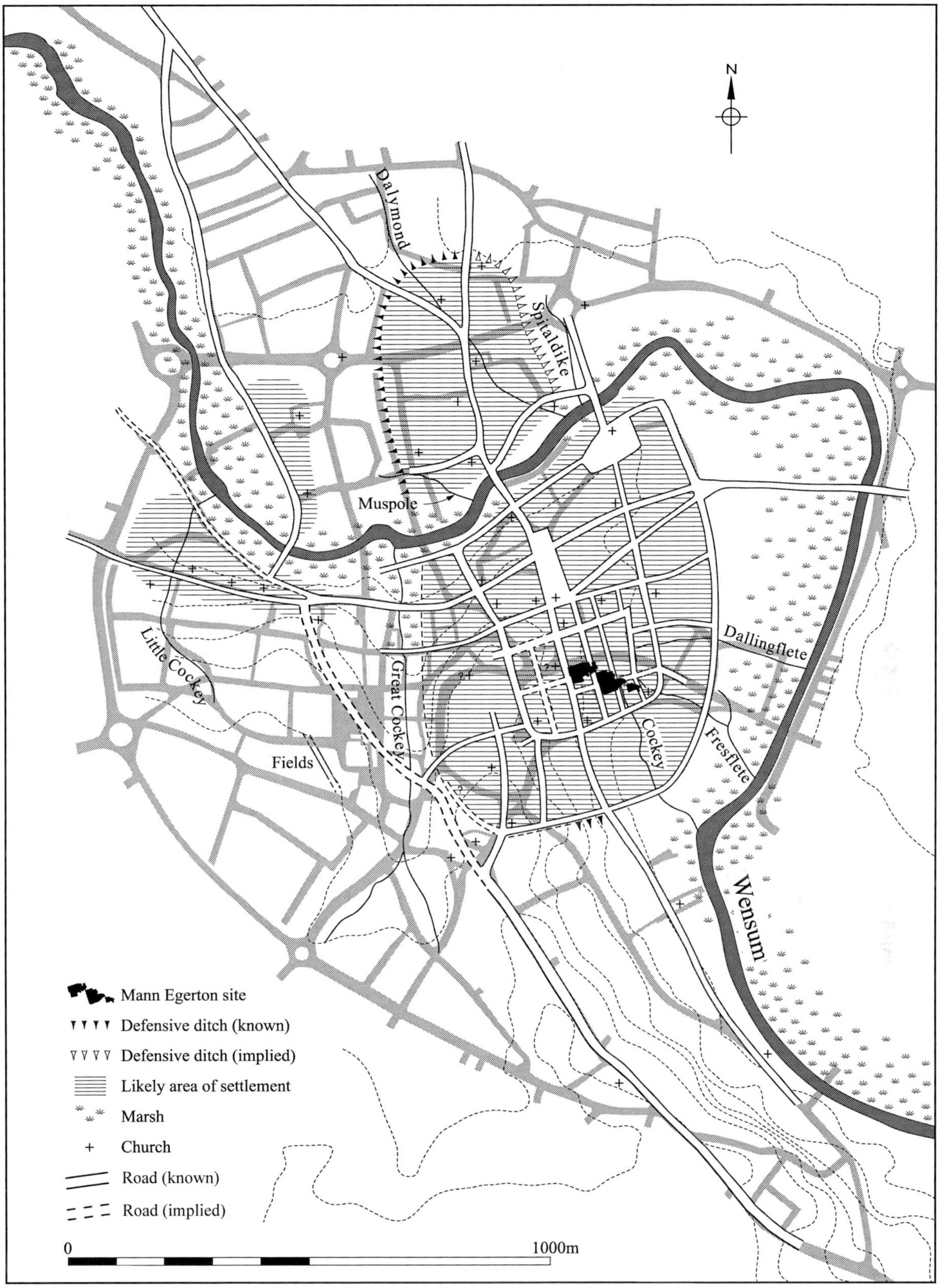

Figure 2.24 Map of Late Saxon Norwich, showing a reconstructed street pattern and the location of probable pre-Conquest churches (after Shepherd Popescu forthcoming, fig. 4.2)

pedestrians and animals is attested by the many hoof impressions that cut deep into the sediment. Interest in maintaining the road continued. A dump of substantial quantities of gravel infilled the hollows and restored a hard running surface (Period 2.3); while ruts created by wheeled vehicles represented the final phase of the road's use. The south wall of the Friary precinct (constructed *c.* 1300), which effectively closed the road, was deflected through an angle of some 9 degrees at the point of the two features' intersection. It is possible that the northern part of Road 1 partially survived enclosure by the Friary precinct, providing an explanation for the longest of the north-to-south dog-leg elements of later Crinkle Crankle Lane/Griffin Lane as shown by Millard and Manning's map of 1830 (Pl. 4.4), although this is offset to the east of the reconstructed alignment (*cf.* Figs 2.1 and 4.1) by *c.* 9.0m.

Projected northwards, Road 1 appears to equate with a vehicle-rutted trackway recorded to the north at St Faith's Lane by Northamptonshire Archaeology (Fig. 2.1) in 1998. This track, however, was interpreted by the excavators as a 14th-century feature associated with quarrying, and apparently overlay three graves associated with the Friary cemetery whilst underlying others (Soden 2001, 18–20, plate 6, fig. 7).

Evidence for what may have been a second pre-Friary road (running east-to-west to the east of the first road: Road 2, Period 2.1) may equate with the thoroughfare that is documented to have led to the church of St Vedast. This lane was apparently aligned east-to-west and adjoined the southern edge of the Friary precinct *c.* 50m north of Rose Lane. It measured 211ft by 12ft and ran from the former highway (*i.e.* Road 1) in 1298. It was probably a continuation of this way that the friars closed in 1285 (Rutledge, above, 10).

Two other minor lanes, neither of them directly attested archaeologically, ran roughly north-to-south on either side of Road 1 (Fig. 2.1). The locations of these routes appear to have been dictated by the position of the local watercourses. Interposed roughly midway between Road 1 and King Street is a dip in the natural ground surface (Fig. 3.22) which correlates both with the projected line of the un-named stream (a remnant of which is shown on Millard and Manning's map of 1830: Pl. 4.4) and the suggested line of the western minor lane. No trace of this lane was found during the excavations, although a Period 2 ditch (*30964*: Fig. 2.12) corresponding closely to its position confirmed the existence of a property boundary on this alignment. The ditch cut across the postulated early part of the cemetery of St John the Evangelist, which had apparently contracted westwards by this time. To the east, the position of the Fresflete appears to have influenced the curious curving alignment of the eastern minor lane apparent in Fig. 2.1. The line of this lane is reflected in the northern section of a line of trees on Millard and Manning's map (Pl. 4.4). Its southern course towards the east, dictated by the position of the stream, is echoed in the alignment of the eastern section of modern Rose Lane (*cf.* Figs 1.2 and 2.1; Pl. 4.4). It is possible that the streams may have been diverted into the roadside drains, as was perhaps the case with the Great Cockey stream to the west of the castle (Shepherd Popescu forthcoming). The influence of streams on the street plan has been noted elsewhere within Norwich (Ayers unpublished) and the new evidence provides a significant addition to this line of research.

Another east-to-west road (taken over by the Greyfriars in 1297) is documented as having lain on the north side of the friars' dwelling place. It ran between the north edge of the precinct and the southern edge of St Cuthbert's churchyard (*i.e.* beyond the limits of the archaeological excavation) and was called Neugate/Bugate in *c.* 1400. Additional evidence for local street pattern comes from recent NAU excavations beneath the cathedral refectory (Site 226N: Wallis in prep. b), which indicate the presence of another Late Saxon road running diagonally from the south-east corner of Tombland (Fig. 2.24), in a position which indicates a route leading to a junction with Bishopgate and thence to the ford over the River Wensum (now Bishop Bridge).

The position of churches and cemeteries can assist the hypothetical reconstruction of local street patterns. The fact that churches had to be accessible can give clues as to their surrounding urban geography, even when no evidence for streets or paths survives. In the words of Richard Morris, 'one of the most characteristic positions for an urban church was in the angle of a junction between a major and minor street' (Morris 1989, 209), while cross-roads were also popular positions. Examples of pre-conquest church foundations thus located are numerous and include St Martin in Micklegate, York and St George in Stamford (*ibid.*), along with many parallels in London (Hobley 1988, fig. 31). At the Norwich Greyfriars site, the probably pre-Conquest churches of St John the Evangelist and St Vedast (see below) each lay within blocks of ground defined by major and minor routes (Fig. 2.1), while the churches of St Cuthbert (?pre-Danish) and St Ethelbert (pre-Conquest) further to the north were similarly placed. At Winchester, it was suggested that large blocks within the gridded street system of the Late Saxon burh perhaps initially housed a principal dwelling and a private church (Biddle 1976, 454), the blocks later being sub-divided. A similar phenomenon is demonstrated in the pre-Conquest settlement beneath Norwich Castle (Shepherd Popescu forthcoming).

Based around primary roads, of which at least one is likely to have Roman origins, the newly revised Norwich street-pattern formulated using the recent findings at Greyfriars and adjacent sites (Fig. 2.24) undeniably exhibits a broad regularity, suggestive of some degree of planning during the Late Saxon or early Norman period. The evidence arguably supports the hypothesis that a pre-Conquest 'planned' town, which potentially extended as far south as Rose Lane (Fig. 2.24; Atkin and Carter 1985, fig. 2), developed at Norwich. The pattern demonstrates regularity on the lower ground to the east of King Street, probably the result of the combined effects of local topography and proximity to the economic centre of the town: this flatter ground adjacent to the river was noted by Carter as the 'optimum site for a trading settlement' (Carter and Roberts 1973, 444–8). However, the results of the Castle Mall excavations (Shepherd Popescu forthcoming) have cast doubt on whether the rectilinear plan presented in the Atkin and Carter model continued to the west of King Street.

Current archaeological evidence only supports the presence of a gridded street plan within an area between King Street to the west and the putative north-to-south road alignment to the east, upon which the Cathedral transepts were later superimposed. Whether this regularity was established during the Late Saxon period or was a post-Conquest development remains open to debate, due to a lack of secure dating. It should be noted, however, that such regularity could have resulted from organic development extending out from the primary roads: unplanned settlements (*i.e.* those not deliberately laid out as an entity) 'could also appear regular owing to the constraints imposed by natural or relict features acting as morphological frames' (Biddle 1975, 31). At Northampton, it has been suggested that the approximately rectilinear street pattern 'was probably imposed by the axial streets and the line of the defences rather than being a deliberately planned layout' (Williams J.H. 1984, 31): this may also have been the case at Norwich. While cartographic analysis can reveal patterning within the city's street plan, the extent to which such regularity arose deliberately from a pre-conceived plan is difficult to demonstrate archaeologically and would require accurate dating of the origins of multiple components of the settlement.

In conclusion, it is suggested that development of settlement beyond the rectilinear 'core' plan, extending as far as the line of Mountergate/St Faith's Lane, may have been less structured, reflecting to a greater extent the natural topography. The proposed model of longitudinal rectilinear development flanking King Street would further underline the primary role that this road played in determining the configuration of the Late Saxon town. The early origins of King Street have previously been recognised, with church dedications to St Edward and St Etheldreda being cited as indicative of the antiquity of its southerly section (Carter and Roberts 1973, 446).

Anglo-Scandinavian and Viking influence

A significant research objective relating to the early growth of Norwich is the analysis of Scandinavian — and particularly Danish — influence. Although Vikings had begun to raid England's coast in the latter years of the 8th century, the Danes first arrived in East Anglia in 866: sporadic raiding of Norwich (*Northwic*) continued until the early 11th century. Norwich's emergence as a town may well be rooted in the probable Danish occupation of *c.* 870–917 and in the Anglo-Scandinavian period that followed the re-conquest by the West Saxon kings. To date, however, the archaeological evidence for this period of activity is limited. Although a defended burh on the north bank of the River Wensum may have been established in the late 9th or early 10th century (Fig. 2.24; Carter 1978, fig. 7) the town's major period of growth appears to lie in the 10th century, when it acquired a mint. The lack of emphasis on Norwich as an Anglo-Scandinavian centre has long been noted: this aspect of the development of the town appears to have been neglected due to the brevity of the period during which it was under Danish political control (Evans and Carter 2002, 237). Despite the fact that from the 880s the Anglo-Scandinavian settlement of Norwich may have focused on a defended area on the north bank of the river, there is growing evidence for late 9th- and 10th-century activity to the south. Recent finds reflecting 'Viking' influence from both Norwich and Norfolk (summarised by Margeson 1997 and Penn 2000) have been supplemented significantly by the discoveries at Greyfriars and at the adjacent Castle Mall site (Shepherd Popescu forthcoming).

The Greyfriars site has provided a significant group of 9th-century artefacts, spanning the transition from the Middle to Late Saxon periods. The Late Saxon finds assemblage includes a number of items indicating Scandinavian influence, which was already apparent from the presence of a 10th-century Mammen-style cross fragment relating to the church of St Vedast (Site 395N; above, 9). The most significant of the Greyfriars artefacts is a late 9th-century half-*eyrir* weight of the Vikings of East Anglia bearing the name of Alfred, which was probably struck at Norwich in the earlier 880s (from Area C: Archibald, Chapter 5.II). The possible implications of this find for the location of a Norwich mint — long the subject of speculation — are discussed further below. A zoomorphic buckle of Anglo-Scandinavian design and of possible 9th-century date retrieved during the 1997 evaluation at St Faith's Lane in the northern part of the later Friary precinct (Site 373N; Geake, Chapter 5.IV, 'Cast buckle frame and plate') is of national significance. Other finds include a Viking copy of the coinage of Alfred the Great, dating from *c.* 880–95 (Blackburn, Chapter 5.II).

The discovery of fragments of two steatite stone bowls or dishes of late 9th- or 10th-century date (Areas A and B: Mills with Ensom, Chapter 5.III) is also significant: although not unknown elsewhere in Norfolk, these are rare objects in this part of Britain. Other notable items include a bone ring-headed pin, which may be a local imitation of a Scandinavian form (Huddle Chapter 5.II, 'Pins (bone and antler)'). Four bi-conical spindle whorls found in Area A (most coming from sunken-floored building *10049*) are the first examples of this form from Norwich (Huddle, Chapter 5.II, 'Spindle whorls (ceramic)'. Such objects are often found on Viking Age sites in Scandinavia. Ceramically, however, there appears to be little to confirm intensive settlement on the present site at this early date (see below).

Plots and boundaries

Insights into the extent, orientation and function of plots spanning the Late Saxon to immediately pre-Friary period were gained from analysis of buildings, boundary ditches and associated pitting. Conflicts between the alignments of some of the significant ditched property boundaries and those of the gridded street layout probably reflect the natural relief. Comparison of the configuration of plots reconstructed on the basis of the 1292 license (Fig. 2.3) with that inferred from the archaeological evidence (Figs 2.4 and 2.12) allows a fuller appreciation of the influence of natural topography on land division. The most visible Late Saxon/Early Norman property that lay adjacent to King Street correlates with Plot N on the early Norman conjectural layout. It was represented by a sunken-floored building (Period 1, building *10049*) and associated clusters of pits which were consistent in terms of the antler-working and metalworking waste that they contained (see below). The association between the building and two contemporary pit groups was supported by the extent of a concentration of crucible fragments which substantially overlapped the three elements. From the outer limits of these elements, the minimum extent of the related plot can be postulated (see below and Fig. 5.19).

The southern boundary of Plots N and O (Fig. 2.3) arguably corresponds with a south-west to north-east ditch (*13355*) aligned along the brow of the natural slope. The implied curvature of the ditch's line may have reflected the natural terrain, the feature apparently having been aligned along the brow of the south-facing slope. The postulated rectilinear arrangement of pre-Friary plots presented in Fig. 2.3 may therefore be regarded as a somewhat idealised model compared to the reality indicated by the archaeological remains. Two smaller ditches (*13366* and *13368*) met the main boundary marker (*13355*) at right-angles (Fig. 2.8). This junction could equate with that formed by the meeting of the boundary between Plots N and O and that defining the south edge of the two plots. During the 12th century, the presence of a north-to-south ditch (*13426*, Fig. 2.12) lying some 37m from the King Street frontage (and apparently meeting the southern boundary of Plot N: Fig. 2.3, now marked by ditch *12251*), suggested that the plot had become subdivided by the time of its acquisition by the Friary.

The northern edge of Plot F as indicated on Fig. 2.3 lay *c.* 4m to the south of ditch *30410* (Fig. 2.4). These alignments may, however, both indicate one property boundary which shifted from its original line (the excavated ditch was cut through by many relatively early pits). The southern wall of the Friary precinct broadly respected the southern boundary of the same plot, represented in its early stages by a row of post-holes (Fig. 2.12). The boundary separated Plot F from the churchyard of St John the Evangelist to the south. Plot F extended westward by *c.* 19m across the line the minor road shown in Fig. 2.1 (which the position of ditch *30964* reflects: Fig. 2.12). Further west, boundary ditch *30755* (Fig. 2.4) may have lain immediately downslope of an early manifestation of Road 1, delimiting the western extent of Plot Z (Fig. 2.3).

New boundaries appeared in the eastern part of the site during the 12th century (Period 2.1). Their curvilinear form apparently reflected the local topography, in particular the western limit of the Fresflete's floodplain. The ditches may have defined enclosures and their construction appears to represent an eastward extension (towards the River Wensum) of earlier activity, with gradual colonisation of the river marsh. Redefinition took place during the 13th century (Periods 2.2 and 2.3).

Buildings and dating

Although of a type familiar at many pre-Conquest sites in Britain, the three sunken-featured buildings recorded at Greyfriars are a significant addition to the few known examples from Norwich (three similar structures were excavated beneath the south bailey of the Castle; Shepherd Popescu forthcoming). Not least, the Greyfriars buildings provide detailed information on constructional techniques. Much of the ceramic building material recovered from Period 1 contexts is Romano-British, the majority having been re-used alongside quern fragments to construct hearths in two of the sunken buildings. Similar re-use of materials is well-known in Late Saxon London (Horsman *et al.* 1988, 98) and elsewhere.

Early buildings (Period 1) were diverse in form, ranging from sunken-floored and sunken-featured examples to structures represented by either post-holes or beam-slots. The three structures whose full extent could be determined were the sunken-floored buildings *10049* and *30332* and the sunken-featured building *50242*, whose groundplans are illustrated in Fig. 2.6. Buildings *10049* and *50242* were of similar proportions, length (the former was only 0.36m longer than the latter) and construction, although hut *30332* was considerably smaller (measuring only 2.8m in length). All three of these structures seemed too small to have been dwellings although, despite its small size, the central post-holes within building *10049* were relatively large, suggesting quite a substantial structure and potentially considerable height. These buildings were probably workshops, an interpretation supported by associated finds of manufacturing waste. Huts of comparable dimensions and character to these structures have been recorded at Keston, Kent (Philp 1973, 156–63) and Colchester (Crummy 1981, 1–5): the occurrence of stake-holes in the floors of these particular buildings, together with the presence of finds of weaving equipment, led to their interpretation as weaving sheds. A wide range of items found in the Norwich Greyfriars buildings — including a near-complete pot — was accompanied by evidence for craft activities such as weaving, antlerworking and metalworking (evidence for silver melting was found in one building and evidence for iron-smithing in all three: below, 42–3).

The date of building *30332* is uncertain, although may be indicated by a 12th-century pit within it which contained evidence for bone/antler and non-ferrous metalworking. Finds recovered from buildings *10049* and *50242*, usage of both of which dates ceramically to the 11th century, are summarised in Tables 2 and 3 (below). Small Find and figure numbers are given for those items that are catalogued in Chapter 5. A full discussion and comparison of the ceramic assemblages is given by Lentowicz in Chapter 5.III.

Building *10049* was shown to have been in use for a surprisingly long time by a succession of interior alterations and by the broad date span of diagnostic artefacts, which demonstrated that it only fell from use in the late 12th–early 13th century. A coin of Alfred (887–9) was recovered from a post-hole, although it is probable that this was residual. This discovery is significant for two main reasons. First, it prompts close consideration of the date of use of this structure, which has been deduced primarily on the basis of pottery recovered from its occupation deposits. The mid–late 11th-century date assigned to the pottery from these layers (Lentowicz, Chapter 5.III) is clearly at variance with the late 9th-century date of the coin. This conflict might be reconciled if the coin was regarded as a redeposited item or scrap for recycling, an interpretation supported by the presence of silver-working evidence in the immediate vicinity. It is possible that the coin formed part of an assortment of scrap silver items waiting to be melted down. Coins of Alfred would have circulated during his reign and beyond, to some extent, although Norwich lay outside the zone where Alfred's money would have normally circulated (John Davies, *pers. comm.*). It appears that, the greater the distance from Alfred's Kingdom, the later the period of residual circulation, up to a certain point. In the Danelaw, his coins circulated into the early 10th century. They are also found in slightly later 10th-century hoards in the far north (and

Scandinavia) but would not, however, have remained in use as late as the 11th century. By the 11th and 12th centuries a coin of Alfred would have been monetarily obsolete, but may have been valued instead as a piece of scrap silver. In fact this scenario is quite likely because such coins were made of good-quality silver. Nevertheless, the alternative possibility — that the building was indeed in use in the late 9th or early 10th century — needs to be acknowledged. Ceramic fabrics and forms from the site tend to support a late 10th–11th century date, rather than late 9th–10th. The two major buildings (*10049* and *50242*) both appear to have been in use, and perhaps constructed, in the 11th century, despite the presence of earlier artefacts found in association with them (Lentowicz, Chapter 5.III). This tension between different kinds of dating evidence emphasises the need for a full review of local ceramic chronology (*c.f.* Shepherd and Lentowicz 1998).

The second point of interest is the rare discovery of this Alfred penny (produced between *c.* 880 and 895 and probably lost shortly after 895) in a sealed archaeological context. This may have implications for the understanding both of Norwich in the late 9th century, when the town was under Danish control, and of contemporary coinage in use within the Danelaw as a whole. The period between the early 880s and the mid to late 890s has been described in numismatic terms as an 'imitative' phase. During this time Anglo-Scandinavian coins largely copied those of Alfred, carrying Alfred's name and, in some cases, those of his moneyers (Blackburn 1997, 127).

As noted above, the concentration of early finds in the eastern part of the site (Area C: see above) possibly relates to occupation associated with Middle Saxon *Conesford*. The 880s lead weight was found redeposited in a Period 2.2 deposit adjacent to sunken-featured building *50242*. Middle Saxon finds (including pottery and a copper-alloy dress pin) came from the building itself, despite the dominance of later pottery. Micromorphological samples taken from building *50242* are similar to those recorded within Middle Saxon buildings at West Heslerton, North Yorkshire (Macphail and Cruise, Chapter 6.VIII). Lower fills indicate construction, use and re-use, with upper fills indicating both midden dumping and structural collapse.

The possibly 13th-century timber building represented by a regular arrangement of post-pits at the eastern limit of the site (Figs 2.12 and 2.21–3; Period 2.3) was clearly substantial.

Possible workshops constructed along the King Street frontage in the 12th–13th centuries indicate a change from timber to stone construction, suggesting a revival in importance of the street which was perhaps stimulated by the presence of the Friary from 1226. The succession of later buildings fronting King Street, prior to the acquisition of this area by the friars in 1292, was complex (Period 2; Fig. 2.12). The substantial flint foundation (*10004 etc.*) clearly formed part of a major building but the groundplan and date of this structure were both ambiguous. This building is only tentatively suggested to pre-date the Friary, and might conceivably represent part of the religious house.

Quarries and marginalization

Marginalisation of the area investigated by excavation in the later 12th and 13th centuries is indicated by the absence of buildings and prevalence of quarry pits. This might partly reflect the site's steeply sloping character, which would have hindered the development of plots and buildings. Such recession, which was already well advanced when the Franciscans acquired their site, apparently resulted from the topographically constricting effects of the establishment of the Norman Castle (*c.* 1067–8) and Cathedral (*c.* 1094), and the relatively remote location of the new market. It also accords with the documentary evidence for depopulation of this area: although they had been previously built up, Plots A–J and M–Q (Fig. 2.3) were void by 1292, and the church of St John the Evangelist had disappeared.

The occurrence of large quarries close to King Street in the 12th and 13th centuries (Period 2.2) provides some information about land-use of this area and the configuration of properties. The quarries indicate open ground that was probably not otherwise intensively used, and may have been dug in the backlands of tenements. The line of the early medieval frontage of King Street, however (based on that of the precinct wall of the Friary), lay only 5m to the west of the largest quarry and only 3m west of another. The short distance between the quarries and the inferred early medieval frontage would have restricted the depth of any buildings fronting the road. This implies that structures were sparsely distributed along this part of the King Street frontage and could suggest that, in terms of frontage development, this section of road was not of primary importance. The later appearance of three structures (Period 2.3) may represent an episode of concerted development of this section of frontage, possibly prior to 1292 when this area was acquired by the Friary. The intensification of use of the King Street frontage, indicated by the construction of buildings in an area formerly occupied by quarries, must reflect an increase in its importance.

Further east, the regularity in plan and profile of the grouping of quarries in Area B (Period 2.3) suggests that the cutting of these pits was an orderly process, conforming to surface constraints and perhaps taking place within a rectangular tenement backland. Such organization maximized the yield of sand while allowing space for temporary spoil heaps within a restricted area of working. The presence of multiple cuts in each cluster reflects the working of the available area in stages.

Churches

The site has provided unexpected new evidence for the churches (and cemeteries) of St John the Evangelist and St Vedast, to the south and east of the excavated area respectively. The three coffin slabs, including a noteworthy 12th–13th-century example (Samuel and Ashley, Chapter 5.I, 'Coffins'), that had been re-used in Friary structures may have derived from early churches in the vicinity.

St John the Evangelist

While the approximate extent of the churchyard of St John the Evangelist was inferred from documents (Fig. 2.1), the positions of a 12th-century grave, disarticulated human remains and boundary markers apparently associated with the churchyard provide new insights into its possible extent to the north and east, and also its subsequent contraction. The church had gone by soon after 1272, and certainly by 1287 (Fig. 2.2), although the Franciscans did not acquire this area until the late 15th century (Fig.3.3).

The excavated 12th-century grave (Period 2.1) was located immediately to the north of the property boundary that later became marked by the southern wall of the Friary precinct. It contained not only an articulated skeleton but also disarticulated bone from two other individuals. The implied disturbance of previous burials indicates that the grave lay within a formal and long-lived cemetery, probably that of St John the Evangelist which once stood on the corner between King Street and Rose Lane. The absence of surrounding graves could be explained by truncation, resulting either from landscaping of the enlarged precinct of the Friary and construction of its southern boundary wall, or from later horticultural activity. The nearby row of post-holes may represent a fence defining the northern limit of the churchyard. The eastern boundary of the cemetery may equate with a north-to-south ditch (*30964*: Fig. 2.12, Period 2.3), two discrete sections of which were found to the south of the later Friary precinct (a further section on the projected alignment occurred to the north). The eastern end of the grave cut lay *c.* 3m to the east of this ditched boundary. This might be explained — perhaps — by a westwards contraction of the churchyard, although it also implies that a cockey in the vicinity may have been enclosed within the early cemetery. On the basis of the location of the grave, the burial ground extended at least 65m from King Street and 59m from Rose Lane. The articulated skeleton was that of an adolescent female, who had apparently suffered repeated spinal injury relating to loading with excessive weight (Boghi, Chapter 6.I).

St Vedast

At the eastern end of the site, 45 pieces of limestone, including a shaft and an ashlar block, were recovered from deposits of late 11th–12th-century date (Samuel, Chapter 5.I, 'Structural stonework'). These may have been associated with the construction, modification or demolition of the church of St Vedast, which was located to the east of the excavation. A copper-alloy suspension unit (SF28; see Huddle, Chapter 5.III, 'Lamp/censer fittings'), possibly associated with a censer, was recovered from a post-medieval make-up layer in Area C. It is conceivable that this item, together with a variety of other objects (worked stone, window glass and lead came), also derived from the nearby church of St Vedast, which was demolished in the 16th century.

Craft, industry, economy and trade

The site has provided important new evidence relating to industrial and economic activity in this area in the pre-Friary period. While some of this evidence simply builds on findings from previous excavations, other aspects (including possible minting and metalworking) are highly significant to understanding of the Norwich economy. A range of craft activities demonstrate the daily occupations of the inhabitants of the area prior to the arrival of the Greyfriars, with additional evidence for waste distribution and provisioning coming from the faunal remains. At Northampton, archaeological evidence suggests that buildings were randomly arranged, perhaps in small social and economic groups (Williams J.H. 1984, 31), and a comparable situation is demonstrated within Late Saxon Norwich at Greyfriars and at Castle Mall. At both of these sites the irregular placement of buildings, some of which may have been workshops or storerooms, along with the distribution of craft waste (*e.g.* antler-, bone- and hornworking and metalworking at both sites) and environmental remains (grain storage and processing at the Castle Mall site), indicates settlement of a similar informal character.

Water to support such activity and other processes (such as tanning: above, 12) would have been locally sourced from the three small streams surrounding the site (Fig. 2.1). Although a number of early pits were very deep (up to 5m), the probable lower level of the water table at this time indicates that they were not used as wells. Similarly deep Late Saxon and Norman pits were encountered during excavation at Norwich Castle (Shepherd Popescu forthcoming).

Metalworking

Some insight into the location of different types of metalworking in the 10th and 11th centuries was gained through examination of the distribution of non-ferrous metalworking waste, including slags and crucible fragments recovered during the excavations (Goffin and Doonan, Chapter 5.II). Crucibles, predominantly of Thetford-type ware but including three Stamford sherds, occurred in various parts of the site and were found throughout the pre-Friary period. Amongst the 12th-century assemblage (Period 2.1) examples were found in a pit that produced independent dating evidence in the form of two coins attributable to the reign of Stephen (1135–54) and probably deposited no later than the mid-1150s (Davies, Chapter 5.II). Although the deposition of crucibles continued into the 13th century and beyond, the ceramic types used indicate that this took place residually by this time.

Three significant concentrations of non-ferrous metalworking waste were identified (Fig. 5.19).

1. The first cluster, which was composed of material from twelve contexts, surrounded building *10049*, stretching some 16m to the south-west of the structure (Area A). This group included three crucible fragments (*10619*, *10725* and *12300*) with high concentrations of silver and little trace of anything else, suggesting that silver melting was carried out here. The first two of these sherds occurred within the building itself. This cluster largely overlapped the extents of two 10th–11th-century pit groups. It is perhaps coincidental that the only silver item of this period from the entire excavation was a penny of Alfred of 887–9 (SF756; Blackburn, Chapter 5.II) recovered from the southern main post-hole of the sunken-floored building. It is tempting, however, to speculate that this coin represented a lost element of the material that was being melted down (see above).
2. The second cluster of crucibles lay in the northern half of Area B. Over 85% of the crucibles in this part of the site had been used for melting brass.
3. The third concentration occurred in the southern part of Area C. Here nearly 90% of the crucibles had been used for melting either leaded brass or leaded bronze.

The assemblage of litharge cakes (of which three, from contexts *30331*, *30928* and *50457*, were analysed) with high concentrations of silver indicate that silver refining was carried out in the vicinity (Doonan, Chapter 5.II, 'Litharge cakes'). The presence of silver refining is significant, since it is thought that the most likely reason for such activities is to prepare silver bullion for subsequent inclusion in alloys used in minting (below). One of these fragments (*50457*) was found amongst the cluster of crucibles, close to two sherds that provided evidence for both silver and lead (*50302* and *50042*). These two crucible fragments may well have been associated with cupellation (silver refining), especially given their proximity to the argentiferous litharge cakes. Additionally, and perhaps most diagnostically, a lead disc bearing the devices of an Alfred penny of 871–99 (SF281: Archibald, Chapter 5.II), was found in close proximity to the litharge fragment. This has been identified as a half-*eyrir* lead weight. Further implications of this discovery are considered below and in Chapter 5.II.

The single largest assemblage relating to ferrous metalworking — specifically iron-smithing — was recovered from the earlier features in Area C (Fig. 5.18: see Cowgill and Mills, Chapter 5.II). These included building *50242* and contexts that were either close to or associated with it (in an area bounded to the north-west by ditches *50681* and *50689* and to the south by ditch *50008*). A total of 10.17kg of iron-working slags was recovered from the building and a further 5.5kg from pits to its west. It appears that the debris was redeposited in features dating to the 10th–11th centuries. This same pattern is seen in Area A to a lesser extent: the majority of the iron slag is contained within the post-usage fills of the sunken buildings (*10049* and *50242*). It seems unlikely that smithing was occurring inside these buildings, but it may have happened close by. In Area C it was apparently being carried out just to the west of the structure. This is suggested by the presence of hammerscale in a number of deposits.

Ferrous metalworking in Area B seems to have been associated with a 12th-century 'industrial' pit (*30980*), apparently sited within building *30332*. This pit also produced evidence for bone-, antler- and non-ferrous metalworking.

The occurrence of metalworking in peripheral areas has been interpreted as reflecting a desire to locate noxious processes away from dense habitation. However, the quantities of slags retrieved at Mann Egerton, while significant, do not suggest large-scale production (Cowgill and Mills, Chapter 5.II). Although iron-working waste predominated in terms of quantity, the presence of non-ferrous metalworking hints at a far more complex picture of production activities, all of them probably carried out on a small scale in artisan workshops.

Minting?

Discovery of the 880s half-*eyrir* weight on the same site as 10th–11th-century silver-refining debris has prompted speculation that minting took place in this area. There was certainly minting in Norwich in the Late Saxon period, and discussion elsewhere in this volume suggests that this was probably so at the time of the Greyfriars weight (Archibald, Chapter 5.II). In 11th-century Winchester minting took place in the premises of the individual moneyers, who were probably located in the same area of the town, rather than in one central place. We do not know how minting was organised geographically in Norwich in the late 9th century, but continuity with one of the later locations is possible. It might be expected, however, that silver-working in Norwich was not necessarily confined to places where coins were being produced. Each later moneyer would have been working a considerable amount of silver: in the absence of dies or other diagnostic artefacts, it is probably evidence for large-scale operations which would help identify a mint. Archibald argues that the Greyfriars weight is a unit in the general Viking system of weighing, rather than being specifically designed for weighing convenient numbers of pennies like the Anglo-Saxon die-struck weights. It is an official weight and could possibly have been used at a mint, although it cannot be proved that the use of such weights was necessarily confined to a mint. In conclusion, while there may possibly have been a mint on this site the present evidence, even when taken together, does not require it.

Other crafts

Antlerworking waste was widespread but can mostly be ascribed to three main clusters (Fig. 5.24: see Huddle, Chapter 5.II, 'Antlerworking'). The highest quantity (336 fragments) was recovered from 25 contexts in Area CB and the north-west corner of Area C. The second group occurred in a linear area which contained building *30332* at its east end and extended *c.* 24m to the west of the structure. In total 303 fragments were recovered from this strip, of which 186 were found in the building. Over 60% of the total assemblage came from a single pit *30980* (Period 2.1). Lying at right-angles to Road 1, this linear cluster probably resulted from discard in a yard to the rear of a building fronting the lane. The third cluster, comprising 241 fragments of antlerworking waste, was adjacent to King Street and may have been associated with building *10049*. Much of the material came from two 11th-century pits (*12461* and *11100*). The extent of this group corresponded closely to that of twelve crucible fragments (see above), perhaps implying that occupancy of the plot by artisans changed frequently. Alternatively, the coincidence of different materials may indicate the production of composite items, or simply that a range of crafts was undertaken in the same area.

Comparison of the distributions of iron slags and antlerworking waste affords some insight to the extent to which particular manufacturing processes were carried out in certain areas over long time-spans. It is notable that the iron-slag cluster noted above in Area C and the antlerworking waste concentration in Areas CB and C were mutually exclusive. The boundary between the two groups corresponds almost exactly with the line of successive ditches *50681* and *50679* (10th–11th century/Period 1 and 12th century/Period 2.1 respectively). This strongly suggests that the ditch defined the boundary between two plots that were characterised by different production activities.

It has already been suggested that some of the excavated Late Saxon buildings may have served as weaving sheds, supplementing earlier evidence for this craft in Norwich. Artefacts relating to textile manufacture and processing came from both Late Saxon and Norman deposits (Chapter 5.II, 'Textile-working'). The group includes teeth from carding combs, bone pins (most deriving from the sunken-featured buildings) which would have either been used in netting or with a loom, and a fired clay loomweight. Other objects include a pin beater and spindle whorls of various materials (also from buildings). Shears of varying size may have been used for cutting cloth, shearing and needlework. Flax seeds were recovered from an early medieval cess-pit (Fryer and Murphy, Chapter 6.V).

Documentary evidence suggests that the lower, eastern part of the site may have been occupied by leatherworkers, using water from the Dallingflete (Rutledge, above, 12). There was, however, no direct evidence for this in the excavated faunal assemblage, although butchery and secondary butchery waste was recovered from Saxo-Norman and early medieval deposits (Moreno-García, Chapter 6.II). Micromorphological sampling indicated that pre-Friary deposits in the eastern part of the site had been biologically worked, representing anthropogenic accumulation which had been disturbed, possibly by cultivation (Macphail and Cruise, Chapter 6.VIII).

On the higher ground to the west, among plots acquired by the Friary in the late 13th century, documentary evidence attests to the presence of a painter, glazier, carpenter, farrier, needlemaker and goldsmith. Although it is tempting to suggest that the oyster-shell palette recovered from the site relates to the documented Giles le Peyntour, the archaeological evidence indicates an association with the Friary itself (Howard and Park, Chapter 5.II).

Daily life

The artefactual assemblages from Late Saxon, Norman and medieval deposits at Greyfriars are typical of Norwich sites of the period. Pottery recovered from buildings and associated pits and ditches of the Saxo-Norman period (Period 1) consists primarily of locally produced wares, with lesser quantities of regional and Continental imports (Lentowicz, Chapter 5.III). It includes a significant group of Yarmouth-type ware. Utilitarian kitchen wares dominate the assemblage, supplemented by serving and other domestic vessels, such as lamps. The nature of the early assemblages generally indicates a local *floruit* in the 11th century. Characteristic of the 12th-century assemblage is the increased presence of early medieval wares and the growing range of regional and Continental imports. Pottery from the immediately pre-Friary period sees the increased importance of medieval fabrics. Again, most of the assemblage came from pits and represents domestic refuse.

Items of intrinsic interest include those with possible Anglo-Scandinavian associations, and important individual assemblages came from the sunken-featured buildings. Other than those associated with craft and economic activity, most of the objects recovered relate to domestic settlement (knives, bone spoon, hone stones, bone combs), while dress items include the familiar range (*e.g.* beads, pins, a shale bracelet, hooked tags, buckles and belt mounts) (Chapters 5.III and IV). There is a notable link between the workmanship of the hooked tags from the St Faith's Lane evaluation (Site 373N) and those recovered from Castle Mall (Huddle forthcoming), indicating that they may have been made by the same person. A small but interesting assemblage of horse-harness pendants, mounts and bells was retrieved from 12th–13th-century deposits (Ashley, Chapter 5.V). The group includes an armorial horse harness mount dating to the second half of the 12th century which depicts the arms of Warenne (the Earls of Surrey). Evidence for pastimes during the 13th century includes an antler die and a bone skate (Chapter 5.VII).

A substantial proportion of the faunal assemblage from the Saxo-Norman period came from sunken-featured building *50242*. Pig bones dominating this group indicated the consumption of the best cuts of meat and young animals, and demonstrating the significance of these animals in the economy of early Norwich. Across the site, the quantity of pig declined during the 12th century, however, with the proportion of cattle remaining relatively stable and the consumption of sheep/goat increasing. A number of arrowheads recovered from pre-Friary deposits may have been used in hunting. There was no evidence for the presence of any 'high-status' birds and fish in pre-Friary contexts, while an unexpectedly high proportion of flatfish in the 10th–11th century assemblage may be a site-specific anomaly (Nicholson, Chapter 6.III). A single possible fishnet spacer was recovered.

Plant remains reflect the typical Norwich assemblage of this period and it is clear that crop-processing was taking place on the site (Fryer and Murphy, Chapter 6.V). One 13th-century pit fill contained oats and barley probably indicating malting. A number of quernstones and millstones recovered from the site may have been used in the processing of flour, malt or other foodstuffs. Edible wild taxa included strawberry, apple, damson/bullace, bramble and elder.

Conclusion

The Greyfriars excavations have surpassed all expectations in terms of evidence for pre-Friary activity, indicating that occupation might have begun in the Roman or Anglo-Saxon periods. The Middle Saxon finds provide an important addition to the growing corpus of artefacts of this date from Norwich, and amount to significant new evidence for the possible location of *Conesford*. One of the key research objectives was to increase understanding of Late Saxon and early medieval Norwich and the results relating to possible minting, metalworking and other economic activity are crucial in this regard. Equally significant is the new evidence for the early street pattern, the influence of local topography on urban development, and the position of early churches. In addition, the new research elucidates the immediately pre-Friary settlement pattern in this now-marginal part of the city, which appears typical of the kinds of urban location chosen for occupation by the Greyfriars.

3. The Franciscan Friary (1226–1538)

O dolor, o plus quam dolor, o pestis trunculenta.
fratis minores venerunt in Angliam.
(Oh sorrow, oh more than sorrow, oh cruel pestilence.
The Friars Minor are come to England.)

Florence of Worcestre, 1239

I. ARCHAEOLOGICAL AND HISTORICAL BACKGROUND

Antiquarian observations and documentary historiography

by Elizabeth Rutledge

The most detailed histories of the Norwich Greyfriars (Franciscans or Friars Minor) and their Friary occur in two early 18th-century accounts, the *History of the Religious Orders of Norwich* by John Kirkpatrick, written *c.* 1725 (Kirkpatrick 1845) and *A History of the City and County of Norwich* by Francis Blomefield, written 1745 (Blomefield 1806). Both deal with the subject as a whole and at some length, with Kirkpatrick concentrating more on the physical development of the precinct and Blomefield more on individual friars he believed to be connected with the house. Although he was personally antagonistic to the whole concept of the Friary Kirkpatrick's approach was scholarly, often quoting from documents and giving references, and his conclusions are well argued. Blomefield is more difficult to use. Although a mine of information, he gives fewer references and can make apparently authoritative statements on the basis of limited, or incorrect, facts. His early list of wardens, for instance, appears to be partly based on the assumption that all Franciscans with Norfolk-sounding surnames must have been connected with the Norwich house (*e.g.* Walter de Chatton: Emden 1957, I, 395), while his comments on the pardon cloister (below) imply a misreading of the evidence. In short, while Blomefield is an invaluable source his references need to be checked and any unsupported statements treated with caution.

Most accounts for the next two hundred years added little of substance. Richard Taylor in his *Index Monasticus* (Taylor 1821, 40) relied mainly on Blomefield, though he does describe the current (early 19th-century) status of the site. William Dugdale's *Monasticon Anglicanum* (Dugdale 1830, 1522–3) quotes William Worcestre's description of the Friary church at length and refers to Taylor, but mainly relies on Blomefield. The *Victoria County History* (Doubleday *et al.* 1906, 430–1) uses Blomefield, Kirkpatrick and Dugdale while providing a little extra information on the Dissolution. The only really new ground covered in this period is William Hudson's description of the stone bridge in St Faith's Lane, of the precinct wall as standing, and of the course of the Dallingflete stream (Hudson 1884–7, 117–41). Two more recent studies, however, have dealt with other aspects of the Friary's history. Norman Tanner's *The Church in Late Medieval Norwich 1370–1532* (Tanner 1984) considers the Norwich Greyfriars as an element of the religious life of the city, while *The Greyfriars of Norwich* (Hale and Rodgers 1991) first sets the Norwich Franciscan Friary within a general context and then traces the development of the site during the first hundred years after the Dissolution.

Three sets of documents providing dimensions formed the basis of historical research into the site in the medieval period. These are a mortmain licence for property acquired *c.* 1292 (Table 4), a paced survey of the church and cloister by William Worcestre in 1479 and the city leases of 1565–71 (Table 5). The 1292 mortmain license allowed the arrangement of plots and roads acquired by the Friary to be conjectured, and all three documents were used in reconstructing the internal layout of the Friary precinct.

Previous archaeological work

Prior to the 1990s work, archaeological evidence within the Friary precinct was largely limited to stray finds, along with observations of the precinct wall (Site 394N), the putative medieval stone bridge (Site 26392N) and possible elements of the church (Chapter 1.IV; below). Although there is no documentary evidence for its location, the expectation at the outset of the project that the Friary cemetery lay in the large area to the north of the church rested upon a number of previous archaeological observations. These comprise discoveries of human skeletal remains: numerous skeletons found during extension of the Wallace King showrooms in 1950 (Site 394N), skeletons disturbed at 13 and 22 Prince of Wales Road in 1878 and 1867/1925 respectively, and disarticulated bone excavated at the rear of the Norfolk Club in 1991 (Site 373N).

Previously published ground-plans of the Greyfriars complex include those of Taylor (1821, map opp. 132) and Campbell (1975, maps 2 and 3), although these were largely speculative, being based on topographical, documentary and limited archaeological evidence. A summary of these and other previous interpretations appears on pp.53–5, below.

II. DOCUMENTARY EVIDENCE

by Elizabeth Rutledge
(Figs 3.1–3.6; Pls 3.1 and 3.2)

History of the Norwich Greyfriars

The Franciscans (Greyfriars or Friars Minor) came to Norwich in 1226, the same year as the Dominicans (Black or Preaching Friars) came to the city and just two years after the first arrival of the Franciscan order in England (Campbell 1975, 11: for this section generally see Hutton 1926, *passim.*). While not one of the very first Franciscan friaries in England it was fitting, given the Greyfriars' predilection for centres of population, that Norwich should have been one of their earlier foundations. Within twenty years of their arrival in England in 1224 the Franciscans had settled at the two university towns, at fifteen out of the nineteen cathedral cities and at 25 of the places that were, or were to become, county towns (Knowles 1948, 133).

Many of these early settlements were on low-lying sites, often at the edge of the town. In this respect the original Norwich holding was typical, lying well down the slope, away from the main streets and not far from the church of St Mary in the Marsh. At first the only building needed was an ordinary house, though this would soon have been supplemented with a chapel, probably built of wood. The earliest chapel at Cambridge was said to have been built by one carpenter in a day. In these early days the number of Franciscans at Norwich is likely to have been very small: the Cambridge chapel, for instance, was built for only three friars. By 1255/6, however, there were 1242 Greyfriars in England in 49 houses, giving an average of over 25 friars a house, although there must still have been considerable variation in numbers as London and Oxford had about 80 friars apiece. This increase in numbers as the 13th century progressed was not the only change in the Franciscan friaries. The order of the Friars Minor had been founded on an ideal of poverty and the friars were to maintain themselves in the simplest manner by begging. At Oxford the early Franciscans went without shoes and within the custody of Cambridge (which included Norwich, and was known even within the movement for its want of temporal goods) they owned no cloaks (Knowles 1948, 141).

This attitude of self-denial also influenced early attempts to extend friary buildings. Agnellus of Pisa (d. 1236) held that no ground was to be enlarged or house built except as absolute necessity required: a stone cloister built by the burgesses of Southampton was demolished as unsuitable *c.* 1236, while between 1240 and 1248 decorations were removed from the cloister at London and the stone walls of the dormitory at Shrewsbury were replaced in mud. Before 1260 objections were made to decorated windows and a painted pulpit at Gloucester. The pressure for more satisfactory premises, however, became irresistible. The Greyfriars at York and Bridgewater had moved to better sites by *c.* 1250. Others received permission to move later in the century, while at Norwich the same result was achieved by extending the precinct over the higher ground to the west (Fig. 3.3). At the same time, both in England and abroad, the years 1270–1320 saw an extensive programme for the rebuilding of Franciscan churches and their attendant domestic buildings (Knowles 1948, 187).

By the later 14th and early 15th centuries a number of writers, including Chaucer, Langland and Wyclif, were bringing complaints of luxury and avarice against all the orders of friars, and especially the Franciscans. In the almost complete absence of Friary domestic records it is impossible to test the truth of these 14th- and 15th- century complaints. Two rare survivals are an account book from the Cambridge Franciscan Friary for 1363–6, which lists amounts given in alms, mainly in money but also in kind, such as figs, herring and pork (Moorman 1974, 36), and a fragmentary series of accounts for 1537/8 for the Greyfriars of York, published in 1971 (Dobson 1984, 110). However, although the Greyfriars had undoubtedly fallen from the rigorous standards of poverty practised in the early 13th century, it is unlikely that their life was very luxurious. Various inventories of friary goods made in 1538 testify to their poverty. While, unfortunately, no inventory survives for Norwich, the gift by the Duke of Norfolk at the Dissolution of 20 shillings to 'the worst of the Greyfriars ... for raiments' does not imply much in the way of resources (Hale and Rodgers 1991, 28). In fact, friary income must always have been managed on a fairly day-to-day basis. Unlike the monasteries, the friaries had no extensive endowments of property bringing in a regular rent. By the Dissolution the Norwich house, like some other Franciscan friaries, had assured a small income by leasing part of the precinct (Rye 1905, 32–3) and could probably supplement alms with home-grown produce, pigeons from the dovecotes and fish from the Dallingflete, but it must still have been largely dependant on begging and bequests. On the other hand, the bequests to individual friars given in Appendix 2, together with the payments for anniversary masses and the Duke of Norfolk's gift in 1538, suggest that Franciscans may have been allowed to retain some kind of personal wealth.

Part of the original rule of St Francis required the renunciation of learning. Unlike the call to absolute poverty, this was soon more honoured in the breach than in the observance. One of the earliest actions of the Franciscans after arriving in England was to found a school at Oxford and by the mid-13th century Franciscans and Dominicans were known as great collectors of books (Little 1892, 60–1). Little is known about the Franciscan library at Norwich (Leland only mentions one book by name, Bacon's geographical work *De Locis*: Kirkpatrick 1845, 127), but the friars there showed their interest in education as early as *c.* 1250 when they requested that one Friar Eustace de Normanville be appointed as their lecturer. He declined on the grounds of poor health and lack of experience but subsequently lectured at Oxford and Cambridge (Little 1892, 65, 140). In 1336 Norwich became one of the order's seven friaries in England established as *studia* for the teaching of theology at a pre-university level. As such it is known to have attracted friars from Italy, Westphalia, Austria and Saxony (Appendix 1), and notes on lectures and disputations held at Norwich survive in two 14th-century sources (Doucet 1953, 85–98; Little 1940, 628–30). The large number of Franciscans ordained at Norwich between 1532 and 1535 (35) suggests that the Norwich house remained a *studium* until its Dissolution in 1538 (Appendix 1).

It is difficult to talk about the numbers in any Franciscan Friary, as friars could be peripatetic and not necessarily tied to one house in the manner of monks; the position of Norwich as a *studium* merely compounds this problem. It is known, however, that there were 47 Friars Minor at Norwich in 1326 (Little 1892, 44) — fewer than at London (72) or Cambridge (70) but more than at Lynn (38), Gloucester (40) or Reading (26) — and the house probably remained one of the more populous friaries in the country. Twenty-seven men from the Norwich Franciscan Friary were ordained in 1406–7 and 35 ordained between 1532 and 1535 (Appendix 1). In 1538 21 Norwich Greyfriars received licences to act as secular ministers. Only London (27), Cambridge (24) and York (21) had as many or more Franciscan friars granted licences at the Dissolution (Hale and Rodgers 1991, 28). This is a minimum figure as it only includes those friars who were also priests in 1538, while two more Franciscan friar priests from Norwich are mentioned in a later source (L and P for. and dom. Henry VIII, 16, 499).

Guardians or wardens (heads) of the Norwich Friary and other Norwich Greyfriars are listed in Appendix 1. Of these the best-known is undoubtedly the mid-15th century friar John Brackley. He spent much of his time away from Norwich, preaching in London and acting as confessor to Sir John Fastolf at Caister, and was partisan in his later support for the Paston family. A number of letters from him, in English and Latin, have survived among the Paston letters, though unfortunately the sermon once believed to be his and to have been preached at the Norwich Greyfriars has since been reattributed (Davis 1971, II *passim*, no. 919, plate XV).

Relations with the community

Relationships between all the orders of friars and the population of Norwich seem to have been good. Friars by their nature were an integral part of the local community. Their vocation was to evangelise, both by example and by direct preaching, while their primary means of subsistence was by the begging of alms. While the size of the Franciscan church gives some idea of the expected popularity of their preaching, the attitude of the general population to the Greyfriars can best be judged from testamentary legacies and requests for burial in the church and cemetery. A list of known burial requests, many from Norfolk clergy and minor gentry, and of more substantial legacies is given in Appendix 2. Altogether almost half of all lay Norwich testators between 1370 and 1532 left bequests to the Norwich Greyfriars — an unusually high proportion — and about 3% asked to be buried there. It was also common practice for local non-Norwich testators to leave small legacies to all four Norwich friaries. More surprising, considering the opportunities for conflict over preaching, the right to hear confessions and burial fees, is the fact that almost half the Norwich clerical testators also left legacies to the Greyfriars (Tanner 1984, 119, 189).

There were other ways in which the Norwich Franciscan Friary impinged on the life of community members before death. An unusual one was in the provision of sanctuary. In 1329 a commission of oyer and terminer was issued after Thomas de Thornham had been taken from sanctuary in the church of the Friars Minor at Norwich (Cal. Pat. Rolls 1327–30, 429). Further links would have come from the three gilds attached to the Franciscan Friary church, those of St Barbara, of Our Lady and of St John the Evangelist (Appendix 2). An even closer relationship between the laity and the Friary could result from letters of confraternity. The translation of a letter of confraternity addressed to Thomas Bate and his children and dated at Norwich in 1433 is given in Appendix 3i (cover illustration), and three sisters and one brother of the order were mentioned in wills between 1477 and 1492 (Appendix 2). Finally, it is clear that, while friars from abroad did attend the *studium*, many of the Norwich friars themselves came from the local community. The wills mention brothers, nephews, sons and uncles at the Friary (Appendix 2) and the surnames of about half the Norwich friars ordained 1406–7 — while an unreliable guide to their former parish of residence — suggest a Norfolk or north Suffolk origin (Appendix 1).

The part which the Norwich Franciscan Friary could play in the life of a local gentry family is nicely illustrated by the 15th-century Paston letters (Davis 1971, I, II *passim*). In a dispute between William Paston and Walter Aslake, rhyming bills in English threatening William were posted on the gates of the church of the Friars Minor at Norwich and subsequent arbitration between the parties took place in the church there in 1425. In *c.* 1459 Richard Earl of Warwick asked John Paston to intercede on behalf of the Norwich Greyfriars. Margaret Paston, writing to her husband John in March 1461, described an opponent as the son of William Baxter 'that lyth beryed in the Grey Freres' and a few months later, in July, reported that her cousin Barney had spoken to the undersheriff at the Greyfriars, perhaps after a service there. John Paston was in regular correspondence with Friar John Brackley, former confessor to Sir John Fastolf, and both Brackley and another Norwich Franciscan, John Mowth, were involved in the Pastons' fight for the recognition of Fastolf's will. In due course the grandson of John and Margaret Paston, William Call, joined the order and was the last warden of the Norwich house (Venn 1922, I, 282).

Some towns experienced conflict between the older monastic orders and the friars (Hutton 1926, *passim*) but at Norwich relations between the Franciscan Friary and the Cathedral Priory, as well as the diocese and the city government, appear to have been peaceful. The city authorities apparently supported the extension of the Friary precinct in 1292 and attended services in the Greyfriars in the 15th century (Kirkpatrick 1845, 113–15, 127). When Queen Elizabeth Woodville visited Norwich in 1469 the Greyfriars lent the city tapser (tapestry) work and vestments to help with her entertainment (Harrod 1859, 35). There is no evidence that the Cathedral Priory particularly helped the Franciscans when they first came to Norwich, and the monks certainly expected a proper return for the land conveyed to the friars in *c.* 1292 (Kirkpatrick 1845, 111–15), but neither is there evidence of opposition. As early as 1233/4 it was noted that the Friars Minor were present, together with the Dominican friars and the Prior of Norwich, at an initial hearing of a case accusing certain Norwich Jews of the circumcision of a Christian child (Rigg 1901, xlvi). Friars preached at the cathedral, at least until the monks decided to take over in 1360 (Tanner 1984, 11), the priory master of the cellar provided food for the Greyfriars at Christmas, and in 1493 the Friary was considered sufficiently neutral ground for the settling of disputes between the Cathedral Priory and the city (Kirkpatrick 1845, 123, 127). Relations with the diocese permitted an ordination at the Franciscan church

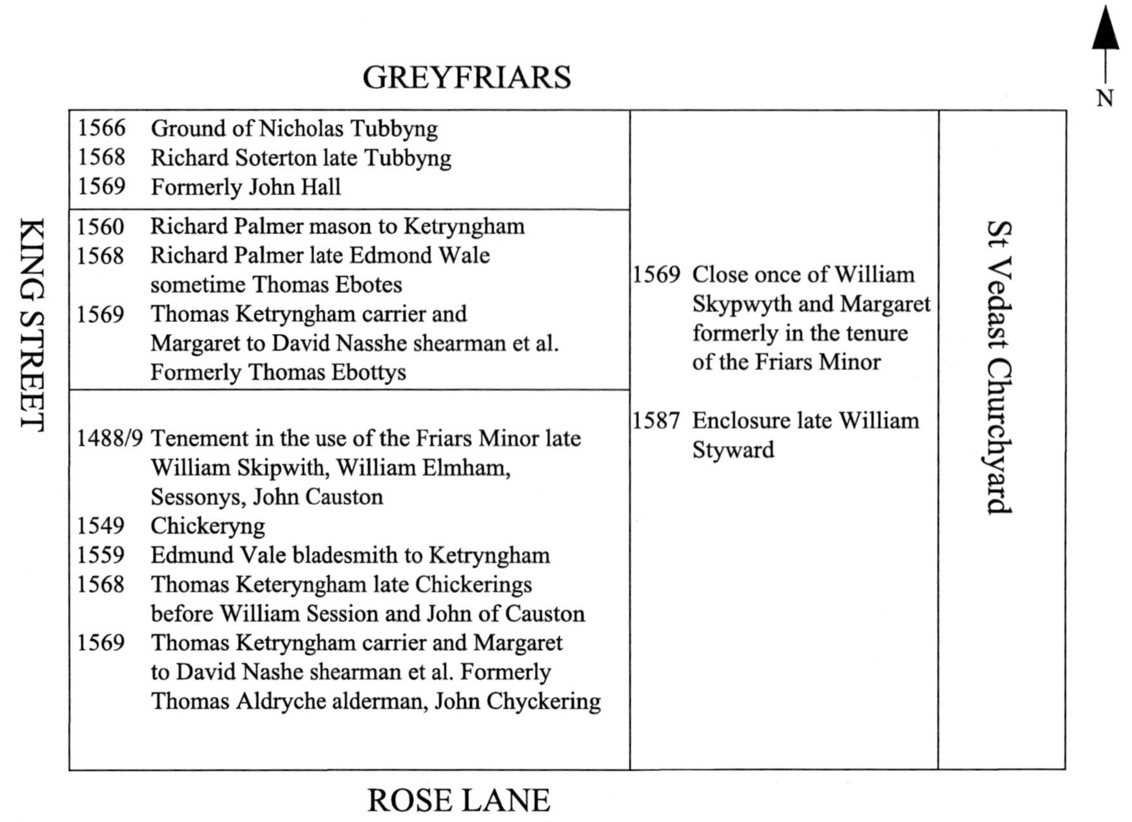

Figure 3.1 King Street/Rose Lane Corner, 16th century. Sources: NRO NCR Ketryngham to Nasshe le (26) m.85; Stanton to Whall lf (29) m.63' 18a Chamb. acc. 1470-90 127; 18d (2) 11; 18d (3) 4: 22g (1) 55–66. Not to scale.

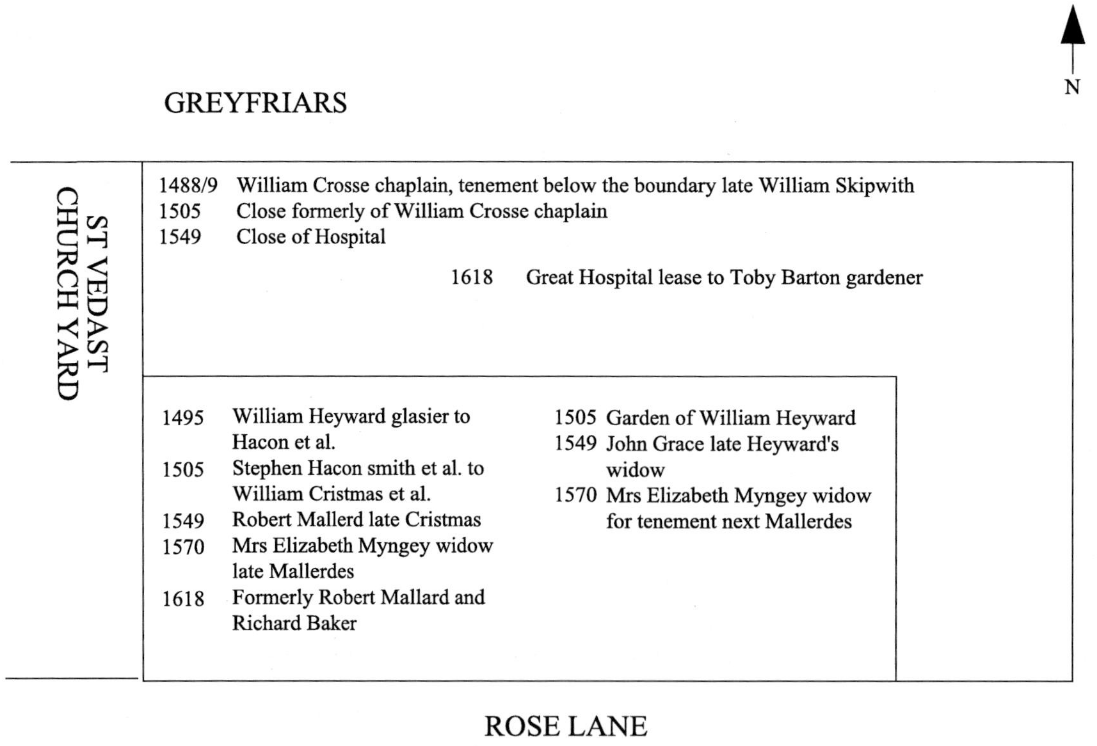

Figure 3.2 Properties east of St Vedast Churchyard (15th–17th centuries). Sources: NRO NCR Hacon to Crismas 1d (20) m. 75; 18a Chamb. acc. 1470-90 128d; 18d (2); 18d 93) 5; 20d (1) 193d. Not to scale.

in 1439 (NRO HMN 7/318 p.115) and the heads of all four Norwich orders of friars co-operated with the diocesan authorities in the cases of the false priest Robert Colynson in 1453 and the martyr Thomas Bilney in 1531 (Cal. Pat. Rolls 1452–61, 98; Blomefield 1806, III, 202).

To all appearances, the popularity of the Norwich Greyfriars continued up to the Reformation. The proportion of Norwich testators leaving legacies to the Friary remained fairly constant until 1517 and then began to fall. This does not mean, however, that such legacies disappeared. Although the proportion had fallen, as many as 39 per cent of Norwich testators between 1518 and 1532 still left bequests to the Norwich Franciscan Friary (Tanner 1984, 222). There is no such direct evidence for the giving of alms before death but it is hard to see how the Friary could have operated as a *studium* into the 1530s, or continued to maintain at least 23 friars until 1538, without popular support. This may have waned, however, in the last few years when confidence in the future of the order must have been shaken by the Dissolution of the more rigorous Observant Franciscan houses in 1534 (Moorman 1974, 92).

Two lozenge-shaped seals (Pls 3.1A and B) relate to the Franciscan Friary (Appendix 3iii).

Development of the precinct

(Figs 2.1–2.3, 3.1–3.6)

The probable development of the precinct is summarised on Fig. 3.3. According to the Norwich monk and chronicler Bartholomew Cotton, the Greyfriars came to Norwich in 1226 and settled between the churches of St Vedast and St Cuthbert on land given to them by John de Hastingford (Hutton 1926, 72). This land must have been in the eastern half of the later precinct, as this is the only area in which they are recorded as holding property before 1292 (in 1288: NRO MC 146/52 plan 100). The original holding therefore lay north of the east-to-west lane shown on Fig. 2.1 and south of the Dallingflete, as other owners are recorded north of the Dallingflete as late as 1325 (NRO MC 146/52 plan 80). There may have been expansion throughout the 13th century but details only become available after the statute of mortmain in 1279 led to the licensing of grants to religious houses and after the start of the series of Norwich enrolled deeds in 1285. For instance, it might have been an extension of the precinct before 1279 that prompted the complaint at the Conesford leet court in 1290 that the Friars Minor had appropriated several tenements accustomed to pay landgable (Hudson 1892, 36), although any early growth would have been limited geographically by the rule that the friars could not acquire property for investment, but only to extend their existing site.

Plate 3.1 Seals of the Norwich Franciscan Friary: A. St Francis at the entrance of a church; B. Coronation of the Virgin with friar praying below. (Reproduced from Blomefield 1806, iii, app. 1)

The earliest known expansion occurred in 1285, with a licence in mortmain to close a lane (211ft x 12ft) adjoining their area on the south side (Cal. Pat. Rolls 1281–92, 155). This was followed in 1292 by a licence to acquire no fewer than eighteen plots of land (Cal. Pat. Rolls 1281–92, 493: there were only eighteen plots although 20 grantors are named). The associated writ and inquisition give the measurements (Table 4) and the properties have been plotted on Fig. 2.3. The sequence has been taken from the writ as the inquisition deals separately with the properties still paying landgable. It has been assumed that the pieces of land were listed in the order in which they lay and that, as far as possible, they abutted onto one of the known highways, either King Street or the parallel former highway shown on Fig. 2.1. The sequence given on Fig. 2.3 takes into account a number of pieces of evidence: Plot E, granted by the Prior of Norwich, adjoins an orchard probably in Norwich Priory hands in 1325 (NRO MC 146/52 plan 80). The building of the new Friary church had started in Plot E by 1292 (Kirkpatrick 1845, 112–3) and this position corresponds with the suggested east end of the choir; Plot F, granted by Mabel de la Cauwec/Cawet, occupies the position of land described as once of Hubert del Carvet in 1285 (Fig. 2.2); according to Kirkpatrick, the abbey of St Benet of Holme (Plot H) was granted a messuage between 1268 and 1275 in the parish of St Cuthbert with a highway to the north (NRO NCR 21f (2) 9); and a deed of 1284 not only shows that Plot L was east of a highway but also gives the relative positions of Plots K, M and G (NRO DCN 45/8/3). Property further south on the King Street frontage was not acquired until after 1302 (Fig. 2.2). Though this is only a hypothetical reconstruction and may be wrong in detail, this summary of the area acquired is likely to be substantially correct.

This major expansion was followed in 1297 by the closure of a lane (100.5ft x 10ft) on the north side of the friars' dwelling place (Cal. Pat. Rolls 1292–1301, 256). This is not long enough to be the whole of the lane to the south of St Cuthbert's churchyard (Fig. 2.1) although it could have been part of it. Two years later, in 1299, the friars received a licence for three more messuages, to be granted by the Prior of Walsingham, Hugh de Rokelund and Roger le Mareschal (Cal. Pat. Rolls 1292–1301, 412–3). The position of Hugh de Rokelund's and Roger le Mareschal's properties appears on Fig. 2.2 and the messuage of the Prior of Walsingham, which paid 1d landgable, presumably filled in the gap along the King Street frontage. There was a little delay in completing the grants. Hugh de Rokelund conveyed his plot to the King and the City to the use of the Friars Minor in 1301 and it was confirmed by his son in 1331 (NRO NCR 1a (3) m.10d; 1b (12) m.31d), while Roger le Mareschal was still in possession of his in 1302 (Fig. 2.2). Roger's grant must have fallen further south than the friars felt necessary for a neat boundary to their precinct, as in 1307 or 1308 John de

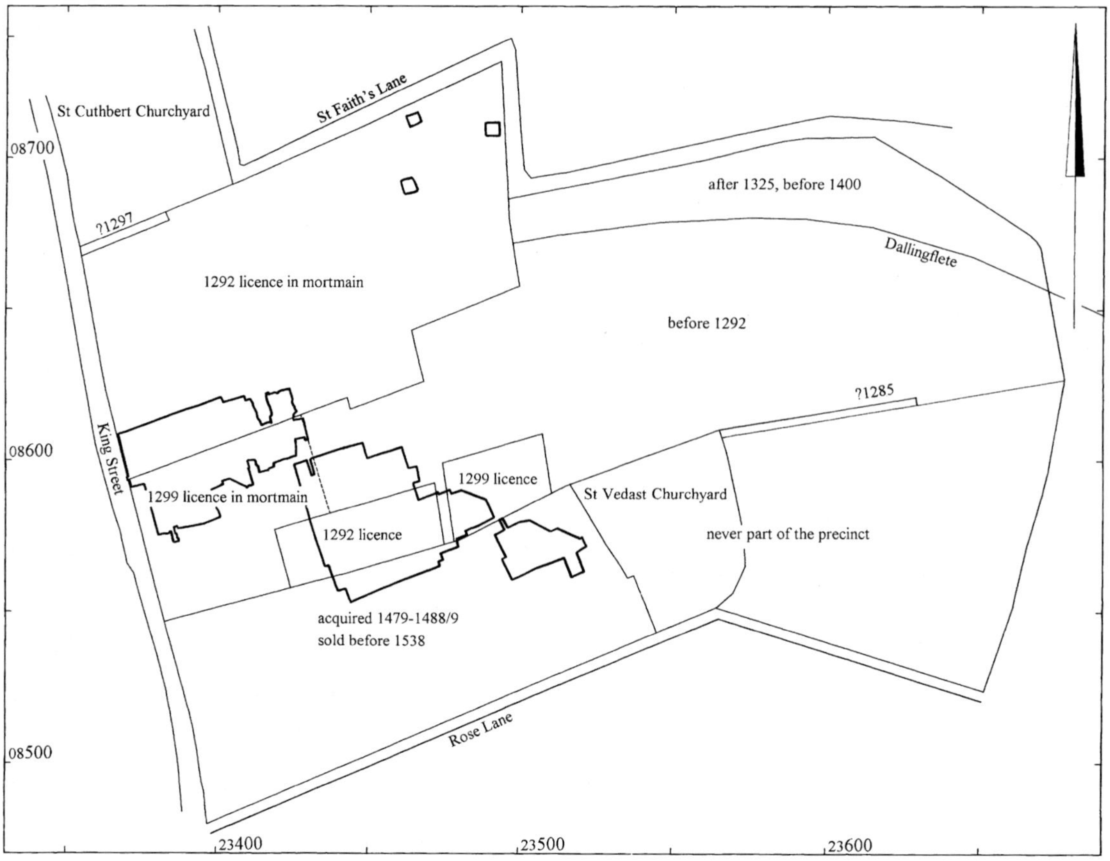

Figure 3.3 Development of the Friary precinct

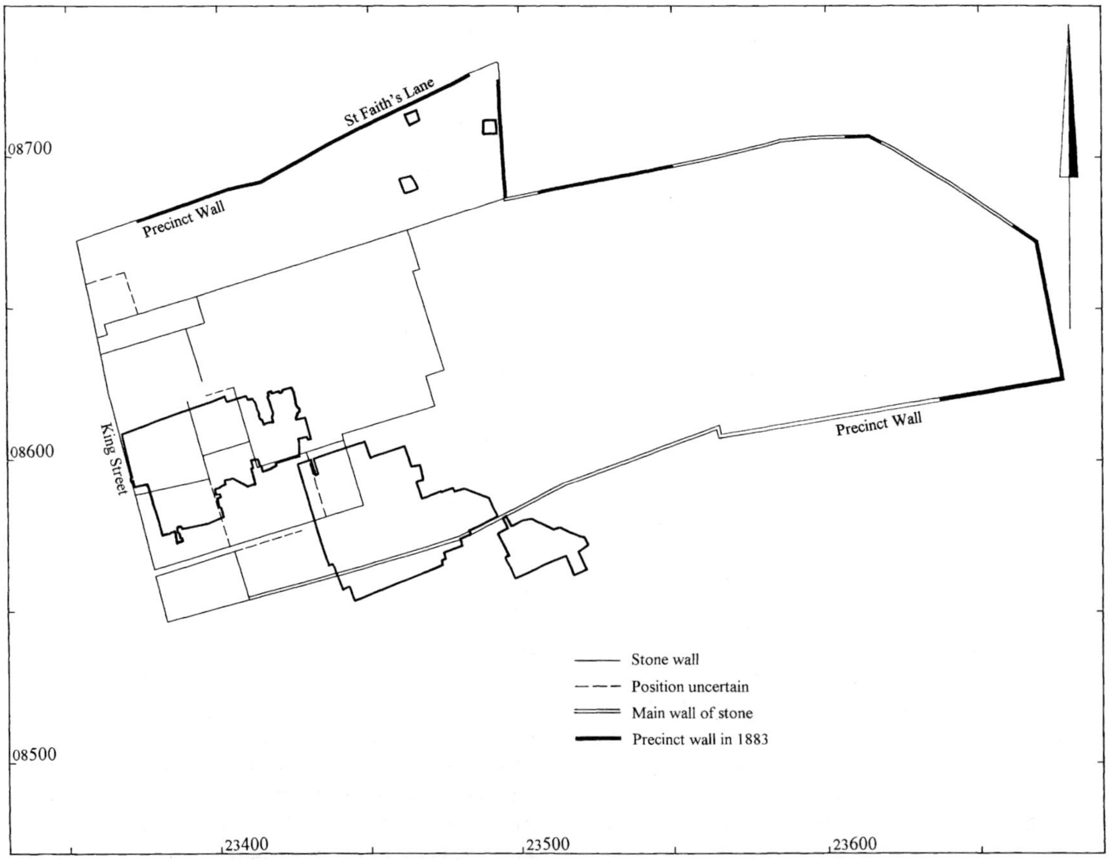

Figure 3.4 Stone walls mentioned in 16th-century leases

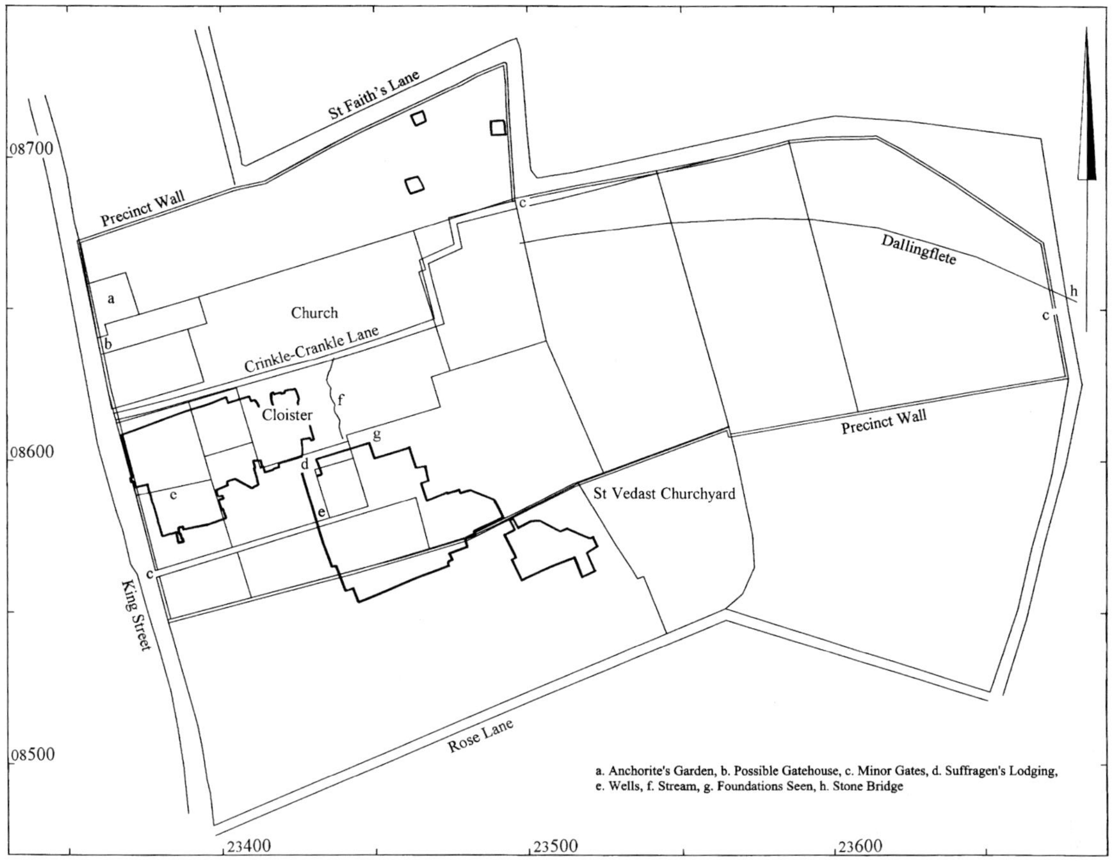

Figure 3.5 Minor features of the Friary

Figure 3.6 Plots leased by the city, 1565–71

Properties in 1292 licence in mortmain (NRO NCR 17b Book of Pleas 51d-52d. Variants show differences between the writ and the inquisition)		
A.	John le Grocer.	Length 9 perches; width 4 perches.
B.	Adam de Stonhous.	Length 9 perches; width 3 perches 7 feet.
C.	Richard de Fornsete.	Length 4 perches 5 feet; width 33 feet.
D.	Prior of St Faith [Horsham].	Length 4 perches; width 33 feet.
E.	Prior of Norwich.	Length 8 perches; width 4 perches 5 feet.
F.	Mabil de la Cauwec (Cawet).	Length 11 perches; width 4 perches.
G.	Thomas de Stanfeld.	Length 7 perches 16 feet; width 35 (30) feet.
H.	Abbot of St Benedict [Holme].	Length 5 perches 3 feet; width 3 perches 15 feet.
I.	Alexander de la Sarteryn and Thomas de Wymundham.	Length 50 feet; width 37 feet.
J.	Roger le Marescall.	Length 6 (7) perches 5 feet; width 4 perches 12 feet.
K.	Godfrey Pikard.	Length 4 perches 5 feet; width 2 perches 6 feet.
L.	Giles Pictor (le Peyntour).	Length 7 perches 16 feet; width 3 perches.
M.	William Justice and Robert his brother.	Length 11 perches; width 3 perches 10 feet.
N.	Roger de Morlee.	Length 11 perches 7 feet; width 5 perches 17 feet.
O.	John de Witton.	Length 3 perches 15 feet; width 30 feet.
P.	Goda de Lodns.	Length 4 perches; width 2 perches 12 feet.
Q.	William de Colney.	Length 7 perches 9 feet; width 3 perches 15 (12) feet.
R.	William Virly (le Wyrly).	Length 7 perches 9 feet; width 3 perches 17 feet.
Property in 1299 licence in mortmain (NRO NCR 1a (3) m.10d; 1b (12) m.31d)		
Z.	Hugh de Rokelund.	Length 113 feet; width 84 feet.

Table 4 Plots shown on Fig. 2.3

A	No dimensions.
B	No dimensions.
C	Length E to W 38½ yards; width at the E end 10 yards, at the W end 6 yards.
D	Length on the N side 32 yards 1 foot, on the S side 34 yards 1 foot; width 20 yards.
E	Length on the N side 26 yards, on the S side 27½ yards; width at the E end 29 yards, at the W end 26 yards.
F	Length on the N side 17 yards, on the S side 15 yards; width at the E end 20 yards 1 foot with a corner at the S 2 yards long, at the W end 20½ yards.
G	No dimensions.
H	No dimensions.
I	No dimensions.
J	Length on the N side 80 yards, on the S side 68 yards; width at the E end 63 yards, at the W end 65½ yards.
K	No dimensions.
L	Length on the N side 66 yards 2 foot 4 inches, on the S side 66 yards; width at the E end 19 yards one foot, at the W end 16 yards 2 foot.
M	Length E to W 68 yards; width N to S 47 yards.
N	Length E to W 36 yards; width N to S 52½ yards.
O	Width at the N end 51½ yards, at the S end 47½ yards 6 inches.
P	Width at the N end 48½ yards, at the S end 46½ yards.
Q	No dimensions.

Source: NRO NCR 22g (1) passim

Table 5 Dimensions used for Fig. 3.6

Morlee bound himself to pay, from a piece of land acquired from the Friars Minor, a rent of 16d formerly paid by Roger (NRO DCN 45/34/4).

By the early 14th century the Greyfriars were in control of a considerable site. It did not yet include the north bank of the Dallingflete, though this was probably in their hands before the end of the century. Nor initially did it extend as far south as Rose Lane (Figs. 2.2 and 3.3; NRO MC 146/52 plan 100). In the late 15th and early 16th centuries, however, the Franciscans also held the block of property lying along Rose Lane from King Street on the west to the churchyard of St Vedast on the east. The evidence for this comes from the city landgable records. The Greyfriars did not pay landgable for their main precinct, not because it was exempt but because other arrangements had been made for the payment (*e.g.* Cal. Pat. Rolls 1292–1301, 412/3). In an account for the receipt of landgable in 1488/9, however (NRO NCR 18a Chamb. acc. 1470–90, 127), two aldermen, John Welles and Thomas Bedefeld, paid for two properties in the use of the Friars Minor. One was described as once of Roger Virly and the other as previously of Sessonys and John Causton (Fig. 2.2). Both were said to have once been owned by William Skipwith and William Elmham. More detail is given in the 1568–70 landgable assessment which describes the properties as 'the tenementes at the south parte of the back gate of the Grey Fryers with a closse ther which grounde in the closse ded sumtyme long to the tenementes … but the Fryers sold parte of the same tenementes to serten persons whereof Richard Soterton holdyth a tenement late Tubbyng, Richard Palmer [holds properties] ... late Edmond Wale and sumtyme Thomas Ebotes, Thomas Keteryngham [holds two] … late Chikeryngs and befor William Session and John of Causton' (NRO NCR 18d (3) 4). Chickeryng is listed in the 1549 landgable list for his tenement on the corner between the common way leading from Over Conesford to Nether Conesford [Rose Lane] on the south and abbutting on the highway on the west (NRO NCR 18d (2) 11). This tenement, and the one to the north, were conveyed by Thomas Ketryngham and his wife to David Nasshe and others in 1569, while a city lease of part of the Greyfriars' ground in 1566 has the ground of Nicholas Tubbyng to the south. The situation is summarised on Fig. 3.1. The whole block, with King Street west, the churchyard of St Vedast east, the Greyfriars north and Rose Lane south, was sold by Thomas Stanton, beerbrewer, and Alice his wife to Augustin Whall, grocer, in 1587 (NRO NCR 1f(29) m.63). It was then described as consisting of five messuages bought from John Peck, skinner, in 1582, an enclosure in the parishes of St Peter Parmentergate and St Vedast (with three tenements) acquired from William Styward of Swardeston, gent., in 1581, and a messuage purchased from David Nasshe, shearman, and others in 1578. The enclosure — that is, the close to the west of St Vedast' churchyard — had been leased out by the friars before it was sold. Depositions taken in 1555 stated that about 40 years previously the warden of the Greyfriars had leased a close with certain tenements to John Hill, roughmason. After Hill's death the lease was taken over by Thomas Pyctow, who married Hill's widow, and the widow had enjoyed the property until her death shortly before. In the meantime, however, the warden had sold the freehold of the close to Mr Augustus Styward (Rye 1905, 33).

These additional properties cannot have been acquired by the Franciscans long before 1488/9 because as late as 1479 the whole block with King Street west, Rose Lane south, the churchyard of St Vedast east and the Friars Minor north was granted to William Skipwith, gent., and Margaret his wife for life (NRO NCR 21f Kirkpatrick (8) 45), while, according to the information given above, they had all been sold again before the Dissolution. The church of St Vedast itself belonged not to the Friary but to the monks of Norwich Cathedral (*e.g.* NRO DCN 45/38/1, 2). Nor did the Greyfriars ever control the land east of the churchyard of St Vedast. The early evidence for this area is summarised on NRO MC 146/52 plan 100. The later information appears on Fig. 3.2.

Friary buildings

The church and cloister: documentary references

All that is known of the earliest Friary buildings at Norwich is that they had suffered a disastrous fire by 1238, when Henry III granted the friars the considerable sum of £20 to help rebuild their houses (Cal. Lib. Rolls 1226–40, 344). The church, as it is not mentioned, may have survived the fire and the friars clearly contemplated a substantial rebuilding of their domestic premises.

The move up the hill towards King Street led to the establishment of the main Friary complex on a completely new site, with the building of the church starting by 1292 (Kirkpatrick 1845, 112–3). It was presumably well advanced by 1329, when Thomas de Thornham claimed sanctuary there (Cal. Pat. Rolls 1327–30, 429). This church would have been in a transitional Early English/Decorated style, with the straight eastern end normal for Franciscan churches. It was dedicated to St Francis and there were at least three chapels to other saints, namely St Ann, St Saviour (on the south side) and St Mary the Virgin (next to the choir). There was an image of St Thomas on the north side of the church, and one of Our Lady in the porch. Little is known of burials before 1370, when the series of Norwich registered wills begins, but among those buried at the Greyfriars — and so possibly in the church — in the early 14th century were friar Roger Merston, Robert Bainard and Roger Bourne, knight, who was buried in the habit of a greyfriar (Kirkpatrick 1845, 118; Kingsford 1915, 192, 199). From 1370 onwards at least 33 lay men and women requested burial in the church. Most would have been buried in the nave but one specified burial in the chapel of St Mary next to the choir. In addition at least two secular clergy were buried in the choir, among the friars. Many of these burials would have been commemorated in some way, as when Thomas Brygg in 1494 required his executors to place a marble slab on his grave within 'le parclos' before the altar on the south side (Appendix 2). A bell tower and bells were included in the grant to the Duke of Norfolk in 1539 (Hale and Rodgers 1991, 32).

The major source for the later church and cloister of Norwich Franciscan Friary, however, is the unusually detailed measurements made by William Worcestre in 1479. These need to be quoted in full. Worcestre wrote that:

> ... the length of the choir of the church of the brothers of St Francis of Norwich contains 60 steps (*gressus*). The length of the interior (*insterticii*) under the bell tower (*sub campanile*), that is of the space between [lit. of] the door of the choir and the doors of the nave of the church, contains 24 steps. The length of the nave of the church from the west as far as the first doors towards the east contains ... steps, and which contains 35 yards (*virgas*) that is 105 feet (*pedes*). The width of the said church contains 32 steps. The length of the cloister on the chapter house side (*ex parte* de le chapiterhouse) contains 61 steps. Note: but the aforesaid width of the church from the west to the first doors of the church contains 35 yards that is 105 feet by my measure with a yard of three feet in length.

The first reference to 35 yards is changed from 34 and the second has 34 written above it. Later Worcestre added:

> ... the length of the nave of the church of the brothers of St Francis of Norwich from the west end of the choir to the west window contains 82 steps. The width of it contains *quoad* the nave 32 [30 deleted] paces (*gradus*).
>
> (Harvey 1969, 236, 238)

This description of the church is consistent with the usual Franciscan pattern of nave, passageway under a central tower and a choir, with a cloister adjoining the church, but there are problems in the interpretation of the details, not least because Worcestre commonly measured in steps or paces. Kirkpatrick satisfied himself with quoting Worcestre in full (Kirkpatrick 1845, 125). Blomefield, however, gives measurements which are often-quoted yet calculated on no obvious basis. They are: a nave 150ft long, nave and aisles about 80ft wide, tower space 50ft long, a choir 150ft long and 50ft wide and a chapter house about 130ft long on the east side of the cloister, the cloister on the side of the church being a square of the length of the nave (Blomefield 1806, IV, 108–9). Richard Taylor probably used these measurements for the cruciform church on his map of Norwich (Taylor 1821). The Victoria County History concluded that 'the dimensions ... are somewhat contradictory; but it is clear that the nave was 105 feet in length and that the cloister on the north side of the nave was a square of its full length' (Doubleday *et al.* 1906, 430). A plan produced by 'Othinel' for the *Eastern Daily Press* in 1925 based the particulars of the church on Taylor but added an extra strip to the chapter house to bring it up to the recorded (*i.e.* Blomefield's) length of 130ft (EDP, 13 January 1925).

The first satisfactory treatment of Worcestre's measurements occurs in Martin's *Franciscan Architecture in England*. He concluded that the average length of Worcestre's step or pace was 21 inches and the same multiple was used by Harvey in his edition of Worcestre's *Itineraries* (Martin 1937, 22–3; Harvey 1969, xv). On this basis the overall length of the Franciscan church at Norwich was between 248.5ft and 252ft, made up from a choir of 105ft (60 x 21ins), tower space of 42ft (24 x 21ins) and nave of either 101.5ft (82 — 24 x 21ins) or 105ft. The Greyfriars church, therefore, was of a similar length to the existing Dominican (Blackfriars) church in Norwich (254ft) and was only rivalled among Franciscan churches by those at London (300ft) and Coventry (254ft) (Martin 1937, 23). These dimensions produce a short nave and an unusually large space under the tower, though part of the tower space might — as at London — have been taken up by chapels such as the chapel of St Mary attached to the choir (Martin 1937, 195).

The width of the Franciscan church is more problematical. Martin, followed by Harvey, takes the references to the width of the church as meaning the width of the nave rather than the choir, and takes both the 105ft measurements as referring to the length rather than the breadth of the nave. This involves interpreting *quoad*, in the sentence 'the width of it contains *quoad* the nave', as 'as regards' and produces a nave 56ft wide (32 x 21ins). Both authors then assume a narrower choir (Martin 1937, 23; Harvey 1969, 237, 239, fig. 1 opp.398). On this basis the nave of the Franciscan church was considerably narrower than that at Norwich Blackfriars (77ft).

This is a plausible interpretation, as the relationship between the length of the choir and nave and their suggested widths would then be similar to those found in many surviving or excavated Franciscan churches (Martin 1937, *passim*). There is, however, no need to assume a narrower choir. It could equally have been of the same width as the nave, as at London (Martin 1937, opp. 22). Moreover it is worth noting, in view of the generally high number of friars at the Norwich house and its continued use as a *studium*, that a quite different reading of the dimensions is possible. This takes both the 105ft references as referring to the width of the nave and interprets the phrase '*quoad* the nave' as meaning 'as far as' in the sense of 'up to', so that the 56ft width only refers to the choir and tower space. This produces a nave 105ft wide, wider even than the London Franciscan church (300ft x 90ft), though the overall size of the Norwich church would have been considerably smaller with a choir only 56ft wide (Martin 1937, 23–4).

In short, there are at least three possible interpretations of Worcestre's dimensions for the width of the church. The two most likely are either an aisled nave 56ft wide with a narrower unaisled choir or a nave 56ft wide with a choir of the same width, both aisled. The third and most unusual would be a nave 105ft wide with a choir 56ft wide, both aisled.

The cloister is rarely mentioned in documentary sources. Worcestre's reference to the length of the cloister on the chapter house side is given above. His '61 steps' (106.75ft) should be taken as referring to the size of the cloister, and probably to the length of the walk on the east side, rather than to the size of the chapter house. The dormitory is mentioned in the will of Alice Brocher, who left 20s for its repair in 1474 (Appendix 2). Apart from the chapter house and dormitory there must have been at least a refectory, an infirmary, a guest house, a schoolroom and a library, though some buildings could have been situated in a second cloister.

Position of the church and cloister

Little has been done hitherto to identify the position of the Franciscan Friary church and cloister within the Norwich precinct. Taylor gives no reasons for the positioning of his cruciform church towards the centre of the precinct (Taylor 1821, map opp. 132) and Taylor was presumably the source followed by the 1885 Ordnance Survey map. The 1925 plan by 'Othinel' used old field boundaries and took recent finds of skeletons into account, but was flawed by over-reliance on Taylor (EDP, 13 January 1925). Campbell, in producing the plans for his Norwich atlas, states that the siting of the Friary buildings within the precinct is hypothetical (Campbell 1975, 17 n.36).

There is no evidence for the site of the pre-1292 Friary church and domestic buildings, although they must have lain somewhere within the eastern half of the later precinct (Fig. 3.3). It is reasonable to assume that the object of the extension of the precinct to the west in the late 13th and early 14th centuries was to build nearer the King Street frontage, and all the available evidence leaves little doubt that this was where the principal buildings lay. The friars started building the east end of their church on land included in the mortmain licence of 1292 (Fig. 3.3; Kirkpatrick 1845, 112–13) and stone walls mentioned in 16th-century Norwich City leases are concentrated in this western half of the precinct (Fig. 3.4). In February 1566 Plot K on Fig. 3.6 lay immediately south of 'the capital messuage or house of the ... late friars'. While the dimensions of K are uncertain, it seems reasonable to equate this with the 'great house of the Greyfriars', which was demolished by the city in 1566 and which must have lain within Plot H since this was the only plot still in the hands of the corporation when the great gable was taken down (Appendix 4; NRO NCR 22g (1) *passim*). Blomefield thought Greyfriars House (the north-west corner of Plot M on Fig. 3.6) was the site of the church, cloister and convent of the Friary, while an unnamed member of the Norfolk and Norwich Archaeological Society believed he had seen the west end of the church here when Greyfriars House was demolished (Blomefield 1806, IV, 103; anon 1924, 139). Skeletons were found at 13 Prince of Wales Road in 1878 and at 22 Prince of Wales Road in 1867 and 1925 (EDP, 8, 9 and 12 January 1925), while the builder of 13 and 15 Greyfriars Road (Plot L, Fig. 3.6) found a quantity of worked stone, including window mullions, when digging out the cellars and used an old flint wall as a foundation (EDP, 9 October 1925).

The more precise identification of individual buildings depends partly on whether the church was north or south of the cloister. Blomefield and Taylor both favoured a southern cloister (Blomefield 1806, IV, 108; Taylor 1821, map opp. 132), while the Victoria County History, followed by Harvey and Campbell, believed it lay to the north of the nave (Doubleday *et al.* 1906, 430; Harvey 1969, fig. 1 opp. 398; Campbell 1975, map 2). As already mentioned, the friars started to build their church within Plot E (Fig. 2.3) but unfortunately this is not conclusive as Plot E may lie further south. To some extent a southern church is supported by the failure of the *Norwich Mercury* to report on the finding of either walls or bones during the building of Prince of Wales Road, though as regards bones the workmen may not have dug deep enough as the six skeletons found in 1925 lay about 9 feet below the ground surface (*Norwich Mercury*, June 1860–October 1862; EDP, 9 January 1925). Further indirect documentary evidence, however, favours a northern church, sited in an imposing position on the higher ground. First, one of the main purposes of a large Franciscan church was for preaching and it seems unlikely that the friars would have started building by 1292 in a part of the precinct where they did not yet have direct access to King Street (Fig. 3.3). Second, early 16th-century deeds for the Suffragan tenements on the other side of King Street describe Bank Street, north-east of the Castle Bailey, as leading from the church of the friars mendicant to the parish of St Michael at Plea (NRO NCR 3/4 box 3). Finally, although the precise position of the main gate on King Street that would have given access to the church is not known, it is clear that it lay on the northern rather than southern King Street frontage. The more southerly entry is described in 1568 as the back gate of the Greyfriars.

If the argument for a northern church is accepted, the pattern of 16th-century stone walls (Fig. 3.4) suggests that it actually lay within Plot J (Fig. 3.6), whose greatest width corresponds well with the measurements for the length of the church given by Worcestre. This plot was further divided by a stone wall, not shown on Fig. 3.4, enclosing an orchard, possibly a section of the church or cloister (NRO NCR 22g (1) f.73–4). In this case, the foundations seen by the Archaeological Society member under Greyfriars House, and the great house of the friars north of Plot K, would represent the domestic buildings of the Greyfriars. With a church in this position the burials under 22 Prince of Wales Road may have overlapped with the tower space, particularly if the tower space is taken to be 56ft wide, but those under 13 Prince of Wales Road would have lain south of the nave. Another factor to be taken into account in considering the precise position of the church is the alignment of Griffin Lane (Fig. 4.1; Pls 4.2–4.4). This way, also known as Crinkle-Crankle Lane because of its abrupt turns, developed in the 17th century and is likely to have taken account of Friary walls still in existence (see Chapter 4, below, 89–92).

Minor buildings

As well as the main claustral ranges, the Greyfriars would have needed a number of lesser domestic buildings, such as kitchen, brewhouse, bakehouse and other outhouses. The grant of the Franciscan Friary to the Duke of Norfolk in 1539 included 'all messuages, houses, buildings, granges, barns, stables, dovecotes, ponds, waters, fisheries, yards, orchards, gardens, lands and ground', while the Duke of Norfolk's lease of the site in 1542 mentioned a stable and brewhouse (Hale and Rodgers 1991, 32, 34). The 1542 lease also included the houses 'called Suffrygans loginge', which had been let for life by the warden of the Greyfriars to the suffragan bishop, John Underwood, who died in 1541 (Hale and Rodgers 1991, 34; Rye 1905, 32; Venn 1922, IV, 289). It was not unusual for a Franciscan precinct to include secular lodgings for important people (Martin 1937, 37–8) and this house should not be confused with the Suffragan tenements, which lay on the other side of King Street and were leased to the City of Norwich for 99 years at a peppercorn rent in 1536 (Hudson and Tingey 1906/10, II, cviii).

There is little documentary evidence for the position of most of these minor buildings. In the later 16th century Plot E contained a house 'sometime used as a bakehouse' with a solar or upper storey, Plot D a little house or stable with a solar, and Plot C a stable with a little chamber (Fig. 3.6). Plot K contained a dovehouse and a ladyng (a shed or storehouse) and Plot L a house used as a stable (NRO NCR 22g (1) *passim*). The Suffragan's lodging and a house said to adjoin it, on the other hand, may possibly be identified with the 'great house of the Greyfriars' that was demolished in 1566 and so lay in Plot H. They are the only substantial buildings mentioned in the lease of 1542: the terms of the lease required their upkeep and there is no other record of their demolition after the site came into the hands of the city (Hale and Rodgers 1991, 34). If this is the case, the apparent willingness of the friars to lease out such a large part of their domestic buildings may imply changes in the domestic arrangements of the later Friary.

Building materials

In 1538 the Norwich Greyfriars was among the friaries described as having no substance of lead apart from some guttering (L and P for. and dom. Henry VIII, XIII pt.2 191). All the buildings, therefore, including the church, must have been tiled or thatched rather than leaded. This does not mean that the buildings were not substantial. It took a tiler and his lad four days' work to remove the (roofing) tile of the great house at the Greyfriars in 1565/6, a carpenter and his servant six days to take down the house (possibly implying some timber framing) and a mason another four days to demolish the gables and buttresses. Other walls were removed by the mason and bricks and stone carried away, and the following year a labourer received the equivalent of a further seven to eight days' pay for felling the great gable (Appendix 4). Accounts of purchases made before the City of Norwich acquired the Friary site mention building materials bought from the Greyfriars. These consisted of *thak* (roofing) tile, paving tile, paving stone, marble, brick, freestone, black (knapped) flint and rough stone (NRO NCR 18a Chamb. acc. 1537–47, 1541–50, 1551–67, *passim*).

Anchorage

The 16th-century Plot B is described from 1611 onwards as the Ankers/Anchores garden (Fig. 3.6). The anchorage itself may have lain on the south side of the garden, next to the proposed main gate, although the only evidence for this is the discrepancy in the east and west dimensions of Plot C (Table 5). The existence of one anchorite at the Greyfriars is well documented (Appendix 1) but there is no evidence to support the suggestion that there was another anchorage connected with the Friary on the site of the church of St John the Evangelist (Blomefield 1806, IV, 111).

Precinct wall and gates

The later extent and history of the precinct wall are discussed below. The only early documentary reference to a wall comes in a grant by William son of Ralph de Thurston and his wife in 1324 (NRO NCR 1b (10) m.7d). The messuage conveyed lay on Rose Lane, between St Vedast's Church and King Street, and had the wall of the Friars Minor to the north (Fig. 2.2). By this date the

Greyfriars had acquired most of their main precinct, with the exception of the north bank of the Dallingflete, apparently still in other hands in 1325 (Fig. 3.3). The line of the wall is shown on Fig. 3.4.

There were at least four gates into the Greyfriars precinct once the wall was established. Kirkpatrick, writing *c.* 1725, said 'one gate remains to be seen at the south end of Sevencote-row'. This would have been the gate giving access onto Griffin Lane from St Faith's Lane (Fig. 4.1). He takes the principal gate to have been at the King Street end of Griffin Lane, opposite the Griffin public house (Kirkpatrick 1845, 108), and there was certainly a gate here by 1608 as the then lessees of Plot J had an obligation to maintain a gate or door and the wall standing at the west end of the lane (NRO NCR 22g (1) 148). While an entry in this position is quite possible, the gate is not mentioned in earlier leases and the whole description is insufficient to imply a gatehouse. Far better candidates for a converted gatehouse would be either the little house with a solar on Plot D or the stable at the west end of Plot C with a little chamber now (1566) used as a dovehouse. Plot C is a particularly strong contender for a main entrance, with its long narrow shape (18ft wide at the west end) and its position next to the anchorite's garden (it being usual for anchorages to be placed near the main gate). Further support for a northern entrance comes from a reference to cleaning out the wells serving the five Suffragan tenements 'next the late gray fryers gate' (NRO NCR18a, Chamb. acc. 1541–50 244). The Suffragan tenements lay on the other side of King Street opposite Plot A. Taking 'next' in the sense of 'nearest to', this description fits well with Plot C, which was only just down the road, as the main entrance, rather than Griffin Lane which was further south. In 1581 Plot C was considered sufficiently 'next' to the Suffragan tenements to be included in one of their leases as a garden (NRO NCR 22g (1) 119–20).

The third gate lay at the entrance of the later Greyfriars Lane between the 16th-century Plots G and I (Fig. 3.6). This entry had stone walls either side in 1566 (Fig. 3.4) and would have led to the domestic buildings and the open ground beyond. It is probably the back gate referred to in 1568, when properties south of the precinct were said to lie 'at the south part of the back gate of the Grey friars' (NRO NCR 18d landgable (3) 4). The final gate led off St Faith's Lane at the east end of the precinct, 18ft south of the crown of the Stone Bridge (Pls 3.2 and 4.1). In the 1880s Hudson described it as a doorway leading into a building 18ft wide (Hudson 1884–7, 121–2).

Cemetery and pardon cloister

The 1539 grant of the Greyfriars site to the Duke of Norfolk included a cemetery (Hale and Rodgers 1991, 32). In fact there are likely to have been two cemeteries, one for the friars and one for laity of insufficient wealth or prestige to request burial within the church itself. There are no specific requests mentioning a lay cemetery, though those asking simply for burial at the Greyfriars or within the precinct may have been buried there. The known requests for burial in the cemetery all come from secular clergy, who are likely to have been buried among the friars (Appendix 2). At London the main cloister was also used for burials (Kingsford 1915, 128ff.) but there is no documentary evidence for this happening at Norwich. Indeed, as lay requests for burial in the church continued into the 16th century there may have been no need to overflow into the cloister. Blomefield, however, states that the Franciscans at Norwich had a special pardon cloister at the north side of St Vedast's church, so-called because of the indulgences granted to anyone buried there and intended to counteract the special indulgences that could be obtained from masses said at the Augustinian Friary down the road (Blomefield 1806, IV, 110). It is fortunate that he mentions two 1485 wills to support this statement. With one of these, that of William Philippes, Blomefield has made a simple mistake, as the request is for burial in the church (Appendix 2). The other will, that of Edmund Albon, is more interesting. He indeed wished to be buried in a pardon cloister, but in 'the pardone cloystre of Poules' [St

Plate 3.2 The stone bridge, St Faith's Lane (reproduced from Hudson 1888, opp. 118)

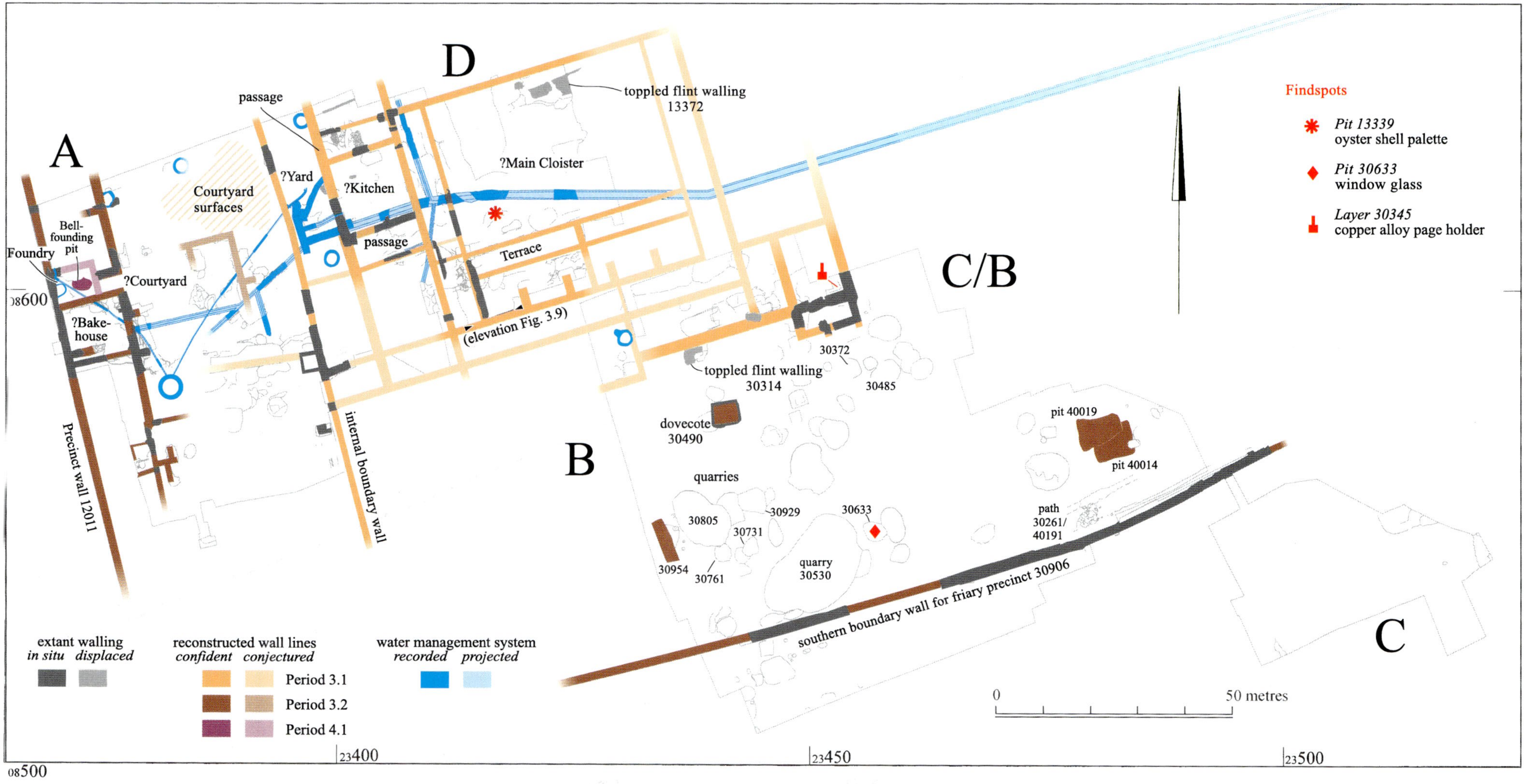

Figure 3.7 Period 3: phase plan — remains of the Franciscan Friary (14th–mid 16th century)

Paul's] as near to the door of St Faith's as possible (PCC 19 Logge). This reference to St Faith's presumably accounts for Blomefield's mention of St Vedast, as the two names were often confused at Norwich (hence St Faith's Lane). The only reference in the will to Franciscans is to a house 'ayens the greyfreres within Newgate in London' and the will has no connection with Norwich.

Water supply

There is no documentary evidence that the Norwich Greyfriars brought in a water supply by conduit, as happened at so many Franciscan houses (Martin 1937, 39). However the precinct as a whole cannot have been short of water. Ponds, waters and fisheries are mentioned in the grant to the Duke of Norfolk in 1539 (Hale and Rodgers 1991, 32). More specifically, no fewer than three cockeys, or small streams, rose within the Friary grounds and ran south and east to the river. Stretches of all three appear on Millard and Manning's map of 1830 (Pl. 4.4). The most southerly ran into the river near the corner. In the 16th century this stream can be traced as far north as Rose Lane and probably ran down to Rose Lane from the precinct between the properties along the King Street frontage and the close once in the tenure of the Greyfriars (Fig. 3.1). Expenses for the cockey in Conesford (the King Street area) in 1561/2 include payment for a post set in the lane against Keteringhams, the property on the King Street/Rose Lane corner, to keep carts out (NRO NCR 18a Chamb. acc. 1551–67 221d). Lanes tended to develop alongside cockeys, and the city authorities tried to discourage this. Part of the stream appears in the western half of the Cooke's Hospital orchard on the Ordnance Survey map of 1883 (Pl. 4.5). The middle cockey, the Fresflete, is not documented in its upper reaches but its presence may account for the curved shape of St Vedast churchyard (Fig. 2.1). The most northerly and largest of the three streams was the Dallingflete. The stone bridge that crossed it at St Faith's Lane needed a span of fifteen feet (Hudson 1884–7, 121).

The Norwich Greyfriars' interest in the Dallingflete did not end at the stone bridge, but extended from St Faith's Lane to the river. In the 14th century Roger Verly, five times bailiff of Norwich between 1335 and 1344, granted the friars the use of the creek for the carriage of their corn and other victuals and goods. This was confirmed by Elizabeth Elmham in 1405, with the additional right to clean out the dike and to fish there for 200 years. In 1466 William Skipwith extended this for another 200 years and added the right to walk eight foot either side of the stream (Kirkpatrick 1845, 115–8). After the Dissolution these rights continued to go with the lease of Plot Q. Hudson, writing in the 1880s, described the stone bridge as lying not far from where the road from Prince of Wales Road bent round towards the Horse Fair and the Dallingflete as running behind the Vinegar Works in the direction marked by a line of trees (Hudson 1884–7, 120), and this section of the stream appears on Millard and Manning.

There is also evidence that water was available within the complex of known Friary buildings. Millard and Manning show water in Plot J (Fig. 3.6) and two wells are mentioned in 16th-century leases of the area (NRO NCR 22 g (1)(2) *passim*: Fig. 3.5). The more northerly lay on the north side of Plot G and the lessees of Plots B, C, D, E, F and J were to be allowed to use it. It was described as a draw well and costs were to be shared. The second was on the south-east side of Plot H. In 1566 the tenant of Plot I also had access and was to pay towards the upkeep of the well, rope and 'stopp' (bucket). Later it came (at least in part) into the occupation of the lessee of Plot M and when Robert Cooke purchased Plots M and K in 1675 the sale included the moiety of a well or pump.

III. ARCHAEOLOGICAL EVIDENCE

Early Friary (1226–*c.* 1290s)

Excavations within the Mann Egerton site provided no direct evidence for the location of the earliest (*i.e.* pre-1292) buildings of the Greyfriars. Although in the early 13th century the Friary may have included the northern part of Area B (Fig. 3.3), the remainder of the excavated area was only incorporated into the precinct by later phases of expansion.

Period 3.1: Friary enlargement and development (*c.* 1290s–1400)

(Fig. 3.7)

Summary

Archaeological evidence indicates that the laying-out of the precinct of the Franciscan Friary and preparation for construction of Friary buildings involved the removal of buildings and infilling of cellars and pits associated with former plots, rationalisation of the sloping ground surface, other landscaping works and — most dramatically — closure of at least one lane and possibly two. In addition, large quarry pits are likely to have been dug to provide sand for major building campaigns in the 13th and 14th centuries, although the dates of these excavations are difficult to establish given the high levels of residual pottery in their fills.

The description of the Friary remains given below is organised with respect to the hierarchical structure of its reconstructed monastic plan (Fig. 3.21). While most of the structures are attributed to the period *c.* 1300–1400 (Period 3.1), a number of buildings and modifications date between 1400 and 1538 and are therefore addressed in the second part of the text (Period 3.2).

Friary structures recorded during the excavations included substantial sections of the perimeter wall of the precinct, an internal boundary wall (aligned north-to-south), extensive remains of buildings that were integral to the cloister, and various outlying structures. Excavation also revealed remains of a water management system comprising a hierarchy of drains, a series of wells and traces of two pipelines that conveyed water from the largest of the wells. This system is described in a separate section and considers elements relating both to the Friary's construction (Period 3.1) and its development (Period 3.2). Also recorded within the Friary precinct was evidence for a pathway running adjacent to the south boundary wall, a pair of large pits containing significant faunal assemblages and a bell-casting pit.

While the ceramic assemblage from this period is relatively substantial (nearly 15kg), over half of it is residual

(Lentowicz, Chapter 5.III). Architectural stonework confirms a major period of construction at the site during the period *c.* 1290–1320 (Samuel, Chapter 5.I).

Archaeological sequence

Final use of Road 1 and its eventual closure
(Fig. 2.9)
Ultimate abandonment of Road 1 was represented by build-up deposits (*30540*, *30753*, *30847*, *30848*: Fig. 2.9) which sealed the latest metalled surfaces. These layers dated to between the late 13th century and the early 14th century. The line of the lane was subsequently cut off completely by insertion of the Friary's precinct boundary wall (see Pl. 2.7 and below).

Quarrying
(Fig. 3.7)
At least some of the earlier quarries (Period 2.3) in the north-central part of the site apparently remained open until this period. A few or all of them may have actually been dug at this date, representing Friary-related extraction of natural materials. From the upper fills of one quarry, with a *tpq* of *c.* 1200 (pit *13339*: Chapter 2.II) came a painter's palette in the form of an oyster shell (SF2621). The pit may have lain open until construction of the Friary buildings *c.* 1300. Further details of this object are given by Howard and Park in Chapter 5.II. Later quarrying is described in Period 3.2 below.

Construction of terraces
(Figs 3.8 and 3.22)
The sloping natural ground surface in the northern part of the site (Areas A and D) was overlain by a succession of dumps of earth (69 contexts, some of which appear in Fig. 3.8) forming a horizontal platform. This construction measured up to 2.8m deep and the terrace effectively extended the area available for building. Pottery from the dumps indicate a 14th century date. The construction of walls on the top of the terrace necessitated a series of deep earth footing trenches (see below, 80, for fuller discussion). This may indicate that the original purpose of the terrace was simply landscaping, the southward extension of the buildings into this area not being anticipated at the time of its creation. The southern extent of the terrace was not established archaeologically, partly due to truncation by construction of the Mann Egerton basement, but also because it extended beyond the southern limit of excavation. There is some evidence to suggest that even after this platform had been created, there was still a need for the made ground surface to be stepped (see below, 65).

Clearance of plots fronting King Street
(Fig. 2.19)
Earlier buildings along the King Street frontage were eventually removed. A north-to-south robber trench (*12252*) indicates the deliberate removal of a wall relating to an earlier cellar (Period 2.3). The cut survived to an elevation of 9.36m OD and the base of the trench was at 8.81m OD, slightly lower than the base of cellar itself (*c.* 8.88m OD). The cellared area was infilled with a mid to dark greyish brown silt sand (*12253*/*12375*/*12376*), the pottery present suggesting that this took place in the late 14th century.

Extant flintwork above and adjacent to the area of the earlier cellar represented at least three buildings that were apparently in use during the life of the Friary (see Chapter 2.III, Period 2.3). All three pre-dated the occupation of this part of the site by the monastic complex in 1292 but may have continued in use during the period *c.* 1290–1400. Although elements of them may have been adapted during this period, they were eventually superseded by the construction of a Friary-related masonry building (see Period 3.2).

Precinct boundary walls
(Fig. 3.7)
The southern wall of the precinct, which lay just over 50m to the north of Rose Lane, was traced for a length of over 60m within the excavated area. Extant walling representing the western boundary of the Friary extended at least 18.5m along the King Street frontage. An internal boundary wall lay approximately 26m to the east of King Street, forming the western limit of the built-up part of the precinct which is here interpreted as the main cloister and associated ranges. Finally, a short length of flint wall, observed during the laying of a new drain immediately to the north of Greyfriars Road, formed part of an eastward return to this wall. This appeared to define the southern limit of the claustral complex.

Plate 3.3 West wall of Friary precinct (*12011*) showing surfaces of King Street

King Street frontage
(Figs 3.7 and 3.15; Pl. 3.3)
From the late 14th century onwards, the King Street frontage was delineated by a substantial wall that was traced over 18.5m (*12011*, Figs 3.7 and 3.15). Its west face, which was composed of knapped flint and *galleted*, was slightly battered; the east face was partially clad with bricks. A succession of undated make-up layers, representing re-surfacing of King Street, directly abutted the west face of the wall (Pl. 3.3). The occurrence of floors to the east of the wall indicated that a building had later been attached to it (see Period 3.2: below).

The maximum recorded thickness of the wall, at a point where an internal addition had been constructed, was 0.94m. Its base was recorded in a slot trench at 9.5m OD. The narrowest section of the wall was flanked to the north and south by buttress-like constructions with chamfered corners. The wall survived to a minimum level of 10.85m OD along this section, no opening that could represent a door or window being apparent in its east face. The ι ppermost related floor surface that survived lay at 9.65m OD, some 1.2m below the top of the extant brick and flintwork.

South wall and adjacent path
(Fig. 3.7; Pls 1.3 and 2.7)
A mortared flint wall, aligned east-to-west and 0.80m wide, surviving to a height of over 2m in places, was traced for 63m (*30469*/*30906*/*40021*/*50630*: Pl. 1.3). Its foundation sloped down to the east in correspondence with the natural terrain. Construction of the wall immediately followed after the abandonment of the north-to-south road (Road 1) described in Chapter 2.III and pottery indicates that it was built *c.* 1300. That the wall's appearance marked the closure of the road was indisputable as there was no trace of there ever having been a break in the structure where it intersected the line of the road (Pl. 2.7). However, a change in the alignment of the wall at this intersection, of some eight degrees, suggests that the road marked a change in the configuration of property boundaries. The length and position of the wall indicate that it was the southern boundary to the Friary precinct.

Immediately to the north of the wall was a layer of sand and mortar (*30262*: see Fig. 2.9). This apparently sloped down to the east, representing a remnant of a deposit that was formed during the wall's construction. Overlying it *c.* 3.25m north of the wall was a linear deposit (*30261*/*40191*) composed of clay and gravel and aligned from east to west. This may indicate the presence of a perimeter path which ran along the inner side of the precinct wall.

Internal boundary wall to west of cloister
(Fig. 3.7, 3.16 and 3.21)
A north-to-south aligned, free-standing flint wall (*212*/*10509*/*11157*/*12054*/*12595*/*12596*), *c.* 26m back from the King Street frontage, was tracked over a distance of 38m across Area A during various stages of the excavation. This wall was separated from the putative west range by a cobbled yard (see below). The upstanding sections of the wall had been concealed by the brickwork of the modern basement. That part of the wall recorded near the north edge of the site stood to a highest level of 9.9m OD, some 1.2m above the contemporary ground surface. This section incorporated a brick culvert (*12390*) that passed through the flintwork of the wall and fell in an eastward direction. The

southern part of the wall was composed entirely of mortared flint. The bottom 0.8m of both of its faces, which comprised knapped flint and was *galleted*, was slightly battered.

The assertion that this wall formed a continuous boundary, breached only by occasional doorways, rests upon the assumption that the sections of its length separated by a gap of *c.* 11m (corresponding with a modern basement) were originally connected. The projected lines of the two sections were at slight variance, indicating that a subtle change in alignment occurred towards the south end of the section that is presumed to have been truncated (Fig. 3.16). If continuous, this free-standing wall would have formed a fundamental component of the ground plan of the Friary complex and as such, is crucial to any attempted reconstruction. Its line coincides with that of a stone wall attested by 16th-century leases to have survived from the Friary (Fig. 3.4).

The north-to-south wall divided the developed part of the precinct into two areas. That to the west appears to have been largely devoid of buildings, apart from the row of premises fronting King Street. The space between the buildings on the frontage and the boundary wall may have been an open courtyard. However, the occurrence of a series of substantial rubble-filled trenches in the centre of this area apparently represented the robbing-out of the foundations of an isolated building, the precise layout of which is unclear. To the east of the major boundary wall evidence of Friary structures is both more concentrated and conclusive. The wall's function seems to have been to delineate the claustral buildings from what appears to have been an open, and maybe publicly accessible, area to the west.

Church

(Fig. 3.21)

The location of the church, and the position of the cloister relative to it, were both unknown prior to this project. None of the structural remnants of the Friary recorded archaeologically could be attributed with any confidence to the Friary church. A substantial east-to-west wall represented by flintwork (*13416*/*13417*/*13372*: Fig. 3.16) and laminated earthen footings (*13468*/*13389*) immediately to the south of the site frontage at Nos 11 and 13 Prince of Wales Road, initially interpreted as the south wall of the nave, is now postulated as the south wall of the north cloister walk (see below). Establishing the position of the church and reconstructing its groundplan have therefore depended almost entirely dependent upon interpretation of William Worcestre's survey and the 1565 leases (Rutledge, above, 46–53). Whilst the measurements recorded by Worcestre indicate the church's dimensions, its position within the large precinct is never made clear by documentary sources. A compelling combination of archaeological, documentary and circumstantial evidence has emerged, however, which allows its location to be suggested. Further details of this are given in the discussion section at the conclusion of this chapter (below, 79–80).

Cloister

(Figs 3.7 and 3.16)

Establishing the precise layout of the cloister was critical, since understanding this element of the plan would help place other buildings in context. Extant flintwork and other remnants of Friary buildings were concentrated into the northern part of the site (in Areas A and D and the northern edge of Area B). The southern limit of this complex lay some 28m to the north of the southern boundary wall, although a single isolated structure — possibly a dovecote — was located further south (see Period 3.2). Reconstruction of groundplans was hindered by the removal of large sections of foundations that had taken place during the Dissolution. Additionally, there was considerable impact from post-medieval disturbance, particularly that resulting from the construction of the buildings fronting Prince of Wales Road in the late 19th century and of the Mann Egerton works in the early 20th century.

The possibility that there was more than one cloister meant that multiple alternative arrangements of adjoining cloisters and courtyards had to be considered. In the idealised Friary arrangement (which that at Walsingham, for example, is assumed to have closely respected), the north walk of the cloister is separated from the south wall of the nave by a narrow yard.

When considering the remains of wall foundations and floors found at Norwich Greyfriars, certain elements emerged as potential elements of the cloister and its surrounding buildings. Closely-spaced pairs of parallel wall foundations, representing corridors, potentially offered the most useful insight into the arrangement of cloister walks. A burial found in 1878, during the construction of 13 Prince of Wales Road, falls within the postulated cloister position outlined below, lying either under the putative north walk or inside the garth.

The extent of the earthen terrace recorded to the south of Prince of Wales Road in Areas A and D indicated that a platform had been prepared in this part of the site in advance of construction of a large group of buildings, including the cloister itself. Evidence of a southward fall in floor level of 0.65m on the west side of the cloister (see below) implies that the ground surface within the garth was stepped. This raises the possibility that a pair of walls retained higher ground to the north.

North side

(Figs 3.7, 3.16 and 3.21)

Excavated evidence of a major west-to-east wall included one *in situ* section of mortared flintwork sitting on a layered earth footing, a further length of masonry lying (together with its compacted earth footing) on its side and an *in situ* portion of the layered footing. The hypothesis that all three pieces of evidence related to a single wall could not be verified because of the retention of the 11a Prince of Wales Road premises. The distance from the western limit of the *in situ* masonry to the easternmost observed point of that which lay on its side was 22.15m.

The *in situ* portion of the wall (*13416* and *13417*: Fig. 3.16) was cruciform in plan, indicating that it formed the junction of two walls. This extant flintwork measured 2.8m east-to-west and 3.6m north-to-south. Since it was cut away to the north by the construction of the 19th-century cellar, the total width of the medieval wall could not be established at this point. However, the section through the piece of toppled flintwork suggested a maximum width of 1.6m at the base. This makes it the thickest wall foundation recorded on this site by far, suggesting that it represented one of the more substantial structures. The section of the wall lying on its side (*13372*: Fig. 3.16) was over 6m long and extended beyond the east edge of the trench.

The compacted layered footing upon which the wall was built was observed at three places: beneath the *in situ* walling (*13468* and *13382*), at the north-west corner of 13 Prince of Wales Road, and (rotated through 90 degrees) in association with the section of wall that had been pulled down (*13389*). It appears to have been a response to the soft ground resulting from earlier pitting in the vicinity.

The east-to-west wall was initially believed to represent the south wall of the nave of the church, on the basis of its remarkable thickness. This interpretation was later rejected, however, after consideration of the archaeological evidence in conjunction with documentary research. It might be interpreted as the inner (*i.e.* southern) wall of the north walk of the cloister.

West side

(Figs 3.7, 3.8, 3.9, 3.16 and 3.21; Pl. 3.4)

A north-to-south corridor — possibly the west walk of the putative cloister — was represented by two earth footing trenches on 3.0m centres, running southward from the major east-to-west wall (*13416 etc.*) described above. These deep, sheer-sided trenches each contained a succession of compacted layers of earth, sand or chalk. The need for such massive footings towards the north of the excavated area was apparently due to heavy earlier pitting. This corridor was 2.8m wide internally. The west wall seemed, on the limited evidence available, to have been significantly wider than that to the east. This disparity supported the interpretation that the corridor was indeed the claustral walk to the west of a cloister garth. At a position corresponding to the internal width of this corridor, there was circumstantial evidence for a doorway in the east-to-west wall to the south (*13149*), this having been robbed out prior to reconstruction of part of this wall after the Dissolution. Assuming that the terminus of the flintwork was abutted by a stone jamb (later robbed), the position of the aperture of the doorway can be estimated (Fig. 3.9).

The exact line of the west wall was suggested by the southward projection from the east-to-west wall *13416*, along which lay wall fragments and the remnants of footing trenches (*13427*, *13407* and *12573*). An additional portion of the same wall (*12608*) was recorded in section during a watching brief. Six rubble-filled cuts with curved ends (*12612*, *12613*, *12614*, *12615*, *12616*, *12589* and *12560*: not illus.) were recorded in a narrow north-to-south trench prior to the construction of a pile-cap just to the west. The eastern extent of the cuts is unknown due to the limits of the excavation trench, and it is therefore unknown whether the features were discrete or linear. However, their close spacing may indicate buttresses or timber piles, presumably supporting the same north-to-south wall (*12608*). The features were cut from the uppermost surviving floor layers, such that the rubble fill of the features was continuous with the dumps of rubble which directly overlay the remains of the floors. Consequently, it seems most likely that the rubble-filled cuts represented the robbing-out of masonry structures between which the floors had been laid. Further north along the same line, three further earth footings (*12582*, *12568* and *12571*: not illus.) were observed in the opposing sides of another narrow excavation trench.

The narrower eastern wall was represented by an extant section of mortared flint foundation (*13287*), 1.4m long, which lay *c.* 9m to the south of the east-to-west wall (*13416 etc.*). Further south was a 6.6m length of this wall foundation (*13018*: Pl. 3.4), leaning over to the east

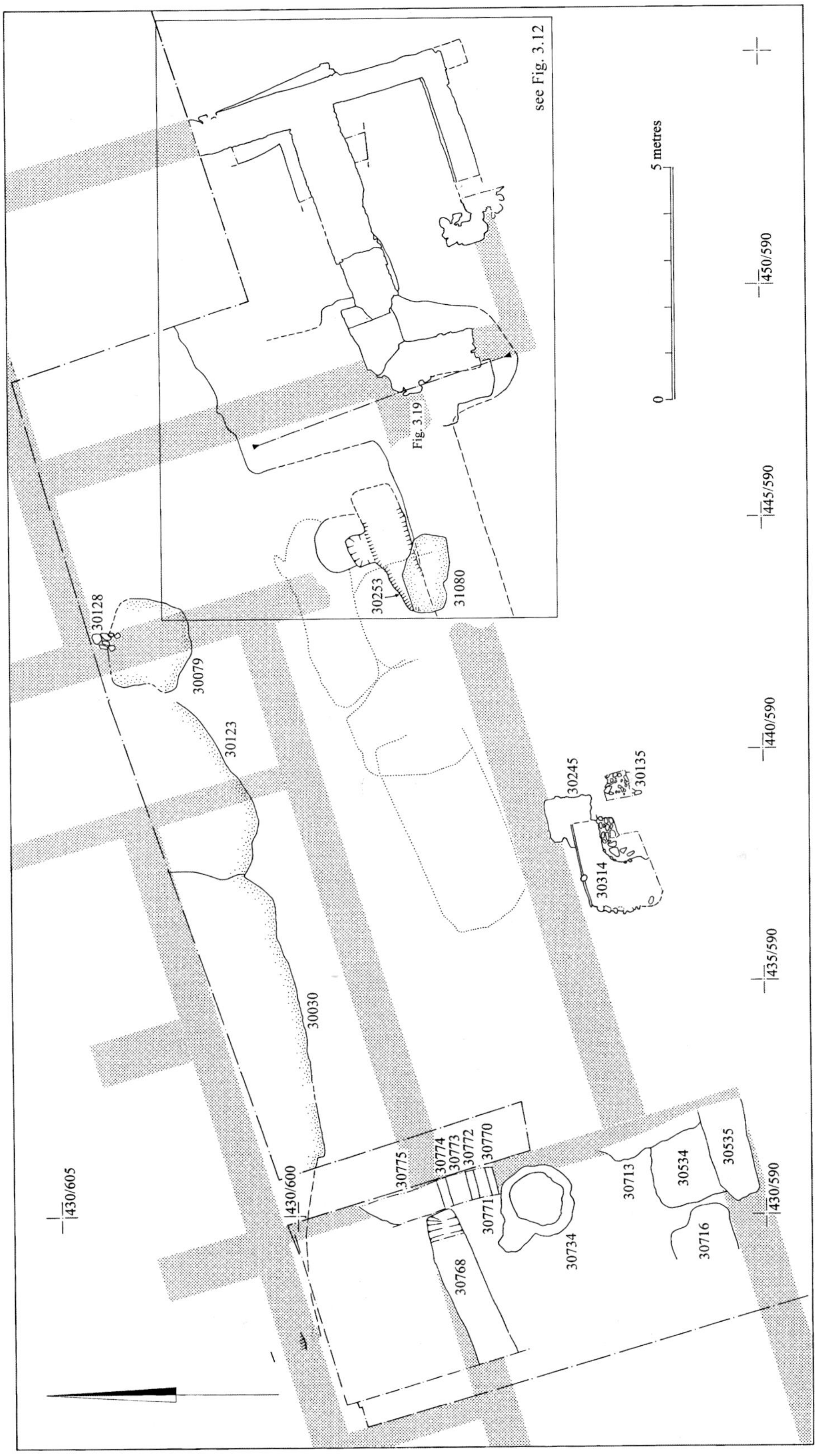

Figure 3.11 Period 3: remains of Friary buildings, Area B. Scale 1:100

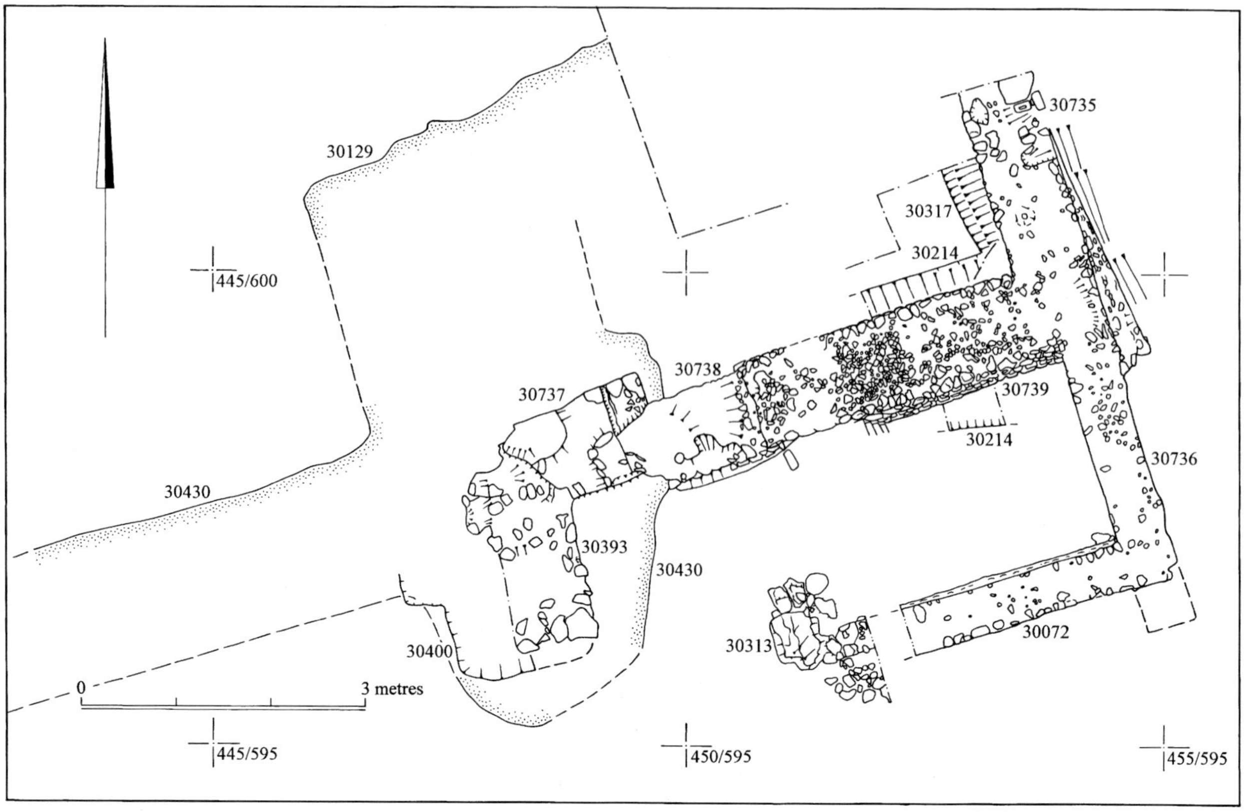

Figure 3.12 Period 3: plan of south-eastern corner of south range and southern end of east range, Area B

and evidently displaced eastward from its original alignment. The south end of this wall formed a T-junction with a major east-to-west wall (*13149*). However, the proposed identification of this east-to-west wall as the inner wall of the south walk of the cloister is inconclusive, as there are clearly remnants of a further corridor *c.* 8.5m to the north. The original position of the north-to-south wall (*13018*) could be inferred from the flintwork of the north face of wall *13149* (Fig. 3.9).

There was no direct evidence for buttresses along the putative west walk facing into the cloister garth. However, a pit (*13123*, Period 4.1: Fig. 3.16) infilled with demolition material (chiefly roof tile) was recorded at the expected position of the southernmost buttress, if such existed. This pit was located at the join between the putative buttress and an east-west wall (inferred from a robber trench, *13107*) interpreted as forming part of a terrace within the garth. An alternative interpretation for this pit is as a soakaway, perhaps receiving water from a down-pipe from the cloister roof. However, the combination of this pit and the dramatic eastward lean of wall *13018* (Pl. 3.4) does suggest that the structure was affected by subsidence on its eastern side. (Wall *13259* may be a post-Dissolution rebuild on the earlier line, sustaining the Friary wall line.)

A tile floor *13019*/*13314* (Fig.3.16, Pl. 3.6) was recorded within the putative west walk near its southern end. The tiles were laid in a chequer-board pattern and were 120mm square. Disturbed tiles recovered from contexts surrounding the patch of flooring were generally unglazed, except for occasional specks of green glaze.

The minimum possible level of the floor surface at the north end of the postulated west walk can be established, from intact constructional deposits, as 8.35m OD. The level of later floors (*10505*/*10507*/*10849*: Period 3.2) in the range to the immediate west was 8.55m OD. This means that the floor within the north part of the corridor was only 0.2m (a fall of one step) below that of the rooms to the west. However, the level of the floor in the southern part of the corridor *13019* was recorded at 7.7m OD, indicating that a series of steps — effecting a total fall of 0.65m — may have existed in the corridor (Figs 3.8 and 3.21). This implies that, in spite of construction of an extensive terrace to the south of the church, there remained a significant fall in the ground surface between the church and the buildings to the south. The obvious point at which to accommodate such a change in level was between the church and the cloister, where a natural break occurred in the building complex (*cf.* Norwich Blackfriars), with further steps coinciding with the terrace across the cloister garth.

South side

(Figs 3.7–3.9, 3.11, 3.12, 3.16 and 3.21)

An extant section of a major wall (*13146*/*13149*: Fig. 3.9), *c.* 5.2m long, at the southern extremity of Area D may represent the remains of the north wall of the south walk of the cloister (but see note above). This wall occurred *c.* 23m to the south of wall *13416 etc.* Further to the west, an additional 2.5m length of flint foundation (*11158*) on the projected line of this wall formed a T-junction with the internal boundary wall (*10509*). This suggests that a corridor, passing along the south end of the west range and to the south of the cloister, may have connected with an open area to the west. Between *11158* and *13149*, the wall alignment passed through the centre of a series of major rubble dumps over 0.7m thick which extended at least 2.5m from north to south. These deposits seem to represent infilling following the quarrying-out of a section of the wall. Further east, the wall had been entirely removed by the construction of the Mann Egerton basement. However, along the northern edge of Area B, a co-aligned series of earth footings for the wall (*30585*, *30030*, *30123*, *30079*; Fig. 3.11: see below), totalling *c.* 17m in length, was also recorded. The various traces of the wall, taken together, indicate that it was at least 46m long.

Wall *13149* incorporated an unglazed window (*13146*: Fig. 3.9) represented by an *in situ* stone sill and west jamb, together with fragments of mullions among material used to block the window after the Dissolution (Samuel, Chapter 5.I). Clear evidence for two northward-projecting buttresses was recorded on the northern side of the wall's line. Each was represented by a rectangular footing (*13064*/*13086* and *13209*: Fig. 3.16), comprising a deep rectangular cut infilled with a succession of very compact alternating layers of earth and mortar. That to the east (*13064*/*13086*) was overlain by extant flintwork (*13108*), slightly displaced by construction of the Mann Egerton basement. The laminated footings were presumed, on the basis of their position relative to the wall, to have provided a firm bearing surface for buttresses. However, removal of both the wall and substantial parts of the buttress foundations by construction of the Mann Egerton basement meant that this could not be verified. These buttresses were calculated to have been located at centres of some 4.82m.

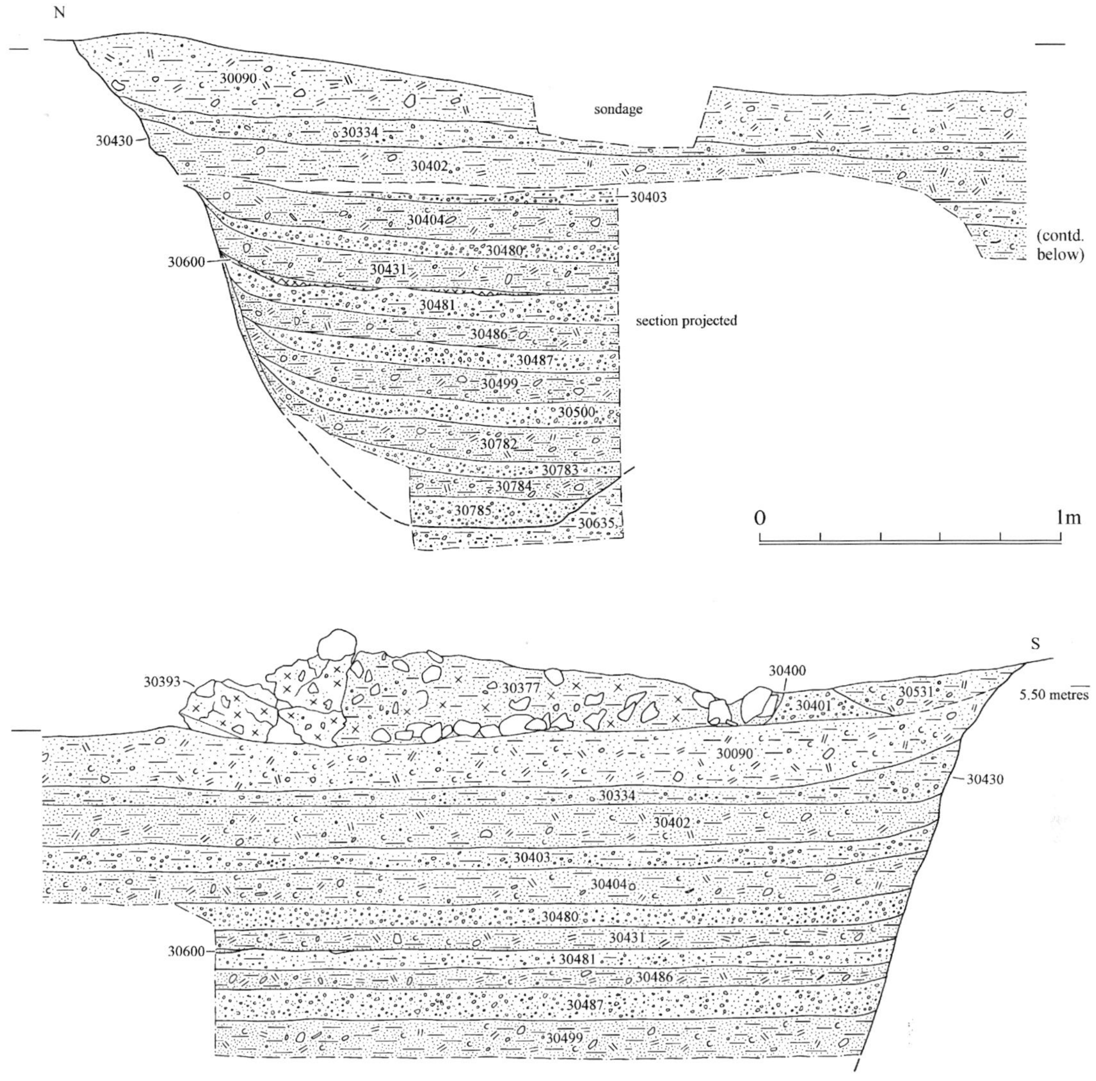

Figure 3.13 West-facing section of earth footing *30430*, Area B

The northern flint face of the east-to-west wall appeared to come to an end to the immediate west of its junction with wall *13018* (Fig. 3.9). This is consistent with there having been a connection between the north-to-south and east-to-west corridors via a doorway.

The footings recorded in Area B consisted of three pits (*30030*/*30585*, *30123* and *30079*) co-aligned on an east-to-west axis and measuring 12.9m in total length (Fig. 3.14). Cuts *30030* and *30123* had been left open for a short amount of time and appear then, given the continuity of their deposits within them, to have been infilled simultaneously. Pottery from the fills of the two features indicated the cuts were infilled some time in the 13th century, which supports suggestions that they were created during the major expansion of the Friary in the late 13th century. The horizontality of the fills, and evidence that compaction of some of them had been promoted by the introduction of large volumes of water, suggested that these features were foundations. By virtue of their co-alignment on an east-to-west axis they clearly relate to a wall running from west to east along the northern edge of Area B. The alternative interpretation — that the features were quarries — could not be reconciled with the quantity of sand occurring in their fills.

A further east-to-west wall — represented by a wall robber (*30768*) and wall footings (*30769–30775*), the layered fills of which were recorded in plan — was found *c.* 4m to the south in Area B (Fig. 3.11).

East side

(Figs 3.7, 3.11 and 3.21)

From this interpretation of the layout of the cloister, it would follow that most of the east walk lay beyond the east edge of excavation. A north-to-south wall, suggested by fragmentary flintwork (*30128*), might have formed the east wall of the east walk of the cloister. On this alignment, projecting southward, a foundation cut (*30831*) with alternating fills of chalk and silty sand was observed in section. This indicated that the wall continued through to the southern limit of the buildings.

Terracing of cloister garth

(Figs 3.8 and 3.16)

Within the area interpreted as the cloister garth were two parallel east-to-west walls on 2.6m centres, represented by footing trenches containing compacted layers of earth and sand (*13029*/*13134*/*13185*/*13306*/*13512* and *13055*/*13275*; Fig. 3.8), and rubble-filled trenches (*13138*/*13186*/*13199* and *13107*) slightly offset to the south of each footing (Fig. 3.16). The base of the northern footing cut sloped from 6.35m OD to 6.60m OD, that of the cut to the south being at 5.30m OD. The rubble-filled trenches may have been created in the process of salvaging facing stones.

These two walls were initially interpreted as forming part of a cloister walk. Consideration of the surrounding complex of walls has, however, cast doubt on this interpretation. A major east-to-west wall occurred less than 16m to the north of the most northerly of the two robber trenches: invoking the cloister plan in interpreting these walls would therefore indicate a cloister that was elongated from east to west, contradicting Blomefield's view that the cloister was square. It seems most likely that the two walls formed part of a terrace, accommodating a fall in ground level of some 1.30m. The difference of over 1m is attributed to the sloping natural ground surface. This interpretation is supported by a corresponding change in level of the north-to-south corridor at the west edge of the putative cloister, which explains why the section of surviving wall (*13018*) terminates at its junction with the northern of the two terrace walls. A further wall, represented by a linear earth footing (*13236*) was at right-angles to the other two, apparently also forming part of the terracing arrangement.

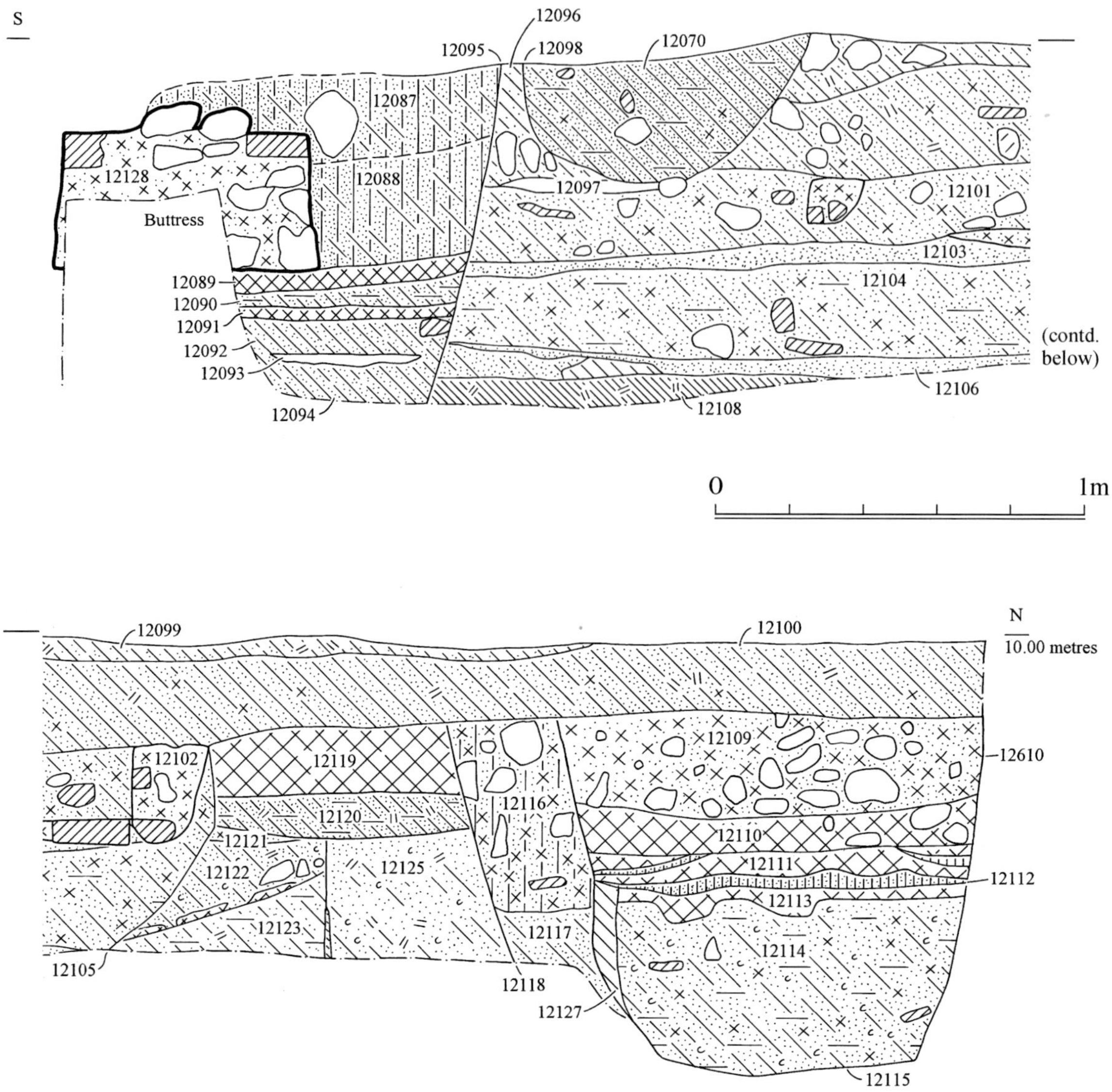

Figure 3.14 East-facing section showing construction of buttresses (*12095* and *12115*), drain (*12102*) and water pipe (*12105*) associated with Friary building fronting King Street, Area A

The rectangular area, *c.* 4.1m wide, enclosed between footing trench *13055* and wall *13146/13149*, contained numerous layers of compact clay apparently forming make-up layers for a floor, suggesting that it had been paved.

Ranges

Substantial parts of the west range and limited sections of the south and east ranges were investigated. The west range may have formed part of the Friary Guesthouse. That to the south may have housed the Refectory and Suffragan's Lodgings, while the Chapter House and Infirmary may have lain to the east. The cloister complex would also have housed the library and *studium*.

West range

?Kitchen

(Figs 3.7 and 3.16; Pls 3.7 and 3.8)

The south-west corner of a building forming part of the west range survived. The room was enclosed by walls *10710* to the west (Pl. 3.7), *10513* to the south, *12528* to the north, and that represented by footing trench *13407* to the east (this wall also forming the west wall of the north-to-south corridor described above). The room created was approximately square, measuring internally 7.2m east-to-west and 7.5m north-to-south.

A large rectangular hearth (*12504*), composed of tiles on edge and measuring 2.1m long (east-to-west) and 1.1m wide (Pl. 3.8), was recorded adjacent to the north wall. The hearth abutted a wall composed of bricks and tiles (*12521*). The top of this construction, which was parallel with the front edge of the hearth, was flat and slightly lower than the surface of the hearth and appeared to represent the foundation of the back wall of the fireplace. On top of the foundation was an additional linear construction of brick and tile, curiously differing in its alignment from that of both the foundation below and the front edge of the hearth by some five degrees. This disparity in alignment seems too great to be explained as a setting-out error by the builder. More likely, the rear face of the fireplace was slightly angled, presumably to help guide smoke up the chimney. Overlying the brickwork of the rear wall of the fireplace (*12513*) was a further section of brickwork (*12514*) which seemed to step over the room's north wall. This appeared to represent the remains of an aperture through the wall, indicating that the fireplace was accessible from both sides. The hearth appeared to have been flanked on its west side by a flint wall or buttress 2m long, only the southern terminus of which survived (*12507*). This was *c.* 0.80m wide (east-to-west) and lay just over 1m to the west of the truncated west edge of the tile construction. If this feature was integral with the fireplace and mirrored by a similar construction to the east, the full internal width of the fireplace may have been *c.* 3.5m.

A succession of thin horizontal layers, representing make-up layers for floors, occurred immediately to the west of the flanking wall for the fireplace. At the southern edge of the room part of a tile floor (*10848*) survived. Elsewhere within the room make-up for the floor took the form

Figure 3.15 Period 3: plan of Friary building fronting King Street, Area A

of spreads of clay (*12522–7*, *12529*, *12530*). A discrete ovate cut feature, containing ash, occurred some 1.1m to the south of the tile construction.

A brick drain, apparently running around the perimeter of the room, was recorded at two points (*12548*). The fill (*12515*) of this structure adjacent to the hearth contained a large number of butchered cattle ribs, and over 3000 fishbones representing over twenty species (Nicholson, Chapter 6.III).

The presence of the tile structure, the ash-filled cut and the drain containing the substantial bone assemblages all support interpretation of this room as a kitchen.

Figure 3.16 Period 3: remains of Friary buildings, Areas A and D

Plate 3.4 West walk of cloister showing leaning wall (*13018*, to right of picture) and connecting east-to-west wall footing trenches *13087* and *13185*, looking south. Rubble-filled pit *13123* lies at centre of photograph

Plate 3.5 Excavation of floors in passage between walls *10506* and *10513*

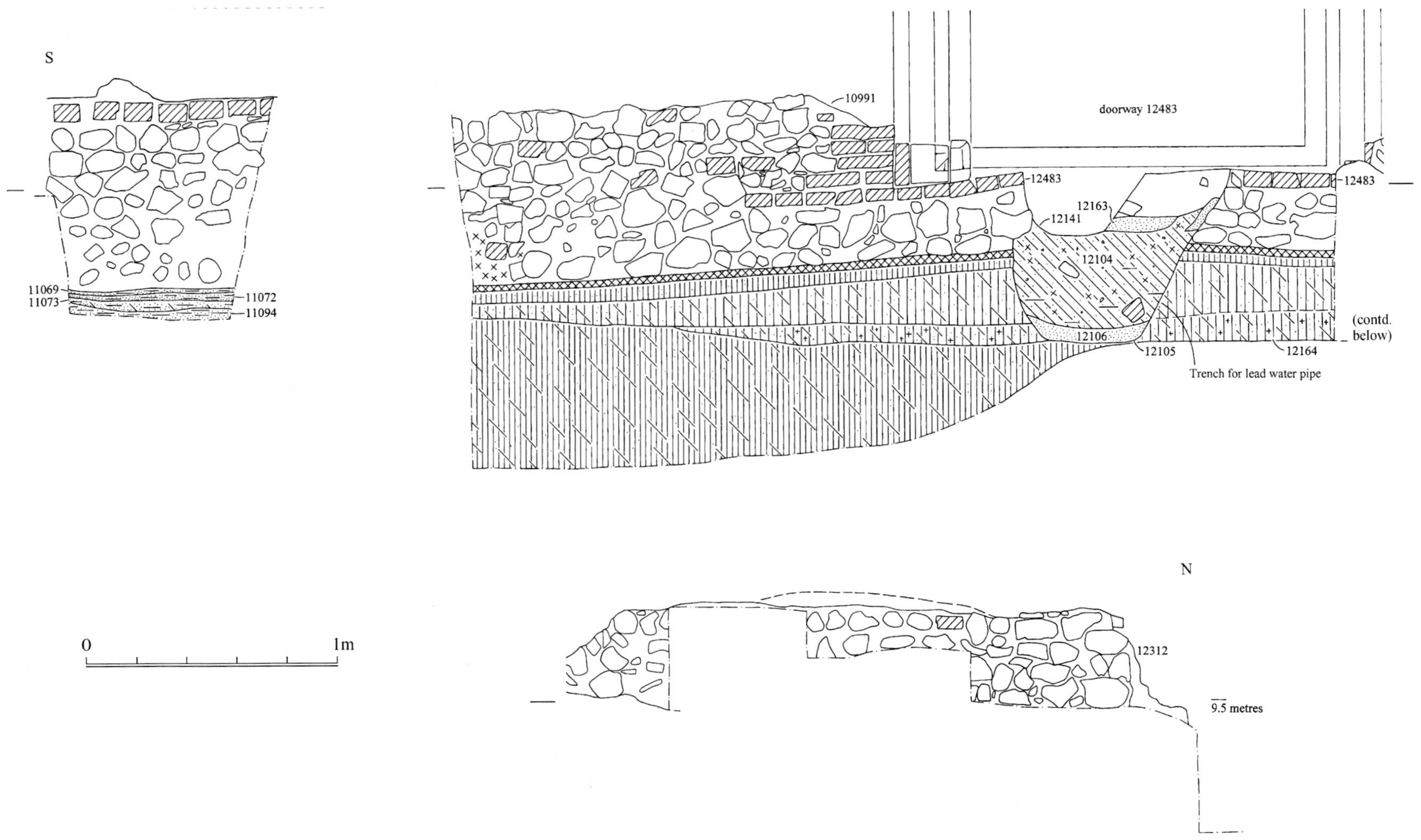

Figure 3.17 Elevation of eastern face of wall of Friary building fronting King Street, showing doorway *12483*, Area A

Plate 3.6 Mortar bedding *13019* with impressions of floor tiles

Plate 3.7 Hearth *12504* composed of tiles on edge, within possible kitchen in west range of cloister

Plate 3.8 West wall (*10710*) of possible kitchen in the west range, viewed from the south

Plate 3.9 Wall *30814* at the southern end of the east range of cloister

To the north of the possible kitchen, an insubstantial wall (*12155*) was traced over *c.* 3m and was inferred to run eastwards from the projected line of wall *10710* to join major wall *13416*/*13417*. This structure may also have formed a passage associated with the kitchen, lying 2.5m to the north of the north wall of the room and with access through it to the substantial fireplace. Later flooring of the passage is described in Period 3.2.

Connecting passage to ?cloister
(Figs 3.10 and 3.16)
To the west of the cloister, immediately south of the possible kitchen area, was a clay and chalk floor (*10515*: Fig. 3.16). This area was later to become a connecting passage between the putative cloister and buildings to its west, although it may have served a similar function from the outset. The floor abutted wall *10513* to the north and sealed make-up layers (*11053* and *11092*) containing 13th–14th-century pottery. A post-hole (*10996*: Fig. 3.10) is likely to have been sealed by this floor. The surface was also recorded to the south of wall *10506* (the construction cut for which had been dug into it), suggesting that the passageway may have been narrowed (see Period 3.2).

Flint-cobbled surface and post-setting
(Figs 3.7, 3.16, 3.19 and 3.20E)
The west range was separated from the free-standing wall described above by a narrow cobbled yard (about 5m wide internally). Only a very small area of the cobbled surface (*10625*) survived, so the extent of this area is uncertain. Within this yard, abutting the north side of a drain running across it (*10857*/*10904*/*10795*; Fig. 3.19) was a chalk block (*10773*; Fig. 3.20E) shaped to form a seating, presumably for a post.

South range
(Figs 3.7, 3.11, 3.12, 3.13, 3.16 and 3.21)
Extant masonry relating to the south range comprised displaced sections of flintwork. Flintwork further east related to the east range and is described in a separate section below. This displaced masonry included a simple rectangular block *c.* 1.7m long and 1.0m wide (*31080*: Fig. 3.11). A larger and more complex piece of flintwork measuring 2.2m long by 1.63m high (*30135*, *30224*, *30243* and *30314*) lay to the south-west. This fragment lay on its side, its flat base clearly visible, having toppled to the south. The fallen position of the piece of flintwork indicated the approximate line of the wall of which this section had formed part. The

reconstructed alignment corresponds to that of an *in situ* wall (*30737 etc.*) to the east. Adhering to the underside of the toppled wall was a layer of mortar which apparently formed a bedding on which it had been constructed. This compares closely with a similar layer recorded beneath comparable walls in the area. The base of the wall appears (on the basis of the varying thickness of the rubble core) to have been wider, the plinth having been some 0.5m high. This large flintwork fragment lay immediately below rubble deposits which may have been disturbed during construction of the Mann Egerton basement in the early 20th century.

To the west, the positions of two east-to-west walls were suggested by rubble-filled linear cuts (*30535* and *30768*). It is possible that these were robber trenches relating to the removal of Friary walls, although dating evidence for this was absent. The eastward projection of the northern trench (*30768*) is interpreted as having represented the south wall of the south walk (see above). No additional remains of walls were found on the projected line of either of these trenches, although the alignment of wall *30746*/*30072* *c.* 19m to the east was offset to the south by only 0.8m.

East range

(Figs 3.7, 3.11, 3.12, 3.13 and 3.21; Pl. 3.9)

The easternmost stone buildings of the Friary encountered during the excavation were located some 80m to the east of King Street, near the northern edge of Area B. The masonry recorded here appeared to represent three phases of building.

Cutting into underlying infilled quarry pits was an extensive feature which contained a series of compact alternating horizontal layers of gravel and earth (*30430*/*30101*/*31038*/*30129*: Figs 3.12 and 3.13). The cut corresponded in plan to the position of masonry foundations which overlay it. This elaborate construction was apparently created to allow the erection of Friary buildings in an area in which the ground conditions had been compromised by intensive quarrying (during Period 2.3). Since the layered fills did not extend throughout the quarry cuts, it would seem that the quarries had already been infilled when this construction work took place. Given the obvious engineering problems that such quarrying would inevitably create, it seems likely that this excavation was carried out prior to the new (post-1292) layout of the claustral buildings being known. The foundations concerned were an east-to-west wall (*30738*) and a north-to-south element (*30393*) which may have represented a buttress (see below). The east-to-west wall extended no further west than a modern stanchion base. The lowest point recorded on the base of the feature was at 3.90m OD (Fig. 3.13), the construction surface for the overlying masonry occurring at *c.* 5.05m OD.

The earliest of the overlying structures was a rectangular building, of which only the south-east corner and adjoining buttresses survived (*30737*/*30393*: Fig. 3.12). Neither the westward nor northward extents of this building could be established since construction of the Mann Egerton basement had removed all of the masonry in these areas. However, the shape in plan of the layered footing, upon which the south and east walls were built, provided some indication of alignment. The second phase comprised an eastward extension to this structure (*30735*/*30739*). The south wall of the addition (*30739*) was *c.* 1.0m thick, battered on its southern side and co-aligned with that of the original building, overlapping the limestone buttress at the join (*30814*: Pl. 3.9). Battering of these foundations on their outside face may have represented a form of continuous buttressing. This may reflect measures by the builders to enhance the intrinsic strength and lateral stability of a flint-and-mortar wall on sloping ground known to have been previously filled and thought to be prone to differential settlement. The final phase comprised the construction of a small rectangular room which was attached onto the south side of the second phase extension (*30736*/*30072*). The resulting composite structure did not entirely conform to a consistent alignment, a noticeable change occurring between the first- and second-phase structures. Given the sloping ground surface and the piecemeal nature of development, extension of the central complex of buildings was bound to entail local adjustments to the alignments of walls in order to maintain the orthogonality of the complex as a whole.

Courtyard between King Street buildings and cloister

The area between the western wall of the precinct (bounding King Street) and the putative guesthouse complex appears to have been substantially occupied by a courtyard, located between buildings fronting the street and the claustral complex.

?Boundary wall

(Figs 3.15, 3.16 and 3.21; Pl. 4.2)

The former presence of a major wall, which may have formed an eastward return of the precinct wall, was suggested by a large robber trench (*11200*/*11220*/*12555*: Figs 3.15 and 3.16) attributed to the Dissolution. A west-to-east aligned flint wall (*11006*), with its base at 8.65m OD and 0.4m thick, was traced over a 1.4m length just to the north of the line of the robber cut, which truncated it to the east. Presumably this wall extended westward to join north-to-south wall *10991*/*12312*/*12483* (Fig. 3.15), although no physical link survived. Both the surviving wall and the robbed out wall may link to the boundary of the southern limit of the courtyard, although variations in position may indicate two phases. The south edge of the robber trench was co-aligned with the north wall of a small, square Friary structure (*11159*/*11177*: Fig. 3.16) attached to the west side of the north-to-south free-standing wall that stood within the precinct (*10509 etc.*: above, 61–2). It also coincided with a 19th-century property boundary that had been perpetuated as a wall line in one of the Mann Egerton buildings, recently demolished. Cleer's map of 1696 (Pl. 4.2) also shows boundaries of plots so orientated. A Friary wall here would presumably have formed the southern end of the building on the King Street frontage as well as having, at one stage, defined the outer boundary of the precinct. The alignment of this boundary is unusual in that it is neither at right-angles to the King Street frontage nor parallel with any other wall lines. This nonconformity with the orthogonal layout of buildings within the Friary suggests that its alignment was inherited from a boundary between pre-Friary tenements fronting King Street.

?Building

(Figs 3.15 and 3.16)

A building to the south of the courtyard was represented only by a series of robber cuts (*10058*, *10111*, *10113*, *10300*, *10414*, *10348*, *10471*, *10842* and *10637*: see Period 4.1). These were generally shallower than those recorded elsewhere on the site, perhaps indicating the presence of a less substantial structure. They indicate the north-east corner of a building, with a possible southwards return from the north wall maybe representing a sub-division. The date at which the building may have been inserted is unknown, although it may have been a later addition to the pre-existing south wall of the courtyard. A sub-circular pit (*10324*), cut by putative buttress robber *10414*, contained large quantities of roof tile. Its position adjacent to the putative buttress and ?later drain suggests that it was a soakaway for a down-pipe from the building.

Flint cobble, gravel and sand surfaces

(Figs 3.7, 3.15, 3.16 and 3.21)

A succession of surfaces and make-ups appeared to represent surfacing within the open courtyard to the north-east of the putative building. Two flint cobble, gravel and sand ?yard surfaces had been truncated by modern basement construction. The lower was 0.1m thick, the surface lying at 8.45–8.60m OD (*10019*, *10512*, *10056*, *10063* and *10719*, *10731*). Post-holes were all cut at this level and were sealed by later levelling/make-up layers comprising mixed sand and mortar and sand and clay (*10012*, *10014*; *10062* and *10011*, *10064*, *10079*, *10095*, *10100*, *10200*, *10264*, *11165*). The upper floor surface (*10040*), which overlay the make-up layers, was 0.1m thick and lay at 8.6–8.7m OD. The west-to-east extent was 10.6m; the north-to-south width 8.0m. The earlier surface may have been associated with surfaces composed of flint/gravel, sand and mortar to the south apparently bounded by the robber cuts of the building. These were similarly overlain by a second floor surface which was also bounded by one of the robber trenches, although the floor probably remained extant or in use after the robbing. Later chalk and flint floor surfaces sealed this second floor, indicating that the ground surface continued to be maintained at this approximate level.

Open ground to the south-east

To the south of the precinct wall was a succession of deposits reflecting horticultural activity, eventually succeeded by a garden or orchard (see Chapter 4). These deposits were encountered during machining in Area C and were largely recorded in section. An accumulation of dark material may indicate, in part at least, cultivation of the area to the south-east of the Friary precinct (see Period 3.2 and Period 4.2). Initial deposits contemporary with the Friary (*50005*; micromorphological sample 5: see Macphail and Cruise, Chapter 6.VIII) indicate the dumping of industrial/hearth debris over the eroded natural sandy soil. These deposits had evidently been subject to strong biological mixing.

Period 3.2: alterations to the Friary (1400–1538)

Summary

Construction work in the period 1400–1538 included the insertion of a new building fronting King Street and subsequent its extensive renovation (apparently prompted by structural problems). Other activity at this time included the establishment of a temporary foundry, additions to the water management system, construction of a dovecote and modifications to the west range. The latter comprised alterations to (or the insertion of) passages to the south and north of the possible kitchen of Period 3.2. Allied to the new works was evidence for the quarrying of sand. Two pits in the eastern part of the excavated area contained waste that may have derived from the Friary kitchens.

The number of features post-dating 1400 seen to cut into natural deposits was negligible. This is a consequence of the degree by which the ground surface had been raised by the end of the 14th century, the natural horizon now lying below the range of most pit-digging. The substantial change in ground level in the southern part of the site may have been associated with the construction of the southern precinct wall of the Friary.

More that 17kg of pottery was recovered from this period, with a considerable reduction in the quantity of residual material and a notable increase in late medieval and transitional types, dating to the late 14th–mid-16th centuries (Lentowicz, Chapter 5.III). The numismatic items from this phase comprise a jetton of Edward II or III (*c.* 1319–43), another of Charles V (1364–80) and a Crown-type jetton (1380–1422) (Davies, Chapter 5.II). Only a few fragments of architectural stonework post-date *c.* 1350, although such absence is not uncommon at monastic sites (Samuel, Chapter 5.I).

Archaeological sequence

Quarrying

(Fig 3.7)

A cluster of pits (*30805*, *30761*, *30929*, *30972* and *30731*) occurred near the western edge of Area B. They were all at least 1.8m across, the largest (*30805*) being some 6.8m long, suggesting that they were quarries. Their probable 15th-century date indicates quarrying relating to the repair of buildings and surfaces within the Friary precinct. One pit (*30633*) contained an important assemblage of window glass dated to *c.* 1330–50 (King, Chapter 5.I).

To the south-east, an extensive cut (*30530*) measuring 12.5m long (north-east to south-west) by 7.3m wide and up to 2.7m deep occurred immediately to the north of the southern wall of the Friary precinct, which it apparently post-dated. The fills of this cut were clean sandy deposits which were dumped rapidly. There was no evidence to suggest that the pit was used for refuse disposal, and it was apparently another quarry. Its siting adjacent to the perimeter wall may reflect the absence of competing land-uses, such as food production, and implies that this stretch of the path running along the inside of the wall was no longer functional.

Modifications to west range

Passage to south of ?kitchen

(Figs 3.7, 3.10, 3.16 and 3.21; Pl. 3.5)

An east-to-west wall (*10506*, *12573*, *12574*, *12606*, *12608*, *12577* and *12571*: Figs 3.10 and 3.16) was inserted *c.* 2.9m to the south of the wall that formed the southern wall of the ?kitchen (*10513*, Period 3.1), forming a passageway. It cut through earlier flooring in the area and presumably ran eastwards to join the putative west walk of the cloister. A robber trench to the west (*12400*) indicated its continuation in this direction, leading into the small cobbled yard to the west of the kitchen.

A succession of floor surfaces interspersed with make-up layers (*10937*, *10938*, *10964*, *10965*, *10505*, *10507*, *10849*, *10855*, *10922*, *10963*, *10927*; *10966*; *12575*, *12584*, *12585* and *12586*: Fig.3.10) lay within the passageway. The earlier flooring was largely of mortar. *In situ* evidence for tile flooring comprised two main patches of tile impressions (*10922* and *10505/10507/10849*: Fig. 3.16; Pl. 3.5). Most of the impressions had been made by tiles that were 120mm square, those recorded along the southern side of the passage (*10922*) measuring 240mm. The tiled areas sealed a layer that contained a Nuremberg jetton (SF270, AD 1500–25). The lowest make-up/foundation deposit for these floors contained early–mid-15th-century pottery. Adjacent to, and contemporary with, the smaller tile impressions were two Purbeck limestone slabs, measuring 900mm long by 580mm wide by 110mm thick. It is likely that these were re-used tomb slabs, although no trace of any inscription was detected on them.

Stratigraphic relationships indicate that alterations to the south wall of the kitchen occurred within the life of the Friary, perhaps for the insertion of a doorway in this wall affording access from this passage into the putative kitchen to the north. This hypothesis is supported by the presence of surfacing (*10510*, *10511*, *10791*, *10845*, *10846*, *10848*, *10850* and *10853*) that sealed the north wall (*10513*) but that did not appear to have overlain the south wall (*10506*).

Passage to north of ?kitchen

(Figs 3.7, 3.16 and 3.21)

Within the passage to the north of the kitchen was laid a floor (*12505/12556* and *12131*), comprising alternating rows of bricks laid longitudinally and laterally (Fig. 3.16). The overlying tread layer (*12130*), which was itself sealed by mortar rubble consistent in character to other Dissolution demolition deposits, contained pottery spot-dated to the mid-14th to 15th centuries.

?Bakehouse fronting onto King Street

The construction of a building with stone foundations on the King Street frontage — against the perimeter wall — appears to date to the late 14th–15th centuries on the basis of pottery recovered from stratigraphically earlier deposits. It lay to the south of an earlier stone building (see Chapter 2.III) and east of another building represented only by robber trenches. This new structure appears to have been built in the angle formed by the western wall of the precinct and its putative eastward return (represented by extant flintwork *11006* and robber cut *12555*: see Period 3.1). Some of the walls of this and other new buildings in this area closely corresponded with the cellar walls of a 19th-century building.

Phase 1: construction

(Figs 3.7, 3.14, 3.15, 3.17 and 3.21; Pl. 3.10)

Definition of the north wall of the building was made difficult by the extent of Dissolution robbing, although it was probably indicated by the position of a robber trench (*12071*: Fig. 3.15). It would be logical for a major wall to have occurred on this line given that the contemporary bell-founding pit *12257*, located immediately to the north, would doubtless have been physically separated from the room to the south. The east wall (*10991/12312*) reflected the pre-existing line of *10004* which perhaps continued northwards as far as the edge of the Mann Egerton basement (where masonry *12033* was recorded on a similar line). The southern limit of the new building may have been defined by the pre-existing east-to-west wall (although a further isolated set of foundations was found to the south: see below).

The eastern wall (*10991/12312*) was constructed upon a 0.7m thickness of layered fills within a construction trench. This foundation design appears to have been a response to the frequent soft ground in this area caused by pitting. The compacted layers of earth formed a raft which reduced the differential settlement caused by disparities in load-bearing capacity between the firm, undisturbed natural and infilled pits. Beneath a doorway through this wall (see below), however, the base of this trench rose by 0.35m. The decision not to dig the trench to the same depth beneath the doorway, together with the cutting of a pipe-trench (*12240/12105*: Figs 3.14 and 3.17) through it, seem to have been

Plate 3.10 Quarter column *12178* abutting wall *10991*, King Street frontage

ill-advised in view of the structural problems that followed in the 15th century (see Phase 2, below).

An internal wall (*12079/12161* and *12261*), aligned east-to-west and less than 3m from the supposed southern end of the building, was separated from the east wall by a robber pit (*12061*, see below). The occurrence of the base of a quarter column (*12178*: Pl. 3.10), bonded to the east wall, immediately adjacent to the north edge of the robber cut, suggests the position of a door-arch. The quarter column would have flanked the east jamb of the doorway. The doorway itself (*12483*: Fig. 3.17) was represented by a chamfered limestone sill-jamb junction (internal width 1.32m, external width 1.93m) which was apparently contemporary with the construction of the surrounding flintwork. The northernmost robber trench (*12071*) terminated some 2m short of the east wall of the building, the gap opposing a putative doorway in the wall to the south, suggesting a third entrance at this point.

The northern 'room' of the building thus enclosed measured 5.5m north-to-south and 6m east-to-west internally. An initial clay floor surface at 9.37m OD (*12156*, *12227*, *12343* and *12344*) sealed the infilling of the earlier cellar (Chapter 2.III). This floor post-dated construction of the east wall and contained pottery of late 14th-century date.

A rectangular base of mortared flintwork (*12317/12376*) *c.* 0.9m long (east-to-west) was built onto the internal (west) face of the east wall (*10991/12312*). A flat pad of brickwork, measuring 0.53m by 0.35m, was built hard-up against the wall on top of this foundation. This appears to have formed the base for a stone column or jamb.

Two features within the building indicated internal structural elements. The first, a pad of flints (*12149*), lay in the south-west corner of the square room and may have formed a base for a flight of stairs. The second, a rectangular robber cut aligned north-to-south (*12075*, Period 4.1), terminated 1.5m short of the suggested north wall of the building. The base of this feature was flat and formed by compacted natural sand, suggesting that a load-bearing upright stood here.

Numerous post-holes were concentrated into the south-east and north-west corners of the room. One series of post-holes formed a north-south line with westward return at its north end (*12195*, *12223*, *12225*, *12248*, *12352*, *12433* and *12435*): given the central position of the north-to-south line in relation to the building, these apparently represent a support for an upper floor. The east-to-west line was later reinstated with a masonry wall represented by robber trench *12071*. A burnt clay floor surface (*12216*) may have been contemporary. This floor overlay make-up dumps (*12177*, *12335*, *12338*, *12339* and *12340*) and established a new floor surface at *c.* 9.5m OD, this elevation representing a 130mm rise above the initial clay surface (*12156 etc.*). Various insubstantial post-holes (*12191*, *12198*, *12200*, *12202*, *12204*, *12206*, *12208*, *12210*, *12212*, *12214*, *12220*, *12346*, *12350*, *12354*, *12356*, *12358* and *12246*), including a cluster in the north-west angle of the room, may have represented internal structures. All of these post-holes had been heavily truncated, presumably during demolition/replacement and disuse of the floor surface. Subsequent making-up of the floor was represented by a succession of clay layers (*12313*, *12302*, *12139*, *12342*, *12323*, *12320* and *12321*).

This small, square building with three entrances and burnt clay floor may equate with the bakehouse with solar above documented by leases (Plot E on Fig. 3.6: this interpretation assumes a continuation of function into the 16th century). No evidence for ovens was found, however, and this suggestion remains tentative.

The remains of an external surface (*10981*), composed of bricks overlying a bedding of orange sand (*10980*), abutted the east face of wall *10991* (Fig. 3.15) and overlay an earlier surface represented by a layer of lime mortar (*11019*) containing brick and tile fragments. This area of flooring formed part of an external yard to the rear of the building.

Phase 2: renovations
(Fig.3.15)
Differential settlement, of the order of 0.25m over a horizontal distance of only 2.5m, was experienced by the section of the building's eastern wall to the south of the doorway. The southern part of this stretch of foundation sunk into a very large infilled pit (*12374/12511*) which measured some 4m in diameter, effectively rotating about the hard peak of undisturbed ground under the doorway. The severity of the settlement must have been reflected by dramatic cracking higher up the wall. Remedial action involved the construction of a buttress (*11097*, *12128*) onto the external (east) face of this wall at the point where the wall had broken its back, which coincided with the centre of the underlying pit. This buttress (*11097/12128*: Fig. 3.14) was built upon a layered earthen footing (*11057/12095*) which cut through the layered footing for the wall and contained alternating horizontal fills of mortar and sandy silt. Its east face was battered. Another external buttress was placed onto the east face of the wall to the north, although it had been almost entirely robbed leaving a projecting stub of flintwork (*12181*).

Part of the internal wall to the south (*12079 etc.*) had been removed by a deep, straight-sided robber pit (*12061*), *c.* 2.5m in length and dating to the Dissolution of the Friary (Period 4.1). This cut represents the removal of a substantial footing that was *c.* 0.6m deeper than the base of the wall (*12079/12161* and *12261*) on the same line. The masonry that stood here clearly formed an important support for the east wall of the building and possibly for an upper floor. Its construction probably formed part of the remedial work following settlement of the east wall and resulting structural damage.

Temporary foundry

Bell-casting and other founding activity took place to the north of the possible bakehouse on the King Street frontage. The northern extent of the area within which the bell-casting pit lay could not be readily defined. A stub of flintwork (*12179*) projecting eastwards from the precinct wall may have been the remnants of the north wall of the foundry. To the east, the workshop was bounded by pre-existing wall (*12490/12594/10004*), the pit being dug against the wall's western end. The southern limit was formed by a wall that had been entirely removed by later robbing (*12071*) and to the west lay the precinct wall. On this basis, the bell-casting area measured 4.0m long (east-to-west) by 3.5m. An adjacent well (*12020*) may have been associated with the founding activities (below, 75).

Bell-casting
(Figs 3.7, 3.15 and 3.18; Pls 3.11 and 3.12)
The bell-casting pit (*12257* and *12489*), containing the *in situ* remains of the pedestal of a bell-mould, lay *c.* 2.8m to the east of the King Street frontage. It was cut into the firm natural sand, was oval in plan, sheer-sided and had an almost flat base (Fig. 3.18; Pl. 3.11). It measured a

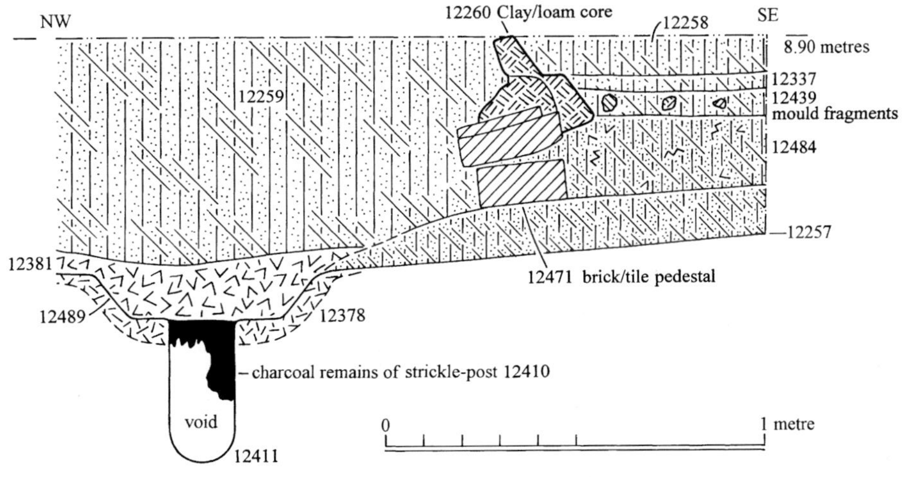

Figure 3.18 Section of bell-casting pit *12257*, Area A

Plate 3.11 Bell pit before excavation

maximum of 1.7m west to east and survived to a maximum depth of 0.5m.

(A glossary of the technical terms italicised below is given in Chapter 5.II.)

A perfectly circular hole, 85mm in diameter and 180mm deep, was cut into the base of the pit and located centrally relative to the *core* (Pl. 3.12). The internal vertical face of the hole, to which charcoal remains of a round timber adhered, was smooth. This timber was the vertical spindle of the *strickle* which rotated in the hole. Given that the hole was perfectly circular in plan and was very smooth it is possible that the timber within was itself the rotating spindle to which the strickle was attached. The hole and charcoal within were sealed by a deposit of ash which lay within a bowl-shaped hollow *c.* 300mm in diameter and 60mm deep. This represented the fire that had been set in order to harden the loam core. The occurrence of the charcoal in the hole indicated that the timber was left *in situ* after use, to be burnt during the internal firing of the core.

Within the cut stood the base of the circular loam core of the bell mould, which was centred on the strickle hole. The core was raised from the base of the cut by a *pedestal* comprising two courses of incomplete bricks capped with roof tiles. A ledge, measuring 22mm in width, was recorded in the profile of the core, some 90mm above its base. The inner, curved edge of this step corresponded to the lip at the mouth of the bell. The *cope* would have located on the outer part of the step. The surface of the core above the ledge was inclined at 45 degrees. This formed the lower, straight section of the *sound bow*. The internal diameter of the mouth of the bell was 0.9m. The sound-bow groove of the pedestal was not centred exactly on the hole for the strickle and dipped to the east at an angle of almost 4 degrees from the horizontal. This indicated that the pedestal, although largely intact, had been bodily moved after use. In profile, the angle of the sound-bow ranged from 110 to 125 degrees.

Further details of dating and the metalworking evidence associated with the bell-casting pit are given in Chapter 5.II.

Adjoining the bell pit to the north was a larger pit (*12217*) which may have been associated with bell-casting (see Dissolution: 1538–65). Also possibly associated pit was a clay-lined pit (*12021*) which was located just under 1m to the south-west (Fig. 3.7).

Building fronting onto King Street

(Figs 3.7 and 3.21)

A set of extant flint wall foundations *c.* 0.3m thick and a robber cut represented a Friary building set back from the King Street frontage, further south than the other recorded buildings. Its association with the Friary is based on dating of a key group of stoneware drinking vessels recovered from the robber fill (*10660*/*10770*: Lentowicz, Chapter 5.III). The north-to-south wall (*11115*/*11117*) lay *c.* 7m from King Street, based on the line of the frontage depicted by the 1885 Ordnance Survey map.

Plate 3.12 Bell pit during excavation, showing central spindle hole for the strickle

Abutting this building to the west was a later structure, comprising walls of brick and flint (*11112* and *11106*) and two flint cobble floors. The floor to the north (*11109*/*11110*) lay at 8.76m OD and that to the south (*11107*) at 8.52m OD, the two separated by a worn step (*11108*) composed of brick and flint. The alignment of these rooms was at variance with that of the building to the east represented by extant walls (north-to-south *11115*/*11117* and east-to-west *11116*). This disparity, together with the fact that the east-to-west wall had clearly been attached to the north-to-south wall, indicated that there were two phases of construction. While the first phase represented by extant flintwork and the robbed foundation appears to have been contemporary with the Friary, the addition of rooms to the west conceivably dates to the post-Dissolution period.

These structures may represent service buildings, the pottery suggesting a connection with the Friary kitchens.

Other Friary structures

Dovecote

(Figs 3.7 and 3.21)

A small, isolated, rectangular, cellared structure (*30490*), to the south of the claustral buildings (*c.* 9.6m to the south-west of the nearest *in situ* Friary foundations) and *c.* 24m to the north of the southern boundary of the precinct, was interpreted as a dovecote. Internally, this structure was 2.5m long by 2.0m wide. The construction cut was 1m deep, the brick walls surviving to a height of 0.5m from their base. The floor, of which no part survived, had probably been removed prior to demolition, which was represented by fills of flint and mortar rubble within the structure. This rubble fill contained pottery dating to the 15th–16th centuries. Association between the structure and the Friary is questionable as it was not aligned orthogonally with respect to the general scheme of Friary walls. However, its alignment was similar to that of a variant north-to-south wall (*30393*), suggesting that its position reflected local variation in the alignments of walls and structures.

Documentary evidence suggests that this structure may have been a dovecote which survived after the Dissolution. Leases of 1565 refer to a 'dovehouse' in Plot K (see Rutledge, above, 55 and Fig. 3.6).

Isolated building

(Fig. 3.7)

A rectangular, sheer-sided cut (*30954*), recorded at the west edge of Area B, appears to have represented a building of some kind, an inner cut (*30959*) containing flint rubble. Less than 1m to the east was a line of four post-holes (*30986*, *31010*, *31012* and *31014*); although undated, they are likely to represent a single structure which may have been associated with that represented by the rectangular cut.

Pitting

(Fig. 3.7)

At the eastern end of the site, some considerable distance from the cloister, lay two Friary-related pits (*40014* and *40019*). These were positioned 6.5m to the north of the southern wall of the precinct. The former, dated to the 15th century on the basis of pottery, was cut by the latter, which was dated by pottery and vessel glass to the early 16th century. Both pits were broadly rectangular and their fills were similar in character, containing large quantities of animal, fish and bird bone and shell (see Chapter 6). The general eastward inclination of the fills indicated that material had been dumped into the pits from the west. While the infilling of the successive pits was separated by a substantial lapse of time, probably a century, the close similarity between the features indicates that they reflect a continuity of land-use of this area from the first half of the 15th century to the Dissolution of the Friary. Both pits contained large quantities of brick and tile (*40014*: 7.7 kg; *40019*: 21.8 kg) in addition to significant amounts of pottery, indicating that refuse from the Friary kitchens was collected together with domestic and building waste.

Open ground to south-east

Earlier dumps recorded to the south-east of the precinct in Period 3.1 were overlain by a humic and charcoal-rich accumulation, containing a high proportion of burned material (slags) and probable wood ash, with a possible cess content (*50024*, micromorphological sample 4: Macphail and Cruise, Chapter 6.VIII). This may have been deposited in more than one dumping episode.

Friary cemetery (Site 373N)

(Fig. 1.2; Pl. 3.13)

Evidence for the Friary cemetery was recorded at the former Wallace King premises on St Faith's Lane (Site 373N) in the most southerly of the three trenches opened during an NAU evaluation (Emery 1997). Subsequent excavation by Northamptonshire Archaeology revealed 137 burials, including the six previously encountered by the NAU (Soden 2001). A dump of yellow brown sand, 0.30m thick, represented levelling associated with the laying out of the cemetery. This layer contained a medieval copper alloy key (373N/SF108: Fig. 5.46). Six graves were partially exposed, cutting into a deposit of grey/brown silty sand representing mixed topsoil and turf. This layer contained two artefacts of particular note: a looped strap-end (373N/SF5; Fig. 5.91) and a square book mount (373N/SF6; Fig. 5.41). The graves recorded in 1997 lay in two north-to-south rows, each comprising three graves (Pl. 3.13). The skeletons were in remarkably good condition. None of the human remains were lifted, due both to the desire to limit disturbance and to the fact that none of the skeletons was completely exposed within the excavated trench, limiting the validity of any osteological study that might have followed.

Plate 3.13 Excavation of late medieval graves within the cemetery of the Francisan Friary (St Faith's Lane evaluation, Site 373N)

None of the exposed graves were intercutting, indicating that in this area at least there was no re-use of cemetery space. Burial plots are likely to have been particularly at a premium close to the church (to the south-west) and at the more public west end of the cemetery, adjacent to King Street. One grave contained an iron nail, perhaps from a wooden coffin, and one was accompanied by a copper-alloy pin adjacent to the right upper arm which may have been used on a shroud.

Overlying rubble deposits associated with the Dissolution contained pieces of painted window glass and lead window came. The occurrence of decorative glass may indicate the presence of a religious building, perhaps deriving from a mortuary chapel within the cemetery or even the church itself.

Water management system (Periods 3.1 and 3.2)

The Greyfriars excavation revealed the substantial remains of a water management system comprising a hierarchy of drains (some of them extremely well-preserved), a series of wells and traces of two contemporary water pipelines. Elements of the system date both from the era of Friary construction (Period 3.1) and from its subsequent development (Period 3.2).

Water supply

Evidence of the supply of fresh water for the Friary consisted of at least eleven wells and traces of lead water pipes, along with a group of ceramic water pipes; at least some of the latter may relate to the Friary.

Wells

(Figs 3.7, 3.19 and 3.21)

Nine of the wells were found in Area A and two in the northern part of Area B. The concentration of Friary wells within Area A is a function of the local topography. It reflects both the higher density of buildings (and thus greater demand for water) in this focal part of the precinct and the advantages of drawing water in the higher part of the site, from which it could be distributed under gravity. As none of the wells were excavated to their bases, their construction could not be dated from finds deposited during their use.

From its scale and probable connection with the pipelines, one well in particular (*11129*: Fig. 3.19) appeared to represent a primary water source. The internal diameter of its lining wall was 1.6m; its outer diameter *c.* 2.5m. This surround was composed of mortared flints and possessed a knapped flint inner face. The internal diameter of the next largest well confidently attributed to the Friary (*12049*), was only *c.* 1.2 metres, its lining measuring ony 0.2m in thickness.

The wells illustrated in Fig. 3.19 are those thought most likely to date to the Friary period on the basis of their exclusively flint construction. An exception was well *12020* which was brick-built, and possibly associated with the use of the foundry and with renovations to the building fronting King Street.

Plumbing

(Figs 3.7, 3.17, 3.19 and 3.21)

The construction trenches and impressions of two lead water pipes were traced for considerable distances across Area A. The first (*12105/12148/12240/12141*) was aligned south-east to north-west and passed under the doorway of a Friary-related building on the King Street frontage (*12483*, Period 3.2: Fig. 3.17). It was apparently inserted immediately following construction of the building. The other pipeline (*10752 etc.*) ran from south-west to north-east. The brick floor within the passageway to the north of the possible kitchen in the west range was traversed by an irregular linear disturbance (*12167*) which probably represents the removal of a section of lead pipe that may have formed the north-easterly continuation of this pipeline. All of the piping had been removed at the Dissolution. The projected lines of the two pipes converged just north of the major well (*11229*), raising the possibility that both pipes had been laid to draw water from this source to supply specific buildings. One of the brick conduits (*10746*) was aligned towards the same well, offering support to the proposal that this particular brick structure housed a water pipe and had nothing to do with drainage.

Drainage and sanitation

Excavation of several well-preserved sections of the system of drains allowed a plan of the overall network to be reconstructed, affording some understanding of the Friary's management of waste water. Elements of this system varied considerably in terms of size and constructional character, indicating piecemeal extension and alteration during the period between the late 14th century and the Dissolution of the Friary. As not all of the recorded drains could be related to each other stratigraphically, the sequence of their construction has been inferred partly through study of the hierarchical relationships between them. This hierarchy was established by comparing internal cross-sectional areas (taken as an indicator of design capacity) and by examining the layout of the network.

The Great Drain

(Fig. 3.8, 3.19 and 3.21; Pls 3.14–3.16)

The highest-order drain within the hierarchy (*10334/10652/10653/10654/11130/13013/13014/13015/13023/13024*) was aligned west-to-east. From its west end this culvert passed beneath a major west wall of the possible kitchen and was traced for some 12m as far as the eastern extent of the excavated area. Beyond this, the structure was traced by electronic probe to a point midway across No.21 Prince of Wales Road, giving a total recorded length of *c.* 144m (Fig. 3.21). A remote-controlled video camera mounted on a crawler tractor unit (Pl. 3.14) provided images of the interior of the drain (Pl. 3.15).

The structure comprised a flat floor of brick, more-or-less vertical side walls and a simply-supported roof (Pl. 3.16). Internally, the culvert measured 0.40m wide and 0.60m high. The floor was generally of brick and the walls, which were rendered internally, were composed of a mixture of flint and brick fragments. The roof consisted of very large flint nodules, pieces of Purbeck marble slab and part of a limestone coffin lid of 12th- or 13th-century date (SF953, Samuel and Ashley, Chapter 5.I).

Tributary drains

(Figs 3.19, 3.20C–E and 3.21; Pls 3.17 and 3.18)

Four secondary drains discharged directly into the main drain. At its west end, a vaulted brick structure (*10335/10708/ 10712/10892/10893/11174*: Fig. 3.19, 3.20C, Pl. 3.17), aligned north-to-south, formed a T-junction. The culvert comprised chiefly complete bricks, but possessed a single course of flint nodules near its base. The maximum internal dimensions of the structure were 0.55m wide and 0.50m high. Oysters had been inserted as wedges between bricks forming the arch of the roof (Fig. 3.20C). The function of the rounded, northern terminus of the north-to-south culvert was suggested by evidence of an adjacent junction in the impression of the lead water pipe that ran east-west immediately to the north. It is conceivable, especially given the absence of any tributary culvert here, that a tap was located at the north end of the vaulted culvert. This, when opened, would have allowed fresh water, perhaps supplied under pressure from a raised cistern, to flush this part of the sewerage system.

Another drain feeding southwards into the main drain (*10707/10786*: Figs 3.7, 3.19, 3.20A and 3.21) lay immediately adjacent to the inner side of the east wall of the possible kitchen (Period 3.1). It was constructed in brick and flowed from north to south, feeding into the main west-to-east culvert vertically via a doughnut-shaped *paramoudra* flint nodule (Pl. 3.18). The interpretation of this vertical connection as a drain represents the most compelling indication that the function of the culvert system as a whole was drainage rather than supply. Along the northern edge of the ?kitchen, a collapsed section of drain (*12548*) of similar construction, composed chiefly of bricks but incorporating a flagstone, was sandwiched between the tile construction fireplace and the room's north wall. The articulated brickwork at the base of this drain occurred at 8.10m OD (0.13m higher than that of the north-to-south drain). It is therefore likely that these two drains connected to run around the perimeter of the northern and eastern sides of the room. The collapsed section of drain contained a loose fill from which 151 square pieces of cattle rib, which had been cut with a knife then snapped, were recovered (Huddle, Chapter 5.II). The deposit also contained 3049 fish bones representing over twenty species (Nicholson, Chapter 6.III). The collapse of the structure may have occurred when the overlying fireplace was constructed: if this were the case, it would preclude any association between its contents and the hearth.

A drain composed largely of architectural fragments deriving from earlier Friary buildings (*13440*: Figs 3.7, 3.19, 3.20D and 3.21; see Samuel, Chapter 5.I) but floored with roof tiles (Fig. 3.20D), ran from north-to-south along the centre of the putative west walk of the cloister. It appeared to have been tunnelled beneath the south wall of the putative north walk. The southern part of the drain had been robbed away (see Period 4.1).

To the south of the main drain was another drain (*12576/12607/13012/13044*: Figs 3.7, 3.19 and 3.21), also aligned north-to-south but falling to the north. It lay at the eastern limit of the 1994 excavation, but was picked up again by the subsequent works in 1995. The floor and walls were in brick and capped by a roof of worked stone blocks. This drain fed vertically into the Great Drain from the south via a mortared brick shaft. This culvert took water from another drain, flowing west-to-east, which ran along the southern, inner, edge of the west-east corridor to the south of the kitchen within the west range (*12573*). The dating of this drain is ambiguous: it may have been constructed after the Dissolution of the Friary and have been associated with a building that incorporated extant elements of the largely demolished complex.

Possible drain running down east side of cloister

(Pl. 4.4)

The stream depicted running from north to south on Millard and Manning's map may well represent the legacy, following its destruction at the Dissolution, of the cockey's diversion into a drain aligned along the eastern side of the cloister. The coincidence of the southern end of this stream with the line of the Great Drain, which is known to have survived intact, may indicate that it had drained into this structure. The post-Dissolution serviceability of the main drain is suggested by the fact that a drain associated with a post-medieval building still fed into it.

Minor drains feeding into vaulted culvert

(Figs 3.7, 3.19, 3.20E and 3.21)

Three tributaries of the north-to-south vaulted culvert (*10335 etc.*), or of its predecessor, were uncovered. The first (*10795/10857/10904*: Fig. 3.20E) was aligned east-to-west and lay to the east of the north-to-south structure. No aperture could be seen in the east wall of the vaulted culvert, on the projected alignment of the smaller drain. This, together with stratigraphic evidence showing the larger culvert to have been built after the smaller, suggests that the vaulted brick structure represented a complete rebuild of a precursor, on the same alignment. Such an interpretation would help to explain the stark difference in design and character between the vaulted brick culvert (*10335 etc.*) and the main east-to-west culvert.

There is a possibility that a robber cut (*11242*) with a rectangular cross-section, located immediately to the south of drain *10904*, represents an additional drain that was removed during the life of the Friary (Fig. 3.20E).

The second tributary (*10794*) was aligned north-east to south-west and fed into the east side of the north-to-south structure via an adjoining chamber (Fig. 3.19). The size and rectangular plan of this chamber suggest that it provided access to the junction of the culverts for inspection and maintenance. A brick wall, which crossed the north-to-south culvert, appeared to be associated with the tributary channel as it lay on the projected line of its north edge. The wall presumably served to aid the flow of water through the junction and also appeared to mark the disuse of the section of the vaulted structure that lay to the north of the wall.

The third culvert (*10524/10746*: Fig. 3.19), possibly discharging into the north-to-south vaulted drain, lay to its west on a south-west to north-east alignment. No evidence of the junction of the two culverts was found. The level of the floor of the tributary culvert at the estimated point of intersection, extrapolated from levels recorded further west, was some 0.25m higher than that of the top of the brick vault. This disparity in levels has two possible explanations. The small culvert either discharged into the larger one via a vertical connection through its roof or by falling to the west of the north-south structure to enter through its west wall, or it passed straight over the larger and was not connected with it at all. A gap occurred in the substantial mortared flint west wall of the possible kitchen, slightly to the north of the projected line of the conduit. The flat base of this opening was some 260mm lower than that of the surviving conduit, *c.* 7.8m to the south-west. It is conceivable, therefore, that the conduit passed through the kitchen wall at this point, which was immediately to the north of the gully on the east side of the wall.

Two smaller culverts were interpreted to have drained into that just discussed (*10524/10746*): one aligned north-to-south (*10542*) which fell to the north and another (*12102*) which ran from the doorway in the east wall of the building fronting King Street. The fact that the west end of the latter was located at the doorway suggests that this culvert took water from a downpipe from the roof of the building. Its level was considerably higher than those further east, suggesting that there was a vertical drop to the west of the junction with the diagonally-aligned culvert.

IV. DISCUSSION: THE FRANCISCAN FRIARY

Introduction

'The friars may be considered as the last wave of the tide of monasticism which had flowed over Europe for almost nine hundred years …' (Knowles and Hadcock 1971, 37). In contrast to the reformed monastic orders of the 12th century, the friars were principally concerned with preaching, evangelism and learning. Their mission was directed to the people of the towns, where the existence of surplus wealth made it possible for the friars to sustain themselves on begging (Lawrence 1994, 102). The towns to which they came were usually densely occupied: sites available for monastic buildings tended to be either constricted or set at the outskirts of settlement. The initial holding of the Norwich Greyfriars is likely to have been modest and also — lying well down the slope in the eastern half of the later precinct (away from the main streets and not far from the church of St Mary in the Marsh) — typically marginal. The imposition of such ecclesiastical establishments and their precincts had a dramatic effect on the shape of medieval Norwich and its street pattern (Ayers 1994, fig. 46). By the mid-14th century about a quarter of the walled city was occupied by religious precincts, this representing a similar proportion to that evident in other towns (such as Chester: Greene 1992, 165). Through a succession of documented enlargements to their precinct dating from 1285 onwards, the Greyfriars had absorbed an area of some 4.2ha (10.4 acres) by the late 15th century.

In 1538 the Norwich Franciscan Friary was surrendered to King Henry VIII and it seems that most of the institution's structures had been demolished by 1542. Despite Dissolution demolition, many of the Friary's key wall alignments were retained as new property boundaries following subdivision of the site after the Reformation. The post-medieval landscape, described by a succession of maps between the late 17th and late 19th centuries, thereby inherited much of the Friary's internal geography (see Chapter 4).

Original Friary precinct

The original site acquired by the Friary prior to 1292 lay to the south of the Dallingflete stream and to the east of the minor lane *c.* 62m to the east of King Street (Figs 2.1 and 3.3). This area represented less than half of that acquired by the Franciscans by 1400. Only a very small part of the pre-1292 site (577m^2) occurred within the area that was investigated archaeologically. Excavated evidence of 13th-century occupation therefore largely related to an urban landscape that had not yet been absorbed into the Friary (see Period 2.3, Chapter 2.III).

Friary expansion

In archaeological terms, the growth in the status and wealth of the Norwich's Franciscan Friary in the second half of the 13th century was most conspicuously expressed in the dramatic enlargement of the precinct and in the new buildings that arose from the extensive programme of construction work and, also, in the impact that this had on the urban landscape (Figs 3.21 and 3.22). The rebuilding of the Friary church on newly acquired land had begun by 1292. Obliterating the pattern of streets and plots that became enclosed by its expanding precinct, the Friary in turn imposed its own internal rectilinear arrangement over a considerable area. Only the precinct's outermost boundary reflected pre-existing alignments to any extent. The impact of expansion of the outward development of the precinct on the existing urban landscape was clear. Buildings fronting onto King Street were demolished and a lane, probably forming part of the pre-Conquest street system, was closed off. The ultimate abandonment of the road was marked by construction of the south wall of the precinct, presumably at the beginning of the 14th century.

The excavated Friary

Layout

Arguably the most significant result of the investigation has been the elucidation of the layout of key elements of the Friary. Prior to excavation it was known from documents that the development site lay within the Greyfriars' precinct, but the precise whereabouts and arrangement of the Friary buildings were unknown. The new interpretation differs considerably from earlier published groundplans (*cf.* Taylor 1821, map opp. 132; Campbell 1975, maps 2 and 3) and offers revised insights into the local topographical context. One major achievement has been to establish the probable position of the late 13th-century Friary church and cloister.

Excavated structural remains that could be attributed to the Franciscan Friary include sections of the precinct wall, an internal boundary wall (aligned north-to-south), parts of what seems most likely to be the claustral complex and associated ranges, a dovecote and at least three buildings on the King Street frontage, one of which may (on the basis of post-Dissolution documents) have served as a bakehouse. Ultimately, the precinct boundary wall measured some 870m in length. The southern wall, which survived to a height of 2.5m, was traced for 60m within the excavation, while some 18.5m length of the west wall was recorded on the King Street frontage.

Despite the limitations noted in earlier chapters, wall alignments inferred from extant masonry, foundations and robber cuts could be correlated with plot boundaries mapped on the basis of 16th-century leases. This integrated plan provided a framework within which the 'floating' church and cloister, surveyed by Worcestre, could be located experimentally and compared with archaeological remains. As part of the process of reconstructing the Friary plan, several alternative schemes (all detailed in the project archive) were explored. This experimentation sought to reconcile potential layouts with the maps of stone walls (Fig. 3.4) and plot boundaries (Fig. 3.6). The plausibility of each hypothetical layout was then evaluated with reference to the known groundplans of other Franciscan houses. However, analogy can only be taken so far as friaries often had to adapt their arrangement to the topographical constraints of their sites. Such restrictions at the Norwich Greyfriars are likely to have necessitated departures from an 'idealised' layout such as that at Walsingham (Dickinson 1961, 147). The possibility that there had been more than one cloister was also considered.

The resulting interpretation of the Friary plan is presented in Fig. 3.21 and a conjectural cross-section of the precinct in relation to the natural topography is given in Fig. 3.22. The ranges surrounding the cloisters would have included a chapter house, dormitory, refectory, infirmary, guesthouse, schoolroom and a library. The excavated west range, comprising two approximately square rooms (including a possible kitchen) and three east-to-west passages, may represent the guesthouse. Its symmetrical layout is similar to that exhibited by the west range of Carmarthen Greyfriars (James 1997, 111). The evidence of leases suggests that the Norwich Suffragan's Lodging fitted in the northern part of Plot H (Fig. 3.6) and seems to equate with the south range. The east range may have housed the chapter house and infirmary.

The proposed arrangement was the preferred interpretation for a variety of reasons. A number of key walls represented by archaeological remains correspond closely to standing walls that were referred to in the 16th-century leases (Figs 3.4 and 3.6). A north-to-south wall forming the east boundary of Plot F could equate with either the inner or the outer wall of the west walk of the cloister in the conjectured reconstruction (Fig. 3.21). Its eastward return seems to conform to the line of the southern wall of the south walk. The line of a wall attested by 16th-century leases to have delineated the eastern edge of Plot K, projected northward, corresponds to the line of the east wall of the east walk of the cloister in the proposed reconstruction. The north-to-south wall line bounding Plots F and H to the west clearly equates with an extant wall. The southern boundary of Plot E was represented only by a substantial rubble-filled cut, assumed to represent the robbing out of a Friary wall. Finally, an east-to-west wall represented by a flint foundation observed during the laying of a drain pipe along the north edge of Greyfriars Road equated with a wall documented to have marked the southern boundary of Plots G, H and K.

It is notable that the southern boundary of Plots N and O in the 1292 mortmain licence (Fig. 2.3) coincides with the northern limit of the artificial terrace created as part of the development of the Friary. The area in which the terrace was constructed, lying immediately to the south of the property boundary and north of Plot F, was acquired by the Friary in 1299. It is possible, therefore, that the construction of Friary buildings within former Plots N and O was already well under way when the terracing was initiated.

Church and cemetery

With the success of their ministry to the townspeople, the size of mendicant communities grew dramatically in the decades after their creation. The expanding congregations combined with a 'hardening of attitude on the part of the secular clergy in the 1240s increasingly debarred friars from using parish churches for preaching' (Lawrence 1994, 109). Encouraged by lay benefactors, friars 'embarked on a programme of enlargement and new building', constructing spacious churches (*ibid.*). The Norwich Greyfriars needed to facilitate public access to the preaching nave, which was designed specifically to accommodate large congregations. The friars would have wished their west door, by which the laity would have entered their church, to lie as close as possible to King Street, the major thoroughfare.

Archaeological evidence indicates that preparation of the enlarged precinct for construction of the new church and claustral complex entailed considerable engineering works. In the vicinity of the modern junction of King Street and Prince of Wales Road the ground was comparatively high and level. This prominent site would have allowed the church to compete visually with other churches in this part of the city, particularly the Cathedral. The shape of the church in plan is debatable. While it is possible that the quire was narrower than the nave, it is equally plausible that a constant width was maintained for the whole length of the church. The dimensions recorded by Worcestre seem to indicate that this was a 'hall' church, in which the nave and its two side aisles were of similar width and height. Tradition dictated that the nave should be a little wider than the aisles (Braun 1971, 217). Such a rectangular reconstruction would give a walking place of more typical proportions, with its long axis at right-angles to that of the church. This layout would resemble that of the London Greyfriars church which was 300ft (91.4m) long and 90ft (27.4m wide) (Martin 1937). The roofs of the nave and aisles would have supported each other laterally, thereby eliminating the need for substantial columns which would have obstructed the view of the preacher. A clerestory would have been unnecessary as sufficient illumination could be provided by high aisle walls.

Although there is no documentary evidence for its location, archaeological evidence has shown that the Friary cemetery lay in the large area in the northern part of the precinct, to the north of the inferred site of the church. Plot A (Fig. 3.6), immediately south of St Faith's Lane and adjoining King Street, was confirmed as the Friary cemetery by the NAU's evaluation of the former Wallace King site on St Faith's Lane in October 1997 (Emery 1997). Subsequent open-area excavation by Northamptonshire Archaeology recorded 131 further burials here (Soden 2001).

Studium and library

In 1336, the Franciscan house at Norwich became one of the order's seven friaries in England established as *studia* for the teaching of theology at pre-university level, evidently achieving international status (Rutledge, above, 49). As early as the 13th century the Franciscans compiled a kind of inter-library catalogue showing in which monastic libraries the various works of well-known authors were to be found (Kelly 1969, 216). The Greyfriars library must have been extensive and a number of metal finds associated with books and writing were recovered from the excavation. These were of types endemic to monastic sites, including copper alloy book fasteners and mounts, along with several lead styli suitable for use with wax tablets: Chapter 5.II. The most significant object in this group is a copper alloy page holder, decorated with arms indicating a connection with the families of Clare and Despencer (SF620, Huddle and Ashley, Chapter 5.II, Fig. 5.41).

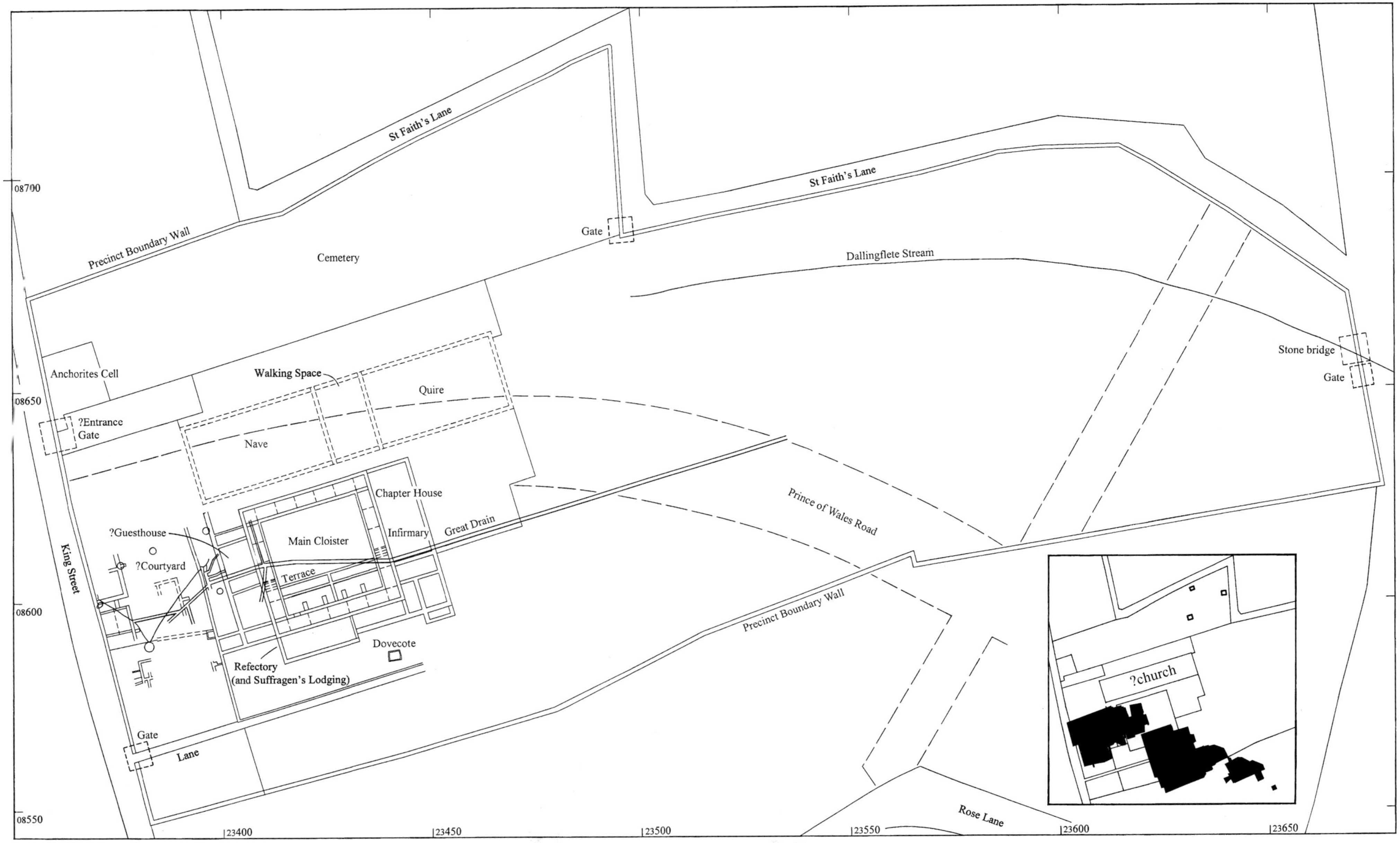

Figure 3.21 Reconstruction of Friary precinct

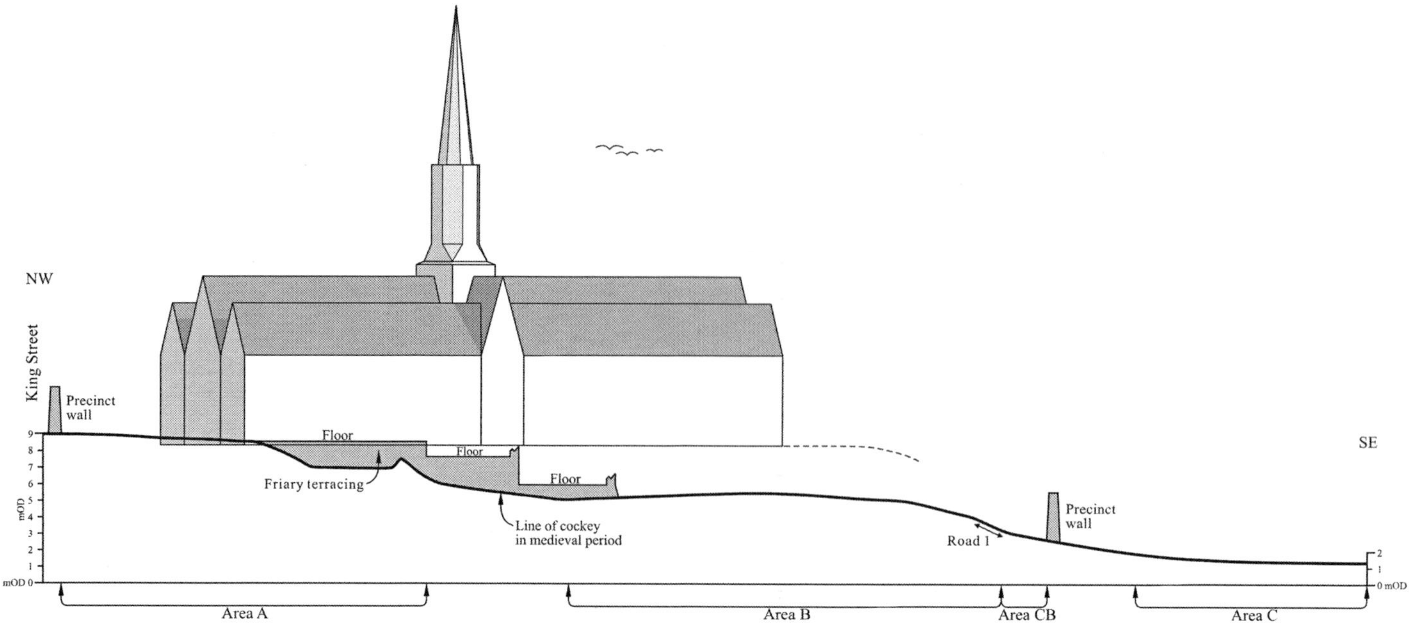

Figure 3.22 Schematic profile across the site, showing the physical impact of Friary constructions

Infirmary

Medical activity is attested by the presence of glass urinals possibly deriving from the monastic infirmary, which may have lain in the eastern range of buildings surrounding the cloister. Further discussion of this group is given by Shepherd in Chapter 5.III.

Dovecote

Identification of a discrete rectangular flint structure as a dovecote was prompted by its location relative to Plot K (Fig. 3.6), which leases of 1565 describe as containing a dovehouse and shed. The dovecote would undoubtedly have supplied doves/pigeons for the Friary community (below, 84).

Construction techniques

Most of the major walls of Friary buildings at Norwich Greyfriars were erected upon earthen footings that consisted of steep-sided trenches infilled with alternating rammed fills. Recognition of the problem of disparate load-bearing capacity of the ground resulting from previous pit-digging seems to have been taken into account. A lack of local freestone has prompted innovative approaches to foundation construction both in Norwich and elsewhere. Salzman notes that 'in places where there was neither rock nor reasonably firm ground to build upon, steps had to be taken to improve the conditions' (Salzman 1952, 83): rammed foundations were employed, for example, during the construction of a tower at Ramsey (Cambs). The repeated use of foundation trenches infilled with sequences of very compact horizontal layers of material, alternating in texture, was observed throughout that part of the Friary precinct examined during the excavations. This laminated type of earthen foundation has been recorded at other medieval sites in Norfolk (Norwich Millennium Library, Bethel Street; Barton Bendish; St Martin-at-Palace Plain). The technique may well have established itself as a local response to the need to provide consistent bearing strength along the length of a wall while minimizing the use of stone. A process apparently producing similar results continues to be used by modern building contractors, involving the repeated flooding and draining of a foundation trench as successive layers of fill are built up in order to enhance compaction of sediment (in a manner similar to that used in setting posts). The apparent waterlaid nature and horizontality of some of the fills of the foundation trenches recorded at Greyfriars suggest that water was used as a compaction agent in the medieval period. In addition, the battering of wall foundations may represent a further measure taken by the medieval builders to enhance the intrinsic strength and lateral stability of flint-and-mortar structures. This technique appears to have been applied particularly on ground that is sloping, known to have been previously filled or perceived to be prone to differential settlement.

The Decorated architectural style (*c.* 1275–1350) is well represented in the worked stone recovered during the recent excavations, leaving no doubt that at least one major phase of construction occurred between *c.* 1290 and *c.* 1320 (Samuel, Chapter 5.I). The stones are unambiguously ecclesiastical in character and the assemblage is notable for its simple and functional nature, perhaps reflecting deliberate policy on the part of the Franciscans. A number of fragments of window tracery survived, allowing partial reconstruction of the relevant schemes. The presence of Purbeck marble elements (including window tracery and floor slabs) indicates the wealth of the order. Upper Greensand fragments — an unusual material in Norfolk, implying long-distance trade — may point to the presence of a free-standing monument. Other decorative stonework includes a corbel depicting a human head (SF2688, Fig. 5.3). Architectural development of the precinct seems to have stopped after *c.* 1400–1450, reflecting a country-wide trend which saw the diversion of devotional legacies away from the monasteries and friaries.

Some indication of the materials chosen for dressing apertures in walls that were otherwise built essentially of flint and mortar was provided by two partial *in situ* survivals: a doorway (*12483*: Fig. 3.17) and a cloister window (*13146*/*13147*: Fig. 3.9). In both cases the use of freestone appears to have been confined to mouldings, such as jamb–sill junctions; otherwise such features seem to have been cased in brickwork.

The use of oyster shells as spacers (as in the vaulted roof of the brick drain *10335*: Fig.3.20C) is directly paralleled elsewhere in medieval ashlar (Salzman 1952, 89).

The ceramic building material assemblage from the site indicates the nature of the roofing and flooring materials used in Friary construction (many of which had been re-used in construction of later Friary-related features such as drains). Purbeck marble was used to provide at least one fine floor within the Friary. Documentary evidence for materials removed at the Dissolution indicates that tiles and thatch were used for roofing rather than lead sheeting (Rutledge, above, 55). Flat peg tiles were the most common roofing material excavated, with lesser numbers of pantiles and ridge tiles (see Huddle and Kemp, Chapter 5.I); only 15% of those recovered were glazed. No decorative elements, such as finials, were found. Brick types are similar to those from other Norwich excavations and had apparently been removed from the site in large numbers after 1538, along with a wide range of other building materials (see Chapter 4).

Decorative detail and furnishings

Insight into the architecture and fabric of the buildings of the Norwich Greyfriars is provided by assemblages of architectural stonework, painted window glass, lead window came, ceramic building materials and structural ironwork. Some of the more diagnostic groups of moulded stonework afforded partial reconstruction of the architectural elements (usually windows) of which they formed part.

An oyster shell which had been used as a painter's palette probably dates to between *c.* 1292 and the early 14th century (see Howard and Park, Chapter 5.II), and may have been associated with polychromed sculpture within the new church. Documentary references confirm that the church contained 'images' (probably sculptures) of the Virgin and St Thomas (Rutledge, above, 53) and other sculptures must have existed. A single sculptural fragment from the Friary was recovered from a post-Dissolution deposit.

The glass included a particularly interesting group of fragments, recovered from a pit in Area B (*30633*), which may have derived from a single window depicting the Crucifixion together with a border of running vine leaf and lion-masks: this theme suggesting that the building involved was both important and ecclesiastical. Associated research (King, Chapter V.1) has identified other surviving glazing schemes, now held elsewhere in Britain, which may possibly be attributable to the Norwich Franciscan Friary. Taken together, the fragments offer a fairly precise date of *c.* 1330–50, linking well with documentary evidence for the construction of the monastic church and other buildings. The glass could possibly have come from the church, which appears to have been completed by *c.* 1330; however, the find was made just to the south of the claustral range, thought to have been built *c.* 1330–50, and it seems more probable that it originated from one of the cloisters, the refectory, library or chapter house. Further details on this group and other important pieces of window glass from the site, as well as evidence for glaziers working at the Friary, is given by King in Chapter 5.I.

The structural ironwork collected includes decorative hinges, as well as latch rests and related hinge pivots which would have been used on doors, gates and windows. Lead items include sheeting that may have been used for drainage/guttering.

Evidence for interior furnishings and fittings includes a decorated cupboard door handle, lock furniture and keys and several curtain rings of similar appearance. A lamp or censer suspension unit was recovered (although this equally well relate to the church of St Vedast: see Chapter 2); other evidence for Friary lighting takes the form of glass lamp fragments.

Water management

Substantial remains of drains, wells and pipelines provided valuable information about the planning, construction and use of a complex water management system within the Friary. The hierarchy of drains ranged from modest tributary gullies constructed of brick and re-used architectural slabs to the Great Drain, internally 0.60m high and rendered, and capped with large tabular flint nodules and a grave slab.

While there are numerous accounts of friaries having their water supplied via 'conduits', it is clear that the majority of the relevant structures excavated at Norwich Greyfriars were drains and sewers. In terms of the long-term history of the site, the development of a communal sanitation system by the friars represented a departure from the *ad hoc* digging of cess-pits characteristic of earlier occupation of the site. The provision of effective sewerage would have been a primary consideration in the laying-out of the Friary and the culverts themselves appear to have formed an integral part of the groundplan. There is some suggestion that the major drains were routed though open areas and along passages and walks to minimise interference with wall foundations.

Lead piping was a common means of distributing water within monastic precincts (Greene 1992, 115). At the Norwich Greyfriars site, the proximity of an apparent junction of a lead pipe, of which traces were recorded, to a cistern at the terminus of one of the major drains, suggested that the system was periodically flushed with water drawn from a large well. This well, which measured 2.5m in diameter, almost certainly equates with one of two wells mentioned in the 16th-century leases (at the northern end of Plot G: Fig. 3.6). Demolition of a building on the King Street frontage may have taken place several years after the Dissolution of the Friary. The postulated continuing use of this structure, and the documented application of the lessee of Plot E to draw water from a well in Plot G, raises the possibility that the lead pipe laid through the building's eastern doorway is of post-Friary date.

Although short lengths of lead piping have been found at many monastic sites, it is rare to find long stretches surviving, due to the value and ease of re-use of the raw material. The few pieces of lead water piping that had escaped robbing at Norwich Greyfriars are detailed by Egan in Chapter 5.I.

Life in the Friary

by Elizabeth Shepherd Popescu with Phillip A. Emery

Intimate insight into the social backgrounds, lives and work of people associated with the Friary is provided by both historical and archaeological enquiry. Individuals, identified in a range of documents, include those requesting burial at the Norwich house, benefactors and Franciscans themselves (Appendices 1 and 2). Artefacts offer a tantalising glimpse into a community which sustained the Friary economically. A fine silver brooch, for example, inscribed IESVS:NAZARENVS: REXIVDEO (Jesus of Nazareth, King of the Jews: SF136, Fig. 5.84; see Geake, Chapter 5.IV), provides a snapshot view of the affluence of the extended community of the Norwich Greyfriars. Was this the possession of an affluent visitor to the Friary, keen to project a pious image, or was it — more controversially — worn by a friar in defiance of the oath of poverty, like Chaucer's prioress?

The diversity of functions and activities associated with various parts of the complex is reflected by the extensive range of fixtures, portable items and waste materials. These finds include culinary equipment such as ceramic and metal cooking vessels, knives, whetstones and mortars. Pottery and glassware vessels were used for lighting, with other glassware utilised for storage, tableware and medical purposes. An evocative assemblage of stoneware drinking vessels from a Dissolution-period robber trench probably indicates clearance from the Friary kitchen during demolition (Lentowicz, Chapter 5.III, Fig. 5.67).

The Friary's growing wealth does not seem to be reflected in the pottery it used. During the life of the Friary, medieval wares are represented by unglazed fabrics, supplemented by small quantities of non-local and regional imports (Lentowicz, Chapter 5.III). Glazed wares make up a much larger proportion of the assemblage. Continental imports continued to be represented, with an increasing range including French vessels. Although medieval wares continued to be used during the later period of the Friary, its needs were increasingly met by late medieval Continental imports. A wide range of kitchen vessels for food preparation and storage were present, many of which would have been produced locally. Pouring and drinking vessels were largely imported.

Some of the copper-alloy vessels and other equipment (including skillets/bowls, skimmer and cauldrons: Chapter 5.III) recovered from Dissolution/post-Dissolution deposits may derive from the Friary kitchens. The presence of numerous repair rivets attests to the re-use of such objects. Other kitchen equipment includes a flesh hook, which would have been used to remove meat from the cooking pot. Four honestones are definitely associated with the use of the Friary.

The assemblages of faunal and avifaunal remains (Chapter 6) combine with artefactual and documentary evidence to provide a detailed picture of provisioning and daily life within the Friary. Two spearheads found during the recent excavations may have been utilised in hunting, while a number of small lead weights may have been used in fishing. Foodstuffs were brought into the precinct via the Dallingflete stream and fishing rights were granted to the friars on the stretch of the stream outside the precinct (Rutledge, above, 58). The house was assured a small income from leasing part of the precinct. Furthermore, it probably supplemented alms with home-grown produce, pigeons/doves, and fish from documented ponds and the three streams which were partially enclosed within the large precinct.

That fish formed an important part of monastic diets, owing to the large number of meat-free fast days each year, is reflected in the increased numbers of fish represented in Friary-period deposits (Nicholson, Chapter 6.III). The species consumed, however, corresponded very closely to that of the other townsfolk, implying that urban markets controlled both supplies, whether directly or indirectly *via* gifts from local people. Both the bird and fish remains associated with the Friary appear to be table waste mixed with bones removed during food preparation. Despite the ownership of fishponds and fish traps and weirs within rivers, freshwater fish never appear to have been more than an occasional resource. While the present excavations provide a glimpse of the profitable business of supplying fish to the region's many religious houses, reconciliation of the archaeological results with the complex picture of hospitality and sustenance painted by documentary research (*cf.* St Giles's Hospital: Rawcliffe 1999, 177–9) is far from straightforward. With regard to samples of food remains recovered from Friary deposits, there are clear difficulties in distinguishing the fare associated with occasional feasts or entertainment of guests from the daily provisions of the residents.

The bulk of the faunal/avifaunal assemblages came from two pits in the eastern part of the excavated area — away from the Friary buildings — and it is possible that these groups indicate foods reserved for secular guests or friary wardens. The large quantity of cattle rib fragments with cut marks from Friary period deposits (particularly those in the putative kitchen in the west range) may be interpreted as a result of butchery for the extraction of marrow by boiling (Huddle, Chapter 5.II, 'Bone-working'). In contrast to the earlier periods, faunal remains from the Friary period indicate that meat played an important role in the diet. Substantial quantities of the best cuts of meat and very young animals were consumed during the later Friary period, in a diet dominated by cattle, sheep/goat and pigs (Moreno-García, Chapter 6.II). Domestic fowl were apparently used for both eggs and meat, while pigeons or doves would have provided another resource. The presence of partridge and swan may suggest that the mendicants did not always follow a life of poverty. While these foods may have been reserved for secular guests or Friary wardens, documentary evidence implies a reduction in the standards of self-denial practiced by the Franciscan order from the later 14th century (Rutledge, above, 46).

Land and freshwater mollusca include species from a range of habitats (Green, Chapter 6.IV; Fryer, Chapter 6.V). A number of burnt examples were probably imported onto the site attached to fuel, litter *etc.* Marine species included the usual range of oysters, mussels, cockles, whelks and winkles. Detailed analysis of the oysters from the site indicates consumption of what may have been cultivated oysters.

A building excavated on the King Street frontage may have served as the Friary bakehouse. During the medieval period, the municipal authorities placed strict controls on the use of querns. Restrictions on townspeople milling their own grain may not, however, have applied to the religious orders and a number of millstones and quernstones were recovered from Friary-period deposits (Buckley, Chapter 5.II), although many had been re-used as building materials. A similar situation is apparent with the mortars (Mills, Chapter 5.III), although a Purbeck marble example dates to the period of Friary use (13th–14th century). The plant macrofossil assemblage included the first example of *Triticum turgidum/durum* (most probably rivet wheat) to have been recorded in medieval Norwich (Fryer and Murphy, Chapter 6.V). One pit indicated malting based on barley, and several others containing stones and seeds including fig, flax, cherry, sloe and grape had apparently been used for sewage disposal.

A number of categories of finds indicate the character of various production activities within the Friary. Lead offcuts and other waste may represent waste from repairs to Friary buildings. Although many of the slags in deposits contemporary with the construction and occupation of the Friary may well be residual, a major construction episode would be expected to include the production of iron nails and fittings by a smith. A few ironworking and woodworking tools were also found (Chapters 5.I and 5.II).

Founding activities took place in a small workshop on the King Street frontage in the immediately pre-Dissolution period (see Chapter 5.II, Period 3.2). This may have been linked to the Friary (*e.g.* for bell-founding) but may also have been making domestic and personal accoutrements for a lay market. Similar results have recently come from excavations at Norwich Castle (Shepherd Popescu forthcoming), where bell-founding activity surrounding the castle precinct has been studied in its wider context.

Bone bead manufacture appears to have taken place on the site during the 14th–15th centuries (Period 3.1), as is witnessed by the presence of a number of waste panels (Huddle, Chapter 5.II). These and other excavated beads may have come from rosaries.

Conclusion

The excavations have clearly done much to address the stated objective of investigating Norwich's Franciscan Friary. Important new evidence for the groundplan has qualified previous interpretations, as well as revising understanding of urban development in this particular area of Norwich. The new socio-economic data is of great significance to the study of monastic sites on a national level and also adds considerably to local knowledge of Norwich's friary sites. Of the city's four major friaries, two others have recently been excavated (the Carmelites/Whitefriars and the Augustinian/Austin Friars: Shelley in prep. a and b), whilst the fourth — the Dominicans or Blackfriars — retains evocative surviving structures on the post-1307 site, forming the most complete surviving friary complex in the country (Ayers 1994, 74).

4. The Dissolution and Afterwards (*c.* 1538–20th century)

I. ARCHAEOLOGICAL AND HISTORICAL BACKGROUND

Very little was previously known in archaeological terms about the development of the site at the time of the Dissolution and afterwards, evidence largely being limited to the recovery of post-medieval pottery and other finds (Chapter 1.IV). Interpretation of the site's post-Dissolution development was partly based on a succession of maps that spanned the late 17th to the late 19th centuries, published by Cleer (1696: Pl. 4.2), Hochstetter (1789: Pl. 4.3), Millard and Manning (1830: Pl. 4.4) and the Ordnance Survey (1885: Pl. 4.5).

II. DOCUMENTARY EVIDENCE

by Elizabeth Rutledge

Dissolution and demolition (*c.* 1538–66)

In September 1538 the Norwich Franciscan Friary surrendered into the king's hands and the site was granted to Thomas, Third Duke of Norfolk, the following March (Hale and Rodgers 1991, 29, 32). Over the next twenty years control of the freehold alternated between the Dukes of Norfolk and the Crown. In January 1547 the Third Duke was attainted of high treason and his lands forfeited. Kirkpatrick's and Blomefield's belief that even before the forfeiture, in 1544, part of the Greyfriars site had been granted by the Crown to Paul Gresham and Francis Boldero for £174 2s 8d (Kirkpatrick 1845, 128; Blomefield 1806, IV, 109) was based on misinterpretation of a grant of the London Blackfriars (L and P for. and dom. Henry VIII, XIX pt.2 412). The Norwich Franciscan Friary was not among the properties alienated by Edward VI and the site reverted to the Duke of Norfolk when he was restored by Mary in August 1553. When the Third Duke died a year later he was succeeded by his grandson, who was still under age, so the duchy lands again came under royal control. The Fourth Duke attained his majority in March 1558 and sold the Friary to the City of Norwich in the following year (Hale and Rodgers 1991, 36–7).

All these changes of ownership did not much affect the actual occupation of the Greyfriars site. In August 1542

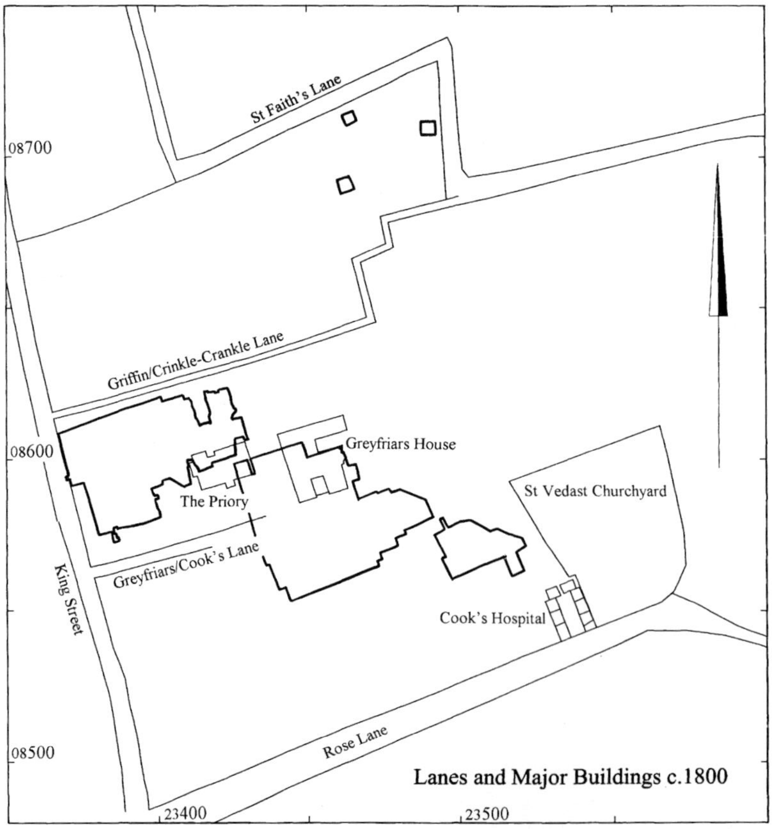

Figure 4.1 Lanes and major buildings *c.*1800

the Third Duke had leased the site to John Bronde the elder of Norwich, beerbrewer, for 40 years at £8 10s a year (Hale and Rodgers 1991, 34). Bronde probably did not remain the lessee for long. John Bassingham is known to have paid rent for the site in 1555 and entries for the purchase of building materials by the city of Norwich suggest that he took over the lease as early as 1544 (AC A935 f.79d; NRO NCR 18a, Chamb. acc. 1537–47 148). Bassingham was still paying the rent in 1557/8 but by the time the city had gained control in early 1559 the lease had passed to Richard Sotherton (AC A1335 m.20d; NRO NCR 18a, Chamb. acc. 1551–67 142).

It seems likely that most of the Friary was demolished in the three years before the lease to John Bronde in 1542. The grant to the Duke of Norfolk in 1539 conveyed 'All the site … church, bell-tower, bells and cemetery … and also all messuages, houses, buildings, granges, barns, stables, dovecotes …'. Three years later the church was not mentioned and the property was described as all the 'site of the late priory of the Greyfriars … with the houses builded within the same called Suffrygans loginge, and one house adjoined to the same, and the stable …' with a brewhouse (Hale and Rodgers 1991, 32, 34). Furthermore, the Duke excepted from the lease the timber, brick, tile and stone of such houses as were already sold or appointed to be pulled down. While Bronde was to leave the remaining buildings standing he purchased part of the store and all three lessees sold materials to the city authorities, who used the Greyfriars as one of several sources of building supplies (NRO NCR 18a, Chamb. acc. 1537–47, 1541–50, 1551–67 *passim*). The purchases began in 1541/2 and continued at a high level throughout the next few years. In 1541/2 the Greyfriars was the source for roofing (*thak*) tile for the repair of a tenement, for small paving tile for the Common Hall at the Blackfriars, for brick to stop up the library windows there and for freestone for the new kitchen. Forty-two great spars for joists for the new buttery and pantry at the west end of the Common Hall had been part of the Greyfriars chancel roof but came, not direct from the site, but via a middleman. In 1542/3 the Greyfriars provided marble for three steps from the Common Hall to the Preaching Yard at the Blackfriars and paving stone for paving the streets near Helle (Heigham) Gate, by the Duke of Suffolk's tenements, at Tombland and at the New Mills. In 1543/4 chalder (small stone) from the Greyfriars was used for street repair and Bronde and Bassingham sold paving tile of various qualities, at 10d, 16d and 5s the hundred and great paving tile, for work on the Common Hall and the infirmary hall at the Blackfriars. In 1544/5 great paving stone was bought at the Greyfriars to pave the south side of the great garden at the Blackfriars, while black flint from the site was used for a wall at St Mary the Less churchyard. There are few later entries that can definitely be ascribed to the Greyfriars, a complicating factor being that all three of the Greyfriars lessees from time to time also leased the lime kiln further down King Street, which was itself a source for flint and chalder as well as lime. It is probable, however, that the main period of clearing the Greyfriars site had come to an end by the mid-1540s, although Bassingham sold rough (*rowe*) stone from there in 1548/9 and even as late as 1564/5 Sotherton was not only

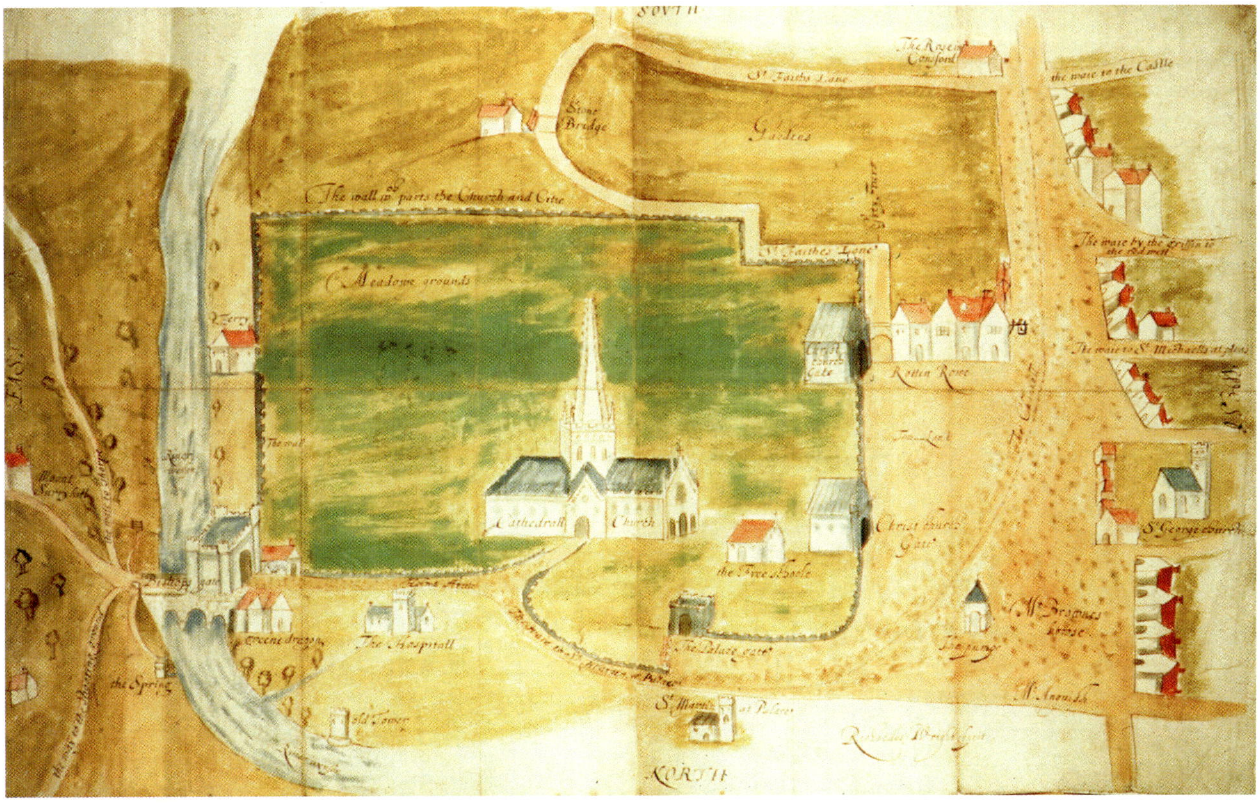

NRO BR 276, reproduced courtesy of Norfolk Record Office; photograph by Jason Dawson

Plate 4.1 Richard Wright's 1630s map of Norwich cathedral, showing the precinct of the Franciscan Friary and the stone bridge

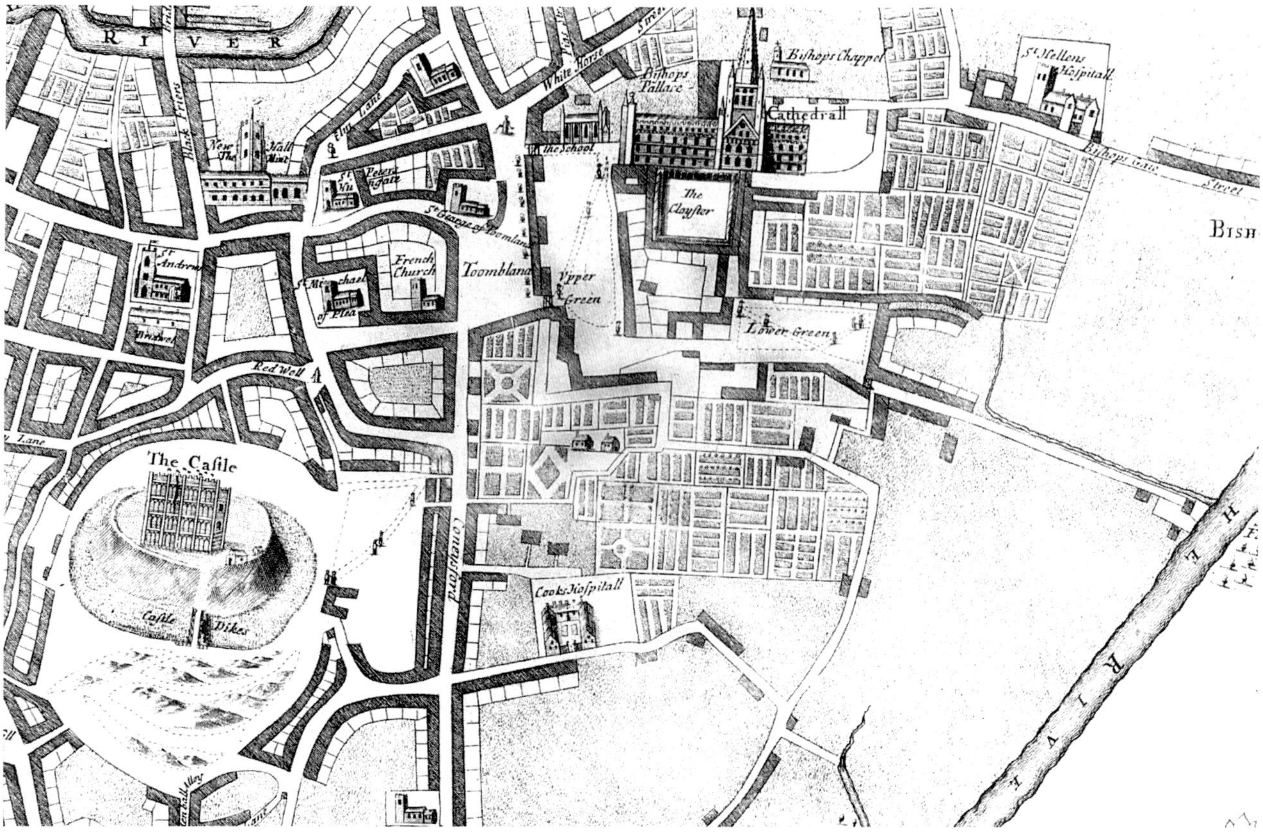

Plate 4.2 John Kirkpatrick's 1720s version of Cleer's map of 1696

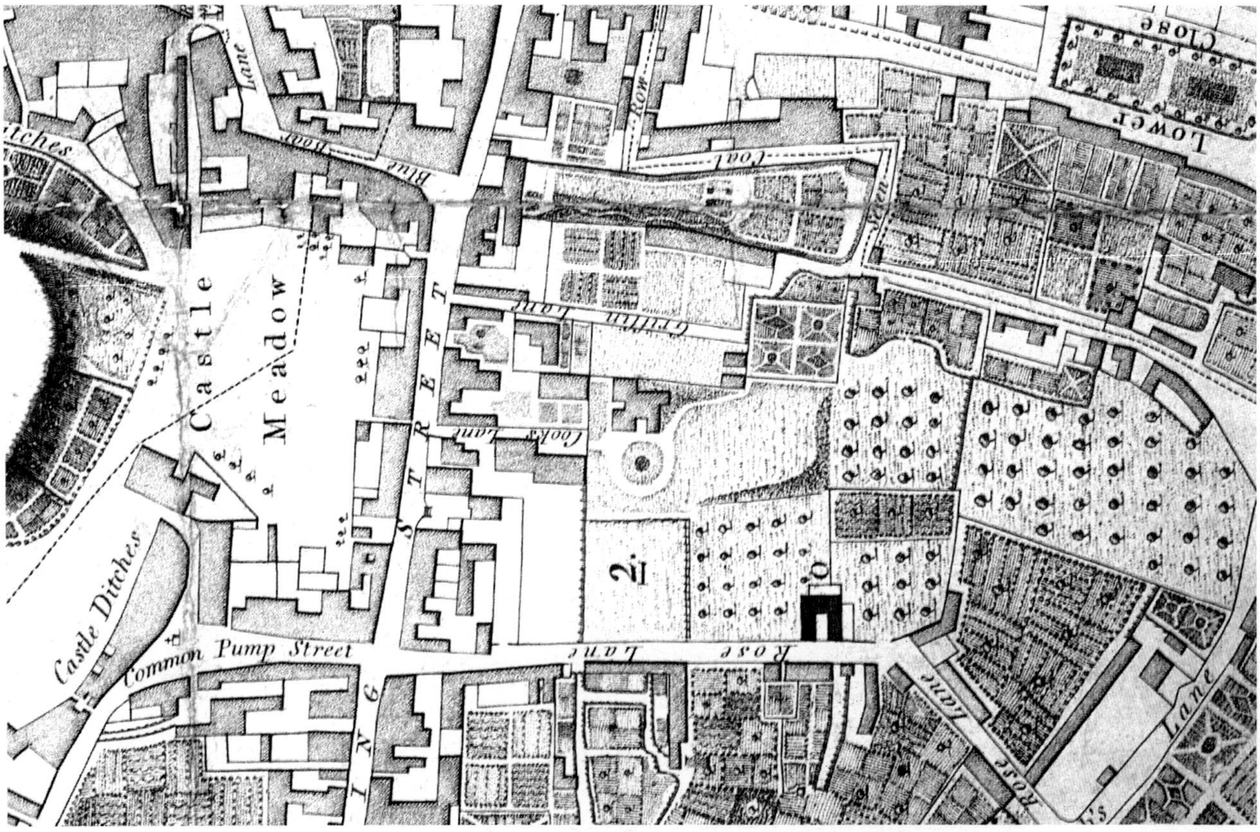

Plate 4.3 Detail from Hochstetter's map (1789, NWHCM Todd 5, 7)

compensated for a standing wall, for stone and for freestone, but also provided paving stone for Fyebridge quay. Bassingham himself may have used a door or gateway from the Greyfriars for his house in London Street but there is no direct evidence to support this suggestion (Barrett 1981, 110). The doorway in question was moved in 1857 to the south-west corner of the Guildhall, where it stands today (Pl. 3.1).

In 1565 the city authorities decided to buy out Sotherton's remaining interest in Bronde's lease. Sotherton was paid £30 and compensated as above and the City undertook the management of the site. In December 1565 and February 1566 new leases were granted for all the plots shown on Fig. 3.6 except for B, F, H and J (NRO NCR 22g (1) *passim*). Some of these plots had certainly been cleared and let to sub-tenants before the City took over. Mr William Farrow was paid compensation for his interest in a lease of part of the Greyfriars, John Wagstaff was remitted half a year's rent for giving up his interest in Plot B, rent was paid for some of the plots before the new leases came into effect and some of the leases mention previous tenants.

In 1565/6 and 1566/7 the City paid for the demolition of the 'great house of the Greyfriars'. This may have been the Suffragan's lodging and house adjoining, the only substantial buildings mentioned in the lease to John Bronde in 1542. The lodging would have been spared earlier because it was held by John Underwood, the suffragan, until his death in 1541 (Rye 1905, 32; Venn 1922, IV 289). The accounts for the demolition are given in Appendix 4.

Development from *c.* 1567 to 1850

(Figs.3.4, 3.6, 4.1 and 4.2, Pls 4.1–4.4)

With the removal of the friars' great house in 1566 the planned demolition of the Friary buildings came to an end and by 1571 the whole site had been leased out in seventeen plots (Fig. 3.6: for most of this section see NRO NCR case 22g (1)(2) *passim*). Little was left standing apart from the boundary walls. Just a few outbuildings remained, mainly along the King Street frontage. On Plot C there was a stable with a little chamber used as a dovehouse, a stable and a solar on Plot D, a house previously used as a bakehouse and a solar on Plot E, a dovehouse with a lading [shed] on Plot K and a stable on Plot L, while a new building was put up for Thomas Elsey on part of Plot J (Table 5). Otherwise all the plots were described as gardens or pieces of ground. In the 16th-century leases Plot A contained walnut trees, the lessees of Plots H, L, N, O, P and Q were to leave fruit trees standing at the end of their terms, and Plot J included an orchard.

Limited redevelopment of the Greyfriars site began in the 17th century. In 1607 the city granted a lease for the building of dwelling houses to the value of £140 on Plots E and G and another for dwelling houses to the value of £30 on Plot N. The latter dwelling houses may never have been built, although Plot N had some kind of building on it by 1648 and again in 1670. In 1630 Plot A was described as containing, not a dwelling house, but a 'banquetting house' (summer house) and another similar building. The first was 11ft 3ins by 6ft 9ins with two 'lucarnes' (dormer windows) and a tiled 'vance' (loft) roof. It had a benched lower room with two windows and a small study adjoining. The second was 16ft square with an upper room, both rooms having a chimney and three windows. The lower room was benched and the roof was thatched with reed. By 1648 there was still a building (not necessarily a dwelling house) on Plot J, while dwelling houses on Plots L and M were leased to Mr Richard Swallowe and Samuell Cooke respectively by 1650 (NRO NCR 18a Chamb. acc. 1643–63 52). In 1651 Plot P, which had previously only contained a shed, now included another banquetting house and £40 was to be laid out on a new dwelling house, while by 1690 John Hunt was expecting to build on an extended Plot F. The 1690 deed also includes the first reference to Griffin/Crinkle-Crankle Lane as a through route, describing it as a passage leading from St Faith's Lane to the church of St Peter Parmentergate.

The information given by the city lease books relates well to Thomas Cleer's map of 1696 (Pl. 4.2). Cleer shows the precinct as mainly open space, with development along the King Street frontage, three detached houses, corresponding to the dwellings on Plots F, L and M, and two elaborate buildings in Plot A, with another smaller one in the corner. There is a large building in the right hand top corner of Plot P but no sign of development in Plot N. South of the precinct, along Rose Lane, there was no building between the King Street frontage and Cooke's hospital. Subsequent maps by Hochstetter (*c.* 1789) and Millard and Manning (1830) show little change over the next hundred years (Pls 4.3 and 4.4). There was new building along the northern side of Plot J and a little development along St Faith's Lane, but most of the area bounded by King Street, St Faith's Lane and Rose Lane remained open ground. By this time not all of the site remained in the hands of the city. Timothy Armitage, preacher, bought Plot E in 1653, Robert Cooke purchased Plots K and M in 1675 and John Hunt bought Plot F in 1690. When Kirkpatrick was writing in *c.* 1725 the anchorite's garden (Plot B) had recently been sold and

Plot	*Occupations*	*Alderman (A); Mayor (M)*
A	Scrivener, mercer	
B	Cordwainer, yeoman, esquire	
C	Goldsmith, plumber	A
D	Grocer, gardener	
E	Hatter, gentleman, preacher/clerk	
F	Tailor, haberdasher, gardener	
G	Grocer, apothecary, gentleman, tailor	
H	Hosier/tailor, musician, apothecary, clerk	
I	Mason, clockmaker, merchant	
J	Scrivener, tailor, tailor, gardener	AA
K	-	
L	Beerbrewer	A
M	Worsteadweaver	AA
N	Worsteadweaver, merchant, gardener	A
O	Tailor, vintner, merchant	AA/M
P	Grocer, gentleman, esquire	
Q	Gentleman, knight, gentleman	AA

Table 6 Given occupations of City lessees, 1565–1660

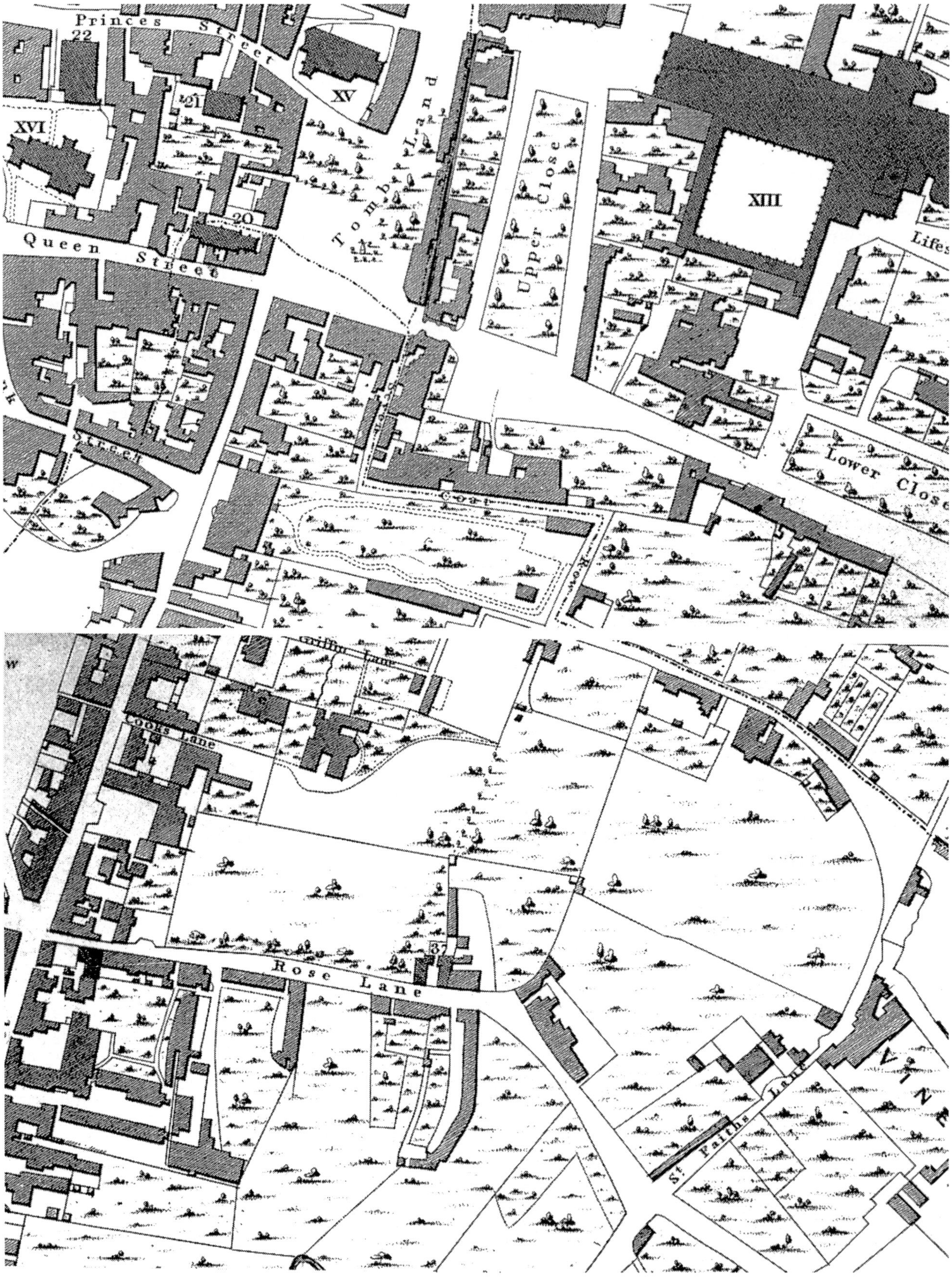

Plate 4.4 Detail from Millard and Manning's map (1830)

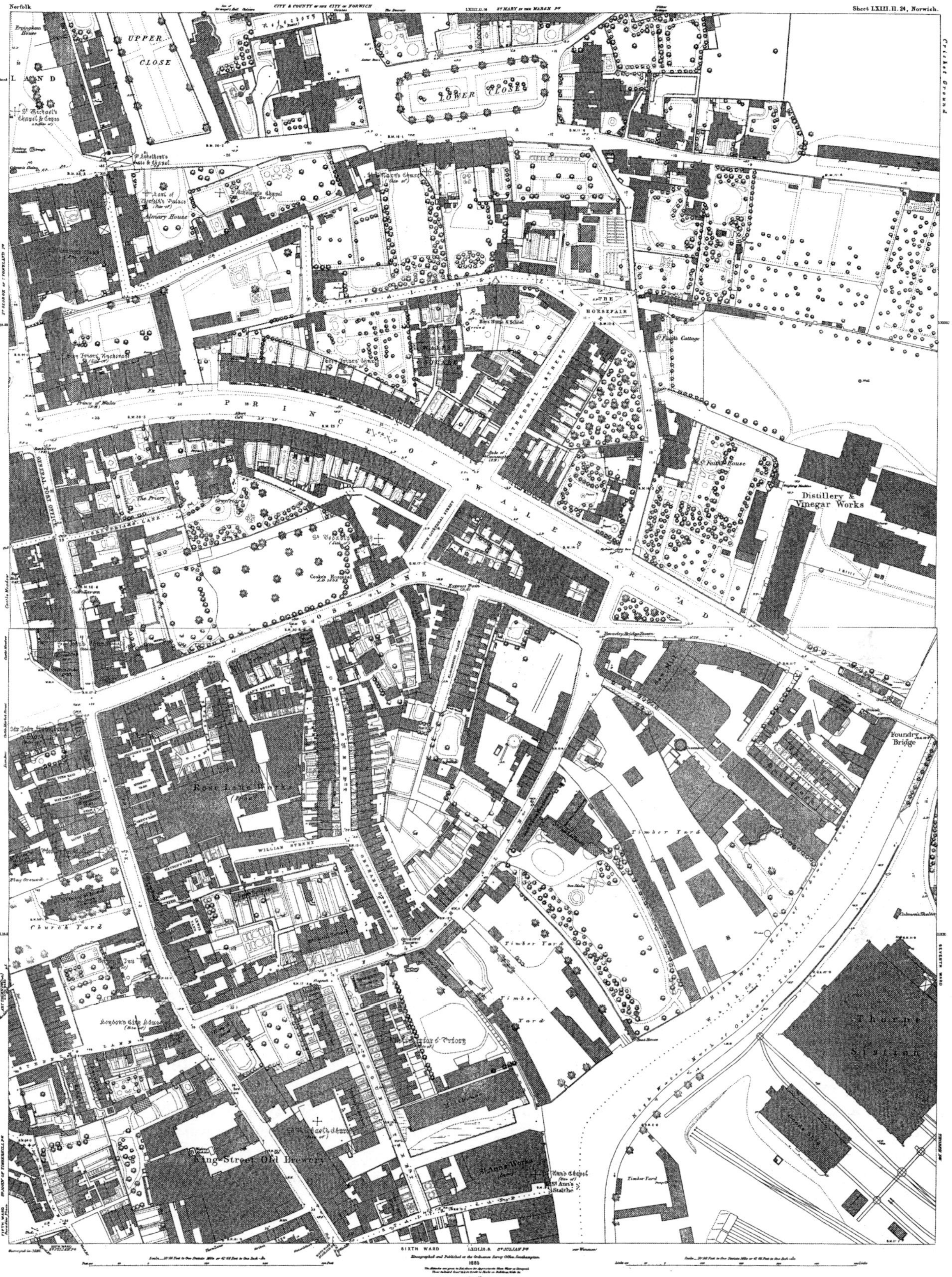

Plate 4.5 Detail from the Ordnance Survey map (1885)

developed (Kirkpatrick 1845, 126). Other plots were let on long leases. In 1726 much of Plot A, described as an orchard, was let to Thomas Maltby for 250 years (NRO NCR N/MC1/64/4). However, the city were still entitled to compensation of £3260 for their interest when the new Prince of Wales Road was built in 1860 (Mackie 1901, II, 97).

Use of the precinct to 1850

(Pls 4.2–4.4)

Apart from quarrying for building materials, the only occupation known to have been carried out on the Greyfriars site from the Dissolution until its purchase by the city in 1559 was brewing. The lease to John Bronde, beerbrewer, in 1542 included brewing vessels belonging to the Duke of Norfolk in the brewhouse (Hale and Rodgers 1991, 34). The subsequent limited development of the site, leaving most of it as open ground, has already been discussed. Table 6 shows the given occupations and status of late 16th- and early 17th-century lessees. The individual occupations are probably not significant since it is unlikely that many of the lessees, apart from the gardeners, used the property for commercial purposes. The worsted weavers, for instance, probably figure not as men engaged in manufacture, but as wealthy members of the community looking for housing and recreation, along with the grocers, merchants and minor gentry. Even on the King Street frontage Plots B and C were initially let as gardens to go with the Suffragan's tenements on the other side of the street. Plots K and M consisted of a substantial dwelling house with domestic gardens and to a lesser extent the same was true of Plots F and H. Cleer's smaller and more ornate map of *c.* 1696 shows almost all of the north and east of the site as gardens (Pl. 4.2). The recreational nature of these is indicated by the presence of the banquetting houses, a type of summerhouse. In addition to two summerhouses Plot A included some type of 'feature' as the lessee in 1630 was to leave 40 fruit trees between the street and the mount and 20 more between the mount and the wall at the east end.

Development and use of the site post-1850

(Pls 1.1, 1.2 and 4.5)

In 1859 Parliament passed the Norwich New Street Bill, giving powers for the construction of Prince of Wales Road (Mackie 1901, II, 82). The effect of the new road system on the former Greyfriars precinct was dramatic. Between them, Prince of Wales Road, Cathedral Street and South Cathedral Street (later St Vedast Street) cut right across the site and took up much of the hitherto open ground. Details are given in the earliest large scale Ordnance Survey map (surveyed 1883, published 1885: Pl. 4.5) and in Jarrold's Norwich Directory of 1885 (Jarrolds 1885). By 1885 two sides of the triangle created by King Street, Rose Lane, South Cathedral Street and Prince of Wales Road were heavily developed. The directory lists eleven properties along King Street between Prince of Wales Road and Rose Lane (uneven Nos 21–41) and 31 along Prince of Wales Road between King Street and South Cathedral Street (uneven Nos 1–61). Four properties are given for the west side of South Cathedral Street, the most southerly being a livery stables. The Rose Lane side of the triangle, however, was still almost empty. Only two properties are listed between King Street and South Cathedral Street, the Rose Tavern on the King Street corner and Foyson the builder next door. The 1885 Ordnance Survey map makes it clear that the whole of the north side of Rose Lane between Foysons and Cooke's hospital was still orchard. North of the orchard the centre of the triangle mainly consisted of Greyfriars House and garden (16th-century Plots K and M) and the house called 'The Priory' and its garden (16th-century Plot H). The 1885 Greyfriars Lane entry came between 25 and 27 King Street and listed four properties along the north side, apart from the two large houses.

Similar entries occur in Jarrolds directories for 1888–95 (Jarrolds 1888, 1893, 1895). The removal of Cooke's hospital in 1892, however, (see below) seems to have acted as a spur for the development of the remaining open space. By 1900 (Jarrolds 1900) Greyfriars Lane (now called Greyfriars Road) had turned a right-angle and extended south to Rose Lane, though it was not yet built up; Maidstone Road had been built with sixteen small tenements, nine on the east side and seven on the west; and the north side of Rose Lane had become fully developed with five properties between Greyfriars Road and Maidstone Road and seven properties and a livery stables between Maidstone Road and South Cathedral Street (now St Vedast Street). The Jarrolds 1905 directory (Jarrolds 1905) lists Child's monumental showrooms on the corner between Rose Lane and the east side of Greyfriars Road. 1905 also sees the first appearance of Mann, Egerton and Co., motor car engineers, at 5 Prince of Wales Road, which they had taken over from George Morris, carriage builder (Pls 1.1 and 1.2). By 1908 (Jarrolds 1908) Mann Egerton had taken over all the old north side of Greyfriars Road, including the Priory house, except for Greyfriars House and Lodge The southern extension of Greyfriars Road now consisted of eleven properties, Nos 2–6 on the west and Nos 1–15 on the east. No change is recorded in 1911, but by 1914 Mann Egerton had taken over even more of the centre of the triangle (Jarrolds 1911, 1914). As motor car engineers they are listed for 25 King Street, 5 and 7 Prince of Wales Road and the whole of the northern section of Greyfriars Road, including Greyfriars House, while as electrical engineers they appear for 21 and 23 King Street. By 1922 (Jarrolds 1922) wholesale grocers had taken over from the livery stables on the Rose Lane/St Vedast Street corner but by 1935 (Kelly's Directory 1935) this property was also occupied by Mann Egerton, as were 13 Prince of Wales Road, 31 King Street and part of the west side of Greyfriars Road. The expansion by the company was almost complete by 1952 (Kelly's Directory 1952), when they held most of the west side of Greyfriars Road and occupied offices at No. 13 on the east. The extent of their garage in 1978 is shown on Fig. 1.3.

Cooke's Hospital

Cooke's hospital was founded before 1701 by the brothers Robert and Thomas Cooke to house ten poor old women. In his will drawn up in January 1702 (NRO NCC 1703 540), Thomas Cooke spelt out the details for the management of the hospital and described it as being situated 'at the lower end of my orchard'. This was not part of the Greyfriars Plots K and M which Robert Cooke bought from the city in 1675, but was the close north of Rose Lane and west of St Vedast churchyard leased to John Hill and then sold to Mr Augustus Styward before the Dissolution. Thomas, the nephew of Thomas Cooke, was the owner of the orchard in 1744, having inherited it among other property from his uncle, and as such had the right to nominate poor women to the hospital (Blomefield 1806, IV, 104–5).

The hospital building was on Rose Lane, next to St Vedast churchyard. Its depiction on Cleer's map of 1696 is misleading (Pl. 4.2): although a tablet on the later 1892 almshouses gave a foundation date of 1692, the actual building may not have been begun when Cleer made his survey. The arrangement shown on his map, with buildings round three sides of a rectangle and an opening in the shorter side onto Rose Lane, is correct but the hospital is at least twice its proper size and has been placed at the western rather than the eastern end of the orchard. The correct size and position are shown on Hochstetter (*c.* 1789), Millard and Manning (1830) and the 1885 Ordnance Survey map (Pls 4.3–4.5). In 1892 the hospital was moved to new almshouses to the south of the Gildencroft and the Rose Lane site was sold (Hudson and Tingey 1906/10, II, cxvi–vii).

The precinct wall

When the city purchased the Greyfriars site in 1559 it was entirely surrounded by a stone wall. All the late 16th-century plots on the King Street frontage had a stone wall to the west, and Plot A also had to maintain the walls to the north and east and Plot I the wall to the south (Figs 3.4 and 3.6; NRO NCR case 22g (1) *passim*). Plots L and M had the 'main wall of stone' and the 'main great wall' to the south respectively and the main wall of stone lay north and south of Plots O and P and north, south and east of Plot Q (Fig. 3.6). The wall round the eastern half of the precinct appears to have been in bad condition, as the city agreed with the lessees of Plots O, P and Q to provide stores for its repair.

The wall along King Street must have been a casualty of the 17th- and 18th-century development along the frontage. Enough was still there in 1640 for a lease to refer to the stone wall standing at the west end of Griffin Lane but sufficient had disappeared by *c.* 1725 for Kirkpatrick not to know where the main entrance had been (Kirkpatrick 1845, 108). Presumably the southern section of wall west of St Vedast church had also gone by this date or Kirkpatrick would surely have qualified his remark that the precinct extended south to Rose Lane (Kirkpatrick 1845, 108). When Robert Cooke purchased Plot M from the city in 1675 it had a stone wall to the south but after his death in the early 18th century both Plot M and the orchard the other side of the wall were owned by his son Thomas, who lived in Greyfriars House (Blomefield 1806, IV, 103–4, 109). The desire to amalgamate these two properties would have been sufficient reason to demolish the precinct wall but it is possible that the original wall, in spite of the reference given above to the 'main great wall', had gone long before. It could have been dismantled when the Friary obtained the properties along Rose Lane in the late 15th century (see above). When the close (later Cooke's orchard) was leased to John Hill, roughmason, by the friars in the early 16th century, a condition of the lease was that Hill should build a stone wall (Rye 1905, 33). John Hill died before the wall was finished and Thomas Pyctow completed it. It is not clear where this wall was, but it might have replaced the original precinct wall. On the other hand, Hill's wall could have been the stone wall mentioned in a grant from Ketryngham to Nasshe in 1569 as dividing the close from the tenements to the west (NRO NCR 1e (26) m.85).

Further sections of the wall were destroyed in the mid-19th century by the building of Prince of Wales Road and Cathedral Street. Nevertheless, when Hudson wrote about the stone bridge in the 1880s he considered that the precinct wall could still be traced for nearly half its circuit. It started at King Street north of Mr Lowe's school (later the County Club), ran along St Faith's Lane past Cathedral Street and continued round two sides of a triangle of meadow west of St Faith's Lane (Hudson 1884–7, 122). The wall as seen by Hudson shows clearly on the 1885 Ordnance Survey map (Pl. 4.5) but the meadow section has since disappeared with further development along St Faith's Lane.

III. ARCHAEOLOGICAL EVIDENCE

Period 4.1: the Dissolution — demolition of Friary buildings and salvage of materials (1538–*c.*1566)

Summary

Both documentary and archaeological evidence attest to the demolition and robbing of the majority of the Friary buildings following the surrender of the site to the king in 1538. The robbing of some structures was so efficient that their presence is only attested by robber trenches. Facing stones and dressed stonework were, unsurprisingly, particular targets. A number of walls had been undermined to bring them down, resulting in the presence of large blocks of collapsed masonry, some with their footings still attached. There is also evidence for the melting down of robbed metal fixtures and fittings for reuse. The following account, rather than offering an exhaustive account of robbing activity, seeks to summarise the main archaeological events connected with the demolition and dismantling of the Friary.

Just over 16kg of pottery was recovered from contexts associated with the Dissolution, largely dating to the early 16th century with occasional sherds attributable to the late 16th–17th century. Two Nuremberg-type jettons, dating to *c.* 1500–50 and 1586–1635, were recovered from deposits associated with this phase (Davies, Chapter 5.II). In addition, a lead token dates to the last quarter of the 16th century (Egan, Chapter 5.II). The presence of items of late 16th- and early 17th-century origin attests both to the duration of elements of the robbing activity and the introduction of intrusive objects.

Archaeological sequence

The cloister and cloister garth

(Figs 3.9 and 3.16)

A 6m length of walling (*13372*: Fig. 3.16) located at the extreme north edge of Area B was found lying on its side. This section of flintwork, which represents a continuation of *in situ* walling to the west (*13416 etc.*), has been postulated as forming part of the south wall of the north walk of the cloister. The presence of a slot trench (*13373*), evidently cut alongside the toppled flintwork during the construction of the 19th-century cellar to establish the extent of the obstruction, indicates that the wall had already been pulled down, probably during the Dissolution of the Friary.

Twenty-four metres due south of this was a substantial stretch of wall (*13146/13149 etc.*), which arguably formed the north wall of the south walk of the cloister. This incorporated a mullioned window which was blocked (Fig. 3.9). This area of the Friary, which may have served as the Refectory and Suffragan's Lodging, is known to have survived the Dissolution.

Rubble-filled trenches within the area interpreted as the terrace across the cloister garth (*13107* and *13138/13186/13199*) appear to have been created in the process of salvaging facing stones.

Ranges
(Fig. 3.11)
Approximately 0.5m to the south of the passage south of the kitchen was an extensive rubble-filled cut (*10504*: shown in section on Fig. 3.10) which was 2.2m wide (north-to-south). Although its base was not reached, the profile recorded in section indicated that the cut was over 1.5m deep. The rubble fill indicates that the cut was excavated in order to salvage stonework. It seems that the Friary complex incorporated a stepped floor level in order to adapt to the southward fall in natural ground level: these steps may have been the target of the robbing.

A layer of cream-coloured mortar rubble (*10285*), some 300mm thick, directly overlay the remains of the floor within the narrow cell that formed part of the putative west range. This deposit contained frequent brick fragments and moderate flints, presumably reflecting the composition of the structure that had been demolished.

Displaced flintwork relating to the south range included a simple rectangular block (*31080*; Fig. 3.11) and a larger and more complex piece of flintwork over 2m long (*30135*, *30224*, *30243* and *30314*). This fragment lay on its side, its flat base being clearly visible, having toppled to the south. It was overlain by rubble deposits.

Building within courtyard
(Figs 3.15 and 3.16)
A building set in the southern part of the courtyard to the west of the main claustral complex was represented only by a series of robber cuts (*10058*, *10111*, *10113*, *10300*, *10414*, *10348*, *10471*, *10842* and *10637*). These indicate its groundplan, including the location of a possible buttress (see Period 3.2, above).

Recycling of metal
Several features and deposits dating to the Dissolution period contained evidence for ferrous and/or non-ferrous metalworking, presumably relating to the recycling of metals robbed from the Friary. An ovate, flat-bottomed pit (*13260*), for example, contained non-ferrous slag comprising two different kinds of metal inclusion (a 99% copper and copper 82%: tin 15%) occurring in close proximity and representing the melting down of various alloys.

Buildings on the King Street frontage
(Fig. 3.15)
A robber cut (*12217*), of which only the southern half was seen, may represent robbing of a structure surrounding the bell-casting pit (Period 3.2). Ceramics present suggest that it was not completely infilled until the 17th century.

A series of north-to-south and east-to-west robber trenches near the King Street frontage represented the salvage of foundations following the demolition of the Friary building in this area (see Period 3.2). This series of layers with a mortar or rubble content represents the surface associated with the post-Dissolution demolition of the Friary. A sequence of mortary layers (*12076*, *12086* and *12138*, *12076*, *12086*, *12138*) occurred immediately to the north of the robber cut which removed the possible doorway in the south wall (*12061*) suggesting that they were deposited during demolition of the upper parts of the structure. A rubble-filled post-hole (*12085*) could represent a temporary prop associated with this activity.

Further south, an elongate rubble-filled cut (*10660/10770*) immediately east of the west wall of the isolated building on the southern part of the King Street frontage may represent the robbing of a wall junction (Fig. 3.7). The frequency of building material (including 6.2kg of brick, 8.8kg of roof tile, 2.3kg of floor tile as well as many knapped flints) supports the interpretation that this cut was a wall robber. A deepening in the north part of the cut may reflect the former presence of a buttress. The occurrence of 5kg of animal bone together with 2.2kg of pottery in the fill indicates that substantial quantities of household refuse, possibly deriving from Friary kitchens, were dumped with the demolition rubble.

The water management system
(Figs 3.19A and B)
One north-to-south aligned drain (*13440*) had apparently been robbed both to the south and north of its extant section. Fire-reddening of its internal surfaces may well date to the Dissolution period — for example, representing the burning of temporary timber props in order to demolish the major building from which the drain emerged. This interpretation is supported by the evidence further east, where both the wall and its underlying earth footing lay on their sides, indicating that undermining had been used to bring down the wall.

To the north, beyond the east-to-west wall (*13416/13417/13481*) beneath which it ran, was a rubble-filled linear cut co-aligned with the drain, indicating that it had been chased as far south as that wall. Two extensive rubble-filled cuts (*13432* and *13439*) occurred to the south of the wall. The former, which measured 2.7m east-to-west and 4.5m long, cut through a north-to-south drain (*13440*). Since the feature extended *c.* 1.4m beyond the east edge of the culvert, and given that the drain was not chased to the north, it appears that it was created by the robbing out of a local masonry construction, rather than the drain itself. The position of the robber cut in the centre of the putative west walk of the cloister makes it unlikely that the robbed construction was a pier base.

Most of the lead piping utilised in the Friary water supply system had been robbed out at the Dissolution.

Open ground to the south-east
Overlying earlier deposits to the south-east of the precinct (Area C), a sequence of dumped deposits and cultivation activities continued into the Dissolution and post-Dissolution periods. Further humic deposits indicate cultivation, with building debris (mortar, plaster, daub and peaty silts) becoming more common (*50041*, micromorphological sample 4: Macphail and Cruise, Chapter 6.VIII). A stony layer within the sequence was overlain by a possible humic soil. The middle part of the layer (micromorphological sample 3) was a soil exhibiting earthworm activity. Within it were bone fragments, chalk, flint, biogenic calcite (slugs?), indicating an anthropogenic accumulation containing high amounts of colluvial material.

Period 4.2 (*c.* 1567–1800)

Summary

Following the Dissolution of the Friary and associated demolition and robbing of buildings, substantial areas of the precinct were given over to horticulture and other cultivation. In Area A, the precinct wall adjacent to the King Street frontage gradually became denuded by a sequence of buildings. To the east of the wall, most of the area of the former Friary courtyard was given over to horticulture from the Dissolution until the 19th century, although a few small buildings may have been present at the outset. In Area D, elements of Friary structures evidently survived to see later re-use (see Period 5). Areas B and CB coincided with the area of the post-medieval Greyfriars House and its grounds, utilising part of the southern wall of the Friary precinct as the estate boundary. To the south of the boundary wall, the land was again given over to horticulture. Further east (Area C) cultivation of the area continued, until the insertion of a formal garden in *c.* 1700. Cooke's Hospital (founded by 1701) lay to the south-east.

Nearly 19kg of pottery was recovered from this phase, including late medieval/transitional and post-medieval types (Lentowicz, Chapter 5.III). Contemporary numismatic items include 16th-century tokens, 17th-century coins and tokens of Charles I, and three George III halfpennies of the 1770s.

Archaeological sequence

Post-Dissolution landscaping
(Fig. 4.2)
Overlying various rubble-filled robber cuts and other dumps of rubble ascribed to the period immediately following the Dissolution of the Friary was a series of layers of dark grey topsoil. Their overall depth, established from various sections in which the deposit was observed, was approximately 1m. Pottery, clay tobacco pipe and vessel glass recovered from this material indicate that it was still subject to disturbance in the late 17th and 18th centuries, although the date of initial deposition is not certain. Given that much of the Friary precinct seems, on the basis of

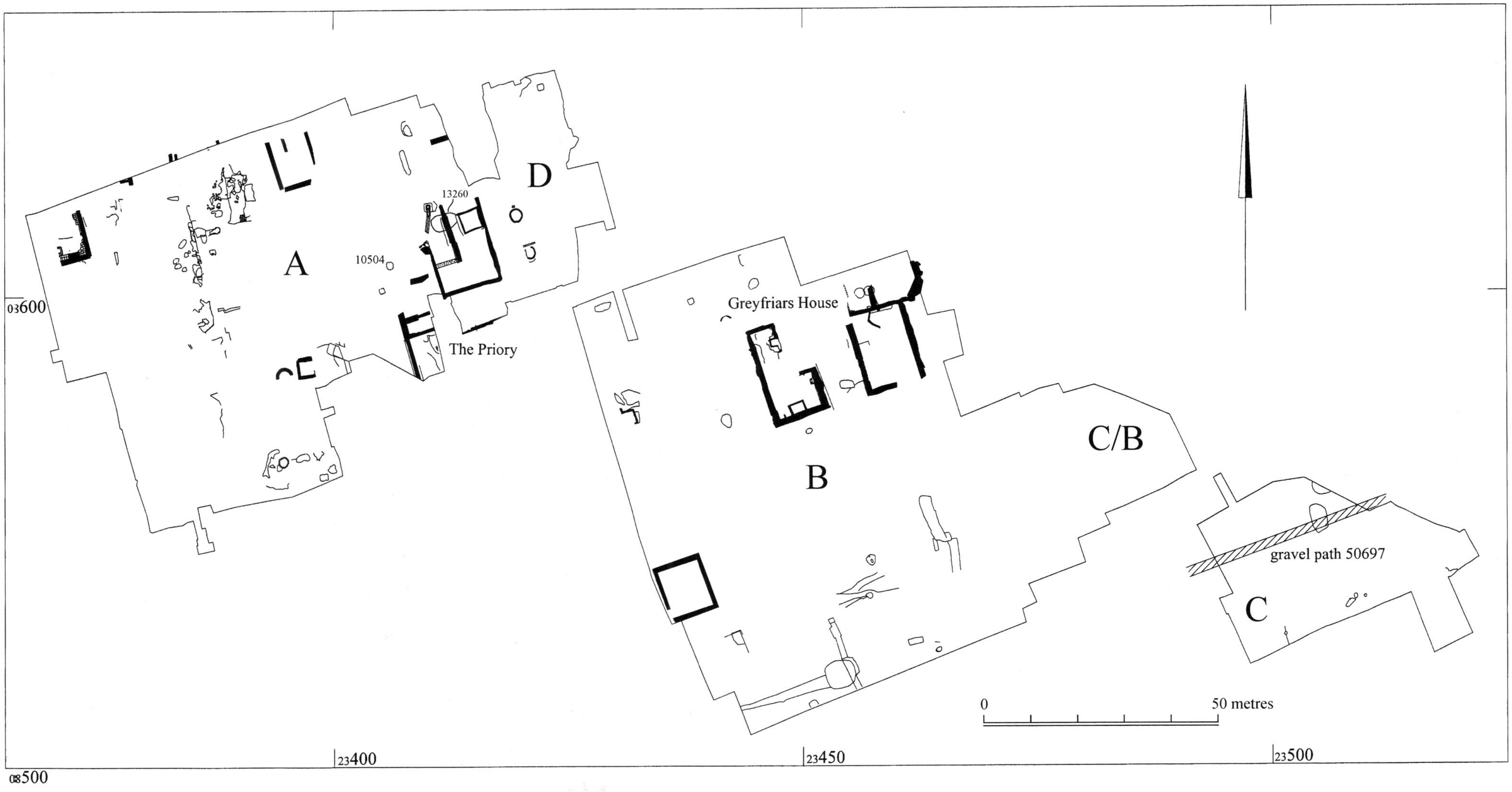

Figure 4.2 Periods 4 and 5: phase plan – Dissolution and afterwards (late 16th–19th centuries)

18th-century maps, to have been given over to horticulture after demolition of its buildings, the topsoil represents levelling of the ground for the laying-out of plots. It was from such levels that most of a significant assemblage of cloth seals was recovered (Egan, Chapter 5.II).

Building on King Street frontage
(Fig. 4.2)
The remains of a post-medieval building which fronted King Street were found in the extreme north-west corner of the excavated area. These included a 5m length of brick wall (continuing northward beyond the excavated area) and its westward return (both 0.45m thick) and a floor composed of pamment tiles (approximately 200mm square). The floor appears to have been that of a cellar. It was overlain by a 0.6m-thick dump of rubble, over which occurred the cellar floor that related to the standing building at the corner of King Street and Prince of Wales Road. Approximately 1.7kg of decorative ceiling plaster recovered from the rubble presumably derived from the building of which the earlier cellar formed part.

Greyfriars House
(Figs 4.1 and 4.2; Pls 4.3–4.5)
The remains of a post-medieval building shown on the 1885 Ordnance Survey map as Greyfriars House were recorded during the excavations (Pl. 4.5). This house is also clearly recognisable on the maps of Hochstetter (1789) and Millard and Manning (1830) (Pls 4.3 and 4.4). Cleer's earlier (1696) map shows three large discrete buildings in the area between Cook's Lane and Griffin Lane/Crinkle Crankle Lane (Pl. 4.2). Comparison with the later maps suggests that the easternmost of these is Greyfriars House and that the central one is 'The Priory' (see below).

The two 19th-century maps indicate that Greyfriars House comprised two wings (each 6.5m wide) projecting southward, a bay window to the east and another wing at the north-east corner projecting eastward. The full extent of the building was shown by the 1885 Ordnance Survey map (Pl. 4.5) to have been a maximum of 23m by 23m. It could be accessed from King Street via the lane that was known, by 1789, as Cook's Lane and by 1885 as Greyfriars Lane (Fig. 4.1). Excavation revealed brick walls and floors of the two southward-projecting wings and of the bay window (Fig. 4.2). In addition, the eastern of the two wings incorporated a hexagonal brick structure which had apparently served as a cold store.

Excavation also indicated that the house incorporated within its core a series of medieval flint foundations that had formed part of the cloister of Franciscan Friary and were left standing after the Dissolution. The full extent of a north-to-south wall is shown on the maps of 1830 and 1885 (Pls 4.4 and 4.5). External walls of the eastward-projecting wing forming the northern part of Greyfriars House indicated on the maps of 1830 and 1885 corresponded with the inner and outer walls of the south cloister walk, whose location had been suggested independently on the basis of documentary evidence. These walls lay some 4.5m apart. The presence of medieval flintwork beneath these wall-lines could not be verified as this element of Greyfriars House lay beyond the excavated area.

Formal garden on Rose Lane
(Fig.4.2)
Earlier horticultural activity to the south of the precinct wall was succeeded by a garden or orchard, represented archeologically by a sequence of very dark deposits (*50039*, *50038*, *50037*: Macphail and Cruise, Chapter 6.VIII). The uppermost layer in this sequence, which had a horizontal upper boundary, was a fibrous humic deposit, indicative of open area or turf (micromorphological sample 1). Four halfpennies (two each of 1771 and 1774) found near the surface indicate that it was in use in the late 18th century.

A formal garden was represented by a variety of features. A gravel path (*50697*), c. 1m wide and aligned west-to-east, lay some 6.6m to the south of the Friary precinct wall (*30469*, *30906*, *40021*, *50630*). The path was composed of pale brown to orange gravel and lay on top of the turfed layer. The edges of the pathway were marked with iron prongs (SF505: Fryer, Chapter 5.I) spaced at intervals of *c.* 0.9m. The line of the path lies immediately to the north of a west-to-east wall depicted on the 1885 Ordnance Survey map. Given that the map indicates a section of this wall takes the form of a semicircular southward projection, it would appear that the wall retained a terrace.

To the east of the gravel path was a ceramic water pipe (*50115*), composed of interconnecting sections (Goffin, Chapter 5.I). It was aligned north-to-south in Area C and had been laid within a cut (*50137*). Although dating of this feature is inconclusive, it seems likely that the pipeline was associated with formal gardens in this area that post-date the Friary. Additional fragments of ceramic pipe were recovered unstratified from Area A. While there is a possibility that this material originated from destruction of the Friary, it seems more likely that they were associated with post-medieval gardens in the vicinity.

The turfed surface and gravel path were eventually buried by dumps of various materials dating to the late 19th century, probably associated with the construction of Prince of Wales Road and adjacent properties in the early 1860s.

Period 5 (19th and 20th centuries)

(Figs 4.1 and 4.2; Pls 1.1 and 1.2)

The 19th century saw the increasing development of buildings across the site, including cellared examples along the King Street frontage and eventually along Prince of Wales Road (Areas A and D). These were subsequently replaced by the Mann Egerton showrooms (Pls 1.1 and 1.2). Greyfriars House and its grounds survived until they were subsumed beneath the Mann Egerton factory. Terraced houses fronting Maidstone Road and Rose Lane were eventually constructed above the formal garden to the east (Area C).

The 1885 Ordnance Survey plan shows a rectangular building *c.* 42m east of King Street and 13m north of Greyfriars Lane called 'The Priory'. That an east-to-west wall incorporating a blocked window which originated as part of the Friary, perhaps part of the Refectory/Suffragan's Lodging in the south range of the cloister (*13139*: Chapter 3.III) continued in use after the Dissolution is indicated by the presence of a section of later brickwork comprising 'Norfolk Red' bricks. This wall equates with the north side of 'The Priory' as depicted on the Ordnance Survey map. The house was bounded to the west and south by an L-shaped formal garden; the line of its south wall coincides with that of a foundation (*12622*) recorded in May 1994, during construction of a sewer running out to Greyfriars Road.

IV. DISCUSSION: THE DISSOLUTION AND AFTERWARDS

by Phillip A. Emery and Elizabeth Shepherd Popescu

The Dissolution

Documentary evidence attests to the large quantity of building materials removed from the site at and after the Dissolution. Accounts refer to the sale of timbers, roof and paving tile, paving stone, marble, brick, freestone, knapped flint and rough stone (Rutledge, above, 87–9; Appendix 4). A chronology for the removal of buildings can be established from 16th-century leases and accounts of dismantling. Architectural stone from the Friary had been re-used in properties fronting the junction between King Street and Prince of Wales Road (Samuel, Chapter 5.I). More dramatic evidence for reuse of materials is provided by the possible removal of a door or gateway by Bassingham for reuse in his own Norwich house: this was moved in 1857 to the south-west corner of the Guildhall, where it can still be seen (Pl. 4.6). Some of the window glass from the Friary may also have been removed to be reconstructed elsewhere (King, Chapter 5.I).

Three deposits of Dissolution date attest to ferrous metalworking at this time, probably indicating a short-term operation relating to the recycling of iron fittings from the Greyfriars buildings. Lead melt was also evident in n Dissolution-period deposits. There is also evidence for late/post-medieval iron-smithing (identifiable as slags with coal adhering to or incorporated within the matrix) which may be associated with the Dissolution and the probable destruction of the Friary buildings and the subsequent re-use or recycling of the stone, iron fittings and other materials. Further details of this recycling activity are given in Chapter 5.II.

Crinkle Crankle Lane, as depicted on Millard and Manning's map of 1830 as Griffin Lane (Pl. 4.4; see also Fig. 4.1), describes a series of dog-legs as it passes between a series of plots that came into being in the Dissolution. The longest straight section — that forming a T-junction with King Street — corresponds to the gap between the nave of the Friary church and the cloister in their interpreted positions (Fig. 3.21) and to an alleyway (between Plots D and E/F) reconstructed from 1565 leases (Fig. 3.6). This raises the possibility that the lane has its origins in the Dissolution as an access through the conventual buildings for the transport of salvaged materials. The gap between the church and the cloister represents an obvious breach that would have required minimal demolition to effect. A thoroughfare was similarly created at Winchester Cathedral (Brian Ayers, *pers. comm.*).

Plate 4.6 Bassingham doorway at Guildhall, Norwich

Post-Dissolution

After demolition of the Friary had come to an end in 1566, only boundary walls and a few outbuildings remained. Evidence of re-use of some of these structures — including the incorporation of medieval flint and mortar foundations into the walls of Greyfriars House, which first appears on Cleer's map of 1696 — was recorded during the excavation. The post-Dissolution survival of the major internal Friary wall-line as a property boundary suggests that not all of the standing fabric of the institution was immediately levelled. Particular walls, either free-standing or forming parts of large buildings, may have been retained in the later 16th century because they conveniently sub-divided the site into parcels for later sale. The post-medieval landscape inherited much of the Friary's internal arrangement of boundaries. A conjectural plan of the plots leased by the city in 1565–71 is given in Fig. 3.6 (see Rutledge above).

Although documentary evidence suggests that few of the known lessees of property on the site before 1850 were engaged in commerce, there is archaeological evidence to suggest that this was indeed the case. An assemblage of eleven *c.* 16th–18th-century cloth seals is significant because they are the first found in the important worsted-production centre of Norwich in the course of formal excavations (Egan, Chapter 5.II) and suggest that processing took place in the immediate neighbourhood. Documentary evidence has tentatively attributed some of the seals to the activities of named individuals (Rutledge, Chapter 5.II).

Cleer's late 17th-century map (Pl. 4.2) shows most of the north and east parts of the excavated site as gardens, apparently with a recreational function. The presence of formal gardens to the south of the former Greyfriars precinct into the 19th century was archaeologically corroborated by excavation of a well-dated gravel path, a turfed surface and a sectional ceramic pipe.

The use of most of the site for horticulture, rather than urban settlement, resulted in a relatively small post-medieval artefactual and ecofactual assemblage. Of note amongst the vessel glass assemblage, however, is an unusual white glass vessel of post-medieval date which may have originated in Italy (Freeman *et al*, Chapter 5.III). Other notable finds include an 18th-century miniature cannon, probably used as a toy (Egan, Chapter 5.VII). One piece of lead window came from the site is of interest, since it suggests lead-casting in the vicinity in the post-medieval or modern period (King, Chapter 5.I). A possible explanation for this fragment is the existence of the firm of William Winter, painter, glazier and plumber, from at least 1877 until 1900 at 25 Prince of Wales Road.

Conclusion

Examination of post-Reformation urban development of the site, as envisaged in the original research objectives, has been elucidated as far as the relatively limited evidence will permit. Some linkage is clear between the footprint of the Friary and the urban topography that was to follow. It is now evident that some elements of Friary structures survived the Dissolution to be re-used in later structures and boundaries. While this re-use was already known of, to a certain extent, prior to the recent excavations, the excavation has provided additional detailed information.

5. The Finds

I. BUILDINGS

Structural stonework

by Mark Samuel
(Figs 3.12 and 5.1–5.4)

Introduction

A total assemblage of 204 items of architectural worked stone was recovered from the excavations at Norwich Greyfriars (131 from Areas A–C, 73 from Area D). Most of the larger fragments in the 1992–4 assemblage had been re-used in the walls of properties fronting the junction between King Street and Prince of Wales Road. None of the fragments from this first group were found *in situ.*

The recovery of two *in situ* worked stones (context *13146*: SF2718 and SF2719) is of particular importance in understanding both the date and function of the wall from which they derived (see below). The recovery of related fragments as a blocking to this opening has allowed its partial reconstruction (Fig. 3.12). Additionally, a mass of well-preserved typestones was recovered from the capping of a Friary culvert (*13440*: see Chapter 3.III, 'Water management system'), examination of which suggests that many can be used in the reconstruction of further window tracery.

Stone types present

The number of different stone types present in the assemblage has been tentatively identified through empirical judgement of the apparent weight, texture and colour of the stones.

Shelly oolitic limestone
The *Shelly oolitic limestone* category is a 'catch-all' describing stones that were perhaps quarried from the *Inferior oolite group*, probably in Lincolnshire or Northamptonshire. These were probably selected for their superficial resemblance to Caen stone and were no doubt quarried as cheaper alternatives.

Caen stone
Caen stone, from Normandy, is recognisable by its yellow/buff tint, fine even texture, denseness and lack of fossils. It was expensive to import (Salzman 1952, 136) and it was only used for fine dressings and ashlar where it would be visible. It seems to have been particularly favoured in East Anglia in the 12th and 14th centuries. For example, the Blackfriars' house at Ipswich was dressed almost exclusively with this stone (author's observation). While Caen stone also seems to have been used extensively at Norwich Greyfriars, alternative stone types form a higher proportion of the assemblage than seen at Ipswich Blackfriars. This may partly reflect marginal differences in the economy of transport in relation to Normandy, and also the availability of stone from other sources. The pattern of use of Caen within Norfolk was strongly influenced by differences in the viability of the river transport in particular areas of the county. The south-east part of Norfolk is well provided with rivers, which eased the importation of Caen stone, but the reduced ease of water transport in the west of the county encouraged the use of Barnack (Parsons 1990, 215). The continued use of Caen at Greyfriars, apparently well into the 15th century, is at odds with the declining use of this building stone elsewhere in the county (*ibid.*). This may reflect the wealth of the Order.

Fine grained yellow/brown limestone
Probably Caen stone, this seems to have been used throughout the history of the Friary as the freestone of first choice, but a dating histogram (not illustrated) suggests that other, more local, stones were favoured in the 14th century (see below).

Spar-prominent shelly oolitic limestone
See 'Coffins', below.

Purbeck marble
The use of *Purbeck marble* for a window mullion (SF1025: not illustrated) is unusual and surviving examples are very rare. It was, however, used for the Bishop of Ely's Hall or buildings associated with it in London (author's observation) built *c.* 1286–90, as surviving fragments attest. A solitary fragment of Purbeck marble from the 1995 excavation formed part of a fine pavement. The *Purbeck limestone* was used almost exclusively for paving slabs. It also seems to have been used for one of the mortars (SF859: Fig.5.54: see Chapter 5.III, 'Mortars') due to its hardness.

Upper Greensand
The two fragments of *Upper Greensand* (SF184 and 156: not illustrated) were probably quarried in the Reigate area (North Downs) and it is unusual for such a stone to have been transported so far, although the stone was used intensively in the London area. The fragments could perhaps have derived from a free-standing monument transported from workshops in southern England. Its occurrence does not prove that a large-scale trade in Greensand existed, as such a monument could have been completed to order in the London area and imported in 'kit' form. The discovery of a single indubitably architectural element (SF2704: not illustrated) shows that Greensand quarrystone was imported, if in small quantities. This probably is 'Firestone' from the Reigate area, but scientific examination would be required for a definite provenance.

Grey spar-prominent and oolite-prominent oolitic limestones
This category is a 'catch-all' describing stones that were perhaps quarried from the *Inferior oolite group*, probably in Lincolnshire or Northamptonshire. These seem to have been used alongside Caen stone, which continued to be favoured for work requiring fine carving. The spar-prominent variety was used for the *in situ* opening, which dates to 1325–1450 (see below).

Orange/brown coarse fossiliferous oolitic limestone
See 'Coffins', below. Two instances of tracery worked from a fossiliferous limestone were found during the 1995 work.

Other types
The other occurrences of stone are less remarkable, and reflect the functional properties of these stone types, rather than their date.

Constructional phases

Norman (c. 1066–1180)
(Fig. 5.1)

A chevron-decorated voussoir dating to the 12th century is complete (SF2018). This type of voussoir could have been used in a variety of different architectural applications. A plinth fragment (SF2024: not illustrated) can be tentatively assigned to the 12th century as it was roughly dressed with a jadd pick rather than a chisel, as has the ashlar (SF1262; not illustrated). The latter fragment was one of ten pieces of stone recovered from the fill of a cess-pit in Area C (*50628*) which was dated by two coins of Stephen (1135–54).

In total 45 pieces of limestone, all but two of them small undiagnostic fragments, were recovered from deposits near the eastern extreme of the excavation. The

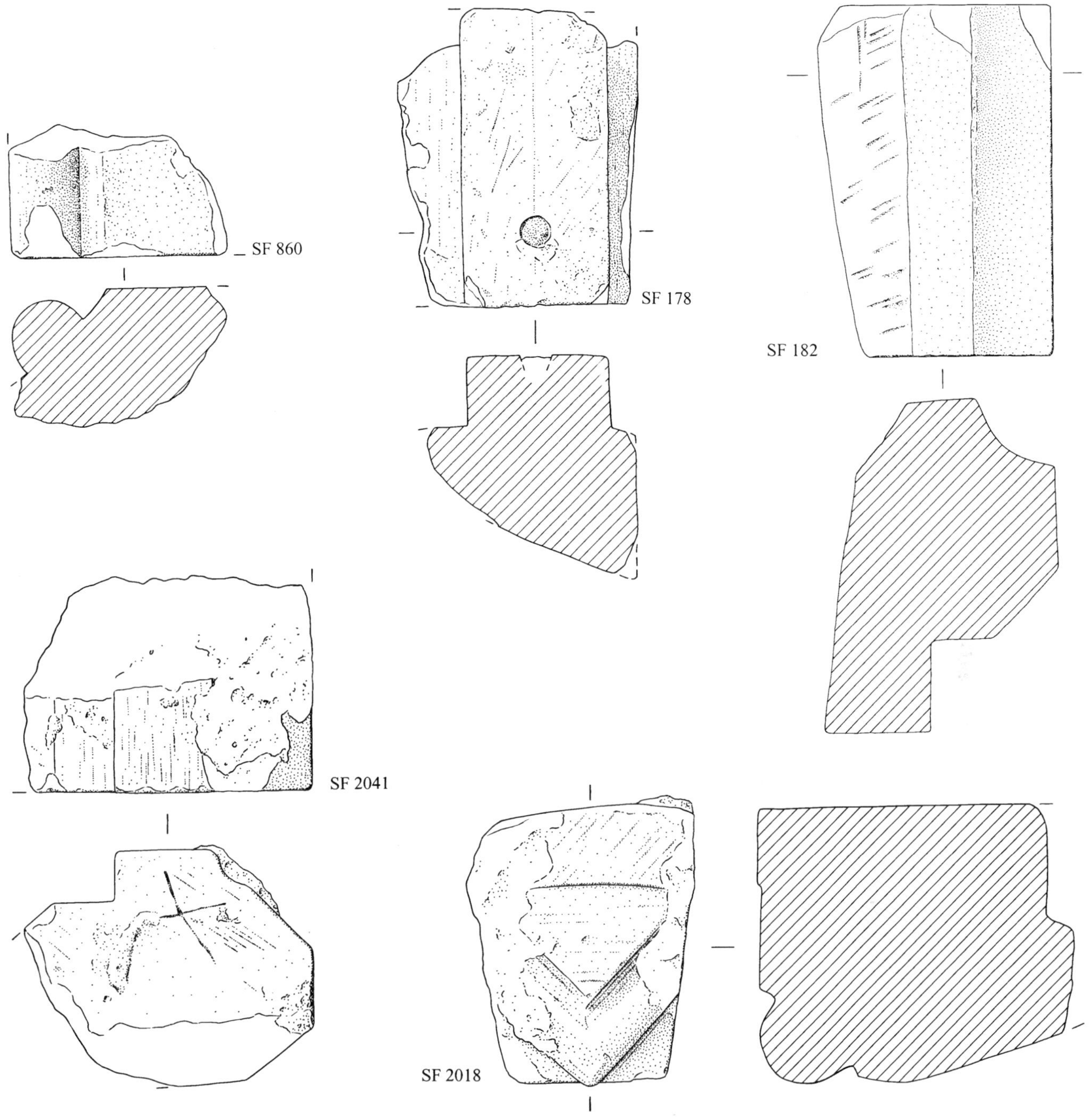

Figure 5.1 Caen stone architectural fragments (SF860, 178, 182, 2041, 2018). Scale 1:4.

more significant pieces consisted of a shaft with keying for stucco (SF1039) and part of an ashlar block (SF1262). The close spatial grouping of these fragments, together with the consistent dating (late 11th–12th century) of the contexts from which they were recovered, implies a common source. The pieces of stone may have derived from building work carried out on the church of St Vedast which was situated to the east of the excavated area.

Early English (c. 1180–1275)
(Fig. 5.1)
Twelve pieces seem to date to the Early English period. A concentration of fragments, mostly dated by their tooling, suggests that a building programme occurred in the first half of the 13th century. These fragments are characterised by the use of the *boaster* chisel to create a regular corrugated finish at 45 degrees to the axes of the stones (ashlars) or parallel to them (mouldings). The mouldings include bowtells (SF860), simple square window jambs with setters' marks (SF2041) and 'peg holes' for glass (SF178) as well as a hollow chamfered window jamb (SF182). The plain, utilitarian nature of the windows perhaps reflects the Rule of the Greyfriars, but they could equally well derive from lay buildings. The lack of distinctive mouldings means that they cannot be dated with any precision. One fragment is a simple Caen stone (?)chamfered plinth

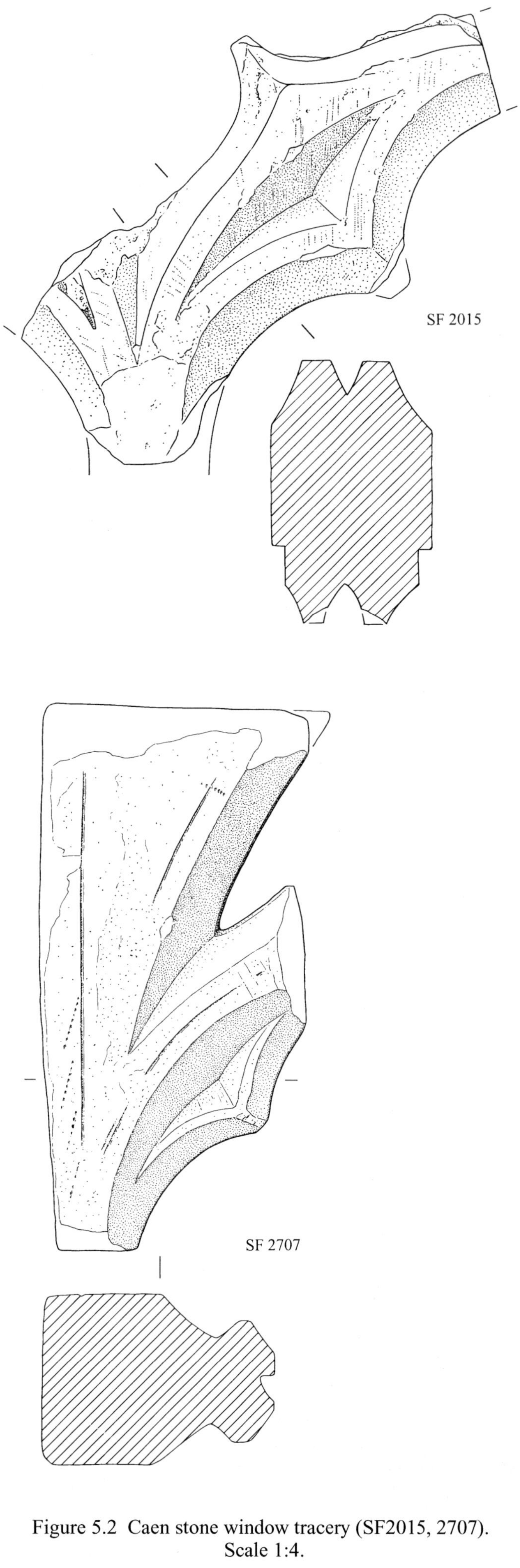

Figure 5.2 Caen stone window tracery (SF2015, 2707). Scale 1:4.

datable by its tooling to *c.* 1225–50, although this and two other tooled fragments (SF2698 and SF2712D: not illustrated) may in fact be somewhat later. The earliest datable moulding is a simple Greensand string course mould with a simple chamfered weathering and a hollow-chamfered underside. This can only be dated to *c.* 1225–1300 because it had been dressed with a serrated claw tool.

Decorated (c. 1275–1350)
(Figs 3.12, 5.2 and 5.3)

This period is well represented and there can be no doubt that at least one major phase of construction occurred *c.* 1290–1320. The stones are unambiguously ecclesiastical in nature. The entire assemblage is notable for the relative simplicity and functional nature of its mouldings, which may reflect deliberate policy on the part of the Franciscans — funds were not to be made available for anything other than basic architectural requirements, even after the Franciscans' abhorrence of masonry structures diminished.

Architectural development of the precinct seems to have stopped after *c.* 1400–50, reflecting a country-wide trend whereby devotional legacies tended to be diverted away from monasteries and friaries towards collegiate churches, song schools, chantries and almshouses.

Windows

Three pieces (SF2015, Fig. 5.2; SF2017 and SF2034, not illustrated) derive from one or more fine traceried windows dressed from Caen. These were cusped and foliated and exhibit the flowing lines associated with the Decorated period. A large fragment of Caen stone tracery (SF2707; Fig. 5.2) found in Area D exhibits the same glazing rebate, suggesting that this fragment relates to the others. SF2707 incorporates part of the jamb, a falchion (a type of tracery opening) and one side of a cusped archlet. Partial reconstruction of the adjacent scheme of tracery can be achieved from these fragments. The form of the glazing rebate (which permitted removal of the glass) indicates a date of 1290–1350. The chamfered mullion moulding was very straightforward, and the common re-use context suggests that this tracery is associated with the hood mould SF2689. The best-preserved fragment (SF2015) probably rested (when complete) on the top of a mullion at the springing line of the tracery and it diverges to form the base of a cusped *oculus*. The smaller fragment (SF2017) is clearly related. The glass was held in place by a glazing rebate rather than a groove, allowing it to be removed. Grooves seem to have been universal after *c.* 1350. The window can be dated quite closely to *c.* 1310–1340.

A re-cut Caen stone window jamb SF2700, a cusped stilted (segmental) archlet SF2702 and a voussoir from a segmental window arch SF2701 were found in drain culvert *13440*: all probably derive from the same window. The glazing groove (imprisoning the glass) can be dated to *c.* 1300–1400. The simple chamfered moulding follows the same form as SF2707.

A small fragment of fossiliferous limestone moulding (SF2711, not illustrated) can be dated to 1250–1325. SF2679, 2681 and 2682 (not illustrated) all can be dated to the period around 1300, but as they all seem to be part of the same broken-up Caen stone window moulding, the apparent peak at 1300 is misleading. All three of these fragments bore traces of red paint.

The Greensand label (?) mould (SF2695, not illustrated) must date to after 1275 because an ogee (wave) mould is present. SF2689 (not illustrated) has a very similar but better preserved moulding, remarkable for its bulk and simplicity. It was dressed from hard spar-prominent oolitic limestone, perhaps because the dressing was an external window label mould requiring a weather-resistant stone. This stone derived from the pointed apex of a two-centred opening. The fragmentary string SF2716 (not illustrated) is apparently dressed from the same type of stone and follows the same moulding theme, but also has a beak mould separating the label from a casement mould.

Contexts *13147* and *13056* contained a mass of spar-prominent oolitic limestone fragments which were re-used from the window that they blocked (*13146*: Fig. 3.12):

SF2709	S-shaped tracery element with glazing grooves.
SF2666	ped glazed vertical jamb (fossiliferous limestone?)
SF2647, 2648, 2664	Unglazed mullion fragments with provision for horizontal irons.

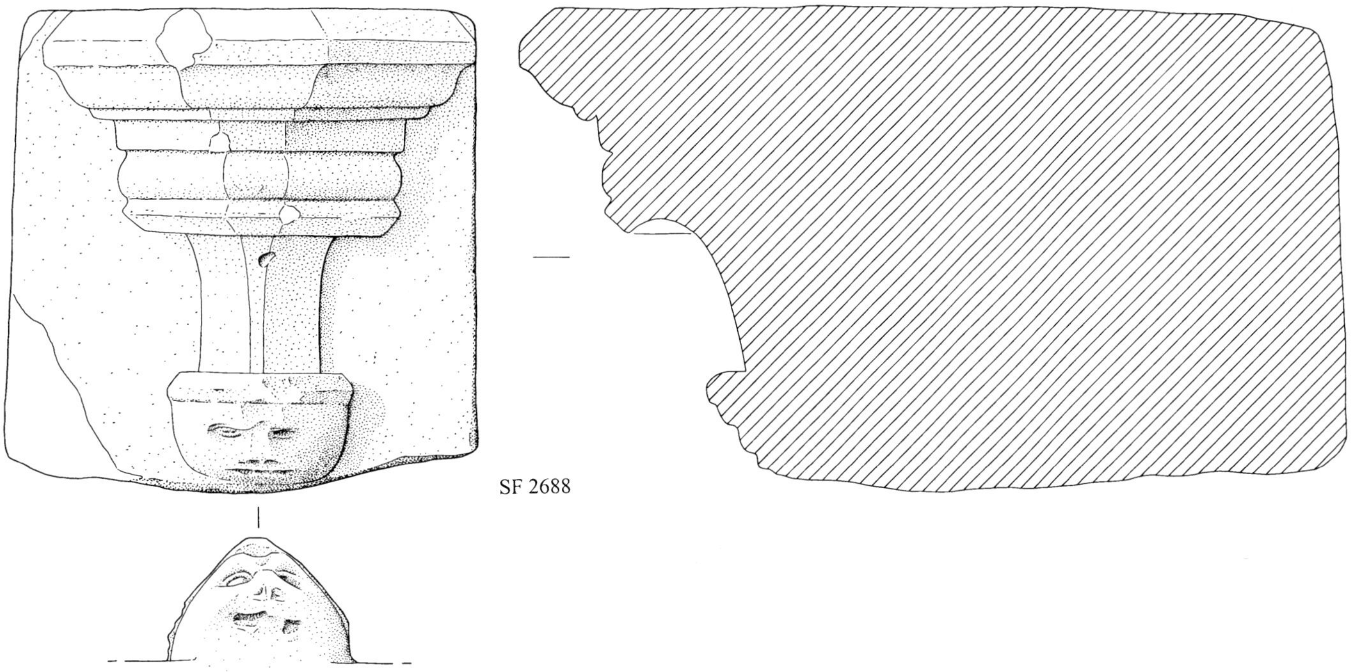

Figure 5.3 Spar prominent oolitic limestone corbel (SF2688). Scale 1:4.

2725, 2720, 2726, SF2649, 2665	Internal? external? radiused glazed window arch with chamfered label.
SF2718	*in situ* unglazed sill/jamb junction
SF2719	*in situ* unglazed jamb

Although two of the pieces were found *in situ,* the lack of tracery fragments means that a complete reconstruction of this window cannot be attempted. Its width, now lost, can be determined from the excavated buttress foundations and their relation to the surviving reveal. The absence of glazing and the ground floor position of the window indicate that the wall is quite likely to be part of a cloister. The splayed embrasure would, of course, point to the interior of the cloister garth. The hollow-chamfered moulding is unfortunately difficult to date more closely than *c.* 1325–1450. The window may have lain adjacent to a doorway forming the southern entrance to the western side of the cloister (see Chapter 3.III, 'Cloister and cloister walks').

A large voussoir cut from spar-prominent limestone (SF2703: not illustrated) probably derives from the splayed and pointed rerearch of a window (being cut to meet the pointed apex). The double-ogee indicates a date after 1350.

Other architectural features

Fragment SF2065 (not illustrated) is part of an ornamental buttress probably deriving from a chapel screen, tomb monument, reredos or similar structure.

Several fragments of Caen stone ashlars indicate the quality of the buildings constructed in this era, as only very prestigious structures would have been ashlared with this stone. They were dressed with a serrated clawtool, unlike the Early English fragments. The use of this tool seems to have fallen out of favour after *c.* 1350 (author's observation).

Other fragments (none illustrated) that may derive from this period include a heavily weathered hood mould (SF179 and SF2025) as well as a weathering from a buttress (SF2022). A Caen stone corner plinth (SF2644) probably dates, judging by its tooling, to 1350–1400.

The spar-prominent oolitic limestone capital (SF2688: Fig. 5.3) was structurally a corbel with an ornamental engaged pilaster below it. It either supported the springer of a ribbed vault or the wall riser of a roof truss. Unusually, polychrome paintwork survives on the capital. The moulding is unlikely to pre-date 1350.

Perpendicular (c. 1350–1485)
(Fig. 5.4)

Very few fragments recovered are definitely later than 1350. The handful that were are dated by their tooling. The beds were dressed with a 'blunt' claw tool, where the chisel was sawn with slits at regular intervals. The 'claws' are therefore rectilinear rather than pointed. This tool was widely used after the Black Death, largely replacing the serrated claw tool (author's observation).

No mouldings could be dated to this period stylistically, apart from a small moulding fragment incorporating an ogee (SF1036: not illustrated). An intriguing astylar door jamb (SF22: Fig. 5.4) may date to this period although the possibility that it is post-Dissolution cannot be ruled out. The door jamb incorporated two reveals and the presence of sockets for pintles indicates that there were two doors, perhaps suggesting that this doorway was used in a strongroom. A small 'veneer' fragment of Caen stone (SF2012: not illustrated) may have formed part of the cladding on a tomb monument or a similar church furnishing.

The scarcity of worked stone from the 200-year period 1350–1550 is surprising yet remarkably similar to the situation at Ipswich's friaries, where very few worked stones of the period were recovered from the Blackfriars or Whitefriars (Samuel 1992 4, 7). It would seem either that the Friars were content with their buildings, or were too poor to commission alterations in line with changing architectural taste. While Tudor work (post-1485) appears entirely absent, the sample is too small to draw definite conclusions.

SF22	**Architectural fragment**. Astylar door jamb. Patch of white pigment on open face. Limestone. *post-pad 10059, Period 5*
SF178	**Architectural fragment.** Incomplete sub-rectangular block with two corners cut out, forming a T-shape in section. All faces including one end are flat. One end is

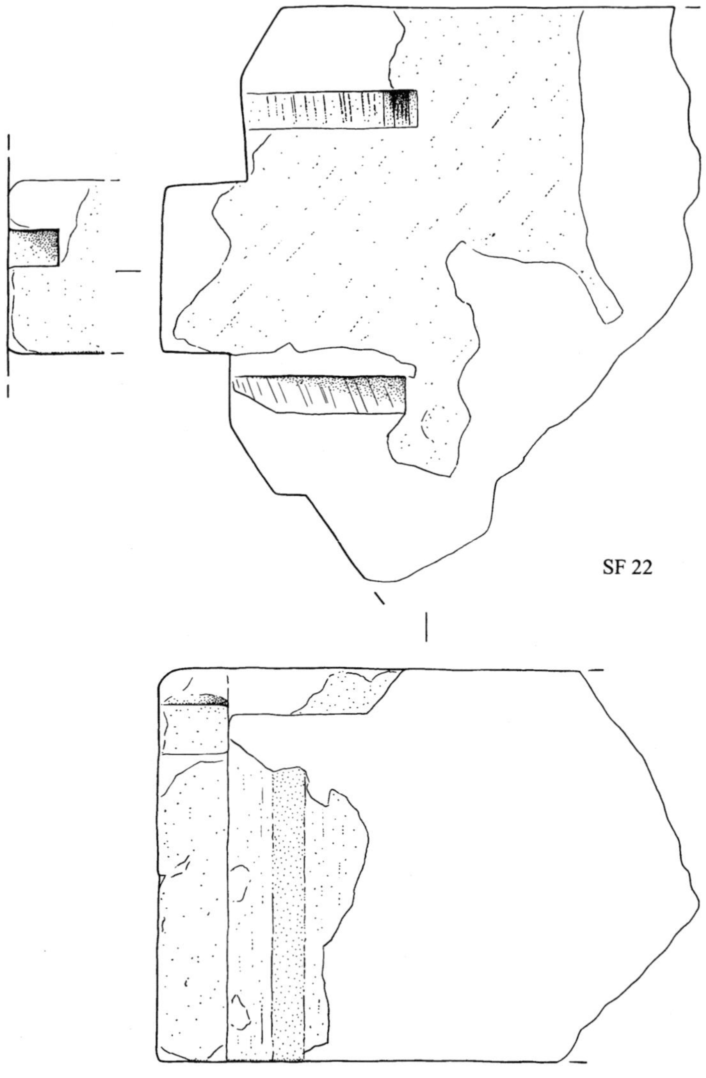

Figure 5.4 Limestone astylar door jamb (SF22). Scale 1:4.

broken. Surfaces ?whitewashed. L: 190mm, W: 140mm, T:130mm. Caen stone.
10109, unstratified

SF182 **Architectural fragment.** Hollow chamfered window jamb. L: 225mm, W: 210mm, T: 150mm. Caen stone.
bedding 10091, Period 5

SF860 **Architectural fragment.** Incomplete quoin, with bowtell mouldings. Remains of whitewash on carved face. L: 130mm, W: 75mm, T: 95mm.
layer 10294, Period 4.1

SF2015 **Architectural fragment.** Window tracery fragment, re-used. L: 390mm, W: 200mm, T: 200mm. Caen stone.
wall 12035, Period 4

SF2018 **Architectural fragment.** Complete chevron-decorated voussoir. L: 200mm, W: 120mm, T: 150mm. Caen stone.
wall 12035, Period 4

SF2041 **Architectural fragment.** Incomplete square window jamb with setter's marks. L: 180mm, W: 140mm, T: 140mm. Caen stone.
foundation 12362, Period 3.2

SF2688 **Architectural fragment.** Decorative corbel with an ornamental engaged pilaster below it, depicting a grotesque human head. The corbel either supported the springer of a ribbed vault or the wall riser of a roof truss. Polychrome paint-work survives on the capital. Spar-prominent oolitic limestone.
culvert 13440, Period 3.2

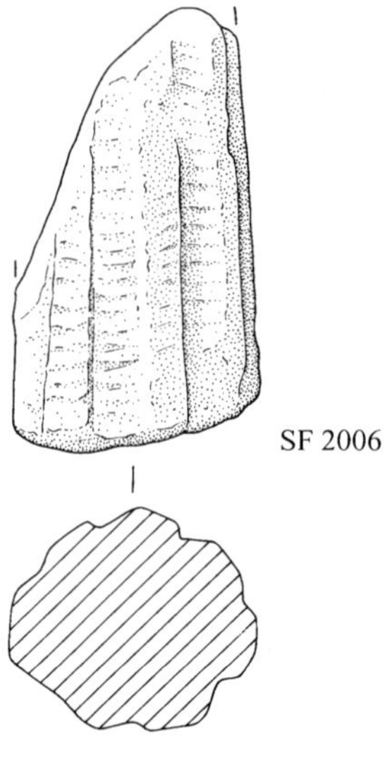

Figure 5.5 Sculptural stone fragment (SF2006). Scale 1:2.

SF2707 **Architectural fragment.** Large fragment of tracery. Incorporates part of a jamb (a falchion) and one side of a cusped archlet. Caen stone.
culvert 13440, Period 3.2

Sculptural fragment

by Mark Samuel
(Fig. 5.5)

A single sculptural fragment (SF2006), apparently representing part of drapes from a figurative carving, was recovered from a post-Dissolution layer (12151) in the north-east corner of Area A. The abraded condition suggests the fragment was residual within the deposit, which also produced clay tobacco pipe. It is therefore likely to have derived from demolition of the Friary buildings.

Coffins

by Mark Samuel and Steven Ashley
(Figs 5.6 and 5.7)

Three coffin slabs had been re-used in later constructions: two came from the monastic drainage system and the third from a wall. Spar-prominent shelly oolitic limestone (Barnack rag?) and orange/brown fossiliferous oolitic limestone were both used for stone coffins at Norwich Greyfriars. Porous coarse-textured fossiliferous limestones seem to have been favoured for this purpose in medieval south-east England (perhaps due to their high lime content). They were exported all over south-east England, probably ready-worked, for this express purpose (author's observation). Both the 1994 and 1995 excavations produced coffin fragments of the orange/brown variety.

It is unusual to see spar-prominent shelly oolitic limestone used for a relief-carved lid (SF953). Although only a very small part of the original decoration of the upper surface of coffin lid SF953 has survived, the 'double-omega' motif clearly shows it to be a product of

Figure 5.6 Coffin lid (SF953). Scale 1:5.

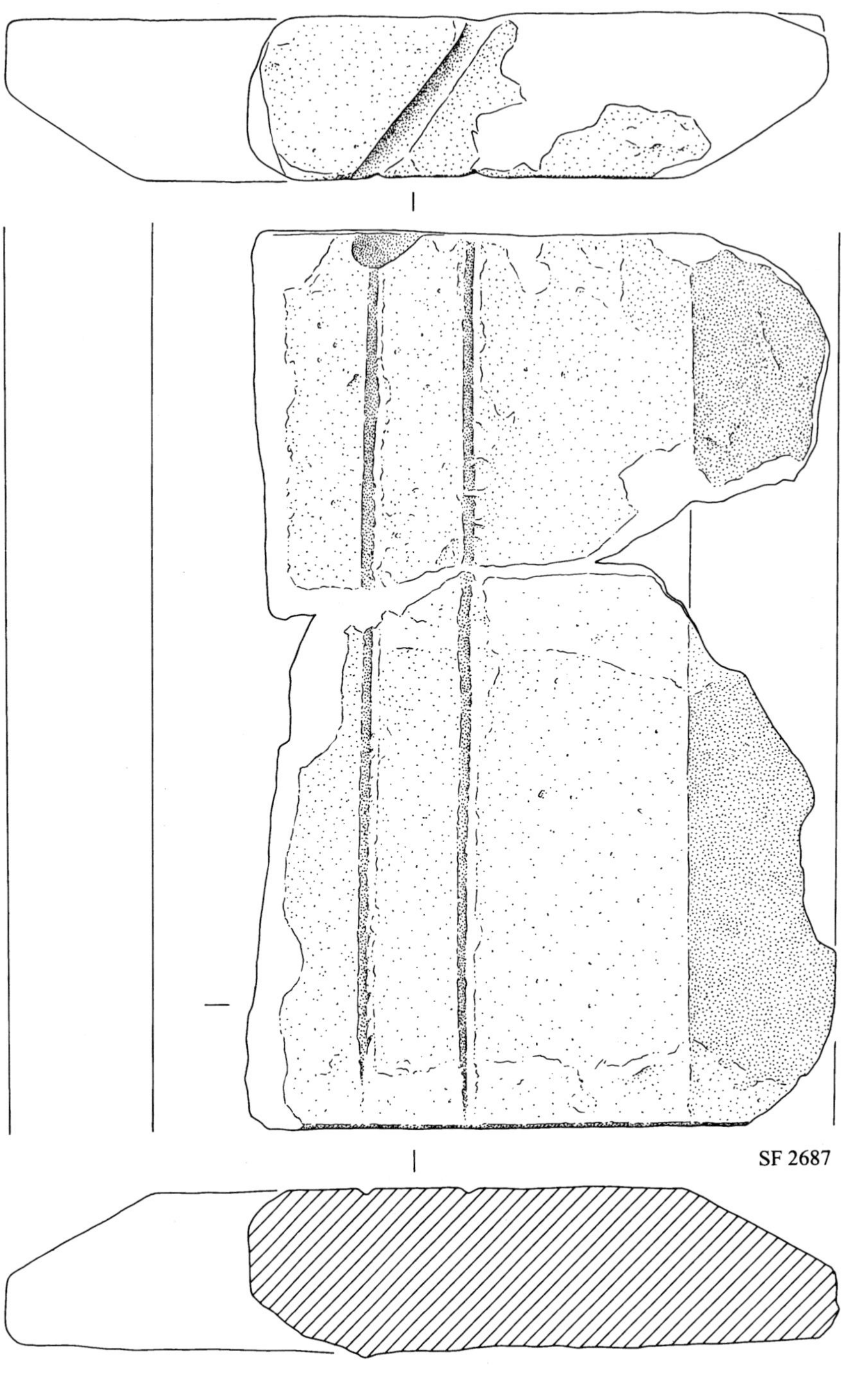

Figure 5.7 Coffin lid (SF2687). Scale 1:4.

the Barnack School of carving and to have been made in the 12th or 13th century (Butler 1957, 92; Butler 1964, 121–2).

SF953 **Coffin lid.** A slab in two joining fragments of shelly limestone, the foot and lower half of which are missing, is min. 870mm long, coped, varying in thickness from 140mm max. to 110mm min., and tapers from 540mm at the head to max. 470mm. The relief decoration, although mostly removed, survives in part to a maximum of 10mm proud of the surface. A 'double-Omega' motif is visible on the small area of surviving upper surface, which also carries traces of diagonal tooling. An incised line runs parallel to the edge, framing the decoration. Another incised line runs around the top of the surviving two sides and head. Much mortar adheres to the sides, head and edges of the base. Spar-prominent shelly oolitic limestone.
drain capping 10334, Period 3.1

SF2687 **Coffin lid.** Chamfered edges, with two incised lines running parallel down centre of slab. Spar-prominent shelly oolitic limestone.
drain 13440, Period 3.2

Fabric	*Drury Match*	*Type*	*Qty (no. fragments)*	*Wt (kg)*	*% total assemblage (by wt)*
102	LB 1, 3 & 4	brick	89	37.420	3.59
106	none	brick	54	17.650	1.69
107	EB 2,3 & 8	brick	714	318.254	30.52
110	EB 3, & 6	brick	225	56.084	5.38
112	EB 5	brick	76	23.003	2.21
113	EB 1	brick	27	26.075	2.50
115	none	brick	47	11.490	1.10
118	EB 7	brick	215	60.253	5.78
134	LB 2	brick	13	10.659	1.02
202	-	?brick	486	20.292	1.95
114	FT 9 & 10	floor tile	125	23.735	2.27
133	FT 18	floor tile	42	10.488	1.01
100	RT 2 & 3	roof tile	5079	287.922	27.61
103	none	roof tile	115	11.023	1.06
135	? R1	tile	137	16.950	1.63
300	-	unidentified	4054	15.730	1.51
TOTAL			**13,171**	**1042.669**	**100.00**

Table 7 Ceramic building material forms by fabric, weight and total number of fragments (Areas A–C). Only those fabrics which account for 1% or more of the total assemblage by weight are presented here.

Ceramic building material

by Julia Huddle with Richard Kemp
(Pls 3.7 and 3.9)

Introduction

A total of 1120.1kg of ceramic building material was recovered from the entire site, of which 1042.7kg (93% by weight) came from Areas A–C (Table 7) and the remaining 77.44kg (7% by weight) from Area D. The earliest material recovered is Roman and had been re-used, notably in the hearth(s) of a Late Saxon building or buildings. The bulk of the assemblage dates to the medieval or post-medieval periods and includes glazed and unglazed flat roofing tile, glazed and unglazed ridge tile, glazed and unglazed floor tile and brick. Also recorded were fragments of daub and fired clay.

The following text discusses the assemblage by fabric and form, followed by a consideration of the material by site period. The latter places the group in its archaeological context, drawing on the evidence from selected features such as those relating to the Friary. The methodology for analysis of the material is detailed in the project archive.

Fabrics and forms

A range of fabric types are represented. Detailed fabric analysis was not undertaken for material retrieved from Area D, although type and subforms were noted. (This material is not detailed further here.) The main fabrics recognised in all areas were types 100 and 107 (catalogued below). Type 100 is mainly associated with the roofing tiles, although other fabric variations were also noted. A number of the floor tiles recorded (*e.g.* those with distinctive nail marks, glaze, fabric *etc.*) may be attributed to the Low Countries, with others that are lacking these characteristics probably from a localised production source (Drury 1981). Some of the non-local floor tile that occurred on the site (fabrics 114 and 133) resembles material recovered from the Norwich Castle Mall excavation (Lentowicz and Kemp forthcoming).

Where possible, the Greyfriars fabric series has been linked to Paul Drury's Norwich type series (Drury 1993, 168). Other fabric codes relate to the NAU's in-house fabric series and are detailed in the project archive.

Medieval and post-medieval roof tile

A total of 6750 pieces of roof tile (weighing 337.308kg) was recovered. The tile is fragmentary, weighing an average of 0.50kg per piece. No complete tiles were recovered, although in one case all three complete dimensions were available, and for another 35 the complete width and thicknesses were recorded. The roof tile assemblage has been divided into thirteen fabrics.

Apart from fragments of possible pantile recovered in Periods 3–5, all medieval and post-medieval tiles recovered are flat peg tiles. Peg tiles were the norm in the medieval and the early post-medieval periods, although when they were first introduced is uncertain. They were made at Orford Castle, Suffolk, *c.* 1165–73 (Drury and Norton 1985) and appeared at Kings Lynn *c.* 1200 (Richmond *et al.* 1982, 122) and in Norwich by the 13th century (Drury 1993, 168).

Of the whole assemblage only seven tiles recovered have complete widths surviving at the 'pegged' end, all of which have two peg holes. Peg tiles previously recovered on sites in Norwich generally have two peg holes (Drury 1993, 168), as opposed to one central peg hole. The types present at Greyfriars appear to indicate a 13th-century production date, possibly continuing into the 14th century. Similar tile types have been recorded from early 13th-century deposits at Borelli Yard, Farnham, Surrey (Riall and Shelton-Bunn 1989).

Peg tiles first appear at Greyfriars during the period *c.* 1290–1400 (Period 3.1). The tile is residual and was mainly recovered in pit fills. However, many of the tile fragments were re-used as wall and floor packing, as well as in the construction of drains and culverts. An indication of the likely extent of their re-use at this site is shown by the quantity of fragments recovered with mortar attached (2719 pieces/56% by weight) of the total.

All systems of tiling the ridge of the roof would have used ridge tiles. These are distinguished from curved tiles by the fact that the edges of the tile are parallel ('curved' tiles used with flanged tiles are tapered). Twenty-five tile fragments from Greyfriars are curved and, although none of the pieces have surviving edges, it must be assumed that these are fragments of ridge tile. No flanged tiles were recovered.

Of the tile fragments recovered 15% (by fragment count) are glazed. The glaze is generally dark green, although some brown glazed fragments are also noted. Where enough of any one tile survives for its distribution to be observed, the glaze occurs towards the lower end of the tile.

Apart from the glazed tile, no other decorative features such as crested ridge tile or spinning top finials were present. The lack of decorative tile within the medieval and early post-medieval assemblage is reflected in collections from other sites in Norwich, where only one example is known of a crested ridge tile, from 33–55 Pottergate (149N, Atkin, Carter and Evans 1985, 93) and one or two ridge tile with holes for spinning-top finials from 70–80 Oak Street (351N), 5–7 Timberhill (345N) and St Martin-at Palace-Plain.

Of the medieval and post-medieval tile assemblage, fabrics 100, 103, 104, 105, 108, 111, 116, 117, and 123 all occur during the active life of the Friary (Periods 3.1 and 3.2). Of these, fabrics 100, 104 and 111 occur in contexts pre-dating *c.* 1400 (Period 3.1).

Fabric 100 is the principal tile used at Greyfriars during the 13th to early 16th centuries, accounting for 27% of the total site assemblage. It was probably first used on the site during the 1300s, since fragments are first encountered in Period 3.1. The majority of the fragments occur in Period 3 (*c.* 51% of the total fabric 100 group), this figure falling to 18% in Periods 4.1 and 4.2, and to 4% in Period 5 (a pattern reflected in the other fabric types). The quantity of other tile fabrics present is so small in comparison that they may simply represent minor repair works, rather than major roofing material used during the Friary period.

Apart from a few fragments of fabric 141 in Period 3, fabrics 141 and 142 were only recovered in post-Friary contexts.

Fabric 100: Peg tile

Hard orange/red sandy fabric, with common clear quartz inclusions and rare flint (up to 5mm). Occasionally the core is reduced. 16% of the fragments are glazed, usually dark green, but occasionally brown. The fabric is comparable to Drury types RT 2 and RT 3; both of which occur on Westwick Street (159N) in the 13th century, and on Oak Street (351N) in the 14th century.

Medieval and post-medieval brick

A total of 2358 bricks, mainly fragments (weighing 607.456kg), were recovered from Areas A–C. They were retrieved from deposits of all periods.

Bricks recovered from contexts assigned to Periods 1 and 2 are thought to be intrusive here, since no great bricks were recovered. Great bricks were used in Essex and Suffolk from the third quarter of the 12th century onwards (Drury 1981, 126–7). None, however, have so far been recovered from Norwich. The medieval bricks recovered at Greyfriars are comparable in form and fabric to those recovered from the Castle Mall excavations (Lentowicz and Kemp forthcoming). Large quantities of bricks reached Norwich towards the end of the 13th century, primarily for use in the castle and city defences. They were also used opportunistically elsewhere, and appear in archaeological deposits from the late 13th century onwards.

The use of brick in Norwich had started by 1263, as is attested by the name of Geoffrey the Tiler appearing as a witness of several property deeds from that date. The bricks he used were probably imported from Flanders (Tillyard 1988, 193), though by the end of the 14th century it is likely they were made locally. An entry in the Norwich Chamberlain's book, mentioning both 'bricks and Flemish bricks' supports this view. Flemish-type bricks were probably first introduced to the city *via* the Royal Works at the Castle in 1268–70 (Drury 1993, 164).

No medieval brick kilns have been found in the vicinity of the medieval city, though there were large post-medieval brickyards immediately to the west near present-day Queen's Road. The provenance of medieval bricks in Norwich is uncertain. In 1388/9, a last of 'Tyle' was brought from St Benet's, the Benedictine Abbey east of the city on the River Yare where both tileries and brick kilns were probably sited (Tillyard 1998, 197).

East Anglian and Flemish bricks were both made from essentially indistinguishable clays, and petrological analysis of the Greyfriars assemblage has not assisted in differentiation between the Flemish-type and Norfolk brick fabrics.

Paul Drury has divided the brick from the Norwich Survey excavations into 'Early' brick (EB) and 'Late' brick (LB). Although Drury's typology is not adhered to here, his division between the 'early' and 'later' bricks is ceramically distinctive and the Greyfriars fabric series equates to these definitions. Drury divided his 'Early' bricks into two groups (A and B) on the basis of details of manufacture. The group 'A' bricks were made in a sanded form and on a surface covered in sand; the group 'B' bricks were made in an unsanded form and on a surface covered with vegetable matter. The Greyfriars brick was not categorised in this way since different methods of production were noted, often within the same fabric.

Fabric 107 bricks form the largest individual assemblage, accounting for 52% of the site collection. Fragments first occur on site in Period 2.2, although the majority (65%) occur in Periods 3.1 and 3.2, where they represent 55% of the fabrics recovered. This fabric continues to dominate the assemblages in all periods, although the actual fabric totals diminish in later periods. Fabric 107 was matched to Drury types EB2, 3 and 8. EB2 bricks were used in the Wilderness Tower and adjacent sections of the City Wall of *c.* 1270–1300, and also in the vaulting ribs of Becket's chapel in the Blackfriars, provisionally dated to 1270–1307. EB3 bricks appear by the later 13th century. EB8 bricks were used for the vault of a passage at St Gregory's Church built in the 1380s or 1390s, and were found on Westwick Street (159N) in contexts dated to the end of the 14th century.

Fabric 107: early brick

This fabric appears to be made of a mixture of two clays, one fine and silty, the other sandier with occasional red/brown iron-rich inclusions. The colours vary greatly from acid yellow and purple to creamy yellow and orange/red. Quartz – rare (up to 0.5mm), mica – rare (up to 0.01mm), shell – very rare and brown/red oxide – rare. The bricks were made in a sanded form on a sanded surface, in a sanded form on a surface covered in vegetable matter, or in a non-sanded form on a surface covered in vegetable matter.

Medieval and post-medieval floor tile

Altogether 225 fragments of floor tile (47.918kg) were recovered. The vast majority came from Area A (Period 3) and the quantities recovered decrease significantly in Areas B, C and CB and Periods 4.1 and 4.2. None was recovered from deposits assigned to Period 5.

Floor tiles reached many religious and large secular houses in south-east England from the late 13th century, from a wide variety of sources (Drury 1981, 134). No relief tiles such as those made at Bawsey (Eames 1955), or inlaid tiles as were used at Horsham St Faith Priory (Sherlock 1976), both in Norfolk, were recovered. The medieval floor tiles from Norwich Greyfriars are generally plain glazed types, usually green but occasionally brown. In addition, twelve fragments displayed a glaze over a white/cream slip.

About a third of the tiles are thought to have been made locally, many being comparable to those recovered from Norwich Survey Excavations 1971–78, which Drury (1993) describes as 'of local origin ... poor quality plain coloured tiles'.

The remaining tiles had been imported from Flanders, although there is a possibility that some may have been made by Flemings settled in England (Drury 1981, 130). Kiln sites producing such copies are known in Essex at Radwinter and Blackmore in the 15th century (Cherry 1980, 262; Drury 1978, 235).

Only 23 post-medieval floor tile fragments were recovered. Examples occurring elsewhere on Norwich sites are dated to the late 16th century and later. The assemblage from Greyfriars includes seven fragments of Dutch tin-glazed polychrome tiles.

Ceramic building material by site period

Period 1: Late Saxon/Norman (10th–11th centuries)

Of the building material recorded within Period 1 contexts, 87% (by weight) is Romano-British and consists entirely of fragments of bonding tiles. Although the quantity of this material is very small in relation to the total assemblage, the provenance is significant. The majority of the material was recovered on Area A both from use fills and/or structural elements of sunken-floored building *10049*. External surfaces of the tile, including broken edges, are invariably burnt and most of the contexts producing this material relate to a hearth, hearth surrounds and hearth rake-outs (*cf.* re-used lava quernstone fragments used here also as fire pad/surrounds). The re-use of Roman ceramic building material is well documented in medieval Norwich (Drury 1993, 163).

One other concentration of Roman tile was recovered from this period, from disuse fills of the sunken-featured building recorded in Area C (*50242*). Although there were no surviving floor levels within the building, some of the tiles here also show signs of burning and one has a vitrified surface, indicative perhaps of re-use as hearth pads or fire surrounds.

Other material recovered in this phase includes fired clay/?brick (fabrics 300, 136, 202 and 201: all undated). The majority of these pieces weigh less than 1g. These fabrics can only be discussed in very general terms since they lack any specific characteristics (except occasionally where they have impressions of wattle), other than the fact that they are probably the result of brickearth or clay that has been directly or indirectly heated. An example of where this is likely to have occurred is within the building in Area A, where over 200 pieces of fabric 300 were recovered, mainly from contexts associated with its hearth.

Period 2: pre-Friary (12th century–c. 1290)

Some of the material included in this period is later than 1226, post-dating the establishment of the initial phase of the Friary, but recovered from areas that had not yet been absorbed into the precinct at this time. This group includes roof tile (fabric 100), medieval brick (fabrics 107 and 110) and Flemish floor tile (fabric 114).

All the material recovered is from Area C, mainly from pit fills but also from ditch *50661*. The majority is fired clay (fabric 129 and 136), significant quantities of which occur in fills of pit *50628*. The third largest group of material recovered here is fabric 300 (unidentified). Very small, these are probably pieces of fired clay or brickearth: such material, if recovered in large enough quantities, is a good indication of fires in the near vicinity. Pit *50444* and dump *50427* both produced over 100g of this material.

Roman material recovered here includes imbrex fragments (fabric 132), and bonding tiles (fabric 127 and 135). These came mainly from pit and ditch fills, where they are likely to have been redeposited during the 12th century (Period 2.1).

Periods 3.1 and 3.2: Friary (c. 1290–1538)

Medieval structures that included ceramic building material in their build were all found in the western part of the site (Area A), and the majority (86% by weight) of the assemblage from the whole excavation was recovered here. These structures included the Friary culvert system, brick and/or flint/stone walls, brick and tile floors, a well, a cellar, a bell-pit and elements of the building sequence on the King Street frontage. Impressions of floor tiles were also apparent in the west walk of the cloister (Pl. 3.7). Much of the material from Friary-related features was sampled individually and the salient points drawn from its analysis are presented below. No ceramic building material was recovered from structures in Areas B and CB at this date, the majority of the material recovered coming from the fills of pits and quarries (no details of this group are given here).

The dominant material within the Friary culvert system was fabric 107. A total of 45 bricks (82.205kg), many complete, were recovered. Other brick types present are fabrics 118, 110, 112 and 113. Two 'later' bricks (fabrics 102 and 134) came from culvert *12102*. A considerable proportion of the fabric 102 bricks occur in Period 3 contexts, providing the earliest known date for these bricks in Norwich. Elsewhere in Eastern England bricks of this type were introduced by Flemish and German craftsmen in the mid-15th century (Drury 1993). The lack of this type of brick from other sites in Norwich before the latter half of the 16th century, however, led Drury to suggest that it was the domination of earlier brick-making traditions in the city which excluded these 'later bricks' from earlier contexts. Four complete bricks in fabric 134 (representing over 74% of the total fabric recovered on site) also came from culvert *12102*. This brick is similar to some of Drury's type LB2 bricks which appear on the Duke's Palace site (169N) in contexts probably as early as the first half of the 16th century.

Fragments of roof tile were also recovered from other elements of the culvert system (fabrics 100 and 104 from *10652 etc.*, *10713 etc.*, *10712 etc.* and *10524 etc.*). One fragment of floor tile fabric 125 was recovered in drain *10712*, context *10752*.

Within the possible Friary kitchen in the west range were the remnants of a brick and tile floor (*10848*, Period 3.2). The majority of the ceramic building material was Flemish floor tiles (fabric 114), with a total of 13 pieces (2.150kg) being recovered. Two English tiles were also present (fabric 101), along with brick fabric 107 and fragments of roof tile (fabric 100). The large hearth (*12504*: Pl. 3.9) was mainly constructed of bricks (fabrics 107, 100, 115 and 118), with a single fragment of Flemish floor tile being recovered (fabric 133) and one piece of roof tile (fabric 100).

A brick and tile floor was constructed in the passage to the north of the kitchen (Period 3.2). Thirteen brick fragments were collected from the floor and its make-up, along with eleven floor tiles (four of them almost complete) and four roof tile fragments. The floor itself (*12131*) consisted of plain glazed local tiles (fabric 128) and Flemish tiles (fabric 114), as well as brick fragments (fabrics 107 and 110). The floor was evidently patchy and the presence of a variety of constituents may imply repairs.

The passage to the south of the kitchen also had a tiled floor (*10849*, Period 3.2) consisting of English and Flemish floor tiles (fabrics 101 and 133 respectively). Another area of flooring in the same passage consisted largely of Flemish floor tiles (*10511*/*10791*, Period 3.2). Thirty pieces were recovered (fabrics 114 and 133: 7.775kg). One English tile was recovered (fabric 128). The remaining material is fragmentary, consisting mainly of roof tiles (fabric 100). Only one small early brick fragment was found (fabric 107).

In *c.* 1400, a stone building and associated culvert system were constructed in the western half of Area A (Period 3.2). Approximately 24% of all ceramic building material recovered in Period 3 came from these contexts alone, many of the retained pieces having been selected on site as representative examples. The retrieved material therefore forms a sub-sample of the total assemblage recorded on site.

The majority of the ceramic building material recovered from the building sequence on the King Street frontage (Period 3.2) is early brick (notably fabrics 107, 113, 106 and, to a lesser degree, fabrics 110 and 118). Later bricks were recovered from the pad of bricks within one building which may have formed the base of a staircase (*12149*), indicating that this may have been a later addition. Roof tiles were also recovered, having been re-used to construct walls. One medieval English floor tile was used in a remedial buttress to wall *10991*.

Building materials were recovered from construction, use and disuse deposits relating to the bell-founding pit (Period 3.2) on the King Street frontage. A total of 2.215kg of brick fragments came from construction and use deposits, and were mainly in fabric 107. Other, smaller fragments included fabrics 110 and 115. Two of the fabric 107 fragments are shaped, one with a rounded moulded end and the other with a chamfered corner, suggesting that they were re-used from elsewhere. Bricks with such mouldings would have been used in decorative brickwork such as windows or door jambs. Six fragments of roof tile (fabric 100) may have been used to level the construction of the bell mould. One brick (*12381*) is over-fired, indicating exposure to intense heat.

Disuse deposits within the bell-pit included 96 fragments of ceramic building material (7.809kg), although many were too small for identification. One complete brick was recovered (fabric 112) and small pieces in fabrics 107, 115 and 121 were present. Two late brick fragments (fabric 102) may have been misidentified due to their small size. High temperatures often change the appearance of fabrics, and eight of the recovered pieces were burnt. Mortar was found on many fragments. Twenty-nine fragments of roof tile were recovered (fabrics 100, 103, 104, 105). Of note was the recovery of 51 pieces of fabric 300, with an average weight of 1.2g. These small pieces are clearly the result of an adjacent fire, representing either burnt brickearth or splinters of brick and tile.

Period 4.1: Dissolution (1538–66)

The majority of ceramic building material recovered from Dissolution-period deposits came from Area A, with the remainder from Area B. This distribution is unsurprising given the location of Friary buildings. Most of the brick types present are consistent with those occurring in Friary-related deposits, including some of the later types.

All of the roof tile types reflect those present in the Friary period (coming from Areas A, B and C/B). Although fabric 100 was clearly the dominant fabric it was invariably found alongside other roof tile fabrics, including 103, 104, 105, 108, 111, 116 and 117. Again, the majority of the floor tile came from Area A, including a few pieces of post-medieval tile. The majority of the tiles are Flemish, with a few English types.

Structural metalwork

Door and window fittings
by Val Fryer
(Fig. 5.8)

Hinge

Goodall (1993, 148) states that hinge straps with ornate scrolled or bifurcated terminals, such as the example from Greyfriars, are of high quality and reminiscent of medieval ecclesiastical fittings. A similar piece from Alms Lane, Norwich (*ibid*., fig. 112 no. 1186), is from a late 13th-century context.

SF2636 Broad iron **hinge strap** with bifurcated terminal. Four surviving attachment holes.
pit fill 13379, Period 2

Latch rests

Two complete latch rests (SF294 and 946) and hinge pivots (SF335 and 1930) were recovered, along with several possible fragments. The latch rests are of a simple form with tapering straight shanks. The hinge pivots would have been used for doors, shutters or gates and vary in size accordingly. Both of the examples from Greyfriars are of the simple L-shape.

SF294 **Latch rest**
pit fill 40024, Period 3.2

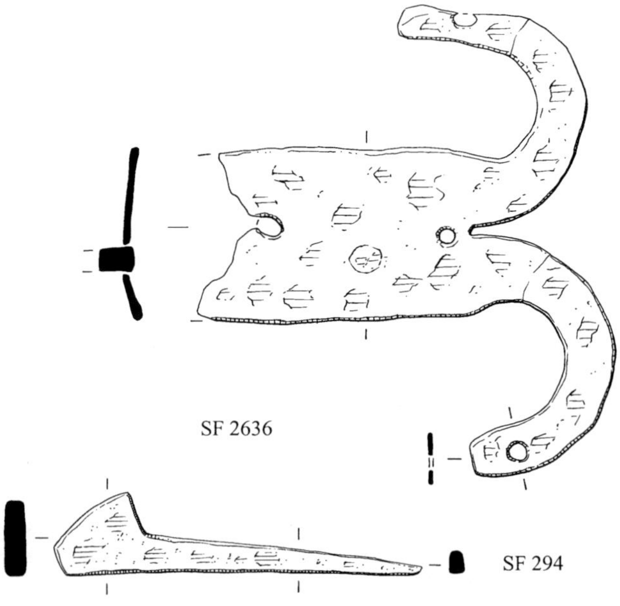

Figure 5.8 Iron door/window fittings: hinge (SF2636), latch rest (SF294). Scale 1:2.

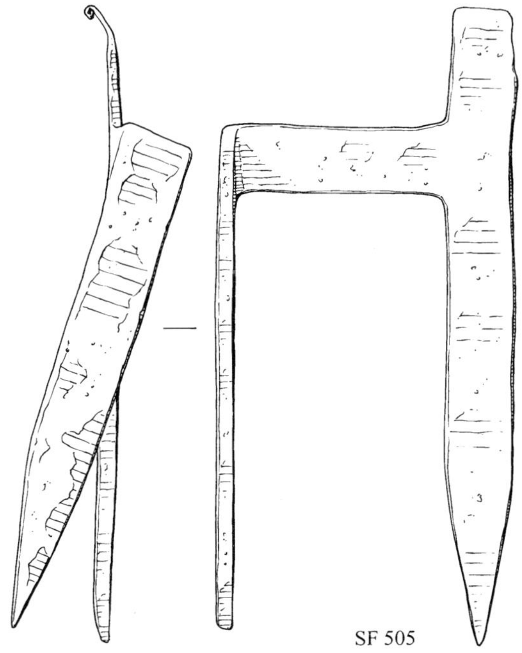

Figure 5.9 Iron fence post base (SF505). Scale 1:4.

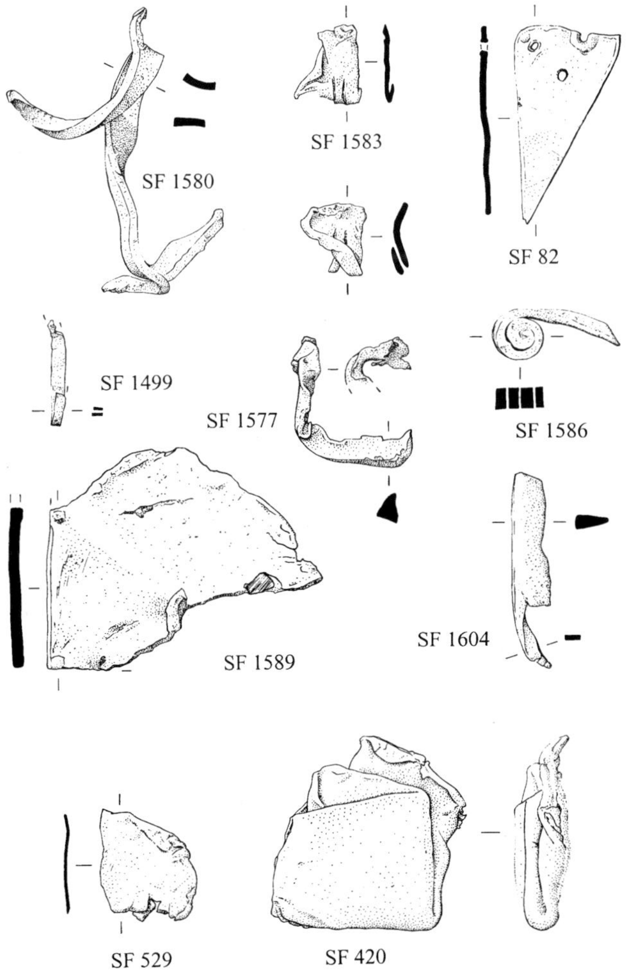

Figure 5.10 Leadwork (SF1580, 1583, 82, 1499, 1577, 1586, 1589, 1604, 529, 420). Scale 1:2.

Garden ironwork
by Val Fryer
(Fig. 5.9)

Fence-post base

This type of fence base is known from other 18th–19th-century contexts, including formal gardens. The shape would facilitate the positioning of the fence and ensure a firm setting if placed within a solid footing. Its archaeological provenance indicates a direct link with an excavated pathway, running along the outside of the southern wall of the former Friary precinct.

SF505 Probable iron **fence post base**, 'h' shaped with shorter arm set at 90 degrees to the main upright. Latter cut/snapped at top.
path 50697, Period 4.2

Leadwork
by Geoff Egan
(Figs 5.10 and 5.11)

The following three categories of finds attest to leadworking, including casting and possibly soldering, though none of them is definitive of a specific product. Many of the sheet offcuts, trimmings and runnels are likely to represent construction or maintenance and repair of roofing and drainage provision such as guttering. They probably represent construction or maintenance and repair of major buildings, perhaps relating to the religious institution. Some of these items could relate to metal-working for the production of saleable goods and sheet fragments could be from coffins, although in the absence of any specific indication they are catalogued together here.

Runnels/spillage

(A further 37 runnels and three droplets are not catalogued below. The 20 runnels from Period 4.1 and 4.2 and four from Period 5 are not catalogued here.)

SF1580 Small **trimming**
fill 11227, Period 3.1

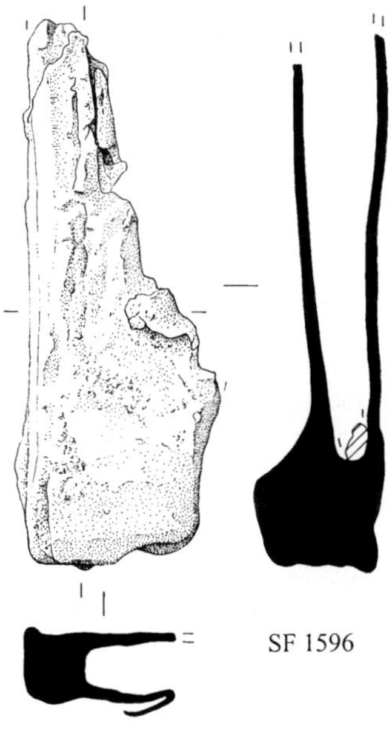

Figure 5.11 Lead setting (SF1596). Scale 1:2.

SF1583 A & B Two fragments partly cut into strips along one edge, presumably to facilitate the use of small pieces, perhaps for soldering (*cf.* ingot SF530 and sheeting SF265).
pit fill 11099, Period 2.3

Sheeting

Forty-one pieces of lead sheeting were recovered from a range of contexts of Periods 3–5 (Period 3 x 11; Period 4 x 6; Period 5 x 7; and 17 other contexts). Most pieces are offcuts of under 100mm x 100mm; surfaces are rough (uneven from having been cast on a sand bed) on one side only, though abrasion sometimes makes this unclear. The largest fragment from Period 3 measured *c.* 80mm x 14mm, from Period 4 *c.* 73mm x 73mm and from Period 5 110mm x 47mm. Some pieces appear to be offcuts resulting from removal of irregularly cast edges. Only the illustrated pieces are catalogued below.

SF82 Triangle 52 x 27mm; two holes, one at the edge
surface cleaning 40005, Period 3.2

SF1499 Narrow strip/trimming
fill 30200, Period 2.3

SF1577 Offcut of irregularly cast edge
pit fill 30470, Period 2.3

SF1586 Rolled-up strip
fill 30100, Period 3.1

SF1589 Offcut of irregularly cast edge
pit fill 11060, Period 3.1

SF1604 Offcut of irregularly cut edge
pit fill 10783, Period 3.2

Setting

A setting, presumably for holding an iron bar in masonry, is similar to lead spindle whorl SF635 (below, p.136).

SF1596 make-up *10753*, Period 1

Miscellaneous

A number of lead items were recovered from unphased contexts. Two items of particular interest are catalogued here and may relate to building maintenance and repair.

SF420 Piece of **sheeting** crumpled into a tight ball, perhaps in preparation for the melting pot.
unstratified

SF529 Piece of **sheeting**, partly cut into strips along one side, presumably to facilitate the use of small pieces. *cf.* SF1583 and 530.
unstratified

Window glass and came

Window glass

by David King

(Figs 5.12 and 5.13)

A total of 249 fragments of window glass were recovered, a full catalogue of which is given in the project archive. Small find numbers were allocated to groups of glass on site and are therefore referenced below with additional reference to analysis catalogue numbers for clarity. The catalogue numbers relate to individual glass fragments.

Glass from pit 60633

Forty-one fragments of window glass were recovered from two fills of pit *30633* (*30007*/*30632* and *30006*/*30631*), which was located near the centre of Area B (Period 3.2). Many are painted and include some of the most significant pieces found on the site. Several of the pieces can be allocated a particular date range within the medieval period. Three fragments (SF1078 and SF1385, cat. nos 94–6 and 166: not illustrated) have smear shading, a technique with a relatively short span of usage of *c.* 1330–80, when it was replaced by stipple shading.

Two fragments (SF1385, cat. nos 164 and 168) have naturalistic foliage characteristic of the period *c.* 1280–1350 while another (SF1078, cat. no. 92) is a magnificent lion mask of a type current in the 14th century. Other contemporary pieces are the fragment of a small crucifixion (SF1078, cat. no. 93), the hawthorn diaper fragment (SF1081, cat. no. 103) and the relieved foliage fragment (SF1385, cat. no. 163). The other fragments are also consistent with a date in the 14th century. If these fragments were from the same window or group of windows, as their style suggests, the combined dating evidence would give a fairly precise date of *c.* 1330–50. The glass was found in association with 15th–16th-century pottery, indicating that deposition may have taken place during the Dissolution.

The proposed date-range for the glass fits in well with the documentary evidence for the construction of the monastic church and other buildings. The glass could possibly have come from the church, which appears to have been completed by *c.* 1330, but the location of the find is just to the south of the claustral range of buildings, thought to have been built in the period *c.* 1330–50, and it seems more likely that the glass is from this complex.

Although these fragments were found in association with the same feature, it is of course not possible to say with certainty how many windows they came from, although their stylistic homogeneity would point to them being from either one window or a number of related windows. The presence of the Crucifixion fragment would suggest that the building involved was an important one and also had a religious function. This suggests strongly that the glass from pit *30633* was from the Greyfriars monastic buildings, possibly the church but more probably the cloister, refectory, library or chapter house.

It is possible to imagine a context for the present fragments within a single window which contained figured glazing including the Crucifixion, against a background of hawthorn diaper, with other relieved foliage in the tracery and a border of running vine leaf and lion masks, a band of naturalistic leaf grisaille at the bottom, and canopy work at the top of the main lights.

This type of 'band' window, combining areas of solid coloured glazing with a band of lighter grisaille, was current at this period, and an almost-complete example of *c.* 1340–50 can be seen in the west window of the church of St John the Baptist, Mileham, Norfolk, although here the border motif is different (King 1974, 32). The motif of lion mask with vine stem does appear in roughly contemporary Norfolk glass, however, notably in excavated glass from the church of All Saints, Barton Bendish, where the vine stem comes from the mouth of the lion. This glass is dated on heraldic evidence to *c.*1350–70 (King 1987, 34–9, fig. 32). A lion mask from a border without the vine stem is recorded in a drawing of the glass of *c.* 1345 in the church of St Mary, Elsing, Norfolk (G.A. King Coll.).

The precise iconographic function of the small Crucifixion is not clear in the absence of further evidence. A single small votive figure may have been the context, but it could also have formed part of a representation of the Trinity of the type known as an Italian Trinity, with Christ on the Cross supported by God the Father and the Dove hovering between them. Such a representation was to be found in glass of *c.* 1380–1400 in the church of St Peter, Ringland, Norfolk: this is now lost, but is recorded in a drawing (G.A. King Coll.). It could also, in a Franciscan context, have been part of a representation of St Francis of Assisi receiving the stigmata. A later fragmentary panel with this subject survives in the church of St Peter Mancroft, Norwich (King forthcoming). It probably came from a window in the north chancel chapel given by Robert Ryngman, suffragan Bishop of Gathy, in 1453. He was appointed by Bishop William Alnwick of Norwich in 1426 and died in 1453, asking to be buried in the Franciscan house in Norwich. His donor portrait in the glass shows him dressed as a bishop, with a knotted rope around his waist showing that he was a member of the Third Order of St Francis. He may, of course, also have provided a window for the Greyfriars church, but no trace of any glass of that date was recovered.

The finely drawn fragment with a lion mask has the lion looking to the left, and was therefore presumably part of the right-hand border of the window. Fourteenth-century border motifs in English painted glass consisted normally of foliage, heraldry or grotesques, but the possibility must be raised that the combination here and at Barton Bendish of lion mask and vine stem may have had a religious significance. The vine stem is associated in medieval art and theology with Christ, as for example in the Tree of Jesse iconography which shows the ancestry of Christ leading from Jesse to Christ set in a tree, regularly shown as a vine at this period, from the words of Jesus in St John's Gospel XV 1, 'I am the true vine'. The lion is linked with David, the lion of Judah, and thereby to Jesus his descendant, and both are linked in the Revelation of St John V 5: 'And one of the elders said unto me, Weep not: behold, the Lion of the tribe of Juda, the Root of David, hath prevailed to open the book, and to loose the seven seals thereof.' If this connection was intended, it may support the idea that at least the lion mask, vine stem and Crucifixion were in the same window, since a border with Christological symbolism would have been suited to a window containing a Crucifixion.

It is just possible that other glass from the Norwich Greyfriars remains extant. Around 1815 the antiquary Revd David Powell came to Norwich and bought a panel of glass depicting the Crucifixion and was told by the vendor, Stevenson, that it came from the Norwich Greyfriars. Powell's antiquarian manuscripts were sold in 1848 by Thomas Dodd and Thomas Thorpe, but what became of the glass is not known to the present writer (British Library, Additional MS 17462, f.334). What may be the most significant Franciscan glass in Great Britain is the earliest extant donor panel in England, showing Beatrix van Falkenburg (d. 1272). This is now in the Burrell Collection, and is generally thought to have come from the Franciscan house in Oxford (Marks 1993, 11, pl. X), but research in progress is beginning to suggest that this and a number of other panels of glass in museums and parish churches may have come from the Norwich Greyfriars. Details of these attributions must await a subsequent publication. A small amount of glass was found in an excavation of the Oxford Franciscan church ranging in date from the 13th to the 15th century. A much larger amount of glass was recovered from the site of the Cambridge Franciscans in an excavation in 1958. Most of it dated from the second half of the 14th century, a little later than the glass from pit *30633*. As in the present glass, part of a Crucifixion and also a lion mask were found. In addition there were parts of an Annunciation, Virgin with Child and a female saint, angels, a friar, canopy work and a ruby diaper with a pattern showing a monkey with a tambourine (Salway 1996, 19–20, pls I and II).

Excavated glass from the Walsingham Greyfriars was published in 1933. Here a large quantity of small fragments were found, which are described as being mainly of 15th-century date. However, the published drawings of 24 pieces would suggest a date in the second half of the 14th century (Martin 1933, 265–6). A few fragments of much lesser interest have also been found on the sites of the Franciscan houses at Grantham (Rogerson in prep.) and Lincoln (Lincoln Archaeological Reports, forthcoming; further glass from this site excavated by the City of Lincoln Archaeological Unit will be recorded archivally). Christopher Woodforde (Woodforde 1937) published a number of other panels of glass which had Franciscan associations, if not actually coming from Franciscan houses.

Other window glass

A few fragments of glass found in other contexts deserve mention. Catalogue nos 43 (SF741, context *50042*: not illustrated) and 226 (SF2579, context *13016*) are painted with the cross-hatching characteristic of stiff-leaf grisaille glazing which is mainly of the first half of the 13th century, although it can occur later. This type of glazing was very common (Marks 1993, 124–36) and is found in many excavations. Its relative scarcity *in situ* in extant glazing in Norfolk is due partly to the extensive rebuilding of churches which occurred in the 14th and 15th centuries, although small quantities survive at (for example) Drayton, Saxlingham Nethergate and Pulham St Mary the Virgin. Interesting fragments of this type were found at Horsham St Faith's Priory and at St Olave's Priory. Catalogue no. 18 (SF707) is a piece from grisaille glazing without cross-hatching, which most often dates from *c.* 1250–80 but which can be found until *c.* 1300. A similar fragment has been found at Langley Abbey. In the first half of the 14th century, and sometimes a little earlier, grisaille glazing used naturalistic leaf forms, and these are to be seen on catalogue nos 16 (SF704, context *30027*) and 224 (SF2575, context *13124*). Sometimes the foliage designs were painted on diamond quarries with strapwork borders, and quarry fragments with strapwork occur as catalogue nos 18 (SF707, context *40026*) and 64 (SF916, context *30296*). Catalogue nos 217 (SF2561, context 13001) and 237 (SF2675, context *13422*) have designs associated with late 13th–14th-century glass. The grisaille glazing of both 13th- and 14th-century date is a type of decoration which was used for less important windows in churches and monastic buildings, although it could also be combined with figured panels. Catalogue no. 126 (SF1215, context *30834*) is a fragment of canopy probably of late 14th-century date, and would have been placed over some kind of figured glazing.

Norwich's medieval glaziers

Immediately following the period to which the glass from pit *30633* is dated, glaziers from many parts of England were impressed to work on the glazing of St Stephen's Chapel, Westminster, for Edward III. These included Adam Hadesco of Norwich who was paid sixpence a day for breaking and fitting glass in 1351. He was one of a small group of glaziers who lived in Norwich around the middle of the 14th century and who owned properties next door to each other at the top of Conesford and backing onto the Castle Meadow, and who were thus more or less opposite the west end of the Greyfriars church. It is possible — perhaps probable — that at least one of them was involved in the glazing of the Friary buildings. The earliest reference to Adam Hadesco is that in the accounts for 1351 of St Stephen's Chapel (Woodforde 1950, 10).

Presumably Hadesco was already an active and fully-trained glazier when he was impressed by the king, and could therefore have been available to do work just before this date on the Friary windows. The latest reference to him during his life is in 1384–5, when the city court rolls for Norwich record that he sold a property to John de Aylesham, furbour, which can be shown to have been on the corner of Conesford at the point where the road called Boar Lane, which also bordered onto the Castle Meadow, joined that street (NCCR, 14m.21). If this sale marked the end of his working life, and if it had begun as suggested just before 1350, this would correspond quite closely with the average working life of 35 years which has been found to be the case for Norwich medieval glaziers for whom both the date of their enrolment as freemen and of their will is known. (These calculations do not count the apprenticeship which would have preceded the enrolment.) Adam Hadesco was presumably related to John Hadesco, who was employed at Westminster working on the glass for Windsor Castle in 1352–3 (Woodforde 1950, 10). He was dead by 1377–8, when Agnes de Hengham, his late wife, sold a property in the parish of St Michael at Plea. This was next door to another property which she owned, which had formerly belonged to her husband (NCCR, 14m.1d). The dates suggest that John was either an elder brother or the father of Adam.

The earliest reference to any of the glaziers in this mid-14th-century group is in a deed of 1348, when Gilbert Sadler, elsewhere referred to as a glazier (*vitrarius*), is mentioned as the owner of a tenement in King Street which was very probably the one immediately to the south of that of Adam Hadesco, since his son and heir Henry sold that property in 1377–8 (Kirkpatrick MSS and NCCR 14m.3.). In that same year, Henry also sold the property on the west side of Adam's messuage together with Agnes, late wife of Gilbert Sadler (NCCR 14m.1.). Gilbert and Agnes had also bought a nearby shop on Tombland next to the cemetery of St Mary the Less in 1357, which lay immediately to the north of their house and workshop (Cal. Nch. Deeds, Priv. 92). The sandwiching of the property of Adam Hadesco between those of Gilbert and Henry Sadler suggests that they may have worked together, perhaps in the workshop in St Mary the Less. John Hadesco may have also been part of the same team of glaziers.

There is one more glazier who is known to have lived in Norwich at this time and who may have played an even more important part in the glazing of the Franciscan Friary, as he is documented as being a glass painter. It is often impossible to tell from the documentary sources whether a person designated as a glazier, verrer or glasswright was engaged in the leading functions in a workshop of producing designs for windows and painting them, or whether he or she was performing one of the less important tasks such as cutting the glass or leading it up.

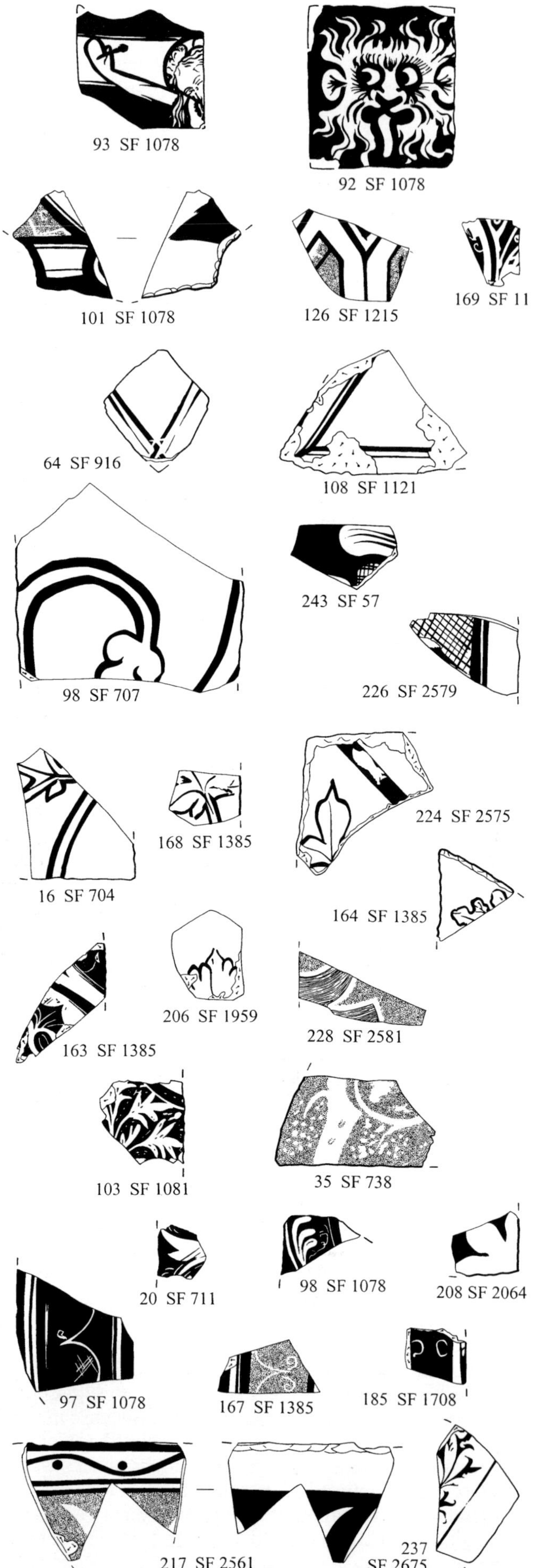

Figure 5.12 Window glass (cat. nos 93, 92, 101, 126, 169, 64, 108, 98, 243, 226, 16, 168, 224, 164, 163, 206, 228, 103, 35, 20, 98, 208, 97, 167, 185, 217, 237). Scale 1:2.

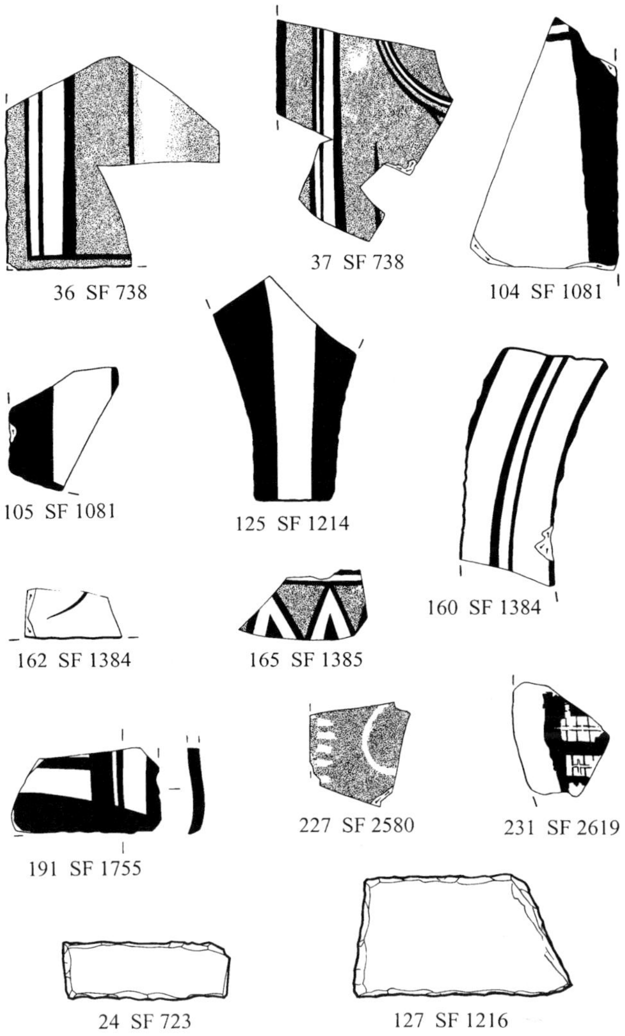

Figure 5.13 Window glass (cat. nos 36, 37, 104, 105, 125, 162, 165, 160, 191, 227, 231, 24, 127). Scale 1:2.

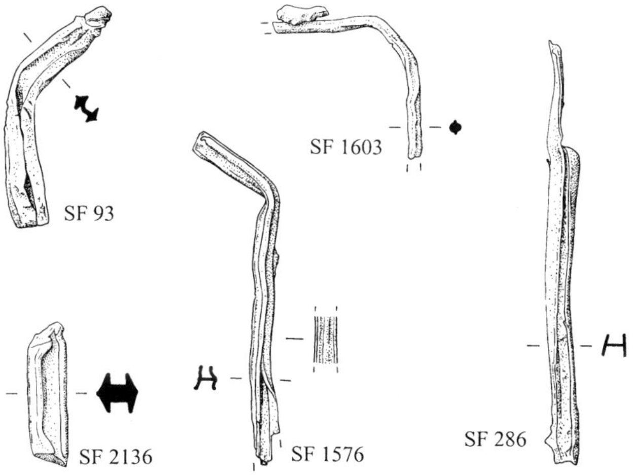

Figure 5.14 Lead window came (SF93, 1603, 2136, 1576, 286). Scale 1:2.

However, Robert of Norwich was one of those recorded as working in 1351 in St Stephen's Chapel, Westminster, where he was paid 7d a day for painting glass. He was presumably the same person as Robert Glaswright, who in 1397 was recorded as the former owner of a property within the Castle Fee (Woodforde 1950, 10), which property was in 1457–8 mentioned as being in the parish of St Peter Parmentergate (C.A.R.). Thus, although he did not live in the cluster of properties opposite the Greyfriars church at the top of King Street, he did own a property a little further down, possibly the messuage with shops and gardens which was bought in 1384–5 by William de Senneed (St Neots), glazier, and sold in 1388–9 to Robert Frenge, painter (N.C.C.R., 14m.29d and 30). In the 15th century, the part of King Street in North Conesford was an important centre for glass-painting (Wallace 1992, 19–29).

It is of course not possible to know for certain which, if any, of these glaziers worked on the Franciscan Friary, but the fact that they existed where they did and that some of them are known to have worked immediately after the probable date of the glass on buildings of royal patronage, combined with the lack of any references to any other glaziers at this time in the city, argues strongly that the Friary would have looked to these glaziers rather than to any further afield. An additional support to this idea is that these glaziers may have lived where they did precisely because of the work available nearby.

Illustrated items are listed as follows: cat. no.; SF no.; context; size in cm; date.

Period 3.1: Friary
24 SF723, *40127,* 3.5, medieval
160 SF1384, *30941*, 4, medieval
162 SF1384, *30941*, 2.5, medieval
208 SF 2064, *12582*, 3.5, C14

Period 3.2: Friary
35 SF738, *30006*, 3, C14/15
36 SF738, *30006*, 4.5, 1330–80
37 SF738, *30006*, 2.5, C14/15
97 SF1078, *30632*, 3, C14/15
98 SF1078, *30632*, 3.5, C14
104 SF1081, *30632*, 4, medieval
105 SF1081, *30632*, 2.5, medieval
125 SF1214, *30834*, 2.5, medieval
127 SF1216, *30834*, 5, medieval
165 SF1385, *30632*, 2, C14/15
167 SF1385, *30632*, 2, C14
169 SF1385, *30632*, 2, C14
185 SF1708, *30632*, 2.5, C14/15
191 SF1755, *30646*, 3.5, C14/15
206 SF1959, *2130*, 2.5, C14/15

Period 4.1: Dissolution
108 SF1121, *30015*, 2, C14
227 SF2580, *13016*, 1.5, medieval
228 SF2581, *13017*, 2, 1330–80
231 SF2619, *13222*, 2, medieval

Period 5: modern
20 711, *10346*, 2.5, C14/15

Unstratified
243 57, u/s, 3, 1200–80

Lead window came
by David King
(Figs 5.14 and 5.15)

The occurrence of two types of medieval came — A and C (King 1987, 39) — may suggest that at least two different workshops were involved with the glazing carried out on

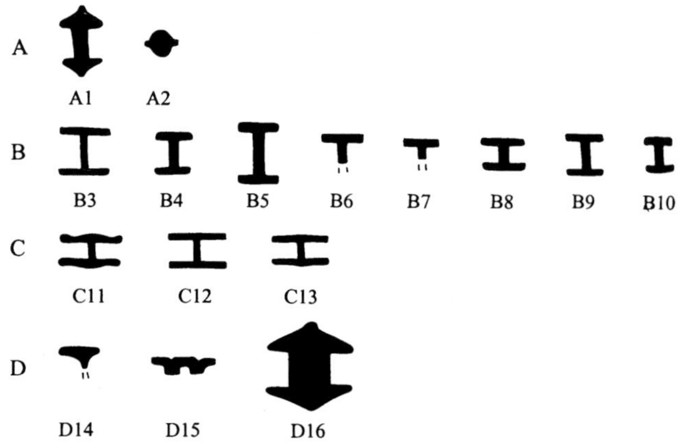

Figure 5.15 Typology of lead window came (types A–D). Scale 1:1.

the site. The came is consistent with the window glass finds, which are mainly dateable to the period 1280–1380, but with a few earlier fragments. Whether this suggests that type A is the earlier of the two types cannot be definitely established, however. The post-medieval leads have a very variable tooth-count of the milling. At Barton Bendish, the later post-medieval leads have a reduced tooth-count, but it is not certain whether this can be applied to the leads here.

One item (SF2136) is of particular interest, as it suggests that lead-casting was carried out on the site or nearby in the post-medieval or modern period. A possible explanation for this fragment is the existence of the firm of William Winter, painter, glazier and plumber from at least 1877 until 1900 at 25 Prince of Wales Road. The garden of this property on the 1885 Ordnance Survey map is about 11.5m from the north-east corner of Area B, and thus near enough for this unstratified object, found in Area C, to have been a stray discard from there, particularly since the ground to the south of No. 25 was open garden in the 1880s.

SF93 A section of medieval lead **window came** *c.*650mm long, type A. The heart is 3.5mm wide and the flange 5mm.
unstratified

SF1576 Three sections of post-medieval **window came**, 140mm in total length, with a heart 2mm wide and flange 6.7mm. The tooth count on the milling is 15 per 20mm.
demolition debris 30553, Period 4.1

SF1585 A section of split **window came**, possibly from a tie, probably medieval. The flange is 5mm wide.
fill of pit 30284, Period 1

SF1603 Two sections of medieval split **window came** type A, with a flange 3.5mm wide but squashed. One piece has a blob of solder attached. Total length 95mm.
unstratified

SF2136 Section of post-medieval/modern **window came** cast from mould before being passed through a lead-mill. The profile is similar to type A. The heart is 4mm wide and the flange 9.5mm. The piece is 37mm long and is chopped off at each end by a heavy knife or shears.
unstratified

Water pipes

Lead water pipes

by Geoff Egan
(Fig. 5.16)

Traces of a lead water pipe system supplying the Friary had survived robbing during the Dissolution period (see Chapter 3.III, 'Water management system'). Such lead piping appears to be a characteristic find at the sites of religious houses (*e.g.* Egan forthcoming d, with references).

SF628 Lead **water pipe**. Offcut from end; flat along one side; squashed (restored in Fig. 5.16 to D: 25mm). ?Cut off during maintenance.
make-up 11163, Period 3.1

SF1573 Lead **water pipe**. Slightly curved, D: 10mm, surviving length 140mm.
demolition debris 30911, Period 5

Ceramic water pipes

by Richenda Goffin
(Fig. 5.17)

Sixty-one fragments of hollow cylinders were identified as water pipes, all of late medieval/post-medieval date. The fabric is hard and well-fired with creamy-buff surfaces and an oxidised pinkish-orange core; the inner and outer margins are buff. Both the inner and outer surfaces are smoothed. None of the pipes is glazed. Dimensions are given in Table 8. The tapering shape would have enabled the pipes to be fitted together to produce a continuous pipeline. The flanged pipes are similar to Williams type H, with a deep up-curving flange near to the cylinder top (Williams D. 1984, fig. 17). No evidence of sealing of the joints was noted. It is unclear whether such ceramic pipes were used in drains or for water supply. Either way, such pipes are not common finds, although they are known from other ecclesiastical sites in the region. Twenty-nine fragments of drainpipe recovered from two drains excavated at Thetford Priory were of an earlier date (Coppack 1976). They were made from an orange-brown sandy fabric, and were tapered with a flange at one end and slightly flared at the other. The pipes had been made in two lengths, 340mm and 235mm, both of which were shorter than the Greyfriars examples.

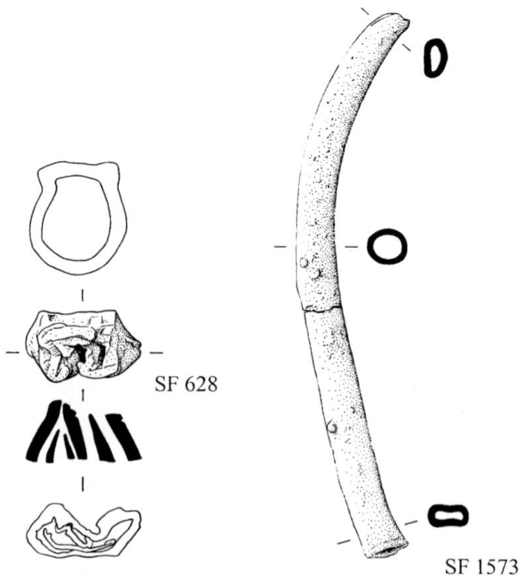

Figure 5.16 Lead pipe (SF628, 1573). Scale 1:2.

Figure 5.17 Ceramic water pipe (from context *50115*). Scale 1:4.

The two drains were associated with a piscina inserted into the wall of the southern presbytery aisle and with the rebuilding of the infirmary, both dating to the 15th century (Coppack 1976, 90).

A survey of comparable sectional ceramic water pipes has been produced by D. Williams (1984, 145). Ceramic drainpipes have also been recovered in Norwich from the recent excavations at Dragon Hall, King Street (Anderson 2005). These were made from a post-medieval red sandy fabric, but were both longer and of greater diameter than those from the Greyfriars excavations. They also had a flange at one end, with a slightly thickened other end with no actual flange. The drain containing the pipes at Dragon Hall was sampled *in situ,* and was associated with deposits containing 18th-century pottery.

At Norwich Greyfriars, 46 fragments were recovered from a pipeline relating to a formal post-medieval garden (*50115*, Period 4.2), including three pipes that were substantially complete. All were made from the same hard, well-fired fabric and were creamy-buff in colour, sometimes with an inner core which was pale orange-pink. The fabric was comparatively fine with moderate quartz inclusions up to 0.5mm in length, and moderate black and red ferrous inclusions up to 1mm in length. One of the pipes was uniformly orange in section but had a buff and pink/orange external surface. The pipes were unglazed, with smooth external surfaces. Such an off-white fabric with grog and ferrous inclusions is indicative of a late medieval or post-medieval date (similar to fabric 9 of Anderson's Dragon Hall fabric series: Anderson 2005).

Further fragments of drainpipe were found unstratified. A single piece of pipe made from a wider diameter than those identified from *50115* was found in context *12563*. It was made from a buff/orange pink fabric which was slightly sandier.

Twelve fragments from a minimum of two pipes were also found in context *12057*. These were more finely made than those recovered from *50115*, and had a slightly larger diameter. They were also made from a sandier fabric. Two joining rim fragments of water pipe recovered from *12152* were also made in a buff-pink yellow fabric similar to the above.

The pipes from context *50115* all had the same form, although their diameters varied (Table 8). At the broadest

	Length	*External diameter (narrow end)*	*External diameter (wide end)*
Water pipe 1	465mm	64mm	92mm
Water pipe 2	462mm	58mm	90mm(?) broken
Water pipe 3	464mm	62mm	96mm
Water pipe 4	330mm (broken)	-	96mm
Water pipe 5	440mm (broken)	-	93mm
Water pipe 6	360mm (broken)	-	93mm
Water pipe 7	332mm (broken)	-	90mm
Water pipe 8	330mm (broken)	62mm	-
Water pipe 9	209mm (broken)	58mm	-

Table 8 Dimensions of water pipes recovered from *50115*

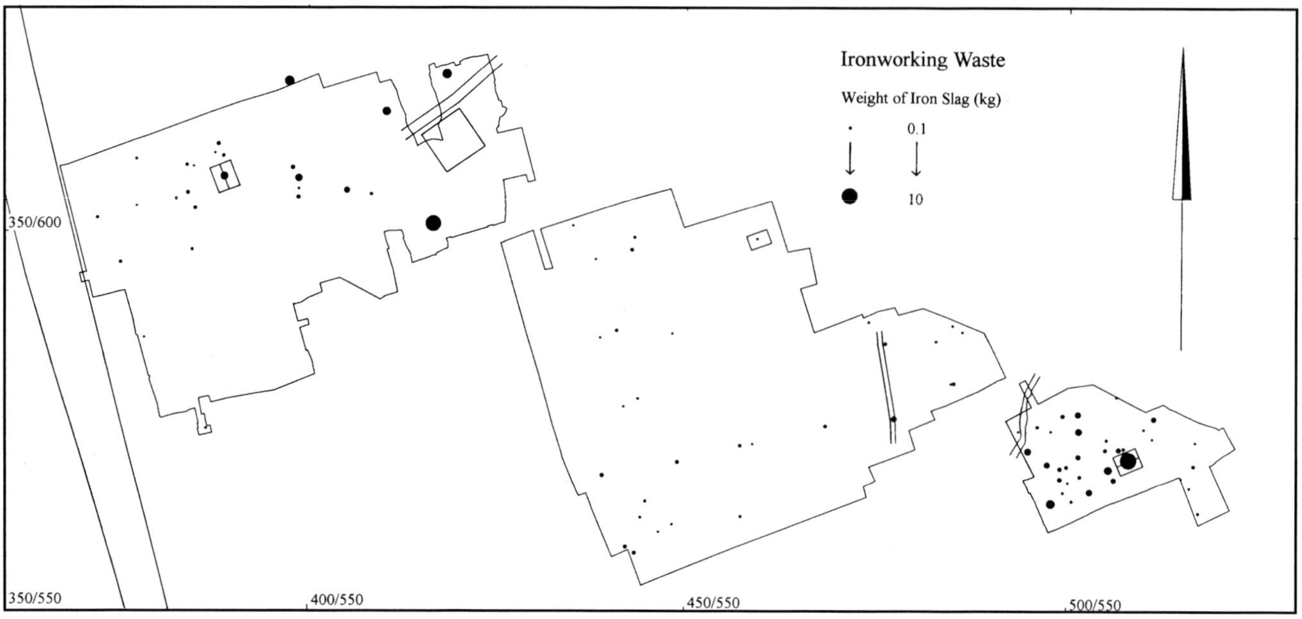

Figure 5.18 Distribution of ironworking waste. Scale 1:1000.

end of the pipe there was an internal recess into which the next piece of pipe would have fitted. The external flange at the other end fitted into another pipe opening.

The fragments of water pipe recovered from the other contexts were simpler in form. Three rims from context *12057* had a slightly thickened edge with no internal or external flange and a diameter of 120mm. There was some evidence of mortar on the top of the rim, which may suggest that individual pipes were butted against each other in the ground. The two joining fragments from *12152* were also of this type, having a simple thickened rim with a diameter of 100mm.

II. OCCUPATIONS, INDUSTRY AND CRAFTS

Ferrous metalworking

by Jane Cowgill and J.M. Mills
(Fig. 5.18)

Introduction

A total of 68.321kg of metalworking slag was recovered from the excavation, the majority of which is probably medieval in date on the basis of both its general appearance and ceramic dating. Given the partial excavation of many features, the recorded slag must be considered an unstructured sample of the material that originally existed on the site. Less than 50% of the slag which must have been present within the excavated area was recovered, and although it is likely that smithing occurred on the site it is therefore difficult to locate the foci of activities. A distribution plot of ironworking waste is presented in Fig. 5.18.

The majority of the recorded slag is either associated with iron-smithing or is of undiagnostic type. There are fifteen small pieces of tap slag (353g; 0.52% of total assemblage). This type of slag is usually associated with smelting but may also be generated in small quantities during smithing. The latter is the most likely source for this material.

The smithing slags have been sub-divided into the following categories:

plano-convex hearth bottoms;
secondary smithing lumps;
cinder;
modern-type secondary smithing lumps.

Nature of the assemblage

Much of the slag was encrusted and had amounts of soil/sand adhering due to the soil conditions. The slag recovered from the samples was often very small in size, individually weighing less than 1g, resulting in a high count compared to the weight. The assemblage came from a total of 437 contexts of which only 121 yielded more

Size range	*Length*	*Width*	*Height*
20–30mm			3
30–40mm	2		4
40–50mm	2		11
50–60mm	1		1
60–70mm	4	2	4
70–80mm	5	3	2
80–90mm	5	6	6
90–100mm	2	2	
100–110mm	4	1	1
110–120mm	1	3	
120–130mm		2	
130–140mm	1	3	
140–150mm		2	
TOTAL	**24**	**28**	**32**

Table 9 Dimensions of hearth bottoms

than 100g of slag (12 with over 1kg); the total weight from these contexts is 55.654kg. Only the groups with more than 100g were used for the following analysis. An explanation of the terms used follows.

Plano-convex hearth bottoms

These are formed in the hottest part of the hearth, just below the tuyere. The terminology should not be taken literally since they do not form in the base of the hearth. The classic shape is a convex base with a flattish top often with a shallow depression formed by the blast of air from the bellows. The examples from this site show the expected diversity in form. Some are elongated, many are part-formed and a few appear to have been re-heated, suggesting that they had been left in the hearth for more than one operation. There is also a considerable diversity in consistency, ranging from the 'normal' black/dark grey dense pieces to lighter green/grey examples high in silica. The weight of the 20 complete hearth bottoms ranges between 63g and 1482g, with the majority weighing between 100g and 400g. Approximately one third of the total assemblage of hearth bottoms has hearth lining attached. Some also contain surprisingly large pieces of stone (usually flint) which must have been introduced into the hearth with the fuel, since the hearth lining seems free from such large inclusions. The dimensions of the hearth bottoms from this site do not have a statistical central tendency but produce a bi-modal distribution (Table 9). While there does not seem to be any chronological or technological explanation for this, the total numbers under consideration are very small.

Secondary smithing lumps

These are defined as part-formed hearth bottoms and develop as slag within the hearth, rather than attached to the hearth wall. They are randomly-shaped pieces of iron silicate generated during the smithing process.

Cinder

This material is silica-rich and represents an intermediate product between the hearth lining and smithing slag.

Modern-type secondary-smithing lumps

This is the relatively vesicular and lighter type of slag often produced when coal or coke is the fuel used for smithing.

Hammerscale

The soil in all the bags containing quantities of slag was checked with a magnet for hammerscale (small flakes or spheroids of iron oxide or slag produced during iron-smithing), which was noted in a number of contexts in moderate quantity. Some contexts produced only single or a very few pieces from samples, but in all these instances only the flots had been checked for the evidence (most hammerscale does not float). The significance of this evidence is that it is considered to be a good indicator that a smithy is present, since it has extremely few secondary uses and its presence on the floor of the smithy is not a hazard.

Fuel

Both charcoal and coal were found incorporated within the slags. The use of charcoal can be inferred from the form of the voids present within the material, which are sometimes quite large. The coal appeared to be of poor quality in all instances, often seeming to be 'shale like'.

Hearth lining

The vitrified clay from the hearths was also analysed. The hearth walls appeared to be constructed from a local sandy clay. A number of possible tuyere fragments were identified but none could be positively confirmed as such.

Chronological discussion

Pre-Friary (Periods 1 and 2)

Only five pieces (0.277kg) of slag came from the sunken-floored building in Area A (*10049*, Period 1), including a hearth bottom weighing 0.133kg from hearth *10439*. The hearth bottom was recorded as being abraded and is therefore unlikely to have been associated with any activity occurring on the hearth. The largest concentration of metalworking waste in Area A is from the post-usage fills of the sunken-floored building, which yielded 1.393kg of smithing slags. This material is fairly mixed, some pieces being recorded as abraded and therefore probably redeposited while others had a more vesicular and 'modern' appearance; the fuel used, however, continues to be charcoal.

Three pieces of slag (0.317kg) came from the construction and use of the sunken-floored building recorded in Area C (*50242*) with a further 4.759kg of smithing slag, hammerscale and 0.162kg of vitrified hearth lining from the backfill. The hearth lining includes one very vitrified fragment which may be part of a tuyere. Associated with the slag is a quantity of both spheroidal and plate hammerscale, suggesting that iron-smithing once occurred in the immediate vicinity of the building, but probably not within it. An adjacent pit (*50458*, Period 1, 0.258kg) also contained small quantities of iron slags. The other large groups are all from pits to the west of this structure, some from fills identified as relating to the use of pits (pit *50311*, Period 3.1, 0.634kg; pit *50616*, Period 2.1, 1.628kg). None of these quantities are particularly noteworthy and therefore the existence of a smithy operating in this building is unlikely. It does seem plausible, however, that some occasional smithing activity was occurring. A possible focus for the activity could be in the area to the west of the building.

A partially-excavated pit in Area B (*30980*; 0.791kg) which lay within the confines of possible building *30332* (Period 1) yielded three possible crucibles, 0.133kg of smithing slag, hearth lining and fuel-ash slag and a large assemblage of bone-working waste. This mixture of craft and industrial waste products has been noted at other urban sites of this date, including Flaxengate, Lincoln (Perring 1981) and Coppergate, York (Bayley 1992).

Evidence for Period 2.1 is scant. Smithing slags are mixed with evidence for non-ferrous metalworking in the form of crucibles and fuel-ash slag incorporating copper droplets. The section across ditch *50492* in Area C produced 1.557kg of slag and both plate and spheroidal hammerscale in some quantity.

Further discussion of pre-Friary metalworking across the site may be found in Chapter 2.IV.

Friary (Period 3)

A pit from this period yielded an interesting assemblage of iron smithing slag. Pit fill *12058* (Period 3.2) contained 3.353kg of smithing slag, three pieces of which were stained extensively by copper alloys and a number with 'shaley' coal or clinker incorporated into the matrix. This material is markedly different to that apparent within the post-usage fills of the earlier sunken-floored building.

Dissolution and later (Periods 4 and 5)

The majority of metalworking waste dating to the Dissolution and later was recovered from Area A (2.713kg), a small amount being recovered from Area B (1.304kg). Most of the metalworking debris is from horizontal deposits, although one sizeable group was found in pit *10651* (Period 4.2; 1.958kg of smithing slags).

Much of the slag from these contexts is described as 'modern-type' and all evidence for fuel suggests that by this date the smiths were using a low quality 'shaley' coal for fuel in the forge. The large amount of clinker present also supports this.

Three deposits dating from the Dissolution period (Period 4.1), excavated in Area D, contained significant quantities of iron-working waste.

13124 (9.764kg): iron slags (including 20 plano-convex bottom fragments), vitrified hearth lining, coal and hammerscale.
13345 (3.185kg): iron slags and coal.
13411 (2.486kg): iron slags; vitrified hearth lining and hammerscale.

The assemblages were all recovered from contexts associated with post-Dissolution robbing of the Friary buildings. Deposits *13124* and *13411* are probably primary dumps of smithing waste because the slags have a fresh appearance and have quantities of hammerscale attached. The slag from *13345* has a more leached and abraded appearance. This may be due to post-depositional factors; alternatively it might (along with the lack of hammerscale) indicate that the slag has been redeposited in a secondary context. A 'shaley' coal was used to fuel the smithing operation, which was probably short term and concerned with the recycling of iron fittings from the Greyfriars' buildings. It is possible, however, that this material was imported onto the site from elsewhere as dumps or levelling.

Non-ferrous metalworking

Ceramic crucibles and litharge cakes

Crucibles
by Richenda Goffin
(Figs 5.19 and 5.20)

Altogether 88 crucible fragments were recovered from the excavation, deriving from contexts assigned to Periods 1–4.2. The metallurgical residues from the crucibles are described by Doonan, below; further broad comments on the crucible assemblage are given by Lentowicz in Chapter 5.III. Two main fabric groups were identified, consisting of TTW and Stamford wares. In addition a small quantity of sherds whose appearance had changed through heat, as well as some sandy variants (including some which were similar to TTW), were also present. Amongst the diagnostic fragments, two different forms of TTW crucibles were recorded and have been catalogued using the typology established for material from excavations in Thetford (Rogerson and Dallas 1984, 156).

The best preserved example from Greyfriars is hemispherical, with a base which has been pushed out by hand. It has an upright but slightly recessed rim with a diameter of 110mm. The remains of the pouring lip from two other vessels were also found in the same context (*50302*: Fig. 5.20 no. 1). Several body sherds of the TTW crucibles have an additional layer of clay, which has subsequently vitrified, applied to the outside of the vessel. Such a layer would have improved the properties of the crucible (Bayley 1992, 755).

Another fragment indicates that smaller crucibles with a U-shaped profile are also present in the assemblage. This rim fragment, recovered from pit fill *30238* (pit *30237*, Period 1), is made from a hard, grey and semi-vitrified fabric which also has an additional layer of vitrified clay still adhering to the exterior (Fig. 5.20 no. 2). The crucible is likely to be a TTW vessel whose appearance has been altered by heat. Similar crucible forms were identified at Thetford, with fabrics described as 'sandy and similar to medium Thetford-ware' (Rogerson and Dallas 1984, 156). A further rim from a more globular vessel was found in context *30558* (pit *30559*, Period 2.3). Although less vitrified, the fabric is still hard to identify with precision, but once again it may have been TTW.

Two fragments from a partially wheelthrown crucible made from a very sandy pale grey fabric were recovered from *50304* (pit *50303*, Period 2.2). The vessel is hemispherical with a slightly recessed rim (Fig. 5.20 no. 3). An additional fragment from a larger vessel from *50302* (pit *50320*, Period 2.2) is made from an off-white sandy fabric of the same shape which also has a slightly recessed rim (Fig. 5.20 no. 4).

Several fragments of Stamford ware crucible were also identified. Five sherds recovered from *11143* (pit *11145*, Period 1) include one which has the remains of an added clay layer still adhering to the exterior, as well as visible evidence of a residue inside. A second fragment has a rounded base with some external sooting, probably

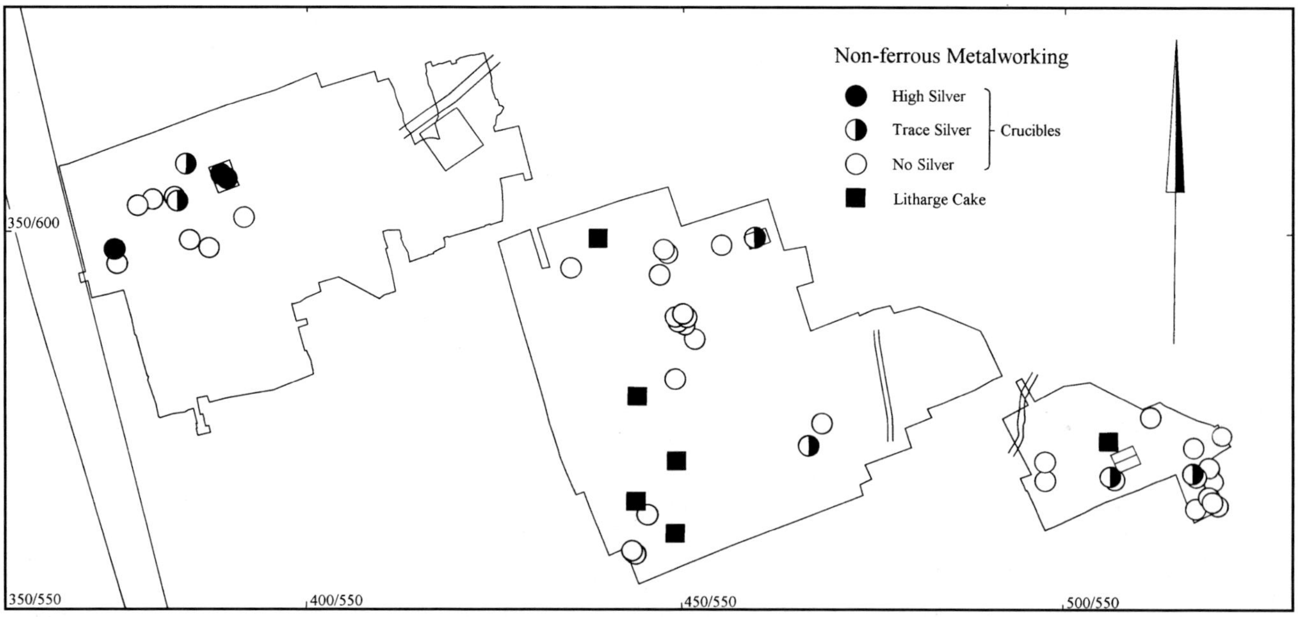

Figure 5.19 Distribution of non-ferrous metalworking waste

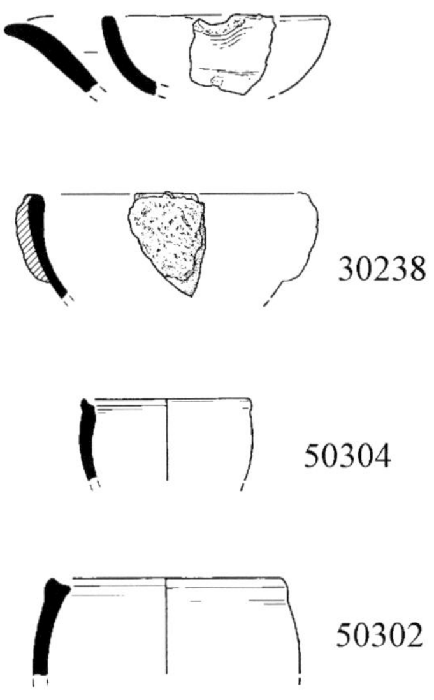

Figure 5.20 Ceramic crucibles. Scale 1:4.

part of an ovoid vessel (Kilmurry Form 19: Kilmurry 1980), which has been used as a crucible. In addition, a single rim sherd from a crucible/ovoid lamp was recovered from this context.

Small globular crucibles made in Stamford ware and dating from the early 10th century onwards have been found on sites in Lincoln (Kilmurry 1980, 142). The larger ovoid form can be dated from the middle of the 11th century, increasing in frequency during the 12th century (*ibid.*). As well as to Lincoln, and also York, Stamford ware crucibles travelled further afield, with many examples recovered from sites in London. Here analytical work on the associated residues from the crucibles has shown that such vessels were particularly used for the melting of silver (Bayley 1991, 405).

Crucible fragments have been recovered from other sites in central Norwich, although usually in smaller quantities. At least one Stamford crucible was recovered from the excavations at Dragon Hall, King Street (Anderson 2005). Excavations nearby at the former Ben Burgess site at 51–53 King Street yielded six fragments of Thetford-type crucible fragments, or TTW variants, but no Stamford ware examples (Goffin forthcoming). Other crucible fragments including examples of Stamford ware were identified at Castle Mall (Lentowicz forthcoming a).

The distribution of non-ferrous metalworking waste (crucibles and litharge cake: see below) is given in Fig. 5.19 and has also been considered further in Chapter 2.IV. Fragments of both main types of fabric were recovered from the earliest phase of activity (Period 1). Sixteen fragments, which were mostly found in a series of pits, were attributed to this earliest period. They included the U-shaped crucible with an added clay layer.

A further 41 fragments came from deposits associated with Period 2 (12th–13th century); these were mostly of TTW or sandy wares. In addition, sherds of Stamford ware from layer *10725* showed high concentrations of silver (see below). These fragments were found in features interpreted as being associated with the disuse of sunken-floored building *10049*.

An additional 27 crucible fragments were recovered from deposits of Period 3 (early 14th–early 16th centuries) and later. By this time the TTW material was residual. Some fragments were recovered from post-Dissolution deposits, such as horticultural features south of the precinct wall.

Catalogue of illustrated sherds
(Fig. 5.20)

1 Thetford-type ware crucible with pouring lip from pit fill *50302* (pit *50320*, Period 2.2)
2 Thetford-type ware crucible fragment with vitrified clay layer from pit fill *30238* (pit *30237*, Period 1)
3 Sandy ware crucible from pit fill *50304* (pit *50303*, Period 2.2)
4 Sandy ware crucible from pit fill *50302* (pit *50320*, Period 2.2)

Metallurgical analysis
by Roger C.P. Doonan
(Fig. 5.19; Pl. 5.1)

Correlations between melt composition and sherd distribution were investigated by the use of cluster and spatial analysis. Such statistical investigations were designed to test hypotheses relating to specialisation and the organisation of metalworking crafts. It is assumed that the findspots recorded for the crucibles correspond with the area in which they were used, although at present there is no direct archaeological evidence which relates findspot to usage.

Numerous sherds excavated from 47 different contexts were submitted for analysis. The crucible fragments were derived from vessels with diameters ranging from 40mm to 120mm. The most common diameter was *c.* 60–80mm; thickness of the fabric ranged from 3mm to 6mm. Some sherds had had their external surface covered in a less refractory coating, although this was not general. Such a layer would have improved the properties of the crucible (Bayley 1984, 107), increasing its thermal capacity and protecting against extremes of temperature and failures brought about by stresses induced by thermal shocks (Bayley 1992, 755). The fabrics represented in the assemblage were either TTW or Stamford wares (see Goffin, above). Both fabrics exhibit excellent refractory properties as there is little evidence of bloating or slagging, deformations typical of ceramics high in quartz temper and with a matrix with high aluminium and low iron and alkali metal contents (Freestone and Tite 1986). Although the refractory properties of Stamford wares have long been acknowledged (Bayley 1992, 754), hand-made TTW has been considered less refractory (Bayley 1984, 107). The sherds in this study described as TTW are wheel-made and have good refractory properties. The lack of evidence for vitrification or slagging on the sherds often made it difficult to determine whether or not they had been used as crucibles. However, close inspection frequently revealed a residue on the sherd which subsequent XRF analysis showed to be rich in metals.

Chemical analysis concentrated on identifying sherds which showed evidence for use as metallurgical crucibles and of the type of metal that was melted. For vessels which had no visible evidence for usage as a crucible, a comparison of XRF spectra of the internal and external surfaces was made to identify any enhanced metal residue on the internal surfaces. There are many problems associated with inferring the composition of an alloy from the composition of the residue on a crucible, especially when the analysis is determined by qualitative XRF analysis. These problems are considered by Bayley (1992, 817–18), to which the reader is directed for a detailed overview.

The absence of slag on the internal surfaces of the crucibles suggests that melting took place under reducing conditions, so that metals did not oxidise and hence flux the crucible fabric. This indicates careful manipulation of the bellows and fuel height to avoid wasting metal in a crucible slag. The low levels of iron in the crucible fabrics meant that it was difficult to infer the redox conditions by the colour of the fabric (red — oxidising, grey — reducing).

Qualitative XRF analysis of the crucible fragments was carried out using a LINK QF200 EDS with a rhodium X-ray tube running at 35KV, with a 4mm collimator and a live time of 50s or 100s. Surfaces were not prepared and comparability is therefore complicated by irregular sample geometry. By noting presence or absence of various elements — specifically iron, copper, zinc, lead, arsenic, tin and antimony — coupled with the relative peak heights for these elements, it was possible to comment on what alloys were melted. These results are listed in Table 10 and for specific sherds in Table 11.

The metals melted at this site were copper alloys, lead and silver. It is possible to be more specific about the copper alloys: XRF results show that brasses, leaded brasses and leaded bronzes were all melted here. It is noted that the crucible debris offered no evidence for simple tin-bronzes, gunmetal or leaded gunmetals. The most common alloy melted was leaded brass. This range of alloys seems to be in agreement with general trends observed for the pre-Conquest period (Blades 1995, 38–42), except perhaps the absence of tin-bronze. The prevalence of leaded copper-based alloys suggests that the most common mode of manufacture was casting, since leaded alloys are known to have unsuitable properties for wrought manufacturing processes.

The eight groups of results shown in Table 10 were formed by cluster analysis performed on relative peak height intensities for elements detected. The most obvious result is that sherds from Group 7 provided no evidence for being used as crucibles. Sherds from this group were found in all areas of the site but the largest concentration came from Area C. Groups 1–6 all represent copper alloys, namely brass, leaded bronze, and leaded brass. Tin was rarely detected above trace levels but this may be due to the poor sensitivity of the XRF in this region of the spectra rather than the absence of the element itself. Based on the results of XRF, the alloys melted in the crucibles were predominantly leaded bronzes and brasses. The size of the crucibles suggests that the metals were probably used for the fabrication of small castings. Area C contained the highest proportion of crucible fragments (44%) whilst Area B contained 36%. Over 85% of crucibles in Area B had been used for melting brass and only 10% for leaded bronze, whereas in Area C nearly 90% of crucibles had been used for melting either leaded brass or leaded bronze, with just over 10% having been used for melting brass. It is possible to relate alloy composition to the manufacturing technique because leaded alloys are only useful for casting whereas unleaded alloys can be wrought. Therefore — based on the distribution of alloy

Group	*Description*	*Metal type*
1	very high Zn. Cu present. Trace Pb	brass
2	very high Pb. Trace Cu/Sn (e.g. Ag (*12300*))	leaded bronze
3	very high Pb. Cu present. Trace Sn. No Zn.	leaded bronze
4	Zn present. Some Pb. Trace of Cu.	brass
5	Zn, Cu. both present. Trace of Pb	brass
6	Cu, Pb, Zn all present	leaded brass
7	Nothing	none
8	High Ag	silver

Table 10 Metal groupings based on qualitative XRF results

Plate 5.1 Litharge cake fragment (SF2328: A), showing scoring caused by removal of silver with a knife (B)

Context	Fabric	EOL	Cu	Sn	Zn	Pb	Ag
Area A							
10136	TTW		+	nd	+++	tr	tr
10386	TTW		nd	nd	tr	+++	nd
10619	TTW		nd	nd	nd	nd	+++
10655	TTW		tr	nd	++	+	nd
10725	TTW		nd	nd	nd	nd	+++
10923	TTW		++	nd	++	++	nd
11101	TTW		nd	nd	nd	nd	nd
11143	Stamford		+	nd	++	tr	nd
11144	Stamford		tr	nd	++	+	tr?
12072	TTW	present	tr	nd	+++	nd	nd
12300	uniden		tr	tr	tr	+++	tr
Area B							
30026	TTW		tr	nd	tr	tr	nd
30126	TTW		tr	nd	tr	tr	nd
30229	TTW		tr	nd	++	nd	nd
30238	TTW		tr	nd	+++	nd	nd
30282	TTW		tr	nd	tr	nd	nd
30303	TTW		tr	nd	tr	tr	nd
30404	TTW		+	nd	+++	+	nd
30434	TTW		+	nd	tr	tr	nd
30437	TTW		tr	nd	+++	tr?	nd
30470	TTW	present	+	nd	+++	tr	nd
30543	TTW		+++	nd	+	tr	nd
30588	TTW		tr?	nd	+	nd	nd
30697	TTW		tr?	nd	nd	nd	nd
30743	TTW	present	+	nd	tr	+++	?
30858	TTW		+	nd	++	tr	tr?
30900	TTW		tr	nd	tr	+	nd
30937	TTW		+	+	tr	++	tr
30937	TTW		+	nd	+++	+	nd
Area C							
50005	TTW		tr	nd	nd	tr	nd
50042	TTW		+	nd	+	nd	++
50168	Stamford		tr?	nd	tr?	tr?	nd
50241	TTW		+	nd	+	tr	tr
50259	uniden		nd	nd	tr	nd	nd
50287	TTW		nd	nd	nd	nd	nd
50295	TTW	present	tr	nd	tr	tr	nd
50302	TTW	present	+	tr	nd	+++	++
50302	TTW		+	tr	nd	+++	++
50304	TTW		nd	nd	tr(?)	nd	nd
50304	TTW	present	nd	nd	++	+	nd
50308	uniden		+	nd	++	+	tr
50341	TTW		+	nd	+	nd	nd
50380	TTW		++	nd	tr	+++	+
50386	TTW		tr	nd	tr	tr	nd
50386	TTW		nd	nd	tr	tr	tr(?)
50437	TTW		tr	nd	tr	tr	nd
50639	TTW		tr	nd	tr	nd	nd

Key: + = weak, ++ = present, +++ = strong, tr = trace, nd = not detected, EOL = extra outer layer

Table 11 XRF results for crucible fragments

compositions as inferred from crucible analysis, and assuming these figures are based on a representative sample from contemporary contexts — it appears that casting was carried out in a separate location (Area C) from wrought-based techniques (Area B).

Three crucible fragments (*10619*, *10725* and *12300*: see Goffin, above, p.118–19) displayed high concentrations of silver and little trace of anything else. It is significant that these were all found in Area A, the first two having been recovered from the fills of sunken-floored building *10049*. This suggests that silver-melting was localised and only undertaken in this area (Fig. 5.19). Silver refining, indicated by the presence of litharge cakes, may have been concentrated in the eastern part of the site in the vicinity of sunken-featured building *50242* (see below).

Litharge cakes
by Roger C.P. Doonan
Three fragments of litharge cakes (*50457*, *30928* and *30331*: Pl. 5.1), chosen from a total assemblage of six fragments, were analysed by XRF. The presence of high silver concentrations is evidence that these were derived from a silver-refining process. These high concentrations of silver were detected at the rim of a depression formed where the pool of silver would have collected during the refining process.

Cupellation is the process used to refine base silver. The metal to be refined is melted alongside some lead and then an air blast across the surface of the melt oxidises the lead. The formation of lead oxide (litharge) is important to the process as it acts as an oxidiser and transforms other base metals, *i.e.* copper, into oxides which then dissolve readily in the litharge. Frequently the hearth lining is made of bone ash, which can absorb several times its own weight of litharge (Bayley 1991). Bone-ash linings thus act as a sink for litharge and the base metals dissolved in it so that a fresh surface of the melt is maintained to facilitate further oxidation. The litharge cakes are the remains of these litharge-impregnated bone-ash linings.

In the examples from Area B and C the rim round the central depression, which represents the zone where the refined silver would have solidified, can be seen to have been chiselled at with a sharp implement so as to ensure maximum retrieval of refined silver.

The evidence for silver-refining at the site is significant since it is thought that the most likely reason for such activities is to prepare silver bullion for subsequent inclusion in alloys used in the minting of currency, although silver was also widely used in making religious objects such as chalices (Theophilus, trans. Hawthorne and Smith 1979, 99, 103). The distribution of non-ferrous metalworking waste (represented by crucibles and litharge cake) is given in Fig. 5.19 and considered further in Chapter 2.IV, 'Metalworking'.

Bell-casting

The bell and bell-casting pit
by Phillip A. Emery and Paul Cattermole
(Fig. 3.18)
A pit (*12257*) containing the *in situ* remains of the pedestal of a bell-mould was found *c.* 5m to the east of the King Street frontage which, from 1292, defined the western limit of the Friary precinct (Fig. 3.18). It was located within a small foundry immediately to the north of a Friary building and (on the basis of documentary research) south-west of the west end of the Friary church. Further details of the pit's constructional details are given in Chapter 3.III. XRF testing by the Ancient Monuments Laboratory of a sample of non-ferrous metalworking waste from the disuse fills of the bell-pit indicated an absence of copper-tin rich alloys that would characterise bell-casting (Doonan, below). However, metals suitable for making domestic vessels and small objects, such as buckles and other belt fittings, were present (Justine Bayley, *pers. comm.*). A *runner* was also found. Although it appears that items other than bells were being cast in the pit, its constructional details indicate that it was also used for bell-founding. Plant macrofossils from the pit are detailed by Fryer in Chapter 6.V and Appendix 13.

On the basis of the bell's diameter, and by analogy with the North Burlingham St Peter tenor bell (late 15th century), the height of the bell (not including the *canons*) is estimated to have been about 0.69m (2ft 3ins). Comparison with the Ormesby St Michael No. 2 bell (*c.* 1500), which was cast in Norwich, suggests a weight of around 225kg (4.5 cwt.).

Glossary
Canons: suspension loops by which the bell would be attached to a beam.
Cope: outer portion of the two-part mould, which formed the exterior shape of a bell.
Core: inner portion of the two-part mould, which formed the interior shape of a bell.
Loam false bell method: a casting technique involving the following stages: 1. The core is built up (using a strickle); 2. A 'false bell' of clay is made, again using the strickle, to the precise form of the intended bell; 3. The cope is built up over the false bell, and is then heated to harden it. This can then be lifted off, the false bell removed, and then the cope replaced in its exact position for casting; 4. The mould for the canons is placed on top of the cope, and then molten bell metal is poured through channels in rammed sand in a box in a single continuous casting operation. The displaced gases and excess metal can escape through the central vent at the top. (Greene 1989, 119).
Lost wax method: casting technique by which the form of the bell was modelled in tallow. On firing the clay mould, the tallow melted and ran out before the molten metal was poured in (Bayley and Richards 1993, 193).
Pedestal: annular foundation of the core.
Runner: metal which solidifies in channels inside the mould leading to the object matrix (Bayley 1992, 779).
Sound bow: the thickened part of the bell struck by the clapper.
Strickle: a revolving template, comprising a timber blade, pre-cut so as to conform to the intended inner or outer profile of the bell, which was attached to a rotating, vertical spindle.

Metallurgical debris
by Roger C.P. Doonan
The mould material from the bell-casting pit was clearly from a substantial casting and was initially thought to be for a bell or cauldron. The mould pieces examined were about 40mm thick and there was no evidence of separate layers. The mould appeared to be constructed of a single layer of sandy fabric heavily tempered with pebbles (4–12mm) and an organic component (traditionally animal dung would have been added: Theophilus 1979, 132). The parallel striations on the inner surface of the mould suggested that it had been made by the use of a strickle board (see Theophilus, trans. Hawthorne and Smith, 1979, 169; Biringuccio, trans. Smith and Gnudi, 1990, 260–77).

Although green corrosion products were present on the surface of various mould fragments (*12439*, *12377*, *12385*, *12258*) further investigation showed that no metallic copper survived. This meant that it was not possible to determine the original composition of the metal cast from the XRF analyses. The corrosion products comprise lead and tin oxides in a matrix of cuprite (copper oxide). Since both lead and tin occur in high yet equal proportions, it appears that the corrosion products were derived from a high-tin bronze which must also have been highly leaded. This does not conform to the composition expected for either a bell or a cauldron.

Fortunately, accompanying the mould material from the casting pit were solidified spillages of metal, some of which were uncorroded. XRF analysis of such material (*12258*) showed that the alloy was a leaded bronze with some arsenic and antimony. This alloy is specifically of the type that was used for casting large domestic vessels such as cauldrons and mortars (Brownsword and Pitt 1981), the analysis proving that cauldron- or mortar-type vessels were cast in the pit. Unlike a casting pit found in the immediate vicinity of a church, it is probable that this casting pit was used repeatedly as there is evidence for continued metalworking at the site. For this reason it is impossible to exclude the possibility of bells having been cast in the pit, though the evidence available indicates only domestic vessels.

The standard alloy for cauldron manufacture is highly leaded bronze containing small amounts of arsenic and/or antimony. These alloys are often referred to as grey coppers and represent imported copper smelted from *fahlerz* ores (Brownsword and Pitt 1981, 185), probably from the Rammelsberg region of Germany. These alloys have excellent properties for casting, which meant that fewer castings suffered defects attributable to problems in the filling of the mould cavity. However, as well as being virtually impossible to use in wrought processes, these metals are also of questionable suitability for their intended application. Blair and Blair (1991) warn that some cauldrons or mortars were such that when left on a fire they were eaten by the flames until reduced to a molten mess. A further problem encountered with highly leaded bronzes is that when they are heated in a fire the lead may melt out or oxidise, leaving behind a porous copper 'skeleton' which is easily broken. This probably explains why so many mortars are found with one or more feet broken off (Brownsword and Pitt 1981).

While the results of the pilot XRF analysis indicated that the non-ferrous metalworking waste tested was not consistent with bell-casting, the interpretation of the pedestal (approximately 0.9m in diameter) as supporting a bell-mould rather than that of a cauldron can be fully justified. The occurrence of waste that can be attributed with certainty to the casting of small objects (*e.g.* runner from *12259*) supports a picture of a versatile metalworker who was chiefly producing household/personal items but who was occasionally commissioned to cast bells. The absence of bell-metal waste could be due to a combination of the care taken to conserve the relatively expensive alloy and the relative infrequency of bell-casting.

Archaeomagnetic and radiocarbon dating

by Paul Linford, Mark Noel and Alex Bayliss

Samples for archaeomagnetic dating were taken from two places: the base of the feature, which had been reddened by firing of the loam core, and the pedestal itself, which had been in direct contact with the molten bell-metal. This analysis indicated that the bell-pit was in use between 1490 and 1525. Radiocarbon dating of the remains of the strickle gave a date of 1470–1620 at 68% confidence:

Laboratory no.: UB-4130
Radiocarbon age (BP): 363±21
δC(%): –25±0.2
Calibrated date range (68% confidence): cal AD 1470–1620
Calibrated date range (95% confidence): cal AD 1450–1630

The conventional radiocarbon age (Stuiver and Polach 1977) has been quoted in accordance with the Trondheim convention (Stuiver and Kra 1986). The calibrated date range was calculated using the maximum intercept method of Stuiver and Reimer (1986). It is quoted in the form recommended by Mook (1986), with the end points rounded outwards to five years. The probability distribution has been calculated using OxCal (v.2.18; Bronk Ramsey 1995) and the usual probability method (Stuiver and Reimer 1993). Calibrations have been calculated using the data published by Stuiver and Pearson (1986).

While the archaeomagnetic dating suggests that the bell pit was in use at some time between 48 and 13 years before the Dissolution of the Friary, radiocarbon results on their own are not conclusive as to whether this feature was associated with the institution or with post-Dissolution occupation of the site.

Discussion

by Phillip A. Emery and Paul Cattermole

Although the lost wax method (see glossary above) of casting bells was used as late as the 15th century (Bayley and Richards 1993, 190), this bell-pit represents use of the *loam false bell* process (Trevor Jennings *pers. comm.*, and glossary above). Langerwehe pottery from the disuse fills suggested that the pit was in use after 1350, although two brick fragments of a 'late' type would support a post-1500 date. A pre-Dissolution date would be consistent with the view that bell-founding was a relatively rare activity after the Reformation when a surfeit of second-hand bells was available.

Assuming that it is associated with the same workshop, the waste metal suggests the founder produced a range of household and personal items but was also occasionally commissioned to cast bells. Salzman (1964, 145) remarked that the demand for bells could hardly have been large enough to enable a founder to specialise entirely in that branch of work. Archaeological evidence from workshops in a number of cities has shown that cauldrons and other domestic vessels represented the major products of urban foundries (Bayley and Richards 1993, 192). It has been noted that the absence of bell-metal waste may result either from the curation of this costly alloy and/or the sporadic nature of bell-casting. It also raises the alternative possibility that the mould was for an unusually large, flared-rimmed vessel rather than a bell. However, the feasibility of casting a cauldron of this size, upside down, must be questioned (Jennings, *pers. comm.*).

The location of the bell pit raises an interesting problem. On the one hand, its occurrence within the contemporary precinct suggests that the pit was associated with a one-off casting of a bell for the Friary itself. The bell-founder, commissioned by the friars, would have set up a foundry as near as possible to the building for which the bell was to be cast, to minimise the distance of its transport (Greene 1989, 119; detailed examination of the itinerant bellfounder's methods is provided by Jennings 2006). However, the proximity to the King Street frontage,

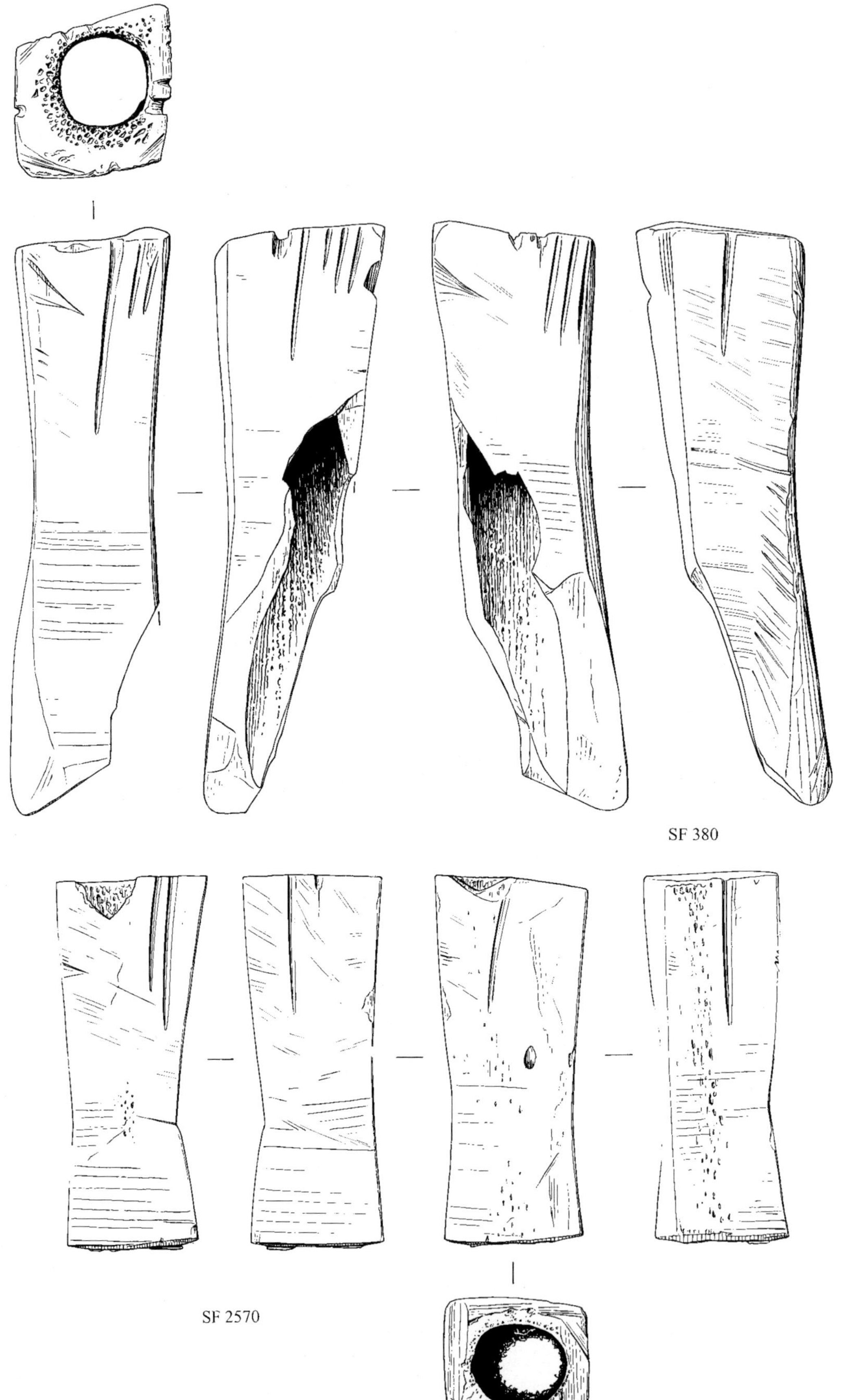

Figure 5.21 Pinner's bones (SF380, 2570). Scale 1:1.

together with the frequency of metalworking waste not derived from bell-casting, hints instead at a more permanent foundry. Such a workshop may have been tied to the Friary but could have been making domestic and personal accoutrements for a lay market.

The archaeomagnetic dating (1490–1525) is sufficiently precise for an identification of the particular bell-founder to be attempted. The bell-foundry owned by the elder Richard Brasyer, until his death in 1482, was probably located on the north side of Westlegate. These premises, together with instruments of the founder's craft, were left to his son (also Richard). It appears that the output of the foundry was not limited to church bells, as pot-metal and brass pots are also mentioned in the will (Cattermole 1990, 151). The younger Richard Brasyer wrote his will in 1505, requiring 'his executors to retain the bell-foundry, so that one of his apprentices could assume control and enable outstanding contracts to be completed' (Cattermole 1990, 152). On the death of Richard Brasyer in 1513 the foundry was left in the hands of John Aleyn, a former apprentice. Described as a bell-founder in deeds of 1523, 1524 and 1528, Aleyn is also known to have cast a bell for Hanworth church in 1521 and a treble and a tenor bell for Castle Rising church in 1530/31. Additionally, he was entrusted with remodelling the pewter belonging to the Gild of St George in 1544.

The death of Richard Brasyer in 1513 appears to have marked a major disruption in bell-founding in Norwich, as the quality of bells produced after that date is noticeably poorer. It is possible that between 1513 and John Aleyn's first documented casting in 1521, the Westlegate foundry was not being used. A 'one-off' casting within the Franciscan Friary, using temporary plant, may well have taken place during this period.

Pin-making

by Julia Huddle
(Fig. 5.21)

Wire (copper alloy)

The fourteen pieces of wire (SF2566) and others recovered from Friary and post-Friary deposits (31 in total, not catalogued here) may have been discarded from the manufacture of drawn copper alloy wire pins, which were manufactured from the medieval period to the early 19th century (Biddle and Barclay 1990, 564).

Pinner's bones

Two pinner's bones, used to hold the pin in position whilst a point was filed onto the end, were found.

SF380 Incomplete section of sawn cattle or horse metatarsal shaft, socketed and roughly facetted to form four flat faces. At one (surviving) end, on each face, are between one and four grooves cut with a saw blade in the long axis; diagonal file marks visible on all faces.
fill 10724, Period 4.2

SF2570 Cattle or horse metatarsal shaft fragment, socketed and roughly facetted to form four flat faces. Complete length survives and only one to two grooves are cut on each face. Green (copper oxide) staining on two sides.
fill 13124, Period 4.1

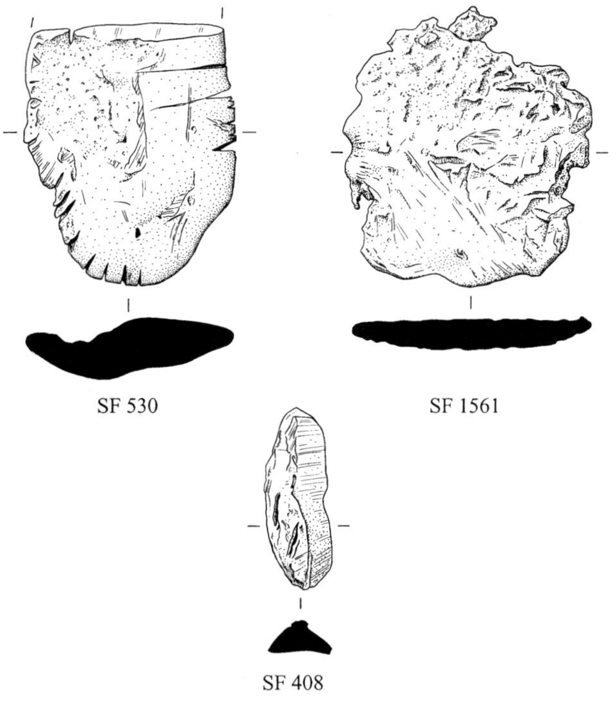

Figure 5.22 Leadworking waste (SF530, 1561, 408). Scale 1:2.

Leadworking

by Geoff Egan
(Fig. 5.22)

Two possible lead ingots, used in the leadworking process, were recovered. In addition, three post-Dissolution contexts in Area D (*13009*, *13021* and *13051*) contained lead melt, perhaps representing the re-cycling of lead fittings from the Greyfriars buildings. Two other examples are illustrated. (Four further pieces from various contexts are not catalogued here.)

SF1561 Possibly a rough-and-ready **ingot**; 70 x 55 x 8mm
fill 30201, Period 2.3

SF530 **Lead melt.** Sub-oval, with one end cut off, 69 x 55 x 14mm; series of nicks around edge — perhaps to facilitate removal of small pieces (*cf.* runnels SF 1583 and sheeting SF529)
pit fill 50358, Period 2.2

SF408 **Lead melt.** Triangular-section fragment *c.*8 x 8mm, surviving length 48mm; cut along one face with a blade
gravel path 40002, Period 4.2

Miscellaneous tools

by Val Fryer
(Fig. 5.23)

The iron head of a punch or chisel (SF816), probably for use in metalworking, was recovered from the fill of a culvert.

SF816 **?Punch/chisel**
culvert fill 10778, Period 3.2

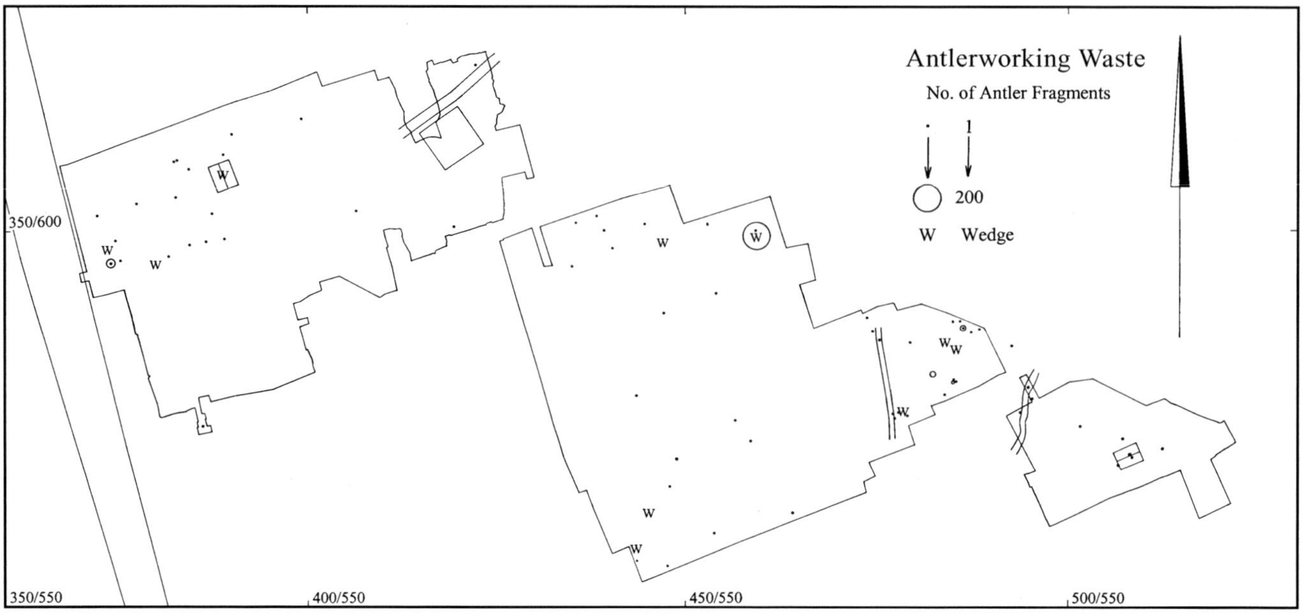

Figure 5.24 Distribution of antlerworking waste

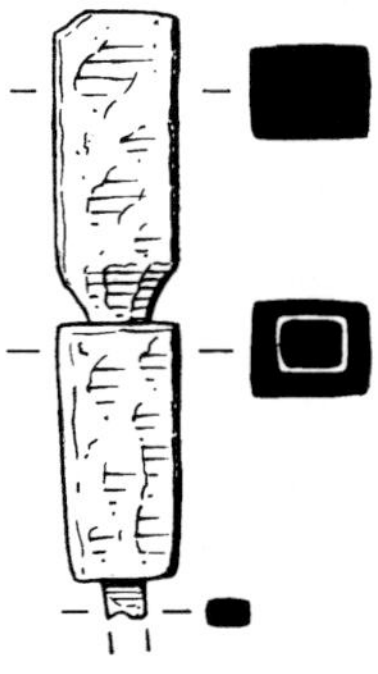

Figure 5.23 Iron punch (SF816). Scale 1:2.

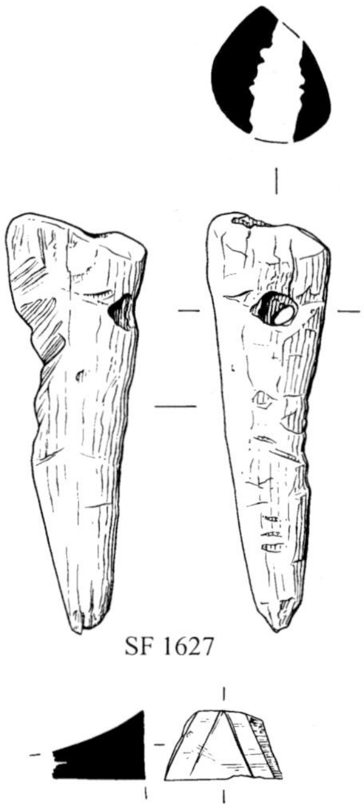

Figure 5.25 Antler wedge (SF1627), antler ?comb waste (SF877). Scale 1:1.

Antlerworking

Tools

by Julia Huddle, with species identification by Ian Riddler (Figs 5.24 and 5.25)

A total of eleven antler wedges was recovered. Two are from Saxo-Norman deposits. Of these, one came from pit *30937*, where considerable quantities of antler-working waste, including comb manufacturing debris, were found. The others are mainly from Friary levels but are likely to be residual. They include one (SF259) recovered from a disuse fill (*10337*) of the sunken-featured building *10049* in Area A.

Antler wedges used in the splitting of thick beams of antler are known from Late Saxon contexts from Norwich and elsewhere in England, as well as on the Continent. One Viking-age antler beam from Haithabu (Hedeby), in present-day Germany, was found with a wedge driven in at one end of the beam (MacGregor 1985, 57, fig. 34).

The wedges are fashioned from sawn antler tine ends and in each case the tip has been modified with several oblique cuts forming a facetted point. Three of the wedges from Greyfriars also have a V-shaped notch cut into one side, towards the middle or lower half of the implement. One of these (SF1627) is also perforated laterally at the wider end. This notching is also seen on three of wedges from Castle Mall (Huddle forthcoming) and some from York (Tweddle 1986, 229, 230, cat. 746) and Hedeby (Ulbricht 1978, 83, plate 45 nos 6, 7 and 15). The notching, at least on the examples from Norwich, seems to

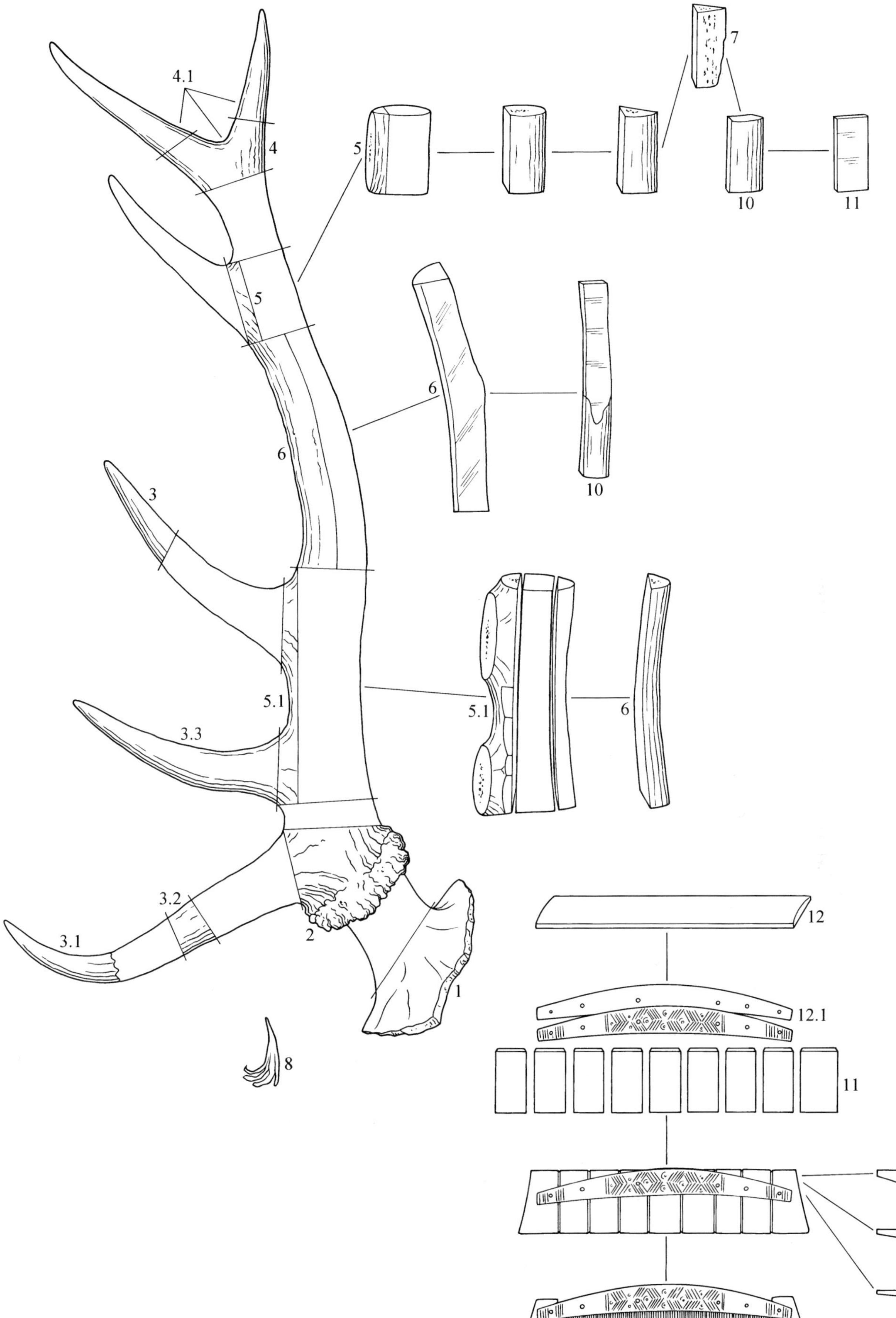

Figure 5.26 Antlerworking diagram (not to scale)

	Stages of antler primary waste (after Ulbricht)								Stages of antler secondary waste (after Ulbricht)				
	1	*2*	*3*	*4*	*5*	*6*	*7*	*8*	*10*	*11*	*12*	*13*	*Total*
Period													
1	1	4	16	6	4	19	118	134	4	14	2	19	341
2	1		4			11		5		9		7	37
3	2	1	14	1		15	2	9	1	12	2	4	63
4	1		3			2		1		3			10
u/s			2				1						3
Total	**5**	**5**	**39**	**7**	**4**	**47**	**121**	**149**	**5**	**38**	**4**	**30**	**454**

Table 12 Total quantity of antlerworking waste by period

be deliberate, although its function is not clear. Ulbricht notes that the notched wedges from Hedeby frequently bear hammer-marks on the sawn surface, suggesting they must have been used as wedges. The notching, she suggests, may have been caused when the wedge was driven in so tightly that it was subsequently caught by the saw (Ulbricht 1978, 83). The function of the perforation on SF1627 is also uncertain, although this may simply be a suspension hole enabling the object to be hung for safe keeping.

The assemblage of antler wedges recovered complements other evidence for antler-working recovered across the site (the distribution of which is indicated in Fig. 5.24). A wedge (from pit *30937*) was found in association with other antler waste from the manufacture of composite combs in the Late Saxon period. Further discussion on antler-working appears in Chapter 2.IV.

SF1627 **Perforated antler wedge**, sawn antler tine end; the tip has been modified with several oblique cuts forming a facetted point; a V-shaped notch has been cut out on one side and it is perforated laterally towards the top.
pit fill 30543, Period 2.3

Primary and secondary waste

by Julia Huddle, with species identification by Ian Riddler (Fig. 5.24–5.26)

Antlerworking waste was recovered from all areas and, with the exception of Period 5, from all periods (amounting to 454 pieces in total). All identifiable pieces are of red deer antler. Post-cranial fallow deer, however, was the only deer species identified amongst the faunal assemblage and derived entirely from Friary contexts, in particular those dated to Period 3.2 (see Moreno-García, Chapter 6.II, where the contribution of deer to the meat diet of the Friary inhabitants is also considered). The availability and distribution of antler in England is discussed by MacGregor (1985 32–8).

The Greyfriars waste provides evidence in particular for the making of single-sided composite combs, of the kind that can be dated to the late 10th and 11th centuries. Other artefacts made of antler (such as a spindle whorl (SF108), needle (SF54) and single-pointed pin-beater (SF114)) may also have been made here during the Late Saxon period. The antlerworking waste recovered from later contexts is likely to be residual given the general transition from antler- to boneworking apparent from the 11th century onwards (MacGregor 1991, 366).

The various stages of antler-working (some of which are encountered at Greyfriars) are described by MacGregor (1985), where he includes summaries of analytical work on excavated material by Ulbricht (1978), Ambrosiani (1981) and Christophersen (1980). Most recently in England, there has been a detailed study of antler waste from Fishergate, York (Rogers 1993), where a considerable quantity of comb waste was recovered. Many of the various stages of antler-working recorded at Fishergate can also be seen in the assemblage from Greyfriars.

The Greyfriars material has been divided into two categories: primary and secondary waste (Table 12). The primary waste covers antler shavings and all split and or sawn antler. The secondary waste is sawn and further modified, often reflecting the finished items from which they have been separated. The stages of antler waste found at Greyfriars have been highlighted on the schematic diagram (after Ulbricht), and this shows the methods of cutting-up and utilising the antler for the production of composite combs (Fig. 5.26). One example of each type encountered at Greyfriars is described below and the figures in brackets alongside these descriptions correspond to those given in the diagram.

A total of 377 pieces of primary waste was recovered at Greyfriars, of which 84% was recovered from contexts of Periods 1 and 2. The remainder was recovered mainly from Friary levels. The secondary waste, all of which has been identified as comb-manufacturing debris, amounts to 77 pieces in total. Once again the majority (70%) comes from Periods 1 and 2.

Only two segments of sawn-off pedicle and part of calvaria (skull) were recovered from contexts ascribed to Periods 1 and 2. No other post-cranial deer bones were recovered from these periods, suggesting that the antlers were collected off-site, the majority probably being naturally shed. This pattern is seen elsewhere at contemporary sites on the Continent and Fishergate, York, for example (Ambrosiani 1981, 99; Christophersen 1980, 156; Rogers 1993, 1257).

Antler waste recovered in deposits later than those of Period 2 is thought to be residual and was mostly recovered as single pieces, indicating secondary deposition.

The antler waste provides evidence for the manufacture of antler composite combs on site during the 10th to 11th centuries. As MacGregor points out, composite combs accounted for the bulk of the output of the pre-Conquest antler industry (1991). One object (SF877; Fig. 5.25) that has fractured at either end originally formed part of a mount of rectangular form with parallel or near-parallel sides. The simple, incised decoration frames each of the angled upper faces. The object is not paralleled amidst the series of bone and antler caskets of early medieval date, which customarily include decorated rectangular mounts (SF1183) of flat or lightly-rounded section (Elbern 1955, 1962, 1971; MacGregor 1985, 197–203; Gabriel 1988; Riddler forthcoming a). Its section and decoration recall a number of antler connecting plates for combs of early medieval date; amongst them combs from York and Ipswich (Waterman 1959; Riddler forthcoming a). The Norwich fragment has near-parallel sides and no trace of saw-marks from the cutting of comb teeth, suggesting that it may have belonged to an unfinished comb, or possibly to a comb case.

As noted elsewhere, other artefacts made of antler may also have been made alongside the manufacture of combs, such as needles, spindle whorls and pin-beaters. However, these simple antler tools require little expertise to make and might have been made by the weavers themselves as and when required (MacGregor 1985).

Elsewhere in Norwich evidence for antler-working during the Late Saxon period comes from Fishergate (Williams 1994a), the north-east bailey of the Castle (Margeson and Williams 1985) and Castle Mall (Huddle forthcoming). The evidence from each of these sites is provided by only a few pieces of secondary waste, which was identified as comb manufacturing debris. In all of these cases, only a fraction of the waste was recovered from Late Saxon contexts. The assemblage of antler-working material recovered at Greyfriars is considerably larger than any other previously recovered elsewhere in Norwich.

Waste was recovered from all parts of the site, although the majority came from Area B. It is notable that 61% of the waste came from the fills of one pit (*30980*) in Area B (Period 2.1). Apart from pieces of pedicle and calvaria, all the stages of antler-working recovered on site were present in this pit and this would seem to represent a small fraction of the debris produced by a single craftsperson in the manufacture of composite combs. Further discussion of spatial and stratigraphic distribution of antlerworking waste is given in Chapter 2.IV and Fig. 5.24.

Period	*Context*	*No. rib frags*	*No. frags*
1	30937	1	
	12519	1	
2.3	30900	1	
	12137	1	
3.1	30941	3	
	12475	1	
3.2	30003	37	2
	30579	4	
	30575	8	
	30835	1	
	30757	1	
	30646	3	
	10743	2	
	12515	151	2
4.1	12064	2	
4.2	30804	2	
Total		**219**	**4**

Table 13 Knife-cut and finally snapped-off bone strips; rib and scapula, by sub-period

SF877 A small section of an **antler mount** of triangular section, which has been neatly fractured at each end. It is decorated by single incised lines along either side of the central ridge, and close to each edge. L: 23mm, W: 10mm
fill 30297, Period 2.3

Primary waste
(bracketed numbers refer to elements shown in Fig. 5.26)

Pedicles and calvaria (No. 1)
Segment of sawn off pedicle and part of calvaria (skull). A total of five pieces was found. The calvaria has been detached from the skull with a knife.

Burrs (No. 2):
Naturally shed antler burr, with the beam and brow tine sawn off close to the burr at an oblique angle. There are four complete examples from the site as well as one sawn segment.

Tines (Nos 3, 3.1, 3.2 and 3.3)
Sawn-off tines and tine ends. There are 39 sawn antler tines from the site. These include 32 sawn-off tine ends (3), three tines sawn off close to the beam (3.3), three sawn sections of tine (3.2) and one ?broken-off tine end (3.1).

Offcuts of crown (Nos 4, 4.1 and 4.2)
Sawn sections of crown and sawn-off crown tines. The seven offcuts of crown from the site include four sections of sawn antler crown tines (4), of which one has one of three tines sawn off (4.1), and two sawn crown tines (4.2).

Offcuts of beam (Nos 5 and 5.1)
Sections of antler beam sawn at the junction of one or two tines. A total of four offcuts of antler beam were identified, of which three pieces have been sawn at the junction of one tine (5) and one has been sawn at the junction of two tines (5.1). The latter includes one tine that has been partially sawn then hacked off with a knife.

Segments of antler beam and tine (No. 6)
Segments of sawn and split antler, with outer (medullary) surface and inner (cortile) tissue present. There are 47 segments from the site, a few of which are quadrants, a number of which have knife marking-out points at one sawn end. The majority are notably smaller at one end, and most of these pieces were presumably discarded because they were too small and/or irregularly shaped to be of any use.

Cortile tissue (7)
Sawn and split segments of antler, consisting mostly of cortile tissue. A hundred and twenty-one pieces were found. Due to the soft nature of the tissue, many pieces retain little (if any) of their sawn end(s). These pieces have been stripped off the outer compact antler tissue.

Shavings (8) etc.
Knife-cut antler, consisting mainly of the outer (medullary) tissue. There are *c.* 149 pieces of antler shavings from the site. Each piece generally retains several knife-cutting marks at the splayed end.

Secondary waste

Half flattened strips (10): tooth or connecting-plate fragments
Sections of sawn and split antler, with only one side flattened. Five pieces were recovered from the site, and are presumably unfinished fragments of either tooth or connecting plates.

Flattened strips (11): tooth plate offcuts
Section of sawn and split antler of rectangular section, flattened on both sides and finished off with the use of a file. Thirty-eight strips were found on the site, some of them incomplete. Due to their size and shape these pieces are likely to be fragments of tooth plates.

Plano-convex strips (12, 12.1): connecting plate offcuts
Section of sawn and split antler of plano-convex section. Four pieces were recovered from the site. One piece has two rivet holes, one across each broken end (12.1). These are identified by their plano-convex section (as seen in composite combs), and occasionally by the presence of rivet holes along the length of the strips.

Small strips (13): tooth plate trimmings
Small strips flattened on both sides, sub-rectangular or trapezoidal in shape and mostly with a small projection on one side. A total of 30 pieces

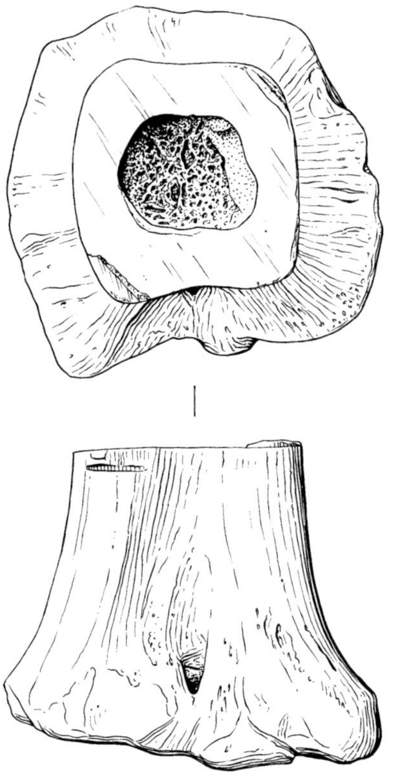

SF 142

Figure 5.27 Primary boneworking waste (SF142). Scale 1:1.

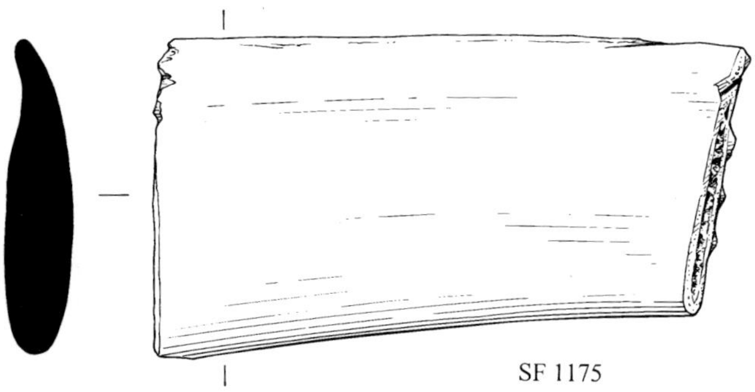

SF 1175

Figure 5.28 ?Butchery waste (SF1175). Scale 1:1.

were found. Once the comb has been assembled the top edges of the tooth plates are cut off flush with the connecting plate, resulting in these small trimmings. The small projection seen on these strips is apparently caused by the sawn edge being ultimately snapped off at one end of the tooth plate (Rogers 1993, 1260).

Boneworking

by Julia Huddle

Primary waste and ?butchery

(Figs 5.27 and 5.28)

Discarded articular ends of cattle and horse long bones (*cf.* SF142; Fig. 5.27) are known from Middle and Late Saxon sites, sometimes accompanied by evidence of bone comb making (MacGregor 1985, 46–7) or ring-making (Biddle 1990, 1130–1; Pritchard 1991). Several rubbish pits at *Hamwic* (Late Saxon Southampton) were filled with sawn-off articular ends of cattle metapodials (Holdsworth 1976, 45). A few examples are also known from Castle Mall, Norwich (Huddle in prep.) and Fishergate, York (Rogers 1993, 1260, cat. 5515–6). Metapodia also provided raw material for handles and beads and a range of other objects during the post-medieval period (Ian Riddler, *pers. comm.*).

At Greyfriars, a total of 219 bone strips was recovered from Areas A and B, the vast majority (94%) from culvert *12548* (Period 3.2) and pit *30008* (Period 3.2). A further two pieces are from Period 4.1, six are from Period 3 and one is from Period 3.1.

Apart from four pieces of scapula the assemblage comprises of animal rib, mostly cattle-sized, although a few sheep-sized ribs are present. Each strip is neatly cut apparently with a knife (rather than a saw) almost to the base, using a straight edge. The ends are finally snapped off, leaving a small burr or ridge along the base. The vast majority are apparently complete, because they are neatly cut on both ends, which suggests they are blanks rather than offcuts. With the exception of three pieces of secondary bone waste recovered from pits *30980* and *30942* (SF1432, SF1436 and SF1747) the assemblage comprises unworked blanks, displaying no attempt to split the ribs or flatten the sides. Both the choice of animal rib and the way in which they have been cut might at first suggest these are blanks for bone horn-comb connecting plates or box mounts. Both of these object types had, however, effectively become obsolete by the 12th century (Ian Riddler, *pers. comm.*) and, given that 99% of these pieces are from Friary deposits, it seems highly improbable that they are all residual here. The most likely interpretation is that the rib segments were the result of butchery for the extraction of marrow by boiling (Rebecca Nicholson, *pers. comm.*). This suggestion is supported by the fact that over 150 of the bones were recovered within the possible kitchen in the west range of the cloister (context *12515*).

SF142 Sawn off **articular end** of cattle metatarsus (proximal end).
build-up 50031, Period 4.2

The following catalogue entry is for one group of bone strips (SF1175) from which one typical piece is illustrated (Fig. 5.28). Table 13 (above) shows total quantities recovered on site and their provenance.

SF1175 **Bone strips** x39, knife-cut, apparently using a straight edge; 37 are cattle-sized ribs, 2 are scapula. The majority of the strips are complete, *i.e.* they are cut at both ends. The average length (from complete sample of 35) is 62mm (four are incomplete).
pit fill 30003, Period 3.2

Secondary waste

?Composite combs
(Fig. 5.29)

Alongside the 219 pieces of knife-cut and finally snapped-off bone rib recovered (above), three further pieces of modified split rib were found. Two of the strips (SF1432 and SF1747) are flattened on one side and the third (SF1436) is also perforated. These can be compared to 186 pieces recovered from the Castle Mall excavations from mainly Late Saxon contexts (Huddle forthcoming) and 600 from Late Saxon deposits at Thetford (Rogerson

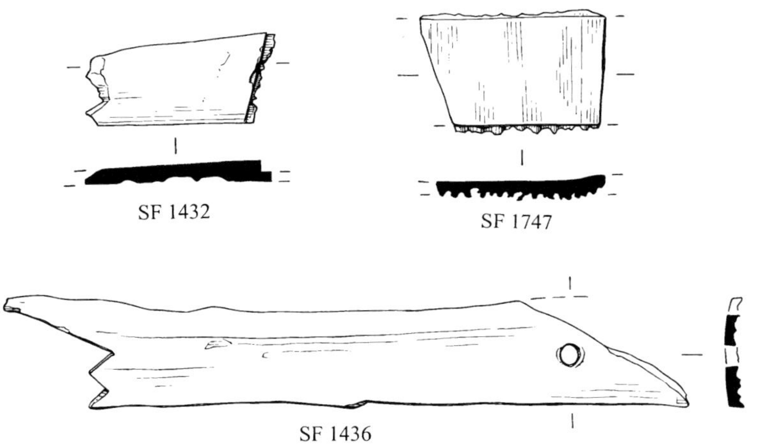

Figure 5.29 Secondary boneworking waste: bone and horn comb manufacture (SF1432, 1747, 1436). Scale 1:1.

and Dallas 1984, 190–2), where they were unidentified. As with the pieces from Greyfriars it is likely that these bone strips are the waste product of horn combs (which have connecting plates made of animal bone, attached to either side of the horn comb by two or three widely spaced iron rivets). Similarly assemblages from both Thetford and Castle Mall also contain a proportion which are perforated and generally broken on or near the holes (presumably being discarded as a result). The piece from Greyfriars pit *30942* (SF1747; Period 3.1) is likely to be residual since horn combs are thought to have become obsolete by the 12th century (Margeson 1993, 66).

A tiny fragment of bone strip (SF1621, not illustrated) is likely to be a fragment of a connecting plate, due to its plano-convex profile. There are no traces of tooth saw marks and cannot therefore be assigned to either a single- or double-sided type. Late Saxon composite combs are usually made of antler (MacGregor 1985, 28), although bone is occasionally used for single-sided composite combs (particularly for the connecting plates), as at Fishergate, York (Rogers 1993, 1402).

SF1432 Incomplete **bone strip**; section of sawn and finally snapped-off cattle-sized rib, split and flattened on the back. L: 25mm, W: 12mm, T: 2mm.
pit fill 30937, Period 1

SF1436 Incomplete **perforated bone strip**; section of split cattle-sized rib, with neat perforation close to one broken end. L: 90mm, W: 14mm, Diameter of perforation: 1.8mm.
pit fill 30937, Period 1

SF1747 Incomplete **bone strip**; section of split cattle sized rib, sawn on both edges and flattened on the front. L: 25mm, W: 15mm, T: 3mm.
pit fill 30941, Period 3.1

?Whistle
by Ian Riddler

A relatively short length of goose ulna (SF1192) is damaged at one end in a manner which suggests that it may originally have been intended to be a small bone whistle. A similar trimmed section of a goose ulna is known from *Hamwic* (Riddler forthcoming b).

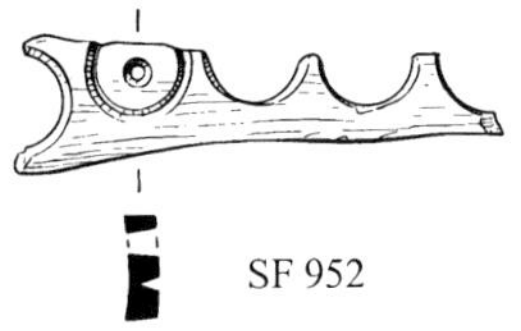

Figure 5.30 Secondary boneworking waste: bone bead manufacture (SF952). Scale 1:1.

SF no.	*Context*	*No. holes*	*Hole diameter*
100	10028	9	7mm
1064	10029	10	6mm
1065	10029	2	6mm
1102	10029	5	6mm
952	30179	5	6mm

Table 14 Bone bead waste from pits *10027* and *30123* (Period 3.1)

Bead manufacture
(Fig. 5.30)

Bone waste panels from the manufacture of buttons, counters or beads, such as SF952, are familiar from late medieval and later contexts (MacGregor 1985, 101–2) and one is known from a 15th–16th century context on Botolph Street, Norwich (Margeson 1993, 193, fig. 143 no. 1508).

Five bone waste panels came from two pits at Mann Egerton (*10027* and *30123*), in Areas A and B respectively. The ceramic evidence points to a late 14th–15th century date for these two groups. One incomplete perforated bone disc from pit *30123*, thought to be a (broken) bead (SF 1610), fits neatly into any of the cut-out holes from these waste panels. It may have been discarded when broken (see Huddle, Chapter 5.IV, 'Beads').

The diameter of the cut-out holes range from 6–7mm, which suggests that they represent bead-making since they appear too small for buttons or counters. If this is the case, it is suggested that since necklaces of beads were not fashionable in the medieval period (Margeson 1993, 5) these may have been from the production of beads for rosaries, which are made of all materials. London has produced similar waste panels of bone, recovered mostly from late 13th- to early 14th-century contexts, and these are also identified as waste from the production of beads (Egan 1991, 311–14, fig. 207, nos 1557–71). The hole diameters on the London waste panels are similar to those at Greyfriars and range from 4.5mm to 8.5mm, with the majority being 6mm.

All the above items are made from split cattle-sized rib with one side (the medullary surface) flattened. SF1610 is an incomplete circular perforated flat disc, probably a bead (not illustrated).

SF952 **Waste panel** from the manufacture of bone beads; strip fragment with four cut-out circular holes, and one partially cut-out disc, with an extended central marking-out point which has penetrated the bone to the other side.
pit fill 30179, Period 3.1

Textile-working

Tools

Carding combs
by Val Fryer
(Fig. 5.31)
Two teeth from combs associated with the manufacture of textiles were recovered from Period 1 contexts, of which one was recovered from the St Faith's Lane evaluation. Contemporary parallels occur at, for example, Thetford, Norfolk (Rogerson and Dallas 1984, fig. 119). Carding combs were used to remove impurities from wool prior to spinning. For a discussion on the construction and function of these combs see Goodall 1993, 182.

SF480 Iron **heckle tooth** from a carding comb.
disuse fill of SFB 50242, 50263, Period 1

373N /SF121 Iron **heckle tooth** from a carding comb
layer 62, Period 1

Thimbles
by Julia Huddle
(Fig. 5.32)
Medieval thimbles are hand-made, often conical in shape with uneven punching applied in a spiral. Margeson discusses a group of hand-made thimbles recovered from mid-17th-century rubbish pits (1993, 187), which were probably made in Nuremberg in the 16th century. These, like SF2557, are highly decorated with elaborate borders and often have a maker's mark at the start of a spiral punching. The unstratified 'ring' thimble (SF2611) from Greyfriars may be compared to one from a 17th-century context at Botolph Street, Norwich (Margeson 1993, 187, fig. 139 no. 1461).

SF789 Copper-alloy conical **thimble** (now distorted) with slightly pointed top, and spiral rectangular punched dots; border of stamped four-pointed motifs.
unstratified

SF2557 Copper-alloy **thimble** with fine circular punched dots and border of roundels containing crosses and vertical lines. Maker's mark ?letter 'S' on its side.
make-up 13051, Period 4.2

SF2611 Copper-alloy **'ring thimble'** with circular ?drilled dots.
unstratified

Needles (copper alloy)
by Julia Huddle
A needle (SF354, not illustrated) is similar to one made of iron from a late 12–13th century context on Lower Close, Norwich (Margeson 1993, 187, fig. 137 no. 1455).

Pins (bone and antler)
(Fig. 5.33)
Eleven pins and pin fragments were found, of which ten are bone and one is antler (copper-alloy pins are presented in Chapter 5.IV, 'Dress accessories'). Six came from the use or disuse fills of sunken-floored building *10049* in Area A and two are from the disuse fills of sunken-featured building *50242* in Area C. Another is from a pit in Area A which produced a large proportion (82%) of residual pottery. Two are from Area B, one unstratified and the other from a post-Dissolution context (Period 4.2) where the vast majority (97%) of the pottery is also residual.

Nine of the pins are made from pig fibula and, with the exception of one fragment of a carved ornamental head, they are undecorated. One other pin is made from the longbone of a large animal, with a gradual swelling to the eye and incised circumferential lines around the shank and

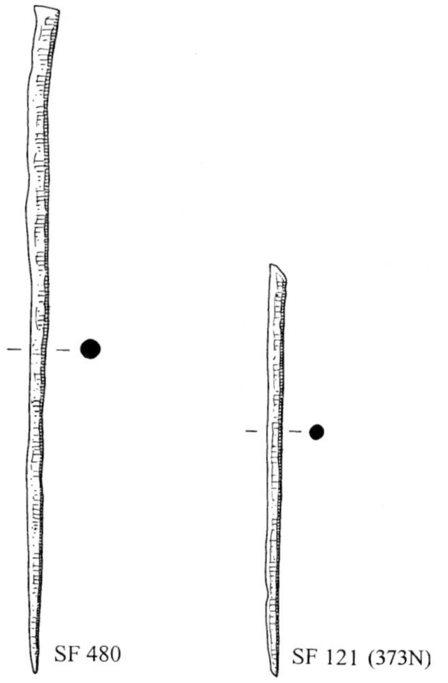

Figure 5.31 Iron heckle teeth (SF480, 121). Scale 1:2.

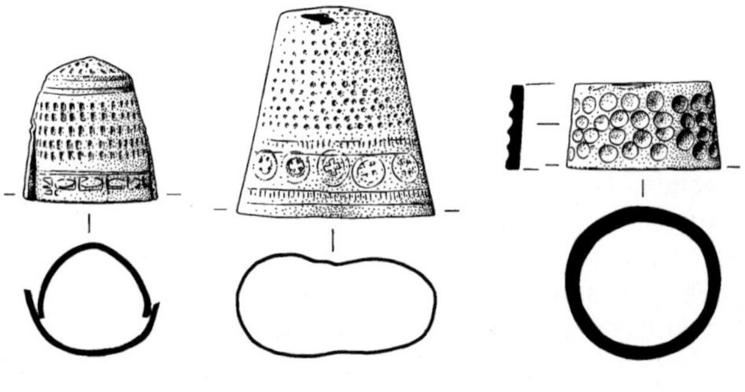

Figure 5.32 Copper alloy thimbles (SF789, 2557, 2611). Scale 1:1.

SF no.	Context	Associated with	Period	Material	Decoration
326	30000	unstratified	N/A	pig fibula	plain head
616	10856	SFB 10049	1	bone	incised
1210	10827		2	pig fibula	plain head
269	10337		2	pig fibula	plain head
613	10725		2	pig fibula	plain head
615	10619		2	pig fibula	plain head
379	10619		2	antler	plain
291	50263	SFB 50242	1	pig fibula	plain head
591	50263		1	pig fibula	plain head
765	10082	pit 10135	3.1	pig fibula	carved head
1193	30319	pit 30322	4.2	pig fibula	plain head

Table 15 Number of bone and antler pins with perforated heads

head. The antler pin is quite plain. All the pins have polished surfaces and the degree of polish appears to be identical above and below the eye. The edges of the eyes are rounded-off and smooth. The exposed half of one eye on a broken pin (SF615, not illustrated) is polished throughout.

Apart from the pin fragment with a carved head (SF765), all the pig fibula pins have plain heads (formed from the distal end of the bone) which are rounded-off, resulting in a smooth contoured surface with a curved transition from shaft to head. Three of the pig fibula pins were initially thought not to have any shaping around the head, but on closer inspection (under magnification) these too were seen to have had their articular surfaces trimmed, to produce more or less rounded heads. Elsewhere perforated pig fibula pins are found with no modification to the head, for example at Fishergate, York (Rogers 1993, 1368, fig. 667 nos 5537 and 5552), and at Ipswich (Riddler forthcoming a).

An example of each type recovered is catalogued below and illustrated. Totals are given in Table 15, showing the period and group/subgroup from which they derive. All the pins have shanks of circular or sub-circular section.

Pins with expanded perforated heads are well known from Late Saxon sites, for example Flaxengate, Lincoln (Mann 1982, 10, fig. 6), Fishergate, York (Rogers 1993, 1368, fig. 667), Northampton (Oakley and Harman 1979, 310, fig. 138), London (Vince 1991, 203 and 207, figs 3.85 and 3.89) and Thetford (Rogerson and Dallas 1984, 167–70, figs 189 and 190). Examples recovered elsewhere in Norwich come from Late Saxon and early medieval contexts such as those from St Martin-at-Palace Plain (Williams 1988, 100–4, fig. 80 nos 7, 8, 10 and 12, fig. 81 no. 19 and fig. 82 no. 23).

Various suggestions have been put forward for the use of these pierced implements. MacGregor describes how perforated pig fibulae may have been used to secure articles of dress, either in pairs or singly with a cord passed through the perforation and tied around the tip (MacGregor 1985, 120–1). Alternatively, these items may have been utilised in the production of textiles. Elisabeth Crowfoot comments on a similar range of implements at Thetford as being 'used for netting and looped needle-netting' and mentions an additional use with the

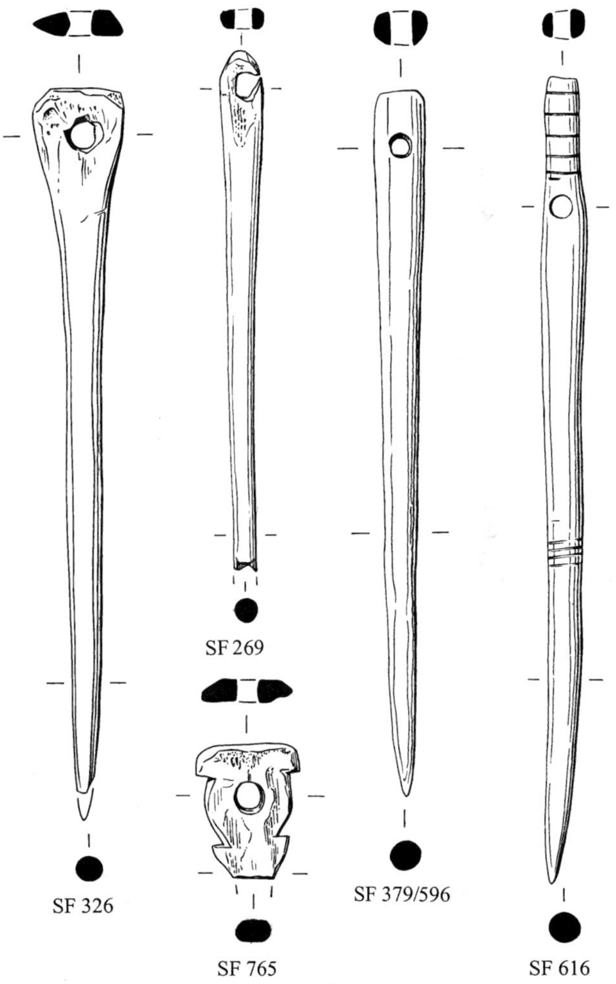

Figure 5.33 Bone pins (SF326, 269, 379/596, 616, 765). Scale 1:1.

warp-weighted loom, whereby the needles were 'placed at the selvage and held the cords which were used to fasten the uprights in order to maintain an even width' (Crowfoot 1984, 167).

The pig fibula pin with simple carved head (SF765) is very crude in comparison to any of the dress pins with hipped shafts (such as the one found at Castle Acre). Simple decoration is often seen on other textile manufacturing tools such as spindle whorls (see SF895) and pin-beaters. Other comparable Late Saxon assemblages often include several pins which have simple carved heads similar to SF765, such as at Thetford (Rogerson and Dallas 1984, fig. 189 cat. 33) and Lincoln (Mann 1982, 10, fig. 6 no. 51). Pin SF765 is similar to Øye's type F needle, which she thought could not have been used, on the basis of the shape of the head, for sewing, single-needle knitting or netting. Øye suggests however they might be suitable as shuttles, bodkins, distaffs or pin-beaters (Øye 1988, 101).

Antler pin SF379/596 has a relatively small head that runs more or less straight down into the shaft. This could have been used for sewing on finer material or for embroidery.

Although bone pin SF616 could have been used for sewing it may have served another purpose. Similar pins, known as loose ring-headed pins, are found with rings inserted through the eyes (Ian Riddler, *pers. comm.*). Loose ring-headed pins are found mainly on the continent from Viking Age sites and examples are known in copper alloy and bone. MacGregor cites two examples in bone from York, one of which is still fitted with its bronze ring (MacGregor 1985, 120, fig. 64 no. 32). Other examples are known from Hedeby and Birka where rings of bronze wire or loops of leather or other organic material were inserted (Jankuhn 1943, 135, fig. 70 no. l; Schwarz-Mackenson 1976, fig. 10 nos 6 and 7). As with the Greyfriars pin, examples are shown where the shaft swells slightly around the eye (see for example Schwarz-Mackenson 1976, fig. 10 no. 9). Many of the bone loose ring-headed pins are decorated around the shaft, generally close to and above the eye. Often the decoration is in the form of concentric lines (*e.g.* Jankuhn 1943, 137, fig. 70 no. l). These objects are dated to the later 9th or the first half of the 10th century. The decorative incised lines around the shank could also have served a more practical purpose, that of preventing the pin from slipping out of position. The ornament on most of the continental bone examples is far more decorative and neatly executed than on the Greyfriars pin. However, this pin could be a locally made copy of the rather more decorative continental examples.

SF326 **Bone pin** with pierced and slightly trimmed head, made from pig fibula, tip missing; entire surface slightly polished.
unstratified

SF269 Incomplete **bone pin** with pierced and slightly trimmed head, made from a pig fibula, tip missing; the head is trimmed slightly to produce a gradual swelling to the top; one side of the head has worn away exposing part of the eye; entire surface slightly polished.
fill 10337, Period 2

SF765 Pierced carved head from **bone pin.** Pig fibula.
pit fill 10082, Period 3.1

SF379/596 **Antler pin with pierced head**; the shaft expands evenly to the top of the pin; polished surfaces.
backfill 1061, Period 2

SF616 **Decorated bone pin, with pierced head**; and fine point; made from the long bone of a large animal. Mostly of even and gradual swelling to the eye, slight swelling of shaft around the eye; above the eye the head is slightly tapered. The head is decorated with five circumferential incised lines, faint (?originally circumferential) lines around middle of the shaft; highly polished shaft. L: 105mm.
beam slot fill 10856, Period 1

Pin-beater

A single pointed pin-beater (SF1988, not illustrated) was recovered from a context ascribed to Period 1. Similar examples, some of which are decorated, are well known from Late Saxon contexts elsewhere in England. Examples from Norwich have been found at St Martin-at-Palace Plain, Fishergate and Castle Mall. Seventeen single pointed pin-beaters were recovered from Thetford, Norfolk, a number of which are decorated (Rogerson and Dallas 1984, 170–5, figs 191–3). David Brown discusses the possible use of these items with the two-beam loom, where he refers to them items as 'pricker-cum-beaters' to reflect their dual purpose (Brown 1990, 227–8).

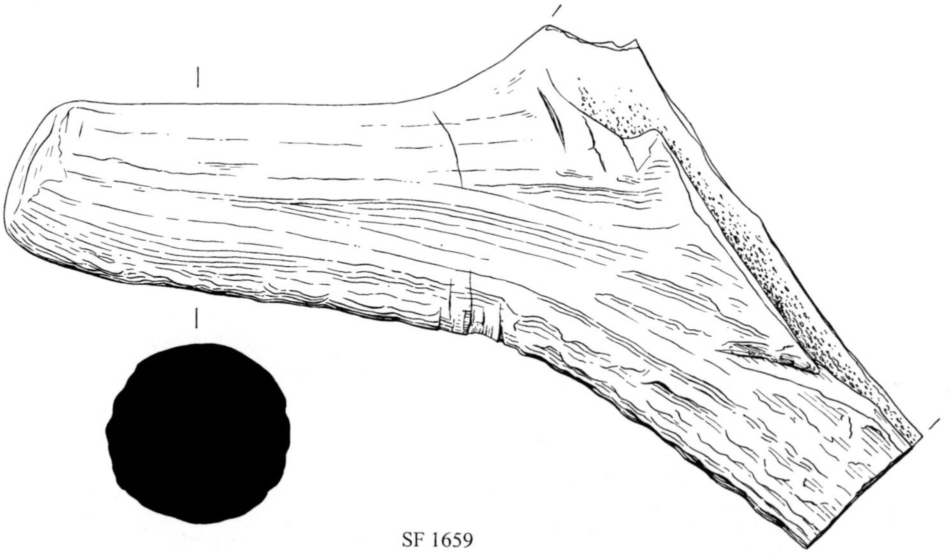

SF 1659

Figure 5.34 Antler ?linen smoother (SF1659). Scale 1:1.

The notched effect seen on SF1988 may be compared to that seen on a single pointed pin-beater recovered from St Martin-at-Palace Plain (Williams 1988c, 103, fig. 81 no. 16), which Elisabeth Crowfoot suggested may have been the result of abrasion by threads.

Possible linen smoother
(Fig. 5.34)
A section of sawn antler beam and tine (SF1659) has its end rounded off and smoothed, suggesting this piece was put to some use. One possibility is that it was used as a linen smoother (Ian Riddler, *pers. comm.*), although if so more attention might have been paid to the rest of the antler, especially around the beam, where presumably it would have been held.

SF1659 Section of sawn and split antler beam with tine, the tip of which has been removed and the end rounded and smooth through ?wear. Several knife marks at junction of beam and tine. Possible **linen smoother.**
fill 30281, Period 3.2

Ceramic spindle whorls
by Julia Huddle
(Fig. 5.35)
Five ceramic spindle whorls, three of which are incomplete, were recovered. Four are bi-conical and one is spherical. The bi-conical spindle whorls are all from Area A, three of them from groups connected with the backfilling of sunken-floored building *10049*. The other is from Period 4.2. Ceramic bi-conical spindle whorls are common on Viking and early medieval sites in Scandinavia (Waterman 1959, 93). Ceramic forms of this type are previously unknown from Norwich. Other ceramic forms are also rare in Norwich, although a discoidal spindle whorl was found at in north-east Castle bailey (Margeson and Williams 1985, 44, fig. 37 no. 1). The other ceramic form found at Greyfriars is spherical (SF204) and was recovered from the disuse fills of the sunken-featured building in Area C (*50242*, Period 1); it is similar to one found in the fills of a Late Saxon 'hut' in Thetford (Rogerson and Dallas 1984, 117, fig. 152 no. 4).

SF590 Small fragment of an asymmetrical (truncated) bi-conical ceramic **spindle whorl**.
backfill 10725, SFB 10049, Period 2.1
SF594 Fragment of an asymmetrical (truncated) bi-conical ceramic **spindle whorl**.
backfill 10619, SFB 10049, Period 2.1
SF595 Fragment of an asymmetrical (truncated) bi-conical ceramic **spindle whorl** (in two pieces).
backfill 10725, SFB 10049, Period 2.1
SF509 Spherical ceramic **spindle whorl**, central hole punched through from one end to the other.
disuse fills 50263, SFB 50242, Period 1

Antler spindle whorl
by Ian Riddler
(Fig. 5.35)
A discoidal antler spindle whorl (SF895) was found in a Period 2.1 pit fill in Area A. A small quantity of objects of this type are known from Middle and Late Saxon contexts; most are not yet published, but they include examples from *Hamwic*, Ipswich and London (Riddler forthcoming a). Previously, they have been regarded as gaming pieces, but they are now considered to be spindle whorls (Ambrosiani 1981, 132 and fig. 82; MacGregor 1985, 137; Margeson 1993, 185). They are customarily decorated on the broad faces, and may include additional designs around the circumference. Linear designs cut with

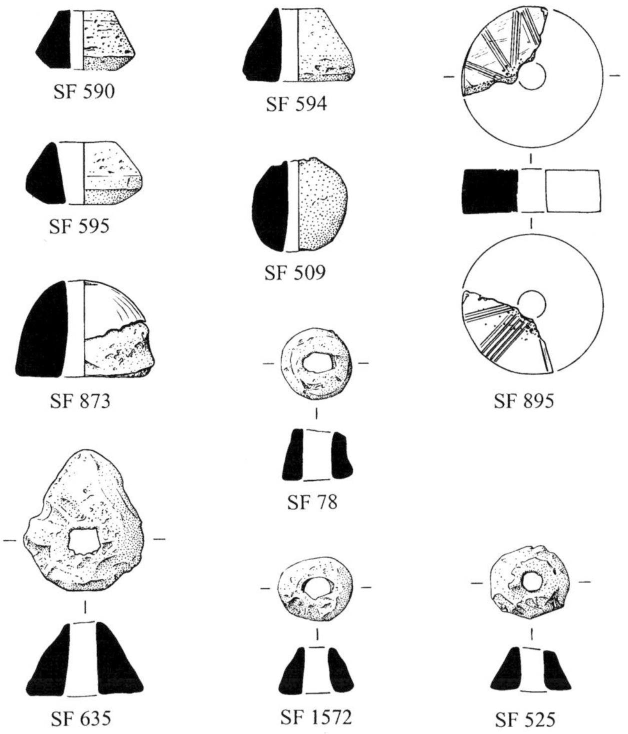

Figure 5.35 Spindle whorls: ceramic (SF590, 594, 595, 509), antler (SF895), bone (SF873), lead (SF635, 1572, 525). Scale 1:2.

a saw form the most common element of their decoration. Numerous examples of such objects have been published from continental sites, including Dorstad, Haithbu, Menzlin, Quentovic and Ribe; they are also known from Frisia (Roes 1965, 52–3 and plates XXI and XXII; Ulbricht 1978, 76–8 and taf 32; Roes 1963). Their frequency on the Continent, and their comparative rarity from Anglo-Saxon contexts where other forms of spindle whorl are known, suggests that they may reflect Frisian presence or influence.

SF895 A fragmentary antler **discoidal spindle whorl**, cut from an antler burr. It has been slightly damaged by fire. It is decorated on each broad face by groups of incised lines cut by saw. On one face these radiate outwards from the central perforation. On the other they circumvent the perforation.
pit fill 10422, Period 2.1

Bone spindle whorl
by Julia Huddle
Simple bone spindle whorls of the type made from the perforated head of a cattle or horse femur, such as SF873 (pit fill *30257*, Period 2.3), are well known from Norwich and elsewhere. They have been recovered from Late Saxon contexts at, for example, York (Walton Rogers 1993, 1268), Lincoln (Mann 1982, 22), Winchester (Woodland 1990, 217), Ipswich (Riddler forthcoming a) and Norwich (Williams 1987, 104; Huddle forthcoming). Those from the Norwich Survey excavations are from 13th–15th century deposits (Margeson 1993, 185).

?Limestone spindle whorl
by Julia Huddle
A ?limestone spindle whorl (SF205, not illustrated) can be compared to two from Late Saxon contexts at Thetford

(Rogerson & Dallas 1984, 117, fig. 152, nos 3 and 4). Similar examples of limestone spindle whorls from the Norwich Survey excavations were found in medieval and post-medieval contexts (Margeson 1993, 185, fig. 136 nos 1442–6).

Lead spindle whorl
by Geoff Egan
(Fig. 5.35)
The following lead objects are rather rough, but the identification as spindle whorls has been made, very tentatively, for similar items excavated at Winchester (Biddle 1990, 1128, nos 4343–4, fig. 368, listed among unidentified material). While this function does not really seem appropriate, particularly for very uneven versions like SF635, these objects are discussed here in the absence of any more satisfactory explanation.

SF635 Sub-conical, very irregular, with rectangular hole; maximum dimension 34mm, height 20mm, Wt: 81.5g. Possibly a setting to secure an iron item in masonry etc. (see SF1596).
make-up 11163, Period 3.1

SF1572 Conical, maximum diameter 20mm, height 12mm; Wt: 19.3g. *cf.* SF1846.
make-up 30484, Period 2.3

SF525 Sub-conical, maximum diameter 11mm, height 6mm, Wt: 18.8g. See SF78, 635, 1572. See also 'Unused seals', below.
build-up 40003, Period 4.2

Loomweight
by Alice Lyons
A fired clay loomweight of the 'bun-shaped' type was recovered from a ditch fill (*30592*, Period 2.1; internal D: 20mm; external D: 93mm; H: 31mm). This object would have been used in conjunction with a warp-weighted loom of a type that had been in use in Britain since the Iron Age (Rogers 1997, 1753). Although Roman examples are known in Norfolk (Darling 1993 fig 62 cat. nos 335–7), loomweights of this type are more commonly found in Late Saxon and Early Medieval deposits (Rogers 1997, 1753) consistent with the date of the deposit from which this object was retrieved. Other loomweights of this type have previously been found in Norwich (Wallis in prep. a and b).

Cloth seals
by Geoff Egan
(Fig. 5.36)
Cloth seals were put on individual, newly-woven textiles by those who manufactured them or were responsible for the workmanship, and also by alnage officials, who monitored standards in the industry. The seals were intended to attest that the quality of the fabric was good enough for the market (Egan 1994).

The eleven seals listed below are a heterogeneous group and they have the significance of apparently being the first found in the important worsted-production centre of Norwich in the course of formal excavations (*cf.* Ayers 1991, 3–5 and 8). Norwich/Norfolk seals are widespread, common finds in Britain and on the Continent, and they have occasionally been found at colonial sites in the USA, though relatively few have been published (see Egan 1994, 43–50, nos 70–95 with references; Egan 1995, 316; Egan forthcoming b).

The present small group, perhaps spanning the 16th to 18th centuries, emphasises local, Norfolk products (the origin of 18th-century issues is, as is frequently the case, difficult to establish), while the three unused blanks suggest weaving or processing in the immediate neighbourhood — although no documentary reference to this has been found (see Rutledge, below). The used seals also provide a hint that the pattern of textile consumption in the city was probably comparable with that now evident from groups of seals found at Salisbury, Gloucester and (although less clearly, because of the presence of major finishing industries like dyeing, and of important national and international markets) London. For each of those centres there is an emphasis particularly on local products, along with seals from important but more distant English and continental centres (Egan 1995, 315; Egan forthcoming b and c).

-	no stamp
//	next part
/	next line
..	single character missing
...	two or more characters missing

Unused seals
The first of these is a seal of the most common and widespread form, from a two-part mould (*cf.* Egan 1994, 5, fig. 4 and 119 nos 344–5), but the other two are of a particular lightweight form that was appropriate for the sometimes very flimsy worsteds of Norfolk (*cf.* Egan 1994, 4–5); the latter were produced from three-part moulds. These two seals are the only unused ones of the type so far known; they are the sole evidence for the precise form as cast, as well as corroboration for its place of origin. The three blanks together strongly suggest local manufacture of textiles, whether this involved weaving or one of the finishing processes.

Alnage seals

SF68 Rectangular 25 x 18mm // missing: (integrally cast) XVII/XVIIII, (stamped) H, S..A(R)CHE.. around // (missing). *Pro forma* seal for textile of standard specifications 17 and 19 — presumably yards length and pounds weight, though which is which is uncertain; these measurements are confirmed by 'searched' (*i.e.* checked) with the initial H, presumably that of the alnager or his assistant, stamped when the seal was attached to the textile; ?late 16th centuries/first decade of 17th century. Several seals from this series are known in London and elsewhere (Egan 1994, 58–9, nos 117–19, with references).
unstratified

SF2524 D: 21//21mm: ornate shield with arms of London (pointed shield base, stranded cross and the sword looks like a cross with ball terminals), (6/R) ..(R) to sides, ... PANNIS quatrefoil LANICIS around // NOT / WAD/ ..E.. (initial N reversed, horizontal lines divide legend). London seal, presumably an alnage issue; the first stamp has several parallels from the capital and Salisbury, and single comparable finds from elsewhere in England — these have ER (the Monarch's initials) in place of (?)RR and show the legend would have begun LONDINI PRO (*i.e.* 'at London for woollen cloth'); some are dated 1564 or 1573 and the present 6.. probably indicates the 1560s. The second stamp — ? 'not woaded' (?WADDED) — here replaces the more common arms of Tudor England with a legend referring to the alnage. If the interpretation is correct, the significance of the negative specification may have been to indicate that the blue colour (or possibly a shade from a combination of dyes) of the cloth to which the seal was attached was not from using woad, the usual colorant at the time for achieving this result; late 16th century.
unstratified

SF206 D: 16mm// (missing) (abraded) ? crown // (missing). Presumably an alnage seal from the royal symbol; the crown appears large enough to be the main device, either alone or with another (it appears larger than those on series

exemplified by Egan 1994, 59 nos. 120-1, for example, which probably includes Norfolk issues); ?late 16th–early 18th century. Norwich Worsted Weavers' Company Seal.
unstratified

SF262 D: 23mm // 23mm (incomplete discs): — (?obliterated by imprint from textile) // (doublestruck) ..(R) /MS... The stamp on the second disc is a series of initials, characteristic of Norwich seals for worsteds from the mid-17th century to 1705, when the control system in this form was ended for the city (Egan 1994, 46–7. nos 81–4). This particular series of seals had 'Norwich' on one stamp, and on the other the surname initials of the twelve annually elected wardens of the Company for the year, given in the same order as they appear in the yearly lists in the Mayor's Court Books. Although only three initials are fully discernible on the present find, and the lists of wardens have not survived for a small number of years, the available indications are consistent with the initials for 1680 (Court Book fo. 64V): AC/DRFG/MSSR/GB (underlined letters correspond, and there are parts of FG and the second G) – *i.e.* wardens John Ryle, Jo Morew jnr and Jo Shepheard. A parallel with more complete stamps was found at Chelsea in London (private collection).
build-up 40003, Period 4.2

Unused seals

SF243 D: 12mm//16mm; discs folded together, but rivet upstanding (*i.e.* unused); 16th–18th century.
unstratified

SF264 D: both 17mm; first disc is clipped and has on reverse a diametrical mould seam, which runs around the edge of the flat, triangular rivet; late 16th–early 18th century.
unstratified

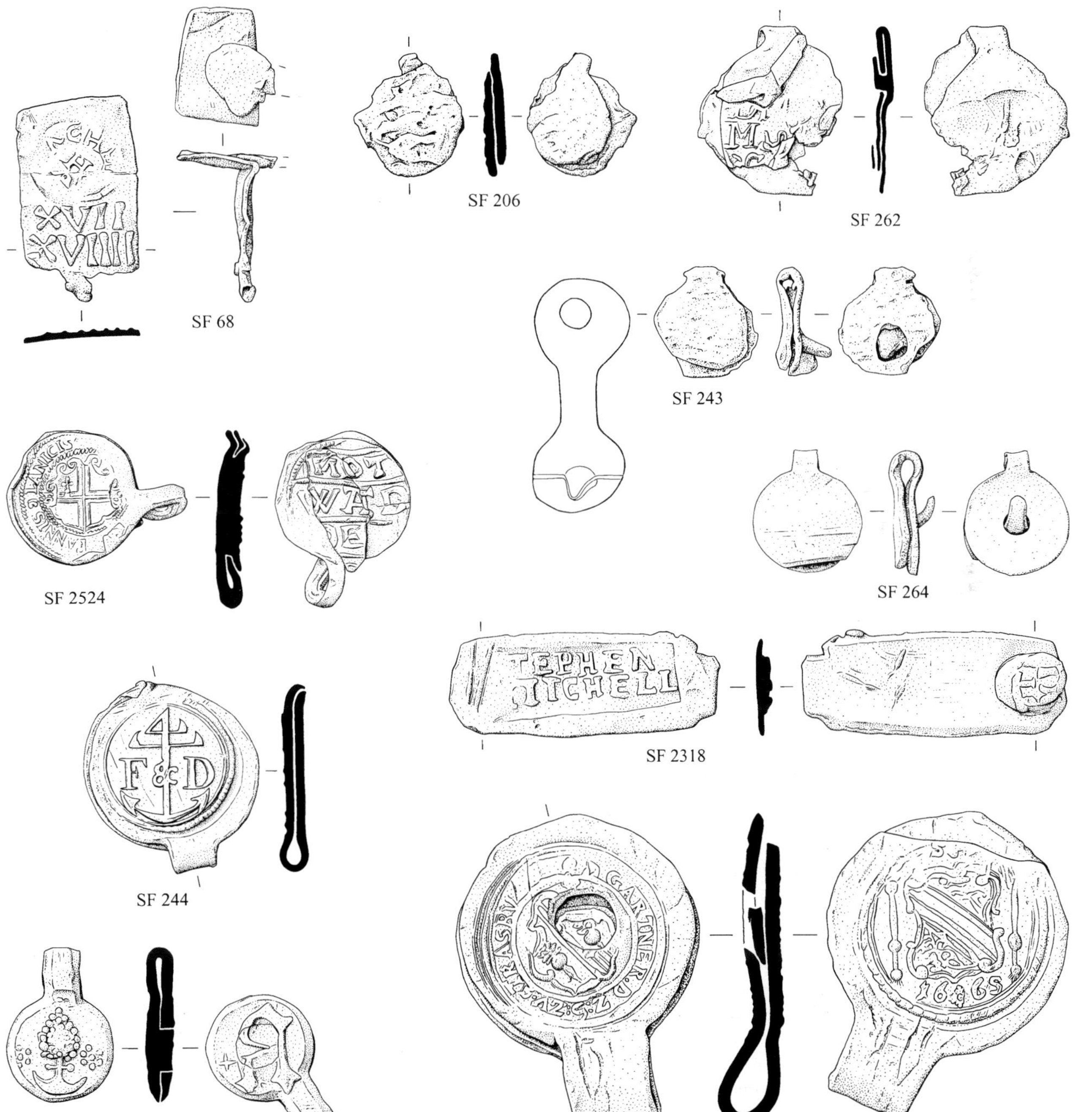

Figure 5.36 Lead cloth seals (SF68, 206, 262, 243, 2524, 264, 2318, 244, 2525, 2531). Scale 1:1.

Weavers'/clothiers' seals

SF244 D: 26mm//25mm: (?) – // anchor with finial in form of 4 instead of loop, F & D in front of bar, husk border. The adapted finial is similar to that on a number of conventional privy marks; identification is, as usual with personal devices on cloth seals, extremely difficult (*cf.* Egan 1994, 11 and nos 206–43); ?18th century.
unstratified

SF2318 Rectangular strip seal; 38 x 16mm // missing: ..TEPHEN/MITCHELL//(on rivet) ST.../MI... (*i.e.* same stamp as on first part). Stephen Mitchell, presumably a weaver or clothier, has not been traced in documentary records and so it remains unknown whether he was based in Norwich; this may well be a post-alnage era seal (*i.e.* 1724 or later); *cf.* Egan 1994, 87, no. 245; ?18th century.
build-up 40003, Period 4.2

Foreign seals

SF2525 D: 17mm//17mm: pine cone made up of dots, on rounded base with crosspiece terminating in dots, rosettes of dots to sides // blackletter A, cross to left. Augsburg seal, the pinecone being the city arms; the A is the initial of the city of origin. Augsburg in southern Germany was the main European centre for the production of fustians — mixed linen and cotton fabrics — and its seals are the most widespread of all in northern Europe, accounting for over 30% of all imports in England in the 16th and early 17th centuries (Egan 1995, 319; *cf.* Egan 1994, 106 nos. 308–10 and Egan forthcoming b). A probable close parallel has been found at Turku, Finland (Taavitsainen 1982, 28 no. 6 fig. 6); the present seal may be among the earliest of the series; (?) early 16th century.
layer 13006, Period 4.2

SF2531 D: 38mm//36mm: S(?fleur de lis)S over ornate shield with scrolling and bend, (?) baton to each side, 16 cross crosslet 65 below // fleur de lis over ornate shield with bend and grenades fired at both ends, (?rosette) D:GARTNER:D:Z:S:ZV: STRASBV... around. Strasbourg seal, the notable heaviness of which (47.75g: *cf.* Egan 1994, 2) implies a thick, robust textile, possibly a tapestry; the legend is in German because the city was part of Germany until 1681; the first arms are said to be those of the Gartner family (as in the legend) and the second ones are those of the city, which produced a variety of serges, bays, says and tapestries (Kerridge 1985, 7, 96 and 221–3); imports to England were called 'broad Strawsbrough linens' in a 1660 customs list. Several Strasbourg seals are known in England, with various dates between 1605 and 1715 (Egan 1994, 104, no. 305) — the present one is the first recorded for 1665; the particular fabric to which it was attached was presumably not available from English looms.
unstratified

Clothworking in Norwich in the late 16th–18th centuries
by Elizabeth Rutledge

Clothworking was probably not a very important industry in this area of King Street at the end of the 16th century. A reconstruction of the street's inhabitants for *c.* 1570 found only two weavers within the northern King Street parishes of St Cuthbert, St Vedast and St Peter Parmentergate, both on the western side of the highway. There were also two shearmen (one poor) on either side of Rose Lane (unpublished reconstruction by the King Street Group, Wensum Lodge, Norwich). While north King Street was never the major clothworking area of the city, textiles may have become more important by the late 17th/early 18th centuries. Probate inventories and other sources for the period 1650–1750 show strong evidence of worsted-weaving in the parishes of St George Tombland (by now incorporating the parish of St Cuthbert) and St Peter Parmentergate (incorporating the parish of St Vedast) (Priestley 1985, 196). Similarly a Norwich poll book of 1714, listing the freemen voting in the same two parishes, has worsted-weavers heavily outnumbering all other given occupations put together (80 to 66: Crossgrove 1714).

While this information shows the growing importance of worsted-weaving within the neighbourhood, it is only of limited relevance when considering the presence of cloth seals within the excavated site. Here the areas within and outside the main Greyfriars precinct need to be treated separately. The alnage seal found south of the former precinct (SF68) may be connected with the activities of David Nasshe, shearman, who acquired the property on the corner of King Street and Rose Lane in 1569 (see Fig. 3.1). When he resold the property in 1579 it included a long house called 'a workehouse'. Nasshe did not himself own the enclosure within which the seal was found but the next owner of his property held all the land as far east as St Vedast's church (NRO NCR Stanton to Whall 1f (29) m.63). During his working life Nasshe took on apprentices and had a son who also became a shearman (Millican 1934, 119).

It is unlikely, however, that such industrial activity was carried on inside the former precinct. Right down to the 19th century much of the area remained as open ground, apparently used as pleasure gardens (see Rutledge, Chapter 4.II). Any worsted-weavers mentioned as city lessees (Table 6) are likely to have been cloth merchants, more involved with marketing than with the day-to-day process of manufacture (Priestley 1985, 188, 190). Both clothier worsted-weavers and tailors, however, might have had occasion to store cloth on the premises and here the known occupations of lessees are of interest. The London and both foreign cloth seals were all within plot J, which was leased by tailors from about 1566 to 1608 (though this would be too early for the Strasbourg seal) (SF2524, SF2525 and SF2531: Fig. 5.36). The area between plot J and King Street, where cloth seal SF206 was found, also included late 16th- and early 17th-century tailors on plots F, G and H. The largest concentration of cloth seals, however, was within plot M (SF262, SF243, SF244 and SF2318). By 1650 this plot included a dwellinghouse and was in the hands of Samuell Cooke, worsted-weaver. Robert Cooke, who bought the property from the city in 1675, and his son Thomas Cooke esq., who was living there in 1744 (see Chapter 4.II; Blomefield 1806, IV, 109), also took up the freedom as worsted-weavers even though Robert was the wealthiest man in Norwich by the end of the 17th century (Millican 1934, *passim*; Corfield 1972, 243). SF264 may also be related to Cooke activities, as the orchard south of the precinct belonged to Thomas Cooke by 1704 (Blomefield 1806, IV, 104). If the Cookes were putting out work (see Priestley 1985, 192) they may have held a stock of unused seals.

No clothworking connection is known for plot L (the find-site of seal SF292). A limited search has found no information on Stephen Mitchell. No will, administration or inventory survives; he was not a freeman up to 1752 and does not appear as a city official (Millican 1934 and 1952; Hawes 1989).

Woodworking

Tools (iron)

by Val Fryer
(Fig. 5.37)
Auger bits, of which spoon bits are the most common, were used for boring holes in wood. Contemporary examples were found at, for example, Thetford, Norfolk (Goodall I.H. 1984, fig. 117 nos 14–17).

SF942 **Spoon bit** with lanceolate terminal.
pit fill 11143, Period 1

SF2651 Large **spoon bit** with lanceolate terminal.
pit fill 13250, Period 3.2

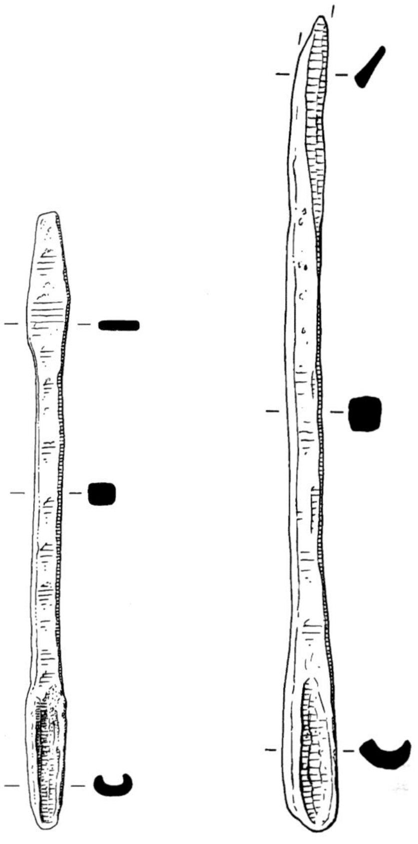

Figure 5.37 Iron spoon bits (SF942, 2651). Scale 1:2.

Painting

Medieval oyster shell palette

by Helen Howard
(Pls 5.2 and 5.3; Fig. 5.38)
An oyster shell palette (SF2621) retaining considerable remains of paint was excavated from quarry pit fill *13325* (Period 3.1). Pottery accompanying the palette suggests a *terminus post quem* of *c.* 1200, while other evidence indicates that the palette was probably associated with the Friary itself and may well have been used in work undertaken in the church *c.* 1300.

Scientific examination undertaken at the Courtauld Institute of Art shows that the pigments include natural azurite and vermilion, and that some of the original binding medium — identified as gum — also survives. Some preliminary analysis was undertaken by Catherine Hassall of UCL Paint Analysis.

Original materials
The oyster shell, which is slightly damaged around the edge, measures 65mm x 53mm. It contains several small islands of predominantly blue and red paint around its perimeter, with additional zones of brown and pinky-brown material (Fig. 5.38, Pl. 5.2).

Analysis of a series of paint samples confirmed the presence of the following pigments: natural azurite ($2CuCO \cdot Cu[OH]$), vermilion (HgS), and a black material which has not yet been fully classified. A brown material, found both in isolation and mixed with vermilion, was identified by FTIR microspectroscopy as a gum.

The blue pigment is natural azurite of average particle size 5 x 7 µm, and with a small number of larger particles of approximately 45 x 25µm (Fig. 5.39, Pls 5.3A and B). Some smaller rounded particles were also found and identified as the synthetic equivalent of natural azurite. When viewed in transmitted light, the combined aggregate structure of this synthetic pigment is easily distinguishable from the angular particles of the natural mineral (Pl. 5.3A). The admixture of the synthetic pigment would have the effect of bulking out the more expensive mineral blue.

The red pigment is vermilion. The average particle size is extremely small (2 x 3µm), although there are a few larger particles of *c.* 15 x 12µm. In a few areas the colour is slightly pink or brown/red, owing to the mixture of vermilion and gum (Pl. 5.3C). The brown material surviving elsewhere in the palette was identified as gum unmixed with any pigments (Fig. 5.40). In both cases the gum must be the remains of the original binding medium. Gums are water-soluble or water-dispersible polysaccharides of high molecular weight (Mills and White 1994, 76), and clearly distinguishable from proteinaceous binders such as animal glue which have been more commonly identified in medieval painting.

A black material which may have been used as a pigment is also present in the palette. Its average particle size is 7 x 12µm, with the largest particles approximately 60 x 110µm. This material has not yet been identified, though analysis by SEM/EDX indicates that the elemental constituents include lead, calcium, phosphorus and silica.

Sample No./ Accession No.	*Description*	*Original materials*	*Analytical method*
1/1877	Blue pigment	natural azurite	PLM & FTIR
2/1878	Brown material	gum	FTIR
3a/1879	Red/brown material	vermilion combined with gum	PLM, FTIR, SEM/EDX
3b/1879	Red pigment	vermilion	PLM, SEM/EDX
4/1880	Black material	containing lead, calcium, phosphorus and silica	PLM & SEM/EDX

Table 16 Materials present in oyster shell palette SF2621

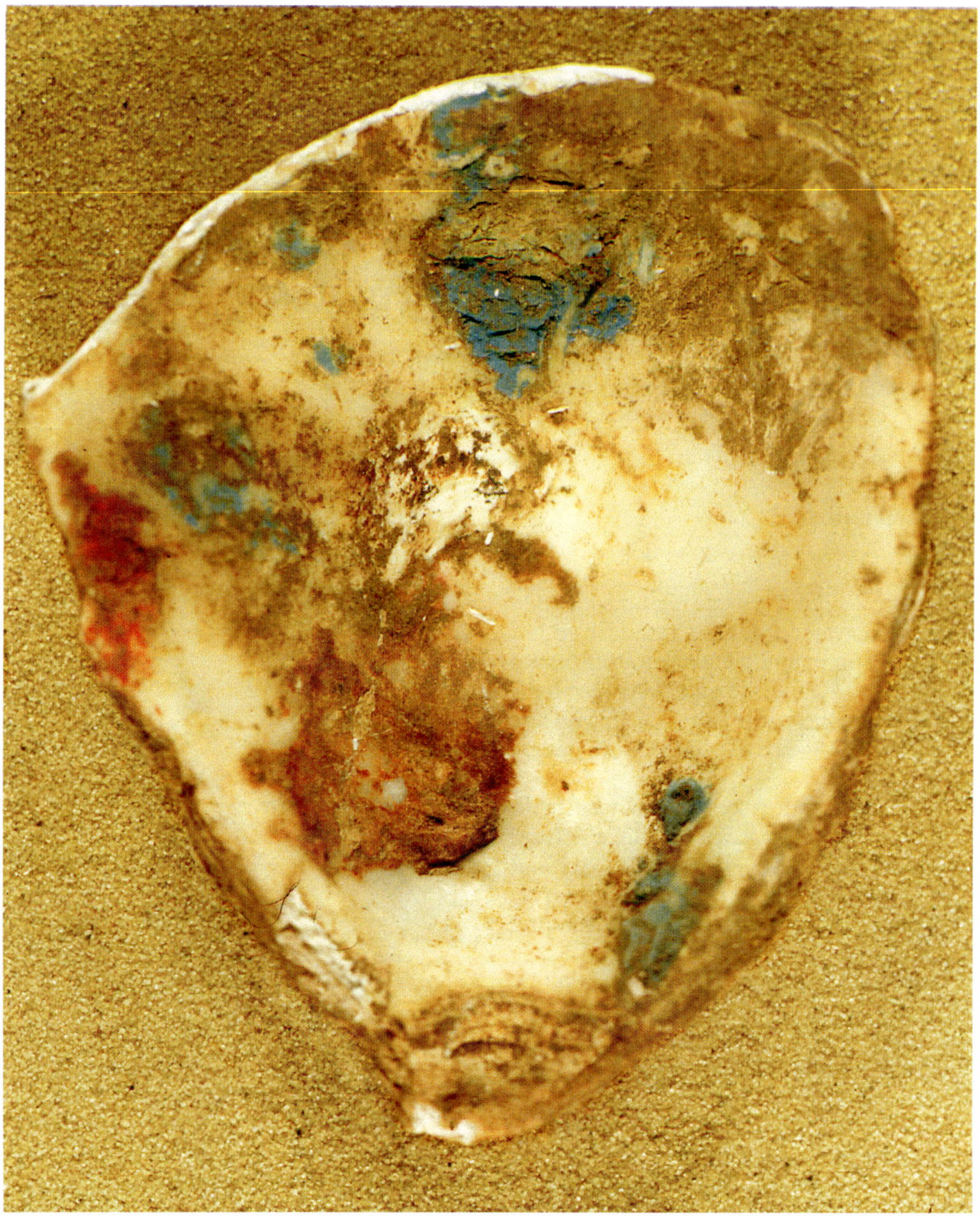

Plate 5.2 Oyster shell palette (SF2621) showing original pigments and binding medium: approximately four times actual size (photograph by Helen Howard).

Discussion

Shells have been used as pigment containers or palettes not only in the medieval period, but from antiquity to modern times. Thus, an oyster shell containing red paint has been found in a Roman context at Witcombe, Gloucs (Davey and Ling 1982, 61, 221), while mussel shells have been used into the 20th century to contain powdered gold combined with a medium, known as 'shell gold' (Gettens and Stout 1966, 310). During the Middle Ages, it is clear that shells were employed in all types of painting. For example, in the 12th century Theophilus describes their use in the application of gold in book illumination (Dodwell 1986, 28), while shells of various types are frequently depicted in medieval illustrations of artists at work (*e.g.* Egbert 1967, plate xxxi, showing panel painting at the beginning of the 15th century).

Surviving shells containing pigment are known from about twenty medieval and Tudor sites in Britain, and these are listed in Appendix 5. Examples from approximately half of these have now undergone scientific examination. Howard forthcoming provides up-to-date information on this analysis work. In most cases precise dating is not possible, nor is it normally clear for which type of painting the shells were employed. Exceptions include the shells found at Oxford and Boynton (Wilts.), the former clearly used for manuscript illumination, and the latter almost certainly for painting the tomb next to which it was found. The majority of the shells were probably used for large-scale painting, and this seems particularly likely in the case of the Clarendon Palace example, found in the excavation of a chamber known to have been painted for Henry III in 1251. Some of the shells only contain a single pigment, and can therefore be regarded as containers, while others — including the Greyfriars example — were clearly used as palettes. Only one of the shells shows evidence of a previous, different

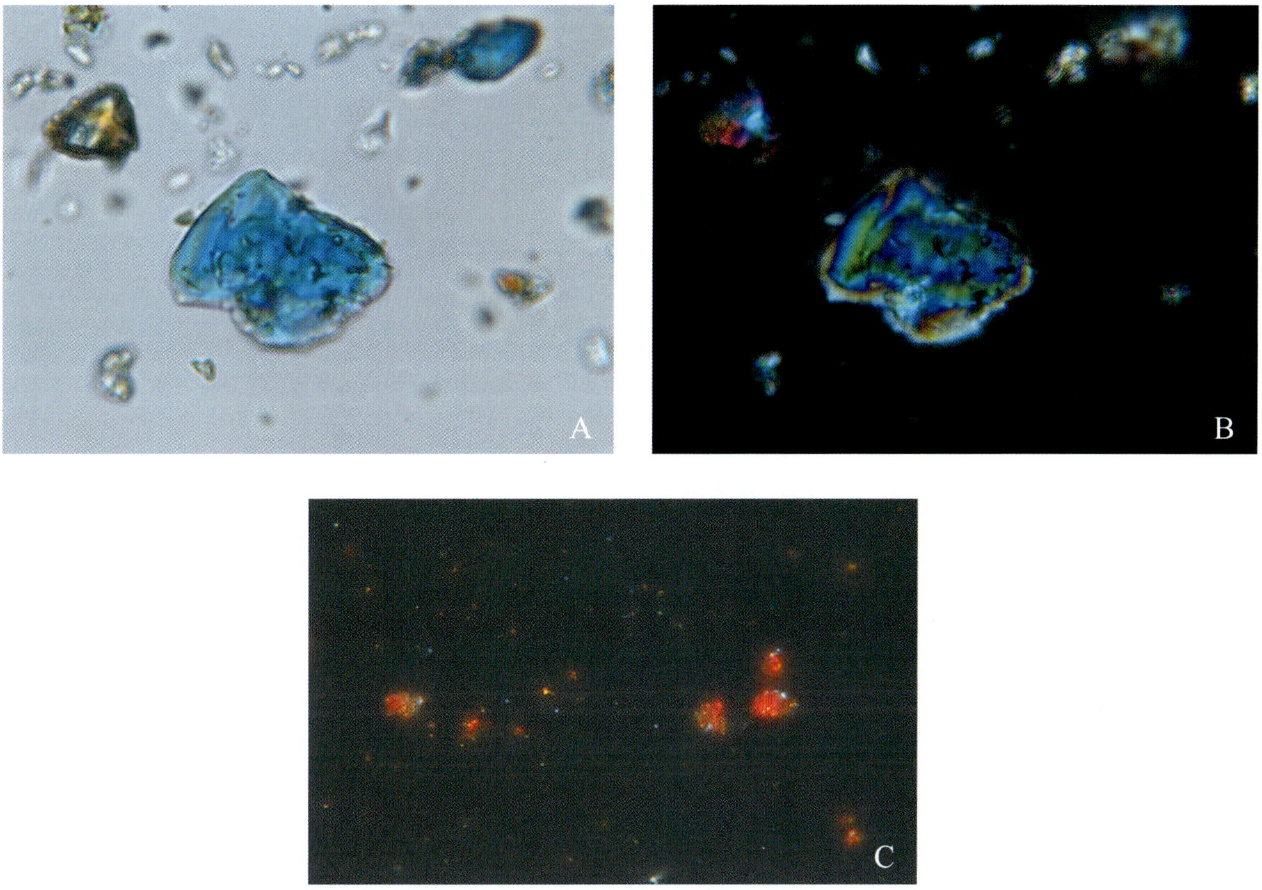

A, B: Dispersion of a particle of natural azurite from Sample 1 (original magnification 1000x). In A the particle is photographed in plane polarized transmitted light. The striations within the angular structure indicate its mineral origin. With crossed polars (B) the particle exhibits strong birefringence.

C: Dispersion of Sample 3 photographed in transmitted light with crossed polars, showing tiny particles of vermilion (original magnification 1000x). Analysis by Fourier transform infra-red microspectroscopy (FTIR) confirmed that this red pigment was combined with gum to form the red paint in the palette.

Photomicrographs Helen Howard, 2007.

Plate 5.3 Oyster shell palette (SF2621): photomicrographs

Figure 5.38 Diagram showing location of pigment samples taken from oyster shell palette (SF2621)

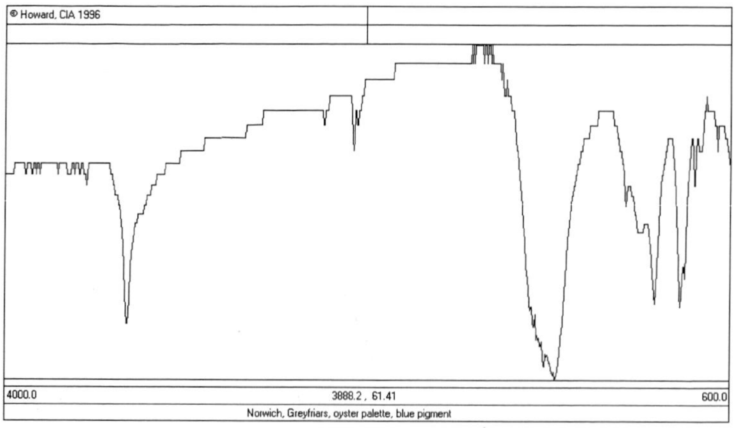

Figure 5.39 FTIR spectrum of the blue paint from oyster shell palette SF2621 (Sample 1/1877). Bands at 3429 cm, 1400 cm^{-1} (CO), 952 cm^{-1}, 837 cm^{-1} and 818 cm^{-1} are indicative of azurite.

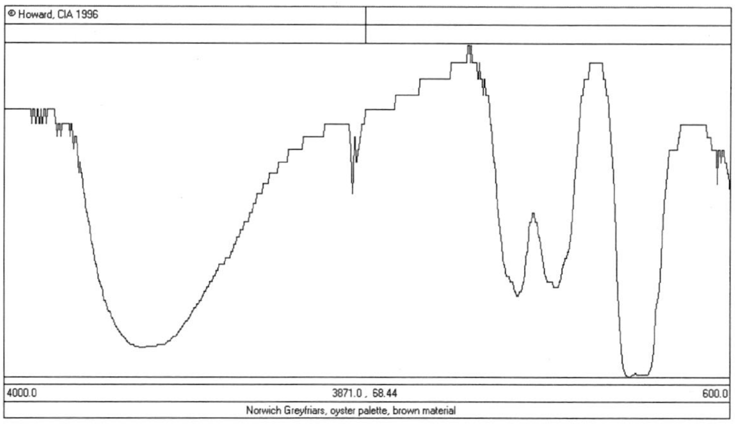

Figure 5.40 FTIR spectrum of the gum (a polysaccharide) from oyster shell palette (SF2621)

use: the Clarendon example is pierced for suspension, and had therefore presumably been used as a pilgrim badge. Similarly perforated shells have been found elsewhere, including Norwich (Margeson 1993, 8), while an example of *c.* 1200 from Keynsham Abbey is even said to be painted with a pilgrim's scrip (Spencer 1985, 293).

The Greyfriars palette is of particular interest since it provides the first case in which the binding medium has been identified. To date, gum has rarely been identified in large-scale medieval painting, although it was commonly employed for manuscript illumination (Mills and White 1994, 76). It is unlikely, however, that the Greyfriars shell was used for this purpose: the Franciscans' general council of 1260 prohibited members of the order from writing books or having them copied for sale (Branner 1977, 9 n. 41), and the Order typically obtained rather plain books for its own use from professional suppliers. There is, in fact, some evidence for the use of gum in large-scale painting. Analysis suggests that it may have been employed in the polychromy of *c.* 1230–50 on the west front of Wells Cathedral (Roy and White 1982), and examination of the painted effigy on the coffin lid of Archbishop Walter de Gray (d. 1255) in York Minster indicated that gum was used both as the paint medium and as an adhesive for the gold leaf. Other evidence includes the recommendation by Peter of Saint-Omer, in his treatise of *c.* 1300, of gum as a binding medium for red lead on walls (Merrifield 1849, 140), while 4lb of gum mastic were among the materials bought for painting the interior of the central tower of York Minster in 1473 (Tatton-Brown 1989, 145).

The pigments found in the Greyfriars palette would also have been suitable for large-scale painting, and have been identified in some of the other surviving shells. In wall painting, azurite was the most commonly employed mineral blue from the beginning of the 13th century (Howard 1988, 19–35). In the Middle Ages, important deposits of the mineral were located in Hungary, and it was imported into England (Gettens and Fitzhugh 1993, 25). The pigment was priced according to the intensity of its colour, which depended on the particle size; the particles in the Greyfriars palette are of average size, with a few larger inclusions. It is of particular interest, however, that the natural mineral here appears to have been adulterated with its cheaper, synthetic equivalent, presumably by the artist or the merchant. Synthetic copper blues have been identified in English wall painting from the 13th century onward, and the use of this pigment to bulk out natural azurite has also been identified in one of the narrative scenes of *c.* 1250 at Horsham St. Faith Priory, near Norwich (Howard 1988, 33).

Vermilion was commonly used for all types of painting in the Middle Ages (Hluvko 1991, 30–44). The Exeter Cathedral accounts for the 1320s provide information regarding its cost, which varied widely (Erskine 1981, 128, 144); the disparities must relate either to its quality, or to whether the natural mineral or its synthetic equivalent were purchased. The small quantity of black material in the Greyfriars palette has not been fully classified. In only one of the other surviving shells has a black pigment been identified: a carbon black pigment in the palette from the Carmelite Friary at Coventry.

It seems most likely that the Greyfriars palette dates to *c.* 1300. The context from which it was excavated was a fill of a quarry pit that had been left open for some time. The pottery accompanying the palette merely suggests a *tpq* of *c.* 1200, and it is conceivable that the palette was used by 'Giles le Peyntour', who owned a plot a short distance to the north-west of the Friary by 1284 (see Rutledge, Chapter 2.II). However, the quarry lies in an area which was apparently acquired by the Friary in 1292, in order that its church could be re-sited. The quarry was sealed by an earth terrace dateable probably to the 14th century, and therefore after the building of the new church was begun by 1292. It seems most plausible, therefore, that the palette dates from between 1292 and some time in the early 14th century, and was associated with the church or one of the other buildings whose construction began towards the end of the 13th century. The church would seem the most likely candidate, and since the Franciscans are unlikely to have had an elaborate scheme of wall paintings it is more probable that the palette was used for polychromed sculpture. It is known from documentary references that the church contained 'images' (probably sculptures) of the Virgin and St Thomas (see Rutledge, Chapter 3.II) — although their dating is uncertain — and doubtless other sculptures also existed.

A date of *c.* 1300 would accord very satisfactorily with the materials identified in the shell palette. Elsewhere in Norwich itself, recent scientific examination has shown that both azurite and vermilion were used extensively in the paintings of *c.* 1300 in the Ante-Reliquary Chapel of Norwich Cathedral (Park and Howard 1996, 396), while the sacrists' rolls of the cathedral priory reveal that blue ('azur') and vermilion were purchased in 1276–7 for work that seems at least partly to have concerned polychromed sculpture, and also that vermilion was employed in the decoration of the shrine of St William in 1304–5 (Park and Howard 1996, 401). Further analysis may provide evidence of the use of gum in surviving paintings at Norwich. Its identification in the Greyfriars palette suggests that it may have been a more common binding medium in English medieval painting than has previously been supposed.

Book fittings and writing implements

Book furniture

Book fastener
by Julia Huddle with Alison Goodall
(Fig. 5.41)
A 'book fastener' (SF200) was recovered from a make-up dump (Period 4.2). Parallels suggest that the raised loop near the closed end of the fastener may have had a chain attached to lock the book. A similar example was recovered from excavations in St Ebbes, Oxford (Goodall 1989, 226, fig. 62 no. 96). A fitting with projecting loop but without a hook at the closed end, also from St Ebbes, is described as a book-fastener (Goodall 1989, 226, fig. 62 no. 137).

A comparable clasp (to SF200) was found at the Austin Friars, Leicester in a mid-14th century context (Clay 1981, 133, fig. 48.33). Two came from the chapter house at St Albans Abbey. One is simple with a trefoil opening at the end and comes from a 19th-century context. The other is made from a single piece of sheet folded round a spacer plate and tapered to form a hook at the folded edge. It is decorated with traced lines and the loop contains the remains of a scrap of rolled leather — perhaps a thong for securing the fastening. Various forms of straps and ties were used for fastening book covers from the 12th century onwards.

Although these objects are sometimes identified as strap-ends, there is no reason why they should not also have been used for fastening books. It is significant that virtually all the examples known come from ecclesiastical and monastic sites, in other words places where books would have been used.

SF200 **Book-fastener** made of two copper-alloy plates attached to fragment of surviving leather. One of the plates has a projecting hook at the closed end. Copper-alloy rivet close to open end and projecting loop near closed end which is riveted to both plates.
make-up 10279, Period 4.2

Book mounts
by Julia Huddle with Alison Goodall
(Fig. 5.41)
Copper-alloy book mounts such as SF643, SF1891 and 373N/SF6, which would have been riveted to the covers of books, are known elsewhere from late medieval and early post-medieval periods. They are often decorated with stamped concentric circles and engraved zig-zag lines. A late 16th-century book in Norwich Castle Museum has similar mounts *in situ* on the binding (Margeson 1993, 74–5). Similar square bossed mounts to Site 373N/SF6 are known from Amsterdam in contexts dating to the 15th–17th centuries and are interpreted as book mounts to protect the leather binding from rubbing (Baart *et al.* 1977, 400–4).

SF643 Incomplete copper-alloy **cruciform book mount**, with two rivets. Single domed boss on each (surviving) arm.
build-up 11234, Period 4.2

SF1891 **Corner mount** from a book, with three copper-alloy tacks. The front is decorated on the inside and outside edge with engraved zig-zag lines and the head of each tack is surrounded by two incised rings.
fill 12143, Period 4.1

373N/SF6 Copper-alloy **square mount** with four V-shaped cut-outs along each side and central circular boss with large perforation. Rivet hole at each corner.
layer 8, Period 3.2

Page holder
by Julia Huddle and Steven Ashley
(Fig. 5.41; Pl. 5.4)
A copper-alloy page holder (SF620) was recovered from a context assigned to Period 3.1. A similar example was found in an early–mid-13th-century context in Winchester and it is suggested that this and other examples from both ecclesiastical and non-ecclesiastical sites are likely to be

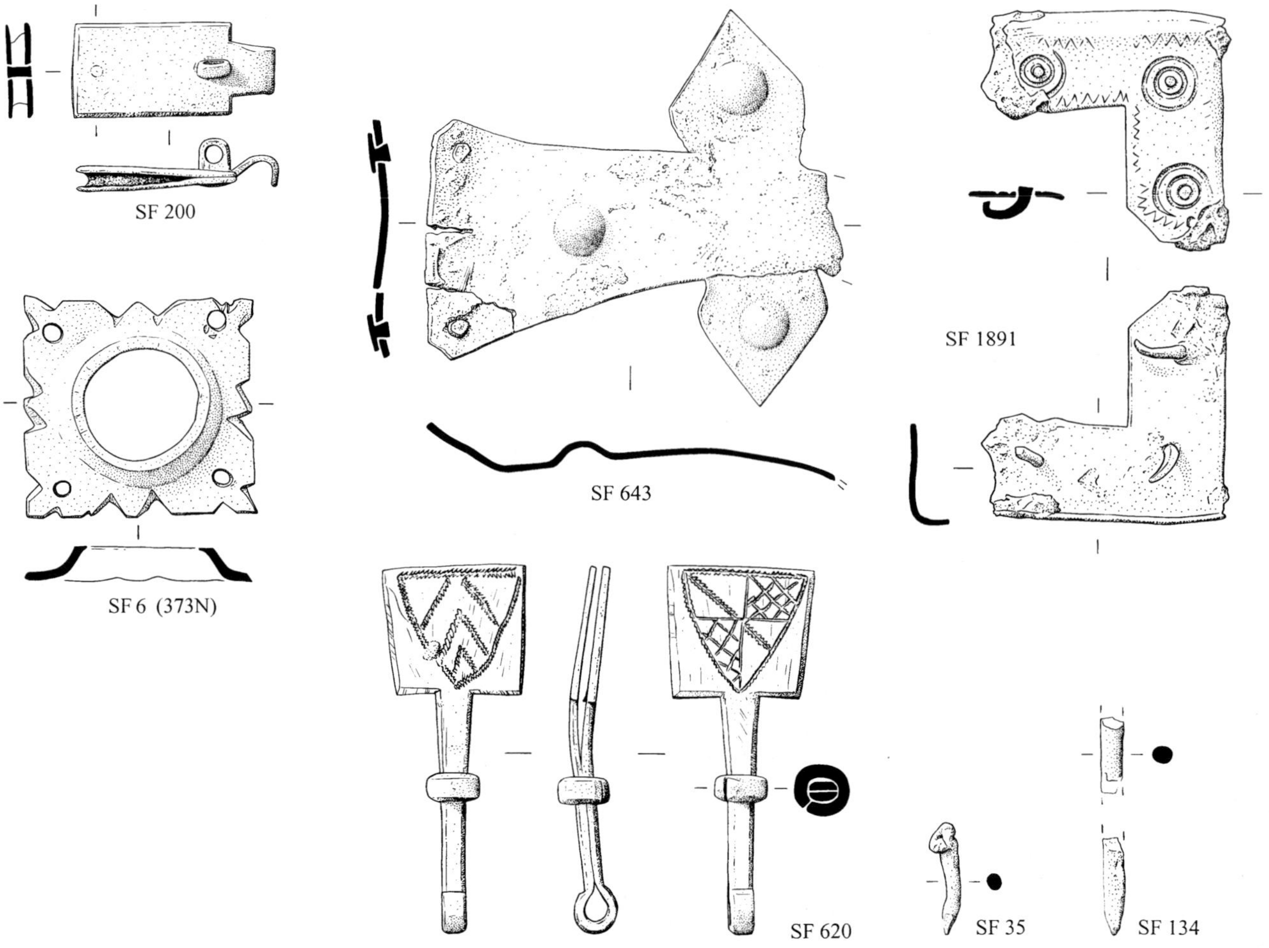

Figure 5.41 Copper alloy book fastener (SF200), copper alloy book mounts (373N/6, 643, 18910, copper alloy page holder (SF620), scale 1:1. Lead rods/stylii (SF35, 134), scale 1:2.

no earlier than the 12th or 13th century (Biddle and Hinton 1990, 757, fig. 215 no. 2326A).

The Norwich book holder displays two coats of arms of purely linear design, therefore lacking tinctures. Any attempt at the identification of the families represented is open to some doubt. The number of families bearing *Three chevrons* (differently tinctured), for example, runs well into double figures (Woodcock *et al.* 1996, 514–22). That said, the majority of examples of arms employing *Three chevrons* represent, or are closely associated with, the family of Clare (*Or three chevrons Gules*), Earls of Hereford and Gloucester. This identification is supported to some extent by the arms shown on the other face of the page-holder *Quarterly one and four [Argent] a bend [Sable] two and three [Gules] a fret [Or]*, the arms of Despencer, a family with strong dynastic links with the Clares in the 14th century.

Plate 5.4 Copper alloy page holder (SF620)

SF620 Copper-alloy **page holder**; front and back plates are square, expanding slightly towards edge, arms folded to form a spring and fastened by a sliding ring. Both plates decorated with rocker-arm ornament in the form of a shield. The arms displayed on the two engraved shields are: *Three chevrons* and *Quarterly one and four a bend two and three a fret*.
layer 30345, Period 3.1

Stylii and other rods (lead)
by Geoff Egan
(Fig. 5.41)

A stylus with a flat, wedge-shaped eraser at its other end (SF35) would have been suitable for use with a wax tablet. A further seven objects, which may or may not have been used for a similar purpose, lack one or both of these defining traits.

SF35 Incomplete; pointed end intact, other damaged; surviving L: 30mm, D: 4mm.
build-up 50031, Period 4.2

SF134 In two pieces; one end pointed; surviving L: 40mm, D: 5mm.
unstratified

Millstones and quernstones

by David Buckley
(not illustrated)

The assemblage of grinding stones was recovered from 73 contexts. Most, if not all, pieces are believed to derive from quernstones and millstones. One had been re-used as flooring (SF1261) in the late 12th century. It is not possible to be precise about the number of stones represented since some contexts produced fragments from more than one stone: numerous fragments can be produced and dispersed from a single stone. The fragments from 34 contexts comprise no more than splinters or are so small as to have no distinguishing features. Of the remaining 39, most are from the body of the stone providing evidence of the grinding surface and opposed surface representing the top or bottom of the original stone. In only a very small number of cases is there additional evidence for the original form, dimensions, dressing of the stones and other tooling. Only five fragments of stone are of sufficient size to provide a diameter (SF1769, SF1261, SF1929, SF1956, SF333). One fragment (SF1760) possibly displays part of the flange around a hopper that may identify it with the forms of flat upper stones from Dorestad classified by Parkhouse (1976, figs 3 and 4). Another comprises a small fragment to the edge of a pot quern lowerstone (SF1929), the rim of which is decorated with faint cross grooves.

The stone from Greyfriars, like previous finds from Norwich, is a grey vesicular lava for which the precise origin cannot be confirmed without petrological examination of each fragment. It is probable, however, that this group is all of Rhenish origin. There is some confusion over the naming of this lava (Biddle and Smith 1990, 881), which has been identified variously as coming from Andernach, Niedermendig and Mayen (all in Rhineland-Pfalz). The Mayen quarries are the most extensive of these and Röder believes, on archaeological grounds, that all the material dating from before *c.* 1500 came from there (Hörter *et al.* 1951). It was not considered appropriate to embark on petrological examination as part of the Greyfriars post-excavation programme since the value of such an exercise would need to be assessed within the context of a much bigger national research project. In this respect, should such a project be undertaken it is worth noting that the quantity of lavastone from Norwich (largely held in the Castle Museum) is considerable and this, coupled with the location of Norwich relative to the Rhine and its importance in the medieval period, makes it an obvious candidate for more detailed examination.

The absence from Norwich of other stone types such as Puddingstone and Millstone Grit was specifically noted by Smith (1993, 202). This is also true of sites in Norwich that have since been excavated, such as Dragon Hall, Castle Mall and the Millennium Library. Despite the scale of the Greyfriars excavations these are again absent, thereby reinforcing these observations in respect of use and trade of these stone types.

Period	*Date*		*No. millstones/ quernstones*
1	10th–11th century	pre-Friary	19
2.1	12th century		7
2.2	12th–13th century		6
3	1300–1538	Friary	14
3.1	1300–1400		2
3.2	1400–1538		17
4.1	1538–1566	Dissolution demolition	1
4.2	1567–1800	Post demolition	5
5	after 1800		1
			1
Total			**73**

Table 17 Quantification of millstones and quernstones

The dating for contexts producing lava is provided in Table 17. This indicates that nineteen of the fragments derive from 10th–11th-century contexts. Trade in lava querns, which appears to have ceased at the beginning of the Saxon period, was re-established during the Middle to Late Saxon period (Parkhouse 1976, 1977). Elsewhere it has been shown that some querns recovered from contexts of this date are in fact Roman, but this does not appear to be the case at Greyfriars. The finds from the site can therefore be added to the evidence from Norwich for an increase in the lavastone trade into the Anglia region during the Late Saxon period, which is supported by the evidence from Thetford (Rogerson and Dallas 1984), Norfolk (Rogerson, Ashley and Penn forthcoming), Ipswich (Keith Wade, *pers. comm.*) and Colchester (Buckley and Major 1987).

The flat quern which possibly had a collar around the hopper (SF1760) is from a Period 1 context, which accords with recognition that these are early medieval querns of a form which, according to Roder, were in use until *c.* 1000 (Hörter *et al.* 1950–1; Crawford and Röder 1955, fig. 1.7). Its recovery from a 10th/11th century context is entirely reasonable and it is likely that many of the fragments, in later contexts, would have derived from similar forms of stone since a larger time-span for their use is recorded in Southampton (West *et al.* 1975, 307–11). The diameters of these flat stones have been found to vary widely, but it is generally accepted that stones up to *c.* 650mm could have been hand-turned rotary quernstones (SF 1769; SF 1956). Stones greater than this are considered too large for hand turning and are therefore attributed to mechanically-turned millstones (SF1261; SF333), possibly powered by animal or water mills.

The pot quern (SF1929) is a form which appears, according to Röder, about 1000 (Crawford and Roder 1955, fig. 1.8). These are known from various widely separated locations and museum collections in Britain (Buckley and Major 1987, 36–9). The number of published examples is small and the trade in medieval lava pot querns has received little attention: many Norwich households will have had them, however, and it is likely that they were traded through the city. One recovered from the Pottergate excavations was taken to be an indication of the relative affluence of the houses in that area (Margeson 1993, 239), while a further example came from the recent excavations at Dragon Hall (Buckley 2005). Some of the fragments from flat stones, particularly those of smaller diameter, could derive from pot quern upperstones.

There is nothing inherent in the Greyfriars finds to suggest a particular purpose, and there is no reason to assume that all of the quernstones were used for the production of flour, a variety of grinding purposes being possible. Smith and Margeson (Smith 1993, 202) concluded that a significant number of the quernstones from the Norwich Survey excavations were used for the grinding of malt for the brewing industry. Since several of the Greyfriars querns are of Late Saxon date they could pre-date the tight control placed on the use of querns by the municipal authorities in the medieval period. In addition, restrictions on the people of the town for milling their own grain may not have applied to the religious orders.

The re-use of stone, indicated by mortar adhering to fragments (*e.g.* SF333) and burnt fragments indicating re-use as hearthstone (*e.g.* SF1261), is not unusual in an area lacking plentiful building stone. The re-use of lava querns for hearths or as building material has been noted elsewhere in Norwich (Margeson 1993, 239; Buckley 2005) and the splintered nature of much of the lava from Greyfriars also indicates stone re-use.

Commercial activity

Numismatic items

Coins
by John A. Davies and Martin Allen
(Pls 5.5 and 5.6)
A total of 34 coins and an unstratified 15th-century coin weight were recovered from the Mann Egerton site and are listed in the project archive, with notable examples catalogued below. An important late 9th-century weight struck between coinage dies is described by Archibald, below. The earliest numismatic item is an Anglo-Saxon 'Runic' type 'sceat', of the first half of the 8th century. Few *sceattas* have been found in Norwich. Others were recovered during excavations at St Martin-at-Palace Plain and at Fishergate (Williams 1988a and 1994b; Gregory and Metcalf 1994, 13). Series R *sceattas,* such as the Greyfriars example, are one of the commoner types to be found in Norfolk.

There is a single penny of the 9th century, a Viking copy of the coinage of Alfred the Great, dating from *c.* 880–95. This coin is discussed by Blackburn, below. Although Anglo-Saxon pennies were found nearby at Castle Mall, none of those dated to earlier than the 10th century (Davies forthcoming).

Thirteen coins date from the 12th to the end of the 14th century. These begin with one penny and two cut halfpennies of Stephen, from the mints of London, Norwich and Oxford. It is interesting to note that of the five Anglo-Saxon pennies recorded from Castle Mall, two of the three that are legible also belonged to the Norwich mint. It appears from this small sample that the local mint was supplying a substantial proportion of the coin in circulation. There is a single Scottish issue, a penny of William I. Such foreign coins comprised a small but steady component of the coinage pool in medieval England.

The three coins of Stephen (1135–54) were all minted before *c.* 1150, and they were probably deposited no later than the mid-1150s, as the issue of Stephen's *BMC* type vii in *c.* 1154–8 seems to have generally eliminated earlier coinage from circulation, although some coin hoards deposited after *c.* 1154 have a residual element of earlier coins. The probable *terminus ante quem* for the Henry II *Cross-and-Crosslets* (*Tealby*) penny, struck in the 1160s, is the end of the recoinage of pre-1180 coins in 1182. The Short Cross penny of Richard I or John and the coin of William I of Scotland were probably deposited no later than the end of the recoinage of 1247–50, and the Long Cross penny of Henry III or Edward I has a probable *terminus ante quem* of 1281, when the recoinage of the Long Cross coins of 1247–78 ended. The deposition of one of the pennies of Edward I or II (SF98), which has only slight signs of wear, may be dated to the first half of the 14th century, but the other Edward I or II penny (SF284) and the coin of Edward II (SF1879) are more worn, and they may have been deposited in the mid- or late 14th century. One of the Richard II pennies of York (SF512) has moderate signs of wear and may have been deposited in the early or mid-15th century, but the other coin (SF784) is heavily worn and clipped, and its deposition should probably be dated between the mid-15th century and the mid-16th century. The Henry VI penny (SF79), minted in the 1430s, is also heavily worn and may be a late 15th-century to mid-16th-century loss. The debasement of the coinage in the 1540s effectively eliminated pre-1544 silver coins from circulation.

SF1244 Anglo-Saxon 'sceat', Series R5 *c.* 710–*c.*750
BMC 2b North 157
O Radiate bust right. MGF before bust.
R Standard containing annulet and symbols; symbols around.
Moneyer: Epa. Wt: 0.90g
pit fill 50477, Period 2.2 (Pl. 5.5)

SF756 Vikings of the Southern Danelaw, penny, anonymous issue, *c.*880–95, with the name of Alfred, moneyer Wigmund
O [+]EL FR ED [RE], small cross
R [ ] / ·:· :· / VND / ·
Die-axis: 90 Wt: 0.69g
post-hole fill 10457, Period 2.1 (Pl. 5.6)

SF1446 **Stephen** Cut halfpenny, *BMC* type i, *Cross Moline* or *Watford*, 1135/6–*c.*1145
O [ ]REX
R [ ]N:ON:O[ ]
Mint: Oxford. Moneyer: Gahan. Wt: 0.27g (chipped).
fill 30414, Period 2.3

SF1194 **Stephen** Penny, *BMC* type ii, *Cross Voided and Mullets, c.* 1145–50
O +STIEFNE
R +DE[ ]N:ON[ ]
Mint: London. Moneyer: Dereman. Wt: 1.11g
50639 pit fill, Period 2.1

SF1195 **Stephen** Cut halfpenny, *BMC* type ii, *Cross Voided and Mullets, c.*1145–50
O +STIEF[NE]
R +ST[ ]NOR:
Mint: Norwich. Moneyer: Stanchil. Wt: 0.52g (two fragments).
pit fill 50639, Period 2.1

SF1832 **Henry II** Penny, *Cross-and-Crosslets* (*Tealby*) class C1, early–mid 1160s
O [hENRI R]EX[ ]
R Illegible.
Mint and moneyer uncertain. Wt: 0.95g
demolition debris 12077, Period 4.1

SF76 **Richard I or John** Penny, Short Cross class 4a, 1194–*c.*1200
O hENRICVS REX
R MEINIR·ON·CANT
Mint: Canterbury. Moneyer: Meinir. Wt: 1.29g
12077 demolition debris, Period 4.1

SF75 **William I of Scotland** Sterling, Short and Stars coinage, phase B, *c.* 1205(?)–1230

Plate 5.5 Middle Saxon 'Runic' type sceatta (SF1244)

Plate 5.6 Alfred the Great penny (SF756)

O LE REI WILAM
R +hVE W[ ]ERI:
Moneyers: Hue and Walter. Wt: 1.08g
unstratified

SF355 **Henry III or Edward I** Penny, Long Cross class 5g or 5h, *c.* 1258–early 1270s
O [HE]NRICVS REX III'
R RENAVD ON LVND
Mint: London. Moneyer: Renaud. Wt: 1.30g
pit fill 30028, Period 4.2

373N/SF310 **Edward I** Penny, 1279–1300
O: EDW R ANGL DNS [HYB]
R: CIVITAS LONDON
Mint: London.
unstratified

SF98 **Edward I or Edward II** Penny, class 10cf3a1, c.1307–09
O EDWA R ANGL DNS hYB
R CIVITAS LONDON
Mint: London. Wt: 1.30g
30978, Period 2.3

SF284 **Edward I or Edward II** Penny, class 10cf3a3, c.1307–09
O EDWA R ANGL DNS hYB
R CIVITAS CANTOR
Mint: Canterbury. Wt: 1.11g
unstratified

SF1879 **Edward II** Penny, class 11b1, c.1312–14
O EDWA R ANGL DNS hYB
R CIVITAS LONDON
Mint: London. Wt: 1.20g
unstratified

SF784 **Richard II** Penny, York local dies, Group C, 1380s–90s
O RIC[ARDVS REX] ANGIL[E]
R [CIV]ITA[S EBORACI]
Mint: York archiepiscopal. Wt: 0.77g (clipped).
unstratified

SF512 **Richard II** Penny, Type III, 1390s
O +RICARD[:REX]:ANGL:[Z:FRAN]
R [CIVI]TAS EBOR[ACI]
Mint: York archiepiscopal. Wt: 0.85g
unstratified

SF79 **Henry VI** Penny, Rosette-Mascle or Pinecone-Mascle, mullets by crown, c. 1430–mid-1430s
O Illegible.
R [C]IVI[T]AS [EBO]RA[CI]
Mint: York archiepiscopal. Wt: 0.87g
unstratified

Coin weight

SF949 English uniface coin weight for gold quarter-noble of 1344–1465, 15th century.
Wt: 1.67g
unstratified

Vikings of the Southern Danelaw penny
by Mark Blackburn

A Vikings of the southern Danelaw penny (SF756; catalogued above; see also BNJ 1992, 221, no. 263, where it appears as an official issue of Alfred), with the name of Alfred, moneyer Wigmund, was found in a post-hole associated with building *10049* (Period 1). Two other coins of this moneyer are known. One from the Morley St Peter hoard (SCBI 26, East Anglian Museums 59) is struck from the same obverse die, but a different reverse with three simple pellets across the centre. The second coin, described without illustration, from the Carlyon Britton collection (Sothebys, 20 November 1916, lot 941 (part)) has similar decoration on the reverse to this piece. The weight and style of the Morley St Peter coin suggests that it is a Danelaw imitation, but the moneyer's name is not recorded among Alfred's official coins and probably represents a real moneyer Wigmund, working at a mint in the Danelaw (Blackburn 1989, 346). This class of coinage was well represented in the Ashdon (Essex) hoard, deposited *c.* 895. A number of mints may already have been operating in the Southern Danelaw by the 880s or early 890s, and it has not yet proved possible to assign individual coins to a mint.

This coin would have been produced in the period *c.* 880–95, and it would probably have been lost shortly after 895 at the latest with the introduction of the St Edmund coinage.

Jettons
by John A. Davies

The jettons from this site comprise a substantial proportion of the numismatic collection, amounting to fourteen items, which are catalogued in the project archive. They can be broken down into three main series. The earliest comprises four English type jettons. These were all produced during the reigns of Edward I, II and III, between *c.* 1280 and 1343. The four French types are slightly later and belong to the second half of the 14th and the 15th centuries. The largest group is that of Nuremberg jettons, which were all produced during the 16th century.

Tokens
by Geoff Egan
(Fig. 5.42)

A lead token recovered from a Dissolution-period pit (SF759) is from a series issued in the last quarter of the 16th century and which has been found mainly in London (Roach Smith 1854, 160 no. 781; North 1975 (2), 116 no. 2062). Single finds are known from Canterbury and Bassingbourn, Cambs., as well as two from the colonial site of Jamestown, USA (Archibald 1995, 953 no. 2, fig. 400; Fitzwilliam Museum 1982, 234 and plate u; Kelso 1995, 15–16, fig. 24: the last, from a site founded in 1607, shows that the series continued in use at least into the first

Figure 5.42 Copper alloy tokens (SF759, 2510). Scale 1:1.

decade of the 17th century). A second lead example displays the initials 'IB' (SF2510) and could date from any time between the mid-16th to early 18th centuries. An additional five plain copper-alloy discs (not illustrated or catalogued here) may also have served as tokens.

SF759 D: 21mm (portion corroded away), Wt: 3.30g: crown over rose, E (R) to sides, (? GOD SA)VE THE QUE(?NE) around // double-headed eagle displayed (parallels allow the edge legend to be restored, as well as the right-hand letter R on the first side).
pit fill 10385, Period 4.1

SF2510 D: 13mm, Wt: 2.60g; uniface: IB — the first of these initials is the three-bar form of I.
layer 13049, Period 4.2

Weights

Half-eyrir lead weight
by Marion Archibald
(Fig. 5.43)

A half-*eyrir* lead weight (SF281) was found re-deposited in a build-up relating to the Friary (context *50025* in Area C). A recent corpus of coin-related lead weights concluded that those struck between coin dies are typically Anglo-Saxon and those set with actual coins, Viking (Williams 1999). The Greyfriars weight bears the name of Alfred and is of the former type, but identifying it as an official weight of Alfred would present considerable historical difficulties since East Anglia is believed to have been under the control of the Danes at this time. It is not necessary to debate this question, however, because the internal evidence of the weight itself demonstrates that it is Viking.

It is well-established that the Vikings in the Danelaw struck copies of Alfred's coins before they began to produce coins naming their own rulers (Blackburn 1989) and the presence of Alfred's name has no direct political significance. Some have the names of real Danelaw moneyers who never worked for Alfred. The copies range from those which are illiterate and gross in style to others which reproduce accurately not just the names of Alfred and his moneyers but closely follow the various styles of the originals. The condition of the Greyfriars weight, where the outlines of the letters are somewhat flattened and corroded, makes it difficult to compare the minutiae of style, but its dies seem closest to those identified with Canterbury.

The reverse inscription is clearly essaying a moneyer whose name has the deuterotheme –VALD. However, the L is retrograde and the D is represented by only the upright, while the prototheme EAF– is a blundered form and not viable as it stands. While inscriptions even on Alfred's official dies are not always perfect, these points taken together indicate that this is an imitative Viking die copied from a genuine coin of one of Alfred's moneyers who used Canterbury-style dies. Of the relevant moneyers in -VALD the most likely, requiring only one letter-change is Eadwald, an apparently prolific moneyer well-represented in the Cuerdale hoard (BMC 272-85), the major source of coins of this period. (A moneyer of the same name for Edmund of East Anglia, d. 869, is not relevant here.) Although no die-identity has been found, some of his coins are significantly below the *c.* 24.5gr/1.60g weight standard of Alfred's official Two Line types, being instead around the Viking standard of *c.*21.0gr/ 1.35g (for these standards see Blackburn 1989, 344). While some of the latter are letter-perfect, one of his low-weight coins has P for D in the king's name (BMC 273), and a further example has the top line of the moneyer's name retrograde (BMC 274). It would appear that a significant number of his extant coins are Viking copies rather than true coins of Alfred. Another of Alfred's moneyers, Elfwald/Ælfwald, seems less likely as he does not use Canterbury-style dies, but a coin in his name could have influenced the copyist. The letter-perfect obverse of the weight does not speak against a Viking attribution since the king's name is more often transcribed correctly on imitations than the varied and less familiar moneyers' names.

The four known Anglo-Saxon weights struck between coinage dies all appear to represent convenient multiples of pennies of the same coin-type, indicating that they were intended to weigh coins (Williams 1999, 20–3). The extant coin-set Viking weights are instead multiples or sub-divisions of the general Viking units of mass with no direct correlation to current coinage standards (Williams 1999, 23–36). At 12.1g, the present weight does not fit the Anglo-Saxon pattern: with the contemporary coinage standard at *c.* 1.60g it is the equivalent of about eight pence, which is not a plausible unit; nor does it correspond convincingly with likely multiples of the standard of the Viking imitations in Alfred's name of around 1.35g. It is, however, strikingly close to the half-*eyrir* unit based on an archaeologically-established *eyrir* standard or standards in the range 24–6g. The Viking *eyrir* and the Anglo-Saxon ounce were equivalents but, for the numismatic reasons outlined above, the present example is unlikely to be an official Anglo-Saxon half-ounce weight which, while theoretically potential, is not yet known in a die-struck form. The Greyfriars weight shows that when the Vikings were beginning to follow the Anglo-Saxon example of striking coins, they also adopted Anglo-Saxon practice in the manufacture of official die-struck weights but adapted to their own system of weight units.

There is one related Viking lead object from an unknown findspot, in the British Museum since 1876, weighing 3.86g and struck between two reverse dies of Regnald II Guthfrithsson and Anlaf Sihtricsson at York, probably *c.* 943-4. These dies were used for coins which both have a Cross Moline type regal obverse. The status of this object — which until now stood alone in a Viking context — has hitherto been unclear. It was catalogued as a weight without discussion of its denomination in the 1986 *Sylloge* (BMS 1255), but was described neutrally as a 'lead piece' in *CTCE* in 1989; it was associated with the plentiful die-struck lead pieces of irregular lighter weight identified as customs tickets (Archibald 1991), and was excluded from Williams' 1999 corpus of weights. The discovery of a cognate piece from Norwich supports its

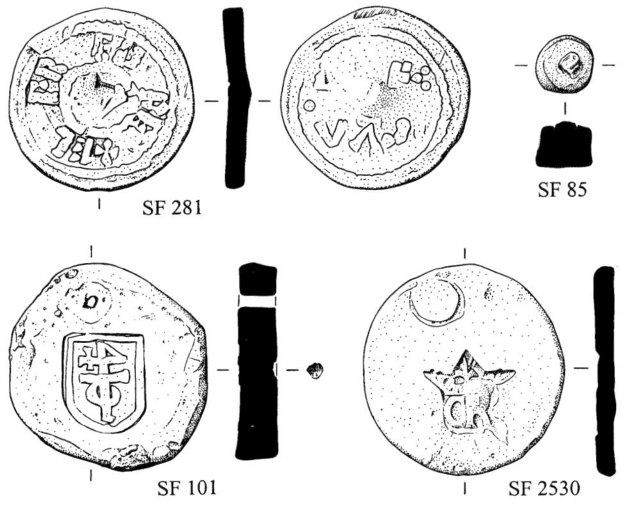

Figure 5.43 Half-*eyrir* lead weight (SF281). Other lead weights (SF85, 101, 2530). Scale 1:1.

identification as a weight and despite the fact that it is not struck from a pair of dies including a regal obverse, this is not a reason to exclude it from the canon of Viking weights. It can be identified as a half-*ertog*, another well-attested Viking unit. Allowing for condition, it fits well with the weight unit of *c.* 4g established from finds at Birka and Hedeby, and with the figure suggested for the *ertog* (one third of the *eyrir*) by Neilsen (based on surviving weights) of 8.1±0.40g and by Lundström (based on ingots) of 7.78–8.64g (for a discussion of the extensive literature on Viking weight systems see Williams 1999, 32–4). It was produced some time after members of the Hiberno-Norse Viking dynasty had begun striking coins in their own names in England but, like the Greyfriars example, it still represents one of their own weight units rather than being a multiple of the weight of the current pennies like the Anglo-Saxon die-struck examples. The function of such Viking weights was to weigh bullion, which still formed a significant part of circulation in the areas of Viking settlement in England; they were struck from coin-dies, as were the Anglo-Saxon weights, to demonstrate their official status in a way which would be recognisable by all. They were no doubt used at the mints, but probably also elsewhere when the rulers or their officials were collecting dues. Viking weights which are multiples of the weights of contemporary coins, and Anglo-Saxon die-struck ounce weights for that matter, remain theoretically possible, but the die-struck weights extant fall into the two categories along ethnic lines and this division may perhaps be generally applicable.

The four Anglo-Saxon die-struck weights were all found at or near their place of manufacture and, while this need not necessarily limit the range of the Greyfriars Viking piece, it is probably indicative. There is no direct evidence that Norwich was a mint for Viking imitations, or for the following coinage of Guthrum/Athelstan, but some rare coins of the late 9th-century St Edmunds issue with a blundered moneyer's name on the reverse have, on the obverse, the inscription 'NORDVICO'. While it has been suggested that this inscription may just denote a personal name Nordvic (Smart 1985, 86), its identification with a mint signature for Norwich at least remains open. It would be possible that the Greyfriars weight was made elsewhere in Viking East Anglia, or even further afield in the Danelaw, and brought to Norwich by traders or others. Some doubt must remain, but Norwich seems the most likely mint. If some of the Viking imitations were in fact made at Norwich or elsewhere in East Anglia, their issue is likely to have ceased when a coinage in the name of its king Guthrum/Athelstan was introduced. If so, this weight was probably produced in the earlier 880s. The sharp-edged damage to the centre of the obverse of this weight was probably not accidental but a deliberate defacement. Three of the Anglo-Saxon weights of this category show intentional damage, suggesting that new weights were made to the current standard each time the coinage types were changed and that the then redundant weights with the old types were deliberately defaced to cancel their official status and validity (Webster and Backhouse 1991, 286, no. 264). It would appear that this further aspect of Anglo-Saxon practice was adopted by the Danes and the mark on the Greyfriars weight inflicted when the imitative coins in Alfred's name were superseded by the coinage of Guthrum/Athelstan. Further discussion of the possibility of the presence of a mint on the Greyfriars site is given in Chapter 2.IV.

SF281 Half-*eyrir* **lead weight** of the Vikings of East Anglia, probably struck at Norwich in the earlier 880s from local dies copying coins of the Two-Line type of Alfred of Wessex, 871–99, probably of the Canterbury moneyer Eadvald.
O +EL FR ED RE around central cross
R EAF followed by trefoil of pellets . . [.] VALI (L retrograde) (a knock at the centre of the first side has made the reading of both sides here difficult)
Weight: 12.1g
D: 25mm, thickness 3mm
Ref. prototype as North 1, 1994, no. 635
build-up 50025, Period 2.2

Other lead and copper alloy weights
by Geoff Egan and Julia Huddle
(Fig. 5.43–44)

Twelve lead weights of varying type and function were recovered. (SF281 is from an earlier era than that of the religious house and is detailed by Marion Archibald above.) SF85 is a cylindrical weight, which cannot be related to any of the main standards in use for weighing. Measured weights are accurate to 0.05g.

Copper-alloy nested cup-weights from England are dated from 1588, although these are unlidded. When lidded cup-weights (such as SF514) first appeared is uncertain. However, they were apparently forbidden by the beginning of the 20th century (Houben 1984).

Several roughly conical items (like SF1557 and SF1846, Fig. 5.44) are known; all are cast, but their crudeness and failure to respect an obvious weighing standard makes their function uncertain.

Some or all of seven further lead weights (SF101, SF1875, SF2513, SF2529, SF2536, SF2559 and SF2530, not illustrated) may be classed as household items or fishing weights but have been grouped together here for simplicity.

SF85 Cylindrical **weight**, H: 12mm, D: 15mm; iron rod in top; Wt: 17.1g. The rod is presumably the remains of a loop for suspension from a balance arm. *cf.* SF2529 and Margeson 1993, 205–6 no. 1585 fig. 157.
ditch fill 50663, Period 2.2

SF101 Slightly uneven **disc**, D: 58mm, T: 10mm, Wt: 29.6g; shield-shaped stamp with (?Lombardic-style) initials ?TP;

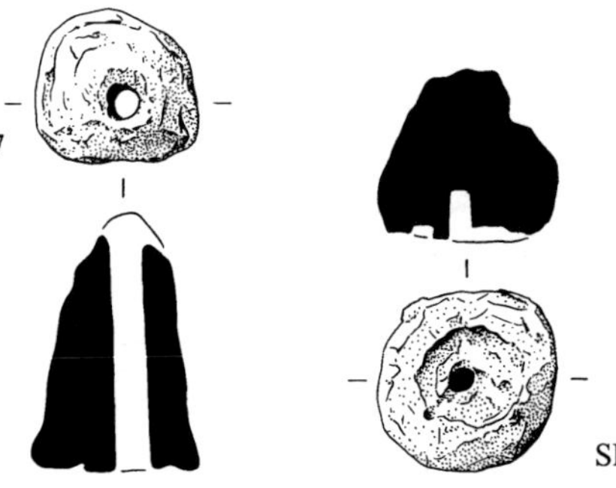

Figure 5.44 Conical lead weights (SF1557, 1846). Scale 1:1.

pierced at top.
floor 10024, Period 4.2

SF2530 Disc, diameter 27mm, thickness 2.5mm, Wt: 13.3g; stamped crown over CR. Half-ounce **weight** with regulatory stamp of Charles I. *cf.* Biggs 1992, 46, for weights with similar stamps, including two from (or believed to be from) Norwich.
make-up 13008, Period 5

SF1557 **Weight**, 152.5g, roughly conical, D: 36mm, H: 31mm, central hole in abraded base.
pit fill 30467, Period 2

SF1846 Hexagonal conoid **?weight**, H: 41mm, maximum D: 28mm, Wt: 124g.
unstratified

Scales
by Julia Huddle
(Fig. 5.45)

Two balance pans (SF2552 and SF358) were found. It seems likely that the former, being a rather fine example, may well have been used in the Friary period, for either domestic or commercial purposes. Margeson discusses the various uses of balance pans (1993, 203).

SF2552 Copper alloy **dished pan**, with three perforations, one with iron rivet *in situ*, for attachment to chains. Embossed motif on base in the form of four short radiating lines, between which are four incised lines which cross in the centre. The shallow rim of the bowl is highlighted by two incised concentric lines and the outer edge is punched to form a raised 'lip'.
fill 13010, Period 4.1

SF358 Hemi-spherical copper alloy **dished pan** made of sheet metal, with two opposing holes near top for missing rivets; the sides are distorted.
unstratified

III. FURNISHINGS AND HOUSEHOLD EQUIPMENT

Furniture fittings

Box/casket mounts

Box/casket mounts (bone and antler)
by Julia Huddle with Ian Riddler
(Fig. 5.46)

The simple ring-and-dot decoration applied to thin strips of bone and (less frequently) antler is typical of the design found on mounts recovered from Norwich and elsewhere in 10th–12th-century contexts. These strips are usually

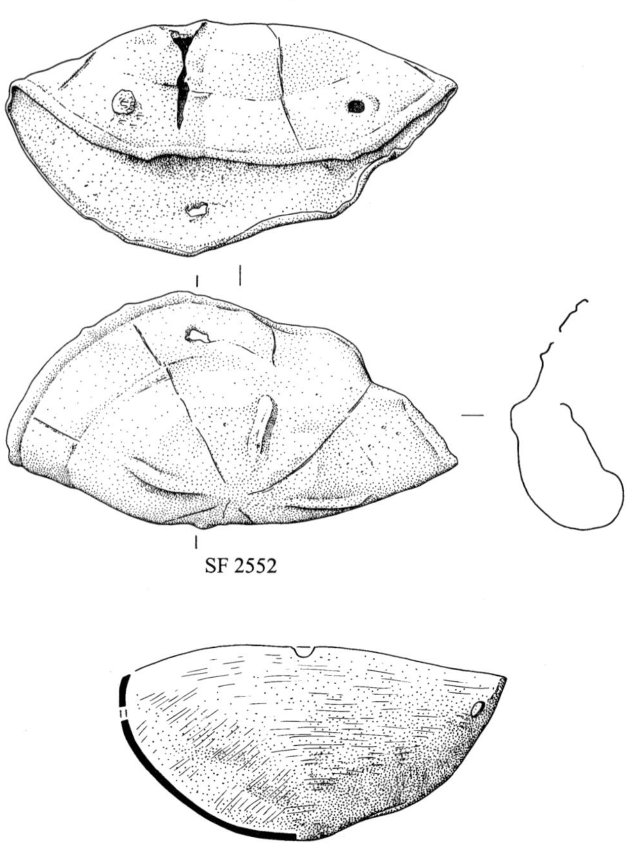

Fig. 5.45 Copper alloy scale pans (SF2552, Scale 1:2; SF358, Scale 1:1)

perforated for attachment (to a box or casket), and one from St Martin-at-Palace Plain (Williams 1987, 104, fig. 82 no. 28) was found with an iron rivet *in situ*. The bone mount found at Greyfriars (SF1183) is residual, whilst an antler ?mount (SF1641) is from an 11th-century pit.

SF1641 Section of sawn and split antler, flattened on both sides; two circular holes one at either end, one with iron nail or rivet *in situ*. **Possible box or casket mount**. Length of shank 21mm.
pit fill 30937, Period 1

Casket/coffer mount (iron)
by Val Fryer
(not illustrated)

SF845 is the pierced terminal of a perforated strip mount with a convex profile, flattened back and traces of white metal coating, probably tin, on the upper surface. Similar mounts are common on domestic sites of the 12th and 13th centuries (*e.g.* Goodall 1993, fig. 46 nos 492–505) and would probably have been used on caskets or coffers.

Handles
by Julia Huddle
(Fig. 5.46)

A copper-alloy mount similar to SF801 was found in a mid–late 15th-century context at Alms Lane, Norwich (Margeson 1993, 78, fig. 43 no. 485). Loop-handles for cupboard doors, some of which like copper-alloy example SF1100 are heart-shaped, have been recovered elsewhere from medieval and early post-medieval contexts.

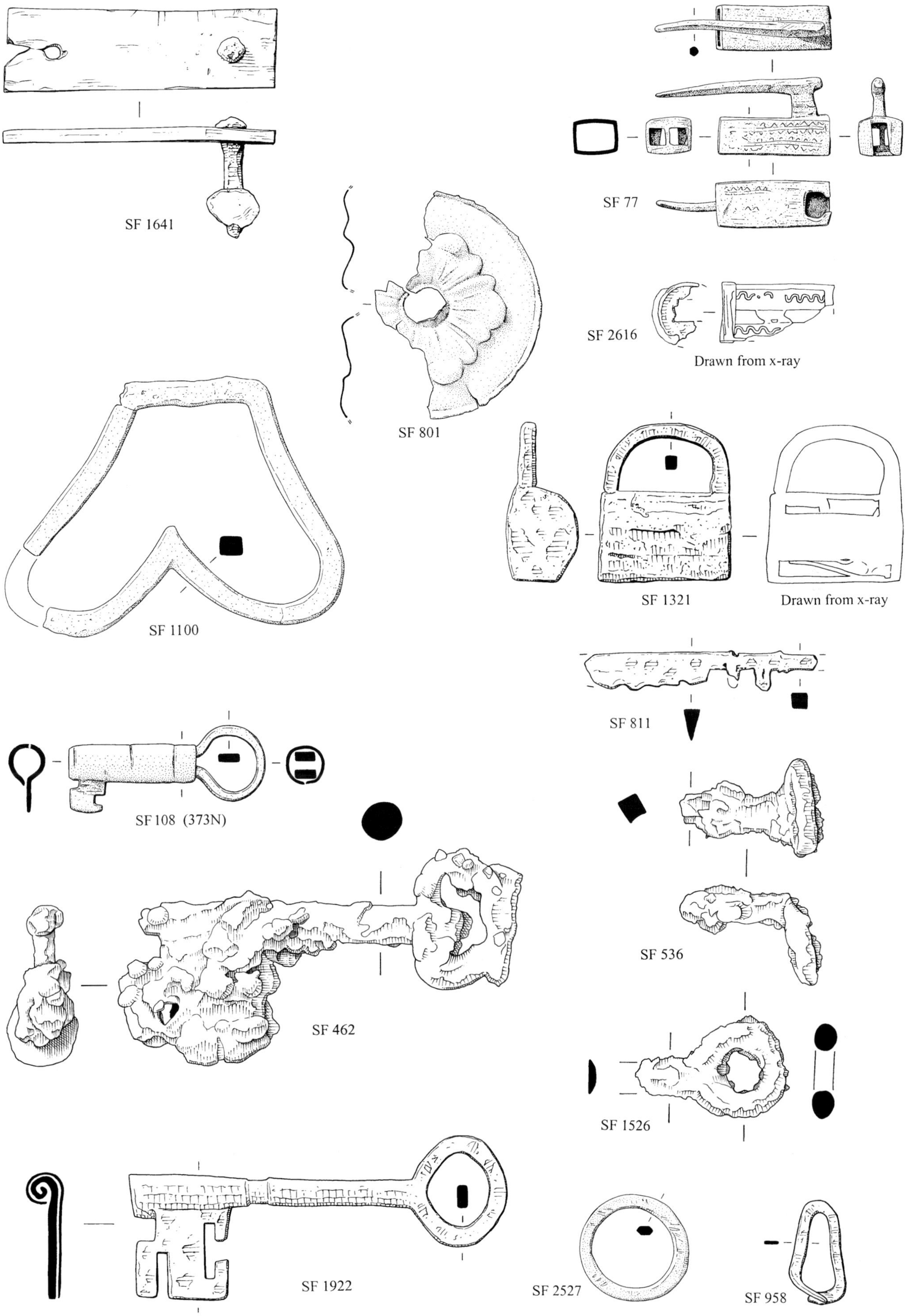

Figure 5.46 Antler box fitting (SF1641), copper alloy handles (SF801, 1100), locks (copper alloy SF77, iron SF2616, 1321, 811) and keys (SF108, 462, 536, 1526, 1922). Iron hasp (SF958). Copper alloy curtain ring (SF2527). Scale 1:1.

SF801 Copper alloy **backplate** for handle, incomplete circular mount with central hole surrounded by pinnate leaves, three of which survive out of five originally. Decorated in repoussé technique.
fill 10346, Period 5

SF1100 Heart-shaped copper alloy **loop handle**.
ditch fill 30524, Period 3.2

Lock furniture, hasps and keys

Padlocks
by Julia Huddle and Val Fryer
(Fig. 5.46)

The typology of locks and keys used here is based on chronological range and form types by Ian Goodall (see Biddle 1990, 1001). The Greyfriars copper alloy barrel padlock (SF77) is very similar to one found at Winchester from a 15th-century context (Type C), although the Winchester piece has a perforation on the L-shaped arm which may have been for the attachment of a chain to hold the various parts together (Goodall 1990, 1001, cat. no. 3666). Barrel padlocks, according to their size, would have been used for a variety of functions but were mainly used to secure doors, chests *etc*. The example from Greyfriars, being very small, was probably used for securing a small item of furniture such as a chest or casket. Although known from pre-Conquest deposits, examples similar to the iron barrel padlock case (SF2616) are more common in contexts of the 11th century and later, for example at Goltho, Lincolnshire (Goodall 1987b, fig. 158 nos 101–3) and St Martin-at-Palace Plain, Norwich (Williams 1988b, fig. 58 no. 7). The copper-alloy strips and wires used on the Greyfriars example served both to strengthen and decorate the padlock case.

SF1321 is an iron box padlock with a ?hinged shackle. The internal mechanism is masked on the x-ray by a heavy rectangular plate attached to the exterior of the case. Box padlocks were introduced at the end of the medieval period and a similar example from Pottergate, Norwich (Goodall 1993, fig. 115 no. 1240) is from fire deposits dating to 1507.

SF77 Copper-alloy **barrel padlock**, with L-shaped arm, cast in one piece. Rectangular case with decoration on sides and underside (and ?originally the top) tall narrow key hole, bolt missing.
unstratified 40005, Period 3.2

SF2616 Fragment of end and side of iron **barrel padlock case.** Remains of T-shaped key slot in end plate. Copper alloy strips running around end and longitudinally along case with areas between latter decorated with wavy lines of applied copper alloy wire.
pit fill 13256, Period 2

SF1321 Iron **box padlock**.
pit fill 30501, Period 4.1

Lock bolt
by Val Fryer
(Fig. 5.46)

SF811 is an iron lock bolt with a pair of teeth on the underside and the remains of a stop on the upper edge, from a stock-lock of medieval or post-medieval date. For parallels and a discussion about lock types see Goodall 1993, 157, fig. 116 nos 1257 and 1259.

SF811 Iron **lock bolt**. Possible traces of plating around teeth.
pit fill 40027, Period 3.2

Hasps
by Val Fryer
(Fig. 5.46)

Hasps were used to secure doors, gates, box-lids *etc*., the exact function being determined by the size of the hasp. A single sub-oval iron hasp with lapped flattened terminals at the wider end (SF958) was one of only five iron artefacts recovered from the disuse fill of the sunken-featured building *50242* in Area C.

SF958 Iron **hasp**.
disuse fill of SFB 50242, 50263 Period 1

Keys
by Julia Huddle and Val Fryer
(Fig. 5.46)

Two keys (373N/SF108 and SF1922) are both made with the stem and bit being rolled out of a single sheet and are of Ward Perkins Type II, which may dated to as early as the late 11th century (Ward Perkins 1940, 136). Those from recent excavations in London are from late 13th–14th-century contexts (Egan 1998, 113–17, nos 314–21). The example from St Faith's Lane is of copper alloy and is unusual in that the bow is made separately and inserted into the top of the shank, presumably making it even less robust than keys made in one piece.

373N/ SF108 Copper-alloy **key** of Ward Perkins (1940) Type II, stem and bit rolled out of a single sheet of metal with asymmetrical clefts. Ring bow made from strip of copper alloy and inserted into the hollow stem, which is decorated with three circumferential grooves, one of which may actually be a crimping to secure the bow. Presumably for a casket lock.
make-up 56, Period 3.1

SF536 Iron barrel padlock **key**
50024, Period 3.2

SF462 Iron **key**
50040, Period 4.2

SF1526 Iron **key**
30034, Period 5

SF1922 Large iron **key**
fill 12336, Period 5

Curtain rings

by Julia Huddle
(Fig. 5.46)

Five copper-alloy curtain rings (or simple buckle-frames) like the illustrated example (SF2527) were found in Dissolution or unstratified contexts. They are uniform in appearance, with a rectangular section, bevelled edges and characteristic file marks, produced as a result of filing the edges down. As with the vessel fragments from post-Dissolution contexts, these rings may well belong to the Friary period. Elsewhere in Norwich these items have previously been found in contexts dated from the mid-15th century, as well as a 16th–early 17th-century context (Margeson 1993, 82, fig. 47 nos 522–4). A ring found on Oak Street, Norwich, with thread wound round one part, suggests these may have been used as curtain rings or similar. However, they may equally have been used as a simple buckle frame (Sue Margeson, *pers. comm.*).

SF2527 Copper-alloy **annular ring**, rectangular in section with bevelled edges; surfaces covered in file marks. Simple buckle-frame or curtain ring.
layer 13001, Period 4.1

Annular fitting
by Val Fryer
Iron fitting SF804 is a severely corroded and very fragmentary annular fitting with four evenly spaced nails/studs which have had their shanks bent over as a means of attachment. Its exact function is uncertain.

Lighting

Lamp/censer fittings
by Julia Huddle
(Fig. 5.47)
A copper-alloy suspension unit (SF28) is similar to an example from a post-medieval context from the late 11th-century church of St Peter, Guestwick (Williams 1987, 73, cat. 2, fig. 50), and others are recorded in the HER (Sue Margeson, *pers. comm.*). Further examples are known from London (where Alan Vince has suggested that these are likely to be for lamps or censers). Given the ecclesiastic contexts for both the Norfolk examples, a unit for a censer seems probable here.

SF28 Copper alloy **suspension unit**, possibly for a lamp or censer. Three radial arms project from central arm; all have pierced terminals. Central arm has pierced terminal for suspension and secondary fastening point at base.
build-up 50031, Period 4.2

Stone lamp
by J.M. Mills
(Fig. 5. 48)
A stone lamp fragment, which is not closely dateable, was recovered from disuse fills of sunken-floored building *10049* (Period 2.1).

SF1041 Fragment of a stone **lamp**. The rim is plain and flat-topped and the external face almost vertical and smooth. The lamp is made from a fine sandstone, pale pink in colour and discoloured grey by burning to a depth of at least 15mm from the internal surface. The internal surface is slightly pitted. Not closely datable. External diameter *c.* 80mm (25% extant), wall thickness at rim c.20mm, extant height 63mm.
backfill of SFB 10049, 10725, Period 2

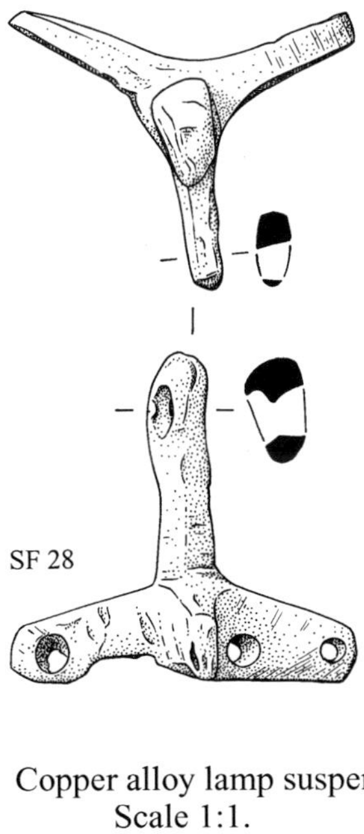

Figure 5.47 Copper alloy lamp suspender (SF28). Scale 1:1.

Fabric type	*Period 1*	*Period 2.1*	*Period 2.2*	*Rest*	*Total*
Thetford-type	1	1	1	2	5
Early med ware	-	-	1	1	2
Total	1	1	2	3	7

Table 18 Frequency of ceramic lamp fragments by fabric type

Ceramic lamps
by Richenda Goffin
(not illustrated)
Fragments of seven ceramic lamps were recovered from the early phases of the excavation (Table 18). The majority of them were made in Thetford-type ware, and were represented by the spiked lamp type (Dallas type DA: Rogerson and Dallas 1984, 156), and the baluster pedestal variety (Dallas type DB). In addition two fragments of EMW lamps were also identified. Both vessels were thin-walled with a slightly curving profile; one had a slight internal lip and the other a thickened rim.

Glass lamps
by John Shepherd
(Fig. 5.48)
The type of lamp with a flared, cup-shaped bowl and a pointed, tapering stem is frequently depicted in medieval manuscripts and sculpture. It was a purely functional form that could have been used for both ecclesiastical or secular purposes, either singly or with others in a frame. The stub-shaped ends, as here at Greyfriars (SF714 and SF1378), are the most easily recognisable parts of such vessels.

Examples of the lamps, identified by their bases, are numerous. For instance, a complete example, probably of 13th-century date, comes from Winchester (Harden *et al.* 1968, fig.4) and examples from early 14th-century contexts at Southampton (Charleston 1975, 205 and 216,

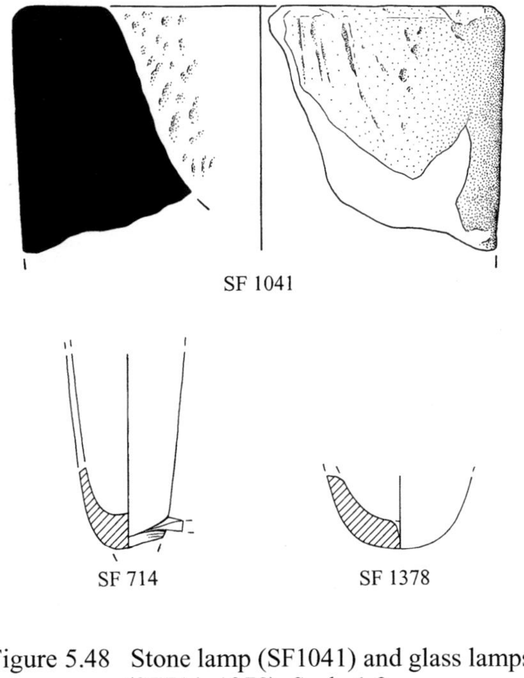

Figure 5.48 Stone lamp (SF1041) and glass lamps (SF714, 1378). Scale 1:2.

no. 1502; see also 205, no. 11 for reference to a 13th- or 14th-century lamp from Goldsborough, West Yorks, and an example in a context dated *c.* 1350–70 at Northolt Manor House). They occur also on the 'early' (*i.e.* 14th-century) glassworking sites in the Weald such as at Hazelbridge Hanger, Wephurst and Gunter's Wood (Kenyon 1967, 166, 181–2 and 193 respectively), Chiddingfold (Winbolt 1933, fig. on p.11) and Blunden's Wood (Wood 1965, 65–6, fig. 6B).

SF714 The base of a glass **lamp**. Free-blown, natural green glass with deep surface decomposition. Rounded point of base with residue of pontil mark adhering to the base.
pit fill 40024, Period 3.2

SF1378 The base of a glass **lamp**. Description as SF714.
pit fill 30804, Period 4.2

Vessels

Cauldrons (iron)

by Val Fryer
(Fig. 5.49)

Parts of two cast iron cauldrons are of probable 18th-century or later date. The more complete example (SF1865) has two of three circular section legs surviving, crooked handles and a sagging base with a carination between base and body. The other (SF2036, not illustrated), from an unstratified context, is very fragmentary but appears to have had a rounded base without legs and an everted rim.

SF1865 Cast iron **cauldron**.
fill 12144, Period 4.2

Vessels of copper alloy

by Julia Huddle
(Fig. 5.50)

Several fragments of copper-alloy cooking vessels were found and include three cauldron or possibly skillet legs (SF65, SF603 and SF1831). Other fragments include part of a cast vessel comprising part of the rim and vessel wall (SF1952), representing either part of a skillet or large bowl. Fragments from a bowl of hammered sheet metal were found (SF419), the rim having been formed by turning over the edges. SF2558, which is heavily sooted on the exterior, was probably used as a cooking vessel which was hung from a chain over a fire.

Copper-alloy vessels are comparatively rare from archaeological deposits in Norwich and the majority of those previously recovered are from the early 16th-century fire debris on Pottergate (Margeson 1993, 90–3). The Greyfriars material is all from post-Dissolution contexts, but is likely to be residual within them. Similar fragments of cast and hammered copper-alloy bowls were recovered from post-Dissolution contexts at the Austin Friars, Leicester (Mellor and Pearce 1981, 130–2).

SF65 Copper-alloy **cauldron leg** with three-toed foot.
build-up 50039, Period 4.2

SF603 Part of copper-alloy **cauldron leg** and foot with flat back and convex front.
unstratified

SF1831 Incomplete copper-alloy **cauldron leg**, surfaces are sooted.
demolition debris 12077, Period 4.1

SF2558 Cast rim fragment of copper-alloy **bowl**, (now in two pieces), with a copper-alloy rivet and two holes for ?missing rivets on a broken edge; the outer surfaces are heavily sooted.
make-up 13051, Period 4.2

Vessel repairs

by Julia Huddle
(Fig. 5.50)

Vessel repairs known as 'paper-clip' rivets were used to hold small repairs in place on copper-alloy vessels (*e.g.* SF986). They are well known from medieval and early post-medieval deposits. Previous examples from the Norwich Survey excavations come from 16th- and 17th-century contexts, and one is from a 13th-century

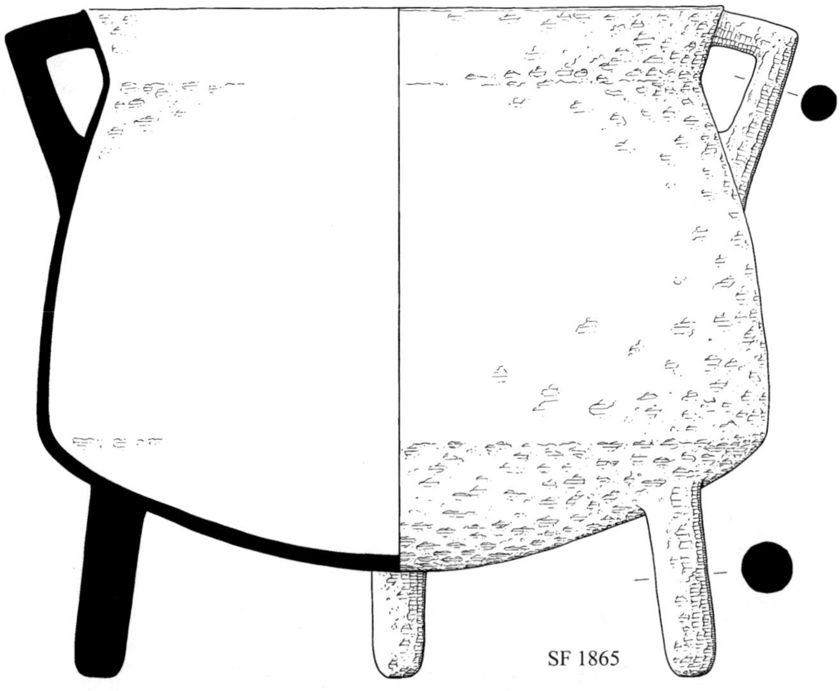

Figure 5.49 Iron cauldron (SF1865). Scale 1:4.

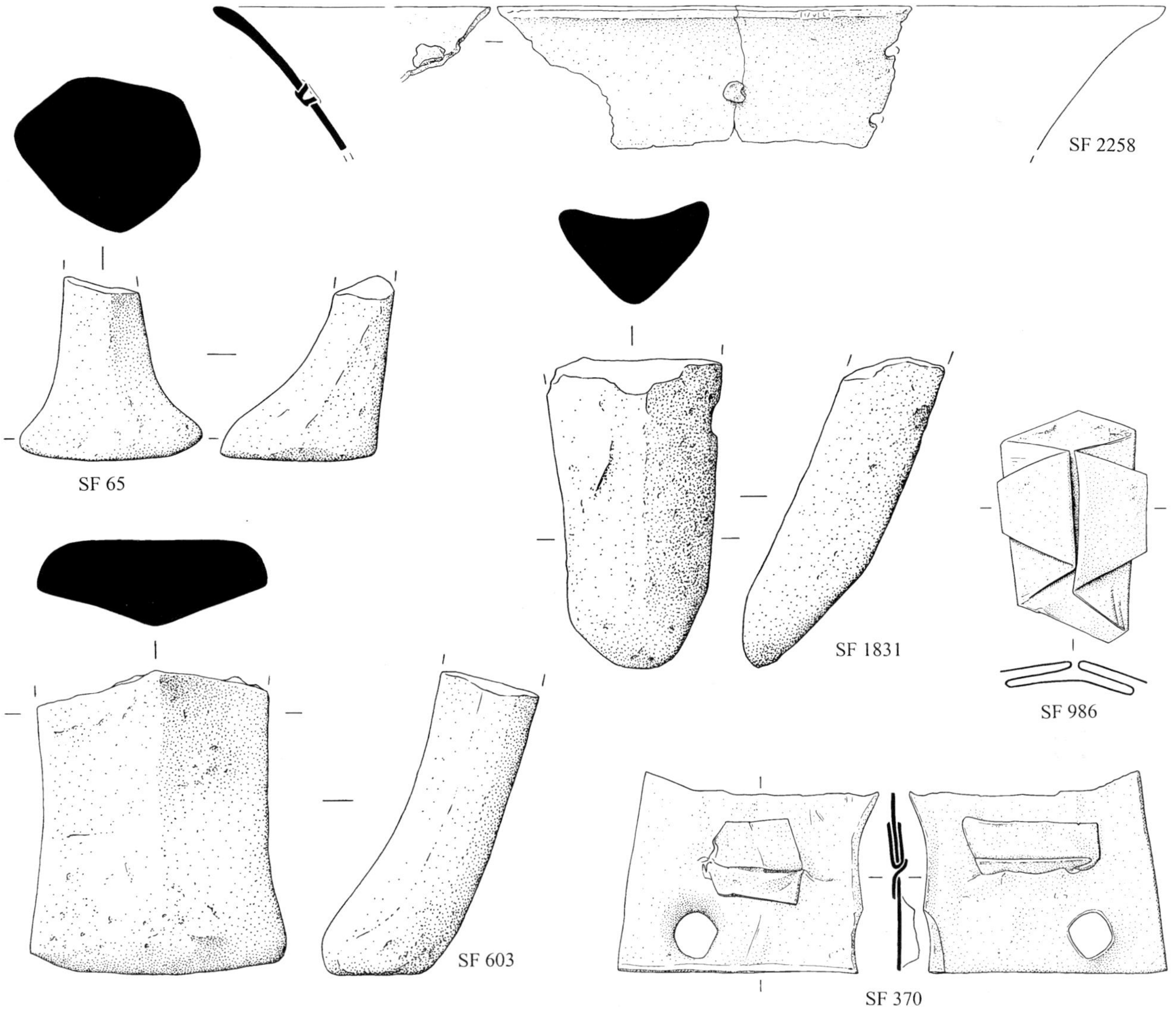

Figure 5.50 Copper alloy vessels (SF2558, 65, 1831, 603) and 'paper-clip' rivets (SF986, 370). Scale 1:1.

context on Alms Lane (Margeson 1993, 93). Several were found from the backfills of the barbican well at Castle Mall, Norwich, provisionally dated to the 15th–16th centuries (Goodall forthcoming). Two examples from Greyfriars are attached to small rectangular copper-alloy sheets (the repair patches: see SF370). The presence of these patches and the 'paper-clip' rivets illustrates the value given to copper-alloy vessels, which are normally associated with wealthier households.

SF370 Perforated sub-rectangular copper-alloy sheet, with copper-alloy **'paper-clip' rivet** patching up a tear.
layer 10597, Period 3.2

SF986 Copper-alloy **'paper-clip' rivet**; six-sided sheet, two opposite ends are folded over to meet in the middle and then folded back to the outer edge.
pit fill 30488, Period 4.2

Skimmer

by Julia Huddle
(not illustrated)

Copper-alloy skimmers (or strainers) used to skim fat from food are well known from early 16th- and 17th-century contexts. Previous examples from Norwich come from the fire deposits dated to 1507 at Pottergate, and from 17th-century contexts on Heigham Street and Oak Street (Margeson 1993, 118). One was also found in the backfill of the barbican well at Castle Mall, which has been provisionally dated to the 15th–16th centuries (Goodall forthcoming); another, from a moated site at Wimbotsham, Norfolk, was from a deposit of similar date (Shelley 2003). Part of a similar skimmer to SF1834 was found (with handle) in a 17th-century deposit on Heigham Street (Margeson 1993, 119, fig. 84 no. 744). Margeson notes that the presence of such objects on other Norwich sites reflects their key role in the medieval kitchen.

Stone bowls/dishes

by J.M. Mills, with stone identification by Paul C. Ensom
(Fig. 5.51)

Fragments of two stone dishes or bowls are likely to be residual items within the pit fills in which they were found. They are of a type commonly found in Viking levels in Scotland's northern islands (*e.g.* Jarlshof, Shetland:

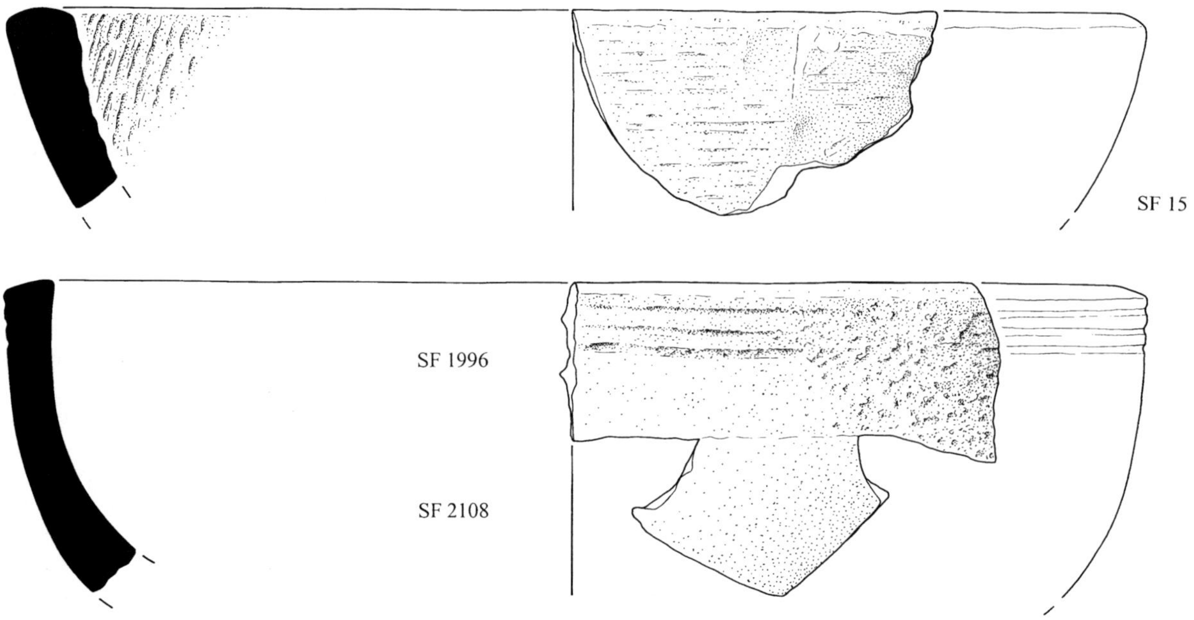

Figure 5.51 Stone vessels (SF15, 1996/2108). Scale 1:2.

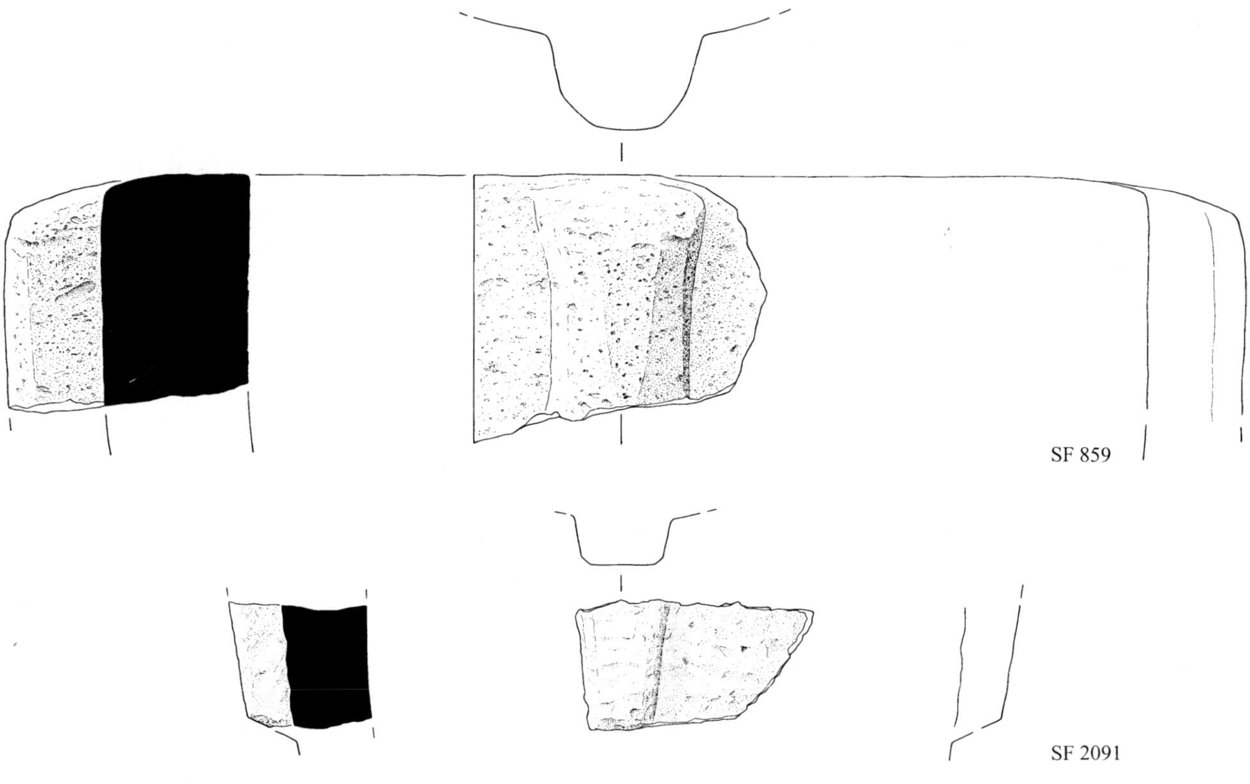

Fig. 5.52 Stone mortars (SF859, 2091). Scale 1:3.

Crawford 1987, 152 and fig. 51) and are probably of late 9th or 10th century origin (Fiona Roe, *pers. comm.*). One of the Greyfriars examples is steatite (soapstone: SF15); the other, slightly larger, example (SF1996/2108) is probably a calc-chlorite schist. Although soapstone vessels are not frequent from Late Saxon sites in England, examples are known from York (MacGregor 1982), Lincoln and Thetford (Rogerson and Dallas 1984, 115). Geologically, the source for the Greyfriars examples could have been Shetland, Scandinavia (possibly Norway) or the south-west of England. Given the known existing trade with Scandinavia, either Shetland or Norway seems most likely. It is probable that the bowls came to Norwich as finished items.

SF15 Rim of a stone dish or bowl with fine tooling around the external surface and heavy, almost vertical, scoring of internal surface. The exterior is blackened and retains some heavy sooting deposits, although these appear to have been washed off to some extent. The rim is plain. The stone is a soft, pale grey, metamorphic rock, in part composed of talc suggesting that it as steatite (soapstone). Internal diameter c.280mm (10% extant), wall thickness at rim 17mm.
pit fill 711, Period 2.3

SF1996/2108 Two (joining) fragments of the same stone vessel, a large bowl with a plain, sloping rim. The vessel is made from a dark grey/green metamorphic rock, probably a calc-chlorite schist. It is very smooth internally and heavily sooted on the exterior and less so on the rim. The vessel was quite large and appears to have been used as a cooking pot, or for other purposes over a fire. Internal diameter *c.* 300mm (10% present), wall thickness 12mm.
SF1996 pit fill 12482, Period 1
SF2108 fill 12397, Period 3.1

Mortars

by J.M. Mills, with stone identification by Paul C. Ensom
(Fig. 5.52)

Fragments of seven stone mortars were recovered, of which three are catalogued below. One had been re-used in a Friary-period wall foundation (SF2091). Fragments were also recovered from Late Saxon buildings *10049* and *50242*. Medieval stone mortars are commonly made from limestone. There being no local stone suitable, all mortars recovered from excavations in Norwich are from non-local stone. The Greyfriars examples are from Dorset, all deriving from the Purbeck series; two are broken shell limestones, probably Burr stone (SF471 and 859), and one comes from the Upper Purbeck Beds (SF2091). Although the mortars cannot themselves be dated, it appears that the main period of stone mortar production in Purbeck during the medieval period was in the 13th and 14th centuries (Dunning 1977, 324). There was, however, trade between Norwich and Purbeck at an earlier date, as indicated by the presence of Purbeck marble columns in Norwich Cathedral.

The stone types and morphology of medieval mortars are fully discussed by Dunning (1961, 279–84; 1977, 320–47), who suggests that they were used both for grinding and pounding. One of the Greyfriars examples (SF859) had been worn to a heavy internal polish through use. The two Burr stone mortars are probably larger than any illustrated by Dunning (1961, 279–84; 1977, 320–47) and are certainly larger than any previously excavated in Norwich. Although the exact forms of the Greyfriars vessels are unknown, given the degree of fragmentation, the rib on SF2091 can be compared with a similar example from Southampton (West *et al.* 1975, 2212).

SF859 Less than 25% of a large stone mortar rim with heavy rib. The stone is a coarse, shelly limestone similar to SF471, although without the iron-staining, and is also probably Burr stone. The rim is plain and heavily worn. The internal surface is worn to a polish although the stone type means that this surface, like all others, is pitted. Internal diameter 300mm, wall thickness 50mm, rib at rim 65mm wide projects *c.* 40mm.
unstratified

SF2091 Fragment of the wall and rib from a stone mortar. Rib and interior finely finished although no real 'polish' observed on the internal surface. Wall thickness 25–35mm, rib (width 25–38mm) projects 20mm. The stone, containing fossils of *Viviparus* and broken shell debris, is comparable with stone from the Upper Purbeck Beds, the level from which Purbeck marble comes. This fragment, with mortar adhering, was re-used in stone wall foundation dating to the late 14th–15th century.
wall 12312, Period 3.1

Glass vessels

by John Shepherd
(Figs 5.53–5.55; Pl. 5.7)

Introduction

A total of 237 fragments of vessel and window glass from the excavations at the Greyfriars site were examined. This total contained fragments dating from the medieval period through to the modern, which may be summarised as follows:

Nineteen fragments of diagnostic medieval and early post-medieval (16th- or early 17th-century) glass came from contemporary contexts with a further seven appearing as residual fragments in later contexts. A number of indeterminate body fragments also came from medieval and early post-medieval contexts but the presence of some intrusive post-medieval and modern fragments makes an 'early' identification difficult to justify on a visual basis alone.

One hundred and seventeen fragments of glass were identifiable as being of later post-medieval and modern date. These appear in contemporary contexts and as intrusive fragments in the earlier contexts referred to above. Apart from a few drinking vessel fragments, the great majority of these fragments are from common bottles dating from the late 17th century to the modern day. The earliest 'English' wine-bottles are very fragmentary; apart from one with a double-matrix seal, none are of intrinsic importance. The later bottles for beer, sauces, oils, medicines and mineral waters are all machine-made, many bearing makers' marks and advertising slogans.

The following report concerns the glass closely associated with the life and demise of the Friary. The glass here is arranged by perceived function: that is, glass for medical purposes, storage and tableware. Glass lamps are described separately above. It is evident that the quantity of glass found in Friary contexts was not great, indicating perhaps the paucity of glass in use, although the range of vessels certainly suggests a wide range of use of glassware, in keeping with many late medieval religious houses in Great Britain.

Each catalogue entry briefly describes the extant fragment, the technique of manufacture of the vessel(s) and the colour and quality of the glass. Many of the fragments are in a poor state of preservation and almost opaque, as should be expected for the majority of the glassware of the period, so details of seed and batch inclusion (air-bubbles and solid, unmelted particles of the batch) are not given. Indeterminate fragments and intrusive post-medieval fragments are retained in the archive.

Medical

(Fig. 5.53)

Irrespective of its fragility, the many practical qualities of glassware (light weight, easy to clean, good conductor of heat) made it an important and useful component in the apparatus used in medieval medicine and science. Glass lenses appear in spectacles from the late 13th century and from the 15th century at the latest glass alembics and cucurbits came into use for distillation purposes. Also from the 13th century uroscopy — an important ancillary of medical diagnosis — benefited from the use of purpose-made urinals. Fragments from the rims of at least four urinals are recorded here, together with one base. Three were retrieved from the same fill of one Period 3.2

pit (SF1018, SF908 and SF703). Urinals are common finds on medieval sites and those fragments which survive here are characteristic of the form. It should be pointed out, however, that the rims and bases of urinals were much thicker than the rest of the vessel and so tend to survive disproportionately in the archaeological record. The fragility of these vessels overall has resulted in a paucity of complete and reconstructable examples.

Three main shapes can be distinguished amongst urinals recorded in Britain. Two share a thickened, convex base with a pontil mark projecting on the external surface, as well as a horizontally-flared rim with a slightly upturned lip, but have different body forms. The first is a thin-walled bulbous-bodied vessel with a cylindrical neck (*e.g.* Southampton: Charleston 1975, no. 1486). The second, also thin-walled, is pyriform in shape with a conical neck narrowing slightly towards the rim (St Swithins House, Walbrook, London: Museum of London Acc. No. 18399). These two shapes are universal, the bulbous form being the more common. Three rims (SF730, SF1018, SF908) belong to these forms, but without any body fragments it is not possible to identify the specific shape to which they belong.

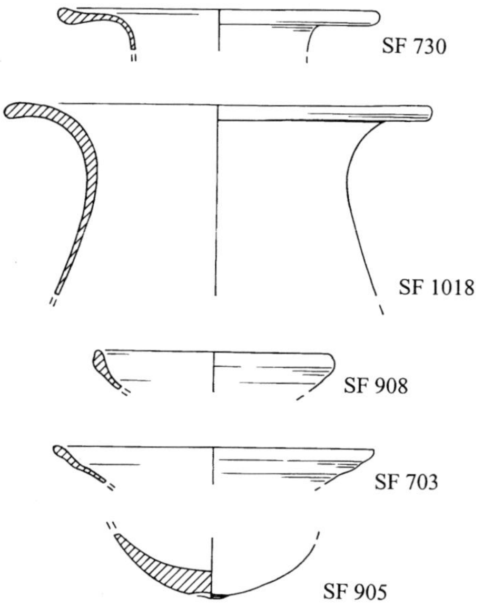

Figure 5.53 Glass urinals (SF730, 1018, 908, 703, 905). Scale 1:2.

The third shape was only identified in the early 1980s by Robert Charleston. At Bayham Abbey, Sussex, he identified a vessel with a heavy base, a globular body and a flared, but not horizontal, rim (Charleston 1983). Other similar fragments from Battle Abbey, Sussex, permitted Charleston to reconsider the evidence for the shape and character of medieval glass urinals (Charleston 1985, 139–42: his observations are summarised below). A similar flared rim fragment comes from Greyfriars (SF703).

The scene of a doctor or monk holding a urinal up to the light to examine its contents is a universal theme in illuminated manuscripts and carvings of the 13th and 14th centuries and of the graphic arts from the 15th–17th centuries. For example, an illumination in a 14th-century Book of Hours (Ms. Lat. 9473, fo.II, vo, Bibliothèque Nationale, Paris: Foy and Sennequier 1989, 332, no. 373) showing a monk examining a urinal while a student or assistant takes notes. The vessel itself even appears as the symbol of the doctor-saints Cosmas and Damian (Charleston 1984, 32–3). In many of these scenes, the doctor is accompanied by the patient who holds a long and thin wicker box in which, one suspects, the urinal could be stored and transported to the doctor. This implies that urinals were not just owned by those practising medicine but were also private possessions.

Charleston noted that a number of these contemporary illustrations show doctors holding up a roughly bell-shaped vessel with a flared rim (see Charleston 1985, 141, for references). These, he came to understand, corresponded with the Bayham Abbey and Battle Abbey vessels, and so were an addition to the canon which already included the two shapes with horizontally flared rims. Furthermore, he noted that the glass of these flared-rimmed urinals appeared to be thicker than those of the other two forms. Considering the function of the urinal as a diagnosis vessel, this obvious observation is very important. It would suggest that these flared rim vessels may also have been made for use as simple chamber-pots. Such vessels were known in the medieval period as 'jordans' (Amis 1968, 6–9). Charleston noted the lines in Chaucer (in the 'wordes of the Hoost to the Phisicien'):

I pray to God so save thy gentil cors,
And eek thyne urynals and thy jurdones.

This, he points out, suggests that 'although parallel in function the two types of vessel may not have been identical' (Charleston 1985, 141). The presence of this shape in the hands of doctors and physicians in the representations referred to above probably suggests that it was made in different thicknesses. Without a doubt, thin-walled vessels could have functioned both as jordans and uroscopic urinals.

As mentioned above, uroscopy was an important ancillary of medical diagnosis in the medieval world and, no doubt, the presence of such thin-walled vessels must have encouraged its practice. Diagnosis did not have to be carried out by doctors or physicians alone, and self-diagnosis was also recommended. The poet and colonial pioneer William Vaughan writing in 1602 urged: 'In the morning make water in an urinal: that by looking on it, you may ghesse some what of the state of your body' (*Naturall and Artificial Directions for Health*, 1602).

Colour-coded diagnosis charts were also available. The 15th-century *Tractus de Pestilentia* of Albik (University Library, Prague: see Foy and Sennequier 1989, 332, no. 374, plate XXIX) contains part of such a chart. The extant fragment shows twelve glass urinals with the contents coloured according to specific diagnoses. These range from normal to hues indicating abnormal digestion and inflammations. Three urinals with their contents coloured in varying shades of dark red or brown indicated mortification (*Iste tres urine significant mortificationem*) — a state where part of the body has died while the rest is still living.

Although three basic forms of urinal (or jordan) can now be identified, it is not possible to differentiate any chronological difference between them. The form first appears in stratified contexts during the 13th century. Many have been found in London, the earliest coming from a mid-13th-century context at Milk Street (MLK76 *25*,).

SF730 Fragment from the rim of a **urinal**. Free-blown; natural green glass with deep surface decomposition. Outsplayed, almost horizontal, rim with a slight upright lip. Medieval.
fill 10777, Period 3.2

SF1018 Two fragments from the rim and neck of a **urinal**. Free-blown; natural green glass with deep surface decomposition. Fire-rounded, outsplayed, almost horizontal rim.
fill 40103, Period 3.2

SF908 Four fragments and numerous splinters from the rim of a **urinal**. Natural green glass with deep surface decomposition. Fire-rounded upright rim.
fill 40103, Period 3.2

SF703 Seven rim fragments and numerous splinters from the upper part of a flared-mouthed **urinal**. Free-blown; natural green glass with deep surface decomposition. Medieval.
fill 40103, Period 3.2

SF905 The base of a **urinal**. Free-blown; natural green glass with deep surface decomposition. Rounded base with pontil mark.
unstratified

Storage
(Fig. 5.54)

SF2571 and SF2572 come from bottles — possibly the same bottle (not illustrated) — of a simple form well-known in late-medieval and Tudor assemblages. SF257 comes from the body of an indeterminate form. Once again there is the possibility that it comes from the same vessel as SF2571 and SF2572.

The base fragment (SF900) is the only other identifiable late medieval/early post-medieval bottle fragment from this site. These bottles, in production from the 15th century until the 17th century when they were displaced by the common 'English' wine bottle, were bulbous in shape with a pushed-in, domed base, as seen in this example. The necks tapered in slightly to a fire-rounded outsplayed rim. Both plain and wrythen examples are known on many sites in England The example here is of the latter variety.

Another type of bottle which appears during the mid-16th century and continues into the 17th is represented by fragments SF905 and SF731. This was a small ribbed flask which was made in two parts, or double-gathered. The first gather fashioned the neck and then a second gather of glass was added up to the neck, blown into a ribbed mould, twisted and flattened. Examples are fairly common in England, but whether this is a true indication of their contemporary frequency or merely because they are easy to identify is not, at present, certain. Three examples were found on the Mary Rose, which sank in 1545 (Charleston 1984, 91).

Included in this catalogue are three fragments (SF1012, SF1067 and SF187) from the rims and necks of those common 'English' wine bottles referred to above, which are 'type fossils' of the late 17th century onwards, and five fragments from pharmaceutical phials of the late 16th or 17th centuries. They are not, therefore, directly associated with the Friary or Dissolution phase on this site but are included because they are virtually the only identifiable vessel glass, along with the opaque white jug below, which dates to the century-and-a-half after the Dissolution.

The small bottles or phials (SF489, SF712, SF257 and SF748) with long necks and squat bodies date from the late 16th or early 17th centuries. This type was superseded by the more cylindrical type so common in 17th- and 18th-century contexts.

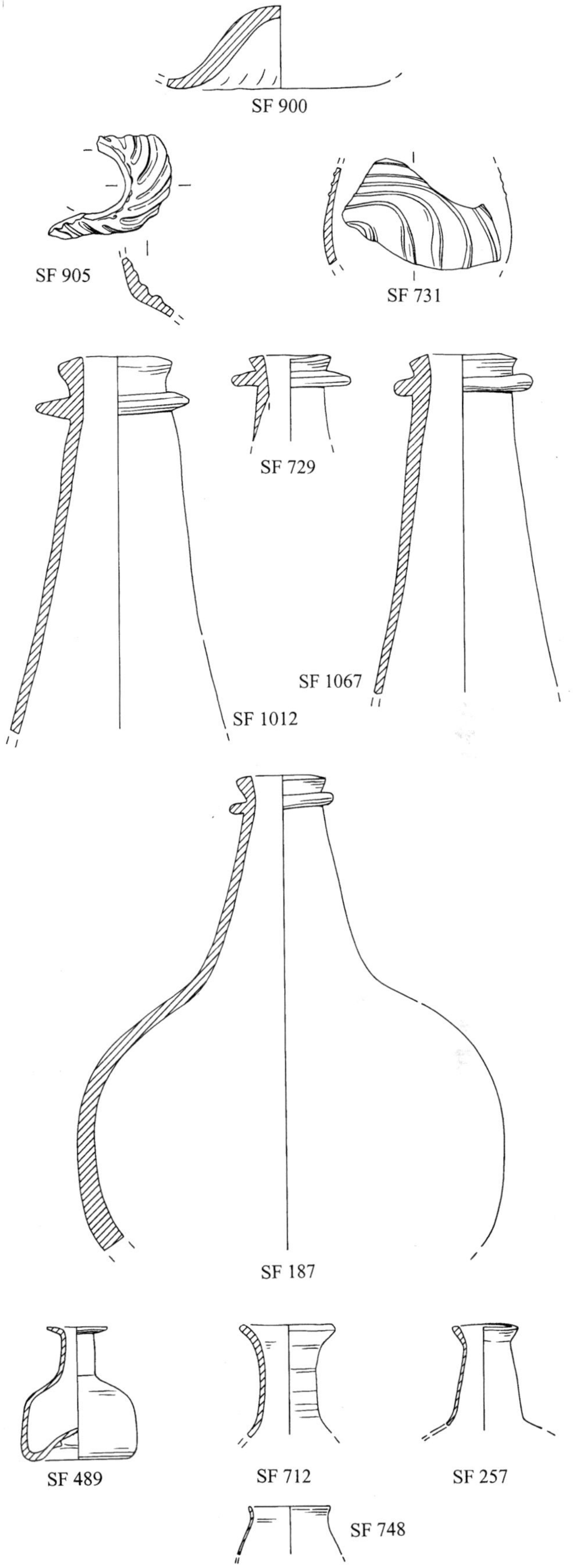

Figure 5.54 Glass storage vessels (SF900, 905, 731, 1012, 729, 1067, 187, 489, 712, 257, 748). Scale 1:2.

The bottle-shaped phial (SF729) was in use during the late 17th and early 18th century. Although the form and finish is similar to that of the common wine bottles, the metal is a good natural green, similar to pharmaceutical phial glass. Its volume — much larger than a pharmaceutical phial but smaller than the bottle — and its form would suggest that it represents some kind of container intermediate between these. Two examples from a domestic refuse dump at Billingsgate, London (Gibson and Evans 1985, 151), deposited *c.* 1700–30, retained residues of their original contents. One residue contained 'magnesium sulphate solution, similar to Epsom salt, the other contained antimony, possibly as a tartrate and most likely used as an emetic' (*ibid.*, 154). A similar bottle, unfortunately without contents, came from a rubbish dump dated to the second quarter of the 18th century in the cellar of the Broad Arrow Tower, Tower of London (Shepherd forthcoming).

SF900 Fragment from the base of a **bottle**. Optic blown; natural green glass with deep surface decomposition. Underside of domed base decorated with low-relief vertical ribs. 15th- to early 17th-century.
unstratified

SF905 Fragment from the shoulder of a small double-gathered **bottle**. Mould-blown; natural green glass with surface decomposition. Mould-blown body decorated with wrythen high relief ribs, plain neck on separate gather. Mid 16th–17th-century.
unstratified

SF731 Fragment from the lower part of a flattened double-gathered **bottle**. Natural green glass of good quality. Vertical high relief ribs on lower part of fragment, becoming wrythen towards the top. Mid 16th–17th-century.
unstratified

SF1012/ SF1067 The rims and necks of common English **bottles**. Free-blown; thick natural green glass. Plain rim with rounded string-rim on a tall neck. Late 17th century.
SF1012 pit fill 30087, Period 4.2
SF1067 unstratified

SF729 Fragment from the rim of a bulbous-bodied pharmaceutical **phial**. Free-blown; natural greenish-blue glass. Plain rim and rounded string-rim as for common bottles. Late 17th-century.
10257 make-up, Period 4.2

SF187 The upper part of a common English **bottle**. Free-blown; thick natural green glass. Squat neck with a plain rim and rounded string rim. Late 17th- or early 18th-century.
make-up 10257, Period 4.2

SF489 A small **phial**. 16th- or 17th-century.
unstratified

SF712 The rim and neck of a small **bottle or phial**. Free-blown; natural green glass with slight surface decomposition. Fire-rounded outsplayed rim. 16th- or 17th-century.
pit fill 40027, Period 3.2

SF257 The rim and neck of a small **phial**. Description as for SF712.
pit fill 10386, Period 3.2

SF748 The rim and neck of a small **phial**. Description as for SF712.
pit fill 10705, Period 3.2

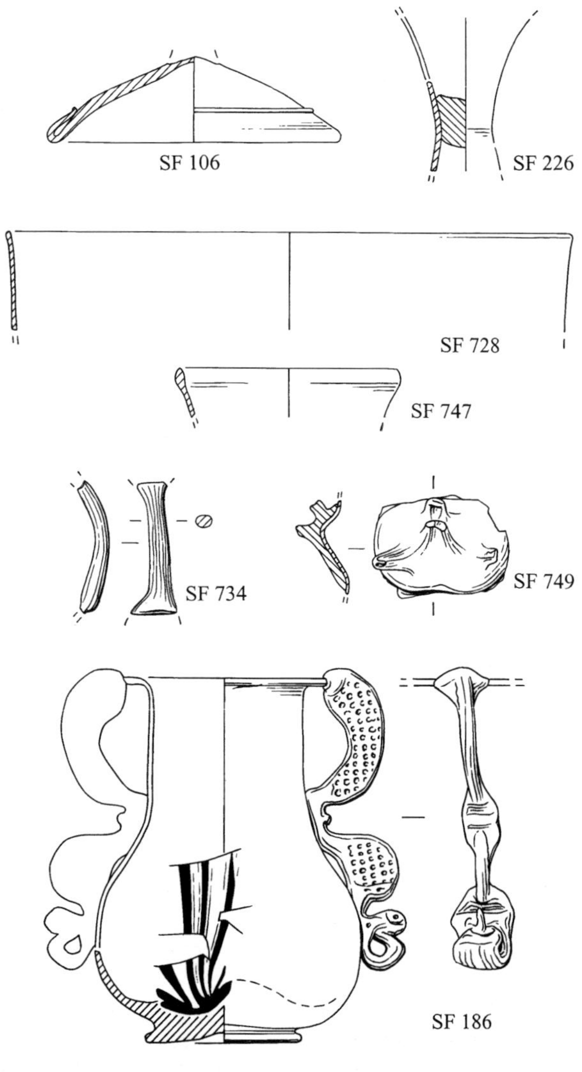

Figure 5.55 Glass tableware vessels (SF106, 226, 728, 747, 734, 749, 186). Scale 1:2.

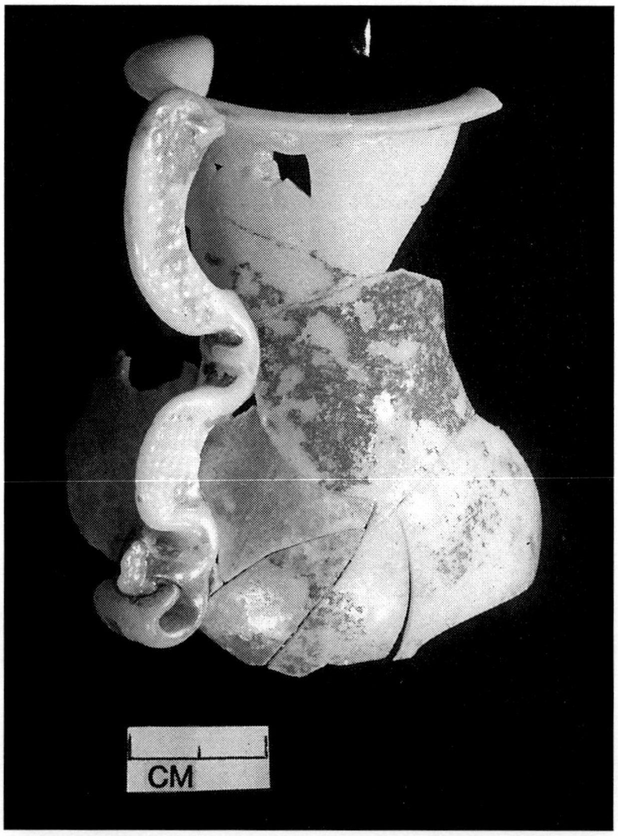

Plate 5.7 White glass vessel (SF186)

Tableware
(Fig. 5.55; Pl. 5.7)
Very few fragments of tableware were recovered from this site and only one of these (SF106) can be dated to the medieval period. All of the others belong to the 16th or 17th centuries, although some may be as early as the late 15th century. The base fragment SF106 comes from either a bulbous-bodied flask or a hemispherical bowl. Unfortunately it is not possible to be more precise. The base finish, pushed-in to form a flattened hollow tubular base ring, is a common medieval design. The pedestal beaker SF226 (the rim SF728 probably comes from the same or a similar vessel) is more diagnostic. Parallels for such ribbed beakers are known in early–mid-16th-century French contexts, especially La cour Napoleon du Louvre, Paris (Foy and Sennequier 1989, 381f) where they are said to have appeared at the end of the 15th century and remained in use during the first half of the 16th century.

Finally, two vessels are of particular interest (see SF186 below). One is represented by just a single fragment, a triple-spur prunt (SF749). Beakers decorated with applied prunts are well-known in continental and English assemblages (where they are probably imports) from the late 15th and 16th centuries. The prunts on these, however, tend to be simple, flattened blobs of glass, sometimes with just a slight spur where the glass has pulled up when the tool applying the prunt was removed. Multi-spurred prunts on vessels, where the prunt has been tooled, are not so common. For similar triple-spur prunts on vessels see Baumgartner and Krueger 1988, 356, no. 436 (possibly Anderlach, early 16th century); 357, no. 437 (Munsterplatz, Bonn, opaque red glass, early 16th century); and no. 438 (Schillerplatz, Mainz, blue glass, early 16th century).

White glass vessel
by I.C. Freestone, C.P. Stapleton and S.G.E. Bowman, with John Shepherd
(Fig. 5.55; Pl. 5.7)
An opaque white glass vessel (SF186) with translucent dark blue glass decoration seems exceptional and has proved most difficult to identify. It was suggested that the vessel was manufactured in Europe during the late 16th or 17th centuries. However, it has typological and decorative characteristics which can be attributed to several different regions and time periods. A loose fragment of the white glass with blue decoration was chemically analysed to help identify its origins.

Scientific examination
The opaque white glass and blue decoration were analysed in the scanning electron microscope with energy dispersive X-ray analysis. They are potash-lead-silica glasses of the English crystal type, and the opacifier in the white glass appears to be arsenical. These characteristics suggest that the vessel is of English origin, post-dating 1680.

Analytical methods
The fragment available for analysis was relatively large, so a small portion was removed for examination. In preparation for analysis in the scanning electron microscope (SEM), this sample was mounted in an epoxy resin block, ground flat and polished with diamond pastes down to 1μm, then coated with a thin layer of carbon. In the SEM, it is possible to examine the microstructure and to identify sub-microscopic inclusions. A quantitative elemental analysis was carried out using the energy dispersive X-ray analyser (EDXA) with Oxford Instruments GEM germanium detector and ISIS processor attached to the SEM.

In order to determine components present at levels of between about 0.01 wt% and 0.20 wt% (which is the approximate limit of detection of SEM-EDXA), the qualitative analytical technique of air-path X-ray fluorescence (XRF) was used.

Opaque white glass body
The white glass contains *c.* 42 wt% silica (SiO), 48 wt% lead oxide (PbO) and *c.* 6 wt% potash (KO). Arsenic, as As0, the only other major component, occurs at *c.* 3 wt%. There are minor amounts (less that 1 wt%) of alumina (AlO), Manganese oxide (MnO), magnesia (MgO) and chlorine (Cl).

A backscattered electron image (BSI) taken in the SEM of the blue and white glasses showed that the white glass is relatively homogeneous. There is no obvious evidence in the image of a colouring or opacifying agent. However, in a lead-rich glass such large amounts of arsenic may precipitate as lead oxyarsenate (3Pb(AsO).PbO), a white crystalline material (Rooksby 1962). Rooksby has shown that lead oxyarsenate particles smaller than 1 gm are responsible for the opacity of some English and Venetian white glasses, while McCray *et al.* (1995) find that lead-arsenic-rich particles around 50mm (0.05μm) are responsible for the opalescence of Venetian girasole glass. At high magnification in the SEM it should be possible to resolve particles down to *c.* 1μm, but no particles were seen in the Greyfriars glass. It is possible therefore that the opacification is of the type that McCray *et al.* (1995) report.

Translucent dark blue glass decoration
The blue is also a potash-lead-silica glass with a composition similar to that of the white: potash, 6 wt%; lead oxide, 45 wt%; silica, 44 wt%. The blue glass, however, contains c. 1 wt% arsenic oxide, only about one-third the amount in the white. There are significantly higher levels of manganese oxide and iron oxide in the blue. In addition, traces of cobalt and nickel were also detected using air-path XRF. The remaining components, which are present at less than 1 wt% or are below detection limits, may occur at different amounts than in the white; but this is not considered significant.

The dark blue colour is due to the small amount of cobalt detected by XRF. Cobalt is an extremely effective colorant so that concentrations in the vicinity of 0.1 wt% are sufficient to produce a deep blue colouration. Iron can also colour a glass blue, but it is a much weaker colorant than cobalt and gives much paler colour. Elevated levels of manganese, iron and nickel in the blue glass are likely to be related to the presence of the cobalt, as they sometimes occur with cobalt in geological deposits.

Relatively pure potash/lead/silica glasses, such as those under consideration, are of the English crystal type and are generally held by English authors to have been first developed by Ravenscroft in England in the late 17th century (Thorpe 1935, Watts 1974, Moody 1988). In fact, lead- and potassium-bearing glasses were in use in Italy much earlier. Lead-rich glass was used for the production of artificial gems and is mentioned by Neri in 1612; McCray *et al.* (1995) drew attention to a Tuscan recipe for glass of 1470 which mentions the use of saltpetre (potassium nitrate) in the batch. Saltpetre is the most likely source of a pure potash component and its use in English glass is, again, usually attributed to Ravenscroft. Moretti and Toninato (1987) present Italian recipes for potash-lead crystal with added arsenic, dating to 1697. They differ from the present glass, however, in having only about 20 wt% lead oxide, as opposed to 40–50%. Even so, it is clear that potash/lead/silica glasses were known in Italy in the late 17th century, although as yet no analytical evidence has been produced for the types of vessels, if any, that were produced from this glass.

It is therefore possible that the Greyfriars vessel is in an Italian glass of a little-known typological and compositional group dating to the late 17th century. However, given the rapid adoption and growth of the use of lead crystal by English glassmakers in the late 17th and early 18th centuries, perhaps a more probable explanation is that the glass is English, a product of the flourishing lead crystal glass industry there, or possibly one of its continental offshoots. Following Ravenscroft's successful development of lead crystal by *c.* 1675, the formulation was taken up by other English glassmakers and, soon after, by glassmakers in the Low Countries and France. Charleston (1960) lists a number of continental glass-houses which were producing lead crystal 'à la façon d'Angleterre' by, at the latest, the third quarter of the 18th century. Even so, as late as 1772 a Frenchman, Libaude, was awarded a national prize for discovering how to make lead crystal (Moody 1988: 204). This suggests that if, as has been indicated, typological considerations suggest an early date (16th–17th-century), then an English origin is more probable.

Available analyses of 17th- and 18th-century English lead crystal glasses are few, but they lead to some interesting conclusions for the present vessel. Specific gravity (S.G.) measurements of glasses dated to the 1670s and around 1680 suggest that the lead oxide content was moderate, at well under 20 wt% (Watts 1974; King, quoted in Charleston 1960, 2). Analysis of lead in two Ravenscroft pieces — a cup (M&LA 1910, 10–17.1) and a bottle (M&LA OA.110), both dated to *c.* 1680 by M.J. Hughes of the Department of Scientific Research, British Museum — gave lead oxide contents of 15.27% and 17.8% respectively, in agreement with the S.G. results (DSR file nos. 2172, 2173). The high lead contents characteristic of typical English crystal, and of the present vessel, do not appear to have been introduced until well after 1680.

Even in terms of English crystal, for which a lead content of around 30 wt. % is considered typical (Cable 1987, Moody 1988, Charleston 1960), the lead contents of the present glasses are extreme. However, there are parallels. In glass waste from a glasshouse at Bolsterstone, Yorkshire, which ceased production in 1758 (Ashurst 1987), fragments of a 'white enamel' have a similarly high level of lead to the present glasses (see table in archive; Cable 1987, analysis 8). In addition, lead crystal glass coloured by cobalt is known from Bolsterstone and also in the glass ingots from the wreck of the *Albion,* an East Indiaman which sank in 1765 (Redknap and Freestone 1995).

Although arsenic as an element was first isolated in 1675, according to Thorpe and Whitely (1937, 468), and its use as a glass opacifier has not previously been confirmed earlier than the 18th century (Turner and Rooksby 1959; Rooksby 1962), its potential as an opacifier was demonstrated at the Royal Society in 1673 (Moody 1989). Furthermore, its earlier use in Venetian glass is indicated by the examination of glassmakers recipes (Moretti and Toninato 1897; McCray *et al.* 1995). However, opaque white and cobalt blue lead crystal glasses do not appear to have become at all common in England until the mid-18th century, and a glasshouse producing opaque white glass was still a matter for comment by Dossie in 1758 (Thorpe 1935, 200–3).

In conclusion, the white and blue glasses are of the English crystal *type.* If made in England they are likely to be later than 1680, on the grounds of their particularly high lead content. Indeed, the fact that these glasses are coloured and opaque lead crystal tends to favour an even later date. An origin on the near Continent would imply a later date still, well into the 18th century. An Italian origin must remain a possibility, as potash/lead/silica glass in Italy was developed by the end of the 17th century, but there is as yet no evidence to indicate that glass of this particular composition was made in Italy, whereas it can be closely paralleled in the compositions of 18th-century English glasses.

SF106 Fragment from the base of a **bowl** or, more probably, a **flask**. Free-blown; natural green glass with deep surface decomposition. Pushed-in pointed base forming a flattened hollow tubular base-ring. Medieval.
unstratified

SF226 Fragment from the pedestal base of a **goblet**. Optic blown; natural green glass with slight surface decomposition. High, pushed-in pedestal base, decorated with low relief optic blown vertical ribs.
pit fill 10332, Period 3.2

SF728 Fragment from the rim of a conical bodied **beaker**. Fire-rounded and slightly outsplayed rim. Probably from same class of vessel as the pedestal base fragment above.
pit fill 40027, Period 3.2

SF747 Small fragment from the rim of a **beaker** of indeterminate form. Natural green glass with deep surface decomposition. Fire-rounded, slightly outsplayed rim.
layer 10597, Period 3.2

SF734 A rod handle from a **vessel** of indeterminate form. Natural green glass of good quality.
pit fill 40024, Period 3.2

SF749 An applied prunt from a **vessel** of indeterminate form but probably a beaker. Natural green glass with deep surface decomposition. The prunt has been pinched and tooled into three spurs, two single spurs above a double-pinched spur.
fill 10600, Period 4.2

SF186 A small **jug or vase**. Free-blown; opaque white glass with golden iridescence. Outsplayed, horizontal fire-rounded rim, cylindrical neck, bulbous body on a heavy pad base. Elaborate applied handle, tooled into three wings. Body decorated with marvered blue trails in spray/foliage design. 17th–18th century (see discussion above).
make-up 10257, Period 4.2

Pottery

Introduction

Excavations at the Greyfriars site produced a total of almost 30,000 sherds of pottery weighing *c.* 210kg. Pottery was recovered in differing quantities from all five excavation areas (Table 19) and from all site periods (Table 20). In terms of weight, the majority of the assemblage was recovered from Areas A and B (33.8% and 31.1% respectively), with a smaller quantity coming from Area C (19.4%) and significantly smaller proportions from Area CB (7.9%) and D (7.8%).

The methodologies for the analysis of the pottery are described in the project archive. The pottery has been described in different reports divided chronologically into prehistoric, Roman, Middle Saxon and Late Saxon to post-medieval periods. Other ceramics, such as crucibles and lamps, have been described under the appropriate functional categories elsewhere in this report.

Prehistoric pottery

by Sarah Percival

(not illustrated)

Five sherds of prehistoric pottery weighing 13g were recovered from three contexts. All appeared to be residual and were small, undecorated body sherds. The largest of the sherds (from context *30027*, unstratified), has quartz-sand and flint temper, and is hard-fired and finished with rough wiping of the outer surface. This sherd appears to be of Iron Age date. Three sherds (context *50342*, pit fill Period 2.2) appear to be of Bronze Age date, being tempered with quartz-sand, flint and grog. The remaining sherd (context *50218*, post-hole fill, Period 2.1)

Area	*Qty (no. sherds)*	*Wt (kg)*	*% Qty*	*% Wt*
A	7531	70.920	25.4	33.8
B	11274	65.322	38.0	31.1
C	6841	40.695	23.0	19.4
C/B	2696	16.562	9.1	7.9
D	1356	16.338	4.5	7.8
Total	**29698**	**209.835**	**100**	**100**

Table 19 Quantity and weight of pottery by area

Period	*Qty (no. sherds)*	*Wt (kg)*	*% Wt*
1	**3587**	**28.848**	**13.7**
2	**15567**	**76.643**	**36.4**
2.1	2957	18.734	8.9
2.2	3228	14.758	7.0
2.3	9382	43.151	
3	**5103**	**32.272**	**15.3**
3.1	2398	14.843	
3.2	2705	17.429	
4	**2811**	**35.004**	**16.6**
4.1	2126	18.811	
4.2	685	16.193	
5	**1160**	**17.752**	**8.4**
Other	**1584**	**19.617**	**9.3**

Table 20 Quantity and weight of pottery by period

was recovered from a sample and is too small to be closely datable.

Roman pottery

by Alice Lyons

(not illustrated)

By comparison with other Norwich sites, excavations at Greyfriars yielded a relatively large residual assemblage of Romano-British pottery, comprising 69 sherds (weighing 0.836kg). The fabrics present are listed in Table 21 and detailed in the project archive. The majority of the vessels are flagons and narrow- and medium-mouthed jars produced in coarse ware fabrics of local manufacture. Several sherds were identified as originating at Colchester (Essex), Hadham (Herts) and in the Nene Valley (Cambs), all of them large regional pottery production centres that commonly traded material into Norfolk. No pottery imported from the continent (such as amphora or samian) was retrieved. The assemblage is very abraded and seldom datable more closely than to the late 1st–4th centuries AD, this date-range being ascribable to most undiagnostic Romano-British coarse wares. The few more diagnostic sherds suggest a mid-Roman date with some later pottery, possibly transitional to the Anglo-Saxon era. Further discussion of the relevance of this material in a local context is given in Chapter 2.IV.

Middle Saxon pottery

by Richenda Goffin

(not illustrated)

Nineteen fragments of pottery of Middle Saxon date were recovered, weighing 0.539kg (Table 22). All were made from Ipswich ware, mainly of the Sandy variety, although five sherds of Gritty Ipswich ware were present. Jar rims and bases were the only identifiable forms recorded. No decorated sherds were found. The pottery was not associated with any features of Middle Saxon date.

The largest quantity of Middle Saxon pottery was recovered from contexts of Period 1. In addition to two body sherds recovered from the natural subsoil of Area C (*50013*), four residual abraded fragments of Ipswich ware were found in dump *50263*, associated with the disuse of the sunken featured building *50242*. One of these was a jar rim made from a slightly gritty fabric variant. The disuse fills also contained Thetford-type wares and small quantities of Early medieval wares (see below). A large unabraded rim sherd and a fragment from second vessel, both made from Sandy Ipswich ware, were found in the fill of cesspit *30237*. A single fragment of an Ipswich ware jar base was recovered from a backfill of medieval date (*10619*, Period 2.1). Five other sherds, including the rims from two other jars, were found associated with Period 2.2 (12th–13th century). Two further sherds of Ipswich ware were present in deposits of Period 3 and Period 5. Three more were unstratified, these including a large and very abraded body sherd.

The nature of the Middle Saxon settlement of Norwich is a subject of much discussion and any new evidence provides a valuable contribution to the overall distribution

Fabric	*Qty (no. sherds)*	*Wt (kg)*	*Vessel type*	*% of total wt*
Colchester white ware	3	0.304	2.5, 6.	36.36
Hadham Oxidised red ware	1	0.003	4.5.2	0.36
Micaceous oxidised ware	7	0.095	4.1, 4.6.1.	11.36
Unsourced oxidised ware	1	0.005		0.59
Micaceous reduced ware	29	0.179	4.1, 4.6.1, 4.13.	21.41
Nene Valley colour coat	1	0.010		1.20
Red Ware	4	0.038	1.9.1	4.55
Sandy grey ware	17	0.162	1.9.1, 4.1, 4.5, 4.13.	19.38
Sandy oxidised ware	5	0.034	4.4.	4.07
Visible clay relict grey ware	1	0.006		0.72
Total	**69**	**0.836**		

Table 21 Roman pottery

Period	*Feature*	*Context*	*Fabric*	*Form*	*Qty (no. sherds)*	*Wt (kg)*
1	Natural	50013		BODY	2	0.020
1	Dump	50263	Gritty/Sandy	JAR	4	0.085
1	Pit	30238		JAR	2	0.114
2.1	Backfill	10619	Gritty	BASE	1	0.052
2.2	Build-up	50004		BASE	1	0.023
2.2	Dump	50457		JAR	1	0.017
2.2	Post-hole	50295		BODY	1	0.012
2.2	Pit	50238		BODY	1	0.051
2.2	Pit	50244	Gritty	JAR	1	0.011
3	Pit	30452	Gritty	BODY	1	0.027
5		30034		JAR	1	0.017
-	Sondage	50222	Gritty	BODY	1	0.065
-	-	50003		BODY	1	0.032
-	-	50600		BODY	1	0.013
Total					**19**	**0.539**

Table 22 Middle Saxon pottery

pattern for this early part of the history of the city. Archaeological evidence for this period within Norwich is very sparse, so that the presence of concentrations of Middle Saxon material are themselves significant, although they may not be associated with actual features of this date. The fragments of Middle Saxon pottery from this site, together with the presence of other artefacts of comparable date, are therefore of considerable interest (see Chapter 4.IV).

The majority of the Ipswich ware recovered was found in the eastern part of the Greyfriars excavation (Area C) which lies closest to the west bank of the River Wensum, and is also near Rose Lane. This has previously been an area from which artefacts of Middle Saxon date have also been recovered (Ayers 1994, 24 and map 8). Small quantities of Middle Saxon pottery have also been found from other sites along the main north-to-south axis into Norwich, King Street. The excavation at the former Ben Burgess site at 51–53 King Street, immediately to the south, provided one further fragment of Middle Saxon pottery (Goffin forthcoming). Further along King Street to the south, beyond the site of the Austin Friary, the larger excavation at Dragon Hall produced a total of seven fragments (Anderson 2005). In addition, seventeen fragments of Ipswich ware were recovered from excavations at Castle Mall, to the south-west of Greyfriars (Lentowicz forthcoming). As many as seven sherds (the identification of two is unconfirmed) occurred residually in later deposits at Busseys garage, Palace Street (Emery 2000b). Five sherds of Ipswich-type ware were recovered during the excavation at Whitefriars Car Park in 1979 (Ayers and Murphy 1983) and seven were found by excavation at St Martin-at-Palace Plain in 1981 (Ayers 1988). During the 1996 evaluation trenching adjacent to Pigg Lane (on the Busseys premises), twelve sherds were recovered (Lentowicz 1996). This brings the current total for the southern part of Norwich (at the time of writing) to 76 sherds.

The main concentration of Middle Saxon pottery, however, is to the north of the river, on either side of Fye Bridge Street and from the associated streets along the river margins (Ayers 1994, 24). The relatively large quantity of Middle Saxon pottery (119 Ipswich-type ware sherds, alongside other hand-made wares which may be of a similar date) recovered from Fishergate in 1985 was found with other artefacts of Middle Saxon date (Dallas 1994, 20, 27–8). Although recovered from secondary deposits, this material suggests activity in the vicinity. By comparison with this, the assemblage recovered from south of the river is far more more modest, suggesting (on the basis of current knowledge) that occupation on the south bank was peripheral to the main settlement in the 8th–9th centuries. It is possible that an area of Middle Saxon settlement was focussed near Rose Lane, although more positive evidence for this is needed.

Late Saxon, medieval and post-medieval pottery
by Irena Lentowicz
(Figs 5.56–5.73)

This pottery report is divided into three sections relating to the chronological chapter headings in the archaeological narrative sections of this volume (Chapters 2–4). Each section begins with an overview of fabrics and forms of the pottery of the period under discussion. It includes all the pottery recovered (including residual pottery) with an emphasis on contemporary material. This is followed by a discussion by feature and function corresponding to stratigraphic periods and their phases (Table 20), where the pottery from illustrated groups is discussed in relation to the development of the site. The sections then conclude with a short, period-specific summary.

Throughout the text the major quantification used is weight; where cited, average sherd size refers to hand retrieved material only. Unless specifically indicated, all percentages refer to weight. Where discussion of forms by fabrics mentions rim numbers, this refers to the actual number of vessels represented by rim sherds. Thus, in cases where two or more rim or other sherds come from a single vessel, these are counted as one rim.

Where possible, rims were allocated to a typology or type series relevant to the fabric. For Thetford-type ware this is Dallas 1984; for Early Medieval ware and Local Medieval Unglazed ware the proposed fabric series from the Norwich Calvert Street analysis was used (Lentowicz forthcoming b), while for Grimston Glazed ware the type series was Little 1994. Further details of the methodologies used during analysis are given in the project archive.

Period 2.3 was effectively contemporary with the earliest phase of the Friary, which lay outside the excavated area until expansion in the late 13th century. Generic references below to 'Period 3' effectively span the whole of the Friary period from 1226 to 1538 (*i.e.* Periods 2.3, 3.1 and 3.2).

Pre-Friary (10th–13th centuries)

Pottery allocated to pre-Friary activity (Periods 1 and Periods 2.1–2.2) is presented sequentially in the main part of this section and is discussed together, although Period 2.3 is tabulated separately.

Almost a third of the pottery from the site was recovered from contexts allocated to Period 1, Period 2.1 or Period 2.2. The assemblage from Period 1 is dominated by TTW domestic vessels, mostly jars and cooking pots, with some storage and serving vessels, with lamp fragments representing lighting. Craft activity in the vicinity is attested by small quantities of crucibles, not only from locally produced fabrics but also specialised vessels from Stamford (see Chapter 5.II, 'Non-ferrous metalworking'). The character of the assemblage as a whole appears to be 11th-century rather than late 9th–10th-century. This is confirmed not only by the range of vessels and rim types recorded but also by the paucity of other Late Saxon regional and continental imports: only a small quantity of St Neot's-type ware was noted, and Stamford ware (Fabric A) is represented by a few sherds, while Pingsdorf-type ware was much more common in later periods. Early medieval wares from Period 1 were also restricted to domestic vessels. EMSW was, surprisingly, more common than EMW. Yarmouth-type ware, though not recovered in great quantity, has a definite presence. Stamford ware (Fabric B) and Andenne-type ware are again represented by a small quantity of sherds.

Although TTW is still dominant in Period 2.1 (12th-century) assemblages, early medieval and medieval pottery account for a far larger proportion than in Period 1. It is possible that supplementary products in local and regional wares, such as EMW and Yarmouth-type wares, were required for functional vessels not present in the range of TTW. TTW is represented by many later 'high' forms (Dallas 1984, 125–6), and many of these later rim forms can be paralleled with EMW. EMW is more common than EMSW and 'fossil'-type ginger jars make their first appearance. Both Yarmouth-type ware and LMU become much more frequent. Glazed wares are represented by imported Andenne-type and Pingsdorf-type wares although local products from Grimston do make an appearance towards the end of the period. This period assemblage does show that TTW, early medieval and medieval wares were being used concurrently into the 12th century.

Since the date range for Period 2.2 is so wide-ranging (12th–13th centuries), it is not surprising that TTW and EMW still makes up a major component of this period assemblage and it is difficult to assess to what extent these fabrics are residual. Undoubtedly some vessels were probably long-lived and survived into the 12th century. However, the wares were no longer being produced and the development of LMU means that the products from earlier ceramic phases were on the wane. Glazed wares are present, but still make up only a small proportion of the assemblage.

Later deposits contained a small quantity of Developed Stamford ware (Fabric C) and a single Scarborough-type ware body sherd. Continental imports are similarly represented by small numbers of body sherds of Andenne-type and Aardenburg-type wares, and the first occurrence of Siegburg and Langerwehe stonewares. More unusually, a single sherd from a Rouen/North French-type jug represents continental trade from the south as well as from the east.

Features and deposits assigned to the immediately pre-Friary period (Period 2.3) clearly contained a large proportion of residual earlier material, as TTW and other early medieval wares are definitely residual finds by this date. Yarmouth-type ware is also now either residual or beginning to decline. Local fabrics still dominate the assemblage, and LMU rims develop into the 13th–14th-century incipient and defined 'hammer-head' rims, although there are still many simpler upright and everted rims in the assemblage. LMU is supplemented by regional imports such as Grimston Coarse ware and Cambridge-type wares although not in any quantity. A few LMU jug rims were recovered, but tablewares introduced in the previous periods become established. Grimston Glazed wares are supplemented by non-local and continental products, again in small quantities. These include jugs of Developed Stamford ware (Fabric C), Hedingham-type and Scarborough-type wares, as well as Andenne-type wares and Aardenburg vessels. While products from France are less common on Norwich sites, a single Saintonge vessel is present. Late Medieval/Transitional wares make their first appearance, and include not only cooking vessels represented by LMT and DREW, but also Rhenish drinking vessels imported from Siegburg and Langerwehe.

Late Saxon fabrics and forms

Late Saxon fabrics make up over a third of the entire ceramic assemblage. They are dominated by Thetford-type ware with only small quantities of regional imports such as St Neot's-type ware and Stamford ware (Fabric A), while continental imports are represented by Pingsdorf-type ware. Quantification of the pottery from Periods 1–2.2 is presented in Table 23, with pottery from Period 2.3 in Table 24.

Thetford-type ware (TTW)

Thetford-type ware is well-fired and wheel-thrown, with a grey colour. It was produced in large amounts at several towns in East Anglia (specifically Ipswich, Thetford and Norwich) and is currently thought to date to the Late Saxon/Norman period (10th–12th centuries). Thetford-type ware was also produced at rural sites such as Langhale (Wade 1976), Grimston (Clarke 1970, 79–95) and Bircham (Rogerson and Adams 1978, 33–44). Although most of the pottery recovered from Norwich sites was probably made locally, the fabrics from all three towns are very similar and have been given a generic name. The range of forms include cooking pots, bowls, jars, spouted pitchers, large storage jars and lamps. The production of Norwich Thetford-type ware is currently thought to have begun in the late 9th century (or *c.* 900), but may have tailed out towards the end of the 11th century (slightly earlier than previously thought). By the 12th century, Early Medieval ware takes over as the dominant fabric.

Only 28.3% of the TTW recovered at the Greyfriars site came from Period 1 (10th–11th centuries), with a further 11.6% from contexts assigned to Period 2.1 (12th century) and 7.6% from Period 2.2 (12th–13th centuries); the remaining 52.5% was recovered as a residual element in later contexts (including Period 2.3, 13th century). TTW makes up a large proportion of the period assemblages, but is most common in Period 1 where it makes up 88.9% of the material recovered. By Period 2.1 it has dropped to just over half (54.1%) and to just less than half in Period 2.2 (45.1%). However, it continues to make up a large proportion of the assemblage as a residual element through Period 3 (44.2%), dropping in Period 4 (12.1%) and rising slightly in Period 5.

Fabric	Period 1 Sherds	Wt	% Wt	Period 2.1 Sherds	Wt	% Wt	Period 2.2 Sherds	Wt	% Wt	Total assemblage Sherds	Wt	% Wt
Residual	29	0.228	0.8	15	0.103	0.5	34	0.257	1.7	*145*	*1.276*	*0.6*
Residual Middle Saxon	129	0.540	1.9	-	-	-	5	0.112	0.8	*145*	*0.919*	*0.4*
Thetford-type ware	2864	24.864	86.2	1702	10.137	54.2	1550	6.663	45.1	*13,834*	*87.661*	*41.7*
St Neot's-type ware	13	0.248	0.9	16	0.043	0.2	4	0.013	0.1	*84*	*0.469*	*0.2*
Stamford ware (Fabric A)	2	0.028	0.1	1	0.004	<0.1	2	0.012	0.1	*11*	*0.084*	*<0.1*
Pingsdorf-type ware	2	0.016	0.1	6	0.350	1.9	7	0.036	0.2	*80*	*0.995*	*0.5*
Misc. Late Saxon wares	-	-	-	-	-	-	-	-	-	*1*	*0.012*	*<0.1*
EMW	342	1.097	3.8	410	1.205	6.4	547	1.111	7.5	*3458*	*8.889*	*4.2*
EMSW	122	1.274	4.4	68	0.701	3.7	111	1.885	12.8	*733*	*8.311*	*4.0*
EMSSW	3	0.025	0.1	6	0.030	0.2	2	0.021	0.1	*39*	*0.195*	*0.1*
Stamford ware (Fabric B)	11	0.154	0.5	6	0.032	0.2	4	0.015	0.1	*47*	*296*	*0.1*
Early Medieval Shelly ware	-	-	-	-	-	-	-	-	-	*3*	*0.080*	*<0.1*
Yarmouth-type ware	28	0.149	0.5	155	0.791	4.2	157	0.881	6.0	*1077*	*5.497*	*2.6*
LMU	25	0.056	0.2	459	2.531	13.5	769	3.489	23.6	*6323*	*23.843*	*11.3*
Non-local Unglazed wares	2	0.036	0.1	3	0.028	0.1	-	-	-	*78*	*0.507*	*0.3*
Grimston Glazed wares	1	0.004	<0.1	13	0.133	0.7	12	0.125	0.8	*1026*	*10.824*	*5.1*
Medieval Glazed wares	-	-	-	10	0.087	0.4	6	0.029	0.2	*193*	*1.509*	*0.7*
Andenne-type ware	11	0.104	0.4	11	0.039	0.2	15	0.087	0.6	*117*	*0.634*	*0.3*
Intrusive	3	0.025	0.1	76	2.520	13.4	3	0.022	0.1	*82*	*2.567*	*<0.1*
Total	**3587**	**28.848**		**2957**	**18.734**		**3228**	**14.758**		***27,476***	***450.27***	

Table 23 Quantity and weight of pottery by fabric and period for Periods 1, 2.1 and 2.2 (see Table 24 for Period 2.3)

TTW is represented by a wide range of vessel forms, almost exclusively household and kitchen wares (Table 25). Jars and cooking pots are the most common forms recorded, with jars making up nearly three-quarters of vessel forms identified by rim (73.9%) and cooking pots accounting for 16.5%. Medium-sized jars and cooking pots (type AB) are by far the most abundant. While small (type AA) and large (type AC) rims are also present in some quantity it is noticeable that cooking pots tend to vary less in size, with many fewer smaller and larger-sized vessels. Therefore it appears that medium-sized vessels were preferred for use over fires. This would seem plausible, since smaller vessels had a restricted capacity and larger vessels may have been too heavy and cumbersome to carry with heated contents.

A wide range of rim types was recorded. The most common single rim form is an everted rim with sides expanded to a wedge shape (type AB6: 164 rims) which accounted for 20% of jar/cooking pot rims recorded. Examples of practically all Dallas's rim types are present, at least in the medium-size range, with the exception of rim type AB2. Some attempt was made to quantify and compare the assemblages of Dallas' 'early' and 'high' level rim forms. In general the 11th-century 'high' level types (types AA1, AB1, AA2, AB2, AB9 and AB10: 94 rims) are more common than the earlier 10th-century rims (types AB7, AB8, AB15 and AB17: 65 rims). Rim types which appear throughout the 10th and 11th centuries are much more prolific: for example types AB13 and AB14 (71 and 118 rims respectively). The general conclusion is that the TTW assemblage seems to reflect a later 10th–11th-century date range rather than the late 9th–10th centuries. This is reflected in other vessel forms also (see below).

In addition, a previously unidentified rim form was noted. A number of rim sherds with everted, thickened rims with no internal hollow were recovered and have been appended to Dallas' typology as type AB18 (Fig. 5.60, a, e–g). Rims with this profile are present in both Period 1 and 2 assemblages on Area B but do not appear in contemporary contexts on other areas of the site, although they are present on other areas as a residual element.

Other rims which could not be allocated to Dallas' typology include those with rounded edges, lid-seated rims with square profiles, upright rims with triangular sections, and everted rims with developed, hook-like exterior pendants. These were recovered in insufficient quantity to be added to the typology.

Other vessel forms were recovered in much smaller quantity and are dominated by kitchen and household wares. These include storage jars and large jars with and without handles. These vessels are characterised

Fabrics	*Sherds*	*Wt*	*% Wt*
Residual	26	0.235	0.5
Residual Late Saxon	4185	22.486	52.1
Residual early medieval	1524	4.509	10.2
LMU	2722	8.082	18.7
Yarmouth-type ware	365	1.397	3.2
Grimston Coarse ware	1	0.015	<0.1
Non-local medieval wares	18	0.077	0.2
Grimston Glazed ware	346	3.907	9.0
Developed Stamford ware	7	0.011	<0.1
Scarborough-type ware	1	0.010	<0.1
Non-local glazed wares	42	0.325	0.8
Andenne-type ware	34	0.161	0.4
Aardenburg-type ware	2	0.144	0.3
Rouen-type/North French ware	1	0.014	<0.1
LMT	64	1.067	2.5
Dutch-type REW	2	0.108	0.3
Siegburg Stoneware	4	0.028	0.1
Langerwehe Stoneware	16	0.124	0.3
Intrusive Post-medieval	5	0.068	0.1
Intrusive Modern	1	0.004	<0.1
Unidentified	16	0.379	0.9
Total	**9382**	**43.151**	

Table 24 Quantity and weight of pottery by fabric and period for Period 2.3

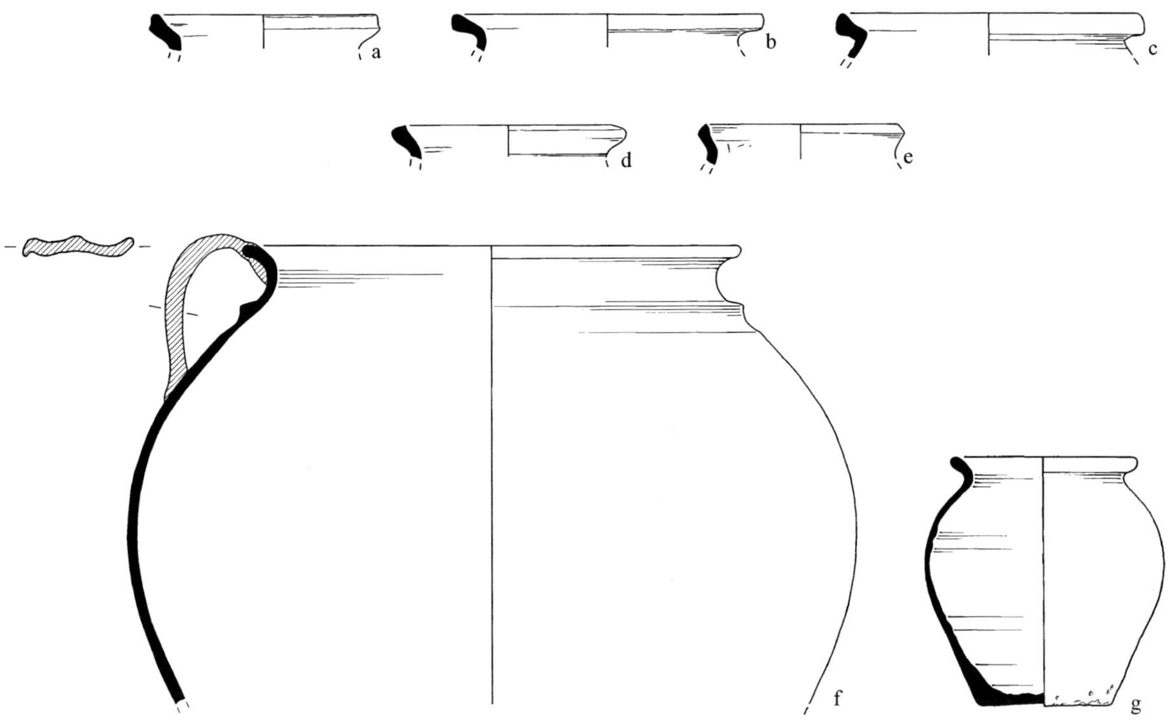

Figure 5.56 Pottery from sunken-floored building *10049* (Area D) (Period 1). Scale 1:4.

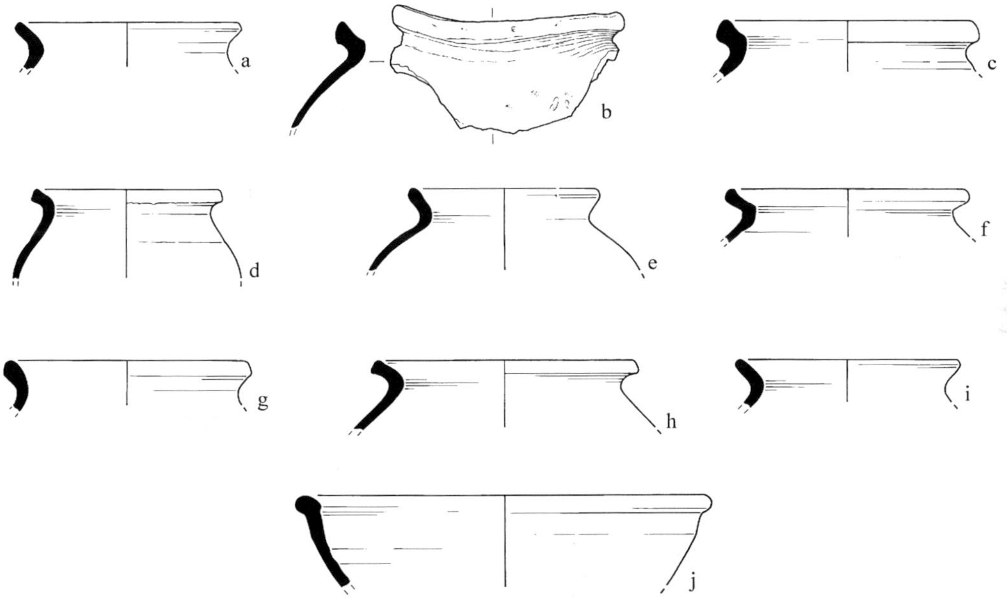

Figure 5.57 Pottery from sunken-featured building *50242* (Area C) (Period 1). Scale 1:4.

by large bases and by body sherds decorated with applied thumbed strips providing reinforcement. The majority have everted rims with parallel or tapering sides or sides expanded to a wedge-shape (Dallas types AF2, AF4, AF8 and AF9) as well as a less common upright rim with internal hollow (Dallas type AF6). Their function was, not surprisingly, storage of grains and foodstuffs. These vessels were large and probably not intended to be moved quickly or conveniently.

A number of rims from ginger jars were recovered, the majority being found residually. Their function is unclear, and many sooted as well as unsooted examples are recorded. They are frequently decorated just below the rim with a variety of motifs, including applied thumbed strips as well as incised and stamped decoration.

Forms which can be identified as table wares are less well represented. Bowls include examples of small, medium and large vessels serving a variety of functions. Small, curve sided bowls (Dallas type BB6) include examples with a plain, internally pulled rim (archive type T6) and plain, upright rim (archive T11), as well as a socketed bowl (Dallas type BD2). Bowls with flaring forms and straight sides and a variety of rim treatments were also present (Dallas types BB2, BB3 and BB4). Large bowls are less common, with a single example of a curve-sided bowl with expanded rim (Dallas type BB7).

Spouted jars, for pouring liquids, are even less common and again simple, less complex rim forms are evident. Plain flared rims (Dallas type AD1) and everted lid-seated rims with sides everted to a wedge shape (Dallas type AD11) are present. Spouted jars are also represented by fragments of spouts and a number of handles.

Other functional vessels were limited to fragments of both pedestal and spike lamps (see Goffin, Chapter 5.II, 'Lighting'). In addition, a considerable quantity of TTW crucible fragments was recovered, some of which retained metalworking residues. These are described in Chapter

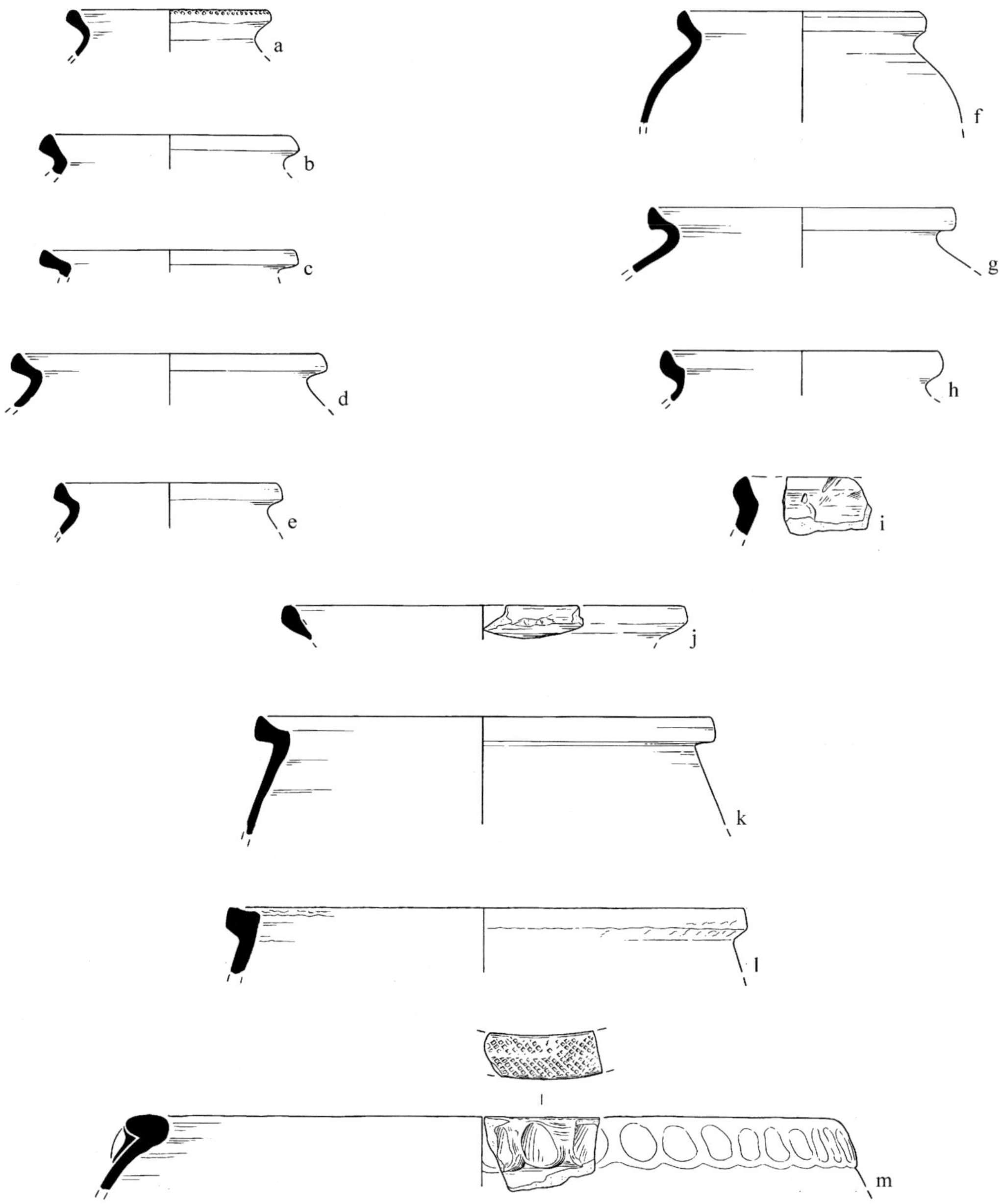

Figure 5.58 Pottery from pit *11231* (Period 1). Scale 1:4.

Vessel Form	*Period 1*	*Period 2.1*	*Period 2.2*	*Rest*	*Total*
Jars	148	78	66	353	645
Cooking pots	66	13	22	63	164
Storage/large jars	3	4	1	7	15
Ginger jars	1	1	-	6	8
Spouted pitchers/handled jars	3	1	1	-	5
Bowls	3	1	-	16	21
Lamps	1	1	1	2	5
Crucibles	-	-	22	6	28
Other	-	-	-	1	1

Table 25 Thetford-type ware forms by rim number (excludes Period 2.3)

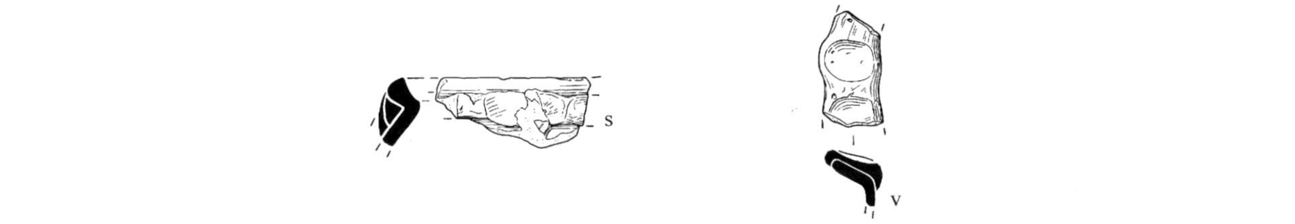

Figure 5.59 Pottery from pit *11145* (Period 1). Scale 1:4.

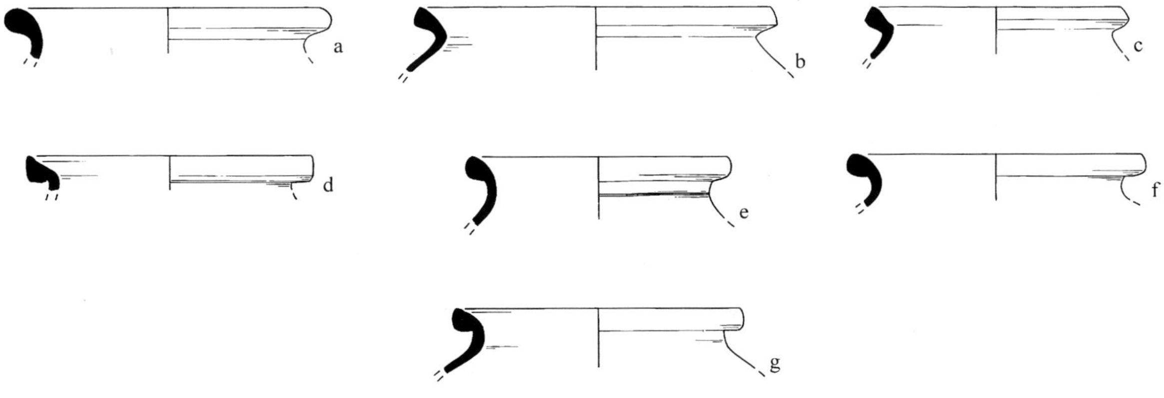

Figure 5.60 Pottery from pit *30237* (Period 1). Scale 1:4.

Vessel Form	*Period 1*	*Period 2.1*	*Period 2.2*	*Rest*	*Total*
Jars	7	7	8	35	57
Cooking pots	8	30	12	26	76
Ginger jars	-	5	2	18	25
Bowls	1	-	1	1	3
Lamps	-	-	1	1	2

Table 26 EMW forms by rim number (excludes Period 2.3)

Vessel Form	*Period 1*	*Period 2.1*	*Period 2.2*	*Rest*	*Total*
Jars	7	2	3	23	35
Cooking pots	5	-	-	-	5
Storage/large jars	-	-	1	1	2
Ginger jars	-	-	-	2	2
Handled jars	-	2	-	3	5
Multi-handled jars	-	-	-	1	1
Bowls	3	-	-	1	4

Table 27 EMSW forms by rim number (excludes Period 2.3)

5.II, 'Non-ferrous metalworking'. In summary, much of the material from Periods 1, 2, 2.2 and 2.3 is typologically characteristic of the 11th century rather than earlier. A comparison of forms with Dallas' 'early' and 'high level' assemblages from Thetford concludes that though some 'early' types are present (*e.g.* rim types AB7 and AB8), these are not recovered in large quantity and later 'high' level 11th-century rim forms (types AB1, AB2 and AB9) and vessels (large type AF9 jars, spouted pitchers) are more common. Other typical early forms such as bowls with carinated profile (type BB12) are not present.

St Neot's-type ware and Stamford ware (Fabric A)

Locally produced coarse wares were supplemented by regional imports represented by small quantities of St Neot's-type ware and Stamford ware (Fabric A). The former is a common occurrence on Norwich sites, but is rarely found in any quantity. This is in contrast with the situation at Norfolk's other large, important Late Saxon settlement at Thetford, where St Neot's-type ware can account for up to 30% of site assemblages (*e.g.* at Redcastle Furze: Little 1995a). This probably indicates that Norwich lay on the periphery of the distribution network, and since the vessels recovered tend to be either jars/cooking pots and bowls the demand for these forms would have been met by the local suppliers. St Neot's-type ware is seen as an indicator of 9th–11th-century occupation and as a Late Saxon rather than an early medieval fabric. This is borne out by the quantities recovered at Greyfriars: less than 0.5kg was recovered in total, and much of this came from Period 1 (0.240kg, 52.9% of the entire quantity), with only 43g recovered from Period 2.1 and 13g from Period 2.2; the remainder was residual in later contexts. Only six rims were recovered, three from jars/cooking pots (two with everted rims coming to a point, and one necked jar with a rounded, slightly lid-seated rim) and one from a bowl (with a flattened, squared rim). More unusually, a rim from a ginger jar was recorded and a putative lid. These are less common but not unknown.

An even smaller quantity of Stamford ware (Fabric A) was recovered and none came from contemporary contexts. This 10th–11th-century coarse ware is usually represented by jars and spouted pitchers (Leach 1987, 70–1), but at Greyfriars is represented by rims from crucibles only (see Chapter 5.II, 'Non-ferrous metalworking').

Pingsdorf-type ware

Imports are not unknown from the Late Saxon period in Norwich, but here are restricted to Pingsdorf-type ware, which from sites in the city can date from the 10th century. A small quantity (two sherds weighing only 16g) was recovered from Period 1 contexts. Larger quantities were recovered from Period 2.1 and 2.2, and it is probable that these vessels continued to be used into the 13th century. The fabric is mainly represented by decorated body sherds and frilled bases from jugs or small jars. Only one rim was recovered, and this was residual.

Early medieval wares

Early medieval wares are frequently hand-made but wheel-finished and broadly date to the 11th to early 12th centuries, after which production develops into Local Medieval Unglazed (LMU) ware. Early Medieval wares therefore effectively breach the transition between Late Saxon wares and truly medieval pottery. In Norwich, they include local products Early Medieval ware (EMW) and Early Medieval Sandwich ware (EMSW), as well as regional wares Early Medieval Sparse Shelly ware (EMSSW), regional imports Stamford ware (Fabric B), and the continuation of continental imports such as Pingsdorf-type ware. They account for *c.* 7% of the entire assemblage, and make up a similar proportion of the Period 1 material (6.8%) and a larger part of Period 2.1 (20.6%). By Period 3, and probably even in the latter stages of Period 2.1, early medieval wares are residual but still account for a sizeable proportion of period assemblages (15.9% in Period 3), although this drops dramatically in later periods (2.4% in Period 4 and 3.6% in Period 5).

Early Medieval ware (EMW)

EMW is usually the most common early medieval pottery recovered on Norwich sites, and makes up 4.2% of the Greyfriars assemblage. The range of forms is limited and only cooking pots and/or jars are found in any quantity, supplemented by ginger jars and small bowls (Table 26). More unusually, two rims from lamps are also recorded in this assemblage. Jars/cooking pots tend to be small with diameters ranging from 13–18cm (type J1); although larger jars with diameters of 20cm are present, these are not common (type J2). Rims tend to be plain and upright (type J1a), everted (type J1b) and everted coming to a point (type J1c). These latter rims are thought to be more 'medieval' and may represent the development of EMW into LMU. Jar/cooking pots with type J1b rims are most common (56% of jars and 72% of cooking pots), but these vessels are relatively standardised.

Ginger jars are the 'fossil' type for EMW and are frequently found in this fabric. Their function is not clear. Some are sooted and many are decorated; motifs vary from applied thumbed strips beneath the rim through incised wavy lines to stamped decoration. Of the 26 examples recovered from Greyfriars twelve rims are decorated. Diameters vary from 10cm to 20cm, within two size groups: smaller vessels ranging from 10–13cm (ten rims) and larger ones from 16–20cm (four rims). (The rims of the remaining twelve ginger jars could not be measured.)

Only two other vessel forms were represented here. The rims from three bowls were recorded, including a small, straight-sided bowl with an everted square rim and a larger example (18cm diameter) with a straight upright rim.

Early Medieval Sandwich ware (EMSW)

The other major early medieval fabric present on Norwich sites is EMSW: the 'sandwich' fabric of dark core and surface and lighter margins is very distinctive and is thought to result from the firing process.

The surface of many sherds is slightly abraded even when the sherds are not considered to be residual, and it may be that the distinctive 'sandwich' appearance is due to incomplete firing which leaves the surface less well-fired and susceptible to wear. EMSW is recovered in a range of forms which have direct parallels with TTW, and may well represent a later, less well-fired development of the Late Saxon pottery industry. It is possible that EMSW is an 11th–early 12th-century version of TTW, but it does not replace TTW. EMSW accounts for 14.6% of the Period 1 assemblage, and its share increases to 31.5% in Period 2.1 as do other early medieval fabrics at the expense of TTW, but since it never constitutes the largest share of the early medieval pottery assemblage it is unlikely that it was ever intended to supersede TTW.

Few forms were recovered (Table 27) but the range extends beyond the usual spouted pitchers (Jennings 1981, 23). Jars are the most common vessel form noted, and although a range of rim types is recorded there is less variation than that exhibited by TTW. Long-lived lid-seated rims which are everted and expanded to a wedge (type AB13) or a degenerate wedge (type AB14) are present, but simpler everted rims are more common. Vessels with plain everted rims with parallel sides (type AB5) or expanded to a wedge-shape (type AB6) are more prolific, while the 'high' level plain, everted (type AB1) and upright (type AB2) rims testify to the 11th-century date for this fabric. It seems that EMSW is not a fabric frequently used for cooking pots, as only five of the rims of this fabric are from such vessels.

The remaining assemblage is made up of storage and serving vessels. Of these handled jars were most common; again these had 11th-century 'high' level rim types with upright rims (type AE2) and everted, parallel rims (type AE4). A single example of a multi-handled jar with an everted, flared rim (type AE1) (Fig 5.63 a) was recovered from a large post-hole or pit of Period 2.1. Other large jars included rims with internal hollow and sides parallel (type AF8) or sides expanded to a wedge-shape (type AF9), but again body sherds decorated with applied thumbed strips were a more common testament to the presence of these large storage vessels. Four bowls were recorded, with flaring form, straight sides and expanded rim (type BB4) and also a small curved-sided bowl (type BB6). Another very fine, thin-walled vessel may come from a small bowl, or possibly a lamp.

Type	*Cooking pots*	*Jars*	*Total*
Y1 (upright)	10	23	33
Y2 (everted)	5	10	15
Y3 (lid-seated)	1	5	6
Total	**16**	**38**	**54**

Table 28 Yarmouth-type ware rim profiles by vessel count

Type	*Y1*	*Y2*	*Y3*
a = plain	8	5	-
b = squared	9	2	-
c = rounded	13	5	-
d = coming to a point	1	1	-
e = slight internal and external projection	1	-	5

Table 29 Yarmouth-type ware rims by type and profile

Type	*Cooking pot*	*Jar*	*Total*
Sagging	6	2	8
Flat	7	13	20
Flat with lip	7	5	12
	20	20	

Table 30 Yarmouth-type ware base by vessel and base type

Type	*Period 1*	*Period 2.1*	*Period 2.2*
Y1	-	2	5
Y2	3	2	2
Y3	-	1	1

Table 31 Yarmouth-type ware rim types by period (excludes Period 3.0)

Yarmouth-type ware

Yarmouth-type ware is a coarse, sandy fabric, comparable with material excavated at Fuller's Hill, Great Yarmouth and is usually paralleled with Mellor's Fabric 3/1 (Mellor 1976, 188). Although Yarmouth-type ware has been found in small quantities on a number of other Norwich sites, at Greyfriars it was recovered in some quantity: 5.5kg, making up 2.6% of the entire assemblage. It was possible for the first time to produce a preliminary rim form series based on phased material. Yarmouth-type ware has been seen as a late 11th–12th-century fabric, but it was noted both here and at Castle Mall that this pottery frequently occurs with TTW and EMW. At Greyfriars the fabric is present as a small element in Late Saxon contexts, and is more common in early medieval Periods 2.1 and 2.2 than later, which would suggest that the *floruit* can be extended into the early 12th century.

The fabric is hard and well-fired, with abundant quartz inclusions and occasional fine calcareous grit. Some sherds are characterised by greater quantities of calcareous inclusions. The surface is orange-grey with patches of fumed darker grey, probably as the result of use over a fire. The core is usually much darker grey with a lighter margin.

With the exception of four bowl rims, the only vessels recovered were rims from jars and cooking pots (Table 28). Three main rim profiles were identified: the most common were upright rims (type Y1; Fig 5.61, i; Fig 5.62, d), while everted rims (type Y2; Fig 5.59, u) were less prolific, and there were fewer everted, lid-seated rims (type Y3; Fig 5.62, e). There does not appear to be any correlation between rim type and a vessel's function as a jar or cooking pot (Table 29).

Diameters are recorded for rims, and these range from 14cm to 27cm; the majority are of 14–18cm (fourteen rims) or 22–26cm (sixteen rims). Rims from type Y1 and Y2 vessels cover the range of sizes, but type Y3 rims are all large and over 18cm in diameter. Table 28 indicates further sub-division on the basis of rim type.

Forty bases with measurable diameters are divided equally (by sherd number) between cooking pots and jars. Flat bases were most common (20 flat and twelve with a lip) and only eight sagging bases were recorded (Table 29). Diameters range from 8cm to 28cm, but the majority come from the 16–20cm range (seventeen bases). Jar bases (or unsooted bases) tend to be smaller in diameter, and include an 8cm base, while cooking pots have one example of 12cm but are mostly from 18cm upwards. The largest base is 28cm in diameter.

In terms of phasing, the earliest rim profiles recovered are everted (type Y2), which are present in Period 1 contexts, while both upright rims (type Y1) and lid-seated rims (type Y3) both first appear in Period 2.1 (Table 31). Although the rim assemblage is not large, and this typology is not exhaustive, it does provide a basis for future research.

As noted above, the Yarmouth-type ware fabric recovered from sites in Norwich resembles Fabric 3/1 recovered from Fuller's Hill, Great Yarmouth (Mellor 1976, 188), hence the attribution. However, no petrological analysis has been undertaken to verify this. The vessels are not ubiquitous enough to be considered an import in their own right, and there are a number of explanations for their presence in Norwich. They may have been brought in as for personal use by people coming from the coast to settle in the city; equally, the vessels may have been used as containers for transporting items and subsequently reused. Residue analysis on the internal surface may eventually answer the question of what, if they were indeed used as containers, they were transporting.

Early Medieval Sparse Shelly ware (EMSSW) and Stamford ware (Fabric B)

Other early medieval wares are represented by a much smaller quantity of pottery. EMSSW is also a regional import and is represented by a small number of jar rims, either plain or expanded to a square-section. Stamford ware (Fabric B) is a mid-11th–12th-century fine ware which is usually represented by pitchers and jars (Leach 1987, 74); however, at Greyfriars the only forms represented by rims are three crucibles (see Chapter 5.II, 'Non-ferrous metalworking').

Medieval

Medieval pottery accounts for a small intrusive element in Period 1 contexts (0.7%), and by the 12th century in Period 2.1 it makes up 14.9% of the period assemblage. It is during Period 2.2 that medieval wares come to represent a significant proportion of the period assemblage (30.6%). This remains high during Period 3 contexts (30.4%) but drops during Period 4 (9.9%).

Local Medieval Unglazed ware (LMU)
LMU is the most common individual fabric recovered and, because of the ranges of the site periods, over 80% came from contemporary contexts. Although LMU appears in small quantities in Period 1, it is in Periods 2 and 3 that the fabric becomes a major part of the assemblage. By the mid-12th century pottery does not appear to have been produced in Norwich itself; possible kiln sources have been proposed to the north-east of the city, at Woodbastwick and Potter Heigham, where fieldwalking has produced wasters.

In Periods 1–2.2, as within the fabric assemblage in general, jars and cooking pots predominate amongst the forms recovered. Only five rims out of the 62 recovered from contexts assigned to these periods (representing four bowls and a curfew) came from other vessels. Of the jars/cooking pots, some twenty rims were recovered from smaller vessels with diameters less than 18cm (type J1), and 37 rims from larger vessels with diameters over 18cm (type J2). Overall the rims are of the less complex forms, typical of earlier, 12th-century vessels. The majority are simple, everted rims (type J1/2b: 22 rims) or everted, coming to a point (type J1/2c: 21 rims). Upright rims are less common (type J1/2A: two rims). Rims which are more developed, with incipient or sharply-defined internal and external projections (known as 'hammer-head', and classified as types J1/2i and J1/2j) were also recovered from these contexts. Those from Period 1, and probably from Period 2.1, are obviously intrusive, but those from Period 2.2 could be contemporary and indicative of a later date. On the whole, however, these LMU jar rims are occurring with Grimston Glazed ware and are dated to the 13th–14th centuries.

Other medieval fabrics
Other medieval wares are recovered in small quantities. Unglazed wares include local regional imports such as Grimston Coarse ware and East Cambridgeshire-type ware, as well as an as-yet unprovenanced Medieval Shelly ware. Glazed wares are represented by a range of local and regional imports, including Grimston Glazed ware, Developed Stamford ware, Hedingham-type ware and Scarborough-type ware, as well as continental imports such as Andenne-type ware. However, these were recovered in much greater quantity from deposits of Period 3.1 onwards, and are discussed in detail in the section on the Friary below.

Discussion by feature and function

Period 1: 10th–11th centuries
(Figs 5.56–5.60; Pl. 2.3)
A total of 3587 sherds of pottery weighing 28.848kg was recovered from contexts assigned to Period 1, accounting for 13.7% of the entire assemblage (Table 23). While a small proportion was residual Roman material (0.804kg, 2.3%) and a smaller proportion intrusive (0.166kg, 0.6%), the assemblage was dominated by Late Saxon TTW, supplemented by other Late Saxon and early medieval wares. There appears to be a concentration of activity around Area C, where 25% of the area assemblage came from contexts allocated to this period. Areas A and B are both also well represented, and while Area D appears less active it is the almost-complete absence of Late Saxon–Norman activity on Area CB which is most noticeable.

Sunken-floored building 10049 (Area A). Most pottery from this feature came from occupational debris retrieved from samples. These sherds, although fragmentary, are comparatively unabraded (2.393kg). Since the material represents occupational debris it has been illustrated (Fig. 5.56). This assemblage is made up mostly of TTW with a small quantity of EMW body sherds. Rims from TTW jars and cooking pots, and a probable spouted pitcher, were recovered. The rim forms include 11th-century types (type AA1 (Fig. 5.56, a) and AB6 (Fig.5.56, b)) as well as more long-lived examples (types AB14 (Fig. 5.56, c) and AB17 (Fig. 5.56, d and e)). Along with the pitcher or handled jar (type AE/AD1 (Fig. 5.56, f), this suggests an 11th-century date for the occupation assemblage. Figure 5.56, g shows a medium Thetford-type ware jar with a plain flared rim (Dallas type AB1) and a flat base, found beneath disuse deposits within the building (Pl. 2.3). The construction of a chalky bank within the sunken-featured building contained a smaller quantity of pottery (*10854*: 0.226kg) but again the TTW and EMW body sherds recovered were large and unabraded. The pottery from post- and stake-holes associated with the building also came from samples and is fragmentary. As well as the small TTW and EMW body sherds, the assemblage also contains small sherds of YT and Andenne-type wares. The range of material recovered from the sunken-floored building dates the use of the building to the mid–late 11th century. Its disuse is detailed in Period 2.1 below. Similar vessels have been recovered from kiln sites at Bedford Street (242N) and Lobster Lane in Norwich (Jennings 1983, fig 40, no 135) and from Thetford (Dallas 1984 and Anderson 2004). These vessels are ubiquitous and broadly 11th-century in date.

Sunken-featured building 50242 (Area C). The construction fills (0.411kg) produced pottery, mostly from samples. Some residual Roman sherds were recovered, but TTW and EMW dominate. Few forms were identifiable but a TTW cooking pot rim (type AC6) and two jar bases are present, as well as a body sherd decorated with rouletting. Associated disuse fills (*50258*, *50263*, *50267*, *50271* and *50272*) produced a larger and more interesting assemblage than that from building *10049* (8.662kg: Fig. 5.57). This includes some residual prehistoric and Roman pottery, and Middle Saxon Ipswich Pimply ware and Ipswich Sandy ware. TTW is the most common fabric and a large number of vessels are represented by rims from jars, some of which have been illustrated. Jar types include AB1 (four rims), AB5 (two rims), AB9, AB11 (six rims), AB13 (five rims), AB14 (three rims), AB16 (four rims), AC6 (two rims), AC16 and cooking pots of types AA1, AA4, AA10, AB1, AB2 (three rims), AB5, AB6 (six rims), AB9, AB11 (two rims), AB13 (four rims), AB14 (three rims) and AB16 (three rims). A socketed bowl was also recorded (type BD2) and other vessels represented by body sherds include a crucible fragment, decorated body sherds from storage jars and sherds with rouletted decoration, as well as a strap handle and numerous bases from jars, cooking pots, pedestal lamps and storage jars. A waster fragment from a Thetford-type jar recovered from one of the fills (*50258*: Fig. 5.57, b) was probably from one of the Norwich Thetford-type ware kiln sites in the vicinity (*e.g.* 2–4 Bedford Street: Jennings 1983, 81–5). Other Late Saxon fabrics present are limited to St Neot's-type ware, and the rest of the assemblage is composed of early medieval wares. EMW is represented by a jar (type J1b). EMSW is, surprisingly, more common than EMW and represented by more vessels including jars (types AB6 and AB16) and cooking pots (types AB1, AB6, AB10, AB13, and AB16), as well as a bowl rim (type BB6) (Fig. 5.57, j) and jar bases. EMSSW is represented by body sherds only. The fills also include some LMU; these jars with later developed rim forms (types J2i and J2j) are intrusive.

Comparison between the two sunken building assemblages is difficult: the only large fill is from the disuse of building *50242*, but only sunken-floored building *10049* yielded occupational debris. The only similar or comparable archaeological events are the construction fills of the chalk bank in building *10049* and the construction fills of sunken-featured building *50242*. Furthermore, most of the material was recovered from samples and is fragmentary — the same is true of the 2.393kg of pottery recovered from occupation debris within this building. The pottery consisted mainly of TTW-type ware jars and cooking pots, although a substantial part of a handled jar or pitcher was recovered in this fabric. In addition a small quantity of EMW body sherds were also identified. The rim forms for the TTW wares include 11th-century types as well as more long-lived examples. No rouletted sherds were recorded. The dating of this material is uncertain, although typologically the pottery from the site appears neither 'early' nor 'late' and may therefore be 11th century. Ceramics from final infilling span the late 12th to 14th centuries (see below), although the building was superseded by another structure in the late 12th–early 13th century.

The range of pottery from disuse fills from building *50242* appears to be much more diverse, although only 0.411kg of pottery (again mainly collected from samples) was recovered from the construction fills. In addition to some residual Roman sherds, TTW and small quantities of EMW were identified. The TTW includes a wider range of vessel forms, not only in the kitchen and tableware assemblage, which includes socketed bowls, but also lamps and crucible fragments (Chapter 5II, 'Ceramic lamps'; 'Ceramic crucibles and litharge cakes'). Forms included a TTW cooking pot rim (type AC6) and two jar bases, as well as a body sherd decorated with rouletting. Although cooking vessels with rouletting on their shoulders are a common feature in the early deposits at Thetford itself (Dallas 1984, 125), they are also found on production sites in Norwich such as 2–4 Bedford Street and 21 Bedford Street, which are likely to be 11th century in date. Rouletted sherds hardly feature at all on the small assemblage recovered from the kiln site at Lobster Lane in Norwich, which is typologically of a slightly later date, a deduction which is supported by a radiocarbon date which is also late (Jennings 1983, 92), although its interpretation is open to question. Early medieval wares are also better represented in building *50242*; while only EMW was recovered from building *10049*, EMSW is more common in building *50242*. St Neot's-type ware was also only recovered from building *50242*, although it was recovered from a refuse pit associated with building *10049* (see below).

Given the limited number of rims present in the two groups, the TTW wares themselves do not provide sufficient characteristics to refine the dating of these features significantly. The small quantities of EMW, however, indicate an 11th-century date for both of these structures' use, and possibly their construction. Building *50242* appears to have gone out of use earlier. What is common to both buildings is that, while domestic kitchen waste was primarily recovered, both also produced small-scale but identifiable evidence of industrial activity in the form of crucible fragments.

Pits associated with building 10049. Over 1.5kg of pottery was recovered from a cluster of pits to the south-west of building *10049* (1.825kg). The largest assemblage came from pit *11231* (1.623kg: Fig. 5.58), and comprises a fine assemblage of TTW, some of which has been illustrated. Vessels represented by rims include medium and large jars (types AB6, AB7, AB12, AB13, AB14, AB16, AB8 and AC15), cooking pots (types AB10 and AB11, as well as a lid-seated squared rim) and bowls (types BB4 and BB7). In addition body sherds decorated with applied thumbed strips from large storage jars and a number of jar bases were also recorded. Most of the TTW is unabraded. Other fabrics present include small but fresh quantities of EMW and EMSW, represented by body sherds and bases only. A small quantity of material is intrusive.

One large rubbish pit, pit *11145* (2.221kg: Fig. 5.59), contained a range of Late Saxon and early medieval pottery. Perhaps most significant is the absence of LMU. TTW makes up over half of the group assemblage; although some of this has been noted as abraded and is probably residual, some is fresher. Forms recovered include jars AC2, AB9, AB10 and AB6 (two examples) and cooking pots (types AB11 and AB6: three examples), as well as large jars (types AF8 and AF9) and a lamp or cup rim. Decorated body sherds from large storage jars and from a bowl are also present, along with six bases. EMW accounts for a quarter of the group and vessels recorded include jars of type J1a (three examples) and J2a, cooking pots of types J1b (four examples), J2a and J2b, and a bowl with an upright, flat rim. EMSW recovered includes a jar base, but most of the sherds are abraded. EMSSW is represented by a jar rim (type AB1). Yarmouth-type ware is also present and includes a cooking pot rim (type Y2c), and non-local Shelly ware (Fabric 21.5) is represented by two jar rims, one with an everted upright rim, and one everted coming to a point. The group also includes forms other than kitchen wares such as crucibles (see Chapter 5.II, 'Ceramic crucibles and litharge cakes').

Cess-pit 30237. Larger groups of pottery were recovered from cess-pits, some of which were selectively sampled. However, some contained distinguishable fills which indicate separate periods of deposition. An example of this was the use and disuse fills of pit *30237* (0.741kg: Fig. 5.60) which contains almost exclusively TTW, except for one sherd of EMSW representing a thin-walled bowl or lamp. TTW forms present include jars (types AB6, AB13, AB15 and AB18: Fig. 5.60, a–g) as well as a spout from a spouted pitcher and a jar base. The disuse fill of this pit produced a much greater quantity of material (1.944kg). The pottery includes residual sherds of Roman and Middle Saxon date. TTW still makes up the greater proportion, and a variety of forms is present including jar rims of types AB1, AB5, AB6 (four examples) and AB18 (five rims), as well as a number of bases, a ginger jar rim and storage jars and crucibles represented by body sherds. Several jars are decorated with square rouletting on their rims or bodies. The remainder of the group assemblage is composed of one vessel of EMSW represented by the rim and base of a jar (type AB5) and four Yarmouth-type ware body sherds.

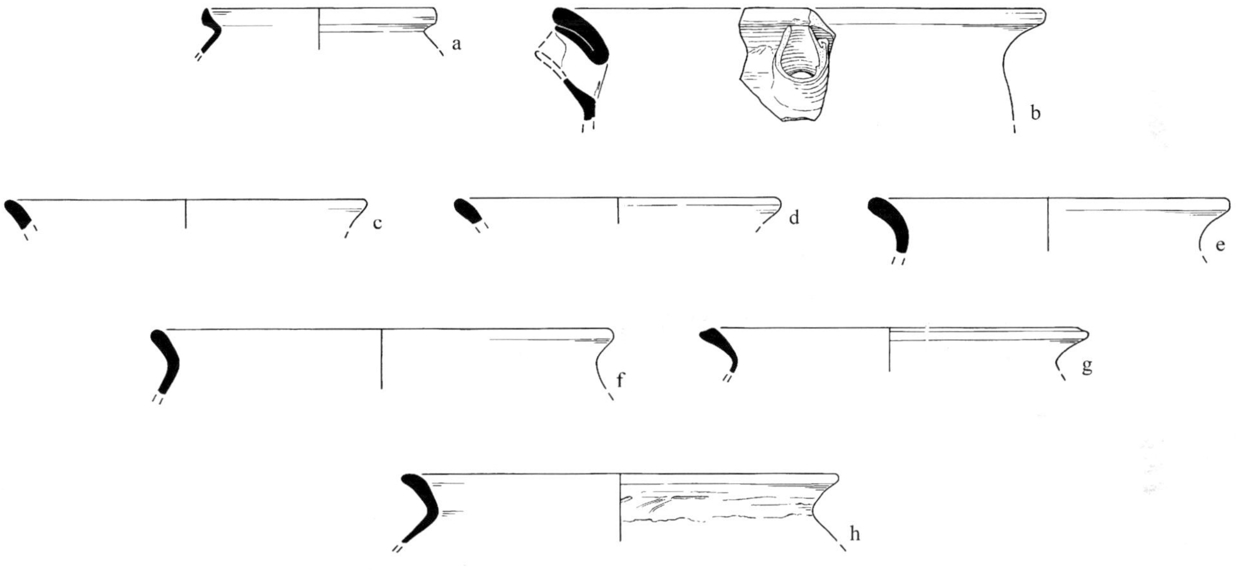

Figure 5.61 Pottery from pit *50628* (Period 2.1). Scale 1:4.

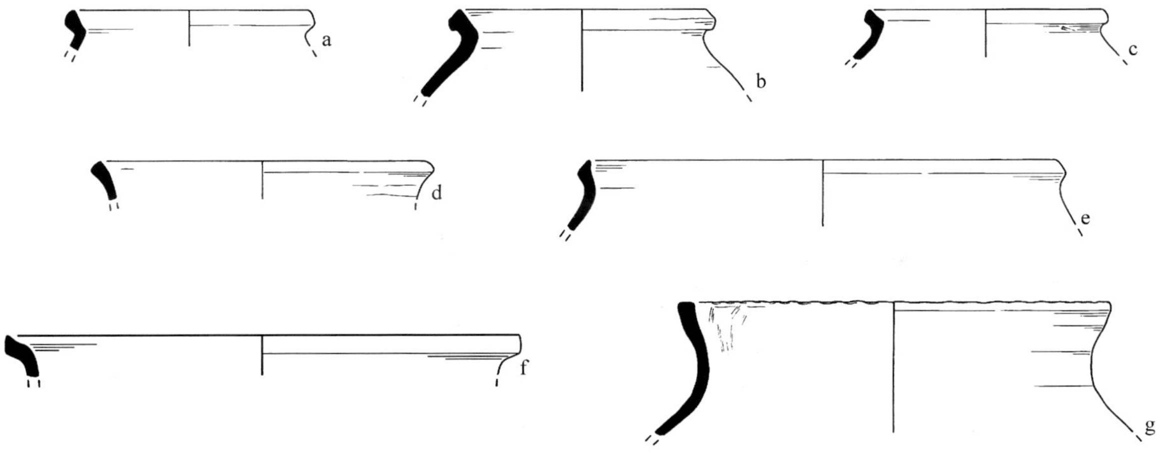

Figure 5.62 Pottery from pit *30485* (Period 2.1). Scale 1:4.

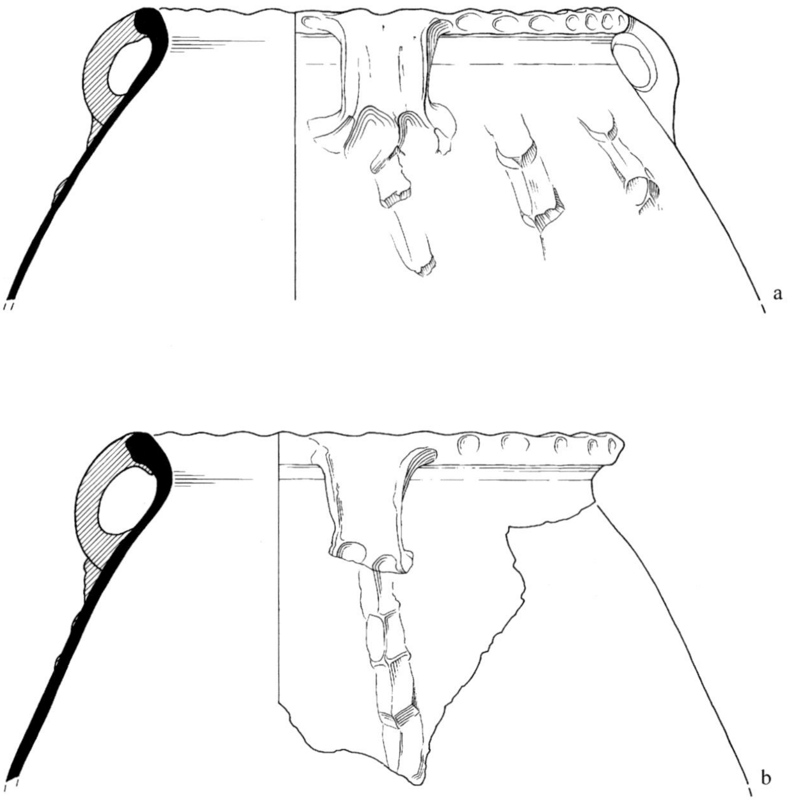

Figure 5.63 Pottery from post-hole/pit *40110* (Period 2.1). Scale 1:4.

These two fills are distinct in character. Only TTW and its derivative EMSW is present in the lower fills, with jars and cooking pots as the only vessel forms represented by rims. A larger range of fabrics and forms came from the later fill, and included EMW and Yarmouth-type ware as well as TTW and EMSW. The vessel forms include ginger jar, storage jar and crucible fragments as well as the ubiquitous jar. It is interesting to note that no cooking pot rims were recorded from either fill. The rim forms from the two fills are not greatly different from each other, and are all of 11th-century date. Rouletting as a decorative technique appears on jar rims and body from only the upper fill, but was recorded on body sherds in the lower fill. The sum of the evidence suggests that the pit was open for some time and the earlier fill dates to the early 11th century and the upper fill to the mid-late 11th century.

Period 2.1: 12th century
(Figs 5.61–5.63)
Contexts assigned to Period 2.1 produced 2957 sherds weighing 18.734kg, making up 8.9% of the site assemblage (Table 23). During this period TTW is still the dominant fabric, making up 54.1% of the period assemblage. However, early medieval wares became more prominent, and EMW and EMSW as well as Yarmouth-type ware form a large proportion of the assemblage (6.4%, 3.7% and 4.2% respectively). Medieval fabrics make a first appearance, with LMU being most common and glazed wares confined to only a few sherds. Residual material, which undoubtedly includes some of the TTW, accounts for only 0.5% (0.103kg), while the intrusive element is much greater at 13.4% (2.52kg), much of which is modern.

Pits. Probably the most important pit assemblage was recovered from pit *50628* (1.179kg: Fig. 5.61). The pit produced additional dating evidence in the form of two coins from the reign of Stephen (1135–54) and an architectural fragment dating to *c.* 1100–1200, as well as metal-working and environmental evidence. Some of the Late Saxon pottery is abraded and probably residual; however, it does not dominate the group assemblage. This includes TTW jars of types AB14 (Fig 5.61, a) and AB16, and a spouted pitcher (type AD1; Fig. 5.61, b), as well as a crucible fragment and a jar base. EMW is represented by rims from jars of types J1a, J1b (two examples) and J2b (Fig. 5.61, c–e) and a cooking pot, and EMSSW by a type J2c jar rim (Fig.5.61, f). Medieval wares mainly comprise LMU body sherds but also cooking pot rims (types J2b and J2c; Fig.5.61, g and h) and a Yarmouth-type jar rim (type Y1b; Fig.5.61, i) and bases. Other medieval fabrics include Stamford ware (Fabric B) and Andenne-type ware (by body sherds only). The coins provide an early–mid-12th-century *terminus post quem* for this group. This is important because it shows (assuming that the TTW is not residual) that the Late Saxon and early medieval fabrics are still in use into the 12th century, although they may no longer be manufactured by this date.

Deep pit *30485* produced a range of early medieval pottery (Fig. 5.62) and *in situ* burning of its primary fills may indicate an industrial process.

A considerable quantity of pottery was recovered from a large post-hole or small pit *40110* (2.301kg: Fig 5.63). The Late Saxon and early medieval material includes the substantial remains of two storage jars, one of them multi-handled (Fig. 5.63 a, b). Both vessels are made in an EMSW fabric. The outer surface has laminated on one of the jars, revealing the orange core, a feature that is characteristic of this fabric. The jars have shallow vertical applied strips with thumbed indentations around the rims. Contemporary pottery includes small quantities of LMU, Yarmouth-type ware and Pingsdorf ware.

Periods 2.2 and 2.3: 12th–13th centuries
(Figs 5.64 and 5.65)
Altogether of 3228 sherds (weighing 14.758kg) were recovered from Period 2.2 contexts, and an additional 9382 sherds (43.151kg) from Period 2.3. TTW is still the most common single fabric recovered in Period 2.2 (1550 sherds, weighing 6.663kg), but its share has fallen to 45% of the assemblage (Table 23). While EMW has increased to claim 7.5%, EMSW (more surprisingly) is more common with 12.8%. LMU now forms nearly a quarter of the assemblage. Although medieval glazed wares are present, they still do not make up a major proportion of the pottery. As well as Grimston Glazed ware, products from Andenne and Pingsdorf continue the tradition of continental imports.

The pottery from Period 2.3 groups is still dominated by residual Late Saxon and early medieval fabrics (62.3% of the period assemblage: Table 24). Most of the rest of the material is medieval with only a small quantity of late medieval and later intrusive pottery. The most common medieval fabric is LMU, which is supplemented by Yarmouth-type ware and a single sherd of Grimston Coarse ware and a number of sherds from unprovenanced medieval fabrics. Other glazed wares are represented by locally produced Grimston Glazed ware, a small quantity of Developed Stamford ware (Fabric C) and a single Scarborough-type ware body sherd. Continental imports are similarly represented by small numbers of

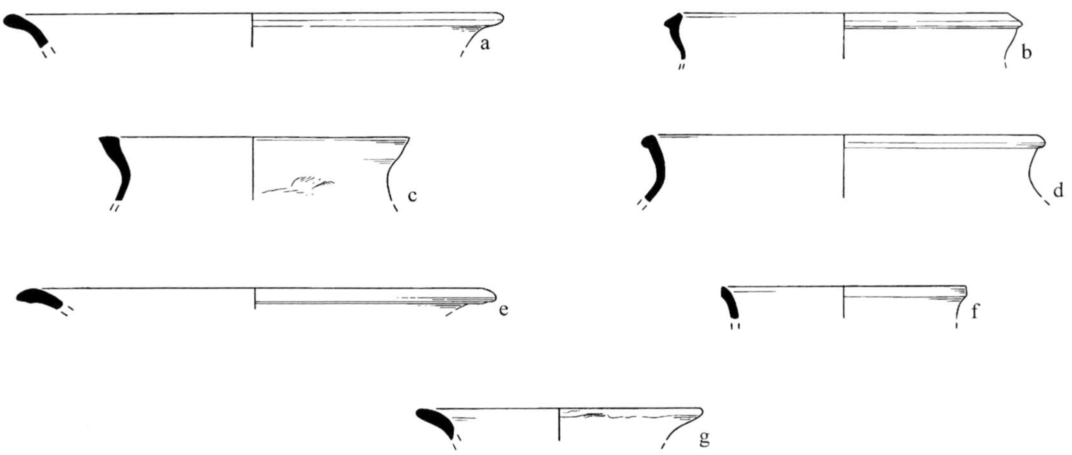

Figure 5.64 Pottery from quarry pit fill *30899* (Period 2.3). Scale 1:4.

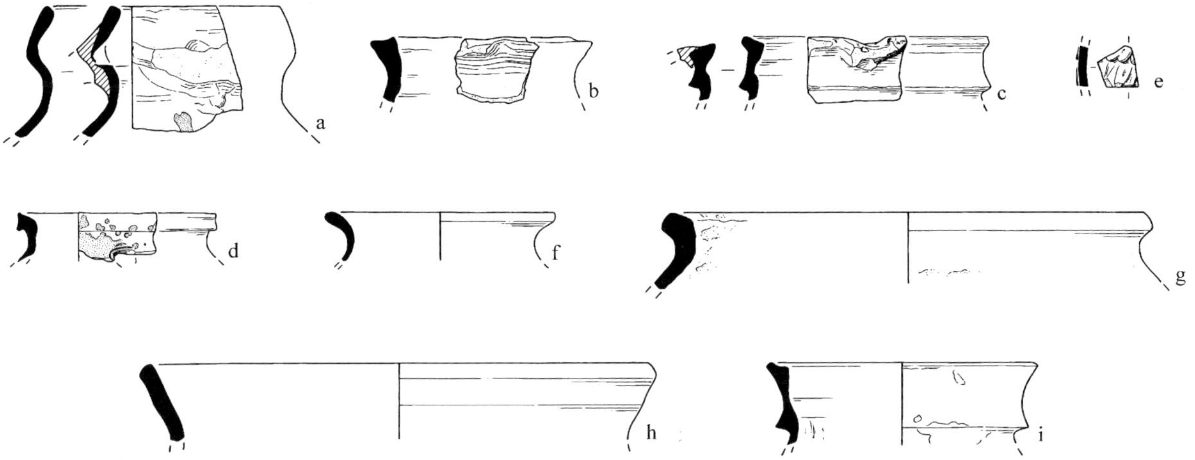

Figure 5.65 Pottery from pit *30213* and pit *30337* (Period 2.3). Scale 1:4.

body sherds of Andenne-type and Aardenburg-type wares, and the first occurrence of Siegburg and Langerwehe stonewares. More unusually, a single sherd from a Rouen/North French-type jug represents continental trade from the south as well as from the east.

Quarries. One of the largest assemblages comes from quarry pit *30899* (1.663kg: Fig. 5.64), the backfill of which incorporated re-deposited natural. The Thetford-type and early medieval wares are residual and account for 55.8% of the group assemblage. The contemporary material is dominated by LMU with a number of vessels represented by rim sherds, including jars and cooking vessels with simple everted rims of types J1b, J2b, J2c, J1e, J2e, J1j and J2j (Fig. 5.64a–c, e, g), as well as bowls (type B1) and a cooking pot base. Other medieval wares include Yarmouth-type ware represented by a jar rim (type Y2c: Fig. 5.64 d), a rim sherd from a local shell-tempered cooking vessel (EMWSS: Fig 5.64 f), a cooking pot base, and body sherds of Grimston Coarse ware. Glazed wares were represented by a handle from a Grimston Glazed ware jug and non-local glazed ware body sherds. A single fragment of a decorated body sherd of Pingsdorf ware is also present.

The fill of quarry pit *30213* produced a larger quantity of material (1.357kg: Fig. 5.65), much of it residual. The contemporary vessels recovered include LMU jar rims (J1a, J1c and J2k) and a cooking pot rim (type J1i) as well as two cooking pot bases, a Yarmouth-type cooking pot rim (type Y1a) and base, Grimston Glazed ware jugs (type GGG: Fig. 5.65, a and e) as well as a more uncommon rim (Fig. 5.65, b), an Andenne ware pitcher (Fig. 5.65, c) in addition to Developed Stamford ware body sherds, and an LMT rim from a jar (Fig. 5.65, d). Again, infilling appears to have continued into the late 14th century.

The Franciscan Friary (1226/1290s–1566)

Although the foundation of the Friary can be dated from documentary evidence to 1226, much of the area covered by the excavations was not incorporated within the Friary walls until after 1292. Periods 3.1 and 3.2 cover the occupation of the site by the Franciscans.

The pottery allocated to these periods of occupation covers two ceramic phases: medieval pottery from the 13th and 14th centuries, and late medieval and transitional wares from the late 14th and 15th centuries. Although early post-medieval fabrics also occur in contexts of these periods, these are discussed in more detail in the next section. While it is possible for the attributes of the medieval fabrics to be described and discussed in some detail, the individual assemblages of late medieval/transitional and post-medieval wares are not large enough to justify comprehensive analysis.

The pottery from Period 3.1 is dominated by a high residual element. Contemporary fabrics consist of LMU and Grimston Glazed ware with small quantities of non-local and continental imports. If anything, the range of contemporary fabrics from this period is more restricted than the previous period, and the paucity of late medieval/transitional wares is conspicuous.

Fabrics	Period 3.1 Sherds	Wt	% Wt	Period 3.2 Sherds	Wt	% Wt	Total assemblage Sherds	Wt	% Wt
Residual	19	0.100	0.6	8	0.073	0.4	*27*	*0.173*	*0.5*
Residual Late Saxon	1195	6.863	46.3	857	4.662	26.7	*2052*	*11.525*	*35.7*
Residual early medieval	325	2.985	20.1	302	0.896	5.2	*627*	*3.881*	*12*
LMU	577	2.066	13.9	826	3.502	20.1	*1403*	*5.568*	*17.2*
Yarmouth-type ware	115	0.604	4.1	109	0.618	3.6	*224*	*1.222*	*3.7*
East Cambridge-type ware	2	0.042	0.3	-	-	-	*2*	*0.042*	*0.1*
Non-local medieval wares	7	0.039	0.3	16	0.083	0.5	*23*	*0.122*	*0.3*
Grimston Glazed ware	131	1.961	13.2	212	2.095	12.0	*343*	*4.056*	*12.5*
Developed Stamford ware	5	0.018	0.1	2	0.004	<0.1	*7*	*0.022*	*<0.01*
Hedingham-type ware	4	0.009	0.1	1	0.003	<0.1	*5*	*0.012*	*<0.01*
Scarborough-type ware	-	-	-	1	0.018	0.1	*1*	*0.018*	*<0.01*
Non-local glazed wares	5	0.120	0.8	33	0.181	1.0	*38*	*0.301*	*0.9*
Andenne-type ware	8	0.020	0.1	17	0.075	0.4	*25*	*0.095*	*0.2*
Aardenburg-type ware	-	-	-	1	0.008	<0.1	*1*	*0.008*	*<0.01*
Saintonge ware		-	-	2	0.022	0.1	*2*	*0.022*	*<0.01*
Rouen-type/North French ware	-	-	-	1	0.012	0.1	*1*	*0.012*	*<0.01*
LMT	2	0.010	0.1	207	2.990	17.2	*209*	*3.000*	*9.2*
Dutch-type REW	-	-	-	14	0.149	0.9	*14*	*0.149*	*0.4*
Tudor Green-type ware	-	-	-	2	0.019	<0.1	*2*	*0.019*	*<0.01*
Siegburg Stoneware	-	-	-	5	0.234	1.3	*5*	*0.234*	*0.7*
Langerwehe Stoneware	1	0.001	>0.1	32	0.990	5.7	*33*	*0.991*	*3*
Raeren-Aachen Stoneware	-	-	-	29	0.449	2.6	*29*	*0.449*	*1.3*
Intrusive Post-medieval	1	0.001	<0.1	26	0.312	1.8	*27*	*0.313*	*0.9*
Intrusive Modern	-	-	-	1	0.002	<0.1	*1*	*0.002*	*<0.01*
Unidentified	1	0.004	<0.1	1	0.032	0.2	*2*	*0.036*	*0.1*
Total	**2398**	**14.843**		**2705**	**17.429**				

Table 32 Quantity and weight of pottery in Periods 3.1 and 3.2

Form	*Period 2.2*	*Periods 2.3, 3.1 and 3.2*	*Period 4*	*Rest*	*Total*
Jar	17	88	12	28	145
Cooking pots	40	78	4	15	137
Bowls	4	12	1	3	20
Large bowls	-	5	4	-	9
Jugs	-	8	-	1	9
Other	1	3	-	1	5

Table 33 Local Medieval Unglazed ware by rim number

Period 3.2 is marked by a decreased proportion of residual material and subsequent marked increase in LMT and other late medieval/transitional pottery types. Medieval wares still make up a consistent proportion of the assemblage: both glazed and unglazed wares probably continued to be used into the 15th century, in particular reflected by late Grimston Glazed ware products. Utilitarian kitchen wares are eventually replaced by LMT and DREW and serving vessels by products from non-local and continental sources. Other contemporary late medieval/transitional wares include Tudor Green-type ware and Langerwehe Stoneware; other Rhenish stonewares from Raeren-Aachen and Cologne are also introduced during this period.

Medieval wares

Medieval pottery accounts for 17.7% of the entire ceramic assemblage, and almost 18% of all medieval pottery came from contexts assigned to Periods 1 to 2.2 where it accounts for varying proportions of the period assemblages (0.7% of Period 1, 14.9% of Period 2.1 and 25.2% of Period 2.2). In Period 3 medieval fabrics make up 30.4% of the assemblage, while in Period 4 they drop to 9.9%.

Local medieval fabrics

The major fabrics represented include local products LMU and Grimston Glazed ware and Grimston Coarse ware, supplemented by regional wares such as Yarmouth-type ware, and small quantities of Developed Stamford ware (Fabric C), Hedingham-type and Scarborough-type wares, as well as other non-local Glazed and Unglazed wares. Continental imports account for the rest of the medieval assemblage, but these are limited to Andenne-type ware and Aardenburg-type ware (Table 32)

Fabrics	Period 3 Sherds	Period 3 Wt	Period 3 % Wt	Period 4 Sherds	Period 4 Wt	Period 4 % Wt	Total assemblage Sherds	Total assemblage Wt	Total assemblage % Wt
LMU	4125	13.650	18.1	511	1.619	4.6	*6323*	*23.843*	*11.3*
Grimston Coarse ware	1	0.015	<0.1	-	-	-	*2*	*0.032*	*<0.1*
East Cambridge-type ware	2	0.042	<0.1	-	-	-	*2*	*0.042*	*<0.1*
Non-local medieval wares	41	0.199	0.3	7	0.022	0.1	*74*	*0.433*	*0.2*
Grimston Glazed ware	689	7.963	0.6	194	1.574	4.5	*1026*	*10.824*	*5.1*
Developed Stamford ware	14	0.033	<0.1	4	0.018	0.1	*19*	*0.061*	*<0.1*
Hedingham-type ware	5	0.012	<0.1	-	-	-	*6*	*0.040*	*<0.1*
Scarborough-type ware	2	0.028	<0.1	1	0.064	0.2	*4*	*0.100*	*<0.1*
Non-local glazed wares	80	0.626	0.8	16	0.133	0.4	*157*	*1.108*	*0.5*
Andenne-type ware	59	0.256	0.3	6	0.029	0.1	*117*	*0.634*	*0.3*
Aardenburg-type ware	3	0.152	0.2	-	-	-	*3*	*0.152*	*0.1*
Saintonge ware	2	0.022	<0.1	-	-	-	*2*	*0.022*	*<0.1*
Rouen/North French-type ware	2	0.026	<0.1	-	-	-	*2*	*0.026*	*<0.1*
LMT	273	4.067	5.4	336	7.611	21.7	*708*	*14.094*	*6.7*
Dutch-type DREW	16	0.257	0.3	110	3.343	9.6	*165*	*4.390*	*2.1*
Tudor Green-type ware	2	0.019	<0.1	2	0.042	0.1	*5*	*0.054*	*<0.1*
Siegburg Stoneware	9	0.262	0.3	6	0.056	0.2	*16*	*0.336*	*0.2*
Langerwehe Stoneware	49	1.115	1.5	38	0.985	2.8	*101*	*2.968*	*1.4*
Raeren-Aachen Stoneware	29	0.449	0.6	82	2.861	8.2	*125*	*3.833*	*1.8*
Miscellaneous wares	-	-	-	1	0.006	<0.1	*3*	*0.022*	*<0.1*
Local EPM ware	3	0.072	0.1	6	0.155	0.4	*12*	*0.244*	*0.1*
GRE	10	0.059	0.1	222	3.892	11.1	*355*	*6.519*	*3.1*
IGBW	1	0.002	<0.1	24	1.017	2.9	*39*	*1.409*	*0.7*
Fulmodestone IGBW	-	-	-	4	0.028	0.1	*5*	*0.068*	*<0.1*
Speckled Glazed ware	-	-	-	11	0.068	0.2	*16*	*0.152*	*<0.1*
West Norfolk Bichrome ware	-	-	-	11	0.093	0.3	*19*	*0.129*	*<0.1*
West Norfolk Bichrome ware/EPM	-	-	-	11	0.142	0.4	*11*	*0.142*	*0.1*
Metropolitan Slipware	-	-	-	6	0.103	0.3	*9*	*0.159*	*0.1*
Surrey White ware	4	0.064	0.1	29	0.119	0.3	*41*	*0.257*	*0.1*
TGE	1	0.006	<0.1	57	1.090	3.1	*88*	*1.961*	*0.9*
Low Countries Earthenware	-	-	-	1	0.018	0.1	*1*	*0.018*	*<0.1*
Dutch White Earthenware	11	0.025	<0.1	2	0.010	<0.1	*15*	*0.059*	*<0.1*
North Holland Slipware	-	-	-	10	0.483	1.4	*11*	*0.565*	*0.3*
Cologne-Frechen Stoneware	6	0.161	0.2	86	1.998	5.7	*113*	*2.760*	*1.3*
Frechen Stoneware	-	-	-	25	0.534	1.5	*36*	*0.696*	*0.3*
Westerwald Stoneware	-	-	-	7	0.155	0.4	*13*	*0.382*	*0.2*
Werra ware	-	-	-	1	0.024	0.1	*1*	*0.024*	*<0.1*
Weser ware	-	-	-	1	0.076	0.2	*1*	*0.076*	*<0.1*
English Stoneware	1	0.002	<0.1	31	1.137	3.2	*127*	*10.469*	*4.9*
Intrusive Modern	1	0.004	<0.1	17	0.138	<0.1			
Unidentified	18	0.415	0.5	2	0.086	0.2			
Total	**14485**	**75.423**		**2811**	**35.004**				

Table 34 Quantity and weight of pottery in Periods 3 and 4

Rim form	*Jar*	*Cooking pot*	*Total*
J1/2a (upright)	7	-	7
J1/2b (everted)	44	46	90
J1/2c (everted to point)	15	49	64
J1/2i (incipient)	21	7	28
J1/2j ('hammer-head')	38	24	62

Table 35 Local medieval unglazed ware rim forms

LMU is the most common individual medieval fabric recovered (11.3% of the entire assemblage, *c.* 64% of the medieval wares). Over a quarter of this comes from contexts allocated to Periods 1 (where it is undoubtedly intrusive), and Periods 2 and 2.2 where it forms a substantial proportion — 13.5% of the Period 2.1 assemblage, rising to 23.6% of pottery from Period 2.2 contexts. By Period 2.3 it makes up 18.7% of the assemblage, rising in Period 3.2 to 20.1% before falling dramatically during Period 4 (4.6%).

Jars and cooking pots account for the majority of the vessel form rims recovered (Table 33). Of the 282 rims identified, 251 (almost 90%) came from five rim profiles (Table 35). Most common were simple everted rims (type J1/2b) and everted rims coming to a point (type J1/2c), which generally seem to be earlier, while later 13th–14th-century incipient and 'hammer-head' rims (types J1/2i and J1/2j) are also common. Although a few examples of the later rim types do appear in earlier contexts, it is not until Period 2.3 that they become very common. Type J1 rims make up approximately a quarter of the jar and cooking pot rims recorded (23.4%), while type J2 rims account for 76.6%. In addition, smaller jars/cooking pots make up 36.4% of the Period 2.1 LMU rims and in Period 3 this falls to 20%. This supports the theory that small jars were introduced before larger jars, although undoubtedly the small forms continued in use after the larger ones were introduced.

Other kitchen vessels include a single ginger jar rim. This is quite an unusual form to be recovered in LMU, and it is possible that it is actually fine EMW. Other diagnostic kitchen forms include two curfew rims with distinctive 'hammer-head' profiles.

Serving and table vessels are more common, and bowls are represented by twenty rims. Most of these are large vessels, with diameters of 18–34cm, and virtually all are deep with straight, sloping sides (type B1: 25 rims). A variety of rim forms was recorded, and 'hammer-head' rims (type B1j: 12 rims) are by far the most common; simpler rims everted coming to a point (type B1c: eight rims) are the next most numerous. It also appears that bowl rims follow the same general rule as jars and cooking pots: type B1c bowls come from Period 2.1 and 2.2 contexts, while type B1j are recovered from Period 3 onwards. A number of smaller, curved-sided bowls (type B2: six rims) were also recorded. These are less standardised: three come from bowls with upright, slightly pointed rims, two with flanged, parallel sided rims and one with a flange-and-bead rim resembling a Roman bowl form.

Only one other form was found in any quantity: the jug (nine rims). These rims tend to be fragmentary and few survive below the immediate rim areas so the profile of the jugs cannot be established. They are classified according to rim profile, and while simpler, everted rims are recorded (two rims) the majority have flattened 'hammer-head' rims.

Other medieval coarseware

Other medieval unglazed wares are represented, in the main, by body sherds only. The exception is a shelly ware which is represented by two rims, one with an everted rim coming to a point and an upright rim: these correspond to LMU types J2c and J2a. Products of Grimston coarse ware and East Cambridgeshire-type ware were identified as body sherds only, but probably came from jars or cooking pots. Unprovenanced, non-local medieval pottery has been amalgamated under the collective term of Non-Local Unglazed wares: these again are mostly body sherds.

Glazed wares

Glazed wares are more prolific, and table/pouring vessels are dominated by Grimston Glazed jugs. Although it occurs in Period 2.2 groups, this is mainly in the form of body sherds from jugs. It is not until Period 2.3 that Grimston Glazed ware forms a larger proportion of the assemblage. Jugs are the most common form and some attempt has been made to parallel the Grimston typology (Little 1994). There are five examples of type GGB, jugs with rim flattened and pulled down (type GGG: five examples) and one example of type GGB (jugs with straight-sided rims, expanded to form flat rim top). A number of jug rims, however, are more unusual and direct parallels could not be found with the published Grimston kiln material. These include rims with a flattened 'hammer-head' and rilled neck (type G1), an upright, thickened rim with a depression on the upper surface (type G6), and a rim from a globular jug with marked carination at the neck and body junction and an inward-curving, rounded rim (type G7).

Jugs are also indicated by bases, handled and decorated body sherds, including distinctive sherds from face jugs. The majority of bases were thumbed and appear to come from 13th–mid-14th-century baluster jugs rather than late 14th–15th-century globular jugs. Decorated jugs are also an earlier, rather than a later, phenomenon. A small number of later vessels were also identified, represented by rims from glazed jars and bowls (including type GBJ) as well as flatware and jar bases.

Other glazed wares are represented only by small quantities of material, all from Period 2.3 groups. Developed Stamford ware (Fabric C), Hedingham-type ware and other unprovenanced, non-local wares are represented in the main by body sherds; these all probably come from jugs. The exception is Scarborough-type ware, which is represented by a jug rim and by a tubular spout which may have come from a Knight jug.

Imported medieval wares

The assemblage is supplemented by continental imports in similarly small quantities. Pingsdorf-type ware continues to be recovered from 13th-century contexts. Andenne-type ware appears in small quantity in Period 2.1 but is more prolific in Period 2.3. Although only 0.6kg of Andenne ware was recovered, five vessels are represented by jug rims. Aardenburg-type ware appears for the first time in Period 2.3, but is represented only by a small number of body sherds. More unusually, small quantities of French imports, namely North French wares and Saintonge Polychrome ware, were identified.

Later Medieval and Transitional wares

The late medieval and transitional wares dating from the late 14th to mid-16th centuries are also dominated by local products. The development from medieval to late medieval/transitional wares is as indistinct as many other ceramic transitions. It occurs during the late 14th and 15th centuries, partly as a result of influence from the Continent when traders and settlers from the Low Countries imported vessels for their own use which were subsequently copied by local potters.

Late Medieval and Transitional ware (LMT)

The most common of these intermediate fabrics, LMT accounts for 6.7% of the assemblage. Although found as an intrusive element in Period 2.1 contexts, it is in Period 3.2 that the fabric first makes an impact (17.2%), coming to the fore in Period 4 (21.7%). It is difficult to pinpoint when LMT takes over from LMU as the principal local coarseware: they co-exist in Period 3.2 groups but by Period 4 LMT has superseded LMU, which increasingly occurs residually. Medieval vessel forms such as jars, jugs and bowls continued to be produced in LMT, but the range of forms extends to include continental forms: two-handled jars, pancheons, storage jars, cisterns, cauldrons, pipkins, dripping pans and skillets, as well as chafing dishes and candlesticks.

Other Late Medieval and Transitional fabrics

LMT is supplemented by a small quantity of Late Grimston wares, including flatwares and open vessel bases. However it is Dutch or Dutch-type Red Earthenwares (DREW) which account for a larger proportion of this ceramic period assemblage (2.1%). Local production of such redware began in the early 16th century when imported vessels were copied for the local market, perhaps stimulated by demand from Dutch immigrants in Norwich. It is virtually impossible to distinguish macroscopically imported DREW vessels from locally produced copies, and therefore these vessels are recorded using one collective term. Forms recovered include cauldrons, handled jars, dishes and pipkins.

A small quantity of fineware is represented by a Tudor Green-type lobed cup and small drinking vessel rim. Rhenish imports make up the rest of the assemblage. Stoneware drinking vessels, comprising jugs and mugs from Siegburg, Langerwehe and Raeren-Aachen appear in Period 3.1 groups and continue to be used into the post-medieval period. Small quantities of Siegburg stoneware were recovered from Areas A, B and CB; Langerwehe was represented on all areas but dominant in Area B, while Raeren-Aachen was common on Area A.

Discussion by feature and function

A total of 5103 sherds of pottery recovered from the excavation (weighing 32.272kg) came from contexts allocated to the occupation of the site by the Friary (Tables 31 and 33). Residual pottery accounts for a large proportion of the material. Medieval wares come to the fore of the contemporary assemblage and the proportion of glazed wares increases to make up a larger proportion. Late medieval/transitional wares make up a small proportion of the Period 3.1 assemblage but a substantial part (17.2%) of the Period 3.2 groups. In addition, the assemblages comprise not only locally produced LMU and Grimston Glazed ware vessels and regional imports, but also LMT and DREW from the Continent, highlighting the first imports on a large scale of Rhenish Stonewares from Langerwehe and Raeren-Aachen. Intrusive fabrics are a small, persistent element.

Period 3.1 (14th century)

Deposits assigned to Period 3.1 produced 2398 sherds weighing 14.843kg, a similar quantity to that retrieved from Period 2.3 contexts (Tables 24 and 31). Residual Late Saxon and early medieval fabrics account for 60% of the assemblage. Medieval wares make up most of the remainder with late medieval and transitional fabrics and later intrusive post-medieval pottery accounting for only a small proportion.

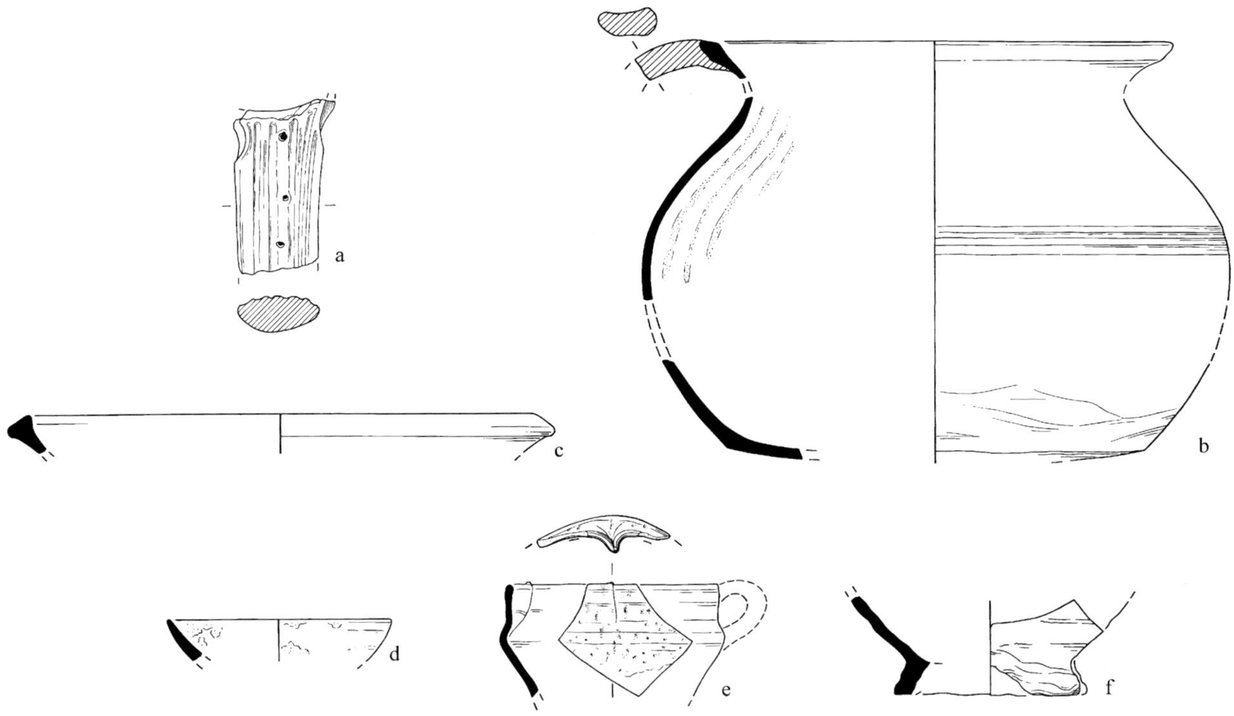

Figure 5.66 Pottery from pit *40014* and pit *40019* (Period 3.2). Scale 1:4.

Period 3.2 (1400–1538)
(Fig 5.66)
Altogether 2705 sherds, weighing 17.429kg came from contexts assigned to this period (23.1%: Table 32). The character of the assemblage can immediately be distinguished from earlier groups. The proportion of residual pottery drops to just over 30% (compared to 62.8% in Period 2.3 and 67% in Period 3.1) and the recently-introduced Late Medieval and Transitional wares form a major element of the assemblage. Medieval wares still account for a similar proportion to that seen in the previous two periods and the range of fabrics is similar (unglazed wares *c.* 20% and glazed wares *c.* 14%). Unglazed wares are dominated by LMU with very few additional wares supplementing the assemblage (by this period Yarmouth-type ware is definitely residual). Glazed wares are represented not only by products from Grimston but also by regional imports such as Developed Stamford and Hedingham-type wares and well-established continental imports from Andenne, as well as the less common Saintonge ware from south-west France.

It is the appearance of LMT and other late medieval/transitional wares that defines this period. LMT is dominant, with only small quantities of Dutch and Dutch-type Red Earthenwares supplementing the kitchen wares. Finer tablewares are represented by small Tudor Green-type ware body sherds, but mainly by imported stoneware jugs and drinking vessels from the Rhineland. Siegburg is present in small quantities, but Langerwehe products are most common while vessels from Raeren-Aachen also appear.

Pits. An interesting assemblage came from two rectangular cess-pits to the north of the precinct wall. Pit *40014* was cut by pit *40019*. In addition to pottery, a significant quantity of brick and tile was recovered from its fills, indicating that rubbish from kitchens was collected together with building waste. Pit *40014* (0.898kg; Fig. 5.66) is the earlier of the two features, both ceramically and stratigraphically. Pottery from the fills were noted as fresh and the residual element is low (7.7%). Medieval pottery is represented by LMU cooking pot base and body sherds, as well as two cooking pot rims (types J2g and J2j: Fig. 5.66, c); no other unglazed ware is present. Glazed wares are also restricted to local products from Grimston and include a jug base and handles (Fig. 5.66, a), as well as a jar base which is slightly more unusual. Later medieval material consists of LMT, including a handled jar (Fig. 5.66, b: *cf.* Jennings 1981, fig. 26 no. 437) as well as body sherds from a jug and jar. Non-local material is represented by Tudor Green-type body sherds and a Raeren-Aachen drinking vessel rim.

Pit *40019* (0.971kg; Fig.5.66) also contained an unabraded assemblage, only a small proportion of which (10%) is residual. The range of medieval fabrics recovered is more varied. Unglazed wares are represented by LMU, including rims from a jar (type J2j) and jug. Glazed wares are present in the form of decorated body sherds from a Grimston Glazed ware globular jug, and supplemented by body sherds from an Andenne-type ware jug. Again, later medieval ceramics are represented by LMT, Tudor Green-type ware and Rhenish stonewares. Forms recorded include an unusual LMT bowl rim (Fig. 5.66, d) and jar base as well as body sherds, a Tudor Green-type lobed cup (Fig. 5.66, e) and various drinking vessels including a Langerwehe base (Fig. 5.66, f) and handle and Raeren-Aachen jug or mug rims. Slightly later pottery is represented by an Early Post-Medieval flatware base.

The Dissolution and after (1538–1800)

These periods encompass the Dissolution of the Friary (Period 4.1) and later activity (Periods 4.2 and 5). The pottery from Period 5 is not discussed in any detail here, since much of the assemblage is made up of late 18th- and 19th-century stonewares, china and creamware (30.7%, 12.1% and 8.8% respectively).

Most pottery recovered from features directly associated with the Dissolution comprises contemporary late medieval/transitional ceramics, and reflects the range of pottery in use in the Friary and environs in the early 16th century. Very little residual material came from groups allocated to Period 4.1, and the medieval pottery recovered may or may not be residual. LMT and Rhenish stoneware dominate, supplemented by Dutch Red earthenware (DREW) and a very small quantity of Tudor Green-type ware. Small quantities of Early Post-Medieval (EPM) and post-medieval wares may be intrusive, or instead early examples of GRE, Iron-Glaze Black ware (IGBW) and Cologne-Frechen products.

The range of pottery allocated to Period 4.2 is similar to that recovered from Period 4.1. The proportion of residual material increases and the number and quantity of contemporary post-medieval fabrics is no longer confined mainly to GRE and Rhenish stonewares. Late medieval/transitional fabrics continue to be used. LMT and

Fabrics	*Period 4.1*			*Period 4.2*			*Total assemblage*		
	Sherds	*Wt*	*% Wt*	*Sherds*	*Wt*	*% Wt*	*Sherds*	*Wt*	*% Wt*
Residual	109	1.416	8.7	824	3.859	20.5	*931*	*5.275*	*15.1*
Residual Medieval	39	0.341	2.1	506	1.544	8.2	*545*	*1.885*	*5.4*
Grimston Glazed ware	68	0.462	2.9	126	1.124	5.9	*194*	*1.574*	*4.5*
LMT	201	5.835	36.0	135	1.776	9.4	*336*	*7.611*	*21.7*
Dutch-type REW	83	2.777	17.1	27	0.566	3.0	*110*	*3.343*	*9.6*
Tudor Green-type ware	1	0.040	0.2	1	0.002	<0.1	*2*	*0.042*	*0.1*
Siegburg Stoneware	6	0.056	0.3	1	0.002	<0.1	*6*	*0.056*	*0.2*
Langerwehe Stoneware	5	0.136	0.8	33	0.849	4.5	*38*	*0.985*	*2.8*
Raeren-Aachen Stoneware	65	2.660	16.4	17	0.201	1.1	*82*	*2.861*	*8.2*
Miscellaneous wares	-	-	-	1	0.006	<0.1	*1*	*0.006*	*<0.1*
Local EPM ware	3	0.119	0.7	3	0.036	0.2	*6*	*0.155*	*0.4*
GRE	13	0.202	1.2	209	3.690	19.6	*222*	*3.892*	*11.1*
IGBW	-	-	-	24	1.017	5.4	*24*	*1.017*	*2.9*
Fulmodestan IGBW	-	-	-	4	0.028	0.1	*4*	*0.028*	*0.1*
Speckled Glazed ware	1	0.035	0.2	10	0.033	0.2	*11*	*0.068*	*0.2*
West Norfolk Bichrome ware	3	0.042	0.3	8	0.051	0.3	*11*	*0.093*	*0.3*
West Norfolk Bichrome ware/EPM	-	-	-	11	0.142	0.8	*11*	*0.142*	*0.4*
Metropolitan Slipware	-	-	-	6	0.103	0.5	*6*	*0.103*	*0.3*
Surrey White ware	26	0.108	0.7	3	0.011	0.1	*29*	*0.119*	*0.3*
TGE	7	0.044	0.3	50	1.046	5.6	*57*	*1.090*	*3.1*
Low Countries Earthenware	-	-	-	1	0.018	0.1	*1*	*0.018*	*0.1*
Dutch White Earthenware	1	0.004	<0.1	1	0.006	<0.1	*2*	*0.010*	*<0.1*
North Holland Slipware	5	0.421	2.6	5	0.062	0.3	*10*	*0.483*	*1.4*
Cologne-Frechen Stoneware	37	1.132	7.0	49	0.866	4.6	*86*	*1.998*	*5.7*
Frechen Stoneware	8	0.248	1.5	17	0.155	0.8	*25*	*0.534*	*1.5*
Westerwald Stoneware	-	-	-	7	0.155	0.8	*7*	*0.155*	*0.4*
Werra ware	1	0.024	0.1	-	-	-	*1*	*0.024*	*0.1*
Waser ware	-	-	-	1	0.076	0.4	*1*	*0.076*	*0.2*
English Stoneware	-	-	-	31	1.137	6.0	*31*	*1.137*	*3.2*
Intrusive Modern	1	0.005	<0.1	16	0.133	0.7	*17*	*0.138*	*<0.1*
Unidentified	2	0.086	0.5	-	-	-	*2*	*0.086*	*0.2*
Total	**685**	**16.193**		**2126**	**18.811**		**2811**	**35.004**	

Table 36 Quantity and weight of pottery in Period 4

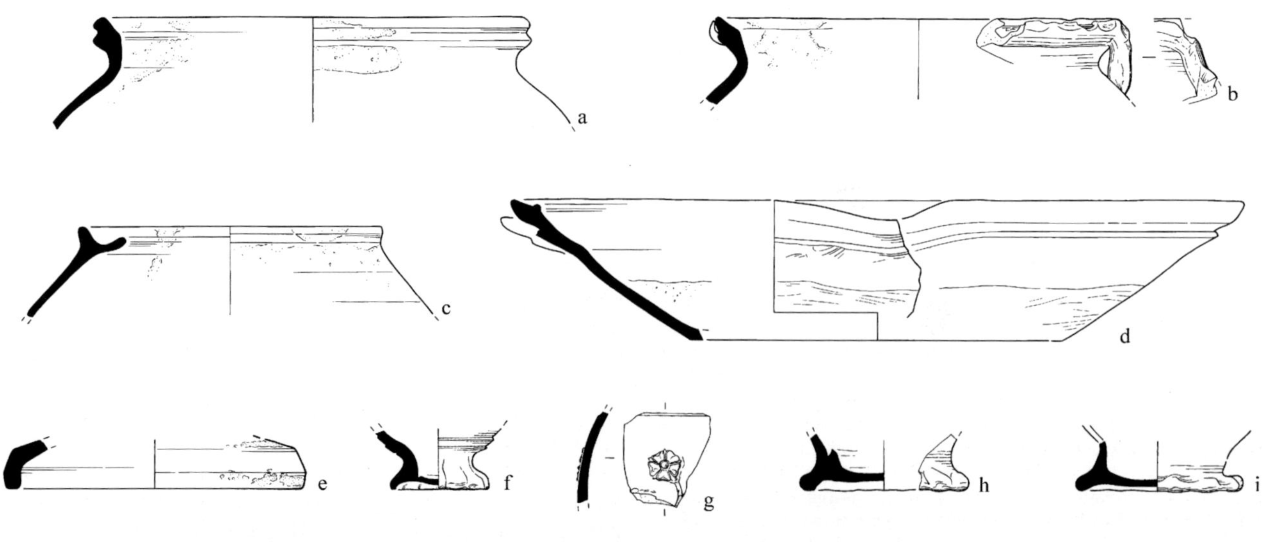

Figure 5.67 Pottery from robber pit *10660* (Period 4.1). Scale 1:4.

DREW are eventually replaced by GRE, and while they never replace Rhenish drinking and pouring vessels, IGBW and Speckled Glazed ware appear in greater numbers. Other local wares include West Norfolk Bichrome ware (WNBC) while regional imports such as Metropolitan Slipware and Surrey White ware appear for the first time. Continental imports include stonewares from Cologne and Frechen, while tablewares are represented by North Holland Slipwares, Dutch White Earthenware and German slipwares from Weser and Werra (Hurst, Neal and van Beuningen 1986, 250–9).

Period 5 contexts produced a range of residual material. Fabrics appearing for the first time include Staffordshire slipwares, Nottingham salt-glazed stoneware, creamware and Westerwald stoneware, as well as modern china and stoneware.

Fabrics and forms

The post-medieval pottery is dominated by locally produced Glazed Red earthenware (GRE) utilitarian kitchen wares and by imported Rhenish Stonewares. GRE is represented by a range of vessels used for food preparation, cooking and warming. The most common by rim number are small, handled jars or bowls which probably served a variety of functions. Other vessels included pipkins, dripping pans, lids, bowls, dishes, pancheons, handled jars, butter jars, jugs and drinking vessels.

GRE is supplemented by other local and regional utilitarian wares, mainly in the form of serving and pouring vessels, since metal vessels were used increasingly for cooking. The exception to this is WNBC, which is present in the form of lid-seated pipkins and cauldrons. Surrey White ware, though seen as a fine ware, also produced two pipkin rims, as well as a bowl and (more unusually) a drug jar rim.

Local jugs and drinking vessels included an IGBW tyg, Fulmodestan IGBW, and a Speckled Glazed ware cup. However, this market was dominated by Rhenish imports from Raeren-Aachen, Cologne and Frechen. Forms are limited to jugs and drinking vessels, until the introduction of the Westerwald chamber pot in later phases.

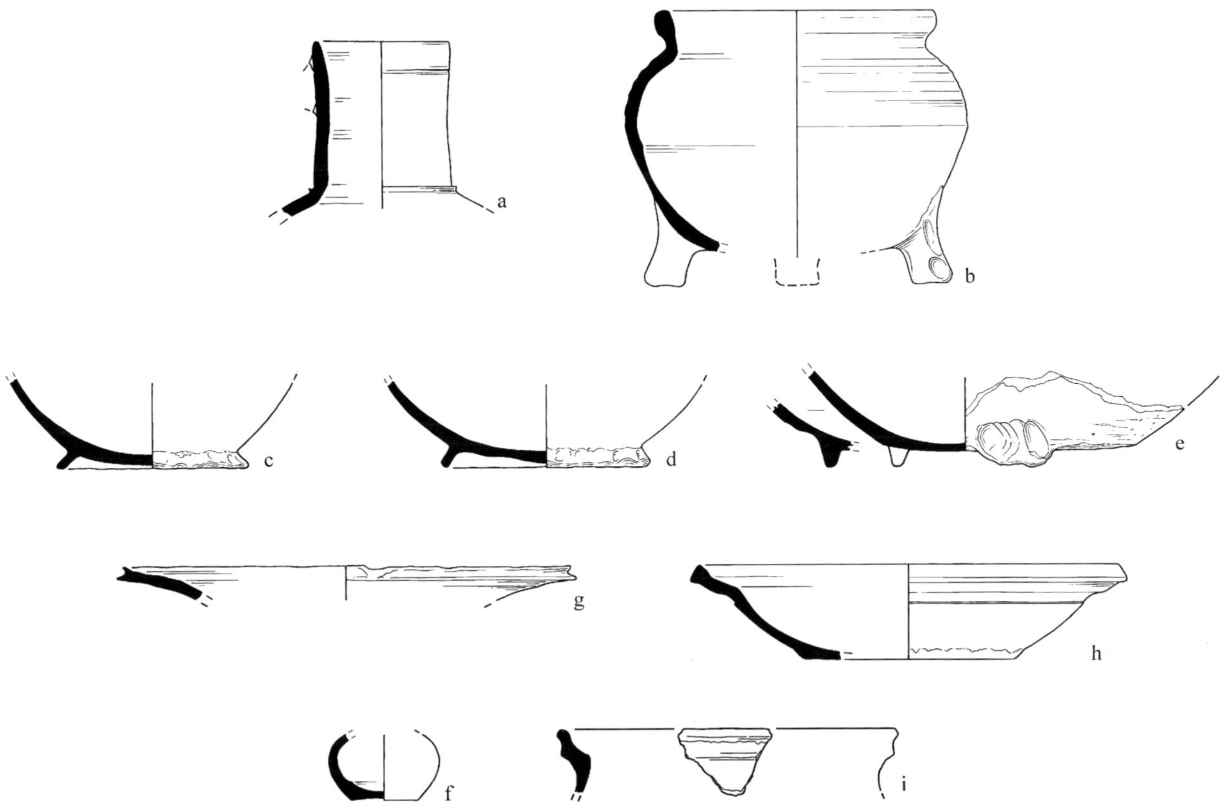

Figure 5.68 Pottery from robber pit *12075* and pit *102/121/10300/10414* (Period 4.1). Scale 1:4.

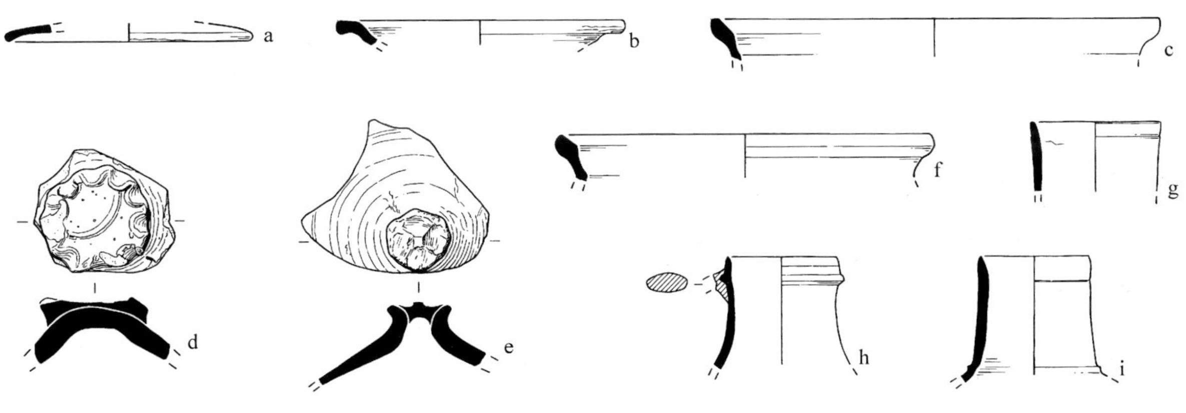

Figure 5.69 Pottery from robber cut *12061* (Period 4.1). Scale 1:4.

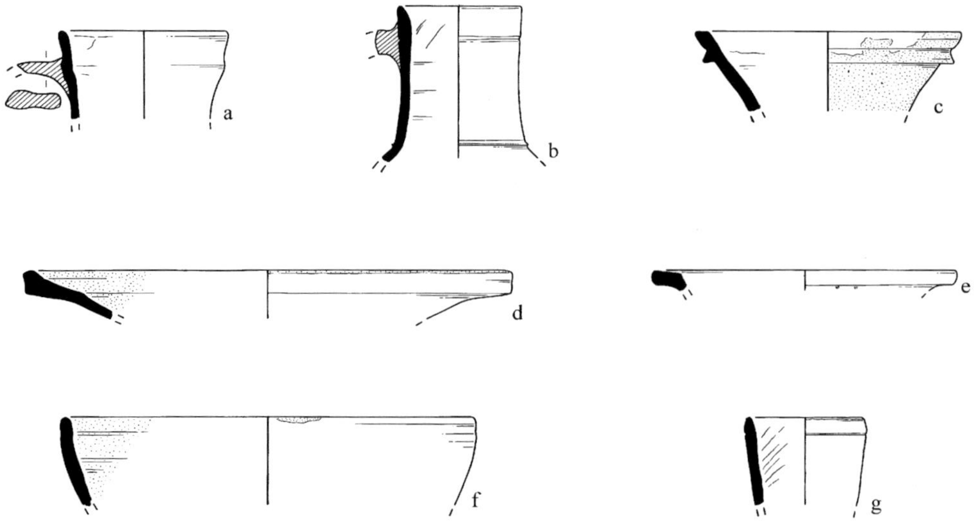

Figure 5.70 Pottery from well *12495/10896* (Period 4.2). Scale 1:4.

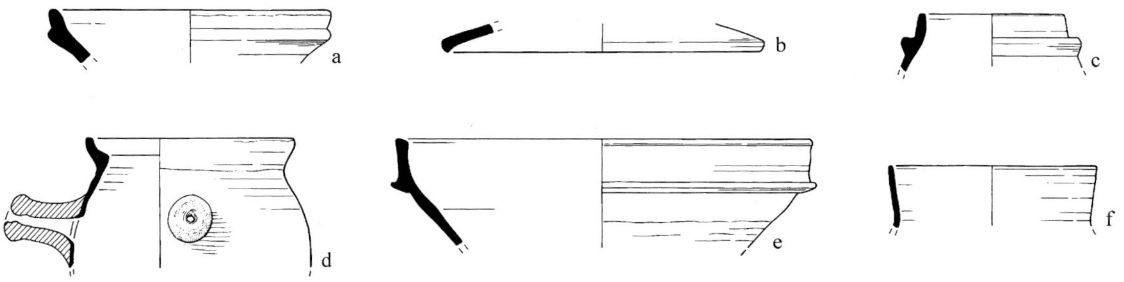

Figure 5.71 Pottery from pit *10111/10113* (Period 4.2). Scale 1:4.

Serving vessels were represented by Metropolitan Slipware dishes and Surrey White ware shallow bowls. Again continental imports supplemented these regional and English wares. Small quantities of Dutch White Earthenwares and North Holland Slipwares were present, as well as single instances of German Slipwares from Werra and Weser. These were represented by rims from bowls and dishes, and in the instance of North Holland Slipware by a distinctive cockerel bowl.

TGE was more common, although again the number of rims was not exceptionally large. Vessels represented included drug jars, bowls, dishes, plates, cups and chamber pots.

Discussion by feature and function

Period 4.1: the Dissolution (1538–66)
(Figs 5.67–5.69)
Only 7.7% of the overall pottery assemblage was recovered from Dissolution contexts (685 sherds: Table 36). The definite residual element is reduced to 12.7% of the assemblage. This does not include medieval wares which may, by the early 16th century, have been in the last stages of contemporary use and account for 2.9% of the pottery. The remaining assemblage is made up of LMT and DREW, and the first early post-medieval ceramics.

In addition to GRE, other local wares present in these contexts include IGBW, West Norfolk Bichrome ware and Speckled Glazed ware, as well as English wares such as Surrey White ware. The greatest proportion of the early post-medieval wares, however, is made up of continental imports dominated by stonewares from Cologne, along with Dutch White Earthenware.

Pits. The majority of the pottery from Period 4.1 groups was recovered from pits. It is immediately striking that these assemblages contain virtually no residual material.

Another group of ceramics of late medieval/transitional or post-medieval date, including a high level of imported wares, was recovered from robber pit *12075* (2.076kg: Fig. 5.68). In addition to an LMT bung-hole cistern, Dutch-type redwares are present and include a cauldron (Fig. 5.68 b). Two other redware vessels have frilled bases and a third has small Dutch style pulled feet (Fig. 5.68, c–e). North Holland Slipware is represented by body sherds only. Additionally, the base of a small Raeren jug was recovered (Fig. 5.68, f) and the upper part of a Cologne/Frechen cordoned plain jug (Fig. 5.68, a).

Pit *102/121/10300/10414* (0.328kg: Fig. 5.68) was also designated as a late 16th-century group. LMT is represented by a lid and dish rims, a jug handle and flatware base; and DREW by two dishes (Fig. 5.68, g and h), and a jar/cauldron rim (Fig. 5.68, i). Post-medieval pottery includes Speckled Glazed ware jug base and Werra ware base sherds.

Robbing. The most interesting group is a fine assemblage from robber cut *10660/10770* (2.067kg: Fig. 5.67). Although a small quantity of earlier residual material is present, the majority of the pottery consists of LMT and Raeren-Aachen stoneware drinking vessels. LMT includes a number of rims from jars: plain jar (Fig. 5.67 a), handled jar (type B2; Fig. 5.67, b) and jar with bifid rim (Fig. 5.67, c) as well as rims from a pancheon (Fig. 5.67, d) and a lid (Fig. 5.67, e). The rims of three Raeren-Aachen drinking vessels are present. In addition there are nine frilled bases from Siegburg and Raeren jugs (Fig. 5.67 h and i). A further small Siegburg stoneware base, probably from a beaker, is also present, and fragments of a Cologne jug decorated with roses (Fig. 5.67, f and g). The group probably indicates a late Friary rubbish disposal pit or clearance from the kitchen during demolition.

A much wider range of pottery — although no GRE — was recovered from robber cut *12061* and its fills (2.33kg: Fig. 5.69), which is dated broadly to the 16th century. The LMT includes a large number of vessels — fragments of two dripping pans, three lids, two with thumbed knobs (Fig. 5.69, a, d and e), rims from two bowls (Fig. 5.69, b and c), a lid and a chafing dish fragment, as well as a pipkin base, a thumbed base of a jar, three flat jar bases and decorated body sherds from a jug. DREW is represented by rims from two cauldrons (Fig. 5.69f), handled jar, a small jar base and body sherds from a drinking vessel. No GRE is present, although WNBC body sherds are included and indicate a 17th-century date. Low Countries imports are represented by DREW bowl rim and a rather fine North Holland Slipware small dish profile.

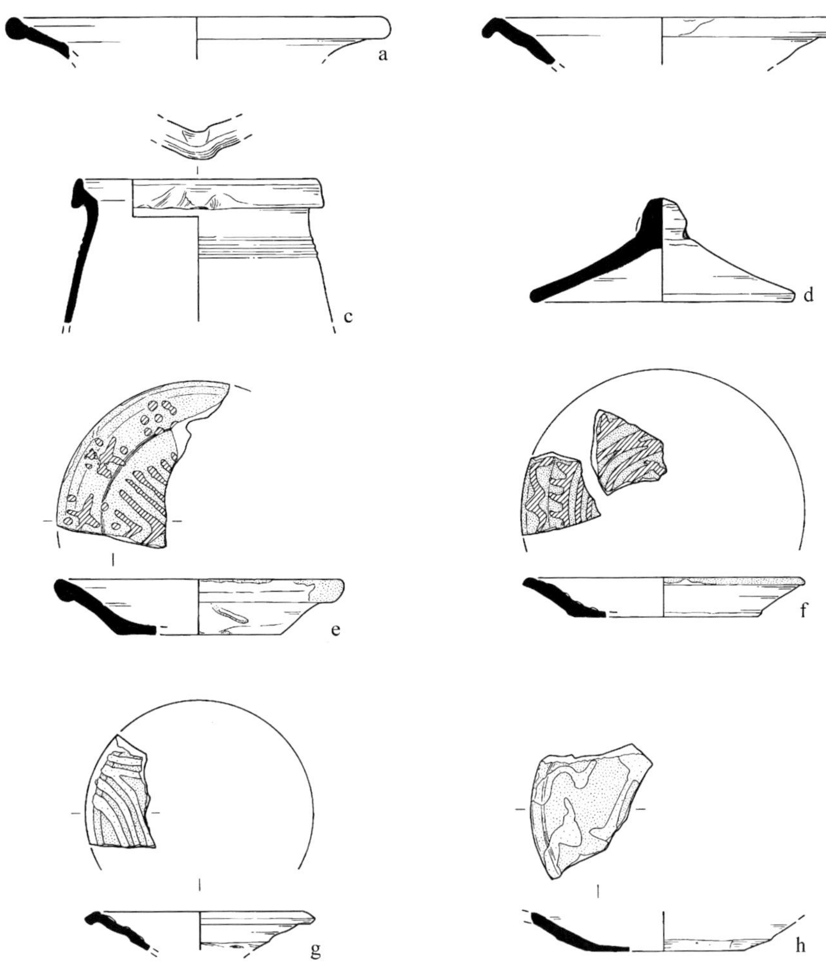

Figure 5.72 Pottery from pit *30686* (Period 4.2). Scale 1:4.

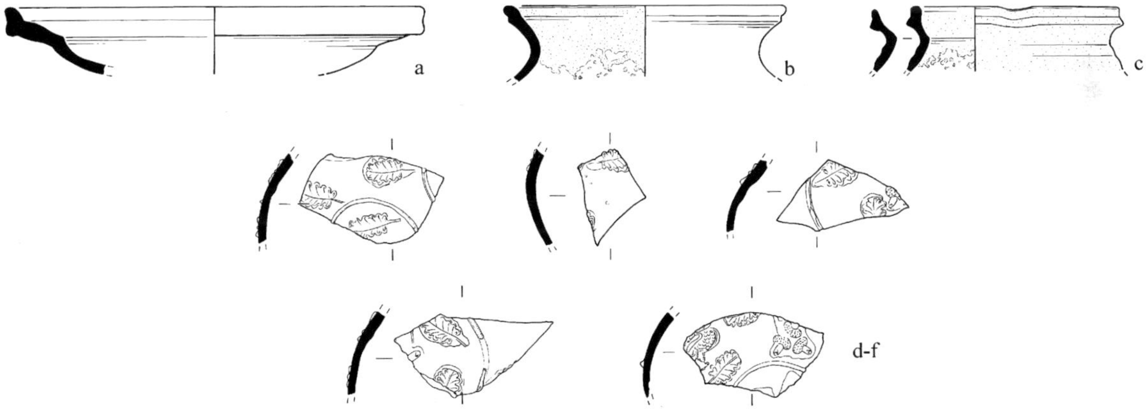

Figure 5.73 Pottery from dumps *10987*, *10989*, *10990*, *12012* and *12040* (Period 4.2). Scale 1:4.

Rhenish stoneware makes up the rest of the group assemblage, with jugs from Cologne and Frechen (Fig. 5.69, g, h and i).

Periods 4.2 and 5: post-Dissolution (c. 1567–1800)
(Figs 5.70–5.73)
A total of 3286 sherds of pottery weighing 36.563kg was recovered from post-Dissolution activity in Periods 4.2 and 5 (Table 36). While the pottery recovered from groups allocated to Period 4.2 is very similar to that from the demolition groups, the proportion of post-medieval ware is greater. The residual element also increases to *c.* 30% of the assemblage (compared to only 12.9% of Dissolution groups). LMT and DREW are still present, although the late medieval/transitional fabrics make up a smaller proportion of the assemblage with the exception of Raeren-Aachen stonewares which are still common. GRE and other local and English post-medieval wares account for the majority of the rest, supplemented by a range of continental imports.

Well (Period 4.2). The assemblage from well *12495*/*10896* (0.834kg: Fig. 5.70) includes LMT jug (Fig. 5.70, a) and dripping pan rims and a pipkin base as well as DREW body sherds. A LEPM bowl was also present in fill *12494* (Fig. 5.70, f). GRE is represented by a bowl (Fig. 5.70, c) and dish (Fig. 5.70, d). The imported ware consists of a North Holland Slipware bowl (Fig. 5.70, e) and fragments of Cologne-Frechen drinking vessels, including a sherd from a jug with part of an inscribed band and two medallions, as well as other Frechen jugs

(Fig. 5.70, b and g). This group dates to the late 16th–early 17th centuries.

Pits (Period 4.2). The assemblage recovered from pit *10111/10113* (0.841kg) was dated to the first half of the 17th century (Fig. 5.71). LMT and DREW are present, by this time probably as residual elements, together with fragments of Raeren-Aachen stoneware. Forms recovered include LMT jug handles and decorated body sherds, a DREW bowl/dish rim (Fig. 5.71, a) and a LEPM cup (Fig 5.71, f). Later post-medieval pottery includes two Border ware pipkins, one with an external lid seating (Fig. 5.71, c) and one with a tubular handle and slight internal lid-seating (Fig. 5.71, d), a GRE lid (Fig. 5.71, b), as well as a North Holland Slipware cockerel bowl (Fig. 5.71, e) and TGE decorated body sherds.

Pit *30686* (1.327kg: Fig. 5.72) contained a fine collection of 17th-century pottery with little residual material (9.6%). Contemporary pottery includes a wide range of GRE vessels represented by a lid profile (Fig. 5.72, d), five pipkins and jars, one of which is illustrated (Fig. 5.72, c), two dishes, a bowl (Fig. 5.72, a and b) and a skillet. Body sherds from IGBW drinking vessels are also present. Slipware dishes are represented by three examples of Metropolitan Slipware, two of which have been illustrated, (Fig. 5.72, e–f) and two dishes of imported North Holland Slipware (Fig. 5.72, g and h). Small quantities of TGE, and a fragment of a Westerwald stoneware jug, were recovered.

Make-up layer. Deposits *10987 etc.* contained a larger and less fragmentary group (62 sherds, 1.636kg: Fig. 5.73). Very little residual material came from this group (0.9%), but the contemporary fills were similar in ceramic terms. These included Grimston Glazed ware jug body sherd, a GRE dish, (Fig. 5.73, a) an LMT pipkin (Fig. 5.73, b), small jug, pancheon, jug and jar rims and bases, and a WNBC pipkin (Fig. 5.73, c). A fragment of a TGE charger with polychrome decoration and a body sherd from a waisted jar with yellow, blue and orange bands, also in TGE, were also recovered. German stoneware was represented by fragments of one or more Cologne drinking jugs with oak-leaf and acorn decoration which date to the first half of the 16th century (Hurst, Neal and van Beuningen 1986, 208–9) (Fig. 5.73, d–h). In addition a substantial part of a Rhenish stoneware jug, which may also be a Cologne product, was identified. It had a dark grey stoneware body with brown wash and salt glaze and was undecorated apart from cordons around the base, waist and neck of the vessel. The base is slightly concave and shows no signs of wire removal marks.

Conclusions

The range of pottery recovered from Greyfriars is similar to that from other sites in the city centre and spans the late 10th to the 19th centuries. While the assemblages from the pre-Friary occupation associated with sunken-featured buildings and domestic and craft occupation of the 11th and 12th centuries are of interest, it is the pottery contemporary with the Friary occupation, and the early 16th-century assemblages from Dissolution contexts, that are of particular significance.

Although Roman and Middle Saxon pottery is present, these sherds are invariably found as residual elements in later contexts. Middle Saxon pottery, in particular, is noted as more common than on other recently excavated Norwich sites (*e.g.* Castle Mall and Calvert Street) and may indicate that a Middle Saxon settlement was located near this part of the river (see Goffin, above, and Chapter 2.IV). However, the quantity is still not large and can only be taken to imply that settlement was in the vicinity rather than on the site itself.

The first evidence of occupation at the site was the establishment of sunken-featured buildings in Period 1 and other pre-12th-century contexts. The pottery recovered from these and associated features is made up primarily of TTW supplemented by small quantities of other early medieval wares, including locally produced EMW and EMSW, as well as regional imports of Yarmouth-type and Stamford-type wares and continental imports from Pingsdorf. Most forms present were utilitarian kitchen wares, supplemented by a few serving and other domestic vessels, such as lamps. While the largest individual assemblages were associated with occupation of sunken-floored building *10049* and disuse of sunken-featured building *50242*, much of the rest of the material came from the fills of various pits associated with rubbish disposal, and the infilling of quarries and cess-pits.

Characteristic of the Period 2.1 assemblage is the increased presence of early medieval wares. Although TTW is still the dominant single fabric, EMW, EMSW and Yarmouth-type ware make up a larger proportion of the assemblage. LMU and other medieval unglazed wares were introduced during this period, as were glazed fine wares such as Stamford ware (Fabric B); Grimston Glazed ware and Hedingham-type ware first occur in late 12th-century contexts. Pingsdorf-type ware continues to represent continental imports, joined by Andenne-type wares; both are represented in small quantities. Again, most of the larger assemblages were recovered from pits of various functions, but ditches also provided some material. Pottery recovered from deposits related to structures tended to be fragmentary.

The assemblage from Periods 2.2 is characterised by the increased importance of medieval fabrics. LMU is the most common medieval ware, supplemented by a small quantity of glazed wares. Whether TTW and other early medieval wares are residual cannot be established. Some of the material is obviously contemporary and groups from this period reflect the range of pottery from different ceramic periods in use at the same time — while early medieval wares (including late TTW) may no longer have been manufactured during this period, these products were still being used. Again, most of the assemblage came from pits and represents domestic refuse. A large number of crucible rims were recovered, including some fine examples from pits associated with a substantial structure. Evidence of metalworking was also noted in a pit that produced independent dating evidence of two coins from the reign of Stephen (1135–54).

Although rubbish and cess-pits, as well as the infill of quarry pits, produced large assemblages of material, pottery was also recovered in some quantity from features related to preparation of the site for construction, including dumps, make-up, levelling and landscaping as well as footings for walls. TTW and early medieval wares clearly become residual items during the span of Period 3, although these fabrics make up a large proportion of the assemblage from contexts of Periods 2.3 and 3.1. During these periods medieval wares are represented by unglazed fabrics dominated by LMU and supplemented by small quantities of non-local and regional imports such as East Cambridge-type ware. Glazed wares make up a much larger proportion of the assemblage and are represented mostly by Grimston Glazed ware, with small amounts of regional and non-local wares such as Developed Stamford ware, Hedingham-type ware and Scarborough-type ware. Continental imports continue to be represented by Andenne-type ware but expand to include Aardenburg-type ware and the first occurrence of Rhenish stonewares, with a few sherds of Siegburg stoneware. More unusual is the presence of French wares represented by a Rouen-type/North French ware jug sherd.

What distinguishes Period 3.2 contexts from their predecessors is the presence of late medieval/transitional fabrics, which were introduced in small quantities in the span of the previous periods but now became a major feature. Although medieval-type wares continued to be used, the needs of the Friary were increasingly met by LMT and continental imports. LMT and DREW provided a wide range of kitchen vessels for food preparation and storage; many of these would have been produced locally. Although some evidence of LMT jugs was recorded, pouring and drinking vessels were mostly Rhenish stonewares from Siegburg, Langerwehe and Raeren-Aachen. These assemblages indicate the range of ceramics being used by the Franciscan friars, and it is noteworthy that the relatively high economic status of the Friary during the late medieval/transitional period is not reflected in the pottery it used.

The pottery recovered from Dissolution pits in Period 4.1 is of note as it includes very little residual material. Much of the assemblage came from infills of robber pits and demolition debris, and is mostly noted as fresh. Medieval fabrics make up a smaller proportion, but by this stage their use would have been dying away. LMT and other late medieval/transitional utilitarian wares dominate the period assemblage, while post-medieval wares such as GRE, IGBW and continental imports such as Dutch White Earthenware and North Holland Slipwares make their first appearance.

By Period 4.2 post-medieval wares dominate the assemblage. A range of local products is supplemented by regional and English imports, while Rhenish stonewares and slipwares from the Low Countries and Germany extended the range of tablewares. GRE and West Norfolk Bichrome ware provide a range of kitchen wares, although, for cooking, ceramic vessels were largely being replaced by metal cauldrons by this date. Jugs and drinking vessels were provided by IGBW and Speckled Glazed ware, but Rhenish stonewares dominate this functional group with products from Cologne and Frechen introduced to add to vessels from Raeren-Aachen. Tablewares were supplied by products from Metropolitan Slipwares and Surrey White wares, supplemented by Dutch White Earthenwares and North Holland Slipwares, as well as TGE and German slipware from Waser. During this period other household wares, such as Westerwald chamber pots and a range of English stonewares, were introduced.

In conclusion, the range of fabrics recovered from the Greyfriars site is consistent with the pattern of ceramics present on many other Norwich sites. What is significant about this assemblage, however, is the opportunity it has provided for attributing groups of pottery to domestic activity in the 11th and 12th centuries, and to the Friary.

Catalogue of ceramic vessels

(Figs 5.56–5.73)

Information on the sherds illustrated in each figure is presented in the following order: identifying letter: fabric/form description; context.

Fig. 5.56: sunken-floored building 10049 (Area D) (Period 1)

a TTW, AA1, small jar, *10631*
b TTW, AB6, medium jar, *10790*
c TTW, AB14, medium jar, *10790*
d TTW, AB17, medium jar, *10790*
e TTW, AB17, medium jar, *10631*
f TTW, AE1/AD1, handled jar/spouted pitcher, *10632*
g TTW, AB1, medium jar, *10632*

Fig. 5.57: sunken-featured building *50242* (Area C) (Period 1)

a, e TTW, AA10, cooking pot, *50263*
b TTW, AB13, waster fragment, *50258*
c TTW, AB13, cooking pot, *50258*
d, i TTW, AB5, medium jar, *50263*
h TTW, AB11, medium jar, *50263*
j EMSW, BB6, curve-sided bowl, *50258*
g TTW, AB9, cooking pot, *50258*
f TTW, AB11, cooking pot, *50258*

Fig. 5.58: Pit *11231* (Period 1)

a TTW, AB16, medium jar, *11230*
b TTW, AB13, medium jar, *11128*
c TTW, AB14, medium jar, *11230*
d TTW, AB13, medium jar, *11129*
e TTW, AB14, medium jar, *11230*
f TTW, AB7, medium jar, *11129*
g TTW, AB8, medium jar, *11128*
h TTW, AB7, large jar, *11129*
i TTW , AC8, Large jar, *11129*
j TTW, AB6, medium jar, *11230*
k TTW, AC15, large jar, *11129*
l TTW, AB10, medium jar, *11129*
m TTW, BB7, bowl, *11129*

Fig. 5.59: pit *11145* (Period 1)

a TTW, AB6, medium jar, *11143*
b TTW, AB6, medium jar, *11143*
c EMW, J2b, plain flared jar, *11143*
d EMW, J2b, plain flared jar, *11143*
e EMW, J1b, plain flared jar, *11143*
f TTW, AB9, medium jar, *11143*
g TTW, AB11, medium jar, *11143*
h TTW, AB10, medium jar, *11144*
i TTW, AB6, medium jar, *11144*
j EMW, J1b, plain flared jar, *11143*
k EMW, J1b, plain flared jar, *11143*
l EMW, J1b, plain flared jar, *11143*
m EMW, J2b, plain flared jar, *11143*
n EMW, J1b, plain flared jar, *11143*
o TTW, AB5, medium jar, *11143*
p TTW, AB9, medium jar, *11143*
q TTW, AB11, medium jar, *11143*
s TTW, lamp or cup, *11143*
s TTW, AF9, large non-handled jar, *11144*
t YT, Y2c, medium everted jar, *11144*
u EMWS, medium jar, *11143*
v TTW, AF8, large non-handled jar, *11143*

Fig 5.60: pit *30237* (Period 1)

a TTW, AB18, medium jar, *30435*
b TTW, AB6, medium jar, *30433*
c TTW, AB13, medium jar, *30435*
d TTW, AB15, medium jar, *30433*
e TTW, AB18, medium jar, *30433*
f TTW, AB18, medium jar, *30433*
g TTW, AB18, medium jar, *30433*

Fig 5.61: pit *50628* (Period 2.1)

a TTW, AB14, medium jar, *50623*
b TTW, AD1, spouted pitcher, *50639*
c EMW, J1a, jar, *50622*
d EMW, J1b, jar, *50623*
e EMW, J2b, jar, *50622*
f EMSSW, J2c, medium jar, *50639*
g LMU, J2b, cooking pot, *50623*
h LMU , J2c, cooking pot, *50623*
i YT, Y1b, medium jar, *50639*

Fig. 5.62: pit *30485* ((Period 2.1)

a TTW, AB14, medium jar, *30467*
b TTW, AB16, medium jar, *30467*
c TTW, AB14, medium jar, *30467*
d YT, Y1, medium upright jar, *30467*
e YT, Y3, medium everted jar, *30467*
f TTW, AB1, medium jar, *30467*
g EMSW, AB2, medium jar, *30467*
h EMSW, AE1, handled jar, *40104*

Fig 5.64: quarry pit fill *30899* (Period 2.3)

a LMU, J2c, cooking vessel/jar, *30900*
b LMU, J1j, cooking vessel/jar, *30900*
c LMU, J1a, cooking vessel/jar, *30900*
d YT, Y2c, cooking vessel/jar, *30900*

e LMU, J2b, cooking vessel/jar, *30900*
f EMWSS, J1c, jar, *30900*
g LMU, J1b, cooking vessel/jar, *30900*

Fig. 5.65: pit *30213* and pit *30337* (Period 2.3)
a GRIM, GGG, glazed jug, *30200*
b GRIMC, coarseware jug, *30200*
c AND, AND1, pitcher, *30200*
d LMT, A, glazed jar, *30200*
e GRIM, jug sherd with applied scales decoration, *30200*
f EMW, J1b, plain flared jar, *30339*
g EMSW, AC9, medium jar, *30337*
h EMSW, AB5, medium jar, *30337*
i AND, AND1, pitcher, *30339*

Fig. 5.66: pit *40014* and pit *40019* (Period 3.2)
a GRIM, GGG, stabbed strap jug handle, *40060*
b LMT, B1, handled jar, *40060*
c LMU, J2j, cooking pot , *40060*
d LMT, small bowl rim, *40017*
e TUDG, lobed cup, *40017*
f LANG, base of jug, *40017*

Fig. 5.67: robber pit *10660* (Period 4.1)
a LMT, jar rim, *10724*
b LMT, B2, horseshoe handled jar, *10724*
c LMT, A, jar with bifid rim, *10724*
d LMT, I, pancheon, *10724*
e LMT, lid, *10724*
f SIEG, base of drinking vessel, prob beaker, *10724*
g KOLN, fragment of jug with rose decoration, *10724*
h SIEG, base of jug, *10724*
i RAER, base of jug, *10724*

Fig. 5.68: Robber pit *12075* and pit *102/121/10300/10414* (Period 4.1)
a KOLN/FREC, rim of plain cordonned jug, *12073*
b DREW, cauldron, *12073*
c DREW, Dutch style base, *12073*
d DREW, Dutch style base, *12073*
e DREW, Dutch-style base with pulled feet, *12073*
f RAER, flat base of small jug, *12073*
g DREW, dish, *10299*
h DREW, dish, *10299*
i DREW, cauldron, *10299*

Fig. 5.69: robber cut *12061* (Period 4.1)
a LMT, lid, *12063*
b LMT, unglazed bowl, *12063*
c LMT, unglazed bowl, *12063*
d LEPM/LMT, lid, *12063*
e LMT, unglazed lid, *12063*
f DREW, cauldron, *12063*
g KOLN/FREC, jug, *12063*
h KOLN/FREC, jug, *12067*
i FREC, jug, *12063*

Fig. 5.70: well *12495/10896* (Period 4.2)
a LMT, jug, *12494*
b FREC, plain cordoned jug, *12494*
c GRE, bowl, *10859*
d GRE, dish, *10859*
e NHS, bowl, *10859*
f LEPM, bowl, *12494*
g FREC, plain jug, *10859*

Fig. 5.71: pit *10111/10113* (Period 4.2)
a DREW, dish, *10182*
b GRE, lid, *10253*
c BORD, pipkin with external lid seating, *10182*
d BORD, lid-seated pipkin, *10142/10253*
e NHS, cockerel bowl, *10253*
f LEPM, cup fragment, *10182*

Fig. 5.72: pit *30686* (Period 4.2)
a GRE, dish, *30670*
b GRE, bowl, *30670*
c GRE, pipkin, *30670*
d GRE, lid, *30670*
e METS, dish, *30670*
f METS, dish, *30670*
g LCSL, dish, *30670*
h LCSL, dish, *30670*

Fig. 5.73: dumps *10987*, *10989*, *10990*, *12012* and *12040* (Period 4.2)
a GRE, dish, *12012*
b LMT, pipkin, *12012*
c WNBC, pipkin, *12012*
d–h KOLN, Cologne stoneware jug fragments with oak leaf decoration, *12012*

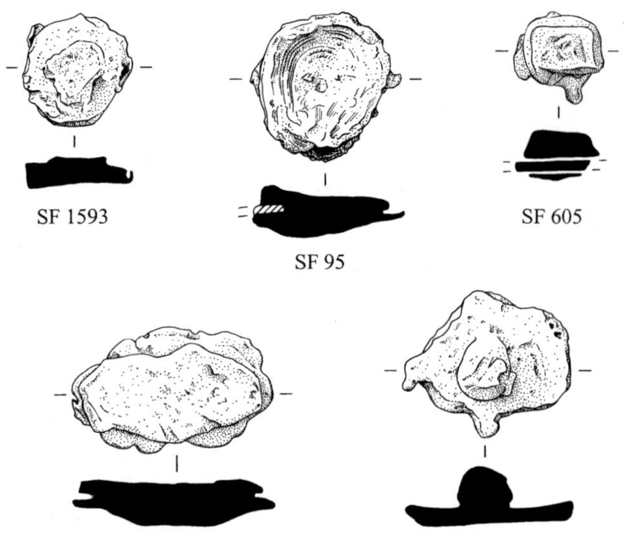

Figure 5.74 Lead vessel repair plugs (SF1593, 95, 605, 52, 2317). Scale 1:1.

Vessel repair plugs (lead)

by Geoff Egan
(Fig. 5.74)

Five lead plugs of varying size had been used to repair holes in ceramic vessels. One example from sunken-floored building *10049* is an early example of the technique.

SF52 Sub-oval lead **plug**, *c.* 50 x *c.* 35mm. Repair for a holed ceramic vessel. Probably residual from the medieval period.
build-up 50041, Period 4.2

SF95 Sub-round lead **plug**, *c.* 20 x *c.* 17mm, retains fragments of Grimston ware (in use mid-12th–mid-16th centuries).
pit fill 30538, Period 3.1

SF605 Sub-square lead **plug**, *c.* 20 x *c.* 18mm.
plotted metal-detector find 30978, Period 2.3

SF1593 Lead repair **plug** for a holed ceramic vessel, 30 x 30mm, roughly round, with raised central area on one face.
hearth debris 10479, SFB 10049, Period 1

SF2317 Sub-square lead **plug,** 44 x 39mm. Repair for a holed ceramic vessel.
unstratified

Implements

Knives and shears

by Julia Huddle and Val Fryer
(Fig. 5.75–5.77)

A total assemblage of 28 knives and knife fragments was recovered from the Greyfriars site, nine of which came from pre-Friary contexts (Period 2.1 – three examples; Period 2.2

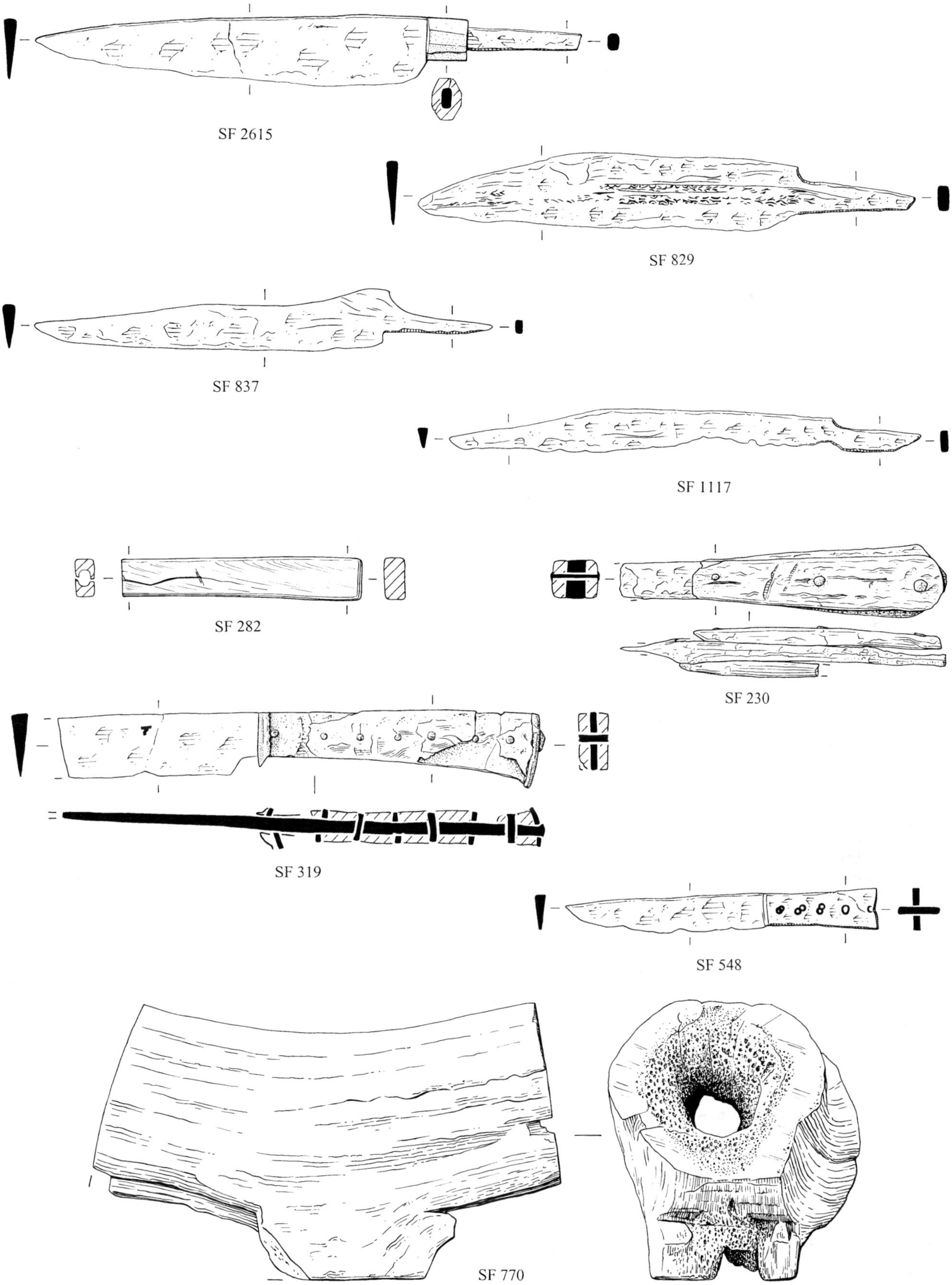

Figure 5.75 Iron and composite knives (SF2615, 829, 837, 1117, 282, 230, 319, 548, Scale 1:2), antler implement handle (SF770, Scale 1:1).

– one example; Period 2.3 – five examples). None were recovered from Period 1 (10th–11th century) contexts, although one (SF844) came from the backfill of sunken-floored building *10049*. A further fourteen knives were attributed to the Friary period and its Dissolution. Most were of scale tang type, and all were probably for everyday use including domestic functions. A sawn antler beam (SF770) may have served as a whittle-tang knife handle (Period 2.1).

One knife (SF2615) was recovered from a 12th-century pit fill. Non-ferrous shoulder plates on whittle-tang knives are very rare before the 14th century, however, and then do not take this form. A whittle-tang knife from a late medieval context in London has ornate non-ferrous fittings (Ward Perkins 1940, plate XI no. 11), while a scale-tang knife from an early 14th-century deposit at Amsterdam has a similar angular shoulder plate (Baart *et al.* 1977, 327 no. 616).

Whittle-tang knives

SF829, SF1117 and SF1349 are of a late 12th-century type with angled backs. SF829, which was found in a 15th-/early 16th-century deposit, has a pattern welded blade, a continuation of 'Saxon' decorative traditions (Cowgill *et al.* 1987, 78). It can be compared to a group from Coppergate and Fishergate, York, characterised by a straight back which is horizontal until the angled tip (Ottaway 1992, 558–99; 1993, 1273–7). SF1117 and SF1349 were both recovered from 13th-century contexts. SF837 was also probably manufactured in the late 12th century, although the back is more sinuous than angled. SF562, SF834 and SF1157 are all 13th–14th-century types.

SF2615 Whittle-tang **knife**. Back and cutting edge slightly curved. Angled shoulder. Octagonal non-ferrous shoulder plate.
pit fill 13224, Period 2

SF829 **Knife**. Pattern welded blade.
fill 30247, Period 3.2

SF837 **Knife**. Slightly sinuous back.
make-up 30234, Period 3.2

SF1117 **Knife**. Damage to blade edge.
pit fill 30452, Period 2.3

SF282 Ivory whittle-tang **handle**, rectangular in section, with rounded edges, tapering slightly at blade (?butt) end.
build-up 50025, Period 2.2

SF770 Sawn section of antler beam longitudinally perforated, from which the tine has been sawn away, forming a tubular ?implement, probably a **handle** for a whittle-tang knife. Red deer antler.
ditch fill 50490, Period 2

Scale-tang knives

Elsewhere, knives with scale tangs first appear in the 13th and 14th centuries. The earliest scale-tang knife at Greyfriars is from a 13th-century context (SF951, Period 2.3) but the majority come from deposits ascribed to Period 3.2 (1400–1538). SF319 and 548 are both probably of 15th–16th-century date, with Norwich parallels from (for example) St Martin-at-Palace Plain (Williams 1988b, fig. 59 no.16) and Alms Lane (Goodall 1993, fig. 95 no. 841). The type is also known from Amsterdam (Baart *et al.* 1977, 332 no.631). SF1361 and SF1362 are possibly components of the same knife.

Two fragmentary knives were recovered from post-Dissolution contexts, one severely corroded blade fragment with inlaid copper-alloy maker's mark and minerally-preserved traces of a leather sheath (SF476a) and one whittle tang, possibly with a bolster, with a minerally-preserved wooden handle *in situ* (SF2060). Utilitarian knives with whittle tangs occur throughout the late medieval and post-medieval periods (*e.g.* Goodall 1993, fig. 92 nos 798 and 799). Knives with bolsters between the tang and blade appear in the 17th century (Goodall 1993, fig. 96).

SF230 **Knife** with incomplete iron blade, scale-tang handle shape. Antler handle, one scale incomplete, attached with three solid iron rivets.
build-up 50019, Period 3.2

SF319 **Knife**. Blade broken. Copper-alloy shoulder plate, tubular rivets and end cap. Remains of wood scales *in situ*. Lead-alloy maker's mark on blade.
drain fill 10800, Period 3.2

SF548 **Knife**. Tang broken. Copper-alloy tubular rivets. Possible traces of wood scales.
pit fill 40017, Period 3.2

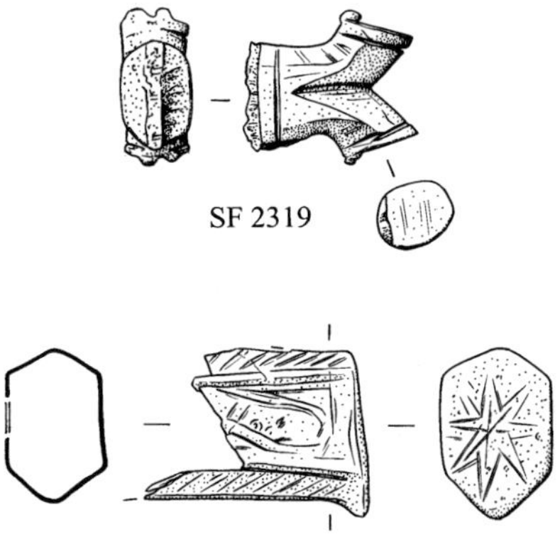

Figure 5.76 Copper alloy knife handle (SF2319), silver alloy knife handle case (SF802). Scale 1:1.

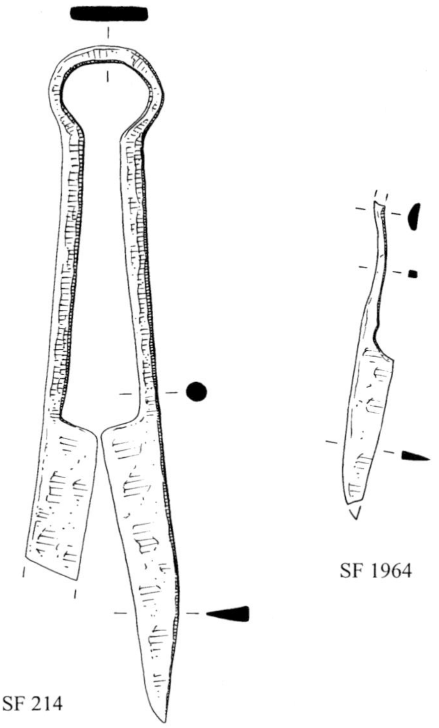

Figure 5.77 Iron shears (SF214, 1964). Scale 1:2.

Knife handle terminal
by Julia Huddle
(Fig. 5.76)
A copper-alloy terminal for a knife handle was recovered. Several of these late 15th–16th-century knife caps, found by metal-detecting, are recorded in the Norfolk Historic Environment Record (Sue Margeson, *pers. comm.*). Another was recovered at Grimston, Norfolk (Leah 1994, 69, fig. 50 no. 7).

SF2319 Copper-alloy **terminal for a knife handle**, iron-stained oval stem with bifurcated end; the two oval terminals apparently representing horses' hooves.
make-up 10257, Period 4.2

Knife handle case
by Julia Huddle
(Fig. 5.76)
A knife handle case made from silver alloy was found unstratified. Few non-ferrous metal handles are known from archaeological contexts. A copper-alloy handle from Trig Lane, London, is from a late 14th-century context and an elaborately decorated sheet copper-alloy handle case of post-medieval date is known from Norwich (Margeson 1993, 128, fig. 93 no. 820).

The style of decoration on SF802 and the subject matter — a hat-wearing human figure — may be compared to two knife handles from Amsterdam, both with engraved decoration depicting, among other things, a man wearing a wide-brimmed hat (Baart 1977, 330 no. 625 and 332, no. 630); the first is dated to the late 15th–early 16th century and the latter, also hexagonal, to the second half of the 16th century. The Greyfriars handle case, made of thin silver alloy sheet would probably have covered a wooden handle, such as the one shown in Baarts' catalogue (no. 630), which is covered at the top and bottom with hammered sheet copper alloy.

SF802 Incomplete decorated six-sided sheet-metal **handle case,** made of silver alloy. Engraved decoration consists of an eight-pointed star at the top, diagonal lines on the two extant sides and on the front a portrait of a ?man wearing a wide-brimmed hat. A small amount of organic material was removed from the inside of the handle-case during conservation.
unstratified

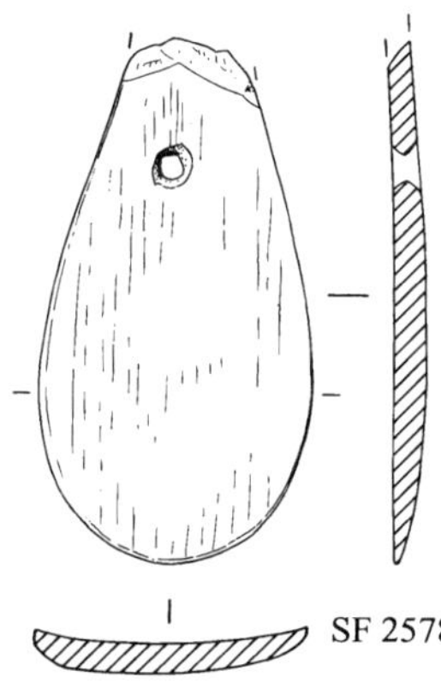

Figure 5.78 Bone spoon (SF2578). Scale 1:1.

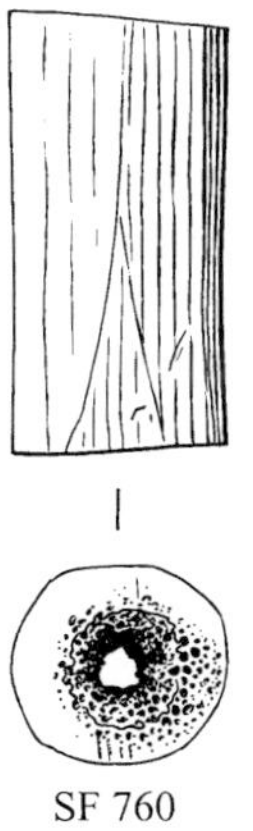

Figure 5.79 Antler tubular object (SF760). Scale 1:1.

Shears
by Val Fryer
(Fig. 5.77)
The large shears SF214, with long handles and blades, were probably used for cutting cloth or shearing sheep. The smaller shears SF1964, with a recess at the junction of arm and blade and a ridged bow, were probably more suitable for sewing/thread cutting. Both are probably of 14th-century date.

SF214 Iron **shears**. One blade broken.
fill 50236, Period 3.1

SF1964 Iron **shears** arm. Broken through bow.
dump 12297, Period 3.1

Spoon
by Julia Huddle
(Fig. 5.78)
A fragment of a bone spoon was found residually in a 15th–early 16th-century context attributed to the Friary (SF2578). Other spoons made of bone and antler, with bowls of a similar form, are known elsewhere from Late Saxon and early medieval contexts. One bone example from Norwich is from a mid-11th century context (Williams 1988c, 100, fig. 81 no. 15) and one of antler from a 10th–11th-century context at Castle Mall (Huddle forthcoming). Such handles can be ornate, including an example from Redcastle Furze, Thetford (Andrews 1995, 116, fig. 87 no. 13).

SF2578 Bone **spoon** fragment. Tear-drop shaped spatulate bowl, handle missing. The bowl has been subsequently perforated. Shaft of longbone, probably cattle.
fill 13061, Period 3.2

Tube (antler)
by Ian Riddler
(Fig. 5.79)
Lengths of shaped antler tine, similar to an example from Greyfriars (SF760), have been recovered from unpublished assemblages at Ipswich and Southampton. Most of these belong to the Late Saxon period, a dating substantiated by continental parallels (Ulbricht 1978, 81 note 223). Ingrid Ulbricht has published a series of antler tine sections from Haithabu which have been perforated and — in some cases — also decorated (Ulbricht 1978, 81–2 and taf 43). Two groups were distinguished, this division based primarily on the degree of care taken over the finished object. The Greyfriars example would belong to the second group, which is less carefully finished (Ulbricht 1978, taf 45.6–12). In this particular case the section of tine has been hollowed; this would have enabled the object to be used either as a simple spacer or a finial,

with a thread or strap passing through the axial perforation. There is no evidence yet for the use of such objects as spacers for fishing nets, although this remains a possibility (Rulewicz 1994). Indeed, Ulbricht has noted that there is no conclusive evidence, invoking archaeological or ethnographic parallels, which would enable these functional options to be distinguished (Ulbricht 1978, 82).

SF760 Part of a red deer antler tine, sawn laterally at either end and hollowed to produce a tube. The outer surface has been smoothed and shows some traces of working; it is undecorated.
backfill of SFB 10049 10725, Period 2

Flesh hook
by Val Fryer
(Fig. 5.80)
A flesh hook with two hooked arms is of a type which originated in the 13th century (Goodall 1987a, 12–13, fig. 8). The handle is broken but both tanged and socketed handles are known. Flesh hooks were used to extract meat and other items from cooking vessels.

SF1098 Iron **flesh hook** head. Handle broken.
pit fill 30646, Period 3.2

Apple-corer or cheese scoop (bone)
by Julia Huddle
(not illustrated)
A bone apple-corer or cheese scoop (SF1185) was found in a mid-16th to 17th-century context. Stratified examples previously found in Norwich and elsewhere are from 17th-century and later deposits. Sue Margeson writes about their various possible uses and includes an interesting transcript from a local television programme, which notes the various purposes people to which these implements were put (as recently as the middle of the 20th century), including cleaning out tobacco pipes (Margeson 1993, 120). The Greyfriars piece lacks any kind of decoration, which is often seen on these items.

Hone stones
by J.M. Mills
(Fig. 5.81)
A group of fourteen hone stones was recovered from the excavations at Greyfriars. Hones would have been needed anywhere that a bladed tool was used and would thus have been required by vast number of trades, crafts and industries, as well as by individuals who needed to keep personal knife blades keen. It is not possible to tell what type of blade was sharpened on a particular hone, although comparison with modern usage suggests that the stones discussed here were for sharpening bladed tools of a type which might include knives, scythes, bill hooks and the like. Chisels and plane irons are likely to have been sharpened on a flat or rotary stone. as the angle of the cutting edge needed to be kept true.

Many of the excavated stones are heavily worn and often broken near to the middle, which had become markedly waisted through use. The majority of hones recovered are incomplete, and several seem to have continued in use after breakage. A single phyllite stone is pierced for suspension (SF279), presumably from a belt. Just two hones have linear grooves in one or more face. It is usually suggested that these grooves are a result of sharpening points, perhaps of needles or awls. It is possible that point-sharpening represents the last phase of use of a hone which has become too worn for maintenance of blades.

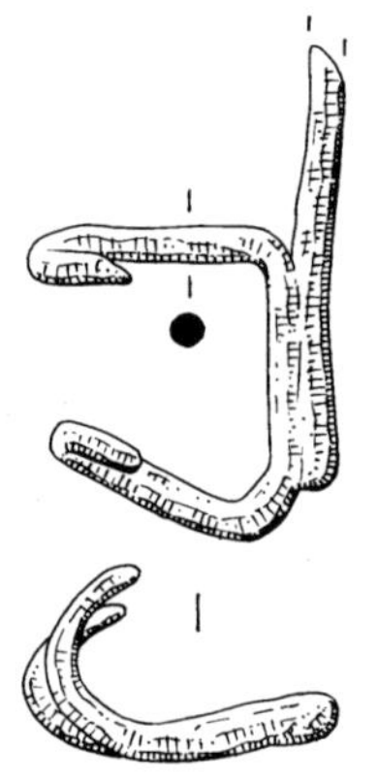

Figure 5.80 Iron flesh hook (SF1098). Scale 1:2.

All the stone used as hones was imported to Norwich. Previous excavations have produced assemblages dominated by Norwegian Ragstone. The hone assemblage from the Greyfriars excavations is slightly different in character from most of those from previous sites in Norwich in that no Coal Measures Sandstone hones were recovered. From previous excavations, the proportion of Norwegian Ragstone is around 80% and phyllite *c.* 12%. At Greyfriars, however, the numbers of Ragstone and phyllite hones represented are equal. While this may have implications in terms of trade patterns, there may be a functional or date-related explanation for the composition of this assemblage.

Hones are seldom intrinsically datable. The shape of most is dictated by the stone type, and thus morphology is no indicator of date of manufacture. The phyllite examples are likely to predate the foundation of the Franciscan friary and three of the Ragstone hones (from 12th-century contexts) are conclusively pre-Friary. Stratigraphically, the earliest hones recovered are three fine-grained fragments, probably from phyllite examples, from 10th/11th-century deposits: fills of sunken-floored building *10049* (SF617 and SF1683) and of nearby pit *10766* (SF1028). The 12th-century deposits yielded three Norwegian Ragstone hones (SF418, SF2641, SF1684). Evidence from London (Pritchard 1991, 155), Thetford (Moore and Ellis 1984) and York (MacGregor 1982, 77–80) suggests that the use of Norwegian Ragstone was

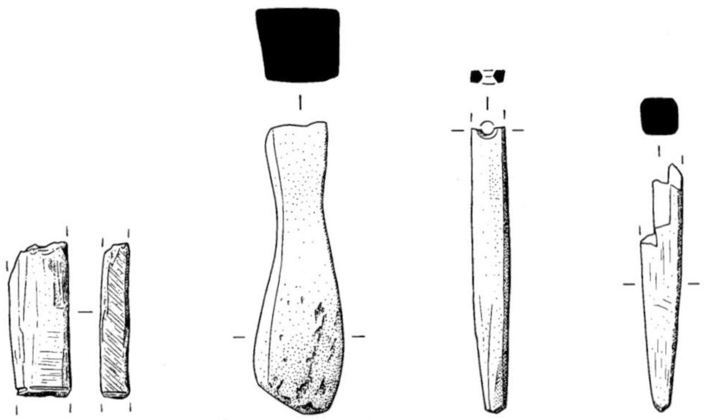

Figure 5.81 Hone stones (SF1028, 418, 279, 1681). Scale 1:2.

widespread before the Norman Conquest and that its use continued throughout the medieval period. Whilst purple phyllite is frequently observed to share its distribution pattern, it has been suggested that this stone ceased to be quarried in the 11th century (Crosby and Mitchell 1990, 292).

Of the seven hone fragments from Period 3 (*c.* 1226–1538) two (SF279 and SF1681) are associated with the pre-Friary period pottery. Both of these are phyllite hones and, as noted above, are therefore likely to pre-date the establishment of the Friary. A further two small fragments of fine-grained (phyllite) hones recovered from Period 3 levels are probably residual. It is worth noting that the two almost-complete phyllite hones are those from Period 3 contexts but are associated with earlier pottery. The Norwegian Ragstone hones from Period 3 and the unstratified Ragstone hone (SF1994) which is associated with 14th–15th-century pottery are typical of the hones known from previous excavations in medieval Norwich.

There remain only four hones likely to be contemporary with the monastic occupation by the Greyfriars. This seems a small quantity when compared to the area excavated and may be due to the function of the areas excavated: for example, few hones would be expected in many areas including dormitories and chapels, whilst the numbers from kitchens or even rubbish disposal areas would be expected to be greater.

SF1028 Fragment of an ?originally rectangular stone. One of the narrow, long sides clearly shows fine saw marks and on the opposite face a small area of the original sawn face remains. Of the wider faces only one is smoothed as if from sharpening/honing. One end has snapped at a point where each side is grooved to a depth of £ 1mm. The stone is very fine-grained and is dark grey; not formally identified but possibly a phyllite. Maximum extant dimensions: 35 x 18 x 6mm.
pit fill 10738, Period 1

SF418 Small **hone**, both ends broken but worn. Heavily waisted by use; maximum cross-section perhaps suggests stone was originally longer, but use continued after breakage. All faces utilised. Norwegian Ragstone (dark grey, hard type). L: 65mm, cross-section tapers from 16 x 18mm to 9 x 8mm.
fill 10136, Period 2.2

SF279 Small **hone** broken at one end across suspension hole, otherwise complete. Very fine-grained; ?purple phyllite. Maximum extant dimensions 67 x 7.5 x 5mm. Suspension hole *c.* 2.5mm diam.
pit fill 50673, Period 3.1

SF1681 Small, incomplete **hone**, square in cross-section and tapering to a blunt point. A fine-grained, pale purple-ish grey stone; possibly a phyllite. This is an unusual stone as most small phyllite hones are rectangular in section. Maximum extant dimensions 57 x 8 x 8mm.
pit fill 30645, Period 3.2

Miscellaneous household items

Nails (copper alloy)

by Julia Huddle
(not illustrated)
Two copper-alloy nails were recovered, one from a medieval context and the other unstratified. Such items may have been used (for example) on small items of furniture (see SF1891: book mount) or horse harness (see SF197, Fig. 5.93: harness mount).

Ferrule

by Julia Huddle
(not illustrated)
SF385 is a copper-alloy ferrule with a flattened base, parallel sides and one attachment pin still *in situ*. Such ferrules were used to protect the ends of staffs *etc.* from wear.

IV. DRESS AND PERSONAL POSSESSIONS

Dress Accessories

Beads

by Julia Huddle
(Fig. 5.82)
Thirteen beads were recovered, all but one from flotation samples. Two came from Saxo-Norman levels, while the rest are from Friary or post-Friary (mainly Dissolution) contexts.

A glass bead (SF1439) from the use fills of sunken-floored building 10049in Area A appears to be a similar size, shape and colour to the type described as *cylindrical* from Anglo-Scandinavian levels from three sites at York: Pavement, 16–22 Coppergate and Fishergate (for a discussion on these beads see Rogers 1993, 1380). SF1616 is an annular bead; a ?burnt annular bead was found at Fishergate, Norwich, in a 10th-century context (Williams 1994c, 19, fig. 13 no. 2). Annular beads are also known from Anglo-Scandinavian deposits in York, and from 12th-century contexts at 34 The Shambles, York (Tweddle 1986).

The beads from Friary and post-Friary deposits display a similar diverse range of materials to those found in medieval and later contexts by the Norwich Survey excavations and also elsewhere — in particular, a collection of 217 beads from London is discussed in Egan and Pritchard 1991. Although necklaces were not in fashion in the medieval period, beads are common on medieval sites and the larger ones in particular are likely to come from rosaries. The tiny beads from Greyfriars (*e.g.* SF882, SF1738 and SF1222) may have been sewn onto elaborate trimmings for dress in the late medieval period (Egan 1991, 305) or used in wire-work jewellery of the late 15th and early 16th centuries. Two glass beads can be seen attached to a copper-alloy pendant made out of two pilgrim badges from Pottergate (Margeson 1993, plate I).

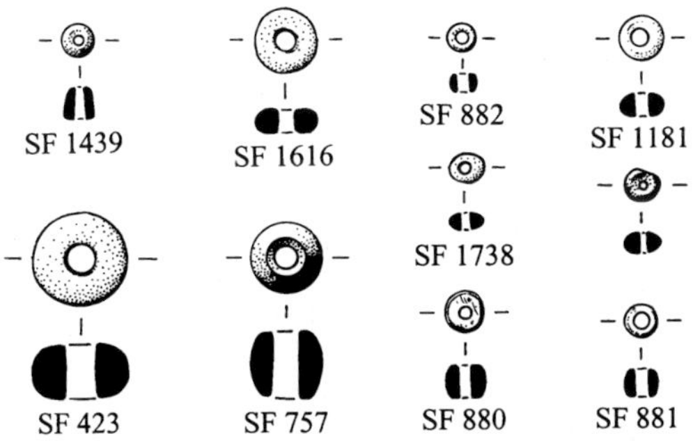

Figure 5.82 Beads: glass (SF1439, 1616, 882, 1181, 1738, 1222), ceramic (SF423), jet (SF757, 880), bone (SF881). Scale 1:1.

Evidence for the manufacture of bone beads was recovered from Friary levels in the form of bone waste panels; interestingly, one discoidal bone bead (SF1610) was recovered from one of the two pits which contained these waste panels. For further discussion see Chapter 5.II, 'Secondary bone working waste: bead manufacture'.

Glass beads

SF1439 Sub-oval (or cylindrical) **bead**, opaque green glass.
fill 10726 SFB 10049, Period 1

SF1616 Annular **bead**, weathered opaque glass with translucent surfaces, pale blue and yellow in colour.
pit fill 40081, Period 2

SF882 Tiny oblate-spheroid **bead**, pale green glass.
pit fill 10385, Period 4.1

SF1181 Oblate-spheroid **bead**, semi-opaque yellow glass.
pit fill 50421, Period 3.1

SF1738 Tiny sub-spherical **bead**, opaque orange glass.
pit fill 30804, Period 4.2

SF1222 Tiny oblate-spheroid **bead**, black ?glass.
pit fill 10688, Period 3.1

Ceramic

SF423 Oblate-spheroid ceramic **bead**, of greyish-brown colour.
layer 50037, Period 4.2

Jet

SF757 Oblate-spheroid jet **bead**.
pit fill 40086, Period 2.3

Bone

SF880 Oblate-spheroid bone **bead**, with pitted surfaces.
pit fill 10385, Period 4.1

SF881 Oblate-spheroid bone **bead**.
pit fill 10385, Period 4.1

Dress pins

by Julia Huddle
(Fig. 5.83; Pl. 5.8)

Pins with solid heads

Two copper-alloy dress pins with large solid heads were recovered (SF25 and 2582). Similar pins have been found elsewhere, predominantly on Middle Saxon sites including Middle Harling (Margeson 1995, 55) and Whitby (Peers and Radford 1943). One at Greyfriars with a facetted head (SF25) was recovered from the disuse fill of sunken-featured building *50242*, dated to the 11th century, and has an almost identical parallel from an early 11th-century context at Fishergate, Norwich, which is provisionally dated to the Middle Saxon period (Williams 1994, 13). At 46–54 Fishergate, York, similar pins with facetted or polyhedral heads have been recovered, many from Late Saxon deposits, although here too they are thought to be Middle Saxon (Rogers 1993, 1363). The second example at Greyfriars (SF2582) has a globular head and collared shaft and is unstratified. An almost identical pin (although with incised decoration around the shaft) was recovered from a Late Saxon context at Redcastle Furze, Thetford (Little 1995, 90, fig. 67 no. 24) and also dated to the Middle Saxon period.

Pins with pierced heads

Two pins with decorative pierced heads and hipped shafts were recovered, one of copper alloy (SF205) and the other of bone (SF1236). This type of pin is known from several Norman sites and the vast majority are bone, although examples of copper alloy are also known. Three similar pins have previously been found in Norwich, one made of bone from a 10th–12th-century context on Botolph Street (Margeson 1993, fig. 4, cat. no. 24) and another of copper alloy from Westwick Street from a late 12th–late 13th-century context (Margeson 1993, fig. 4, cat. 25) and the third from Dragon Hall, made of bone, from a context provisionally dated to the 12th–13th centuries (Huddle 2005, 54, fig. 189). They have been found, and are often associated with, high-status sites: an important group comes from Castle Acre Castle, Norfolk, while they have

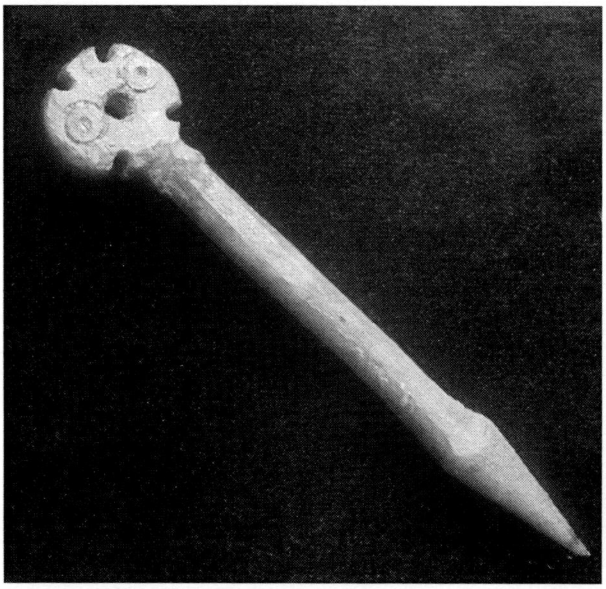

Plate 5.8 Bone dress pin (SF1236)

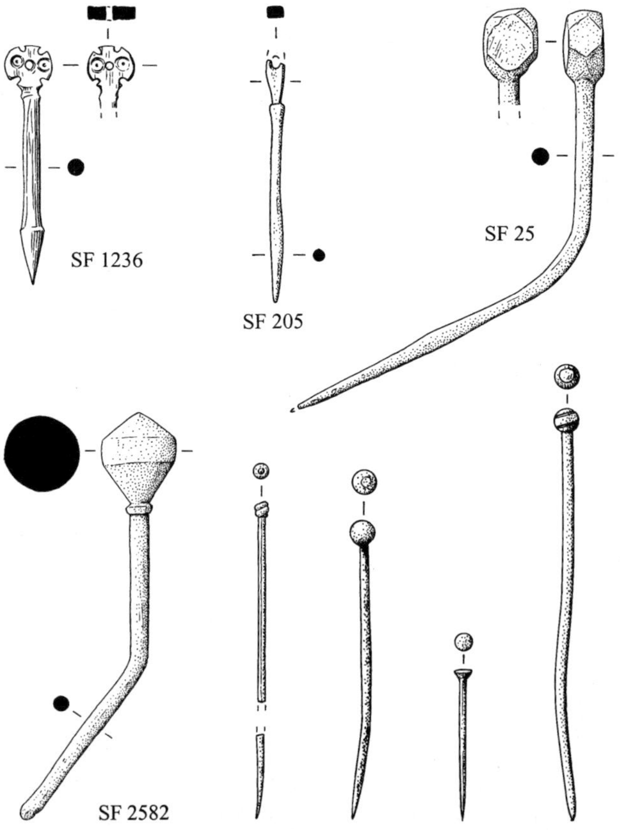

Figure 5.83 Dress pins of bone (SF1236) and copper alloy (SF2582, 25, 205, 237, 368, 1449, 1868). Scale 1:1.

also been found at Richmond Castle and Northampton Castle. A stratified group of 24 hipped pins with decorated pierced heads from Castle Acre indicates a date for these objects sometime between *c.* 1085 and the 1140s (Margeson 1982, fig 47 nos 23–46). Margeson discusses their possible function as head-dress pins with a decorative cord passing through the pierced eye. For a detailed discussion of the function of these hipped pins.

Copper-alloy pin SF205 is from a pit which contains residual 11th- and 12th-century pottery. SF1236, of bone, is from a pit which contains 12th–13th-century pottery and two 13th-century iron arrowheads (SF1531 a and b).

Drawn wire pins

A total of 99 drawn copper-alloy wire pins was recovered from Greyfriars, along with a further seven pins or needles (shafts with missing heads). Three variants of pins were recorded, distinguished from each other by the way the heads are made:

1. With wire-wound spherical heads (92 examples, including SF237 and SF1868).
2. With a spherical head, formed by a single strip wound round the top of the shaft (two found, including SF368).
3. With cap-like or 'blob' heads (five found, including SF1449): two are white-metal coated.

The pins were recovered from Periods 3, 4, 5 and unstratified deposits, with a notable concentration of wire-wound head pins coming from Period 4 (76 examples).

Drawn wire copper-alloy pins with wire-wound spherical heads are known from medieval and post-medieval deposits elsewhere. The evidence at Winchester, for example, shows they were available in the 13th century. Biddle and Barclay discuss many references to drawn wire and pin makers and the methods used to attach and shape the two or more spirals of wire around the top of the shaft to make the spherical heads (Biddle and Barclay 1990, 560–1). Pritchard (1991) discusses more than 800 pins examined from excavations in London, and notes the increase in the use of pins and change of size due to the increased availability of drawn wire by the 14th century. Pritchard also notes the surprisingly small number of drawn wire pins apparently excavated from other towns in England during this period. A total of eight were recovered at Greyfriars, although perhaps given the quantity recovered from site, surprisingly few are from Friary deposits.

Pins with large solid heads

SF25 Copper-alloy pin with facetted head, lower half of the shank bent up. L: 75mm.
fill 50258 of SFB 50242, Period 1

SF2582 Copper-alloy pin with large solid oval head and slightly pointed top. Moulding between shaft and head, point missing. L: 56mm (incomplete), diameter of head 10mm, gauge of shank 2.3mm.
unstratified

Pins with pierced heads and hipped shafts

SF1236 Bone pin with decorated pierced head and hipped shaft. The head is carved in the form of a cross; the front and back of the two side arms are decorated with a single ring-and-dot. L: 32mm, diameter of eye 1mm.
pit fill 50657, Period 2.3

SF205 Copper-alloy pin with pierced (incomplete) head, moulding between shaft and head; hipped shaft. L: 31mm (incomplete), diameter of eye 1mm.
pit fill 50017, Period 3.1

Drawn wire pins

SF237 Copper-alloy pin with wire wound spherical head, L: 26mm, and one pin shank, head missing.
pit fill 10385, Period 4.1

SF368 Copper-alloy pin with strip forming spherical head around top of shaft. L: 40mm.
unstratified

SF1449 Copper-alloy pin with cap-like head, white-metal coated.
demolition debris 30911, Period 5

SF1868 Copper-alloy pin with wire wound spherical head. L: 55mm.
layer 12099, Period 3.2

A further 97 pins, most with wound spherical heads, are not catalogued here.

Brooches

Disc brooch

by Helen Geake

(Fig. 5.84; Pl. 5.9)

The Middle Saxon copper-alloy openwork disc brooch (SF587) recovered from a post-medieval dump (Period 4.2) in Area C is one of a small group which is remarkably homogeneous. Published examples are few, but include one in the Ashmolean Museum thought to be from Suffolk (Hinton 1974, no. 14). All have eighteen lobes around the rim, but some are finished in more detail and have dots or ring-and-dots added to the bosses at the ends of the arms, making them into pairs of eyes. The corpus is a steadily growing one: those known from Norfolk, in addition to the Greyfriars brooch, include examples from Morton-on-the-Hill, Mundham,

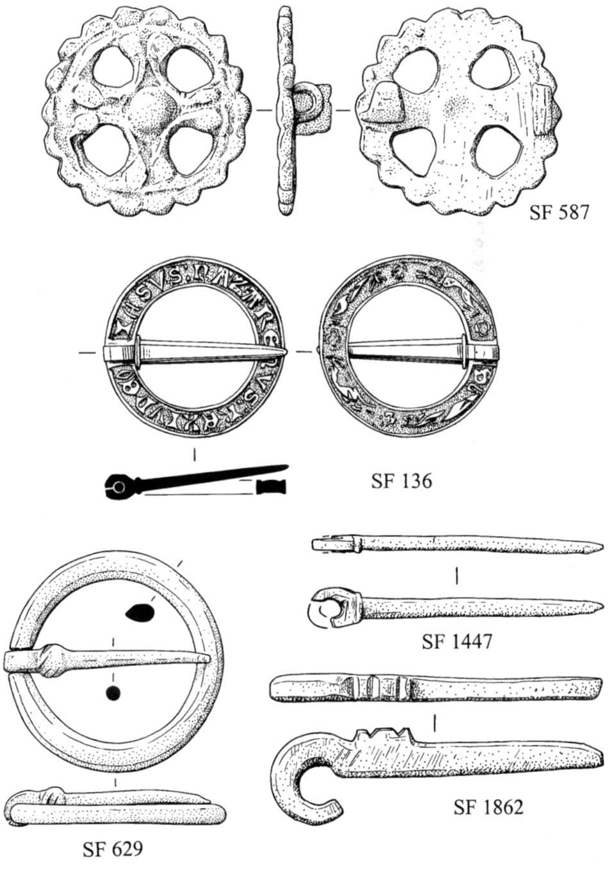

Figure 5.84 Copper alloy openwork disc brooch (SF587), gilded silver annular brooch (SF136), copper alloy annular brooches (SF629, 1447, 1862). Scale 1:1.

Plate 5.9 Copper alloy openwork disc brooch (SF587)

Plate 5.10 Gilded silver annular brooch (SF136)

Redenhall, Saxlingham Nethergate, Tattersett, Tibenham, Great Walsingham and West Acre. The West Acre example has a transverse filed catchplate on the reverse, which shows that despite their homogeneity, the brooches cannot all have been made from the same mould. A slightly different example from Trowse is 27mm in diameter but has a smooth circular shape with no lugs, a single dot at the end of each flat flaring arm and no central boss; this brooch hints that the group may have outliers. The dating of these brooches is by no means secure, most having been found by metal-detectorists, but they are thought on typological grounds to be of the 9th century AD.

SF587 Copper-alloy **openwork disc brooch**. Flat, circular and of 28mm maximum diameter, the rim is scalloped into eighteen little lobes and has a decorative groove running round it. Four approximately D-shaped holes inside make an openwork cross; each arm has a longitudinal groove and ends in a pair of low bosses. The grooves meet to make a lozenge at the centre around a low circular boss. On the reverse is a longitudinal curled-over catchplate and a plain unpierced transverse lug which looks as if it is complete. Either the hole for the pin was never drilled, or the lug was exceptionally long and has broken straight across below the hole.
layer 50584, Period 4.2

Annular brooches
by Helen Geake
(Fig. 5.84; Pl. 5.10)

The distinction used here between plain annular brooches and plain circular-framed buckles follows that given by Egan (1993, 64–5). Where there is a constriction in the frame for a pin, they are described as brooches; where the pin is free to move around the frame then they are described as buckle frames. Examples of simple annular brooches, such as SF629, are well known from medieval contexts from Norwich and elsewhere. They were used for fastening garments at the neck or worn purely as decorative features. Often the pins are found separately. As with the two examples from Greyfriars (SF1447 and SF1862), they often have some kind of moulding around the pin, close to the looped end.

The silver brooch (SF136) is one of a group of 14th-century annular brooches with religious inscriptions which were thought to have apotropaic powers. Sue Margeson, before her untimely death, described this object as 'one of the finest brooches from medieval Norwich' and speculated on whether it was lost by a visitor to the Greyfriars or whether one of the friars was wearing it in defiance of his oath of poverty. Certainly such brooches could have been worn by either a man or a woman. Many parallels are known; nineteen Scottish examples were listed by Callander (1924, 169–79) and there are others in the Museum of London and the Victoria and Albert Museum (Egan and Pritchard 1991, 255). Although some brooches with the INRI legend were said to be made (for magical reasons) from five melted-down pennies (Egan and Pritchard 1991, 255), the Norwich brooch (with its pin) seems to weigh rather more than three 18-grain pennies. A recent York find, from the Merchant Adventurers Hall, at 1.98g also bears little relationship to the weight of contemporary pennies (Kyriacou *et al.* 2004, 46–7).

SF629 Plain annular copper-alloy **brooch**, with constriction for the pin; transverse pin with moulded collar.
make-up 11163, Period 3.1

SF1447 Cast copper-alloy pin from annular brooch with moulded collar. Broken at looped end.
pit fill 30146, Period 3.1

SF1862 Cast copper-alloy pin from annular brooch with moulded collar.
layer 12129, Period 4.2

SF136 Gilded silver annular brooch. The frame is flat and circular, 23 mm in diameter and 4 mm broad. A gilded silver pin swivels on a constriction; it has a projecting moulding at the base of the loop and the loop is open at the back. There is no obvious pin rest. The brooch frame is decorated on both faces. On one, there is a neatly made relief legend reading in Lombardic letters IESVS: NAZARENVS: REXIVDEO (Jesus of Nazareth King of the Jews) — the inscription which was fixed to Christ's cross at the Crucifixion. The other face is decorated with relief flowers and leaves between a dog chasing a hare. Wt: 3.9g (60 grains).
unstratified

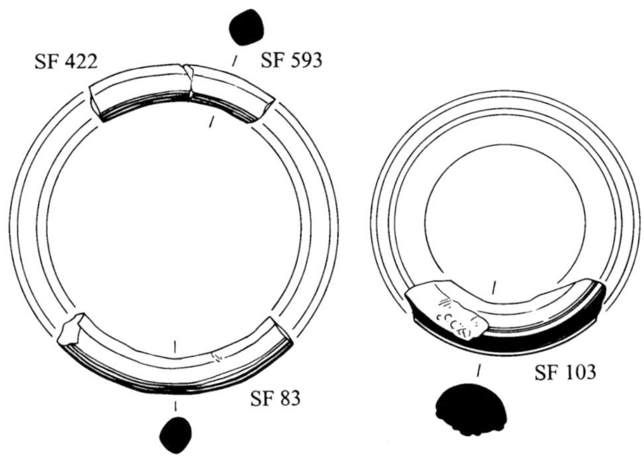

Figure 5.85 Shale bracelets (SF 83/422/593, 103). Scale 1:2.

Bracelets (shale)
by Julia Huddle
(Fig. 5.85)
Four pieces of shale were found, three coming from the same bracelet (SF83, SF422, SF593) and deriving from deposits associated with the backfilling of the sunken-floored building *10049* in Area A. The fourth piece (SF103) was recovered from a cleaning layer in Area C.

The use of shale, and more particularly jet, for jewellery is known in the Late Saxon period. A fragment of a jet finger ring was recovered from an 11th-century context at the north-east bailey of Norwich Castle (Margeson and Williams 1985, fig. 29 no. 1). Jet arm and finger rings from this period are known elsewhere in England, Dublin and the Scandinavian countries (Roesdahl and Wilson 1992, cat. nos 75, 154, 329, 396, and 409). A pit beside Wood Street, London contained waste from the manufacture of shale finger rings and this is provisionally dated to the late 11th or early 12th century (Pritchard 1991, 154, fig. 3.38).

A Roman jet bracelet with similar grooves and ridges to SF103 was found in Anglo-Saxon deposits in Colchester (Crummy 1983, 36, fig. 38 no. 1559). The Greyfriars piece is similar to Lawson's type 41a and b (Lawson 1976, 243). Objects of shale, including lathe-turned armlets, are well known in Roman Britain. The Greyfriars piece is very small, with an estimated internal diameter of 40mm, and may have been a child's bracelet or worn as a hair ring or dress fastener (Lawson 1976, 247). A small quantity of Roman pottery was also found on site, in particular from Area C: this piece may similarly reflect nearby Roman activity in the area of the medieval city, or was perhaps picked up alongside Romano-British ceramic building material used on site in the Late Saxon period, which is thought to have been robbed from nearby *Venta Icenorum* (Caistor St Edmund, a few kilometres south of Norwich).

SF83 Three fragments of a shale bracelet of sub-rounded cross-section. Two pieces adjoining and a third part of the same bracelet.
SF422 Reconstructed external diameter 80mm, internal diameter 60mm.
SF593 SF83 backfill 10618 SFB 10049, Period 2
SF422 fill 10337 SFB 10049, Period 2
SF593 backfill SFB 10049 10725, Period 2
SF103 Fragment of a lathe-turned shale ring of sub-oval cross-section with latitudinal grooves and ridges on the outer half of the ring. Estimated external diameter 70mm, internal diameter 40mm.
surface cleaning 50001

Fasteners
by Julia Huddle

Hooked tags (copper alloy)
(Fig. 5.86)
Hooked tags were probably used to fasten garments and accessories and are known from the 7th century (Webster 1991, 235), but are especially common from the 9th–11th centuries. For a discussion on Late Saxon hooked tags see Margeson and Williams (1985, 29). Margeson considers the three basic types — circular, triangular and lobed — and how they seem to have been used from the 9th to the 11th centuries for a variety of purposes (Margeson 1995, 56). The three hooked tags found at Greyfriars are all are the 'triangular type', rather than the circular-plate type or the type with lobes. Two of the tags are from Area C, one from Period 3.1 (SF37), and another (SF432, not illustrated) found in a pit close to sunken-featured building *50242* from Period 2.2. The other tag (SF618) from Area B is unstratified. Similar tags to the three at Greyfriars have been found elsewhere in Norwich. SF37, with its nicked edges, incised borders and ridged where the hook develops from the plate, is almost identical to one found at Norwich Castle's north-east bailey, which on the basis of a comparison has been given a probable 10th-century date (Margeson and Williams 1985, 28, fig. 24 no. 5). Two from excavations at Castle Mall (one from an 11th-century context) are very similar to (SF618) each being decorated with short punched lines forming a double-line border and further double lines punched on the plate (Shepherd Popescu forthcoming: SF6142 and SF5164) and it is tempting to suggest that these three objects may have been made by the same person.

Three additional hooked tags and one blank for a hooked tag were found during the evaluation at St Faith's Lane (373N). All are unstratified apart from 373N/SF75, which came from a post-Dissolution context. All three of

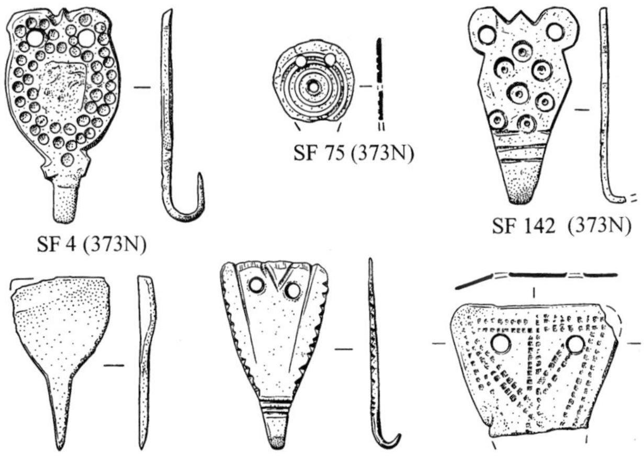

Figure 5.86 Copper alloy hooked tags (SF4, 75, 142, 143, 37, 618). Scale 1:1.

the types noted above were recovered at St Faith's Lane, and these finds form an interesting group. A circular hooked tag (373N/SF75) is similar to several others from Norwich, such as the examples found at Castle Mall (Shepherd Popescu forthcoming) and during the Norwich Survey excavations (Margeson 1993). Further afield in Norfolk, circular tags have also been found at Thetford (Goodall 1984, 69, fig. 111 nos 32 and 33) and Middle Harling (Margeson 1995, 56, fig. 39 nos 35–7), the latter being likened to others from 11th-century contexts (*ibid.*, 56). The two examples with lobes at the top and pierced for attachment (373N/SF4 and 373N/SF142) are the first of their kind (known to the author) found in Norwich. Four lobed hooked tags were recovered at Harling in Norfolk (*ibid.*, 56, fig. 39 nos 45–8) and the ring-and-dot decoration on an example from there, as seen on 373N/SF142, is apparently indicative of a 10th- or 11th-century date (*ibid.*, 56, fig. 39 no. 45). The decoration on 373N/SF4, with stamped annulets, is similar to the 'punched dots' seen on a hooked tag, although with a triangular plate, from Winchester from a late 11th–early 12th-century context (Hinton 1990a). Three unfinished hooked tags like the example from St Faith's Lane (373N/SF143) are known from Late Saxon Thetford (Goodall 1984, 69, fig. 111 nos 37–9).

373N/ SF4 Copper-alloy hooked tag with sub-circular plate with two lobes pierced for attachment and collared hook. In the centre of the plate is a panel, square on the X-ray, with the remains of enamel (?) which possibly originally had silver wire scrolls. The rest of the plate is covered with unevenly spaced stamped annulets.
unstratified

373N/ SF75 Copper-alloy hooked tag with circular plate, decorated on front with three incised concentric rings and central perforation; two attachment holes and scar from missing hook.
layer 7, Period 4.2

373N/ SF142 Copper-alloy hooked tag with sub-triangular plate decorated with stamped ring-and-dots and ridged towards the hooked end; with two lobes pierced for attachment.
unstratified

373N/ SF143 Unused blank for hooked tag. Copper alloy sub-triangular plate, with pointed but straight hook.
unstratified

SF37 Copper-alloy hooked tag, triangular plate, with escalloped end. The sides are decorated with nicked edges and contoured border. The hook is ridged where it develops from the plate; two holes for attachment.
build-up 50005, Period 3.1

SF618 Copper-alloy hooked tag, triangular plate decorated on the front with short punched lines forming a double-line border and double line down the centre and also from both corners towards the centre; two attachment holes. Hook and lower part of plate is missing.
unstratified

Chains (copper alloy)
(Fig. 5.87)

Chains were used for fasteners as well as for household purposes. SF993 and SF1245 are rather delicate and were probably used as dress fasteners. SF993 can be compared, in its method of joining, to three from London, from contexts dating from the late 13th to mid-14th centuries (Egan 1991, 320, fig. 319, nos 1593–5). SF1245 is similar in appearance to a piece of six-strand plaited chain (which is attached by a ring to a rectangular sheet that is hooked at the opposite end) from a late 14th-century context at Winchester. It is thought it may be a chatelaine (Biddle 1990, 655, fig. 178 no. 2102). The chain (SF1245) is not plaited and appears to be made up of a series of interlinking loops, the overall effect, however, being one of a tightly woven chain as with the Winchester example.

SF993 Copper-alloy chain in two pieces, made up of S-shaped links made of wire. One loop is joined onto the adjoining loop of the next link, whilst the other is joined to both loops of the opposite link. Gauge of wire 1.3mm.
build-up 30113, Period 4.2

SF1245 Inter-linked fine copper-alloy wire, forming part of a tightly woven chain. Iron concretion at one end. Gauge of wire *c.* 0.3mm.
make-up 30540, Period 3.1

Twisted fine wire
(Fig. 5.87)

SF584 is possibly braid from edging of a garment (see Crowfoot in Margeson 1993, 51, no. 371).

SF584 Two strands of twisted or plied-together fine copper-alloy wire; the ends are looped and fixed together; considerably

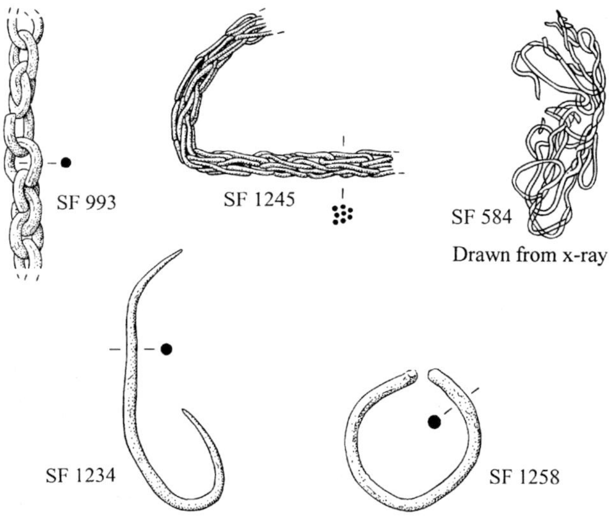

Figure 5.87 Copper alloy chains (SF993, 1245), copper alloy twisted wire (SF584) and copper alloy fasteners (SF1234, 1258). Scale 1:1.

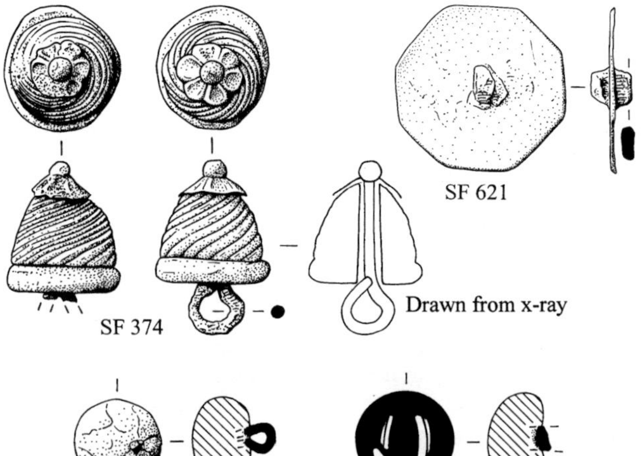

Figure 5.88 Buttons: composite glass/iron/copper alloy (SF374/912), copper alloy (SF621), pewter (SF788), glass (SF922). Scale 1:1.

distorted.
pit fill 10703, Period 3.1

Double-hooked fastener (copper alloy)
(Fig. 5.87)
SF1234, a piece of wire bent at either end with pointed ends, is a simple double-hooked wire fastener. These have been found elsewhere in Norwich from contexts ranging from the 15th to the 18th-centuries (Margeson 1993, 19, fig. 9 nos 82 and 84). Numerous examples were recovered from the Barbican well at Castle Mall, from backfills dated to the second half of the 15th century to the early 16th century (Goodall forthcoming). A possible incomplete wire loop fastener (SF1258), if correctly identified, is thought to be part of a clothes fastener. Margeson (1993) discusses their function as fasteners and their abundance in the late medieval to early post-medieval period.

SF1234 Copper-alloy wire **double-hooked fastener**.
pit fill 50601, Period 3.2

SF1258 Copper-alloy wire **loop**; possibly an incomplete wire loop fastener.
well fill 10859, Period 4.2

Buttons
(Fig. 5.88; Pl. 5.11)
A total of eight buttons was recovered from Greyfriars, all from post-Dissolution contexts. Two are cast, one of these being solid with a separate shank (SF788). Solid cast buttons are known from mid-13th to mid 15th-century contexts in London (Egan and Pritchard 1991, 274–6, cat. nos 1384–95). Metallurgical analysis of SF788 (at the Ancient Monuments laboratory) using XRF revealed high traces of copper, tin and lead. Under the microscope, however, it appears that the button, which is fissured, is pewter (being silvery throughout), and that the copper detected and visible as a green corrosion on parts of the surface of the button has probably leached out from the embedded copper-alloy shank. Many of the cast solid buttons from London with separate shanks are of bronze, with high tin or tin coating, and the shanks, if present, are all of copper alloy.

Three identical composite buttons were found (SF374 — two objects — and SF912: Pl. 5.11), all from a pit dating to Period 4.1. They are very elaborate and may indeed have been purely decorative. These ornate buttons are similar to a ?pendant bead of chalcedony from Winchester: this is suspended on a copper-alloy wire which is hooked at one end for attachment or ?suspension, and expands at the other end to form a hexagon which is set with a garnet. The Winchester item is thought to be from a piece of copper-alloy jewellery of the 14th century (Hinton 1990b, 645, fig. 174 no. 2045).

The glass button (SF922) is similar to two others (one of which still retains an iron wire loop) from Norwich, recovered from 17th-century contexts on Botolph Street (Margeson 1993, 21, fig. 11 nos 105 and 106).

SF374/ SF912 Three composite buttons, each made of moulded or twisted glass forming a spiral effect; iron wire runs through the axis of each button, and is looped at the base to form an attachment eye; a copper-alloy four-petalled finial is attached to the wire at the top of each button.
pit fill 10385, Period 4.1

SF621 Copper-alloy button made from an eight-sided sheet; incomplete loop for attachment on reverse.
floor 30122, Period 4.2

SF788 Cast pewter solid bi-convex button, with separate embedded copper alloy loop for attachment.
pit fill 30028, Period 4.2

Plate 5.11 Composite buttons (SF374/SF912)

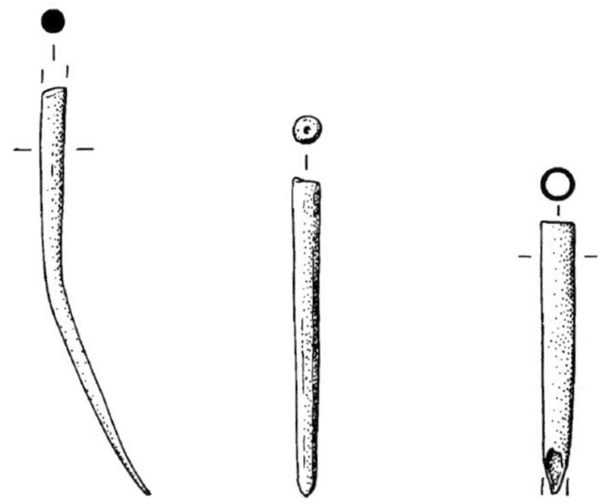

Figure 5.89 Copper alloy lace-tags (SF988, 1239, 1706). Scale 1:1.

SF922 Button, with domed head, green glass; iron stub on reverse from missing attachment loop.
pit fill 10385, Period 4.1

Lace-tags (copper alloy)
(Fig. 5.89)
Twenty-three lace-tags were recovered, of which nine came from Friary contexts, twelve from post-Friary deposits and a further two were unstratified. Margeson discusses fully the various dress functions for lace-tags (or 'aiglets'), made of sheet copper alloy, which were attached to the ends of laces, essentially to stop the ends from fraying (although by the later 16th century many were used purely ornamentally).

The typology used below follows that used by Margeson (1993, 22), which follows and extends Oakley (1979, 262–3).

Type 1: slightly tapering form with a transverse rivet at the top to secure the lace, and the edges overlapping only at the base. One from Greyfriars (SF1706) has two rivets. Mainly 15th-century, but also some 16th- and 17th-century finds (ten examples).

Type 2: cylindrical with both edges folded inwards to grip the lace along its length: date mainly 16th–17th century (SF1239) (seven examples).

Type 3: with edges overlapping along its entire length (SF988). Those illustrated by Margeson (1993, 22–3)

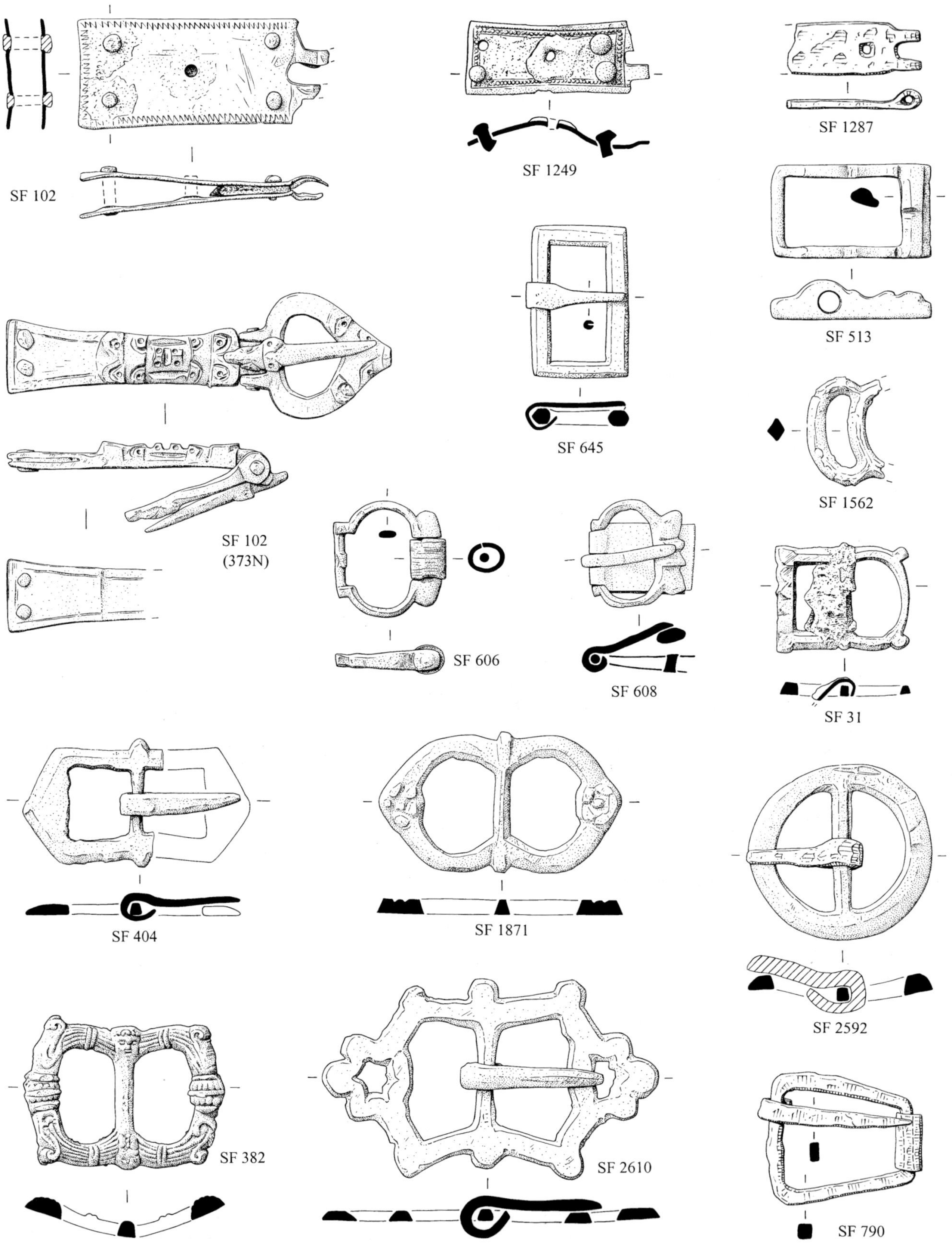

Figure 5.90 Buckles and buckle plates: copper alloy (SF102, 373N/SF102, 645, 513, 606, 608, 31, 404, 1871, 2592, 382, 2610), iron (SF1287, 790), lead-tin (SF1562), gilded copper alloy (SF1249). Scale 1:1, except SF790 (1:2).

are from later 15th/16th century contexts (six examples).

All three types occur in Period 3 deposits, although most of the Greyfriars group came from Period 4 (twelve examples, four of each type). Like many of the other objects found on site, some of those recovered from post-Dissolution contexts may equally have been in use during the Friary period.

Belt fittings and accessories

Buckle plates and buckles
by Julia Huddle and Helen Geake (373N/SF102)
(Fig. 5.90)
Twenty-five buckles or parts of buckles were found at Greyfriars, spanning the 13th century to the late post-medieval period. An important earlier buckle frame and plate came from the evaluation at St Faith's Lane. The vast majority of the examples have close parallels to items from other sites in Norwich and elsewhere. Most of the buckles were used simply as a means of fastening a strap, girdle or belt. One example (SF513) may have held a purse or knife and another, a small lead tin buckle (SF1562), may have been attached to a shoe strap. A particularly fine ornate buckle from Period 4.2 (SF382) has a parallel, dated to the late 15th–16th centuries, from Devon (Read 1995, 109–10). A spur buckle (SF31) is dated to the late 16th or 17th century and a girdle buckle is dated to the 17th century (SF2610). The latter also has an almost identical parallel in Devon.

The buckles are presented below within groups based on their descriptive similarities, and appear, as far as is possible, in chronological order. All are of copper alloy unless otherwise stated. Two late post-medieval buckles do not merit detailed publication and are not catalogued here.

Cast buckle frame and plate
by Helen Geake
The elegant and beautifully made copper-alloy buckle from the St Faith's Lane site (373N/SF102) is part of a growing corpus of Anglo-Scandinavian buckles and strap-ends decorated with multiple stylised animal heads. A close parallel was found residually at Fishergate, York (Rogers 1993, 1346–9, no. 5314). Although this lacks the pin, pin-bar and plate, both frames are similar in size and shape and both have an animal head at the pointed pin rest with nose, dot eyes, engraved eyebrows and moulded dotted ears. Rogers cites a similar example to the Fishergate buckle frame from Meols on the Wirral (Bullock 1960, 25, fig. 7g). Another buckle frame metal-detected from Norfolk, from Whissonsett (NHER 31879), has slightly different decoration; the dotted ears and eyes and engraved eyebrows are present, but there is a line of dots between the ears and above the animal head the frame is decorated with an engraved ladder pattern. The loops on the Whissonsett example are blocked with corrosion from an iron pin-bar. Given the narrowness of the pin-bars on these buckles, the strap must always have been attached by means of a plate; another has been found in Gisleham, north Suffolk (SMR ref: GSE Misc.), with a similar flattened and split attachment end, confronting animal heads and pair of loops for the pin-bar. The Gisleham plate, however, lacks the open jaws of the Greyfriars/St Faith's Lane animals, the snouts and the division between the animals being represented merely by transverse fluting.

Strap-ends of the same type appear to be more common than the buckles. Fishergate, York, has produced a fine example, but again this is a residual find (Rogers 1993, 1350–1, no. 5320). It has an animal-head terminal below two confronting animal heads, each with moulded and dotted ears, dot eyes (with an extra dot in between) and dot nostrils; Rogers cites a parallel from Cheddar (Wilson 1979, 282–3, fig. 95, 90). A 12th-century context at Coppergate, York, yielded a more unusual example with a single animal head modelled in the round (Mainman and Rogers 2000, 268–9, no. 10424). The open jaws on this strap-end mirror those on the Greyfriars/St Faith's Lane buckle plate. Parallels are given by Mainman and Rogers from elsewhere in Yorkshire, and from Northumberland, Norfolk and Scotland. Norfolk finds include a simplified example excavated in 1971 on Bishopgate, Norwich, on the other side of the Cathedral precinct *c.* 450m north of the St Faith's Lane site. This was also residual in a 12th-century context (Margeson 1993, no. 227). The decoration on the Bishopgate example consists of a pair of dots above three transverse flutes, with only the animal head at the terminal clearly defined. Further examples are known from the county's rich resource of metal-detector finds (*e.g.* from Horsham St Faith NHER 35668, Tibenham NHER 28632 and Burnham Market NHER 32087: for the last, see Gurney 2001, 702–3); an incomplete example is also known further south, from Brandon in Suffolk (Suffolk SMR BRD 075).

Mainman and Rogers, in their discussion of the Coppergate strap-end, draw attention to a distribution restricted to the Danelaw. They cite the very persuasive Scandinavian parallel of the strap-ends attached to a strap-distributor from Västergötland, Sweden (Bersu and Wilson 1966, 75, pl. XVIII C). Art-historical considerations, and the earliest contexts of excavated examples, suggest a date in the 9th century for the strap-ends and so it is probably here that we should also place the buckles. The Greyfriars/St Faith's Lane buckle and the Bishopgate strap-end are thus important early survivors of Norwich's Anglo-Scandinavian past.

373N/ SF102 Copper-alloy cast buckle frame and plate. The frame is heart-shaped, with the pointed pin rest decorated with an animal head. The head has a moulded nose, dot eyes, engraved eyebrows and moulded and dotted ears. The underside of the frame is flat and undecorated. The copper-alloy pin has a similar animal head at the loop end. The pin-bar is separate and of a darker metal; it passes through loops in the frame, plate and pin. The one-piece plate is split at the attachment end, with two copper-alloy rivets. As these are rather clumsy, and in a darker metal similar to that of the bar, they may be replacements. The plate tapers from the flatter attachment end to a zone with raised moulded decoration consisting of two confronting animal heads, most clearly seen in profile, with open jaws, turned-up noses with dot nostrils, dot eyes with engraved eyebrows, and moulded dotted ears. The underside of the plate has an engraved border. The hinge is corroded so that the plate and frame are now at an angle.
post-hole fill 48, Period 2.3

Buckle plates
Buckle plates were often attached to the buckles by folding the plate over the pin-bar, with either a slot or holes for the pin. The strap was in turn attached between the folded plate by rivets (see buckle SF608 below). As with the three examples found at Greyfriars, buckle plates are

often recovered without the original buckle. They are frequently found in medieval contexts either plain or with simple-incised or punched decoration.

SF102 Copper-alloy buckle plate on strap. The plate is broken off at the folded end, which tapers slightly; there are five rivets, two are of copper alloy, the rest are iron. The front is decorated with engraved zig-zag lines.
build-up 50042, Period 3.2

SF1249 Incomplete gilded copper-alloy buckle plate broken off at fold, only the front half remains; decorated with a beaded border; holes for five rivets, three copper alloy rivets present.
make-up 30484, Period 2.3

Buckles with plain rectangular frames

Two plain rectangular buckle frames both came from Period 4.2 deposits. A buckle similar to SF645 was found residually at Alms Lane, Norwich in a late 17th–early 18th-century pit. Examples of rectangular buckles from London (Egan and Pritchard 1991, 95, fig. 60 nos 425–33) are generally from mid–late 14th-century contexts.

SF645 Copper-alloy buckle with plain rectangular frame; copper-alloy pin made of sheet metal.
layer 11235, Period 4.2

Buckle with moulded rectangular frame

Buckle SF513 can be compared to a buckle at the British Museum (Fingerlin 1971, fig. 324 no. 229), and one from London (Egan and Pritchard 1991, 97, fig. 62 no. 445), the latter recovered from a mid–late 14th-century context. Similar examples from London discussed in Egan and Prichard 1991 have a combined pin and bar and it is suggested that the frames are similar to the 'locking buckles' with curved arms which may have held a purse or knife (see Ward Perkins 1940, 279–80, pl. LXXVII, nos 11 and 12). An arm from one of these 'locking buckles' has been recovered from a 17th-century context in Norwich (Margeson 1993, 28, fig. 13 no. 139).

SF513 Copper-alloy buckle with moulded rectangular frame and grooved pin-rest. Central bar and pin missing, but pierced holes in frame where central bar fitted.
build-up 40003, Period 4.2

Buckles with single oval frames and offset narrow bars

SF606 is almost identical to a buckle found in a mid–late 14th-century context from Billingsgate Lorry Park, London (Egan and Pritchard 1991, 73, fig. 44 no. 301). The presence of the offset narrowed bar suggests it could originally have had a buckle plate, as with SF608. A similar buckle to SF608 was found on Alms Lane, Norwich from a 13th/14th century context (Margeson 1993, 26, fig. 13 no. 130); Margeson describes this as D-shaped. These buckles, with offset narrowed bars for plates, are known in London from the late 12th to late 14th centuries and their occurrence in London and elsewhere is discussed by Egan (1991, 76).

SF606 Copper-alloy **buckle** with oval frame and offset narrowed bar; two knops and central constriction for the sheet roller; pin missing.
small find reference 30978, Period 2.3

SF608 Copper-alloy buckle with decorative oval frame with offset, narrowed bar and attached plain rectangular plate on leather strap. Four moulded knops on frame; copper-alloy pin.
unstratified

Small shoe buckle (lead/tin)

These small lead/tin buckles seem to have been used as shoe buckles and those from London are, in the main, from early–mid-15th-century contexts. For a full discussion on these buckles see Egan and Pritchard (1991, 86–7). The example from Greyfriars is from a Friary-period pit.

SF1562 Incomplete lead-tin buckle with oval double-looped frame; pin missing.
pit fill 50462, Period 3.2

Buckles with double-looped frames

Eight buckles with double-looped frames were found. All are from post-medieval contexts (Period 4.2) or were unstratified. Many of them can be compared to examples previously recovered in Norwich from early post-medieval contexts (Margeson 1993, figs 16 and 17 nos 167–75). Margeson discusses these buckles with double-looped frames, often with cast rosettes (such as SF1871), or simple mouldings on the outside edges of the frames (for the pin-rests). Often (like SF404) they incorporate lobes at the junctions of the bar and frame.

A particularly fine double-looped framed buckle (SF382) with a ?cherub head at either end of the bar was found also in a post-medieval context. A parallel for this, dated to the late 15th–16th centuries, has been found in Devon (Read 1995, 109–10).

A buckle with an asymmetrical frame (SF31) is likely to be a spur buckle and is of a type dated to the late 16th–17th centuries (Read 1995, 111, nos 696–9 — described as buckles — and 141, nos 890–8 — described as spur buckles).

A large buckle with ornate trapezoidal double-looped frame (SF2610), found unstratified, is almost identical to another from Devon. This is described as a girdle-buckle and dates to the 17th century (Read 1995, 142 no. 925).

SF31 Copper-alloy spur buckle with asymmetrical double-looped frame, one loop D-shaped the other rectangular, V-shaped mouldings on front edge and lobe at corners of back edge; central bar projects slightly at sides. Traces of mineralised leather on iron pin and central bar.
pit fill 50151, Period 4.2

SF404 Incomplete copper-alloy buckle with sub-rectangular, lipped, double-looped frame and central bar which projects at sides (only one loop survives); complete copper alloy pin.
unstratified

SF1871 Copper-alloy buckle, with oval lipped double-looped frame. Rosettes on each lip and lobes at junctions of bar and frame; central bar projects at sides, pin missing.
layer 12151, Period 4.2

SF382 Copper-alloy buckle with ornate double-looped frame, pin missing. The angled frame is ornamented with foliate decoration and a head either end of the bar. The four corners of the frame are accentuated with a leaf-scroll and the pin rests have beading either-side and between ridged mouldings.
layer 10989, Period 4.2

SF2610 Copper-alloy girdle buckle with ornate trapezoidal double-looped frame. Lobes at corners and junctions of bar and frame and three lobes set round an open star-shaped motif at each end; copper-alloy pin.
unstratified

Circular buckle-frames

Two circular buckle-frames with central bars were both found unstratified (SF2592 and SF 2622). Simple circular buckles with central bars are well known from late medieval and early post-medieval contexts from Norwich and elsewhere (*e.g.* Margeson 1993, 28–9, nos 160–1; Egan 1991, 65, nos 215–19). The angled frame, so often seen in

on double-looped buckles, is presumably deliberate, so that the strap passes more easily over the central bar and under the sides of the buckle.

SF2592 Copper-alloy buckle with circular frame and central bar; iron pin looped around bar. Angled frame.
unstratified

Buckle plates (iron)
Two fragmentary and heavily corroded buckle plates (SF1145 and SF1287) are of forms common throughout the medieval and post-medieval periods. SF1287 is tinned/plated.

Buckles (iron)
A tinned/plated trapezoidal buckle with a sheet metal roller has 15th–17th-century parallels at Basing House, Hants (Moorhouse 1971, fig. 25 no.174) and St Benedicts Street, Norwich (Goodall 1993, fig. 18 no. 200). SF810 is probably a small circular buckle but so severely corroded that the possibility of it being an intrusive ring-hook cannot be excluded. Small buckles would probably have been used on shoes (Goodall 1993, fig. 38 nos 55, 72 and 88).

SF790 Iron **buckle**.
fill 10589, Period 4.2

Strap-ends
(Fig. 5.91)

Strap-ends (copper alloy)
by Julia Huddle
Strap-ends attached to girdles, straps or belts appear to become fashionable in London in the 14th and early 15th centuries. SF1238 may be compared to a similar strap-end from Billingsgate lorry park, London (Egan 1991, 127, fig. 83 no. 582) from a mid–late 14th-century context. The form of cut-out ornament seen on the Greyfriars strap-end is similar to that on a belt-mount from Norwich from early 16th-century fire deposits on Pottergate (Margeson 1993, 39, fig. 22 no. 270).

Examples of medieval hinged strap-ends with pierced, often zoomorphic, terminals and projecting loops, are known from Norwich (Margeson 1993, 35, fig. 20 no. 239), France (Fingerlin 1971, 464, fig. 240 no. 521), London (Pritchard 1991, 154, fig. 101 nos 720–6), St Ebbes, Oxford (Goodall 1989, 226, fig. 62 no. 25) and the Austin Friars, Leicester (Clay 1981, 133, fig. 48 no. 28).

There is some debate about the function of these items. Ilse Fingerlin suggests that they are strap-ends which may form pairs which were connected by a hook and possibly a chain (Fingerlin 1971), whilst Alison Goodall suggests the example from Oxford may come from a book-binding (Goodall 1989, 223). Frances Pritchard supports the interpretation of these objects as book fasteners, given the prevalence of these items on ecclesiastical sites (Pritchard 1991, 155).

Strap-ends similar to 373N/SF5 from St Faith's Lane but with openwork decoration are found in France and the Netherlands, and date to the first half of the 15th century (Fingerlin 1971, nos 7, 138 and 139). Looped strap-ends with hinged plates are known from late 14th- and early 15th-century contexts in London (Egan and Pritchard 1991, nos 720–6), where it is suggested that they may have a specialised use on clothing or as book fasteners.

SF1238 Incomplete copper-alloy strap-end on leather strap, made of sheet metal folded widthways. The open end is decorated with grooved trefoil aperture flanked by two holes; there is one surviving copper-alloy rivet. Width of strap 23mm.
pit fill 30806, Period 3.2

SF424 Copper-alloy strap-end on leather strap; made of sheet metal folded widthways with two copper-alloy rivets. On one side the open end is notched and the face is decorated with engraved ornament in the form of dotted lines; the other side is decorated with engraved ornament in the form of illegible garbled ?lettering and 'V's along two sides.
build-up 50040, Period 4.2

SF787 Copper-alloy two-piece strap-end with hinged plate, with pierced terminal and projecting loop at the base in the form of an animal head. There are two copper-alloy rivets near open, slightly concave end; remains of leather or textile strap.
pit fill 40059, Period 3.2

373N/SF5 Copper-alloy looped strap-end. Cast in one piece, it is roughly circular with a flared upper end with facetted decoration, one large rivet hole and one small iron rivet. At the terminal is a moulded collar and then a small loop which is at right-angles to the rest of the strap-end. The strap-end is decorated with ?foliage decoration made up of small punch-marks.
layer 8, Period 3.2

Strap-ends (iron)
by Val Fryer
SF378 is the tongue-shaped terminal of a strap-end with transverse grooves and incised decoration. Traces of tinning survive. SF2124 is a simple folded sheet metal strap-end, broken across the attachment holes and again

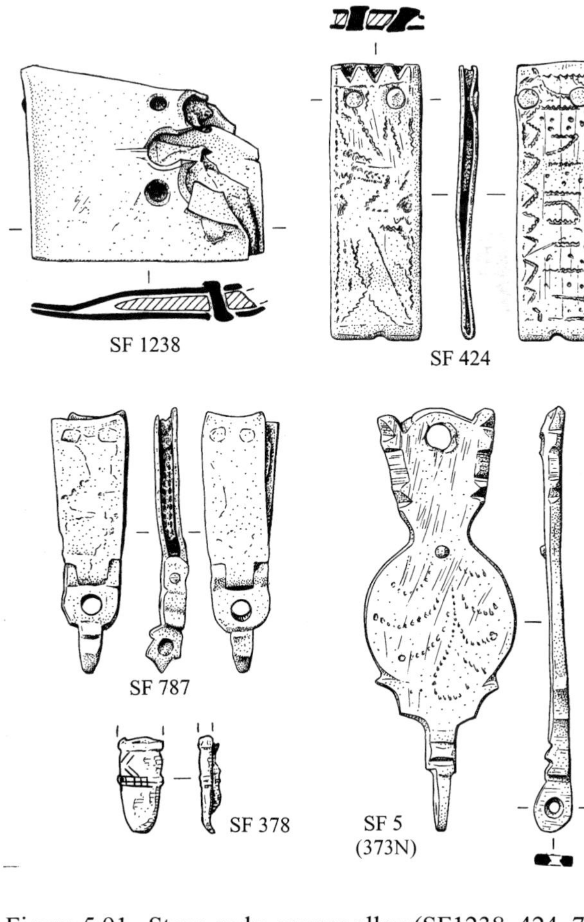

Figure 5.91 Strap-ends: copper alloy (SF1238, 424, 787, 373N/SF5), iron (SF378). Scale 1:1.

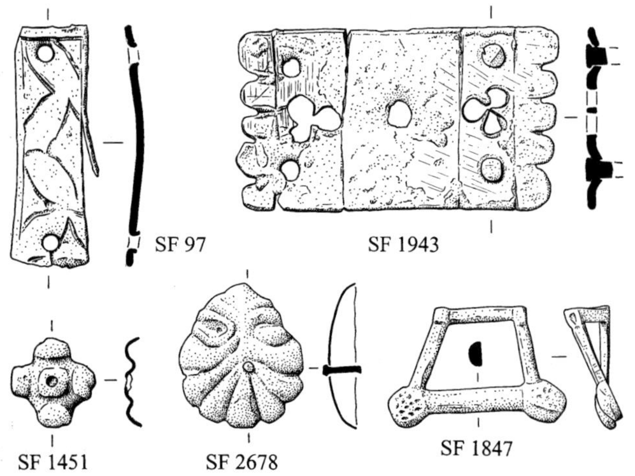

Figure 5.92 Belt mounts: gilded copper alloy (SF97, 1847), copper alloy (SF1943, 1451, 2678). Scale 1:1.

with traces of non-ferrous plating, possibly a tin/lead alloy. Both have parallels at, for example, London (Egan and Pritchard 1991, figs 84 and 85).

SF378 Iron **strap-end**.
backfill 10618 SFB 10049, Period 2

Belt mounts
by Julia Huddle
(Fig. 5.92)

Rectangular belt mounts
Rectangular belt mounts were used for stiffening belts, as well as for decoration. Some are plain but many, like the two examples from Greyfriars, are decorated with incised decoration and/or cut-out ornament. Examples are known from medieval contexts in London (Egan 1991, 196, figs 123–4 nos 1050, 1054 and 1060); those found previously in Norwich were recovered from medieval and post-medieval contexts (*e.g.* Margeson 1993, 38, fig. 22 nos 263–72).

SF97 Gilded copper-alloy belt mount, with two rivet holes. The front is decorated with two engraved four-petalled flowers, both severely truncated by trimming along one side.
pit fill 30971, Period 2.3

SF1943 Copper-alloy belt mount, with four rivet holes two of which contain copper-alloy rivets; the ends are beaded and the front is incised with four transverse lines dividing the plate into five zones; further decoration consists of a central hole and two cut-out trefoils, one towards each end.
layer 12302, Period 3.2

Repoussé belt mounts
Repoussé belt mounts recovered elsewhere in Norwich come from late medieval/early post-medieval contexts (Margeson 1993, 40, fig. 23 nos 273–80). In London, sheet copper-alloy mounts first appear in early 13th century deposits and are common in the late 14th and early 15th centuries (Egan and Pritchard 1991, 162). Two were found at Greyfriars, one in a 13th-century context (SF1451) and the other in a mid-16th-century deposit (SF2678).

SF1451 Copper-alloy quatrefoil repoussé mount, with domed centre, domed lobes and central hole for (missing) rivet.
pit fill 30914, Period 2.3

SF2678 Copper-alloy scallop repoussé mount with rivet.
robber fill 13438, Period 4.1

Pendent loop
An ornate frame (SF1847) is almost identical to one in the National Museum of Denmark, hanging from a bar-mount on a beautiful silk tablet-woven girdle (Fingerlin 1971, 362–3, fig. 409 no. 126). Pendent loops, some still attached to the bar-mounts, are found in London: see, for example, one from a late 13th–mid-14th-century context at Swan Lane (Egan 1993, 219–21, fig. 138 no. 1193).

SF1847 Gilded copper alloy trapezoidal pendent loop with two circular convex lobes, one at each outside corner, and each decorated with small punched dots.
unstratified

Personal possessions

Combs
by Julia Huddle
(not illustrated)
Three fragments of tooth-plates and one incomplete decorated connecting plate were found at the Mann Egerton site, while fragments of what was probably a single comb with simple linear decoration on its connecting plate were recovered from the St Faith's Lane site (373N).The structural terminology used here is that suggested by Galloway (1976), except following MacGregor's more recent study (1985) 'tooth-plate' replaces 'tooth segment'.

All of the Mann Egerton examples are residual from pit fills of Friary or post-Friary date, while the St Faith's Lane fragments were all found in an 11th-century post-hole. All pieces are from composite single-sided combs made of antler. This type of comb is well known from Late Saxon contexts in Norwich and elsewhere. Many examples are decorated with incised linear ornament in a similar style to SF894 and SF373N/138, with lines often occurring in pairs. An example of this decorative technique can be seen on an antler comb found from an 11th–12th-century context at Whitefriars, Norwich (Ayers and Murphy 1983, 20, fig. 19 no. 4). Composite single-sided combs are particularly well represented amongst the combs found at Thetford (Rogerson and Dallas 1984, 167–9, figs 186–7).

Evidence for comb manufacture (using both antler and bone) is presented in Chapter 5.II.

V. HORSE EQUIPMENT

Harness fittings

Side link
by Julia Huddle
(Fig. 5.93)
A side link with non-ferrous plating (SF1835) was found unstratified. Two previous examples from Norwich are both from medieval contexts, one on Westwick Street and one on Alms Lane (Goodall 1993, 225, fig. 172 nos 1820–1). Four iron side-links have been found in Winchester, where they are described as attaching the reins to the bit, from Late Saxon and early medieval contexts — two with non-ferrous plating (Goodall 1990, 1043-4, fig 334, nos. 3880, 3880A, 3881 and 3884). A complete iron snaffle bit dating to the 10th–11th century

was found at Coppergate York. Its side links are engraved and have angular bosses towards the middle (Waterman 1959, fig. 8).

SF1835 Iron with non-ferrous plating. **Side link from bridle bit** with one lozenge-shaped end loop and knop at each corner, circular loop at other end. The circular loop is worn very thin towards the end; central oval boss on stem near circular loop; flat back.
unstratified

Horse harness pendants and mounts
by Julia Huddle
(Pl. 5.12; Fig. 5.93)
The form typology of harness pendants is currently being studied by Robinson and Griffiths. The terminology used here is based on their research (Griffiths 1986).

Elaborate pendants such as SF81 and SF609 were suspended from horse harness from the peytrel (breast band), from the head stall (a fitting projecting above the horse's head) or from the crupper (a strap buckled to the back of the saddle). Fringes of tiny, often gilded, pendants (such as SF654) and bells (such as SF43) were used to decorate reins. The Greyfriars examples come from Friary and post-Friary contexts, although they are all probably 14th- or 15th-century in date (with the exception of SF1452, a possible harness mount, which is discussed separately below).

A small convex mount (SF654) may have been used in the type of 'fringing' described by Griffiths (1986). It can be compared to a ?gilded harness pendant which was recovered from a post-medieval context on King Street (Margeson 1993, 224, fig. 171 no. 1812), where it was residual. Cast mounts, with sturdy integral shanks (such as SF197) may have been attached to horse harnesses (Clark 1995, 70, fig. 53 nos 77–80).

Double-framed pendants appear to be quite rare on archaeological sites in England and none are previously known from excavations in Norwich. An elaborate, single-framed, gilded quatrefoil pendant was found residually in a post-medieval context on Botolph Street (Margeson 1993, 224, fig. 171 no. 1811). Published examples from elsewhere include a single-framed pendant

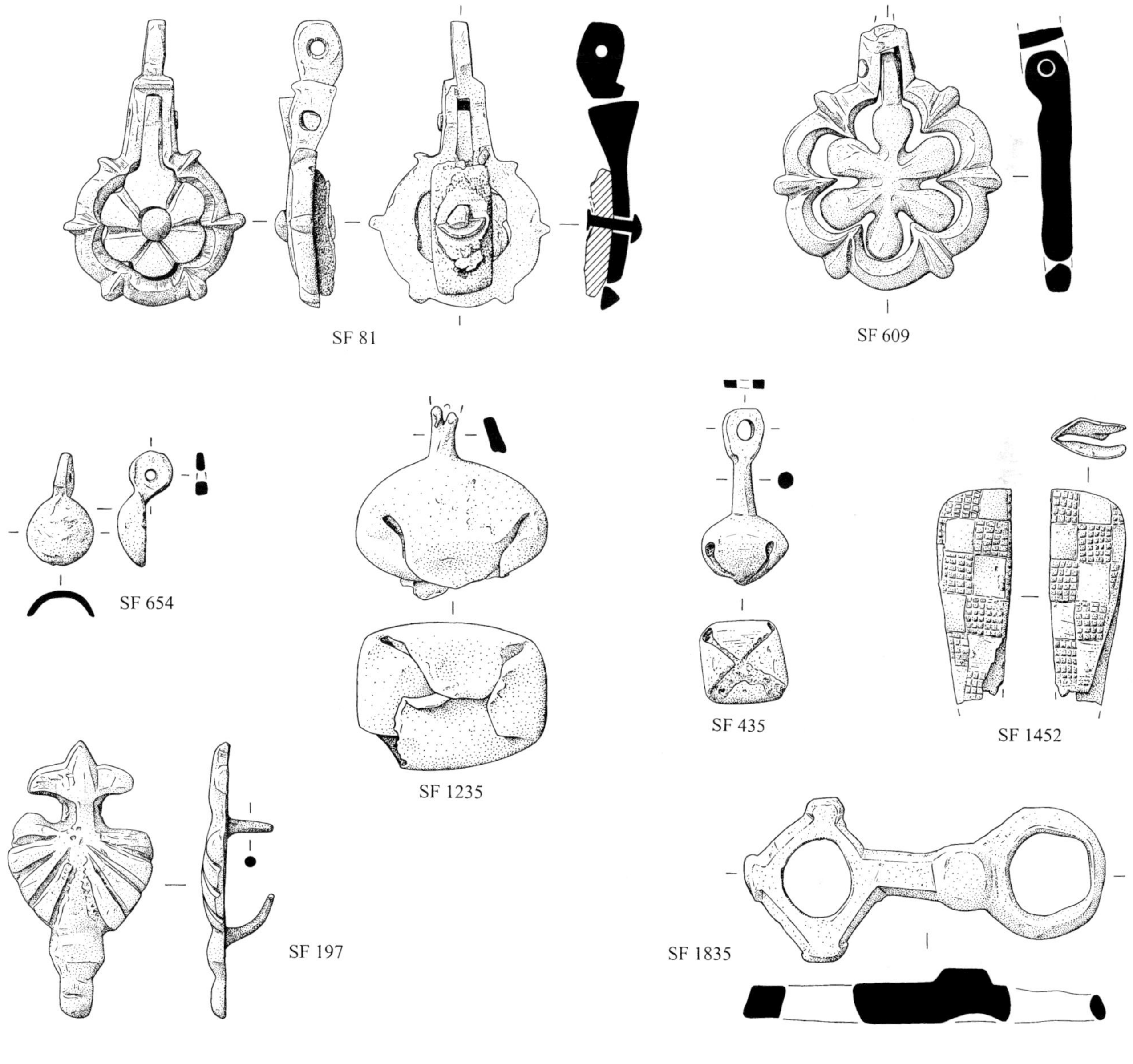

Figure 5.93 Gilded copper alloy harness pendants and mounts (SF81, 609, 654, 197), copper alloy rumbler bells (SF1235, 435), copper alloy shield-shaped mount (SF1452), iron bridle bit side link (SF1835). Scale 1:1.

Plate 5.12 Gilded copper alloy harness pendants and mounts (SF81, 609 and 197)

(Griffiths 1986, fig. 18) and an example at the Musée de Cluny, Paris (Ward Perkins 1940, 119, fig. 39 no. 2).

Two rumbler bells were recovered. The smaller example is gilded and was found unstratified (SF 435). The other is from Period 2.1 (SF1235). Both are made from a single sheet of copper alloy with four petal-like tabs cut out at the lower half, leaving metal lobes which have been pushed in at the base to enclose the iron pea. Each has a suspension arm, ?soldered into position and pierced for attachment. Rumbler bells from the medieval period seem to have been used for several purposes. A bell almost identical to SF435 recovered from excavations at Old Sarum, still attached to its mount with a stud, is dated to the 13th or 14th century. These objects were attached to swivels and hung from horse harness (*e.g.* one from Winchester: Biddle 1990, 1052, fig. 337 no. 3933), or they were used on other animals or as costume ornaments (Pritchard 1991, 336–41). SF 1235 is from a 12th-century context at Greyfriars and is slightly earlier than the London rumbler bells, which are first encountered in the early 13th century (*ibid.*, 219).

SF81 Gilded copper-alloy **horse pendant on strap**. Sexfoil lobed central portion with central copper-alloy domed rivet attached to incomplete strap on the reverse. Central portion attached by copper-alloy spindle to similarly lobed outer frame with projecting knobs and looped terminal.
unstratified

SF609 Gilded copper-alloy **horse pendant**. Sexfoil lobed central portion attached by copper-alloy spindle to similarly lobed outer frame; incomplete suspension arm.
pit fill 30156, Period 2.3

SF435 Gilded copper-alloy **bell** with long suspension arm and pierced circular terminal. The bell has four petal-like tabs; iron pea visible on x-ray.
unstratified

SF654 Gilded copper-alloy miniature convex **harness pendant**, with suspension arm and pierced circular terminal.
well fill 30693, Period 2.3

SF197 Gilded copper-alloy **harness mount** with two integral shanks on reverse; cast in the form of a shell with lobe at base and trefoil above shell.
unstratified

SF1235 Copper-alloy **bell**; slightly distorted, with suspension arm and broken at pierced terminal. The bell has four petal-like tabs; iron pea visible on x-ray.
surface 30752, Period 2

Shield-shaped mount
by Steven Ashley
(Fig. 5.93)

A copper-alloy shield-shaped mount (SF1452) is probably an item of horse furniture. The thickness of the metal and the use of engraved, rather than cast, decoration conforms to other known examples of early horse furniture from Norfolk (Ashley 2002, 5–7, figs 6 and7).

The arms displayed on the shield are *Checky*. The linear decoration, although lacking tinctures, almost certainly represents the ancient and well known arms of Warenne, Earls of Surrey (*Checky Or and Azure*). The shield, when reconstructed, is 'kite-shaped', which, when considered in conjunction with the armorial evidence, indicates a date of manufacture sometime in the second half of the 12th century. Although uncommon, further examples of armorial horse furniture from Norfolk, employing 'kite-' or 'almond-shaped' shields, belonging to the 12th or early 13th centuries, have been drawn and blazoned by the writer (Ashley 2002).

SF1452 Copper-alloy **?mount,** broken, originally shield-shaped, now folded lengthways, with no surviving means of attachment; decorated with incised lines forming a *Checky* field, each alternate square of which is filled with cross-hatched incised lines.
fill 30900, Period 2.3

Spurs

Spur (iron)
by Val Fryer
(Fig. 5.94)

A fragment of a rowel spur (SF1297) is probably of mid–late 16th-century type. The surviving side is slightly curved and missing its terminal. The rowel box is short, and its bosses and the rowel are missing. Spurs of a similar date and shape were found at Pleshey Castle, Essex (Ellis 1977, fig. 40 no. 44) and Basing House, Hants (Moorhouse 1971, fig. 21 nos 85 and 86).

SF2624 Iron **prick spur**. One side and goad surviving. Short straight D-section side with sub-circular riveted terminal. Short goad decorated with three parallel transverse ridges. Extremely short neck Traces of non-ferrous plating/tinning overall.
pit fill 13340, Period 2

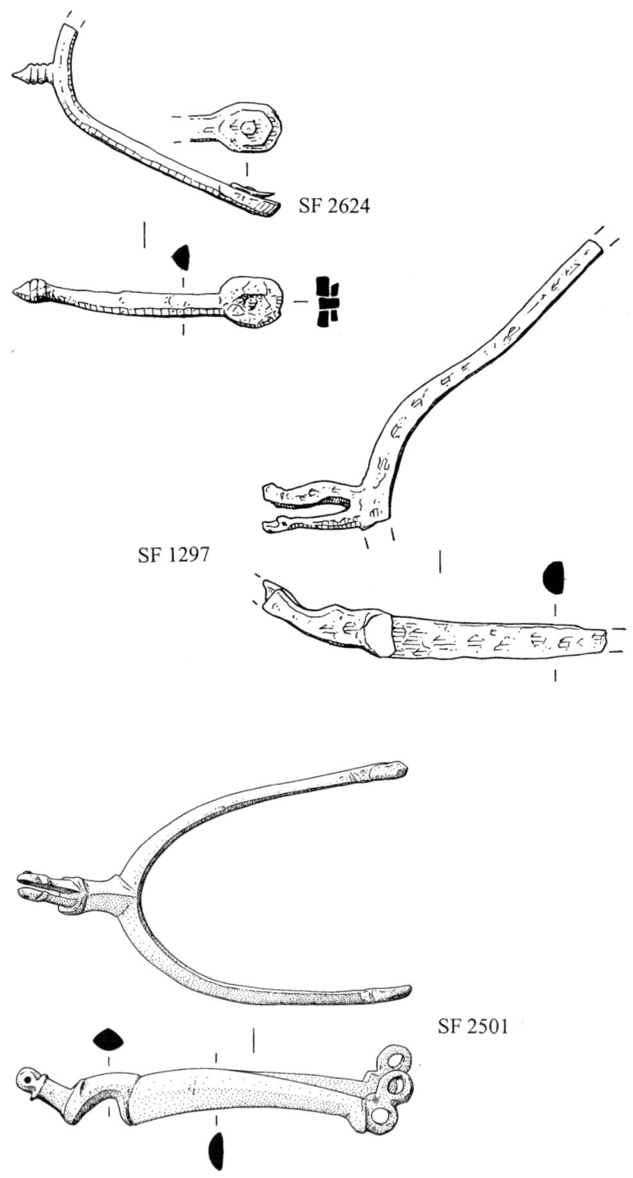

Figure 5.94 Spurs: copper alloy (SF2624, 1297), iron (SF2501). Scale 1:2.

SF1297 Iron **rowel spur**.
pit fill 30804, Period 4.2

Spur (copper alloy)

by Julia Huddle
(Fig. 5.94)

The copper-alloy spur (SF2501) is of similar proportions to two in the *Norwich Households* volume (Ellis 1993, 220–22, cat. nos 1799 and 1800), which Blanche Ellis suggests may have been made for boys. The neck is a form of the angle-neck fashion of the first half of the 17th century. For a full discussion of these rowel spurs see Ellis 1993, 220. A late 16th–17th-century copper-alloy spur buckle (SF31) is described alongside other types of buckles in Chapter 5.IV, 'Dress accessories'.

SF2501 Small copper-alloy **rowel spur**. D-section sides, with figure-of-eight terminals. The neck is a form of the angle-neck fashion, commencing as a rounded U-shaped curve with a simple moulding defining the change into the straight rowel box, a further simple moulding defining the change into the straight rowel box; a further simple moulding is set above the iron rowel pin (broken). Overall length 102mm, length of neck 31mm.
unstratified

Horseshoes

by Val Fryer
(not illustrated)
One complete iron horseshoe and four fragments were recovered. The complete example (SF999a) has narrow webs (*c.* 18mm wide), three countersunk nail holes on each arm, small calkins but little or no sinuous outline and is probably of a late 13th century type (Goodall 1993, 225, fig. 173 no. 1837). SF999b and SF649 may also be of this type. SF650 has a broader web (*c.* 33mm) and four rectangular nail holes and is of a type introduced in the 14th century. SF1389, with a sinuous outline, narrow web and small calkins, is of a late 11th–13th-century type.

VI. WEAPONS, ARMOUR AND HUNTING EQUIPMENT

Arrowheads

by Val Fryer
(Fig. 5.95)

Two socketed iron arrowheads were recovered. SF1531a has an angular blade and appears to be of a 13th- century type (see Ward Perkins 1940, fig. 16 no. 3 and fig. 17 nos 10 and 12). Such examples probably served both for military usage and hunting. SF1531b is a slender bodkin head of 13th–14th-century date, designed for piercing defensive armour. Although SF1468 resembles the form of hunting/military arrowhead which originated in Scandinavia in the 10th–11th centuries (see, for example, Williams 1988b, fig. 59 no. 21), it is impossible to determine either the exact shape or function of the Greyfriars example due to breakage. It is to be noted that the lanceolate terminals of drill bits may also adopt this form.

SF1468 Possible **arrowhead** or terminal.
fill 30275, Period 2.3

SF1531a **Arrowhead**.
pit fill 50657, Period 2.3

SF1531b **Arrowhead**.
pit fill 50657, Period 2.3

Spearheads

by Val Fryer
(Fig. 5.95)

Two iron spearheads were recovered. SF2242 is the socket and base of the blade of a spearhead, possibly of 13th–14th-century date. Although very little of the blade remains, it appears to have been of a flat leaf shape, probably designed for both hunting and military use.

SF1903 is a possible spearhead fragment. A split socket *c.* 19mm in diameter tapers to a broken square section neck. Most ferrules of this period have parallel sides and flat bases and in form this resembles the armour-piercing spear heads of the 14th century and later (see Ward Perkins 1940, pl. XVI nos 1–4). It was probably residual within the context in which it was found.

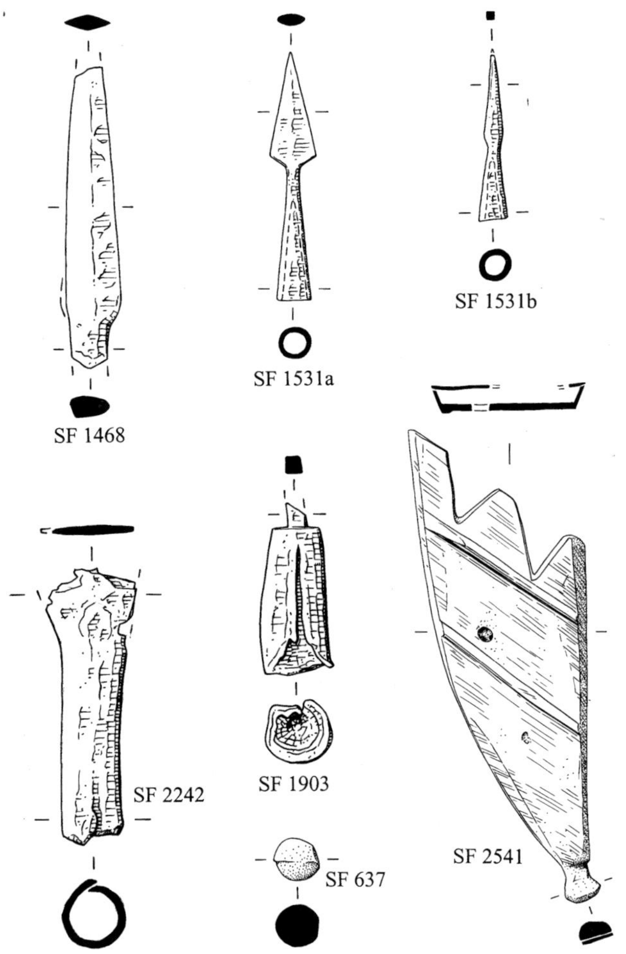

Figure 5.95 Iron arrowheads (SF1468, SF1531 a and b), iron spearheads (SF2242, 1903), copper alloy chape (SF2541) and lead shot (SF637). Scale 1:1, except SF2242 and 637 (1:2).

SF2242 **Spearhead**.
fill 50181, Period 3.1

SF1903 Possible socket of **spearhead**. L: 41mm.
fill 12169, Period 4.1

Chape

by Julia Huddle
(Fig. 5.95)

A chape (SF2541) is very similar to two shown by de Reuck (1991), which are dated to the 16th–17th centuries. The examples from London each have a single ridged diagonal line and the tops are scalloped.

SF2541 Cast, two-piece copper-alloy **chape**, of asymmetrical form. The front is decorated with two diagonal ridges; the flat top has two cut-out Vs. The terminal is knobbed. Both front and sides are covered in file marks. L: 67mm.
unstratified

Shot (lead)

by Geoff Egan
(Fig. 5.95)

Eight examples of lead shot (seven of which are uncatalogued) were recovered, of 11–24mm diameter. They were generally unstratified, although the illustrated example was intrusive in a Friary-period deposit.

SF637 **Lead shot**. D: 11mm.
fill 11204, Period 3.1

VII. DIVERSIONS

Musical instruments

Jew's harp

by Val Fryer
(Fig. 5.96)

A Jew's harp (SF349) came from a Friary-period context. It has a flattened, slightly rounded head and may be compared to several recovered from medieval deposits in London (Wardle 1998, 285, fig. 217 nos 933–6). Jew's harps are known in Europe as early as the 12th century. Parallels dating from the 14th to the 16th–17th centuries are recorded from Amsterdam (Baart *et al.* 1977, 476–7) and from Hales Hall, Norfolk (J. Read, *pers. comm.*). Two are also noted from 17th-century contexts in Paris. SF349 is largely covered in corrosion products but it is likely that a scar exists where the missing tongue would have been attached.

SF349 Iron **Jew's harp** with well formed flattened head, slightly rounded; arms have a lozenge cross-section and are ?incomplete. The tongue is lost.
pit fill 40024, Period 3.2

Tuning peg (bone or antler)

by Ian Riddler
(Fig. 5.96)

This tuning peg is similar to those of Lawson's type A, which are perforated at one end and include a squared terminal at the other (Lawson 1990, 713 and fig. 201.00). Pegs of this type derive from objects tuned from the back on the outside with the aid of a key. In this particular case, however, a key would have been fitted into the recessed hole at one end, and fastened to the copper-alloy bar.

Tuning pegs have previously been considered to originate in the Anglo-Saxon period, although stratified examples come entirely from medieval contexts (Fry 1976; Lawson 1978; MacGregor 1985, 146–7). The earliest examples include several of type A from Wallingstones, Waltham Abbey and Ipswich, which can be dated to the 12th century (Riddler forthcoming a). Thereafter, they continue in use throughout the medieval period. One other tuning peg is known from Norwich: also of Lawson's type A, this comes from unstratified deposits at Castle Mall (Huddle forthcoming).

SF290 An incomplete bone or antler cylindrical **tuning peg** which is broken at one end across a slender lateral perforation. The other end has been perforated axially and includes a small, recessed copper alloy bar of square section.
make-up 10304, Period 5

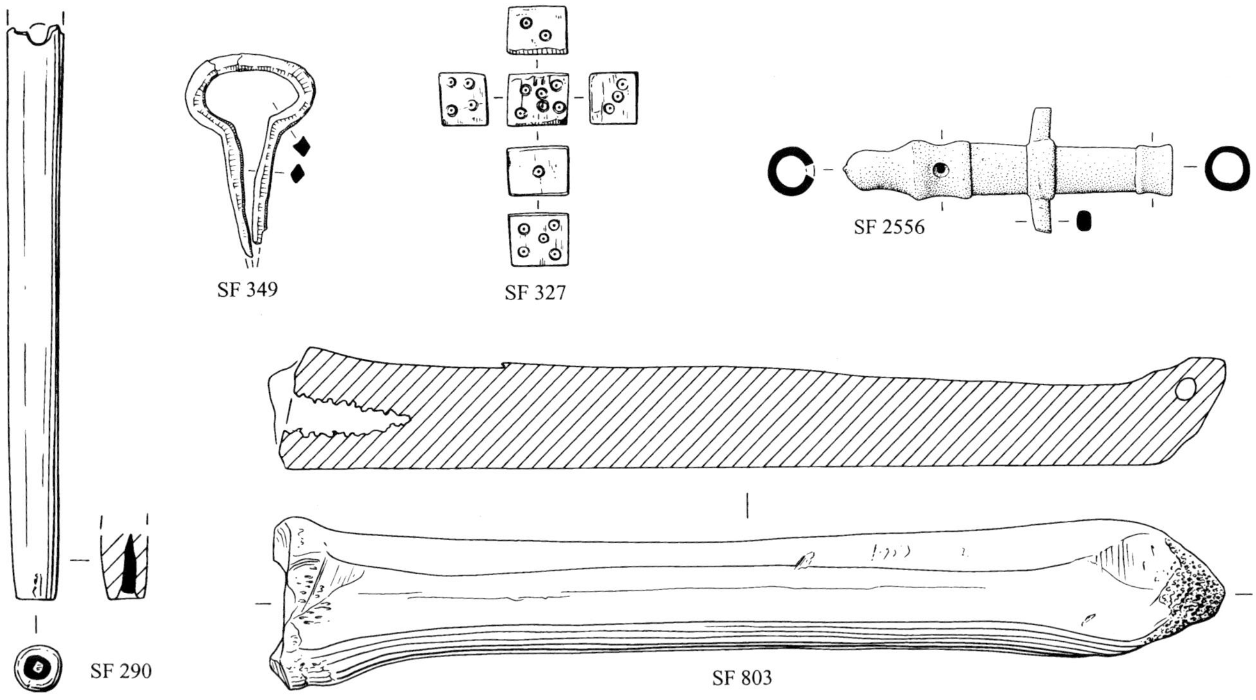

Figure 5.96 Bone or antler tuning peg (SF290, Scale 1:1), iron Jew's harp (SF349, Scale 1:2), bone die (SF327, Scale 1:1), copper alloy miniature toy cannon (SF2556, Scale 1:1), bone skate (SF803, Scale 1:2).

Games and pastimes

Die (antler)

by Julia Huddle
(Fig. 5.96)

An antler die (SF327) was recovered from a 13th-century pit fill. Previous examples of asymmetrical dice from Norwich, numbered this way, come from medieval contexts at Botolph Street, Pottergate and Castle Mall. (For a discussion of these, and of symmetrical dice, see Margeson 1993, 215–16.)

SF327 **Asymmetric die**, made of antler; each unit is represented by a ring-and-dot, arranged so that 1 is opposite 2, 3 is opposite 4 and 5 is opposite 6, the latter two being on the broader faces.
pit fill 30082, Period 2.3

Skate (bone)

by Julia Huddle
(Fig. 5.96)

MacGregor discusses the occurrence of bone skates in the British Isles from the 8th to the 13th centuries (MacGregor 1976, 57–77). Bone skates previously recovered from Thetford and Norwich sites are predominantly from Late Saxon contexts, although two from the Norwich Survey excavations are from 12th–13th-century contexts (Margeson, 1993, 218, fig. 116 nos 1789 and 1790) while one from Castle Mall is from a post-medieval deposit. Much of the pottery from the deposit in which the Greyfriars skate was found is residual (86.3%) and it is therefore possible that the skate is also a residual Late Saxon item within a medieval context.

The Greyfriars skate (SF803) is perforated at both ends to help fasten it to the foot, as are the two from the Norwich Survey excavations. In addition there are transverse grooves cut on the upper side of the skate to improve the foothold of the skater. This grooving is noted on several bone skates, for example some of those reviewed by MacGregor (1976. 59) and one from the Waterfront Bank site, London (Vince 1991, 208, fig. 3.91 no. 253).

SF803 Bone **skate** with pointed upswept toe. Axial hole at heel (proximal) end and horizontal hole at toe (distal) end. The posterior surface is cut with rough transverse lines; the anterior surface is highly polished and flattened. Horse metatarsus. L: 245 mm.
fill 30257, Period 2.3

Toys

Miniature cannon

by Julia Huddle
(Fig. 5.96)

A miniature toy cannon (SF2556) was found unstratified. Geoff Egan discusses the popularity of miniature toy cannons, starting probably from the 17th century and continuing until very recently (Egan 1996). One example from Amsterdam is dated to the first half of the 17th century (Baart *et al.*, 1977, 469, 901). At least two 18th-century (copper-alloy) toy cannons are recorded in the Norfolk Historic Environment Record. The majority of cannons are of copper alloy, although one of iron and some of lead are also known (Baart *et al.* 1977). The Greyfriars example may well date to the 18th century.

SF2556 Copper-alloy cast **miniature toy cannon**, with two trunnions for mounting in gun carriage, ?high tin content. L: 43.5mm.
unstratified

6. Zooarchaeological and Botanical Evidence

Important note: Assessment and related analysis of the faunal and avifaunal remains, as well as plant macrofossils, was undertaken prior to the realisation that archaeological evidence dating to the 13th century did not link directly to occupation by the Friary from 1226, which did not extend into the area of the excavation until the 1290s (see Chapter 1.III). Revision of the relevant reports was proposed but did not prove possible. The texts and data included here therefore include contexts assigned broadly to Period 3, spanning the whole period *c.*1226–1538 (later revised to become Periods 2.3, 3.1 and 3.2).

I. HUMAN BONE

by Francesca Boghi
(Pl. 2.5)

Human remains were recovered from two contexts in Area B: grave cut *31008* (Period 2.1) contained a single inhumation burial (skeleton *30702*) and a few residual human bones found within make-up deposit *30614* (Period 4). Collectively, they represent the remains of at least three individuals.

Skeleton *30702* was recovered in supine position within grave cut *31008*. This was located immediately to the north of the later precinct wall of the Friary (*30906*) and is probably of 12th-century date. The skeleton was partially complete with 50–75% of bone elements present and had well-preserved bone cortex, but was severely fragmented.

The remains of two other individuals were recovered from make-up deposit *30614* which overlay the upper fills of a quarry pit (*30530*: Period 3.1). This context had a late 14th-century *terminus post quem* and was located *c.* 4m to the north-east of the grave. Although it is possible that the human remains from this deposit derived from earlier graves within the Friary precinct disturbed by the quarry pit, they also may have derived from excavation of foundation trenches elsewhere within the precinct. The remains consist of the right forearm bones of a child (3–12 years) and the left femoral head of an adult of indeterminate sex.

Skeleton *30702*

This skeleton was that of a late adolescent female (16–20 years). Although the skeletal development of this individual showed some post-cranial epiphyses still open or partially fused, those of the long bones were completely closed, indicating that she had reached a full adult stature. This was calculated at 1.64m (Trotter 1970).

Despite the fact that the available skeletal evidence gave no clues as to the cause and manner of death of this individual, a number of pathological conditions were recorded. These may be taken as indicators of levels of metabolic stress, health status and activity. A metabolic condition, enamel hypoplasia, was present on 2/7 teeth. Enamel hypoplastic defects are the result of a disruption in the enamel formation process and may be caused by acute stressful episodes such as major febrile infections and/or dietary deficiency of vitamins A, C and D, as well as by a number of other factors including premature birth and stress following weaning (Aufderheide and Rodriguez-Martin 1998, 407). Since enamel formation occurs from birth to about 12 years of age and given that enamel lesions cannot be resorbed, they form a permanent record of episodes of stress occurring in childhood (Larsen 1997, 44; Lewis 2000, 46).

Spinal joint disease was recorded in the form of Schmorl's nodes. They were present on both superior and inferior aspects of 5/23 vertebrae showing a marked to moderate expression. These defects occur as the result of the prolapse of intervertebral disc material into the vertebral body, creating a depression in the articular surface of the vertebral body which is visible in dry bone. They normally reflect traumatic events associated with an overload of the weight-bearing capacity of the spine and/or the weakening of the vertebral bodies as a consequence of ageing, although other factors may be implicated too (Roberts and Manchester 1995, 107). In a young individual, injury following repeated loading activity is the most likely cause.

Slight traces of periostitis were observed on the left fibula. This is a very common skeletal inflammatory response to a bacterial infection which enters the body either near the area of the skeletal change, as in the case of a traumatic injury, or travels through the bloodstream from elsewhere in the body (chest, ears, throat). It may also reflect venous stasis, as in varicose veins (Roberts and Manchester 1995, 126). Infection resulting in periostitis is rarely fatal, especially when localised within a single bone (Larsen 1997, 84). The lack of evidence of remodelling and healing of the lesion indicates a recent event.

Localised hyperostosis of the endocranial surface was recorded on the left parietal bone along the sagittal suture (120mm max. thickness). Hyperostosis of the endocranial surface of the frontal bone has been linked to pituary gland disorders believed to occur shortly following pregnancy (Roberts and Manchester 1995, 182). Unfortunately the absence of all cranial bones apart from one fragment of left parietal bone and one fragment of mandible makes it difficult to diagnose this skeletal variation. A number of other pathological conditions result in localised hyperostosis (see Ortner and Putschar 1981, 294). However, these are associated with extra-cranial manifestations as well as osteo-clastic activity, which were absent in this skeleton.

While the remains lay within the Friary precinct as defined by its southern flint boundary wall, stratigraphic evidence suggests that these remains are associated with the churchyard of St John the Evangelist which lay at the corner of King Street and Rose Lane (see Chapter 2.IV, 'Churches'). The position of the redeposited human skeletal remains in a make-up layer sealing the quarry cut may indicate that the churchyard extended at least 70m from King Street and 59m from Rose Lane at some time in the 12th or 13th centuries. Surrounding graves had presumably been truncated, possibly either during landscaping associated with the laying out of the enlarged Friary precinct (*c.* 1300) or as a result of more recent horticultural activity.

With regard to articulated skeleton *30702*, the lack of skeletal evidence for the cause and manner of death is very common in skeletal material. It reflects the fact that some of the most common causes of death in past populations — such as acute fulminating forms of infection as well as soft tissue injuries — do not leave bone lesions.

II. MAMMAL BONE

by Marta Moreno-García
(Figs 6.1–6.6)

Introduction

A total of 14,565 hand-recovered fragments of mammal bone (weighing 179.5kg) was analysed, spanning Periods 1 to 4.1. This total includes the avian and fish bone

	Period							
	1	*2.1*	*2.2*	*3*	*3.1*	*3.2*	*4.1*	*Total*
NISP	2012	2170	564	4637	236	4179	767	**14,565**
% fragments	13.8	14.9	3.8	31.8	1.6	28.7	5.3	
Wt (kg)	32.208	21.633	7.534	43.220	3.737	56.629	14.612	**179.573**
% Wt	18	12	4.2	24.1	2.1	31.5	8.1	

Table 37 Distribution of fragment numbers and weights by period (see footnote)

	Period															
	1		*2.1*		*2.2*		*3*		*3.1*		*3.2*		*4.1*		*All periods*	
	NISP	*%*	*NISP*	*%*	*NISP*	*%*	*NISP*	*%*	*NISP*	*%*	*NISP*	*%*	*NISP*	*%*	*NISP*	*%*
Mammal	1899	94.4	1650	76	510	90.4	3757	81	220	93	3303	79	749	97.6	12,088	83
Bird	91	4.5	287	13.2	45	7.9	610	13	12	5	766	18	18	2.4	1829	12.6
Amphibian	5	<1	3	<1	-	-	2	<1	-	-	3	<1	-	-	13	<1
Fish	17	<1	230	10.6	9	1.6	268	6	4	2	107	2	-	-	635	4.3
Total (no. frags)	**2012**		**2170**		**564**		**4637**		**236**		**4179**		**767**		**14,565**	

Table 38 Total number of bone fragments for all classes of animal (by period)

	Period						
	1 (<1100)	*2.1 (1100–1200)*	*2.2 (1100–1300)*	*3 (1226–1538)*	*3.1 (1226–1400)*	*3.2 (1400–1538)*	*4.1 (1538–1566)*
Domestic Mammals							
Horse (Equus caballus)	32	2	1	3 (2)	-	6 (1)	3
Cattle (Bos taurus)	220 (21)	237 (44)	83 (8)	356 (60)	32 (3)	470 (29)	292 (21)
Sheep (Ovis aries)	11	3	1	21	1	5	-
Goat (Capra hircus)	1	-	-	18	1	1	-
Sheep/goat (Ovis/Capra)	141 (24)	251 (26)	28 (10)	280 (51)	13 (6)	270 (14)	95 (2)
Pig (Sus scrofa)	265 (26)	130 (19)	59 (16)	290 (43)	19 (2)	212 (26)	28 (3)
Dog (Canis familiaris)	22	9	2	7	-	42 (14)	1
Cat (Felis catus)	4	2	4	129	-	20	-
Total domestic mammals	**696 (71)**	**634 (89)**	**178 (34)**	**1104 (156)**	**66 (11)**	**1026 (84)**	**419 (26)**
Wild mammals							
Red deer (Cervus elaphus)	-	1	-	-	-	-	-
Fallow deer (Dama dama)	-	-	-	1	-	10	3
Deer sp. (Cervus sp.)	1	4	1	3	2	-	-
Fox (Vulpes vulpes)	-	-	-	-	-	-	1
Hare (Lepus sp.)	-	5	-	6	-	2	-
Rabbit (Oryctolagus cuniculus)	1	-	-	16	1	84	1
Badger (Meles meles)	-	84	-	-	-	-	-
Rat (Rattus sp.)	-	1	-	5	-	15	-
Total wild mammals	**2**	**95**	**1**	**31**	**3**	**111**	**5**
Oxo (horse, red deer & cattle size)	14	1	1	36	1	46	-
Lar (red deer & cattle size)	487	395	116	974	67	1068	201
Sma (roe deer, sheep/goat size)	577	387	144	1189	68	797	82
Tim (tiny mammal)	-	1	-	5	-	3	-
Unidentified mammal	123	138	70	418	15	252	42
Total no. fragments	**1899 (71)**	**1650 (89)**	**510 (34)**	**3757 (156)**	**220 (11)**	**3303 (84)**	**749 (26)**

Table 39 Total mammal remains (NISP) from all periods; teeth in brackets.

discussed by Nicholson below. Initial quantification of this material amounted to 1829 bird bone fragments and 635 fish bone fragments, leaving a total of 12,088 mammal bone fragments, alongside 13 amphibian fragments which are analysed here. Table 37 shows the distribution of fragment numbers (NISP) and weights by period, while Table 38 shows the total number of bones for all classes of animal by period (including avian and fish bone). It is evident that Friary deposits (spanning the 14th century to 1538) yielded the majority of bone (nearly 103.5kg: 9,052 fragments); Saxo-Norman/early medieval levels produced 54kg (4,183 fragments) and post-medieval contexts 8kg (767 fragments).

Animal bone fragments were identified and counted by skeletal element for each taxon using the NISP method of quantification (Grayson 1984). Although attempts were made to identify the bone to taxa level, this was not always possible with some skeletal elements such as longbone shafts, ribs, vertebrae and skull fragments. These were recorded under additional categories: for example 'oxo', which comprises animals of large artiodactyl and perissodactyl size (*e.g.* horse, red deer and cattle); 'lar', which includes large artiodactyles (red deer, fallow deer and cattle); and 'sma', representing beasts of smaller size, such as sheep, goats, roe deer, pigs and dogs. Further details of the methodologies used during analysis are lodged in the project archive.

Generally, the assemblage was not very well preserved, with the exception of the remains from a few specific contexts, such as the two pits recorded in Area CB (Period 3.2). Equally the faunal remains from two post-medieval pits in Area D show high percentages of well-preserved bone (cattle 67%; sheep/goat 66% and pig 75%). In addition, bones from Period 3 and 4.1 show the highest rates of recent breakage within the whole assemblage. Thus, cattle bones have suffered much damage during excavation (27% and 20% of the total cattle bone fragments for Periods 3.2 and 4.1 respectively were recently broken).

Gnawed bones were recorded in all periods and for all taxa. All the gnawing seems to have been by carnivores, particularly dogs, although rodent tooth marks were observed on some sheep/goat bones. The highest incidence of gnawed marks was recorded for cattle during Period 3.1 (16%) and sheep/goat during Period 2.1 (12%). Among pigs, the incidence of gnawed marks was low. This may relate to the fact that most of the pigs consumed at Greyfriars were still juveniles and it is likely that their bones would have been consumed totally by dogs (Stallibrass 1990).

The species

The distribution of animal bone fragments by taxa has been calculated for Periods 1 to 4.1 and tabulated in Table 39. The 'lar' and 'sma' categories are the most abundant bone fragments in period assemblages except within Period 4.1. Since the identifiable fraction of the assemblage is dominated by the three main domesticates (cattle, sheep/goat and pigs), and since wild animals are very scarce, it can be assumed that the 'lar' and 'sma' categories mainly represent cattle and sheep/goat, respectively. Horse, dog and cat are the other domestic taxa present. The wild mammals identified are red and fallow deer, fox, hare, rabbit, badger and rat. It is only the rabbit which seems to have made a contribution to the diet in Period 3.2. The partial skeleton of a badger recovered in context *13271* (Period 2) had been thrown into a cess-pit after having been skinned (indicated by the fine knife cuts displayed on several anatomical elements).

Bones identified to taxa make up over one-third of the total number of fragments from all periods, except for Period 4.1 where they represent more than half the total sample. The other two-thirds comprise mainly fragments from the 'lar' and 'sma' categories. These results indicate that most of the assemblage is probably domestic rubbish. Evidence for antler- and bone-working is presented by Huddle in Chapter 5.II. Four additional sawn fragments of deer antler were recovered from three of the Period 2.1 pits adjacent to sunken-featured building *50242* in Area D.

The highest percentage of unidentified mammal bone occurs in Period 2.2: this may be related to the disturbed nature of many of the contexts assigned to this phase.

In order to estimate the relative importance of the main three domesticates, their remains were analysed using different quantitative methods: the number of identified specimens per taxa (NISP), the minimum number of individuals (MNI) and the indicators (ID) method (Rackham 1986; Moreno-García *et al* 1996). All contexts related to the entire Friary period (Period 3) were considered together (although NB see note above).

On the basis of fragment counts for the Saxo-Norman contexts, pig (41.5%) is the most abundant of the domestic taxa, followed closely by cattle (34%) and then sheep/goat (24%). In the early medieval period, pig declines in favour of sheep/goat and cattle increases slightly. These proportions change again with the establishment of the Friary. Cattle are the dominant species followed by sheep/goat, and pigs remain at a similar level (26%) in relation to the previous period. In the post-medieval contexts of Period 4.1 there is an absolute dominance of cattle (over 70%). Pig is the species that shows an enormous decline with the establishment and development of the Friary, while sheep/goat remain at a similar level.

If these results are compared to those based on MNI, some differences are evident immediately. For Period 1, sheep/goats (37%) outnumber cattle (23%), while pigs are predominant (40%). The MNI results for Period 2.1 support the importance of sheep/goat in relation to cattle. Ovicaprid remains account for nearly half the total sample, followed by cattle and then pig. In the Friary period sheep/goat appear as the most abundant taxa although they are slightly less dominant than in the previous period, with a corresponding small increase in cattle and pig. Despite the small MNI in Period 4.1 (18), the data agree totally with the results from the NISP count method. Cattle are the dominant species followed by sheep/goat and pig.

The different proportions derived from the two quantitative methods are interesting, for several reasons. Firstly, they indicate how recovery biases affect different taxa (Payne 1975). Small bones such as carpals, tarsals, phalanges and even vertebrae were rarely recovered for sheep/goat. Thus, on the basis of the number of fragments, there is a bias towards cattle. Secondly, the results from the MNI method point to sheep/goat bones being less damaged than those of cattle, leading to a bias towards sheep/goat. Since the MNI method is based on the number of right and left bones for each anatomical element, it is clear that fragmented bones are more difficult to assign to one or the other side. As has already been mentioned, recent breakage affected a higher proportion of cattle bones than sheep/goat. In addition, although the types of chop marks recorded are not very different for both taxa, the butchery was carried out in different areas of the bones. Cattle longbones were chopped mainly at the joint, so that proximal and distal epiphyses were highly fragmented and could not be assigned easily to the right or left side. By contrast, sheep/goat bones were chopped mainly through the diaphysis, and if the epiphyses were touched, it was only by a single blow.

If indicators are considered, cattle are the most important taxa (41%) followed by sheep/goat (33%) and then pig (26%) for the Saxo-Norman period. The lack of first phalanges, which count as indicators, has ensured sheep/goat follow cattle closely in this period. In the Friary contexts, cattle have been relegated to second place and sheep/goats are predominant. In this case, the damage caused to cattle bones during the excavation and differences in butchery practices are partly responsible. Relatively few distal ends of cattle bones were intact, so fewer bones could be counted as indicators.

The proportion of pig in the assemblage was not free from bias. Most pig remains were from young animals in all periods. Their bones would have been smaller than those of an adult sheep and this — and their fragility due to being unfused — would have led to poor preservation. However, pig bones can be identified to taxa level more easily than those of ovicaprids and it is likely that most of the fragments recorded under 'sma' belong to sheep/goat, in such a way that if they were added to this taxon the difference between sheep/goat and pig would be smaller. Despite all these problems, it appears that pig was relatively more important in the Saxo-Norman period than in medieval and post-medieval times. According to any of the three quantitative methods used, cattle and sheep/goat outnumber it in importance in the Friary contexts.

To conclude, there is no doubt that the greatest amount of meat consumed at the site in all periods must have come from cattle. However, in order to estimate more accurately the proportions in which beef, mutton and pork contributed to the diet, it is necessary to examine the proportions of skeletal elements that are present in the assemblage (see below). The amount of bone from game species (deer, hare and rabbit) was extremely small, so that their contribution to the diet must have done little more than provide variety.

Skeletal proportions

Skeletal elements were arranged in three categories according to the relative quality of meat yield (Uerpmann 1973). Thus, the high-quality meat bones are scapula, humerus, pelvis, femur, vertebrae and ribs. Meat of lesser quality is provided by tibia, radius, ulna, skull (brain), maxilla and mandible (cheek meat and tongue). Finally, horn cores, metapodia, carpals, tarsals and phalanges are regarded as low-quality meat or waste bones. The same grouping of periods used in the previous section is adhered to below.

Cattle

The anatomical analysis is set out in Appendix 6. 'Lar' bones have been tabulated next to those of cattle, since the probability of them being red deer is very low.

As can be seen, the total proportion of meat and waste bones is very similar among Period 1, 2 and 3. In Period 4.1 there was a much higher proportion of meat-bearing bones than in previous periods. Overall, meat-bearing bones are present in higher proportions than waste bones. Using the meat quality categories, differences become apparent among periods. The high-quality meat percentage for cattle increases over time (26% Period 1; 28% Period 2; 39% Friary period; 47% Period 4.1) while proportions of lesser-quality meat, in particular head bones, were more abundant in the Saxo-Norman and early medieval periods (22% and 23% respectively) than in the Friary (13%) and post-medieval periods (11%). These results can be interpreted in different ways. On the one hand, the larger number of high-quality meat bones in the Friary and Period 4.1 deposits may illustrate that the primary activity contributing to most of these contexts was the disposal of food refuse. As Grant (1988, 149) has pointed out, it is likely that animal remains recovered from monastic sites would reflect what was in the larder. This contrasts with the material deposited in the Saxo-Norman and early medieval contexts, where the proportions of food debris bones are close to those of bones traditionally described as secondary butchery waste (skulls and jaws). Therefore it may be assumed that if animals were slaughtered in the Friary area, most of the butchery waste was deposited somewhere else. Furthermore, the abundance of high-quality meat bones suggests that joints of meat were introduced to the site, rather than whole carcasses. For Period 4.1 contexts this seems to have been the case as well. The scarcity of waste bones (head and lower parts of legs) suggests that the debris derived from meals. By the 16th century carcasses would reach the city dwellers already cut into quarters, or even smaller portions. The butchery waste would have been disposed of in slaughter houses, as ordered by the town regulations. Exactly the opposite situation is apparent in the Saxo-Norman contexts, however, where waste materials derived from the slaughter of animals, processing of carcasses and consumption all seem to have been dumped together.

It is clear that the information derived from the Friary contexts indicates that the friars here consumed meat of very high quality. The data from the Period 1 and 2 deposits cannot be interpreted in the same terms due to its more complex origin. Although there is a large percentage of high-quality meat bones recorded under 'lar' for all periods, the proportion of the best cuts of meat still is slightly lower in the Saxo-Norman and early medieval contexts. However, one cannot assume that, at that time, the inhabitants of this area of Norwich had a more frugal diet than their medieval successors. More information, such as the age of the animals slaughtered, would be needed to be more conclusive concerning the cattle remains from Periods 1 and 2. The practice of butchering carcasses into sides of beef was already common in Saxo-Norman times, since sagitally-split vertebrae were found from this period onwards.

Sheep/goat

The skeletal proportions of sheep/goat and 'sma' bones are shown in Appendix 7. In contrast to cattle, the total proportion of meat and waste bones in Period 1 and 4.1 is considerably different from Period 2, 3, 3.1 and 3.2. The total proportion of meat-bearing bones is larger in the Saxo-Norman and post-medieval periods than in later medieval times, and consequently, waste bones are scarcer in these periods. However, a closer look at the data shows that 32% of the meat-bearing bone fragments dating to the Friary period belong to high-quality meat cuts, as opposed to the high proportion of lesser-quality meat bones from animal heads (42%) in the Saxo-Norman levels. Contexts from Area D dated to Period 4.1 yielded the highest proportion of good-quality meat-bearing bones (43%). Thus, the sheep/goat skeletal element anatomies mirror the findings with regard to cattle. The Friary was consuming not only the best cuts of beef but also of mutton, and the same happened in this quarter of the city after the Dissolution. On the contrary, more than half of the sample of meat-bearing bones for the Saxo-Norman period is comprised by skull fragments, which have been split to remove the brain, and mandible fragments.

For Period 2 there is a remarkable scarcity of vertebral elements and upper limb bones and a bias towards the denser lower limb bones, *i.e.* radius (18%), tibia (12%), metatarsal (17%) and metacarpal (9%). This might indicate that more fragile parts of the skeleton, such as the upper limb bones, had been destroyed by taphonomic processes. During the analysis it was observed that there was a high incidence of gnawing on sheep/goat bones for this period. This may be suggesting that bones were left lying around for a while before they were incorporated into deposits (Lyman 1994). Another hypothesis to be considered is that if the animals were killed on the site, and their carcasses processed, the best cuts of meat could have been sold on the bone and/or taken somewhere else. Therefore, these remains would represent mainly butchery waste. However, these contexts could also be domestic rubbish and the abundance of lesser- and low-quality meat elements can be taken as an indication of the low economic level of the inhabitants of the site, who could only afford the cheapest cuts of meat.

The data recorded under 'sma' can be used to support one or another of the previous hypotheses. For all periods the proportions of 'sma' bones are very similar. Assuming that in Period 2 the upper limbs were badly affected by taphonomic processes (gnawing), one would expect them to be recorded under the longbone fragment category, but Period 2 does not show a remarkable number of 'sma' longbone fragments in relation to the other periods so this hypothesis can be rejected. The relative abundance of low-quality meat bones (*i.e.* metacarpus, metatarsus and phalanges) points to the waste of processing carcasses. Due to the smaller size of sheep/goat it would not have been that difficult to slaughter these animals on site and dispose of the waste in the nearby pits used for the domestic refuse. It would appear that the sheep/goat remains from Period 2 derived from both butchery and consumption.

A total of 20 goat horn-cores were found in different deposits from Period 3. Five of them were chopped at the base and only one displayed knife cuts. This indicates that horns were removed from the skulls. Since they were not concentrated in one deposit but scattered around the site it may be assumed that horning activities were not undertaken at the Friary on an 'industrial' scale. No other skeletal element has been positively identified as goat, so that the presence of this species on the site may be considered marginal.

Pig

Appendix 8 represents the anatomical distribution of pig bones at Greyfriars. As with cattle and sheep/goat, the total percentage of meat-bearing bones outnumber waste bones in all periods, although in Period 2 the proportion of low-quality meat bones (41%) is quite similar to the meat-bearing bones (59%). The highest proportion of the best cuts of meat is present once more in Period 1 (32%), where the number of skull and mandible fragments is large as well (33%), and in Period 4.1 where 50% of the bone sample comprises high-quality meat bones. In particular, it is worth noting the high percentage of femora and humeri. The contribution of pig to the diet is not very important for this period, but practically only the best cuts of meat are present in the sample (14% humeri, 21% femora).

For Period 2, the pig skeletal elements distribution mirrors that of sheep/goat. No vertebrae, few limb bones and a high number of skull fragments, including mandibles, together with metapodials and phalanges, are present in the sample. Although the Friary contexts have a lower total number of high-quality meat bones than that from Period 1 or 4.1, a closer look at the data shows that upper limb bones (with the exception of humeri) are slightly more abundant here than in the Saxo-Norman levels. Also, the number of lower limb bones (radius, ulna and tibia) is larger. As evidenced by the other taxa, it may be concluded that joints of pork were introduced to the site to be consumed by the friars in the medieval period.

Ageing

Analysis of ages at death for the main domesticates allows species kill-off patterns to be reconstructed, and thus conclusions on their role in the economy of the site from Saxo-Norman to late medieval times to be made. In addition, the results can be compared with other sites. The age estimates are based on the data provided by Silver (1969) on epiphysial fusion, and stages of tooth eruption and tooth wear given by Grant (1982).

Cattle

Epiphysial fusion data for post-cranial cattle bones has been split into three fusion stages. The early fusion group contains those skeletal elements which fuse by 1–1.5 years: distal humerus, proximal radius and proximal first phalanx. The second includes the distal tibia and the distal metapodials, which fused by 3 years. The late fusion group consists of those bones which fuse by 4 years: proximal calcaneus, femur and humerus, distal radius, proximal ulna, distal femur and proximal tibia.

The epiphysial fusion data for Period 1 suggests that 6% of the Saxo-Norman cattle died or were killed at 1.5 years, but that 77% survived for more than 3 years. This means that approximately only 17% were killed at between 18 months and 3 years of age, and 42% survived for more than 4 years, suggesting that 35% were slaughtered between 3 and 4 years of age. Thus, the kill-off pattern reflects a population of adult and mature animals. Although the number of complete mandibles available for ageing was very small for this period, it is worth noting that all specimens (three) were older than 4 years of age.

The epiphysial fusion evidence from Period 2 points to 16% infant mortality (*i.e.* deaths of calves). Very few animals were killed between 1.5 and 3 years, and also between 3 and 4 years of age since 75% survived to 4 years of age. Therefore, it can be concluded that in this period cattle were slaughtered at maturity. Only one ageable mandible was retrieved from these contexts. It has a mandibular wear stage (MWS) of 34, with the lower third molar already in wear, indicating an adult animal.

The data from the monastic levels has been split into two periods. Period 3 extends from the establishment (1226) of the Friary to the Dissolution (1538) and any possible changes in the dietary habits of the inhabitants are difficult to track over such a wide time span (NB see note on p.208). Much bone could be phased into the later occupation of the Friary, *i.e.* Period 3.2 (1400–1538), and this was compared with all the bone belonging to Period 3 in order to highlight particular trends evident in Period 3.2.

The evidence from Period 3 shows that 92% of the late medieval cattle survived 18 months of age, while 32% were killed at 1.5–3 years of age. An additional 17% were killed between 3 and 4 years of age, and 43% survived for more than 4 years. In short, at the Friary a greater proportion of cattle was killed between 18 months and 3 years of age. The epiphysial fusion data from Period 3.2 supports this finding. Not only were 12% of animals killed during their first year but also 58% were slaughtered between 18 months and 3 years. An additional 13% were killed between 3 and 4 years of age, and only 17% survived 4 years.

The mandibular data confirm the epiphysial fusion findings, and show more clearly the consumption of very young animals. Eight of the nine ageable mandibles for Period 3.2 have MWS of 2 and represent neonatals and very young calves. The remaining mandible belongs to an adult with a MWS of 45.

After the Dissolution of the Friary, the trend observed since 1400 persists. Now 53% of the bones belong to animals older than 1.5 years: in other words, the inhabitants of the area were consuming veal. Only 19% of the sample corresponds to mature animals.

The kill-off patterns for the different periods reveal variations between the different communities. In the Saxo-Norman and early medieval periods cattle were mainly slaughtered once they have reached maturity. These mature animals would have been primarily bred for draught or milk purposes, with meat a secondary product. Eventually they would have contributed to the diet, after they had completed their working life. In contrast, calves and young adults outnumber elderly animals in the deposits from the Friary era and Period 4.1. The age profile indicates a deliberate slaughter of young beasts, and these would have provided veal and prime beef for the inhabitants of the Friary. In addition, from the skeletal elements distribution (see above) is it evident that the best meat bones were more abundant in the Friary and Period 4.1 contexts than in any other. It may therefore be assumed that the Greyfriars at Norwich were not restricted to a diet poor in meat, but indeed that the opposite applied.

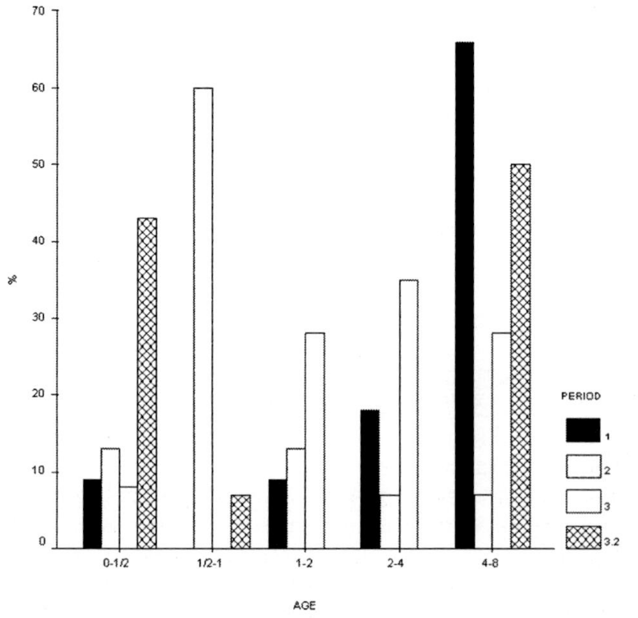

Figure 6.1 Sheep/goat kill-off profile

Sheep/goat

As with cattle, the data on epiphysial fusion for sheep/goat longbones has been separated into three fusion stages. The early fusion group includes those epiphyses that fuse by 16 months of age (distal humerus, proximal radius and first phalanx). The second stage comprises the distal tibia and metapodial which fuse by 28 months. Those elements that fuse by 3.5 years (proximal ulna and femur, calcaneus tuber, distal radius, proximal humerus, distal femur and proximal tibia) form the third group.

According to the kill-off pattern based on epiphysial fusion there were no juveniles present in the Saxo-Norman contexts, and 10% of the sheep/goats were killed between 16 and 28 months. A further 32% were slaughtered by 3.5 years and 58% survived beyond this age. The profile obtained from the mandibular data (Fig. 6.1) shows a similar picture, with 18% killed between 2 and 4 years and an additional 64% between 4 and 8 years of age. There was only one mandible of an animal younger than six months.

In Period 2 deposits, the epiphysial fusion of the longbones shows a high percentage of neonates and young animals (50%) of less than 16 months. Apparently there was no slaughter of animals of 16–28 months. Eighteen per cent of the sample belongs to animals that were killed over 2 years of age, and 40% survived 3.5 years. The results from the tooth eruption and wear method agree with this conclusion. Fifteen mandibles could be aged using Grant's method (Fig. 6.1). Sixty per cent of them correspond to sheep/goat killed between six and twelve months of age. Only 7% were of adult animals older than 4 years.

As with cattle, Period 3 and 3.2 sheep/goat kill-off patterns are examined separately. The epiphysial fusion data for Period 3 shows a small number of animals being killed during the first year (8%) and a large number (67%) surviving 3.5 years of age. The results from the MWS point to 28% of sheep/goats slaughtered between 1 and 2 years and a further 36% between 2 and 4 years, so that only 28% would survive beyond this age (Fig. 6.1). The discrepancy between the results of the two methods can be explained by the taphonomic processes described above. Immature and juvenile limb bones of sheep/goat would be more easily missed in the excavation, as well as being more susceptible to attack by dogs and rodents, and even by acid soil conditions (Lyman 1994). The kill-off pattern derived from the epiphysial fusion data for Period 3.2 mirrors that of Period 3, although it points to a greater proportion (25%) of animals killed between 16 and 28 months. The results from the MWS support the slaughter of very young animals. By the first 6 months, 43% of sheep/goats had been killed and a further 7% by the first year; thus 50% of the sample belongs to very young animals. The other 50% of the mandible sample is aged between 4 and 8 years. Given the taphonomic factors that seem to have biased the results from the epiphysial fusion method, the MWS method provides more accurate data, in that teeth/mandibles survive better than immature long-bones.

The data on epiphysial fusion for Period 4.1 follows the trend observed for cattle bones. The sample is too small to draw general conclusions but it appears generally that neonate and juvenile animals were consumed at this time. Only 45% of the sheep/goat bones belong to individuals older than 3.5 years. Unfortunately, the sample of sheep/goat mandibles for Period 4.1 was limited to three specimens. Two of them were aged to infant individuals and the third one belongs to an individual older than 4 years of age.

Unlike many other monastic orders, friars were forbidden to own land (Moorman 1968). Therefore, it is unlikely they had their own flocks. Since sheep yield their first fleece at about 18 months, it is likely that a good number of the animals represented in the Friary deposits were primarily valued for their meat and not their wool. This trend is supported by the kill-off pattern for Period 3.2. Two clear peaks appear in Fig. 6.1. As much lamb as mutton was consumed in the Friary. These results agree with those obtained from the cattle kill-off pattern, confirming that veal and lamb both played important roles in the diet of the Norwich Greyfriars. On the contrary, the pattern shown in Norwich for Saxo-Norman times follows the general trend observed in other early medieval English towns such as Lincoln (O'Connor 1982), Southampton (Noddle 1975) and King's Lynn (Noddle 1977), where mature sheep were kept mainly for wool, milk and breeding purposes before they were eventually slaughtered. However it is worth noting the abundance of young animals in deposits dated to Period 2.

Pig

The early epiphysial fusion group for post-cranial pig bones includes those skeletal elements which fuse by 1 year of age: distal humerus and proximal radius. The proximal first phalanx, distal tibia and metapodials, and calcaneus fuse by 2.5 years and represent the second group. The elements that fuse by 3.5 years are included in the last group: these are the proximal ulna and humerus, distal radius, proximal femur, distal femur and proximal tibia.

The epiphysial fusion data for the Saxo-Norman period suggests that 83% of the pigs survived their first year, to be slaughtered in their second

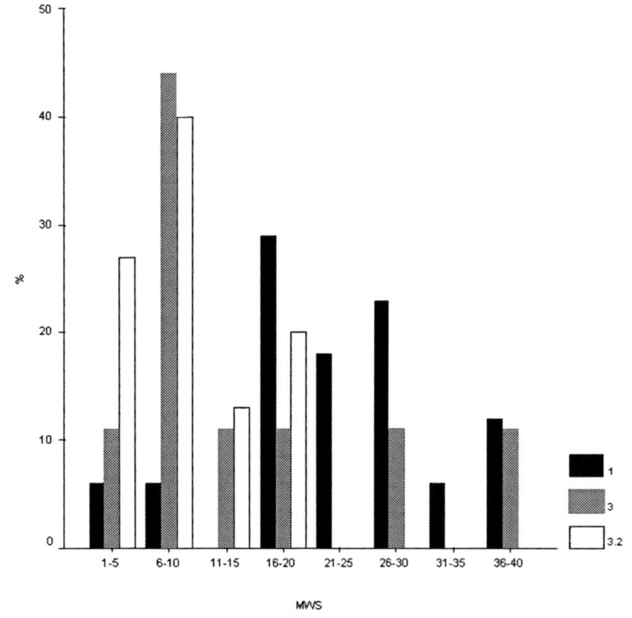

Figure 6.2 Pig kill-off profile

year of life. Only 28% survived 2.5 years, however, and none seem to have reached 3.5 years. This means that 55% were killed at 1–2.5 years, which corresponds to mid-adolescence.

For the same reasons as those described with reference to other species, it seems the evidence for dental eruption and wear provides a better reflection of the kill-off pattern for this taxa. Since some of the mandibles were incomplete, mandibular wear stages were estimated within class intervals of five. Thus, MWS classes 1–5 and 6–10 correspond to mandibles younger than 6 months of age. MWS classes 11–15 and 16–20 correspond to mandibles between 6 months and 1 year. Mandibles aged to 1 to 2 years are included in MWS classes 21–25 and 26–30. The last two classes, 31–35 and 36–40, comprise those mandibles between 2 and 3 years of age. Figure 6.2 presents the kill-off pattern obtained from the mandibular data. It shows that in Period 1 the mortality rate (41%) during the first year, and especially in the second six months, is much higher than that indicated by the epiphysial fusion data. This result attests the consumption of very young pigs at the site during this period. In addition, it points to the underestimation of this species when calculating its relative frequency in relation to other taxa, since 41% of pigs were killed between 1 and 2 years and a further 18% between 2 and 3 years of age.

In Period 2 the peak of slaughter took place between 1 and 2.5 years of age. Only 12% appeared to have survived to 3 years. No mandibles were recovered in the sample for this period. However there was one loose canine that could be sexed as female.

The pattern for the Friary data, with regard both to the epiphysial fusion and the mandibular evidence, indicates a remarkable reduction in the age of slaughter. The epiphysial fusion data suggests that 30% of the animals did not survive the first year, and that only 10% survived the second. Furthermore, for Period 3.2 55% survived the first year, to be killed before they reached 2 years. The dental eruption and wear analysis emphasises these results (Fig. 6.2). About 67% of pigs from 15th-century contexts (Period 3.2) were killed during the first six months (MWS classes 1–5 and 6–10) and the remaining 33% during the second half of the first year (MWS classes 11–15 and 16–20).

The trend towards the consumption of younger animals with time is observed in the kill-off pattern (Fig. 6.2). In the Friary, the tender meat of these very young pigs would complement the 'luxurious' diet of veal and lamb that the friars seem to have enjoyed. In Biddick's (1984) faunal study of Peterborough Abbey it is mentioned that while Benedictine monks were not supposed to eat meat, items such as the 'ten finest suckling pigs' appear in the delivery lists for their monthly food allowances in the 11th century. Also Holmes (1981) reports how pigs of only a few weeks of age were a delicacy at the Whitefriars in Coventry. In the Saxo-Norman period, however, pork could have been the best meat consumed, since the ageing data for cattle and sheep pointed to both taxa being raised to maturity, primarily for other purposes than meat. Grant (1988, 159) has pointed out that average percentages of pigs rose after the Iron Age, through the Roman and Saxon period, to reach a peak in the early medieval period. Although these pigs could have been bought at market, the presence of the

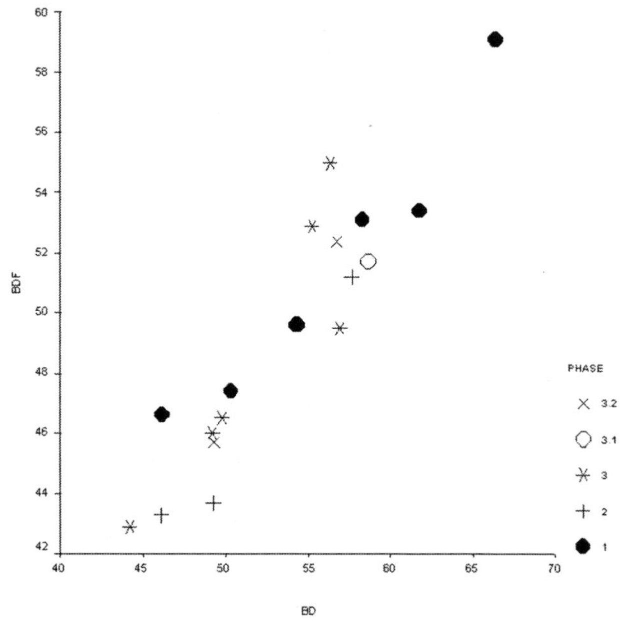

Figure 6.3 Scatter diagram of the distal breadth (BD) against the distal fusion point breadth (BDF) for cattle metacarpi

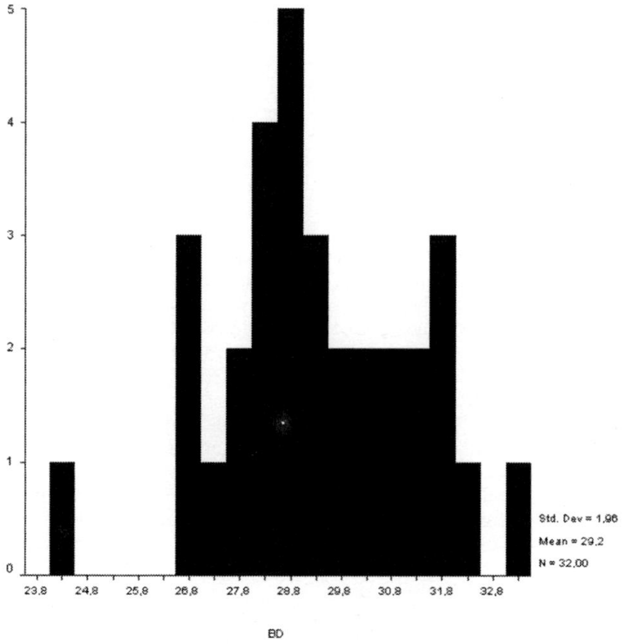

Figure 6.4 Sheep/goat humerus distal breadth (BD) for Periods 3, 3.1 and 3.2

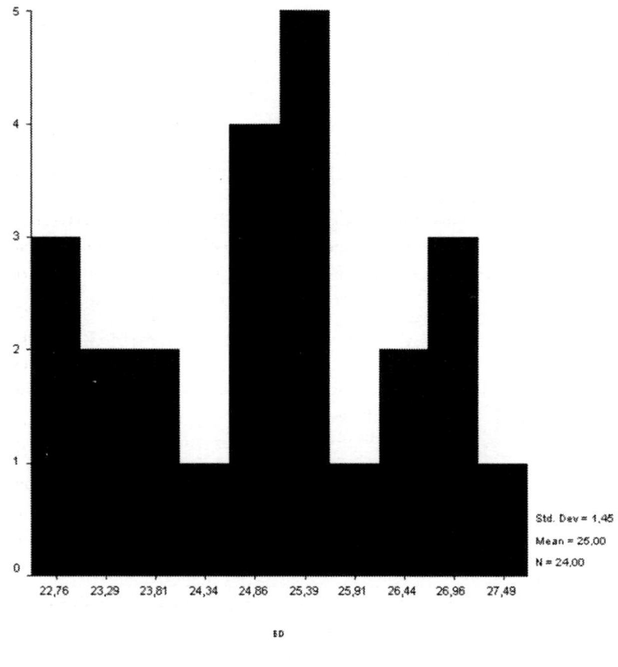

Figure 6.5 Sheep/goat tibia distal breadth (BD) for Periods 3, 3.1 and 3.2

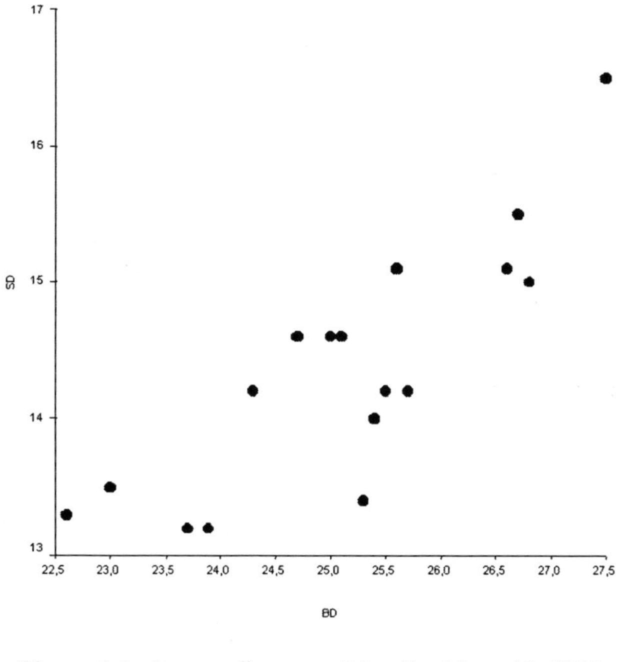

Figure 6.6 Scatter diagram of the distal breadth (BD) against the smallest breadth of the disphysis (SD) for sheep/goat tibiae (Periods 3, 3.1 and 3.2)

bones of one-year-old pigs may indicate pig-rearing within the town boundaries. This would not have been difficult, since they can be fed on spare or waste food (Hudson and Tingey 1910).

The sample for Period 4.1 is very small, but only neonate and infant animals are represented.

Metrical data

Due to the fragmentary nature of part of the assemblage only a limited number of bones could be measured. The measurements follow the standards set out by von den Driesch (1976).

Cattle

Sample numbers for cattle bone measurements are very small (a maximum of nine examples for one measurement) and pairs of measurements (useful for assessing shape) are even scarcer.

Withers height were estimated from metapodial measurements by way of Fock's conversion factors (von den Driesch and Boessneck 1974, 336). A pooled result taken from four metacarpi and two metatarsi for the Saxo-Norman period is compared to the pooled result taken from two metacarpi and two metatarsi for the early medieval period and to three metacarpi and one metatarsus of the Friary levels. No measurements were available for Period 4.1. These give withers heights of 1.15m for the Saxo-Norman cattle, 1.12m for the early medieval sample and 1.11m for the animals consumed at the Friary. Due to the small size of the sample it is difficult to assess if there was a real change in the size of cattle with time.

A comparison of the withers height estimates for Greyfriars cattle with those from other Saxo-Norman and medieval sites in Britain (see Appendix 9) shows a general trend towards a slight decrease in cattle size from the 11th–12th centuries to the late medieval period. If the Greyfriars sample is combined, the mean is very much like that from Lincoln. These measurements compare with the smallest modern breeds.

No cattle pelvis remains were complete enough to measure them for sexual characteristics. An attempt to differentiate between the sexes of cattle has been made from metrical analysis of the metacarpus following the method used by Higham (1969). Plotting the maximum distal epiphysial width (Bd) against the width at the distal fusion point (Bdf), the specimens from the Saxo-Norman and medieval samples fall into two main clusters (Fig. 6.3). One interpretation of the analysis is that the clusters show sexual dimorphism. That at the lower left of the graph would include the females whilst the cluster in the centre is likely to represent the castrates, and the only specimen to the top right a male. The Saxo-Norman and medieval specimens displayed approximately the same range and variation in size, which suggests that there was little change in the size of the stock with time.

Sheep/goat

Most of the measurements indicate a slight reduction in the average size of the animals from the Saxo-Norman to the medieval periods, as seems to be the general trend in Britain (Grant 1988, 176). However, when one compares the Greyfriars Saxo-Norman and medieval means of the distal breadth of humerus and tibia against those for other sites at King's Lynn and Exeter (Appendix 11), it can be seen that the Greyfriars animals were slightly larger. Withers heights estimates (Appendix 10) were calculated from complete humeri, radii, metacarpi and metatarsi. It should be noted that sample numbers are small and that differences between these sites may be due to regional variations in sheep breeds, and not to changes through time. Further measurements are needed to draw firm conclusions.

A reasonable number of distal humeri and tibiae were present for the Friary period. Histograms of the maximum distal breadth of both these bones (Figs 6.4 and 6.5, respectively) reveal a trimodal distribution which may be related to sexual dimorphism. The same result is shown when the maximum breadth of the distal epiphysis of the tibia is plotted against the breadth of the diaphysis (Fig. 6.6). A cluster in the lower left corner of the plot would represent the females, and the bigger one in the centre the castrates; and the points to the top right would be males. Wethers seem to predominate in this period. This could be related to the production of wool, since it is known that the best fleeces come from wethers.

Pig

The majority of pig bones were of immature individuals and therefore very few measurements were available. The mean of the distal breadth of three humeri from the Saxo-Norman period was 38.1mm, whilst the mean for two medieval humeri was 37.7mm. A reduction in size from the earlier to the later period is shown also by the mean of the distal breadth of the tibia. Two specimens of the Saxo-Norman period give a mean of 28.6mm. One specimen from Period 2.1 has a distal breadth of 27.8mm and three specimens in the medieval period a mean of 28.2mm. The sample is so small that these specimens are not worth comparing with any other sites.

Other species present

Horse

Horse bones are extremely scarce. A partial burial of some vertebra, ribs, one scapula and one humerus occurred in dump *50568* (Period 1). No butchery marks were seen on any of the bones. Two more specimens were recovered from deposits of this period, a third phalanx in a fill of sunken-featured building *50242* (context *50258*) and a metatarsal in quarry-pit fill *12276*. Four first phalanges, two femur shafts, one tibia shaft, one astragalus and one whole metacarpal were retrieved from Friary-period contexts; a withers height of 144.2cm was estimated for the metacarpal. The only horse remains in Period 4.1 were one fragment of right pelvis, one complete second phalanx and a fragment of left femur retrieved from pit fill *13124*.

The rarity of horse in the Greyfriars deposits could be accounted for by two factors: that most recorded animal bone deposits at the site derived from domestic and/or food waste, and that the absence of horse remains reflects local land use. Trow-Smith (1951) mentions that Domesday entries for Norfolk pointed to horse-breeding as an industry in decay during the early medieval period.

Dog

Dog remains were occasionally found in the Greyfriars deposits. There was a partial burial in Area B in build-up *30196* (Period 3.2), while dog bones also came from grave fill *30197* (Period 2.3): these latter remains represent 80% of the dog bones collected from medieval deposits. The pathological condition of the only thoracic vertebrae retrieved showed that the animal in question had suffered from osteoarthritis (Baker and Brothwell 1980). The height of this individual at the shoulder was calculated, following the formula used by Harcourt (1974), as 414mm. The remaining dog bones were scattered around in different contexts.

As with horse, the scarcity of dog bone fragments can be explained in terms of the types of deposit recorded at the site. The location of the site in the historic centre of Norwich implies that carcasses of dogs were disposed of away from the inhabited area.

Cat

At least four partial skeletons were retrieved from Friary contexts. Cat remains are very scarce in the Saxo-Norman and early medieval period (four and two fragments respectively). All partial burials occur in Area B, in the following contexts: pit fill *30105* (Period 3.1), build-up *30196* (Period 3.2), pit fill *30200* (Period 2.3), layer *30235* (Period 4.1). These individuals were adults, except for one juvenile individual in context *30196*. It is worth mentioning that there was also a dog burial in this latter context. No knife cuts were observed on any of the skeletons so there is no evidence suggesting that the animals were skinned, like the cat skeletons from Benet Court, Cambridge (Luff and Moreno-García 1995). All the bones belong to the domesticated species. Cats were probably present in larger numbers than shown by this sample. The reasons cited for the scarcity of dog remains may also explain the low number of cat bones present in the Greyfriars assemblage.

Lagomorphs

Just one rabbit bone occurred in the Saxo-Norman deposits, and it was only in the Friary contexts from the 13th century onwards that rabbit become more common. According to Veale (1957, 88–9) at that time they were considered something of a luxury, since they were expensive to purchase. It may be assumed that rabbit provided the monastic order with another delicacy. The scale of the rabbit's contribution to the diet is difficult to assess but it seems that they were of more importance than hare. Only eight fragments of hare were present in medieval contexts, against one hundred fragments of rabbit. Maltby (1979, 61) found that in medieval Exeter rabbit was eaten by few people, and that hare was the more regular source of food. The scarcity of hare in the monastic levels thus supports other indications of the high-status diet enjoyed by the Friary inhabitants.

Deer

Deer antler fragments were scarce in all deposits and only five of the twelve fragments found were sawn. This is not surprising, since these are not 'industrial' deposits (see Chapter 5.II, 'Antler-working').

Fallow deer was the only species of deer that could be identified. The fragments present in contexts from the Friary and dated to Period 3.2 were a scapula and femur in layer *10268* (Area A), along with a metatarsus from ditch fill *30524* and a pelvis from pit fill *30104* (both in Area B). The latter had been gnawed by a dog. The rest of the bones came from cess-pit *40019* in Area CB and include two metatarsi, one astragalus, three first phalanges and one second phalanx. These bones are extremely well preserved and bore no butchery marks.

Three fallow deer bones were recovered from pit fill *13124* (Period 4.1). There was one complete metacarpus with measurements GL – 190.5mm, BP – 28.6mm and SD – 17.7mm. On the shaft near the articulation point this displayed very fine knife cuts resulting from skinning. Two more tibiae were also retrieved from this deposit, one one with knife cuts on the shaft. The distal breadths of these two specimens are BD – 35.0mm and 31.9mm.

The fact that most of the deer bones are from the lower limbs could be explained by the way this taxa would have been introduced to the site. Grant (1988, 165) has pointed out that deer were probably butchered in the forests where they were killed and that the meat, stripped from the main bones of the body, was carried back in, or with, the skin to which the lower limb bones were still attached. The contribution of deer to the meat diet of the Friary inhabitants was not significant since the number of fragments are very low in relation to the three main domesticates. Occasional consumption of deer, however, would have introduced variety into the good-quality fare the friars were already enjoying.

Badger and fox

The partial skeleton of a badger was present in pit fill *13271* (Area D, Period 2). One fragment of ulna, humerus and skull displayed very fine knife cuts, probably the result of skinning. The only fox bone present in the assemblage came from pit fill *13124* (Area D, Period 4.1). It is a tibia with a small knife cut on the diaphysis. In urban contexts the presence of small mammals such as these indicates how they were valued for their skins (Serjeantson 1989).

Conclusions

The analysis of the faunal remains retrieved from the different periods of occupation at the Mann Egerton site has shown a considerable variation in the contribution of the main domestic species to the diet with time.

Nearly half of the sample (48%) of bones retrieved from Saxo-Norman levels came from deposits within sunken-featured building *50242* in Area C. The number of fragments method (NISP) indicated that pig bones predominated, followed by cattle and then by sheep/goat. The skeletal element distribution and the ageing data for the latter two taxa point to a high proportion of lesser-quality meat, and to the consumption of old animals during this period. In contrast, pig was represented by the best cuts of meat and young individuals. It is therefore likely that pigs played an important role in the diet of the inhabitants of this area of Norwich during this period.

An important proportion of the faunal remains dated to Period 2 (12th–13th centuries) come from Area D. As evidenced by the three quantification methods the consumption of ovicaprines increases at this time. Cattle remain at a similar level, with pig the species that declines considerably. The age profile of sheep/goat showed how young animals were dominant in the sample and the skeletal element distribution pointed to all parts of the skeleton been present. This seems to suggest that sheep/goat were killed and consumed at the site. Cattle were slaughtered once they had reached maturity and had completed their working lives. It can be concluded that if cattle were providing most of the meat to the inhabitants of the area, young sheep/goat and pig provided higher-quality tender meat to the diet.

In contrast to the earlier faunal remains, those retrieved from the Friary contexts comprise good quantities of the best cuts of meat and very young animals for all taxa. Cattle, sheep/goat and pigs dominated the diet of the friars. Despite the large number of religious fast days during the year, meat played an important part in the Norwich Greyfriars' diet. According to Dyer (1983, 193), this is one of the distinguishing characteristics of upper-class diet.

Moorman (1945, 1968) describes the severe living conditions of Franciscan friars in England during their early years. Compared with the older religious orders, the friars had very little property and depended upon voluntary contributions. Many friaries received gifts of money, building materials or clothes. The Rule did not allow the possession of land on which to work, but the friars were expected to labour in the fields and received a night's lodging, or a little food, in exchange. However, the second half of the 13th century saw a gradual falling-away from the ideals set by the Rule. In 1349 and 1350 a Royal Inquiry was held into property held by the Mendicant Friars in England (Little 1943). In exchange for burial rights, or to engage the prayers of the friars, owners of property often gave them houses which were then leased in the ordinary way to provide regular rental income. In addition, a system of collecting the gifts was devised in such a way that the collectors, known as limitors or quaestors, were assigned a certain area, outside which they were not allowed to go. They had certain privileges, such as being allowed to eat flesh-meat in the evening if they had been out all day.

As an example of the transactions conducted by these limitors, Moorman (1968) presents the notes from an account-book kept at the Franciscan house at Cambridge *c.* 1366. This records gifts made in kind, including a basket of figs, a barrel of herrings and several gifts of pork. Other accounts of 1356–67 show that the friars bought considerable quantities of foodstuffs that were customary in the houses of the rich, but which rarely appeared on the tables of the poor. Moorman also notes that it had also been customary for a select circle of socially superior or better-educated friars to have their meals apart from the rest of the community, in a different room, where the normal rules and customs about food and conversation did not apply. Thus, the Greyfriars faunal remains can be interpreted as direct evidence for the pattern of meat consumption within the resident community.

Knowles and Hadcock (1953, 192) state that the community at Norwich was a large one since there are said to have been about 50 friars in the early 14th century. Half of the faunal remains from Friary contexts were dated to the 15th century. The results obtained in relation to the kill-off patterns, the skeletal element distributions and the evidence derived from written sources allow us to suggest that the animal bones are associated with the most prosperous period of the Friary.

It is difficult to compare the results from the Norwich Greyfriars with those from other monastic houses, due to the scarcity of faunal studies carried out on these establishments (O'Connor 1993). Armitage and West (1985) report on the late 15th-century faunal remains from the London Greyfriars. Their results indicate that general standards were more austere than in Norwich, with very high proportions of lesser-quality meat indicated by skulls of cattle and sheep. Pork was rather scarce. In addition, the diet was supplemented by small birds (Chapter 6 III, 'Avian and fish bone'). A similar situation is described by Ryder (1956) with regard to late 15th–early 16th-century faunal remains from the Cistercian abbey at Kirkstall (Yorks). This assemblage yielded a large percentage of cattle bones (90%), followed by sheep/goat (5%), pig (3%) and red deer (2%). The majority of cattle and sheep/goat bones came from fairly old animals (5–10 years in the case of cattle) and among the pig and sheep there was a high proportion of skull fragments. Ryder explains that the small numbers of pig bones may indicate that pork was considered a luxury in 16th-century Yorkshire.

Testimony from an earlier period than that represented by the last two examples comes from the Account Book of Beaulieu Abbey (Hockey 1975), dating to the 1270s. The Cistercian diet of this period was almost entirely based on fish, with eggs and spices to help relieve the monotony. When meat was eaten, sheep predominated over cattle. The 14th-century larder account book of the Augustinian Bolton Priory (Kershaw 1973) more clearly resembles the diet at the Norwich Greyfriars. Cows, pigs and sheep for the table came largely from the priory's own stock. The book shows that there were variations in the proportions of sheep and pig. Thus, in 1315/16, when there was a heavy slaughter of sheep due to murrain, no pigs were registered in the book. The same accounts show that although young cattle were seldom slaughtered, a few calves were set aside for the table each year. In addition, prime beef was bought in the market to serve in the refectory. Therefore, it may be concluded that beef consumption outweighed that of any other meat at Bolton Priory. The same happened at the Norwich Greyfriars. Although the MNI method indicated that sheep/goat were slightly more abundant than cattle, the meat provided by one sheep is always less than that from one cow. As far as pig is concerned, since they were eaten very young their contribution to the diet was much lower than that of any of the other taxa. Birds, fish and some game would have complemented the friars' diet (see Nicholson, below).

Levitan (1989, 171) discusses the bone assemblages dated to 1500–30 from two monastic sites in Exeter. The evidence suggested that cattle carcasses were jointed and boned-out in the kitchens. He argues that halved carcasses were introduced in the priory and secondary butchery was undertaken on site. In addition, O'Connor reports on the exploitation of newly-weaned cattle for veal indicated by early 16th-century deposits at St Andrew's priory in York (O'Connor 1993). There may be some analogy in these two later sites with the cattle remains from the Friary in Norwich.

To conclude, the standard of living of the Norwich Greyfriars, assessed in terms of food consumption, was obviously high. After the Dissolution of the Friary, the trend towards the consumption of the best cuts of meat and young animals increases. The sample for this latter period is small, however, and more data would be needed to allow any conclusions to be drawn. There are very few published bone assemblages from urban monastic houses (O'Connor 1993), and the analysis of the Greyfriars material has provided much new information. Excavation of further similar sites would be needed in order to gain a clearer picture of how these communities were integrated in the larger economic systems of medieval towns.

III. AVIAN AND FISH BONE

by Rebecca A. Nicholson

Introduction

A large quantity of both bird and fish remains was recovered from the excavations at Greyfriars, only a proportion of which is considered in this report. Bones were recovered by hand collection (HC) during the excavation, by wet-sieving large volumes of sediment through an 8mm aperture mesh (SRS – soil riddled samples) and by sieving smaller volumes of sediment through a 0.5mm mesh (BS – bulk sieved samples) using a Siraf-type system (detailed in the project archive). This sampling strategy is consistent with that implemented at several sites in Norwich, most recently Castle Mall (Albarella *et al.* 1997), enabling assemblages from the city to be compared with confidence. At Greyfriars, in contrast to the mammal bone, the fish bones (and particularly the bird bones) were well preserved or moderately well preserved through most periods. Methodologies for the identification and recording of the material are presented in the project archive.

Few urban ecclesiastical sites, and even fewer mendicant sites, have produced significant assemblages of bone (O'Connor 1993). By contrast, a number of secular sites in Norwich and urban centres elsewhere have produced large bone groups with which the Greyfriars material may be compared. Both because of the importance of the fish and fowl to the monastic diet, and also due to the discovery of pit-fills rich in small bones from the later Friary occupation (Period 3.2: 1400–1538), this report concentrates to a greater extent on the supply and consumption of fish and fowl in the Friary than on examining changes over time.

Selection of contexts for study

While a large proportion of excavated features was sampled during the excavations at Greyfriars, results from only a small proportion of contexts are presented here. For consistency, the same context groups were considered for both the bird and the fish remains. Contexts were selected according to the following criteria:

1. to include only sampled contexts from securely dated features representing the major periods of occupation at Greyfriars;
2. to include those contexts or context groups containing the greatest numbers of bones from each major period (where possible over 50 fragments of bird and fish).

By far the richest sampled contexts in terms of small bones were from two adjacent pits in Area CB: pits *40014* and *40019*. These pits were closely dated to the later Friary occupation (see below). While many features from other periods produced both bird and fish bone, the amounts of bone in these other contexts were usually, by comparison, fairly small. The context groups used for this study are as follows:

Period 1: Saxo-Norman (pre–1100)

Bones recovered from sunken-featured building *50242* located in Area C, in the south-eastern part of the excavation area. Also bones from cess-pit *12000*, in Area A, at the north-west of the excavated trench: this feature contained fish but no bird bone.

Period 2: early medieval (1100–1226/1290s)

Bones recovered from layer *13379*, contained within a very large pit adjacent to a building consisting of two parallel beam-slots (*13333*/*13334* and *13245*) in Area D. While many contexts from this period contained bone, this was one of the larger assemblages. Unfortunately bird bones were infrequent.

Period 3: Friary occupation (1226/1290s–1538)

Eight pits (*10249*, *10017*, *10737*, *30335*, *30731*, *30008*, *40014*, *40019*) are considered; the fills of each appeared to be primarily domestic in nature. Fills from the first three have been dated to the 13th and 14th centuries (except for the lowest fills of *10737*, which were dated to Period 1 and are not considered by this report). These three pits were located in Area A, to the west of the claustral buildings and two of them (*10017* and *10737*) were in close proximity to each other and to pit *10471* (dated to Period 4.1: see below), possibly forming a pit group. Pit *30335* was located in the south-west part of Area B, just outside the south wall of the Friary precinct. The sub-oval pit *30731* was situated inside the Friary precinct, in the south-west part of Area B and south of the Friary buildings as encountered during excavation. The fills of *30731* are dated to Periods 3 and 3.2 and appear to be domestic in nature. The last three pits have been more closely dated, to Period 3.2. Pit *40014* was cut by pit *40019*; these features have been dated to the 15th century and 1500–38 respectively. The pits were situated in Area CB, within the Friary precinct and to the south of the Friary buildings. Pit *30008* was positioned about mid-way between pits *40014*/*40019* and pit *30731*. The fills of these pits again appeared primarily domestic in nature. Also dated to this period was a group of bones recovered from a Friary-related drain (*12515*) which also contained many butchered cattle ribs (Huddle, Chapter 2.II, 'Boneworking: primary waste and butchery').

Period 4.1: Post-Dissolution (1538–)

This period produced very few contexts containing bird or fish bone. The only context-group considered relates to pit *10471*, which may be associated with pits from Period 3 (see above) and contained no bird bones.

Period	*Period 1*		*Period 2.1*		*Periods 2.3–3.1*		*Period 3.2*		
Date	*10th–11th centuries*		*1100–1200*		*1226–1400*		*1400–1538*		
Collection method	*HC*	*SRS*	*HC*	*SRS*	*HC*	*SRS*	*HC*	*SRS*	*BS*
Litres of earth sieved		*550*		*?*		*130*		*650+*	*150.2**
Domestic fowl (*Gallus gallus*)	8	6	0	17	13	0	157	118	3
Goose (*Anser anser*)	6	3	0	6	7	1	39	59	1
Domestic duck/mallard (*Anas platyrhynchos*)	0	0	0	0	0	0	0	5	0
Small duck	0	0	0	0	0	0	0	1	0
Teal (*Anas crecca*)	0	0	2	1	0	0	1	0	0
Fowl-size	1	3	0	6	6	0	42	20	3
Goose-size	1	0	0	1	2	0	19	5	7
Swan (whooper or mute: *Cygnus sygnus* or *C. olor*)	0	0	0	0	0	0	4	3	0
Godwit (*Limosa* sp.)	0	0	0	0	0	0	0	1	0
Partridge (*Perdix perdix*)	0	0	0	0	0	0	0	9	0
cf. Partridge	0	0	0	0	0	0	0	1	0
Plover (*Pluvialis* sp.)	0	0	0	0	0	0	1	1	0
Snipe (*Gallinago gallinago*)	0	0	0	0	0	0	0	1	0
Curlew (*Numenius arquata*)	0	0	0	0	0	0	1	0	0
Stock/rock dove (*Columba oenas* or *C. livia*)	0	0	0	0	0	0	1	9	0
Crow (*Corvus corone*)	0	0	0	0	0	0	0	1	0
Pigeon-size	0	0	0	0	0	0	1	0	1
Blackbird (*Turdus merula*)	0	0	0	0	0	0	1	1	2
cf. Sparrow (*Passer* sp.)	0	0	0	0	0	0	0	1	0
cf. Song thrush (*Turdus philomelos*)	0	0	0	0	0	1	0	0	0
Unidentified	27	1	2	33	41	4	45	114	13
Total identified	**16**	**12**	**2**	**31**	**28**	**2**	**267**	**236**	**17**

* not all volumes recorded

Table 40 Total number of bird bones (NISP) from selected contexts (by period)

Bird bones

Of 611 identified fragments, most (403) were identified as fowl or fowl-sized (mainly chickens: no other fowl species were identified). A smaller number (157) of geese or goose-sized bones were present (Table 40). The size of the goose bones was generally consistent with the domestic or greylag goose *Anser anser*, but insufficient measurable specimens were present to allow detailed biometrical comparison with wild geese populations. A number of other birds were identified from one or several contexts; most of these species are represented in medieval food inventories and included ducks (both mallard and/or domestic duck *Anas platyrhynchos* and teal *Anas crecca*), swan (whooper or mute swan, *Cygnus cygnus* or *C. olor)*, partridge *Perdix perdix*, plover *Pluvialis* sp(p.), snipe *Gallinago gallinago*, curlew *Numenius arquata*, godwit *Limosa* sp. and stock or rock doves *Columba oenas* or *C. livia.* A few smaller hedgerow birds were identified, including blackbird *Turdus merula* and possible identifications of song thrush *Turdus philomelos* and sparrow *Passer* sp. One scavenger, a crow *Corvus corone*, was recorded.

Of the features selected for this study, pits *40014* and *40019* contained the greatest number of bird bones, and hence the greatest diversity of species. Fowl bones outnumbered geese in all of the periods studied. Small sample sizes in all but Period 3.2 preclude detailed analysis, but there is a slight indication of an increased proportion of fowl in the later Friary occupation (Period 3.2), which would be consistent with the trend observed at Alms Lane, Norwich (Harman *et al.* 1985) and King's Lynn (Bramwell 1977) during the later medieval period. At these sites, however, a much greater proportion of the bird bones were from geese. Insufficient bird bones were identified from Periods 1 and 2 to investigate changes in the sex ratio or age at slaughter of poultry through time. In Period 3 (and mainly 3.2) 24% of fowl and 13% of goose bones were from immature individuals. These proportions do not demonstrate convincingly the move away from egg production towards commercial meat production based around younger birds in the later middle ages that has been identified at Castle Mall (Albarella *et al.* 1997). An increase in the proportion of domestic fowl to goose has also been identified at a number of other monastic sites in the later phases of occupation, including Dominican Beverley, Gilbertine York and Dominican Oxford (O'Connor 1993; Gilchrist 1996).

During Period 3 the ratio of spurred to unspurred fowl tarsometatarsals was approximately 1:5, indicating a policy based upon both egg and meat production (Grand and Delatouch 1950). Medieval levels at Castle Mall showed a similar ratio until the late 15th–early 16th century when, as at the Barbican well, a much higher proportion of adult males was represented (Albarella *et al.* 1997; Moreno-Garcia 1996). If only the bone from Greyfriars pit *40019* (dated 1500–38) is considered, the ratio of about one cockerel to five hens remains true (4:18). Almost all of the unspurred tarsometatarsals were from small birds, many of about bantam size; all had a greatest length of 75mm or below, though a tarsometartarsal with a spur scar had a length of 90.1mm. Spur scars are thought to represent females (West 1982), but this bird — if indeed female — must have been from a breed much larger than the majority at Greyfriars. All spurred tarsometatarsals had a greatest length in excess of 79mm.

Duck was only a minor component of the bird assemblage, a situation seen on most medieval British sites (Grant 1988). Ducks, waders (curlew, godwit, snipe, plover) and swans may all have been commercially available in Norwich, being caught in the nearby fenlands. Geese were bred on the fens (Dudley Stamp 1969), while domestic ducks were kept within the city at least by 1437 (Moreno-Garcia 1996). Fowl were also often bred in urban back yards. Dovecotes are recorded as belonging to Greyfriars, Norwich by the time of its Dissolution (Rutledge, Chapter 3.II). Partridge was particularly prized in medieval times, and its occurrence in several contexts dating to the later Friary occupation may indicate that a life of poverty was not always practised by the mendicants. Swan, too, was a dish of the wealthier classes. While it is possible that these foods were reserved for secular guests or Friary wardens, there is some documentary evidence to support the suggestion of slipping standards within friaries, particularly those of the Franciscan order from the later 14th century (Rutledge, Chapter 3.II).

Despite good preservation, there were few examples of apparently articulated bones, supporting the view that most of the sampled features contained domestic refuse, mostly originating as kitchen and table waste. A small proportion of bones exhibited knife cuts or chop marks, most commonly to the distal femur, distal tibiotarsus and proximal tarsometatarsus of fowl and goose, indicating removal of the lower limb, probably during meal preparation. Several geese fulcrums (wishbones) were also cut; removal of this bone facilitates carving. The numerical dominance of the tarsometatarsus over other fowl elements in some contexts (notably pit *40019*) may indicate that the lower limbs were trimmed away before presentation at table. Crania, mandibles and phalanges were rare despite the sieving of deposits; however, the greater abundance of meat-bearing bones is probably best explained in taphonomic as well as recovery terms. Vertebrae and sterna were also under-represented, and there were insufficient bird bones recovered from sieved samples to examine whether smaller and less robust bones were under-represented when total recovery operated. A very small number of fragments (less than 1%) were burnt. Few bird bones were gnawed, and those which were displayed paired puncture marks typically produced by cats. This, and the generally well-preserved nature of the bird bones, implies that a minimal length of time elapsed before refuse was buried.

Fish bones

Nearly 4000 fish bones were identified from the selected contexts, the great majority from the later Friary occupation Period 3.2 (Table 41). The abundance and diversity of fish bones was clearly affected by recovery biases to a much greater extent than the mammal and bird bones. Only the bulk-sieved residues can be argued to reflect accurately the composition of species in any given deposit, although the hand-collected and soil riddled samples provide larger groups of bones from relatively big individuals such as mature cod *Gadus morhua*, saithe *Pollachius virens*, haddock *Melanogrammus aeglefinus*,

Period	*Period 1*			*Period 2.1*			*Period 2.3–3.1*			*Period 3.2*			*Period 4.1*		
Date	*10th–11th centuries*			*1100–1200*			*1226–1400*			*1400–1538*			*1400–1538*		
Collection method	*HC*	*SRS*	*BS*	*HC*	*SRS*	*BS*	*HC*	*SRS*	*BS*	*HC*	*SRS*	*BS*	*HC*	*SRS*	*BS*
Litres of earth sieved		*550*	*120**		*?*	*?*		*220*	*130*		*650*	*150.2**			*10*
Ray (*Rajidae*)	0	0	0	4	0	0	0	0	0	0	1	1	0	0	0
Thornback Ray (*Raja clavata*)	0	0	0	0	0	0	0	0	0	6	15	0	0	0	0
Elasmobranch (Elasmobranchii)	0	0	0	0	0	0	0	0	1	0	1	4	0	0	0
Eel (*Anguilla anguilla*)	0	0	20	0	0	0	0	0	25	1	118	196	0	0	4
Conger Eel (*Conger conger*)	0	0	0	0	0	0	0	0	2	0	2	0	0	0	0
Salmon (*Salmo salmo*)	1	0	0	0	0	0	0	0	0	1	0	0	0	0	0
Trout (*Salmo trutta*)	0	0	0	0	0	0	0	0	0	0	1	0	0	0	0
cf. Trout	0	0	0	0	0	0	0	0	0	0	0	1	0	0	0
Salmonid	0	0	1	5	0	0	0	0	0	0	0	0	0	0	0
Herring (*Clupea harengus*)	0	0	116	0	0	0	0	0	282	0	721	1206	0	0	5
Sprat (*Sprattus sprattus*)	0	0	0	0	0	0	0	0	2	0	0	0	0	0	0
Clupeid (*Clupeidae*)	0	0	11	1	0	0	0	0	1	0	0	11	0	0	0
Smelt (*Osmerus eperlanus*)	0	0	4	0	0	0	0	0	0	0	0	0	0	0	0
Pike (*Esox lucius*)	0	0	0	0	0	0	0	0	0	17	9	2	0	0	0
cf. Pike	0	0	0	0	0	0	0	0	0	1	0	0	0	0	0
Roach (*Rutilus rutilus*)	0	0	0	0	0	0	0	0	0	0	11	1	0	0	0
Roach/Rudd (*Rutlius/Scardinius*)	0	0	0	0	0	0	0	0	0	1	0	0	0	0	0
Bream (*Abramis brama*)	0	0	0	0	0	0	0	0	0	0	1	0	0	0	0
Tench (*Tinca tinca*)	0	0	0	0	0	0	0	0	0	0	2	0	0	0	0
Cyprinid (*Cyprinidae*)	0	0	1	0	0	0	0	0	6	0	61	14	0	0	0
Cod (*Gadus morhua*)	1	0	1	19	13	0	12	1	9	104	180	78	0	0	7
Whiting (*Merlangius merlangus*)	0	0	0	0	0	0	0	0	3	0	35	18	0	0	0
Cod/Whiting	0	0	1	0	0	0	0	1	0	37	31	0	0	0	0
Saithe (*Pollachius virens*)	0	0	1	0	0	0	0	0	0	0	0	1	0	0	0
Cod/Saithe	0	0	2	0	0	0	0	0	0	4	0	0	0	0	0
Cod/Saithe/Pollack (*Gadus/Pollachius*)	0	0	0	0	0	0	0	2	5	5	3	0	0	0	0
Haddock (*Melanogrammus aeglefinus*)	0	0	0	0	0	0	0	1	2	24	3	0	2	0	0
Ling (*Molva* cf. *molva*)	0	0	0	1	0	0	10	0	3	3	19	0	0	0	0
Gadid (Gadidae)	0	0	13	2	0	0	7	3	12	16	82	33	0	0	0
Gurnard (Triglidae)	0	0	0	0	0	0	0	0	0	0	1	1	0	0	0
Perch (*Perca fluviatilis*)	0	0	0	0	0	0	0	0	1	0	11	0	0	0	0
cf. Perch	0	0	0	0	0	0	0	0	0	0	0	1	0	0	0
Wrasse (Labridae)	0	0	0	0	0	0	0	0	0	0	3	0	0	0	0
Scad (*Trachurus trachurus*)	0	0	2	0	0	0	0	0	0	0	0	0	0	0	0
Mackerel (*Scomber scombrus*)	0	0	3	0	0	0	0	3	0	5	7	0	0	0	0
Plaice (*Pleuronectes platessa*)	0	0	0	0	0	0	0	0	2	0	0	6	0	0	0
Flounder (*Platichthys flesus*)	0	0	2	0	0	0	0	0	0	0	2	0	0	0	0
Plaice/Founder	0	1	2	1	0	0	0	0	1	0	12	5	0	0	0
Long Rough Dab (*Hippoglossoides platessoides*)	0	0	2	0	0	0	0	0	0	0	0	0	0	0	0
Right-sided Flatfish	0	2	21	2	0	0	0	17	0	70	42	0	3	0	0
Sole (*Solea solea*)	0	0	0	0	0	0	0	0	1	0	5	3	0	0	0
Flatfish	0	0	0	0	0	0	2	0	0	0	3	9	0	0	0
Unidentified (estimate)	0	10	264	45	10	4	66	12	922	214	246	2687	2	0	45
Total identified	**2**	**3**	**203**	**35**	**13**	**0**	**41**	**28**	**358**	**295**	**1382**	**1591**	**5**	**0**	**16**

* not all volumes recorded

Table 41 Total number of fish bones (NISP) for selected contexts (by period)

whiting *Merlangius merlangus* and ling *Molva cf. molva*. At Fishergate, Norwich, a positive correlation was demonstrated between the number of taxa represented and the number of samples examined (Jones and Scott 1985, 223). Jones and Scott concluded that periods represented by less than fifteen samples were likely to contain only the most common taxa. At Greyfriars the assemblage reported on here comprised less than fifteen samples for most periods, and clearly a greater number would have to be examined before a detailed study of temporal changes in fish procurement and consumption can be made. It is apparent from Table 41, however, that there is no direct correlation between the volumes of soil sieved and the diversity of taxa. While twelve samples of 10 litres each were examined from building *50242* (Period 1), both the numbers of bones and the diversity of fish taxa were considerably less than from 40 litres of soil bulk sieved from pit *40019* (Period 3.2). Further analysis of additional samples would be required to elucidate whether the apparent increase in fish consumption during the span of the Friary occupation is real.

Very few bones were burnt (less than 1%), and butchery marks were also rare. A very small proportion of bones exhibited crushing or other marks indicative of gnawing or passage through the gut. No contexts could, on this evidence alone, be described as containing cess.

In most of the bulk-sieved residues the most numerous bones were from herring *Clupea harengus*, followed by fish of the cod family (Gadidae) and eel *Anguilla anguilla*. Larger contexts also contained numbers of bones from the Pleuronectidae (right-sided flatfish including plaice *Pleuronectes platessa*), flounder *Platichthys flesus*, dab *Limanda limanda* and long-rough dab *Hippoglossoides platessoides*. This species composition is typical of medieval urban sites, and must reflect the relative availability of species as much as their perceived palatability. The surface-dwelling mackerel *Scomber scombrus* was represented by small numbers of bones in several of the sampled features, both in Period 1 and Period 3, while the mineralised remains of cartilagenous fishes (Elasmobranchs), particularly thornback ray *Raja clavata*, were represented only from Periods 2 and 3. With the exception of salmon *Salmo salmo*, smelt *Osmerus eperlanus* and eel which migrate from freshwater to the sea and back again to spawn, species living in freshwater were almost exclusively represented in deposits from the Friary (Period 3), although the disparity in the amounts of sieved earth and in the richness of the sampled deposits from the different periods must be born in mind. These freshwater fishes included most commonly roach *Rutilus rutilus* but also tench *Tinca tinca*, bream *Abramis brama*, pike *Esox lucius*, trout *Salmo trutta* and perch *Perca fluviatilis*. Most were small individuals, and while undoubtedly adding diversity to the diet were unlikely to have contributed significant calories. The friars' diet also appears to have been augmented by the occasional consumption of a range of other marine species including gurnards (Triglidae), dover sole *Solea solea*, conger eel *Conger conger* and wrasse(s) (Labridae). Smelt and scad (*Trachurus trachurus*) were here represented in Period 1 only.

Despite the sieving of large quantities of earth, Period 1 contexts did not produce large numbers of fish bones. Perhaps the most striking feature of the assemblage was the relatively high proportion of flatfish which, at 13% of the bulk-sieved group, compares with 1% of the bulk-sieved bones in Period 3.2. Gadid bones, by contrast, comprise 8–9% of the bulk-sieved assemblage from both Periods 1 and 3.2. Herring comprises 57% and 76% in the two periods, and eel 10% and 12% respectively. Most contexts from Period 2 were either not bulk-sieved, or produced few fish bones; hence the context selected for study was dominated by fish from the cod family which had been collected by hand. The greatest number of bones, and hence diversity of species, were recovered from 40 litres of earth taken from pit *40019*. Fish formed an important part of monastic diets, owing to the large number of meat-free fast days each year, and this seems to be reflected in the increased numbers of fish represented in Period 3.2. It is possible that some of the bones from small individuals represent fish-gutting activity, although even very small fish such as lampreys and minnows are known from historical records to have been eaten. Very small fish are likely to have been eaten whole, and consequently their bones are likely to have been lost from the archaeological record as only small proportions of bones survive the mammalian digestive process (Wheeler and Jones 1976; Nicholson 1993).

Comparing the fish assemblage from the selected contexts at Greyfriars with assemblages from elsewhere in Norwich (*e.g.* St. Martin-at-Palace-Plain, Locker 1987; Alms Lane, Jones and Scott 1985; Castle Mall, Locker 1996 a and b) it would seem that the species consumed by the friars corresponded very closely to that of the townsfolk in general. Herring appear to have been eaten commonly in pre-Conquest Norwich, and their bones occur in quantity at all sites dating from the Late Saxon occupation where quantities of soil have been sieved to 1mm. The herring fishery off the East Anglian coast has been documented since AD 647 (Cushing 1988, 79) and salted herring and (from the 14th century) smoked (red) herring were an important staple of the poor. Great Yarmouth was one of the major herring markets of Europe by the 13th century, and many monastic houses sent ships there to buy fish (Saul 1981). Ignoring the possibility of differences in the taphonomic histories for the pit fills of Periods 1 and 3.2, which may affect species representation, there would seem to be an increased reliance upon herring in the later period, as well as a reduction in the consumption of flatfish (see above). This may reflect the greater importance of the herring fishery in the medieval period, and the increased commercialisation of fishing in East Anglia. Flatfish are found in inshore waters, and as bottom-dwellers are likely to have been primarily caught by hook and line or shoreline trap in the past. Intriguingly, this trend was not observed at Castle Mall, where herring appeared to comprise a larger proportion and flatfish a smaller proportion of the fish remains in the pre-Conquest period (Locker 1996a), or at Alms Lane (Jones and Scott 1985). The pattern at Greyfriars may therefore be an anomaly produced by different sample sizes or taphonomic histories. Fish of the cod family (particularly cod, saithe and ling) are represented in most deposits at Greyfriars as well as in most contexts from other sites in the city. They were commonly salted or dried for later consumption. Both dry and 'green' (salted) fish of the cod family figure extensively in monastic records (Bond 1988). Documentary data from monastic houses indicates a general decline in the importance of herring from the late 14th century and a concomitant increased reliance on stored cod, a trend reflected in fish assemblages from several monastic houses (Locker 2001, 277).

It may be presumed that most of the fish consumed by both the friars and townsfolk reflected produce caught off the East Anglian coast and seasonally available in the local markets. While friaries were often supplied by alms, most donors would have supplied locally available produce to them. Donations of money also allowed the friars to purchase some food directly. Herring are commonly mentioned in monastic accounts and bequests to monastic houses, including that of the Cambridge Franciscan Friary (Moorman 1974, 36; cited in Rutledge, this volume). They were also some of the cheapest fish on the market (Dyer 1988, 31). At the Cluniac Priory of Bromholm in Norfolk 17% of total food expenditure was for fresh, red and salted herring, while cod, ling, halibut, salmon and sturgeon were also purchased (Redstone 1944). Herrings were also sometimes donated by the Crown to smaller religious houses: in 1260 the king gave 1000 herrings to the Augustinian friars of Clayhanger, Devon (Bond 1988, 77). Interestingly, records from Canterbury Cathedral Priory in *c.* 1300 indicate that the fish dish for one monk should comprise two soles or one plaice, four herrings and eight mackerel (Smith 1943, 42, cited in Bond 1988, 70). Monastic rolls at Winchester Priory indicate that between 50% and 70% of meals were fish-based in the late 15th century (Kitchin 1892, cited in Bond 1988).

Freshwater fish were extremely expensive and consequently highly prized in the medieval period (Dyer 1988). Those represented at Greyfriars are generally small and so perhaps less desirable, though still marketable. The fenland marshlands contained some of the most important monastic fisheries in England, but the Greyfriars may have obtained most of their freshwater fish from their own fisheries in the Dallingflete and in ponds (presumably managed fishponds) documented in the Dissolution inventory of 1539 (Rutledge, Chapter 3.II). Eel, bream, roach, perch, pike and less commonly tench were often kept in monastic fishponds (Bond 1988, 94).

Conclusions

The small numbers of bones studied to date in Periods 1, 2 and 4.1 preclude detailed comparison with the periods of Friary occupation, and so the contention that higher-status food was consumed following the establishment of the Friary can not yet be verified by reference to the avian and fish remains. There is, however, no indication of high status in the types of birds and fish represented in Periods 1 and 2, whereas a range of wild bird species including swan and partridge, as well as a diversity of fish species including more expensive freshwater taxa, were consumed during the later occupation of the Friary. The term 'high-status' cannot be applied convincingly to the Friary in the 15th and early 16th century on the basis of the birds and fish represented, although it would seem that the Franciscan vow of poverty was not uniformly adhered to. It is possible that bones from the pits *40014* and *40019* derived at least in part from food fed to guests rather than representing the friars' fare. Similarly diverse groups of taxa are represented at other sites in the region, including at Castle Mall, where they have been interpreted as representing the diet available to medieval citizens of moderate means (Locker 1996a, Albarella *et al.* 1997).

Refuse disposal at monastic sites was generally an organised affair. By and large, smaller bones are more commonly found associated with monastic structures, larger and more offensive remains having been disposed of away from the habitation area (Gilchrist 1996). Comparing the proportions of fish and bird waste with that of domestic mammals in order to try to establish the proportions of different types of meat in the diet is therefore likely to mislead. At Greyfriars both the bird and fish remains associated with the Friary can be largely interpreted as table waste, mixed perhaps with some bones removed during meal preparation. While the records of religious houses suggest that a greater amount of fish was consumed at monastic compared with secular houses, the range of species recovered archaeologically remains similar for secular and religious sites in the same geographical area, indicating that urban markets controlled both supplies, whether directly or indirectly though gifts from local people. Despite the ownership of fishponds and fish traps and weirs within rivers, freshwater fish never appear to have been more than an occasional resource.

Documentary evidence for exploitation of fish and fowl

by Elizabeth Rutledge

Fish and shellfish

The provision of fish and shellfish was a major occupation in late 13th- and early 14th-century Norwich. Even within the population as a whole, regular fast days made fish a regular item of diet and the Norwich fishmongers were both numerous and (as a group) comparatively wealthy. The major trade is likely to have been in herring from Great Yarmouth, which could be exported further inland when salted or smoked. A number of Norwich fishmongers owned smoke houses and the desire for a good supply of herring was probably behind the presence in Norwich of no fewer than four Cistercian abbeys with property near the river (Warden and Woburn in Bedfordshire, Garendon in Leicestershire and Combe in Warwickshire). The city records also mention shellfish: in 1288 one fishmonger was accused of mixing good and bad whelks, and two more cornered the market by buying oysters en route to Norwich (Hudson and Tingey 1906/10, I, 360–1).

However a more general picture of what was available in Norwich comes from the household accounts of Lady Katherine de Norwich (Woolgar 1992, 203–26). Lady Katherine was the widow of Sir Walter de Norwich, treasurer and baron of the Exchequer. During her residence in Norwich between 13 January and 30 April 1337 Wednesday, Friday and Saturday were the regular fish days, though after the start of Lent fish was eaten every day. Lady Katherine had both red and white herring in store (smoked and salted), as well as cod (*mellvellus, muruca*). In addition she made regular purchases of the following:

> *Fish:* salmon, sprats, ling, pikerel, roach, stockfish, codling, small fry (*menusa*), plaice, burbot, smelts, ruff, sole.

Shellfish: cockles, oysters, crayfish (*skreyth*, *krevycz*), whelks, razors, crabs.
Eels.

She was also given as gifts turbot and conger eel, though these were not necessarily for sale in Norwich.

Birds

There were far fewer poulterers than fishmongers in late 13th- and early 14th-century Norwich and few were wealthy enough to own property. Lady Katherine's household ate hens, and sometimes chicks, cocks or capons, on every non-fish day. These were supplemented on occasion by swans and partridges from gift or store, wild fowl (*volatiles*), geese, gosling and doves. When she gave a feast on the anniversary of the death of Walter de Norwich the fare provided also included mallard, heron, bittern, plover, woodcock, 40 larks and 107 other little birds. No birds were eaten during Lent.

IV. MOLLUSCA

Mollusca (site wide)

by Zena Green

Introduction

An assemblage of 116kg of assorted mollusca dating from between the 11th and the 20th centuries was recovered. The marine molluscs comprised mainly oysters (*Ostrea edulis*), whelks (*Buccinum undatum*), cockles (*Cerastoderma edule*), mussels (*Mytilus edulis*) and pod razor or spout-fish (*Ensis siliqua*). There are also fragmentary pieces of crab (possibly *Cancer pagurus*), including a claw and fragments of eggshell. Included in the sample was a significant number of land and freshwater shells: these were not identified or included in the study as they are unlikely to have made up part of the diet.

The oysters are in a varied state of preservation, some being highly fragmented while others are very well preserved. Others, while whole, are friable. Whelks and cockles tend to be in a slightly better state of preservation, although some are fragmented. In general, the mussels and razor shells are far more fragmented and are rarely whole. Both crab and eggshell are in small fragments.

Results

Quantitative analysis

Quantitative analysis involved calculation of each marine species present: full details of relevant methodologies are provided in the project archive. This analysis showed that there were few shellfish present in Period 1 (Table 42), with a narrow range of species. Oyster was the most prevalent, with one or two instances of whelk and mussel. Razor shell was also present, although there were no cockle shells.

Period 2 shows a greatly increased number of individual shells and species range. There is a large increase in the number of oysters, with the figures for whelks and mussels showing them to be included to a greater extent in the diet.

Period 3 deposits yielded the greatest numbers of shellfish. This period has the highest incidence of oyster shell and displays a huge increase in cockle shell. There is also an increase in whelk, but almost a 50% decrease in the number of mussels. In Period 3.1 there are few shellfish present, with a MNI of only 45 oysters. There are small numbers of whelks and cockles, with no mussels or razor

Period	*Date*	*Oyster*			*Whelk*	*Cockle*	*Mussel*	*Razor*	*Crab*	*Egg*
		Right	*Left*	*MNI*						
1	10th–11th centuries	130	127	174	13	0	11	x	x	x
2.1	12th century	305	341	391	66	2	7	✓	x	✓
2.2	12th century–1290s	59	66	85	6	1	64	x	x	x
2.3	1200–1290s	298	429	478	268	1457	2	✓	x	x
3	1200–1538	92	95	105	15	5	0	x	x	x
3.1	1290s–1400	514	384	591	117	118	15	✓	x	x
3.2	1400–1538	838	940	1051	169	2581	940	✓	✓	✓
4.1	1538–1566	400	341	445	16	79	4	✓	x	x
4.2	1567–1800	131	144	190	10	21	6	x	✓	x
5	19th–20th centuries	383	409	426	254	17	14	✓	x	x
Undated	?	75	63	88	6	5	0	✓	x	x
Total		**3225**	**3339**	**4024**	**930**	**4286**	**1063**			

Table 42 Quantitative assessment of shellfish present

Period	*Mean size*	*Min. size*	*Max. size*	*SD*	*SE*	*No. in sample*
2.1	60.3	40.4	79.0	8.553	1.197	51
3.2	55.3	44.8	75.2	8.269	1.169	50
4	55.0	43.8	77.2	8.062	1.140	50
5	51.5	34.6	64.3	6.385	0.903	50

Table 43 Mean oyster size, range of sizes, standard deviations (SD) and standard errors (SE) (in mm)

shells. This contrasts with Period 3.2 in which all shellfish are present, including a large number of oysters, whelks and cockles. There is a large increase in the number of mussels which only occurs to any extent in Period 3.2. Also present were razor, crab and egg shell.

Period 4 shows a marked decline of shellfish, particularly in mussels which are of an insignificant number. Whelks, cockles and oysters have all decreased by over 50%. Period 4.1 shows a greater decline, although in a more limited period. Period 5 shows a slight increase in oyster and whelk with a slight decrease in cockle.

Measurement

The samples of oysters showed a marked decrease in mean size over 15mm between Periods 1 and 5. There is a significant decrease between Periods 1 and 2 and a further decrease between Periods 2 and 3.2. This is contrasted by Periods 3.2 and 4, where there is little variation in size, while there is a further decrease in size between Periods 4 and 5. These results are presented in Table 43. Equally, the range of sizes of the oyster shells was more limited and shown to contain more shells of smaller sizes in the later periods.

The standard deviation of each collection of 50 oyster shells was calculated to assess deviation from the mean using the equation of Fletcher and Lock (1991). More detailed analysis proved that there is a significant variation between the sizes of each phase, with each one becoming increasingly different and the actual size decreasing (Green 1997, 22–3).

Age at death

Age estimations followed a similar pattern to size and appeared to be decreasing, with the mean age being 4.6 years in Period 1 and only 2.68 years by Period 5. Older specimens only appeared with regularity in the earlier phases and the majority of Period 4 and 5 oysters fell into the 2- and 3-year age groups.

Signs of infestation and damage

Analysis for encrustation by other organisms proved to show little living on the outer valve of the oysters studied. As a consequence, no quantitative analysis of this could be undertaken. The oysters proved to be far cleaner that had been expected. Similarly, the cockles and mussels also showed no signs of infestation. The whelks, however, did show traces of infestation by several organisms. Within a sample of 34 whelks, six proved to be infested with the organism *Pomatoceros triqueter* (Fish and Fish 1989). This is a tubular polychaete worm with a body up to 25mm in length which produces calcareous tubes with a longitudinal ridge on the upper surface. *P. triqueter* is found in north-west Europe and Britain on stone, rocks and shells. It lives at depths up to 70m. All of the infested whelks came from Period 3.2.

A further encrusting organism on the whelks proved to be *Electra pilosa* or hairy sea-mat. This is an encrusting mat found in seaweeds, stone, shells, hydroids and often on the shells of whelks (Fish and Fish 1989). It occurs from the middle shore to the area just beyond the intertidal zone.

A significant number of the oyster shells were fused together. In the collection studied, this occurred on nine occasions with eighteen oyster shells being joined together. All of these proved to be from Period 3.2, which had a MNI of 97. At the margins of a large number of oyster shells there is a small, roughly square notch missing. This is of a similar, distinctive shape on many of the shells and could indicate the method of opening, possibly with some kind of short, stout knife or an object of similar shape to a knife. The oysters were opened from the margin, not by cutting in from the hinge as is often done today.

Discussion

Due to the large quantity of shell refuse recovered from the Greyfriars site, it appears likely that the shellfish were being eaten. Few oysters were present in Period 1, in relation to the numbers in later periods, and this may result from several factors including the size of the settlement and the distance of Norwich from the sea (30km). The shellfish were probably imported along the River Yare and the cost of transporting them may have made them expensive.

There is a large increase in all shellfish in Period 2, in particular whelks and mussels, and this may reflect an increase in the density of settlement and perhaps improved transportation. The incidence of eggshell is interesting as it is delicate and large amounts are rarely preserved. Its retrieval here is likely to indicate consumption in quantity.

In Period 3.2, there are a very high number of shellfish of all species; in particular, there are high numbers of oyster and cockle shells. This period, which encompasses much of the active life of the Friary, would be expected to produce evidence for such a diet. Of particular note is the number of mussels, which do not appear to this extent in other periods. This may be due to changing tastes and/or availability.

Period 4 shows a dramatic decrease in shellfish consumption at the time of the Dissolution. It appears that the majority of the oyster shells in Period 5 pre-date the 'crash' in the oyster population around 1850, after which oysters became an expensive luxury. This may also explain why the number of whelks suddenly becomes greater, after the reduction in Period 4, as a replacement for oysters was sought.

Crab only appears during Periods 3.2 and 4 and then only in small numbers. This scarcity may be a result of the nature of the shell, which is less robust than those of shellfish and may well have fragmented. If crab were being consumed to any great extent, however, the more robust parts, such as the claws, might be preserved. Since only one claw was recovered from the Greyfriars site, crab appears to have been a relatively high-status commodity.

Razor shell appears in contexts of each period and, although unquantifiable, is quite common. There is little documentary evidence for this species, although it is known to be a delicacy in Orkney (Wilson 1973). It would appear that razor shells formed at least some part of the diet throughout the span of occupation.

The decrease in size of oysters over the thousand-year span studied at Greyfriars is of particular interest and may be due to over-exploitation of the resource. This theory is supported by the reduction in the range of sizes utilised and particular by the reduction in numbers of the larger oysters. Over time, the character of the oyster assemblages appear to diverge from the 'natural' population seen in Period 2. This statistically proves a significant change in the sizes of oysters chosen for consumption. Since human preference is a factor here, it is possible that this alteration in size may be due to changes in dietary habits, with the smaller ones increasingly favoured.

It has often been stated that oysters suddenly became scarce and expensive in 1850. At the beginning of the 19th century they were associated with poverty, however, and even by 1840 they were selling for only 4d a dozen. Following increasing demand and the reckless dredging of natural oyster beds (Drummond and Wilbraham 1939) oysters suddenly became very rare, and a luxury for the wealthy. The Greyfriars study, however, appears to indicate that this scarcity did not emerge suddenly at all but was part of a trend which had been continuing for at least 500 years, with oysters coming increasingly under pressure from intensive collection. The heightened desire for oysters in the mid-1800s could simply have made an impossible demand on an already-weakened resource.

Linked to the reduction in oyster size is a younger age at death, with the mean age being reduced from 4.6 years in Period 1 to 2.68 years in Period 5. This also appears to be linked to over-exploitation as the preferred age for the consumption of oysters given in most relevant literature is 3–4 years old. In Period 2 there are thirteen oysters out of 51 aged 5 and 6 years, but by Period 3, no oysters of this age were present and only five examples out of 50 studied are aged 4 years. Assessment of age, however, can be problematic and growth rings are subject to fluctuations in climate.

All of the oysters, cockles and mussels proved to be remarkably clean and free from infestation, with no evidence for damage caused by predators such as star fish. This may indicate human influence such as cultivation: this need not have included the actual breeding of oysters, but could have involved controlling their living environment. If cultivation was introduced during the centuries under consideration, it would be expected that such organisms would appear in earlier phases and then disappear. However, this is not the case, implying either that cultivation had continued into the post-Roman period in some vestigial form or that it was re-introduced earlier than was previously thought. Alternatively, infested shells may not have been included with those to be sold. The infestations evident on the whelk shells include *Pomatoceros triqueter* which lives in deep water, while whelks tend to live on the midshore in rocks and crevices: this indicates that the whelks may have been dead and swept out to sea before being accidentally harvested along with other species.

The large numbers of joined oyster valves could provide evidence for cultivation. One means of encouraging oysters to settle is to increase the numbers of places available, using empty shells put back into the water so spat can settle on them (a method known as clutch). In natural populations, larvae are inclined to settle and grow upon old shells. At Greyfriars joined shells occur only in Period 3.2, possibly indicating the use of clutch and demonstrating an intensification of cultivation. The clutch method, however, usually involves a campaign of removing the spat from the other shells in May, a practice which is known to have been under way in the 16th century. It would therefore be anticipated that the majority of the spat would have been removed to grow freely. Whether the 20% attachment figure noted in the Greyfriars assemblage represents such cultivation or natural occurrence is uncertain.

It has been suggested (Murphy 1995) that oysters with a large mean size and few attachments, other than those of oysters, indicate a natural population. A group with small valve size, but with higher numbers of attachment to other molluscan species, is more likely to be cultivated. The Greyfriars assemblage fits neither of these explanations. It appears that the increased incidence of joined shells noted in Period 3.2 represents an intensification of cultivation, or some other change. Cultivation may also be suggested by the similar size of oysters evident after Period 2, this being one of the features of a cultivated group (Winder 1980).

The Norwich oyster shells showed some indications of the method of opening, indicating that they were either opened before cooking or were eaten raw (cooked oysters would open naturally). During the Middle Ages, oysters were usually removed from their shells and prepared in a simple broth of their own juice (Wilson 1973), indicating that the Greyfriars group may have been consumed in this way. In later periods, oysters were eaten live.

Mollusca from samples

by Val Fryer

Significant groups of molluscs are indicated by weight throughout Chapters 2 and 3 of this report and detailed further by Green, above. The following information derives from the material retrieved from environmental samples.

Periods 1, 2.1 and 2.2

Shells of terrestrial and freshwater molluscs were noted in several samples at a low density and were of unknown and diverse origin. Taxa present included open country species (*Helicella itala*), catholic/synanthropic species (*Trichia hispida* group, *Helix* sp.) and a single example of a freshwater species (*Anisus leucostoma*). Shells of *Cecilioides acicula* were present but not common and are probably later contaminants since this is a burrowing species.

Periods 2.3, 3.1 and 3.2

Land and freshwater shells, including specimens discoloured to a grey or black colour by burning, were recovered at a low to moderate densities from fourteen samples. Taxa indicative of open habitats (*Pupilla muscorum, Vallonia* sp., *V. costata, V. excentrica*), woodland/shade loving species (Zonitidae indet., *Oxychilus* sp., *cf. Retinella* sp., *Carychium* sp., *Discus rotundatus*, *Clausilia* sp., *C. bidentata*), catholic species (*Trichia hispida* group, *Cochlicopa* sp., *Cepaea* sp.) and marsh/freshwater slum species (*Succinea* sp., *Vertigo antivertigo, Anisus leucostoma*) were all noted. Freshwater species were also present and included *Armiger crista, Bithynia* sp. (including opercula), *Pisidium* sp., *Planorbis planorbis* and *Valvata cristata*. A single limacid plate was also recovered. Shells of *Cecilioides acicula* were present but not common and are probably later contaminants. The burnt specimens were all of woodland/shade or marsh/freshwater species and were probably accidentally imported to the site on firewood, litter, thatch etc. Ostracods were noted in one sample with burnt specimens in another. In view of the complex taphonomy of urban assemblages, quantitative analysis has not been undertaken.

Marine molluscs from the site generally comprised oysters (*Ostrea edulis*), mussels (*Mytilus edulis*), cockles

(*Cerastoderma edule*), whelks (*Buccinum undatum*) and winkles (*Littorina littorea*), represented in the bulk samples by occasional valves, shells and fragments. A notable concentration of shell came from samples of the upper fills of a well (*10017*, Period 2.3). Taxa present comprised *Buccinum undatum, Neptunea antiqua. Cerastoderma edule, Ostrea edulis, Ensis siliqua* and one shell of *Hydrobia ulvae*. The latter, a small intertidal species, presumably reached the site accidentally with edible shellfish. *Ensis siliqua* (razor shell) has also been reported from Castle Acre Castle and Fishergate, Norwich (Murphy 1987, 1994); it seems to have been an edible species of minor importance in medieval East Anglia.

V. PLANT MACROFOSSILS

by Val Fryer and Peter Murphy

Introduction and methods

Five hundred and fifty-eight bulk samples were taken from a wide range of contexts including the fills of pits, ditches, post-holes, wells, linear features, stake-holes, culverts, drains, beam-slots and foundation trenches, the construction, use and disuse fills of sunken-featured buildings, contexts associated with a bell-founding pit and from dumps, horticultural deposits, make-up layers, burnt deposits, hearths and surfaces.

The samples were processed on site by bulk flotation, collecting the flots in a 500µ mesh sieve. The residues were collected in a 1mm mesh and sorted when dry. All flots were scanned under a binocular microscope at low power during the assessment and 56 (10%) were selected for analysis. The samples selected fell into two categories:

1. Those with relatively high densities of plant material, representing assemblages potentially interpretable in terms of activities or processes;
2. Those from contexts considered by the excavator to be of particular significance for site interpretation.

All samples selected were from contexts of Period 1, 2 or 3 (in this section, 'Period 3' includes Periods 2.3, 3.1 and 3.2: see note at the start of this chapter). Macrobotanical and other remains extracted from selected samples are listed in Appendices 12 and 13.

Most deposits were well-drained and preservation of plant macrofossils was primarily by charring and mineral replacement, though in a few contexts there was preservation by waterlogging. Since the taphonomy of charred and non-charred assemblages differ, these two categories of plant macrofossils will be considered separately in this report, which is primarily concerned with remains of crop plants, fruits and seeds of edible wild species and weeds. Charcoal fragments were present at varying densities in all samples. Other plant macrofossils included root/rhizome/stem (charred, waterlogged and mineral replaced), silica skeletons (which were especially common in sample 878: pit fill *30579*, Period 3.2), waterlogged wood fragments, and indeterminate buds, culm nodes, inflorescence fragments, leaf fragments, thorns and twigs.

Charred plant material

Periods 1 and 2 (pre-1100–1226/1290s)

Crops and other food plants

Cereal grains and/or chaff were present in all samples and included *Hordeum* sp. (barley), *Triticum* sp. (wheat), *Avena* sp. (oats) and *Secale cereale* (rye). *Hordeum* sp. was predominant. Floret bases of both *Avena fatua* (wild oat) and *A. sativa* (cultivated oat) were present. During the assessment, a single glume base of *Triticum spelta* (spelt) was noted in the fill of a Period 1 ditch (*50682*). Other food plants included *Pisum sativum* (pea) and *Vicia faba* (field bean). Rare fragments of *Corylus avellana* (hazel) nutshell were present in nine samples.

Wild flora

Charred seeds/fruits were present in all but one sample. Weed species were predominant and included *Agrostemma githago* (corn cockle), *Atriplex* sp. (orache), *Bromus mollis/secalinus* (lop-grass/rye-brome), *Centaurea cyanus* (cornflower), *C. nigra* (lesser knapweed), *Cerastium* sp. (mouse-eared chickweed), *Chenopodium album* (fat hen), *C. ficifolium* (fig-leaved goosefoot), *Fallopia convolvulus* (black bindweed), *Galium aparine* (cleavers), *Geranium* sp. (cranesbill), large and small grasses, *Lapsana communis* (nipplewort), *Malva* sp. (mallow), *Medicago/Trifolium/Lotus* sp. (medick/clover/trefoil), *Plantago lanceolata* (ribwort plantain), *Polygonum aviculare* (knotgrass), *P. persicaria/lapathifolium* (redshank/pale persicaria), *Raphanus raphanistrum* (wild radish), *Rumex* sp. (dock), *Silene* sp. (campion), *Sinapis arvensis* (charlock), *Spergula arvensis* (spurrey), *Stellaria* sp. (chickweed), *Vicia cracca* (tufted vetch) and *Vicia/Lathyrus* sp. (vetch/vetchling). *Rumex acetosella* (sheep's sorrel) and *Tripleurospermum maritimum* (scentless mayweed) are species common on light, sandy soils, while *Anthemis cotula* (stinking mayweed) is indicative of heavy, damp clay soil. Damp grass/wetland species included *Montia fontana* (blinks), *Carex* sp. (sedge), *Eleocharis* sp. (spike rush) and *Ranunculus acris/repens/bulbosus* (meadow/creeping/bulbous buttercup). The seeds of *Brassica* sp. (cabbage/swede/turnip) may be either from a cultivar or a weed species. Charred seeds of *Sambucus*

	Period 1 (SFB 50242)	*Other Period 1/2*	*Period 3*
Hordeum sp(p) (barley)	+	++	+++
Triticum aestivum/ compactum (bread/club wheat)	+	+	++
Triticum turgidum/durum (rivet or macaroni wheat)			+
Avena sp(p) (wild or cultivated oats)	+	++	++
Avena sativa (cultivated oats)		+	+
Secale cereale (rye)	+	++	+
Pisum sativum (pea)	+		++
Vicia faba (horsebean)		+	+

Table 44 Synopsis of distribution of charred crop remains.

nigra (elderberry) were present in two samples. Charred Ericaceae stems and bracken (*Pteridium aquilinum*) pinnules were noted.

Period 3 (1226/1290s–1538)

Crops and other food plants

Cereal grains and chaff were present in all but two samples. As in the Period 1 and 2 samples, *Hordeum* sp., *Triticum* sp., *Avena* sp. (including *A. sativa* but not *A. fatua*) and *Secale cereale* were all present, with *Hordeum* sp. predominant. Four asymmetrical grains probably of *H. vulgare* (six-row barley) were recovered from the primary charcoal fill of large pit *50459* (Period 3.2). In addition, rachis internodes and rachis fragments of *Triticum aestivum/compactum* (bread/club wheat) and *T. turgidum/durum* (rivet wheat type) were recovered from nine samples.

Internodes from a short section of *T. aestivum/compactum* rachis were 1.8mm long by 1.5mm broad, and were therefore either from the base of an ear or represented a very dense-eared form. The general predominance of very short *Triticum* grains certainly implied a dense ear type. The record of *Triticum turgidum/durum* (most probably rivet wheat) is the first from medieval Norwich.

Seeds of *Pisum sativum* and *Vicia faba* and nutshell fragments of *Corylus avellana* were also present.

Wild flora

As in Periods 1 and 2, weeds were predominant. A similar range of species was present with, in addition, *Anagallis arvensis* (scarlet pimpernel), *Bromus sterilis* (sterile brome), *Chrysanthemum segetum* (corn marigold), *Euphrasia/Odontites* sp. (eyebright/red bartsia), *Lamium* sp. (deadnettle), *Lithospermum arvense* (corn gromwell), *Prunella vulgaris* (self-heal), *Scleranthus annuus* (annual knawel), *Sherardia arvensis* (field madder), *Stellaria graminea* (lesser stitchwort), *S. media* (chickweed), *Valerianella dentata* (cornsalad), *Veronica hederifolia* (ivy-leaved speedwell) and *Viola tricolor* (wild pansy). Charred seeds of ruderal species included *Conium maculatum* (hemlock), *Hyoscyamus niger* (henbane) and *Solanum* sp. (nightshade). A single seed of *Linum catharticum* (fairy flax), a grassland species, was found. In addition to the damp grassland/wetland species noted in Period 1 and 2, seeds/fruits of *Scutellaria* sp. (skullcap), *Cladium mariscus* (saw-sedge) and *Menyanthes trifoliata* (bog-bean) were recovered from Period 3. A single fruit fragment of *Fraxinus excelsior* (ash) was noted. *Ericaceae* and *Pteridium* were again represented.

Taphonomy and interpretation

Periods 1 and 2: pre-Friary

Samples from contexts of these periods produced generally low densities of charred cereals, pulses and weed seeds. Although indicating that some types of cereal processing were taking place on site, the samples are not generally interpretable: they represent 'background noise' of unknown and probably diverse origin. Exceptions were the samples from fills of pit *11056* (Period 2.1). Most grains from these samples were poorly preserved and unidentifiable, but oats (*Avena* sp.) predominated. The only floret bases were of *Avena fatua*, suggesting that some or all of these grains were of wild oats. Cereal chaff was relatively common and in one sample rye (*Secale*) rachis nodes were abundant. Poaceae culm nodes, probably from cereal straw, occurred consistently and were common in one sample. The samples also included large numbers of weed seeds, in particular *Anthemis cotula, Chenopodium album* and *Rumex acetosella*. There were variations in sample composition between layers, and the material probably derived from more than one source, but the assemblages overall clearly represented charred waste from early stages of crop-processing.

Stem fragments of indeterminate Ericaceae (heath) and pinnule fragments of *Pteridium aquilinum* (bracken) were noted in a number of samples, and were probably imported to the site as litter or flooring material.

Period 3: Friary

This period represented activity encompassing the whole Friary period. Again, many of the samples examined must be considered uninterpretable 'background noise'.

In several rubbish pit fills, markedly higher densities of charred plant material were present. Given the nature of the contexts, it is unlikely that any of the assemblages related to a single activity or event: all appeared mixed in character, and included material derived from a variety of sources. The only process discernible with reasonable confidence is malting. Pit *30032* (Period 2.3) included grains and floret bases of oats (*Avena sativa*) and barley grains associated with charred fragments of plumules and primary roots indicating germination prior to sprouting; and pit *30677* (Period 3.2) included a barley-dominated assemblage, again with cereal 'sprouts'. At the Buttermarket, Ipswich, charred deposits of early medieval malt comprising both barley and oats have been reported (Murphy 1991).

Three samples were examined from fills of the bell-founding pit *12257* (Appendix 13). Cereal grains were virtually absent, but chaff (rachis nodes) of barley (*Hordeum* sp) was moderately common, and grass culm nodes, possibly including straw, were noted. The samples also included moderate frequencies of fruits and seeds of weeds, grasses and wetland plants (Carex, Eleocharis). Charcoal and fired clay fragments were abundant. The significance of the charred plant material is hard to assess, but it would appear that crop-processing waste (chaff, straw and weed seeds) was utilised in the process.

Stem, leaf and floret fragments of Ericaceae and pinnule fragments of *Pteridium aquilinum* were again commonly present in many samples of this period, probably representing the residue of litter or flooring material.

Mineral-replaced/waterlogged plant material

Periods 1 and 2: pre-Friary

Mineral-replaced and/or waterlogged material was present in seven samples. Uncharred seeds of *Sambucus nigra, Geranium* sp. and *Hyoscyamus niger* were common in most deposits: these appear to be durable propagules, persisting in aerobic deposits. They were not quantified unless preserved by mineral replacement or from waterlogged contexts.

Edible taxa
Mineral-replaced seeds/fruits of potential food plants included *Fragaria vesca* (strawberry), *Malus* sp. (apple), *Prunus domestica* ssp. *insititia* (damson/bullace), *Rubus* sect. *Glandulosus* (bramble), *Brassica* sp. and *Sambucus nigra* (elder).

Wild flora
Macrofossils were preserved by both mineral replacement and waterlogging. Weeds were predominant and included *Aethusa cynapium* (fool's parsley), *Anthemis cotula, Chenopodium album, Euphorbia helioscopia* (sun spurge), *Fumaria officinalis* (fumitory), *Hyoscyamus niger,* large and small grasses, *Lapsana communis, Papaver* sp. (poppy), *Raphanus raphanistrum, Silene* sp., *Torilis japonica* (upright hedge-parsley), *Urtica dioica* (stinging nettle) and *U. urens* (small nettle). Seeds of *Papaver somniferum* (opium poppy) were noted from organic fill *10621* within large cess-pit *10620* (Period 1). Wetland and aquatic species included *Carex* sp. and *Lemna* sp. (duckweed).

Period 3: Friary
Mineral-replaced and/or waterlogged material was present in six samples. Uncharred *Sambucus nigra, Geranium* sp. and *Hyoscyamus niger* were again ubiquitous.

Edible taxa
Large quantities of cereal periderm (bran) and rachis nodes of *Hordeum* sp. and *Secale cereale* were preserved by waterlogging in one sample. Other food plants included *Brassica* sp., *Ficus carica* (fig), *Fragaria* sp., *Linum usitatissimum* (flax), *Malus* sp. (including endocarp fragments), *Prunus avium* (cherry), *P. domestica* ssp. *insititia, P. spinosa* (sloe), *Rubus* sect *Glandulosus, Sambucus nigra* and *Vitis vinifera* (grape).

Wild flora
As in Period 1 and 2, weeds were predominant. A similar range of species was noted with, in addition, *Atriplex* sp., *Ballota nigra* (black horehound), *Carduus nutans* (musk thistle), *Centaurea* sp., *Conium maculatum, Galeopsis tetrahit* (hemp-nettle), *Hyoscyamus niger, Lamium* sp, *Polygonum aviculare, Polygonum persicaria/ lapathifolium, Potentilla* sp. (cinquefoil), *Rumex* sp., *Sonchus asper* (spiny sow-thistle), *S. oleraceus* (sow-thistle), *Stellaria media*, and *Thlaspi arvense* (field penny-cress). Abundant testa fragments of *Agrostemma githago* and *Fallopia convolvulus* were noted in some contexts, and probably represented contaminants of wholemeal flour. Seeds of *Papaver somniferum* were recovered, while a single seed of *Lycopus europaeus* (gipsy-wort), a wetland species, was present.

Taphonomy and interpretation

Periods 1 and 2: pre-Friary
Two samples (from the primary fill of ditch *50351* and pit fill *50451*) were both from deposits that were at least partially waterlogged, and primarily consisted of uncharred plant material. The restricted seed assemblages were dominated by weeds.

Two other samples (fills of pits *10737* and *11145*) both contained a low density of mineral-replaced macrofossils, probably derived from sewage residues. The fill of pit *10620* predominantly featured dietary residues (fruitstones and seeds of strawberry, apple, *Prunus* sp., and bramble) probably indicating use of the feature as a latrine pit. Samples from the disuse fill of sunken-featured building *50242* and pit fill *40115* contained extremely low densities of mineral-replaced seeds, possibly contaminants.

Period 3: Friary
Three samples from pit *10429*, the waterlogged primary fill of pit *50311* and the primary fill of pit *40149* contained low to moderate densities of waterlogged and/or mineral-replaced remains, predominantly consisting of dietary residues and probably derived from the deposition of sewage.

Others, from the primary fill of pit *30677* (Period 3.2) and from pit *50628* (Period 2.1) included abundant fruitstones and seeds, indicating the use of the features as latrine pits. One contained an especially high density of cereal bran and testa fragments of corn-cockle (*Agrostemma githago*). Another sample from pit *30677* contained a large quantity of amorphous mineralised concretions incorporating some plant material including silica skeletons, as well as ash, charred material and phosphatic concretions.

VI. OTHER ANIMAL MACROFOSSILS

by Val Fryer

Dietary residues from bulk samples included eggshell, fish bone (common throughout at varying densities: see Nicholson, above) and small fragments of large mammal bone, some of which was burnt. Other animal macrofossils included fragments of coprolite and mineral-replaced faecal concretions, arthropod remains (mineralised and waterlogged) and small mammal/amphibian bones. Occasional large foraminifera were noted.

VII. OTHER MATERIAL

by Val Fryer

Probable industrial residues from bulk samples included hammerscale, metallic globules, copper alloy residues, slag, vitreous material and possibly small coal fragments. Glass fragments were noted in the fill of pits *40103* and *30633* (both Period 3.2) and possible small fragments of amber were present in samples from the fills of pits *11056* (Period 2.1), *11145* (Period 2.1) and *30633* (Period 3.2). Fragments of black, porous 'cokey' material, black tarry droplets and siliceous globules are probably all residues of the combustion of organic material (for example, cereal grains and chaff and grass/straw) at very high temperatures. Charred and mineral-replaced textile/fibre fragments were recovered from the fill of pits *10621* (Period 2), *40014* (Period 3.2) and *50628* (Period 2.1). Other materials included burnt/fired clay, mortar/plaster and probable parchment or bark fragments.

Sample	Depth	Context	Archaeology and Soils	Micromorphology
Area C: Section 5				
1	2.55–2.70m OD	50037 (Period 4/5) 50038 (Period 4) 50039 (Period 4)	?Post-medieval very dark grey to black (10YR3/1–2/1) humic sand.	Not processed
2	2.35–2.50m OD	Top of 50041 (Period 4)	Top of medieval (AD 1450) dark brown (10YR3/2) build up.	Not processed
3	2.06–2.13m OD	50041 (Period 4)	AD 1450 dark brown (10YR3/2) humic sandy build up containing stones, pot etc.	Coarsely earthworm burrowed poorly sorted sand and silt, with abundant fine charcoal; fine and large bone fragments, chalk, flint, biogenic calcite (slugs?) and eggshell present; weakly calcitic (ash?) fine matrix with occasional secondary calcite. Anthropogenic accumulation containing high amounts of colluvial? Soil.
4	1.85–2.00m OD	50041 (Period 4) 50024 (Period 3.2)	AD 1250–1450 dark brown (10YR3/2) sandy humic build up containing stones, pot etc.	Humic and charcoal-rich soil containing high amounts of burned? material (slags), probable wood ash, possibly organised in dumped layers, with building debris (mortar, plaster, daub, chalk, peaty silts) becoming more common later. Possible cess input. Stony layer half way up, with possible humic soil layer developing. Two phases of accumulation
5	1.75–1.82m OD	50005 (Period 3.1) 50014 (natural)	AD 1250+ dark brown (7.5YR3/2) build up with gradual boundary over very dark greyish brown (lOYR3/2) sands. Natural yellowish red (10YR5/8) and yellowish brown (10YR5/8) B(g) horizon sands, with few charcoal and common dark vertical probable earthworm channels.	Strong biological mixing of underlying non-calcareous natural sands with fine charcoal-rich deposit containing bone, large slag, semi-vitrified material, burned soil/daub; deposit is poorly calcareous. Dumping of industrial/hearth debris over eroded natural sandy soil.
North face of section by SFB *50242*				
9	local depth 78–86cm	50026 (Period 2.2)	12th–14th century dark greyish brown (10YR3/2) sand	Charcoal-rich calcitic deposit with bone, mortar, possible ash and coprolitic material; similar to 4 and biologically worked. Some charcoal-rich silty inwash. Anthropogenic accumulation, disturbed, possibly cultivated?
SFB *50242*				
8	local depth 7–15cm	50249 (Period 2.2)	12th–14th century very dark grey to very dark greyish brown (10YR3/1-3/2)-fill of pit 50243	Processed but not sectioned.
7	local depth 14–22cm	50258 (Period 1)	11th+ century abundantly mottled dark greyish brown (10YR4/2) backfill	Strongly heterogeneous very poorly calcareous flu, with high amounts of natural Bs subsoil, and leached sands and silt 'topsoil', sometimes intimately mixed with fine charcoal and infilling hollow bone; patches of possible decomposing woody fragments, possible fine layering in places and a very thin matrix that is very weakly calcareous and contains phytoliths; slag and other burned materials present. Mixture of backfill, natural collapse/slurry of SFB sides?, possible woody structural material and possible cereal processing waste? Surfaces possibly trampled/occupied.
6	local depth 34–42cm	50263 (Period 1)	11th+ century very dark greyish (10YR3/2) fill, rich in charcoal, bone and pot	Heterogeneous fill rich in fine charcoal, phytoliths, amorphous organic (peat/turf?) and charred fragments, with many amorphous (phosphatic)? features; finely ashy, seed?, in situ root remains; mollusc, vesicular slag, bone, natural (Bstg) subsoil and pot present. Cereal processing waste and other midden material fills, in part possibly relating to use and abandonment of SFB?

Table 45 Samples, archaeology and micromorphology

VIII. MICROMORPHOLOGICAL ANALYSIS

by R.I. Macphail and G.M. Cruise

Nine undisturbed samples were taken from the two locations in Area C (Table 45), of which seven were processed for thin-section manufacture. Samples were impregnated with crystic resin and manufactured into thin sections according to the methods of Murphy (1986) and Guilloré (1985). Thin sections were briefly described and interpreted according to Bullock *et al.* (1985) and Courty *et al.* (1989). At Section 5, where there was over a metre of dark soil accumulation, a series of samples were taken from the natural/dark soil accumulation boundary dating to AD 1250+ (Sample 5) through to AD 1450 (Samples 4 and 3, respectively). Samples from the lower (Sample 6) and upper (Sample 7) 11th-century fills of sunken-featured building *50242* were taken, together with one from the fill of a 12th–14th-century pit (Sample 8), and another from a 12th–14th-century dark soil accumulation (Sample 9) seen in a section adjacent to this latter feature.

Field and preliminary soil micromorphological data are presented in Table 45. The natural soils on site are typical brown sandy soils formed in fluvioglacial drift over probable chalky till (Hodge *et al.* 1983). Soil material both from leached (upper subsoil and topsoil) and from iron- and clay-enriched Bs(t) subsoils are present. These originate from possible primary Late Saxon soil disturbance and from the later, more extensively eroded, medieval soil cover.

Building *50242* may contain fill elements relating to its construction, use and re-use. For example, it has a basal fill (Sample 6) rich in ash, charcoal and phytoliths, possibly a relic of cereal processing/storage waste. Similar basal fills have been assessed from Middle Saxon buildings at West Heslerton, North Yorks (unpub. assessment to English Heritage). The upper fill (Sample 7) contains more evidence both for midden dumping and for structural collapse of the feature, while fine layering in the upper part of the deposit might indicate re-use. These fills differ in character from the AD 1250+ deposits found adjacent to the building and at Section 5 (Samples 4, 5 and 9).

It appears likely that pre-existing soils at the site had been heavily truncated by the time the medieval Friary was established. A large proportion of the dark soil accumulation consists of sandy soils with occasional chalk, especially in the AD 1450 deposits (Sample 3). This may suggest renewed disturbance of the natural substrate (sands over chalky till) during this period and hence a rather rapid build-up of these dark soil deposits, probably from upslope. It is possible that midden, hearth, industrial and building debris dumping during the AD 1250+ period was carried out to produce more biologically active and fertile garden soils than would have been possible on the natural acidic sands. It is also likely that a natural humic soil formed during some period between 1250 and 1450 (Table 45, sample 4), when active dumping ceased for a time, if only in the immediate vicinity.

7. Conclusions

This project has highlighted the interdependence of archaeological evidence and documentary and historical sources when considering urban sites and landscapes. In defining the remit of the Norwich Survey, Malcolm Atkin observed that the role of archaeology, as compared to those of documentary research and the survey of standing buildings, depends on the period in question (Atkin 1993, 129). He noted that archaeology was particularly important for the period before 1285, but for the period between 1285 and 1470 there is parity between archaeological and documentary research. Fittingly, the year 1285 saw the first of a series of documented enlargements to Norwich's Franciscan Friary. Mortmain licenses of 1292 and 1299, giving the names of grantors and dimensions of properties, together with excavated evidence of boundaries, have formed the basis of spatial reconstruction of the pre-Friary urban landscape.

The wide-ranging new evidence has done much to address the project's stated objectives, as well as introducing some unexpected interpretative issues. One of the key aims of the recent excavations was to increase understanding of the development of this area of the Late Saxon and early medieval town. The information that the project has yielded regarding street pattern, plot development and associated production activities is invaluable. The new evidence for the layout of Norwich's early roads and lanes provides a framework for the study of the south-eastern block of the historic urban core. Concomitant with this is the evidence for the placement of urban churches. As a result of the Greyfriars project, and adjacent work at Norwich Castle (Shepherd Popescu forthcoming), the relevant sections of previously published maps of early Norwich (*e.g.* Atkin 1993, fig. 8.2; Ayers 1994, figs 18 and 29; Ayers 1996, fig. 10) will need revision.

Archaeology has not only augmented our rather scant knowledge (based on documents) of the internal layout of the Franciscan Friary following its redevelopment at the end of the 13th century, but has also provided an intimate picture of the day-to-day life of a religious community that was also an integral part of the secular society of Norwich until the Dissolution. Details of interaction with the lay community have been established from documentary sources (for example, for burial requests and legacies) and a number of key local individuals have been identified in connection with the Friary, including glaziers and bell-founders.

Although limited in scope, evidence for post-Reformation development of the site has aided definition of the influence of Friary structures and holdings on the city's developing topography. It has confirmed the position of Greyfriars House and surrounding gardens, while important new information (drawn from both excavated seals and documentary sources) has been gained relating to the post-medieval cloth trade.

Having discharged its archaeological obligations, the project's sponsor — the NFU Mutual and Avon Insurance Group — has built its new head office only metres from the site of the Franciscan church. Seven hundred years may have elapsed, but perceptions about the desirability of this northerly section of King Street do not seem to have changed. The only difference is that insurance of the soul, offered by the friars in exchange for gifts, bequests and elaborate requests for burial and anniversary masses, has been replaced by policies of a more earthly nature.

Appendix 1: Franciscans at Norwich

Date	*Name*	*Details*	*Source(s)*
Died about 1303	Roger Merston/Marston	Buried at Norwich, previously at Oxford and Cambridge.	(18)(19)
Died about 1334	Richard de Reppis		(19)
1337	Adam d'Ely	?lecturer at Norwich, later at Cambridge.	(16)
1337	Bartholomew de Repps	Lecturer at Norwich, previously at Cambridge.	(16)
1337	Roger Roseth/Rogeth	?lecturer at Norwich.	(16)
1337-39	[ ] Haverel	Lecturer at Norwich.	(16)
1337-39	Nicholas de Assisi	Took notes on lectures at Norwich.	(2)
mid-14th cent	Adam Wodham/Godham	Lecturer and author, also at London and Oxford.	(17)
after 1357, before 1378	Pietro Philarghi *alias* Peter de Candia	Studied at Norwich before going to Oxford. Became Pope Alexander V 1409, d.1410.	(1)
about 1358	John de Walsham	Questions disputed at Cambridge and Norwich.	(19)
fl. 1362	John Wichingham	Author.	(2)
Died 1369	Simon de Tunstede	Entered Franciscan order at Norwich before going to Oxford. Author.	(1)(2)
1373	Ralph de Castr'	Was bequeathed 5 marks for prayers.	(3)
1373	John de Alby	Was bequeathed 20s for prayers.	(3)
1373	John de Hilton	Was bequeathed 20s for prayers. Died at Norwich 1376.	(1)(3)
1373	Robert Colman	Was bequeathed 20s for prayers	(3) See also 1412
1373	John de Stutton	Was bequeathed 10s for prayers.	(3)
1397	John de Langha[ ]	Was bequeathed vjs v[ ].	(3)
1406	William Beeston (?at Norwich)	Ordained deacon.	(4)
1406	Nicholas de Saxonia	Ordained priest.	(4)
1406	John Pykyng	Ordained deacon.	(4)
1406	John de Wesfalia	Ordained deacon.	(4)
1406	John Todenham	Ordained priest.	(4)
1406	John de Austria	Ordained priest.	(4)
1406–7	John Dounham	Ordained deacon, priest.	(4)
1406–7	Geoffrey Harlyng	Ordained acolyte, subdeacon, deacon.	(4)
1407	John Oxwyk	Ordained subdeacon.	(4)
1407	John Lawynham/Lavenham	Ordained subdeacon, deacon.	(4)
1407	John Walpool	Ordained deacon, priest.	(4)
1407	Thomas Byry	Ordained priest.	(4)
1407	John Ewell	Ordained subdeacon, deacon.	(4)
1407	Theodoric de Saxonia	Ordained deacon.	(4)
1407	William Holkham	Ordained priest.	(4)
1407	Charles Lamb	Ordained acolyte.	(4)
1407	William Sedgeford	Ordained acolyte.	(4)
1407	Gerard Splynter	Ordained acolyte.	(4)
1407	Richard Wynour	Ordained subdeacon	(4)
1407	Simon Hemyngton	Ordained deacon.	(4)
1407	Bartholomew Reppys	Ordained deacon.	(4)
1407	John Bard	Ordained deacon.	(4)
1407	Peter in Ruremunda	Ordained deacon.	(4)
1407	Richard de Norwico	Ordained priest.	(4)
ntbl1407	Robert Langham	Ordained priest.	(4)
1407	John Russell	Ordained priest.	(4)
1407	Robert Botlesham	Ordained priest.	(4)
fl.1410	Reginald Langham	DD, author.	(2)(5)
before 1412–1430	Robert Colman	DTh, author, travelled abroad.	(1)(2)(14) See also 1373

Date	Name	Details	Source(s)
fl. 1418–66	John Brackley	Professor of theology, preacher, confessor to Sir John Fastolf, supporter of the Pastons, mentioned in wills, correspondence survives.	(3)(7)(8)
1431	John Paas	Was bequeathed a psalter.	(3)
1433	Robert de Carlt[ ]	Warden. Sealed letters of confraternity.	(9)
idctlpar1439-60	John Yergeawnt/Master Vergeant	Was bequeathed 33s 4d for half an annual; was not available to preach.	(3)(8, no.705)(19)
about 1440	Robert Finyngham	Author.	(2)
1442	John Pulham	Was bequeathed 5 marks for repair of chapel of St Mary.	(3)
about 1459	[ ] Gurnay	Procurator.	(8, no.581)
1460	[ ] Barnard	Warden. Not available to preach.	(8, no.705)(19)
1464-69	John Mowth/Moghte	?Warden. Supporter of the Pastons and confessor to Friar Brackley. Later at Cambridge.	(8)(19)
1465	Richard Colby	Warden. Was leased fishing in the Dallingflete. Later at Cambridge.	(10)(19)
1467	[ ] Lammesse	Was bequeathed 6s 8d.	(3)
1467	Thomas Poope	Was bequeathed 5 marks to sing for a year.	(3)
1468/9	William Rokewode	Warden.	(10)
1474–80	John Sparke	Received bequests and was made supervisor of wills.	(3)
1477–97	John Fyssher	Received bequests and was asked to go on pilgrimage to Rome.	(3)
1484	[ ] Thornham	Warden. Was bequeathed 20d.	(3)
1488	Nicholas Lucas	Was requested for prayers.	(3)
1494	Thomas Glaunvyle	Warden. Had made agreement for prayers.	(3)
1496	George Muse	Received bequests and was made supervisor of will.	(3)
1497	John Spryngwell	Was bequeathed 20s for prayers and was made supervisor of will. Later at Cambridge.	(3)(19)
1503–15	[ ] Laws/Lausell/Lawsall	Received bequests to himself and to his young friars.	(3)
1520	Master Hugh Kestren	Anchorite defamed by allegation that he had a son.	(11)
1524–39	William Call	Last warden. DD, minister provincial of the Franciscan order in England, received dispensation to hold benefice, rector of Heydon 1538, d.1539.	(5)(6)
1532	Robert Legate	Ordained subdeacon, deacon. Later at Cambridge.	(12)(19)
1532	Augustine Water	Ordained deacon, priest.	(12)
1532	Thomas Wraye	Ordained deacon, priest.	(12)
1532	Henry Howlette	Ordained priest.	(12)
1532	John Tompson	Ordained priest.	(12)
1532	William Russhebroke	Ordained priest.	(12)
1532	Richard Ryse	Ordained subdeacon.	(12)
1532	Robert Morley	Ordained deacon.	(12)
1532–33	Edward Wodhowse	Ordained subdeacon, deacon, priest.	(12)
1532–33	Thomas Skotte	Ordained subdeacon, deacon. Later at Cambridge.	(12)(19)
1532–33	Thomas Whyght/Wythe	Ordained subdeacon, deacon, priest.	(12)
1532–33	Thomas Maxfelde/Maxwell (?at Norwich)	Ordained subdeacon, priest.	(12)
1532–33	John Bull	Ordained subdeacon, deacon, priest.	(12)
1532–33	Richard Alexander	Ordained subdeacon, deacon, priest.	(12)
1532–33	Robert Starke	Ordained subdeacon, deacon, priest.	(12)
1532–34	Thomas Cade	Ordained subdeacon, priest.	(12)
1532–38	Thomas Bent(e)ley(e)	Ordained subdeacon, deacon, priest 1532, received dispensation to hold benefice 1538.	(6)(12)
1532–38	Robert Shereman	Ordained subdeacon, deacon 1532/3, received dispensation to hold benefice 1538.	(6)(12)
1532–41	Richard Sharpe	Ordained subdeacon, deacon, priest. Pardoned for forging letters of dispensation.	(12)(15)
1533	John Fraunces	Ordained subdeacon, priest.	(12)
1533	Edward Pache	Ordained subdeacon.	(12)
1533	John Gumble (?at Norwich)	Ordained priest.	(12)
1533	Thomas Browne (?at Norwich)	Ordained priest.	(12)

Date	*Name*	*Details*	*Source(s)*
1533–34	Humfrey Typpynge	Ordained subdeacon, deacon, priest.	(12)
1533–34	Thomas Feverell	Ordained subdeacon, deacon, priest.	(12)
1533–34	Nicholas Breten	Ordained subdeacon, deacon.	(12)
1534	William Bylyn	Ordained deacon, priest.	(12)
1534	William Canivas/Canvas	Ordained subdeacon, deacon. Later at Cambridge.	(12)(19)
1534	Thomas Cappes	Ordained subdeacon.	(12)
1534	Henry Skytmore	Ordained subdeacon.	(12)
1534–35	Thomas Roche	Ordained subdeacon, deacon, priest.	(12)
1534–35	Peter Wellys	Ordained subdeacon, deacon.	(12)
1535	William Baules	Ordained priest.	(12)
1535	John Vincent	Ordained exorcist and acolyte. Later at Cambridge.	(12)(19)
1535	John Keler	Ordained exorcist and acolyte.	(12)
1538	Richard Morleye	Received dispensation to hold benefice.	(6)
1538	Thomas Godderd	Received dispensation to hold benefice.	(6)
1538	Thomas Foote	Received dispensation to hold benefice.	(6)
1538	Jo. Woode	Received dispensation to hold benefice.	(6)
1538	John Cause	Received dispensation to hold benefice; aged 66 in 1555.	(6)(13)
1538	Thomas Grimston	Received dispensation to hold benefice.	(6)
1538	Edward Wellis	Received dispensation to hold benefice.	(6)
1538	Robert Lakeham	Received dispensation to hold benefice.	(6)
1538	William Harwoode	Received dispensation to hold benefice.	(6)
1538	Thomas Calye	Received dispensation to hold benefice.	(6)
1538	Walter Austen	Received dispensation to hold benefice.	(6)
1538	Barnaby Whiting	Received dispensation to hold benefice.	(6)
1538	Thomas Palling	Received dispensation to hold benefice.	(6)
1538	Jo. Albon	Received dispensation to hold benefice.	(6)
1538	Henry Joynte	Anchorite; received dispensation to hold benefice; rector of Kimberley, 1542; aged 70 in 1555.	(6)(13)
1538	Richard Smyth	Received dispensation to hold benefice.	(6)
1538	Thomas Bowth	Received dispensation to hold benefice.	(6)
1538	Jo. Marsley	Received dispensation to hold benefice.	(6)
before 1541	John Yong	Received dispensation to hold benefice.	(15)

Sources
(1) Emden 1957
(2) Tanner 1984, 34, 192
(3) Appendix 2
(4) Lambeth Palace Library, Arundel 1, 544–9
(5) Venn 1922
(6) Chambers 1966, 160
(7) Blomefield 1806, IV 115
(8) Davis 1971
(9) Appendix 3
(10) Kirkpatrick 1845, 117
(11) Stone 1938, no. 216
(12) NRO DN/ORR/1/1
(13) Rye 1905, 32-3
(14) Cal. pat. rolls 1429—35, 380
(15) L and P for. and dom. Henry VIII, 16 p.499
(16) Doucet 1953
(17) Little 1892, 172–3
(18) Kingsford 1915, 192
(19) Moorman 1952, 146–226

This list does not include friars whose attribution to Norwich depends entirely on Blomefield 1806, IV 111–16. In the absence of evidence to the contrary, friars mentioned in wills asking for burial at the Norwich Greyfriars have been assumed to be Franciscans.

Appendix 2: Requests for burial at, and legacies concerning, the Norwich Greyfriars (1370 to the Dissolution)

Date	*Name*	*Details*	*Source(s)*
1370	Sir John de Haddon of Houton St Peter.	Burial among (*inter*) the friars. Bequest: one *ogum* [?Ockham], a portable breviary or psalter, a copper pot, one blanket *de Reyn'*, fifteen ells of linen cloth.	(NRO NCC 5 Heydon)
1371	Walter Baker, parson of Shropham.	Burial in the cemetery next to where Master Dionisius was buried. Bequest: 15s.	(NRO NCC 10 Heydon)
1372	William de Pulham, mercer, of Norwich.	Burial in the church. Bequest: 20s for prayers.	(NRO NCC 22 Heydon)
1372	Thomas Ladde of Norwich.	Burial elsewhere. Bequest: half a mark for prayers.	(NRO NCC 24 Heydon)
1373	John de Reppes, knight.	Burial at (*apud*) the friars minor next to the burial of Sir John Bauent. Bequest: to friars Ralph de Castr' five marks, John de Alby 20s, John de Hilton 20s, Robert Colman 20s and John de Stutton 10s for prayers.	(NRO NCC 31 Heydon)
1374	Henry Wynke chaplain.	Burial in the burial place (*sepeltura*). Bequest: 40s of silver.	(NRO NCC 47 Heydon)
1385	Lady Petronilla de Hardeshill.	Burial in the church. Bequest: 40s.	(NRO NCC 52 Harsyk)
1397	Henry Oldebek of Great Witchingham, rector of Wramplingham.	Burial among the friars minor. Bequest: 10 marks and to friar John de Langha[ ] vjs v[ ].	(NRO NCC 241 Harsyk)
1418	John Esterford, rector of Bixley.	Burial within the precinct (*infra limites*). Bequest: the best of three vestments then in the custody of the friars minor for prayers.	(NRO DN/REG 4 book 8 f 144d)
1424	Thomas Ocle of Norwich.	Burial in the church. Bequest: 5 marks for prayers.	(NRO NCC 138 Hyrnyng)
1430	Richard Carbonell, knight.	Burial anywhere. Bequest: 20s, two gold cloths with (a) frontal(s) for the altar and one bible.	(NRO NCC 66 Surflete)
1431	Margaret widow of Richard Carbonell, knight.	Burial in the chapel of St Anne in the church. Bequest: 20s and to friar John Paas one psalter.	(NRO NCC 82 Surflete)
1431	Thomas Boys, esquire.	Burial among the friars (*infra ordinem*). Bequest: 20s for burial.	(NRO NCC 82 Surflete)
1437	Henry Walsingham of Trowse.	Burial in church. Bequest: none.	(NRO NCC 34 Doke)
1439	Thomas atte Yates son of Richard lister of Norwich.	Burial in the church. Bequest: £5 for prayers. 10 marks to friar John Brakle, bachelor of theology, my full brother (*germano meo*). 33s 4d to friar John Yergeawnt of the friars minor for half an annual. Appoints friar John Brakle a supervisor of his will.	(NRO NCC 103 Doke)
1442	John Braklee of Norwich, lyster.	Burial in the church. Bequest: half the proceeds from the sale of a tenement in St Swithin, Norwich, for prayers. Appoints friar John Brakle, professor of theology, supervisor of the will.	(NRO NCC 177 Doke)
1442	William Seman of Norwich.	Burial in the church. Bequest: 5 marks and to friar John Pulham 5 marks for the improvement or repair (*ad facturam sive emendacionem*) of the chapel of St Mary within the church.	(NRO NCC 185 Doke)
1445	Roger Totenay.	Burial in the church. Bequest: 10s.	(NRO NCC 37 Wylbey)
1446	Robert Londesdale of Norwich, esquire.	Burial in the church. Bequest: 20s. Property in Norfolk to be sold for the benefit *inter alia* of the souls of Margery and Margaret former wives of John and Richard Carbonell. Both women were buried in the church of the friars minor at Norwich. Appoints friar minor John Braklee, professor of theology, a supervisor of the will.	(Lambeth Palace Library, Stafford 138)
1453	Robert Ryngman, rector of Barnham Broome and suffragen bishop of Graden'.	Burial within the choir of the church. Bequest: 20s for a pittance of food [extra allowance].	(NRO NCC 175 Aleyn)
1459	Alice Preston, widow.	Burial in the church. Bequest: 6s 8d for a pittance and for prayers.	(NRO NCC 176 Brosyard)
1462	Thomas Shyrlok, chaplain	Burial in the cemetery. Bequest: 20s for two trentals.	(NRO NCC 74 Betyns)
1463	John Causton *alias* Julians of Norwich, grocer.	Burial elsewhere. Bequest: 20s for repair of the buildings and 20s to be distributed among the cloister for food and various necessities.	(NRO NCC 161 Betyns)

Date	*Name*	*Details*	*Source(s)*
1467	Richard Hofft of Norwich, mercer.	Burial elsewhere. Bequest: to each of the four orders of friars 26s 6d for repairs and to each house 6s 8d for a pittance for a dirge in the church of St John Maddermarket, Norwich. To each friar at Norwich, doctor of divinity, and to friar Water, bachelor, 20s; to friar Lammesse, friar minor, 6s 8d; to friar Thomas Poope, friar minor, 5 marks to sing for a year.	(NRO NCC 84 Jekkys)
1470	Margery Eton of Norwich.	Burial in the church. Bequest: ? a mark and 8d.	(NRO NCC 185 Jekkys)
1474	Alice Brocher of Norwich, widow.	Burial in the church. Bequest: 20s to the repair of the dormitory. Appoints friar John Sparke supervisor of the will and leaves him 40d for his trouble.	(NRO NCC 61 Gelour)
1477	William Herbert of Swardeston.	Burial in the church. Bequest: 6s 8d for prayers. In addition would like friar John Fyssher, his nephew, to have the job of celebrating mass for two years on his behalf for 14 marks and 10s.	(NRO NCC 180 Gelour)
1477	Sir John Spendlove, chaplain.	Burial elsewhere. Bequest: to each order of friars in Norwich 6s 8d. To Katherine sister of the order of friars minor 8d.	(NRO NCC 183 Gelour)
1478	Joan Cook of North Walsham, widow.	Burial elsewhere. Bequest: to the house of the friars minor in Norwich of which I am a sister (*consoror*) one comb of barley.	(NRO NCC 216 Gelour)
1480	Thomas Spark of Norwich, coverlet weaver.	Burial in the church. Bequest: 20s for his burial. To friar John Spark his son 8 marks for prayers for one year. Appoints John Spark supervisor of the will and leaves him 3s 4d for his trouble.	(NRO NCC 74 Caston)
1484	Margaret Est of Norwich, widow.	Buried elsewhere. Bequest: 6d with her letter of pardon from ('over') the grey friars to the same place 'unto which I am sustyr' and a mass there if her goods be sufficient.	(NRO NCC 203 Caston)
1484	Cecily Shelton of Norwich, widow of Thomas Shelton, gentleman.	Burial in the church next to the tomb of Thomas. Bequest: none.	(NRO NCC 208 Caston)
1484	John Dyghton of Norwich, vintner.	Burial in the north side of the church, before St Thomas. Bequest: 20s for breaking the ground; to each friar a priest 4d, to each other friar 2d and to each friar a master [of arts] 12d; to the friars priests one pipe of red wine to sing mass with; to friar Thornham warden 20d; a stained cloth with the nine worthies.	(NRO NCC 237 Caston)
1485	William Philippes, alderman of Norwich.	Burial in the church by the grave of his wife Kateryn. Bequest: to every friar a priest at his burying and mass 4d, to every other friar 2d; 3s 4d for a pittance and 20s for the repair of the friary.	(NRO NCC 245 Caston)
1486	Margaret Fissher of Norwich, widow.	Burial in the church. Bequest: 10s for one pittance and for breaking the ground. To friar John Fysher her son 6s 6d which he owes her and a further 20s for prayers for three months and one pair of linen sheets.	(NRO NCC 61 Aubry)
1488	Margaret Skipwith, widow of William Skipwith of Norwich, esquire.	Burial in the chapel of St Mary the Virgin next (contigua) to the choir of the church. Bequest: 10 marks. To one friar praying in the chapel for five years, £4 a year, with preference to be given to friar Nicholas Lucas for the first two years. To each friar a priest at her burial 4d, to each novice 2d.	(NRO NCC 18 Wolman) Neither the chapel of St Anne nor the ceiling of any part is mentioned (see Blomefield 1806, IV 110, Kirkpatrick 1845, 121).
1492	Isabell Lyston, widow of Robert Lyston, esquire.	Burial in the church next to the grave of her husband, if she die in Norwich. Bequest: to repair of the friary 33s 4d; for two pittances at two different times 6s 8d.	(NRO NCC 171 Wolman)
1492	William Cusshyn of Hingham.	Burial elsewhere. Bequest: 10s to the greyfriars in Norwich where he is a brother for *placebo* and dirge with a requiem mass.	(NRO NCC 40 Norman)
1494	Thomas Brygg, esquire.	Burial on the south side of the church within 'le parclos' before the altar. Bequest: 100 marks for prayers as specified in an agreement with Thomas Glaunvyle, guardian. 20s to each of the four orders of friars in Norwich. 100s for a marble stone on his tomb.	(NRO NCC 202 Wolman)
1496	John Savage, rector of Forncett St Peter.	Burial in the church among the friars minor. Bequest: 5 marks from his tithes and more if possible. To friar George Muse his best bed, his stained cloth in the hall, a piece of silver and two silver spoons. Appoints friar George Muse supervisor of the will.	(NRO NCC 8 Multon)
1496	John Brasyer, priest of Tacolneston.	Burial elsewhere. Bequest: 13s 4d to be distributed between the four orders of friars in Norwich. 10s for a trental to be sung for the souls of Alice Chawmneys and Kateryn Cony in the Greyfriars at Norwich.	(NRO NCC 31 Multon)

Date	*Name*	*Details*	*Source(s)*
1497	Roger Aylemer, esquire.	Burial within the precinct. Bequest: to repair of books and vestments 40s and 6s 8d for a pittance. To each of the four friars bearing his body to the church 20d. For the repair of the church, for prayers and for an annual requiem mass for four years, £8 from the sale of a house in St Stephens, Norwich. Friar John Fyssher to pray and to go on pilgrimage to Rome on his behalf for 10 marks when he goes and 40s when he returns.	(NRO NCC 49 Multon)
1497	Petyr Peterson of Norwich, hardwareman.	Burial at the friars preachers. Bequest: to each of the other houses of friars 6s 8d. To the gild of St Barbara held in the Greyfriars 40d.	(NRO NCC 55 Multone)
1497	John Spryngwell of Norwich.	Burial in the church of St Francis at the friars minor in Norwich. Bequest: 40s and a pittance. To friar John Spryngewell his son 20s for prayers. Appoints John supervisor of his will to help his mother the executrix.	(NRO NCC 55 Multone)
1498	Herry Barnard of East Dereham.	Burial elsewhere. Bequest: 12d to the gild of our lady at the friars minor in Norwich.	(NRO NCC 91 Multone)
1498	Laurence Williamson of Norwich.	Burial in the church. Bequest: 20s for his burial.	(NRO NCC 97 Multon)
1499	Richard Glawnvile of Norwich, brewer.	Burial at the Greyfriars.	(Kirkpatrick 1845, 122)
1502	Geoffrey Freman of Norwich.	Burial in the church. Bequest: 10s for a trental.	(NRO NCC 150 Popy)
1502	Anastas Elys of Norwich, singlewoman.	Burial in the church. Bequest: 2s to their use and 10s for a trental of St Gregory to be sung in the church on her burial day.	(NRO NCC 239 Popy)
1503	Thomas Hood of Norwich, skinner.	Burial elsewhere. Bequest: to friar Laws 10s.	(NRO NCC 348 Popy)
1504	Geffrey Stywarde, alderman of Norwich.	Burial elsewhere. Bequest: to each of the four orders of friars in Norwich 13s 4d. Four friars from the four orders to take it in turns to sing mass for 32 days after his death, each priest to have 4d for his labour. To the gild of St John the Evangelist held in the Greyfriars 20 shillings.	(NRO NCC 507 Popy)
1505	Nicholas Townlee of New Buckenham.	Burial elsewhere. Bequest: for a trental of St Gregory to be sung for his soul in the Greyfriars and Austin friars at Norwich.	(NRO NCC 139 Ryxe)
1505	Isabell Hoode of Norwich, widow.	Burial in the church. Bequest: a maser, six silver spoons, my best brass pot, my best pan and 3s 4d for a pittance. To friar Lausell a little silver salt, my best featherbed with the 'curynge' and testor or anything in my house. The residue to friar Lausell and to his young friars for prayers. Friar Lausell is to use her husband's legacy to make John his child a friar and maintain him until he be a priest.	(NRO NCC 174 Ryxe)
1505	William Southwode of Norwich, cook.	Burial elsewhere. Bequest: to have four grey friars bear him to church, 4d to each for their labour.	(NRO NCC 230 Ryxe)
1506	William Heyward of Norwich.	Burial elsewhere. Bequest: 20s and to the gild of St John the Evangelist held in the Greyfriars in Norwich 3s 4d.	(PCC 7 Adean)
1511	Robert Barnard of Norwich, esquire.	Burial elsewhere. Bequest: 20s for prayers and a gown of tawny damask to make a chasuble.	(NRO NCC 111 Johnson)
1514	Edward Walshe of Witlingham, gentleman.	Burial in the church. Bequest: 5 marks for prayers and for his burial.	(NRO NCC 18 Spurlinge)
1515	Margerye Havyr of Norwich, widow.	Burial in the church beside her husband John. Bequest: 26s 8d for her burial, to every friar a priest 4d, to every novice 2d and to every servant 1d. A friar to sing prayers in the Greyfriars for 3 years for 4 marks a year. Friar Lawsall to have 5 marks to sing for a year.	(NRO NCC 58 Spurlinge)
1516	Olive Dade of Norwich, maid.	Burial in the Greyfriars. Bequest: 4 marks and 'unto your ladie of pietie' her best frontlet.	(NRO NCC 121 Spurlinge)
1518	Alisander Persan of Taverham.	Burial where god pleases. Bequest: if greyfriars (Norwich not specified) bury him before our lady of pity, 6s 8d to the convent (friary) and 6s 8d to the brethren for their labour.	(NRO NCC 71 Gylys)
1518	William Beisby of Norwich, draper.	Burial elsewhere. Bequest: to every order of friars in Norwich 3s 4d. To the gild of St John held in the Greyfriars in Norwich 2s. 20d to his uncle the anchorite of the Greyfriars to sing 5 masses of the 5 wounds. If he be dead or unable to sing the masses to use some other priest.	(NRO NCC 76 Gylys)

Date	*Name*	*Details*	*Source(s)*
1522	Robert Boys of Norwich, grocer.	Burial elsewhere. Bequest: to each of the four orders of friars in Norwich for prayers 3s 4d. To the gild of St John in the Greyfriars 12d.	(NRO NCC 148 Alblaster)
1522	Agnes wife of John Marchaunde, widow of John Ballis of Norwich, pinner.	Burial elsewhere. Bequest: 3s 4d to the gild of St Barbara held within the Greyfriars.	(NRO NCC 150 Alblaster)
1523	John Burward of Norwich, cook.	Burial elsewhere. Bequest: that Agnes his wife during her lifetime should provide a candle before the image of our lady in the porch of the Greyfriars yearly from 5 weeks before All Saints' Day to 3 weeks after Candlemas.	(NRO NCC 15 Herman)
1529	Roger Appylyarde.	Burial in the Greyfriars. Bequest: £4 for his burial and prayers.	(PCC 14 Jankyn)
1532	Raffe Metcalfe of Swanton Morley.	Burial elsewhere. Bequest: to the box of St Francis' friars in Norwich 12d and to the place there 4s.	(NRO NCC 157 Alpe)

This list makes no attempt to be comprehensive. It is primarily based on printed sources and does not include the many bequests left generally to the Norwich friaries. The dates are those of probate as given in the printed indexes.

Appendix 3: Records of Norwich Franciscan Friary

i) Letter of Confraternity to Thomas Bate and Family, 1433

(frontispiece)

To his most dear in Christ, Thomas Bate and his children, Friar Richard, minister and servant of the Friars Minors in England, wisheth health, and by the merits of this life to receive eternal joys. I, considering and accepting the devotion, which, for the reverence of God, you have to our order, with an affection of sincere charity, and desiring to render to you a salutary recompence, I receive you to all and singular the suffrages of the friars of the English administration, as well in life as in death, by the tenor of these presents; granting to you a full participation of all the spiritual good things, as far as it shall please God, which, by the same friars committed to my care, the clemency of our Saviour shall vouchsafe to be wrought. Adding, moreover, of our special grace, that when your deaths, together with an exhibition of these presents, shall be shewed in our provincial chapter, there shall be done for you by the whole administration of England, that which hath been used to be performed for our friars, and the friends and benefactors of our order deceased, there recommended. Farewell, happily! in the Lord Jesus Christ, and in His Mother, the glorious Virgin. Dated at Norwich, the fourth day of February, A.D. 1432 [1433]. By Friar Robert Carlt[on] [seal].

Translation from the Latin by Kirkpatrick (Kirkpatrick 1845, 124–5). Richard Leak was minister provincial of the order in England. The original document, without the seal, is now NRO Phi 567 578x3.

ii) Chronicles

Mentioned by William Worcestre in 1478 (Harvey 1969, 78–81).

iii) Seals

(Plate 3.1)

Blomefield shows two lozenge-shaped seals on his map of Norwich (Blomefield 1806, III opp.1). The earlier shows the coronation of the Virgin with a friar praying below and the legend *Sig(illum) Fratrum Minorum in Norwico* in Lombardic lettering. The later seal depicts St Francis at the entrance of a church with the legend *S(igillum) com(m)u(n)e prioris et convenc(us) in Norwico Fratrum Francisc(anorum)* in Gothic lettering.

Appendix 4: Payments made by the city for work on the Greyfriars site

(NRO NCR 18a Chamb. acc. 1551–67: not seen)

1565/6 (f.320)

Payed to Fraunces the tyler for fower dayes worke in taking downe tyle of the greate howse at the Graye Fryers at 10d the daye	3s 4d
Item payed to hym for fower dayes worke of his ladde at 8d the daye	2s 8d
Item payed to John Nuby laborer for six dayes worke at 7d the daye	3s 6d
Item payed to Broke laborar for six dayes worke at 7d the daye	3s 6d
Item payed to Cleare laborar for fower dayes worke at 8d the daye	2s 8d
Item payed to Gedge laborar for six dayes worke at 7d the daye	3s 6d
Item payed more to Cleare laborer for six dayes worke at 8d the daye	4s
Item payed to Reason the carpenter for fower dayes worke in making of doores and mending of gates	3s 4d
Item payed to hym for fower dayes worke of his servaunt at 8d the daye	2s 8d
Item payed for nayles	20d
Item payed more to Reason for six dayes worke in taking downe the greate howse at the Graye Fryers at 10d the daye	5s
Item payed to hym for six dayes worke of his servaunt	4s
Item payed to John Hewby laborer for six dayes worke at 8d the daye	4s
Item payed to Palmer mason for fower dayes worke in taking downe gables and butteresses at the greate howse	3s 4d
Item payed for baskettes to carry bryke and stone in	12d
Item payed for a new barrow	3s
Item payed for a barrow spyndell	12d
Item payed for too ropes to take downe the howses	5s
Item payed to Reason the carpenter for six dayes worke as 10d the daye	5s
Item payed to hym for six dayes worke of his servaunt at 8d the daye	4s
Item payed to Palmer the mason for eighte dayes worke in mending of walles and pulling downe of walles at 10d the daye	6s 8d
Item payed more to hym for eighte dayes worke of his servaunt	5s 8d
Item payed to Hothe the laborer for eighte dayes worke	5s 4d
Item payed for thre chalder and one combe of lyme occupyed there	13s
Item for too lodes of sande	20d
Item payed to Hewby laborer for coldering of thirty lodes of stone	7s 6d
Item payed to Quantrell the dawber for fower dayes worke in covering the walles	3s 4d
Item payed to his too laborers for fower dayes worke	5s 4d
Item payed for fower lodes of claye	4s
Item payed for rede to cover the walles	5s
Item payed for cariage of rede	10d
Item payed for stre [straw]	2s 6d
Summa	£6 7s

1566/7 (f.353)

Payed to Reason the carpenter for thre dayes worke of hymselfe in making up a howse for Thomas Elsey at the Graye Fryers (with other minor payments adding up to a total of 27s 1d)	
(f.356r) Item to Huby for fellyng the greate gable at the Graye Fryer	5s

Appendix 5: Medieval paint palettes

Date	*Provenance and description*	*Pigments and media identified*	*Comments*	*References*
Mid/late 16th-century	Acton Court (S. Glos.): oyster shell containing red pigment.	Dry process vermilion was identified by PLM & XRF. FTIR analysis undertaken to determine the presence of original binding media proved inconclusive.	The shell was excavated from the south arm of the moat.	Hughes and Strong 1990.
Before 1338 (?)	Boyton Church (Wilts.): oyster shell found next to tomb probably of Lady Margaret Nevill (d.1338): retains gold, and red and blue pigment.		Examination undertaken by the British Museum indicated that the palette was used in painting the tomb chest.	Richardson 1980, 29; *Age of Chivalry* 1987, 391.
	Canterbury, St. Augustine's Abbey: oyster shell from excavation immediately S. of the Lady Chapel and St. Thomas' Chapel in the Norman crypt. Contains azurite, cinnabar, etc.	Azurite, cinnabar, lead white, lead-tin yellow and a copper green identified by XRF & XRD. No media analysis undertaken.	The palette was excavated from Area 1, layer 1 (probably a levelling layer of 1791). Four layers of colour were found, indicating that the palette had been used several times.	Knight 1988, 200.
1251?	Clarendon Palace (Wilts.), scallop shell found in excavation of Antioch Chamber. Contains blue pigment.	Azurite, identified by PLM & MCT. Media staining tests proved inconclusive.	The Antioch Chamber was painted in 1251 with the story of Antioch and the duel of Richard I and Saladin. The shell was found together with the base of a pot containing red lead.	Hughes and Lewis 1988, 258–60, pl. LVIa.
Between 1342 and mid 16th century	Coventry, Carmelite Friary: oyster shell containing gold leaf and pigments.	Gold leaf, natural azurite, red lake, lead white and carbon black identified by PLM, MCT, SEM/EDX & FTIR.	The Friary was founded in 1342, and the palette was excavated from a rubbish fill associated with the mid 16th-century Grammar School.	Howard 1997.
	Faversham Abbey (Kent): three oyster shells containing red, blue and green pigments.	Vermilion, a copper-based blue pigment, and a green which may have been obtained by mixing the blue with a lead-based yellow pigment, were detected by MCT.	The shells were excavated from fill in the 'workshop area' between the church and cloister; associated pottery indicated that the fill was not undertaken before 1500 at the earliest.	Philp 1968, 27, 51.
	Glastonbury Abbey (Somerset): five oyster shells, two containing blue pigment, two yellow/green, and one pink.		Excavated by Bond in 1915, close to the 'chapel in the monks' graveyard'; colours described by him as vermilion, azure and 'black or neutral colour'. Pigments sampled by J. James in 1986, but results not available.	Bond 1915, 136–7.
	Hardham Church (W. Sussex): shells found in cavity in chancel, N. wall.	Two shells examined by J. Plesters (National Gallery): one contained red iron oxide mixed with chalk and brown earthy material, and the other chalk and brown earthy material.	Red iron oxide, but not chalk, is compatible with the materials of the very complete scheme of surviving wall painting at Hardham, dating from *c.* 1100. However, the present location of the shells and other objects (including a cresset lamp) found in the cavity is unknown, and the dating of the finds is very uncertain; although the balance of evidence suggests they may have been medieval, one reference mentions that a teacup was among the finds.	Letter from J. Plesters (National Gallery) and other unpubl. references in Courtauld Institute archive.
	Haverfordwest Priory (Dyfed): shells containing pigment.		Some four or five oyster shells, all (?) containing remains of pigment, have been found in the excavation of the Priory which began in 1983. They were found in the slype between the chapter house and S. transept.	T. Pestell, *pers. comm.*, 1997.

Date	*Provenance and description*	*Pigments and media identified*	*Comments*	*References*
	Linlithgow (W. Lothian), Carmelite Friary: three shells with traces of pigment.	Traces of red lead identified in one shell, and large particles of vermilion in another.	Found with two pot fragments also with remains of pigment. In analysis, azurite and a synthetic copper green were also identified, but it is unclear from the published account whether either of these pigments are present in any of the shells. Excavated from early post-Reformation demolition layers, in which lumps of red ochre and a lump of indigo or woad was also found.	Lindsay 1989, 153–4, frontis.
12th-century	London, City: two oyster shell palettes with red pigment.	The pigment was identified as probably vermilion by PLM and MCT.	Excavated from pits on the W. side of the City. One is from a pit-fill dated to the first half of the 12th century, while the other is from a fill of date later in the 12th century.	Pritchard 1991, 170–1, 260.
	London, Guildhall yard: four shell palettes with pigment.		Excavated by the Museum of London. Dated to the medieval period.	G. Egan, *pers. comm.*
	Ludgate, London: eight (?) shell palettes with pigment.		Excavated by the Museum of London. Information on the various contexts is not yet available, but they are all broadly dated to the medieval period.	G. Egan, *pers. comm.*
	Merton Priory (Surrey): five shell palettes with red, blue and reddish/purple pigments.		Four shell palettes, and a fragment of a fifth, were excavated by the Museum of London Archaeology Service in 1986-89.	D. Seeley, *pers. comm.*; Miller and Saxby forthcoming.
	Mount Grace Priory (N. Yorks.): shells containing pigment.			Knight 1988, 200.
c. 1300 (?)	Norwich, Greyfriars: oyster shell palette containing pigments.	Natural azurite, vermilion, gum and a black material were identified by PLM, SEM/EDX and FTIR.	Examination undertaken for the Norfolk Archaeological Unit.	See present report.
13th-century	Oxford, St. Aldates: oyster shell palette.		Found with pens and other tools used in book production.	Donovan 1991, 13.
	Salisbury Museum: oyster shell containing red pigment.	Red iron oxide, identified spectrographically and by MCT (British Museum 1958).	No information in analytical record on date or original provenance of shell.	British Museum, unpubl. record, 1958.
	Sempringham Priory (Lincs.): two oyster shells containing pigment.		One shell contains red pigment, and the other what seems to be a buff paint overlain by red.	Park & Stewart 1996, 302.
	Winchester Cathedral: two oyster shells, one containing red and the other yellow 'ochre'.		Current location of the palettes is not known.	R. Lithgow, *pers. comm.*, 1990.

PLM – polarised light microscopy; *MCT* – microchemical tests; *SEM/EDX* – scanning electron microscopy with energy dispersive X-ray analysis; *FTIR* – Fourier transform infra-red microspectroscopy; *XRF* – X-ray fluorescence; *XRD* – X-ray diffraction.

Appendix 6: Percentage number of anatomical elements of cattle and 'lar' bones expressed as a percentage of the total number of bones per period

		Period							
		1		*2*		*3–3.1–3.2*		*4.1*	
		CATTLE (220 nisp)	*LAR (487 nisp)*	*CATTLE (237 nisp)*	*LAR (395 nisp)*	*CATTLE (858 nisp)*	*LAR (2109 nisp)*	*CATTLE (292 nisp)*	*LAR (201 nisp)*
	Bone	*%*	*%*	*%*	*%*	*%*	*%*	*%*	*%*
HIGH QUALITY	Scapula	2	7	7	3	4	5	6	5
	Humerus	3	1	4	3	4	1	11	-
	Pelvis	5	2	7	2	9	2	9	1
	Femur	4	<1	3	2	7	1	7	-
	Cervical vx.	<1	1	2	1	<1	1	3	1
	Thoracic vx.	4	3	3	4	2	6	2	3
	Lumbar vx.	4	3	2	2	1	4	4	3
	Sacrum	1	1	<1	-	1	<1	3	4
	Vertebra frag.	1	9	-	7	<1	8	<1	11
	Caudal vx.	<1	-	<1	-	<1	<1	-	-
	Sternum	<1	<1	-	<1	1	<1	-	-
	Ribs	-	40	-	36	8	43	-	34
	Total	26	67	28	60	39	73	47	64
	Long bone frag.	-	24	-	29	-	20	-	20
LESSER QUALITY	Tibia	6	<1	6	<1	7	<1	13	-
	Radius	7	1	4	1	4	1	6	-
	Ulna	2	<1	2	1	2	<1	1	-
	Total	15	1	13	3	13	2	20	-
	Skull	12	5	14	4	7	3	7	16
	Maxilla	1	-	2	-	1	-	-	-
	Mandible	9	1	7	1	5	1	4	-
	Total	22	6	23	6	13	4	11	16
Total meat-bearing bones		63	99	64	98	65	99	78	100
LOW QUALITY	Horn core	1	-	1	-	2	<1	1	-
	Hyoid	-	<1	<1	<1	<1	<1	-	-
	Atlas	2	<1	1	<1	<1	<1	2	-
	Axis	2	<1	1	<1	1	<1	1	-
	Carpal	1	-	3	<1	1	<1	-	-
	Metacarpal	5	<1	6	-	6	-	3	-
	Patella	1	-	-	-	<1	-	-	-
	Astragalus	2	-	2	-	4	-	1	-
	Calcaneus	4	-	1	-	3	<1	2	-
	Tarsal	2	-	1	-	2	<1	1	-
	Metatarsal	4	-	5	-	4	<1	5	-
	Metapodial	2	-	1	<1	1	-	2	-
	First phalanx	4	<1	5	-	5	<1	3	-
	Second phalanx	3	-	5	-	3	-	1	-
	Third phalanx	3	-	1	-	1	-	1	-
Total waste bones		38	1	36	2	35	1	22	-

Appendix 7: Percentage number of anatomical elements of sheep/goat and 'sma' bones expressed as a percentage of the total number of bones per period

		Period							
		1		*2*		*3–3.1–3.2*		*4.1*	
		S/G (153 nisp)	*SMA (577 nisp)*	*S/G (254 nisp)*	*SMA (387 nisp)*	*S/G (610 nisp)*	*SMA (2054 nisp)*	*S/G (95 nisp)*	*SMA (82 nisp)*
	Bone	*%*	*%*	*%*	*%*	*%*	*%*	*%*	*%*
HIGH QUALITY	Scapula	4	6	3	1	5	3	18	-
	Humerus	8	1	3	<1	9	1	7	-
	Pelvis	5	2	3	1	8	2	8	1
	Femur	1	<1	2	-	2	1	8	-
	Cervical vx.	1	1	-	1	1	1	-	2
	Thoracic vx.	1	4	1	4	3	4	-	5
	Lumbar vx.	4	3	-	3	3	4	1	7
	Sacrum	-	<1	-	<1	<1	<1	-	-
	Vertebra frag.	-	5	-	2	1	7	-	7
	Caudal vx.	-	-	-	<1	-	<1	-	-
	Sternum	-	<1	-	-	-	<1	-	-
	Ribs	-	45	-	50	-	42	-	50
	Total	23	68	12	64	32	65	43	73
	Long bone frag.	-	23	-	25	1	27	-	22
LESSER QUALITY	Tibia	3	1	12	<1	8	1	8	-
	Radius	10	1	18	<1	8	<1	6	-
	Ulna	4	<1	1	-	2	<1	3	-
	Total	17	2	21	1	18	2	18	-
	Skull	21	4	5	7	3	3	11	5
	Maxilla	6	-	4	-	1	-	1	-
	Mandible	15	1	14	<1	11	<1	5	-
	Total	42	5	24	8	15	4	18	5
Total meat bearing bones		82	99	57	98	66	98	79	100
LOW QUALITY	Horn core	4	-	1	-	6	<1	1	-
	Hyoid	-	-	1	-	1	<1	-	-
	Atlas	-	<1	2	<1	1	<1	8	-
	Axis	1	-	1	<1	2	<1	3	-
	Carpal	-	-	<1	<1	-	<1	-	-
	Metacarpal	3	<1	9	-	7	-	1	-
	Patella	-	-	-	-	<1	-	-	-
	Astragalus	1	-	1	-	1	<1	-	-
	Calcaneus	2	<1	2	-	3	<1	-	-
	Tarsal	-	-	-	-	<1	-	-	-
	Metatarsal	5	-	17	-	5	<1	5	-
	Metapodial	1	<1	<1	<1	1	-	2	-
	First phalanx	1	<1	3	-	5	<1	-	-
	Second phalanx	-	-	2	-	<1	<1	-	-
	Third phalanx	-	<1	2	-	1	<1	-	-
Total bone waste		18	1	43	2	34	2	21	-

Appendix 8: Percentage number of anatomical elements of pig bones expressed as a percentage of the total number of bones per period

		Period			
		1	*2*	*3–3.1–3.2*	*4.1*
		PIG (265 nisp)	*PIG (130 nisp)*	*PIG (521 nisp)*	*PIG (28 nisp)*
	bone	*%*	*%*	*%*	*%*
HIGH QUALITY	Scapula	4	1	5	3
	Humerus	5	4	4	14
	Pelvis	1	1	3	3
	Femur	2	6	5	21
	Cervical vx.	2	-	<1	-
	Thoracic vx.	8	-	2	3
	Lumbar vx.	2	1	1	3
	Sacrum	-	-	-	-
	Vertebra frag.	<1	-	-	-
	Caudal vx.	-	-	<1	-
	Sternum	-	-	-	-
	Ribs	6	-	5	-
	Total	32	14	25	50
	Long bone frag.	-	-	<1	-
LESSER QUALITY	Tibia	4	6	6	11
	Fibula	2	2	2	-
	Radius	2	3	4	-
	Ulna	4	5	4	-
	Total	12	17	16	11
	Skull	15	11	13	14
	Maxilla	6	6	5	7
	Mandible	12	11	8	3
	Total	33	28	26	25
Total meat bearing bones		77	59	68	86
LOW QUALITY	Atlas	2	2	1	3
	Axis	1	-	<1	-
	Carpal	2	2	1	-
	Patella	-	-	-	-
	Astragalus	1	1	1	3
	Calcaneus	1	3	3	3
	Tarsal	-	-	<1	-
	Metapodial	9	20	16	3
	First phalanx	2	8	4	-
	Second phalanx	1	2	3	-
	Third phalanx	3	2	3	-
Total waste bones		23	41	32	14

Appendix 9: Comparison of the withers height estimates for the Greyfriars cattle with those from other Saxo-Norman and Medieval sites in Britain

	Mean	*s*	*N*
Greyfriars (Norwich)			
Period 1	115.8	6.5	6
Period 2	112.0		4
Period 3	111.9	4.4	4
All periods	113.2		12
North Elmham			
Saxo-Norman	107.4		4
Medieval	104.4		4
King's Lynn			
1050–1250	108.7		7
1350–1500	103.0		1
Greyfriars (London)			
c. 1480–c. 1500	132.9	15.7	19
Flaxengate (Lincoln)			
c. 870–1500	111.9	59.5	61
Exeter			
c. 1100–c. 1200	107.0		25
c. 1200–c. 1300	105.6		11

Appendix 10: Comparison of the withers height estimates for the Greyfriars sheep/goat with those from other Saxo-Norman and Medieval sites in Britain

	Mean	*s*	*N*
Greyfriars (Norwich)	60.0	1.2	4
Period 1	69.4	-	1
Period 2	56.2	2.8	22
Period 3	54.0	-	3
Period 4.1			
Whitefriars Church (Coventry)	57.7	33.1	37
Mid-16th century			
King's Lynn	55.5		4
1250–1350	57.2		3
1350–1500			
Greyfriars (London)	60.5		
c. 1480–c. 1500			
Flaxengate (Lincoln)	59.5	36.0	170
c. 870–1500			
Exeter	55.1	7.0	17
c. 1100–c. 1300			

Appendix 11: Comparison of the measurement of the distal humeral and tibial breadth on sheep/goat bones from Greyfriars to other sites

	Humerus (Bd)		*Tibia (Bd)*	
	Mean	*N*	*Mean*	*N*
Greyfriars (Norwich)				
Period 1	31.0	7	25.4	3
Period 2	-	-	24.8	4
Period 3	29.2	32	25.0	24
Period 4.1	-	-	25.5	1
King's Lynn				
1250–1350	27.1	4	23.7	3
1350–1500	27.8	3	24.5	2
Exeter				
1000–1200	27.8	13	24.0	8
1200–1300	27.8	41	24.3	61
1300–1500	28.0	10	23.8	16

Appendix 12: Macrobotanical and other material from SFB *50242* (Period 1)

Sample no.	*228*	*368*	*445*	*473*
Context no.	*50267*	*50413*	*50263*	*50550*
Layer within/fill of:	*fill*	*post-hole 50412*	*surface/abandonment*	*post-hole 50549*
Cereals				
Cereal indet. (caryopses)	6	3	33	13
(rachis internodes)				1
Hordeum sp. (caryopses)			1	
(rachis nodes)				
Triticum sp. (caryopses)	1		3	3cf
(rachis nodes)				
Avena sp. (caryopses)	1cf	2	3	1cf
Secale cereale L. (caryopses)	1cf		3cf	2cf
(rachis nodes)			3	
Other crops				
Fragaria vesca L.				
Large Fabaceae indet.				2coty
Malus sp.				
Prunus sp.				
Rubus sect. *Glandulosus* Wimmer & Grab.				
Herbs (weeds/grassland plants)				
Aethusa cynapium L.				
Agrostemma githago L.			1	
Anthemis cotula L.	1	1	2	1
Brassica sp.				
Bromus mollis/secalinus L.		1	1	
Bromus sp.	2cf			1cf
Caryophyllaceae indet.				
Centaurea cyanus L.				
Centaurea sp.			1cf	
Cerastium sp.				
Chenopodium album L.			1scf	
C. ficifolium Smith		1cf		
Chenopodiaceae indet.		1scf	3	
Euphorbia helioscopia L.				
Fabaceae indet.	1	1		
Fumaria officinalis L.				
Galium aparine L.			4	
Galium sp.		2		
Geranium sp.				
Poaceae indet. (small)	1	1		2cf
(large)				
Hyoscyamus niger L.				
Lamiaceae indet.				
Lapsana communis L.				
Papaver somniferum L.				
Papaver sp.				
Plantago lanceolata L.				
Polygonum aviculare L.				1
Persicaria maculosa/lapathifolia L.				1scf
Polygonaceae indet.				1
Raphanus raphanistrum L.				

Sample no.	*228*	*368*	*445*	*473*
Context no.	*50267*	*50413*	*50263*	*50550*
Layer within/fill of:	*fill*	*post-hole 50412*	*surface/abandonment*	*post-hole 50549*
Rumex acetosella L.			1	
Rumex sp.	1			1
Rumex/Carex sp.				
Silene sp.				
Stellaria sp.				
Torilis japonica (Houtt)				
Urtica dioica L.				
U. urens L.				
Vicia cracca L.				1cf
Vicia/Lathyrus sp.	1cf			
Wetland/aquatic plants				
Cyperaceae indet.		1cf		
Lemna sp.				
Trees/shrubs				
Corylus avellana L.	7fgs			1
Sambucus nigra L.			1m	
Other plant macrofossils				
Charcoal	+++	+++	+++	+++
Charred root/rhizome/stem	+	+	+	+
Waterlogged root/stem				
Mineral replaced stem				
Indet. culm nodes				
Indet. inflorescence fgs.				
Indet. seeds			7+1m	3
Animal macrofossils				
Fish bone	++	+	+	+
Mammal bone	+			
Mineralised/faecal concretions				
Mineralised invertebrates			+	+
Small mammal/amphibian bone		+	+	+
Other				
Black porous 'cokey' material	+	++	++	+
Metallic globules				+
Siliceous globules		+	+	
Textile/fibres				
Vitreous material				
% flot sorted	12.5%	100%	50%	100%

+ – present; ++ – common; +++ – abundant; m – mineralised; coty – cotyledons; scf – seed coat fragments; w – waterlogged; cap – seed capsule; pod – legume pod fragments; sil – siliqua fragments; agg – seed aggregate; b – burnt; t – tendril

Appendix 13: Macrobotanical and other material from bell-founding pit *12257* (Period 3.2)

Sample no.	*2001*	*2002*	*2005*
Context no.	*12381*	*12377*	*12337*
Cereals			
Cereal indet.(caryopses)		1	
(basal rachis nodes)			1
Hordeum sp.(caryopses)			1
(rachis nodes)	2	5	36
Hordeum/Secale sp.(rachis nodes)	2		33
Other crops			
Large Fabaceae indet.			1coty
Herbs (weeds/grassland plants)			
Anagallis arvensis L.			2
Anthemis cotula L.	2		10
Apiaceae indet.	1		
Asteraceae indet.	1		
Atriplex sp.	2+1scf	3scf	8+1scf
Brassicaceae indet.	13	12	
Bromus mollis/secalinus L.	2		
Centaurea sp.	1	1	
Chenopodiaceae indet.	4	3	10+2scf
Chrysanthemum segetum L.	1	1	3
Conium maculatum L.	1	4cf	4cf
Fabaceae indet			3
Galium aparine L.	3cf	7+18fg	4
Galium sp.	4fg		
Poaceae indet. (small)	5	3	17
(large)	7		4
Hyoscyamus niger L.		1	1
Polygonum aviculare L.		1cf	5
Persicaria maculosa/lapathifolia L.			
Polygonaceae indet.	2	1	1
Prunella vulgaris L.	1		
Raphanus raphanistrum L.		1stem	3silfg
Rumex acetosella L.	16	2	12
Rumex sp.	2	2	6
Sherardia arvensis L.	4	9	8
Silene sp.	1		4
Solanum nigrum L.	28	4	36
Spergula arvensis L.			6
Tripleurospermum inodorum (L.) Schultz-Bip.			1
Veronica hederifolia L.			3cf
Vicia/Lathyrus sp.	2cf		
Wetland/aquatic plants			
Carex sp.		1	3
Eleocharis sp.			5

Sample no.	*2001*	*2002*	*2005*
Context no.	*12381*	*12377*	*12337*
Other plant macrofossils			
Charcoal	+++	+++	+++
Charred root/rhizome/stem	+	+	+
Indet. culm nodes			7
Indet. inflorescence fgs.	++	+	++
Indet. seeds	25	1	37
Other			
Black tarry droplets	+	+	
Burnt/fired clay	++	+	++
Copper alloy residue			+
Small coal fgs.	+		
Vitreous material		+	
% flot sorted	100%	100%	50%

+ – present; ++ – common; +++ – abundant; m – mineralised; coty – cotyledons; scf – seed coat fragments; w – waterlogged; cap – seed capsule; pod – legume pod fragments; sil – siliqua fragments; agg – seed aggregate; b – burnt; t – tendril

Bibliography

Adams, D., 2002 — *Interim Report on an Archaeological Evaluation at Norwich City Football Club, Carrow Road, Norwich, Norfolk*, Norfolk Archaeological Unit Report 753 (unpublished)

Albarella, U., Beech, M. and Mulville, J., 1997 — *The Saxon, Medieval and Post-Medieval Mammal and Bird Bones Excavated 1989–1991 from Castle Mall, Norwich (Norfolk)*, unpublished Ancient Monuments Laboratory Report No. 72/97, English Heritage

Alexander, J. and Binski, P. (eds), 1987 — *Age of Chivalry* (London)

Ambrosiani, K., 1981 — *Viking Age Combs, Comb Making and Comb Makers in the Light of Finds from Birka and Ribe*, Studies in Archaeology 2 (Stockholm)

Amis, P., 1968 — 'Some domestic vessels of southern Britain; a social and technical analysis', *Journal of Ceramic History* 2, 1–35

Anderson, S., 2004 — 'The pottery', in Wallis, H., *Excavations at Mill Lane, Thetford, 1995*, E Anglian Archaeol. 108, 67–86

Anderson, S., 2005 — 'The pottery', in Shelley, A., *Dragon Hall, King Street, Norwich: Excavation and Survey of a Late Medieval Merchant's Trading Complex*, E. Anglian Archaeol. 112, 129–51

Andrews, P., 1995 — *Excavations at Redcastle Furze, Thetford, 1988–9*, E. Anglian Archaeol. 72

anon, 1924 — 'The Norwich skeletons: an antiquary's opinion', *J. Brit. Archaeol. Ass.* new series 30 (1)

Archibald, M.M., 1995 — 'The lead counters', in Elder, J. (ed.), *Excavations in the Marlowe Car Park & Surrounding Areas (The Archaeology of Canterbury 5, 2)* (Canterbury), 953

Archibald, M.M., 1991 — 'Anglo-Saxon and Norman lead objects with official coin types', in Vince, A. (ed.), *Aspects of Saxo-Norman London: II, Finds and environmental evidence*, London Middlesex Archaeol. Soc. Spec. Pap. 12 (London), 326–45

Archibald, M.M. and Blunt, C.E., 1986 — *British Museum Anglo-Saxon Coins V: Athelstan to the reform of Edgar, 924–c. 973*, Sylloge Coins of the British Isles 34

Armitage, P. and West, B., 1985 — 'Faunal evidence from a late medieval garden well of the Greyfriars, London', *Trans. London Middlesex Archaeol. Soc.* 36, 107–36

Ashley, S., 2002 — *Medieval Armorial Horse Furniture in Norfolk*, E. Anglian Archaeol. 101

Ashurst, D., 1987 — 'Excavations at the 17th–18th century glasshouse at Bolsterstone and the 18th century Bolsterstone Pothouse, Stocksbridge, Yorkshire', *Post-Medieval Archaeol.* 21, 147–226

Atkin, M.W., 1993 — 'The Norwich Survey 1971–1985: a retrospective view', in Gardiner, J.P. (ed.), *Flatlands and Wetlands: Current Themes in East Anglian Archaeology*, E. Anglian Archaeol. 50, 127–43

Atkin, M.W., and Carter, A., 1985 — 'General introduction', in Atkin, M., Carter, A. and Evans, D.H., *Excavations in Norwich 1971–78; II*, E. Anglian Archaeol. 26, 1–6

Atkin, M.W., Ayers, B.S., and Jennings, S., 1983 — 'Thetford-type Ware production in Norwich', in *Waterfront Excavation and Thetford Ware Production, Norwich*, E. Anglian Archaeol. 17, 61–97

Aufderheide, A.C. and Rodriguez-Martin, C., 1998 — *The Cambridge Encyclopaedia of Human Paleopathology* (Cambridge)

Ayers, B.S. and Murphy, P., 1983 — *A Waterfront Excavation at Whitefriars Street Car Park, Norwich, 1979*, E. Anglian Archaeol. 17, 1–60

Ayers, B.S., 1985 — *Excavations within the North-East Bailey of Norwich Castle, 1979*, E. Anglian Archaeol. 28

Ayers, B.S., 1988 — *Excavations at St Martin-at-Palace Plain, Norwich, 1981*, E. Anglian Archaeol. 37

Ayers, B.S., 1991 — 'From cloth to creel — riverside industries in Norwich', in Good, G.L., *et al.* (eds.), *Waterfront Archaeology, Proceedings of the Third International Conference, Bristol, 1988*, Counc. Brit. Archaeol. Res. Rep. 74, 1–9

Ayers, B.S., 1994 — *English Heritage Book of Norwich* (London)

Ayers, B.S., 1993 — 'The urbanisation of East Anglia: the Norwich perspective', in Gardiner, J. (ed.), *Flatlands and Wetlands: Current Themes in East Anglian Archaeology*, E. Anglian Archaeol. 50, 117–26

Ayers, B.S., 1996 — 'The cathedral site before 1096', in Atherton, I., Fernie, E., Harper-Bill, C., and Smith, H., *Norwich Cathedral* (London), 59–72

Ayers, B.S., 2003 — *Norwich: A fine city* (Stroud)

Ayers, B.S., unpublished — *The Influence of Minor Streams on Urban Development: Norwich, a case study*

Baart, J. Krook, W., Lagerweij, A., Ockers, N., Van Regteren Altena, H., Stam, T., Stoepker, H., Stouthart, G., and Van Der Zwan, M., 1977 — *Opgravingen in Amsterdam: 20 jaar stadskernonderzoek* (Amsterdam)

Baker, J., and Brothwell, D., 1980 — *Animal Diseases in Archaeology* (London)

Barrett, G.N., 1981 — *Norwich Silver and its Marks* (Norwich)

Baumgartner, E. and Krueger, I., 1988 — *Phonix aus Sand und Asche: Glas des Mittelälters* (Munich)

Bayley, J., 1984 — 'Metalworking evidence', in Rogerson, A. and Dallas, C., *Excavations in Thetford 1928–59 and 1973–80*, E. Anglian Archaeol. 22, 107–8

Bayley, J. and Richards, J.D., 1993 — 'Medieval founding', in Richards, J.D., 'The Bedern foundry', *The Archaeology of York 10/3* (London), 186–200

Bayley, J., 1991 — 'Processes in precious metal working', in Budd, P., Chapman, B., Jackson, C., Janaway, R., and Ottaway, P. (eds), *Archaeological Sciences '89*, Oxbow Monograph 9 (Oxford), 125–31

Bayley, J., 1992 'Anglo-Scandinavian non-ferrous metalworking from 16–22 Coppergate', *The Archaeology of York 17/7: The Small Finds* (London)

Bayley, J., Bryant, R. and Heighway, C., 1993 'A tenth-century bell-pit and bell-mould from St Oswald's Priory, Gloucester', *Medieval Archaeol.* 37, 224–36

Bersu, G., and Wilson, D.M., 1966 *Three Viking Graves in the Isle of Man,* Soc. Medieval Archaeol. Monogr. Ser. 1

Biddick, K., 1984 'Pig husbandry on the Peterborough Abbey estate from the twelfth to the fourteenth century AD', in Grigson, C. and Clutton-Brock, J. (eds), *Animals and Archaeology: 4. Husbandry in Europe* (Oxford), 161–78

Biddle, M., 1975 'The evolution of towns: planned towns before 1066', in Barley, M.W. (ed.), *The Plans and Topography of Medieval Towns in England and Wales*, Counc. Brit. Archaeol. Res. Rep. 14, 19–32

Biddle, M. (ed.), 1976 *Winchester in the Early Middle Ages: An edition and discussion of the Winton Domesday,* Winchester Studies 1 (Oxford)

Biddle, M. (ed.), 1990 'Unidentified bone objects' in *Object and Economy in Medieval Winchester,* Winchester Studies vol. 7.ii (Oxford), 1129–45

Biddle, M. and Barclay, K., 1990 '"Sewing pins" and wire', in Biddle, M. (ed.), *Object and Economy in Medieval Winchester,* Winchester Studies vol. 7.ii (Oxford), 560–71

Biddle, M. and Hinton, D.A., 1990 'Book-clasps and page-holder' in Biddle, M. (ed.), *Object and Economy in Medieval Winchester,* Winchester Studies vol. 7.ii (Oxford), 755–8

Biddle, M. and Smith, D., 1990 'The querns' in Biddle, M. (ed.), *Object and Economy in Medieval Winchester,* Winchester Studies vol. 7.ii (Oxford), 292–6

Biggs, N., 1992 *English Weights, An Illustrated Survey* (Egham)

Biringuccio, V., Trans Smith, C.S. and Gnudi, M.T., 1990 *De la Pirotechnia* (New York)

Blackburn, M.A.S., 1989 'The earliest coinage of the southern Danelaw late 9th century', *Proceedings of the 10th International Congress of Numismatics, 1986* (London), 341–8

Blackburn, M., 1997 'Expansion and control: aspects of Anglo-Scandinavian minting south of the Humber', in Graham-Campbell, J., Hall, R., Jesch, J. and Parsons, D.N., *Vikings and the Danelaw,* Select Papers from the Proceedings of the Thirteenth Viking Congress, Nottingham and York, 1997

Blades, N., 1995 *Copper alloys from English archaeological sites 400–1600AD: An analytical study using ICP-AES,* unpublished Ph.D. thesis, Royal Holloway College, University of London

Blair, C. and Blair, J., 1991 'Copper alloys', in Blair, J. and Ramsay, N. (eds), *English Medieval Industries* (London), 81–106

Blomefield, F., 1806 *An Essay Towards a Topographical History of the County of Norfolk* (London)

Blunt, C.E., Stewart, B.H.I.H. and Lyon, C.S.S., 1989 *Coinage in Tenth-century England, from Edward the Elder to Edgar's Reform* (Oxford)

Bond, C.J., 1988 'Monastic fisheries', in Aston, M. (ed.), *Medieval Fish, Fisheries and Fishponds in England,* Brit. Archaeol. Rep. Brit. Ser. 182 (ii), 69–112

Bond, F.B., 1915 'Glastonbury Abbey: eighth report on the discoveries made during the excavations', *Proceedings of the Somerset Archaeological and Natural History Society* 61, 128–42

Bramwell, D., 1977 'Bird bone', in Clarke, H., and Carter, A. (eds), *Excavations at King's Lynn, 1963–1970,* Soc. Medieval Archaeol. Monogr. Ser. 7, 399–402

Branner, R., 1977 *Manuscript Painting in Paris during the Reign of Saint Louis* (Los Angeles and London)

Braun, H., 1971 *English Abbeys* (London)

Bronk Ramsey, C., 1995 'Radiocarbon calibration and analysis of stratigraphy', *Radiocarbon* 36, 425–30

Brown, D, 1990 'Weaving tools', in Biddle, M. (ed.), *Object and Economy in Medieval Winchester,* Winchester Studies vol. 7.i (Oxford), 227–8

Brownsword, R. and Pitt, E.H., 1981 'Medieval "bell-metal" mortars — a misnomer', *The Metallurgist and Materials Technologist,* April 1981, 184–5

Buckley, D.G. and Major, H., 1987 'Quernstones', in Crummy, N. (ed.), *The Post Roman Small Finds from Excavations in Colchester 1971–1985,* Colchester Archaeol. Rep. 5

Buckley, D.G., 2005 'Lavastone objects', in Shelley, A., *Dragon Hall, King Street, Norwich: Excavation and Survey of a Late Medieval Merchant's Trading Complex,* E. Anglian Archaeol. 112, 126–7

Buikstra, J.E. and Ubelaker, D.H., 1994 *Standards for Data Collection from Human Skeletal Remains,* Arkansas Archaeological Survey Research Series 44

Bullock, P., Fedoroff, N., Jongerius, A., Stoops, G. and Tursina, T., 1985 *Handbook for Soil Thin Section Description* (Wolverhampton)

Bullock, J.D., 1960 'The Celtic, Saxon, and Scandinavian settlement at Meols in the Wirral', *Trans. Hist. Soc of Lancashire and Cheshire* 112, 1–28

Butler, L.A.S., 1957 'Medieval gravestones of Cambridgeshire, Huntingdonshire and the Soke of Peterborough', *Proc. Cambridge Antiq. Soc.* 50, 89–100

Butler, L.A.S., 1964 'Minor medieval monumental sculpture in the East Midlands', *Archaeol. J.* 121, 111–59

Cable, M., 1987 'Glass technology at Bolsterstone', *Post-Medieval Archaeol.* 21, 217–223

Callender, J.G., 1924 'Fourteenth-century brooches and other ornaments in the National Museum of Antiquities of Scotland', *Proceedings of the Society of Antiquaries of Scotland* 58 , 160–84

Campbell, J., 1975 'Norwich', in Lobel, M.D., (ed.), *Atlas of Historic Towns* (London)

Carter, A. and Roberts, J., 1973 'Excavations in Norwich, 1972. The Norwich Survey: second interim report', *Norfolk Archaeol.* 35, 443–68

Carter, A., 1978 'The Anglo-Saxon origins of Norwich: the problems and approaches', *Anglo-Saxon England* 7, 175–294

Cattermole, P., 1990 *Church Bells and Bell-ringing: a Norfolk Profile* (Woodbridge)

Chambers, D.S. (ed.), 1966 *Faculty Office Registers 1534–1549*

Charleston, R.J., 1960 'Lead in glass', *Archaeometry* 3, 1–4

Charleston, R.J., 1975 'The glass', in Platt, C. and Colman-Smith, R., *Excavations in Medieval Southampton 1953–69, II: The Finds* (Leicester), 204–26

Charleston, R.J., 1983 'The vessel glass' in Streeten, A.D.F., *Bayham Abbey,* Sussex Archaeol. Monogr. 2, 112–16

Charleston, R.J., 1984 *English Glass – and the Glass Used in England, Circa 400–1940* (London)

Charleston, R.J., 1985 'Vessel Glass' in Hare, J.N., *Battle Abbey: The Eastern Range and the Excavations of 1978-80,* HBMC Archaeol. Rep. 2, 139–46

Cherry, J., 1980 'Medieval Britain in 1979: 2 Post-conquest', *Medieval Archaeol.* 24, 236–64

Christophersen, A., 1980 'Raw material, resources and production capacity in early medieval comb manufacture in Lund', *Meddelanden fran Lunds Universitets Historiska Museum* (1979–80), New Series 3, 150–65

Clark, A.J., Tarling, D.H. and Noel, M., 1988 'Developments in archaeomagnetic dating in Britain', *Archaeometry* 15, 645–67

Clark, J. (ed.), 1995 *Medieval Finds From Excavations in London: 5. The Medieval Horse and its Equipment c.1150–c.1450* (London)

Clarke, H., 1970 'Excavations on a kiln site at Grimston, Pott Row, Norfolk', *Norfolk Archaeol.* 35(1), 79–95

Clarke, R. and Shepherd Popescu, E., in prep. *Norwich Whitefriars: Excavations 2002–03,* E. Anglian Archaeol.

Clay, P., 1981 'The small finds', in Mellor. J. and Pearce T., *The Austin Friars, Leicester,* Counc. Brit. Archaeol. Res. Rep. 35, 130–44

Coppack, G., 1976 'Two late medieval pipe-drains from Thetford Priory', *Proc Suffolk Inst. Archaeol. Hist* 33, 88–90

Corfield, P., 1972 'A provincial capital in the late seventeenth century: the case of Norwich', reprinted in Clark, P. (ed.), *The Early Modern Town* (New York)

Courty, M.A., Goldberg, P. and Macphail, R.I., 1989 *Soils and Micromorphology in Archaeology,* Cambridge Manuals in Archaeology (Cambridge)

Cowgill J., de Neergaard, M. and Griffiths, N., 1987 *Medieval Finds from Excavations in London: 1. Knives and Scabbards* (London)

Crawford, B.E., 1987 *Scandinavian Scotland,* Scotland in the Middle Ages 2 (Leicester)

Crawford, O.G.S. and Röder, J., 1955 'The quern-quarries of Mayen in the Eifel', *Antiquity* 29, 68–76

Crosby, D.D.B. and Mitchell, J.C., 1990 'Pottassium-argon age and natural remnant magnetization determination: the metamorphic hones of the ninth to fifteenth century from Winchester', in Biddle, M., (ed), *Object and Economy in Medieval Winchester,* Winchester Studies 7.ii.i (Oxford), 288–92

Crossgrove, H., 1714 *Norwich Poll Book*

Crowfoot, E., 1984 'Comments' in 'Bone and antler objects', in Rogerson, A, and Dallas, C., *Excavations in Thetford 1948–59 and 1973–77,* E. Anglian Archaeol. 22, 167

Crummy, N., 1983 *The Roman Small Finds From Excavations In Colchester 1971–9,* Colchester Archaeol. Rep. 2

Crummy, P., 1981 *Aspects of Anglo-Saxon and Norman Colchester,* Colchester Archaeol. Rep. 1/Counc. Brit. Archaeol. Res. Rep. 39

Cushing, D.H., 1988 *The Provident Sea* (Cambridge)

Dallas, C., 1984 'The pottery', in Rogerson A., and Dallas C., *Excavations in Thetford 1948–59 and 1973–80,* E. Anglian Archaeol. 22, 117–66

Dallas, C., 1994 'The pottery', in Ayers, B.S., *Excavations at Fishergate, Norwich, 1985,* E. Anglian Archaeol. 68, 19–29

Darling, M.J., 1993 *Caister-on-Sea Excavations by Charles Green, 1951–55,* E. Anglian Archaeol. 60

Davey, N. and Ling, R., 1982 *Wall-Painting in Roman Britain* (London)

Davies, J.A., forthcoming 'Coins, jettons and tokens', in Shepherd Popescu, E., *Norwich Castle: Excavations and Historical Survey 1987–98,* E. Anglian Archaeol.

Dickinson, J.C., 1961 *Monastic Life in Medieval England* (London)

Davis, N. (ed.), 1971 *Paston Letters and Papers Of The Fifteenth Century* (Oxford)

Dobson, B., 1984 'Mendicant ideal and practice in late medieval York', in Addyman, P.V. and Black, V.E. (eds), *Archaeological Papers From York Presented To M.W. Barley* (York), 109–22

Dodwell, C.R. (ed. and transl.), 1986 *Theophilus: The Various Arts, De Diversis Artibus* (Oxford)

Donovan, C., 1991 *The de Brailes Hours: Shaping the Book of Hours in Thirteenth-Century Oxford* (London)

Doubleday, H.A. *et al.* (eds), 1906 *Victoria History of the County of Norfolk* II (London)

Doucet, V., 1953 'Le studium franciscain de Norwich en 1337', *Archivum Franciscanum Historicum* 46, 85–98

Driesch, A. von den and Boessneck, J.A., 1974 'Kritische Ammerkungen zur Widerristhohenberechnung aus Langenmassen vor- und frühgeschichtlicher Tierknochen', *Säugetierkundliche Mitteilungen* 22, 325–48

Driesch, A. von den, 1976 *A Guide to the Measurement of Animal Bones from Archaeological Sites,* Peabody Museum Bulletin 1 (Harvard, Mass)

Drummond, J.C., and Wilbraham, A., 1939 *The Englishman's Food: a History of Five Centuries of the English Diet* (London)

Drury, P., 1978 'A Saxon loomweight and medieval tile-kiln at Blackmore,' *Essex Archaeol. Hist.* 10, 234–6

Drury, P.J. and Norton, C.N., 1985 'Twelfth-century floor-and roof-tiles at Orford Castle', *Proc. Suffolk Inst. Archaeol. Hist.* 36(1), 1–7

Drury, P.J., 1981 — 'The production of brick and tile in medieval England', in Crossley, D.W. (ed.), *Medieval Industry,* Counc. Brit. Archaeol. Res Rep 40, 126–42

Drury, P.J., 1993 — 'Ceramic building materials', in Margeson, S. (ed.), *Norwich Households: The Medieval and Post-Medieval Finds from Norwich Survey Excavations 1971–1978,* E. Anglian Archaeol. 58, 163–70

Dudley Stamp, L., 1969 — *Man and the Land* (London)

Dugdale, W., 1830 — *Monasticon Anglicanum* VI (London)

Dunkerton, J., Roy, A. and Smith, A., 1987 — 'The unmasking of Tura's "Allegorical Figure": a painting and its concealed image', *National Gallery Technical Bulletin* 11, 5–35

Dunning, G.C., 1961 — 'Stone mortars', in Hurst, J.G., 'The kitchen area of Northolt Manor, Middlesex' *Medieval Archaeol.* 5, 279–84

Dunning, G.C., 1977 — 'Mortars', in Clarke, H. and Carter, A., *Excavations in King's Lynn 1963–70,* Soc. Medieval Archaeol. Monogr. Ser. 7, 320–47

Dyer, C.C., 1983 — 'English diet in the later middle ages', in Aston, T.H., Coss, P.R., Dyer, C.C. and Thirsk, J. (eds), *Social Relations and Ideas: Essays in Honour of R.H. Hilton* (London), 191–214

Dyer, C., 1988 — 'The consumption of fresh-water fish in medieval England', in Aston, M. (ed.), *Medieval Fish, Fisheries and Fishponds in England,* Brit. Archaeol. Rep. Brit. Ser. 182 (ii), 27–38

Eames, E.S., 1955 — 'The products of a medieval tile kiln at Bawsey, King's Lynn', *Antiq. J.* 35, 162–81

Egan, G., 1991 — 'Beads', in Egan, G. and Pritchard, F., *Medieval Finds from Excavations in London: 3 Dress Accessories, c. 1150–c. 1450* (London), 305–31

Egan, G. and Pritchard, F., 1991 — *Medieval Finds from Excavations in London: 3. Dress Accessories c. 1150–c. 1450* (London)

Egan, G., 1994 — *Lead Cloth Seals and Related Items in the British Museum,* Brit. Mus. Occas. Pap. 93

Egan, G., 1995 — 'England's post-medieval cloth trade: a survey of the evidence from cloth seals', in Hook, D.R., and Gaimster, D.R.M. (eds), *Trade & Discovery: The Scientific Study of Artefacts from Post-Medieval Europe and Beyond,* Brit. Mus. Occas. Pap. 109, 315–26

Egan, G., 1996 — *Play Things from the Past, Lead Alloy Miniature Artefacts c. 1300–1800* (London)

Egan, G., 2001 — 'Lead finds', *Salisbury & South Wiltshire Museum Catalogue* 3, 43–86

Egan, G., forthcoming a — *Lead seals from Kingsholm, Gloucester*

Egan, G., forthcoming b — *Finds from Excavations at the Site of St Mary Spital, London*

Egbert, V.W., 1967 — *The Mediaeval Artist at Work* (Princeton)

Elbern, V.H., 1955 — 'Ein neuer Beitrag zur Ikonographie des Unfigurlichen. Über die bildliche Aussage beinerner Reliquienkastchen des frühen Mittelalters', *Münster Zeitschrift für Christliches Kunst und Kunstwissenschaft* 25, 313–24

Elbern, V.H., 1962 — 'Der fränkische Reliquienkasten und Tragal-tar von Werden', in Elbern, V.H. (ed.), *Das erste Jahrtausend. Kultur und Kunst im werdenden Abendland an Rhein und Ruhr,* Band 1 (Düsseldorf), 436–70

Elbern, V.H., 1971 — 'Das frühmittelalterliche Beinrelief aus Hausen', *Mitteilungen Oberhessiches Geschver,* Neue Folge 56, 73–88

Ellis, B.M.A., 1977 — 'The spurs', in Williams, F., *Excavations at Pleshey Castle,* Brit. Archaeol. Rep. Brit. Ser. 42, 179–82

Ellis, B.M.A., 1993 — 'Horse equipment', in Margeson, S., *Norwich Households: Medieval and Post-Medieval Finds from Norwich Survey Excavations 1971–78,* E. Anglian Archaeol. 58, 220–7

Emden, A.B., 1957 — *Biographical Register of the University of Oxford to AD 1500* (Oxford)

Emery, P.A., 1997 — *Evaluation excavation at the former Wallace King premises, St Faiths Lane, Norwich,* Norfolk Archaeological Unit Report No. 285, unpublished

Emery, P.A., 1998 — 'Riverside Development, Norwich: archaeological investigation', *Journal of the Norfolk Archaeological and Historical Research Group* 31

Emery, P.A., 2000a — 'The Franciscan Friary', *Current Archaeology* 170 (Norwich Special Issue), 72–8

Emery, P.A., 2000b — *Report on an Archaeological Evaluation at Busseys Garage, Palace, Street, Norwich,* Norfolk Archaeological Unit Report 498 (unpublished)

Emery, P.A., and Ashwin, T., 2001 — 'Prehistoric occupation evidence at Busseys Garage, Palace Street, Norwich', *Norfolk Archaeology* 43(4), 670–5

Erskine, A. (ed.), 1981 — *The Accounts of the Fabric of Exeter Cathedral, 1279–1353* (Torquay)

Evans, J. and Carter, A., 2002 — *Excavations in Norwich 1971–78 Part III,* E. Anglian Archaeol. 100

Fingerlin, I., 1971 — *Gürtel des hohen und späten Mittelalters* (Munich/Berlin)

Fish, J.D. and Fish, S., 1989 — *A Student's Guide to the Seashore* (London)

Fitzwilliam Museum, 1982 — *Fitzwilliam Museum Cambridge: The Annual Report of the Syndicate & of the Friends of the Fitzwilliam for the Year Ending 1981* (Cambridge)

Fletcher, M. and Lock, G.R., 1991 — *Digging Numbers: Elementary Statistics for Archaeologists* (Oxford)

Foy, D., and Sennequier, G., 1989 — *A travers Le Verre du moyen age a la renaissance* (Nancy)

Freestone, I. and Tite, M., 1986 — 'Refactories in the ancient and pre-industrial world', in Kingery, W.D. (ed.), *High Technology Ceramics: Past, Present and Future,* Ceramics and Civilisation 3 (Ohio), 35–63

Fry, D.K., 1976 — 'Anglo-Saxon lyre tuning pegs from Whitby', *Medieval Archaeol.* 20, 137–9

Gabriel, I., 1988 — 'Hof- und Sakralkultur sowie Gebrauchs- und Handelsgut im Spiegel der Kleinfunde von Starigard/Oldenburg', *Bericht der Romisch-Germanischen Komission* 69, 103–291

Galloway, P., 1976 — 'Note on descriptions of bone and antler combs', *Medieval Archaeol.* 20, 154–6

Gettens, R.J. and Fitzhugh, E.W., 1993 — 'Azurite and blue verditer', in Roy A. (ed.), *Artists' Pigments: A Handbook of their History and Characteristics* (Cambridge), 23–35

Gettens, R.J. and Stout, G.L., 1966 — *Painting Materials: A Short Encyclopaedia* (New York)

Gibson, J. and Evans, J., 1985 — 'Some eighteenth-century pharmaceutical vessels from London', *Post-Medieval Archaeol.* 19, 151–7

Gilchrist, R., 1996 — 'The animal bones', in Foreman, M., *Further excavations at the Dominican Priory, Beverley. Sheffield Excavation Report*s 4, 213–28 (with a contribution by T.P. O'Connor)

Goffin, R., forthcoming — 'The pottery', in Shelley, A., and Brennand, M., 'Excavations at 51–53 King Street, Norwich', *Norfolk Archaeol.*

Goodall, A.R., 1984 — 'Non-ferrous metal objects' in Rogerson, A. and Dallas, C., *Excavations in Thetford 1948–59 and 1973–77* E. Anglian Archaeol. 22, 68–75

Goodall, A.R., 1989 — 'Copper alloy objects', in Hassall, T.G., Halpin, C.E. and Mellor, M., 'Excavations in St Ebbe's, Oxford, 1967–76: 1. Late Saxon and Medieval domestic occupation, tenements and the Medieval Greyfriars', *Oxoniesia* 54, 223–6

Goodall, A.R., 1991 — 'Copper alloy objects', in Hassall, T.G., Halpin, C.E. and Mellor, M., 'Excavations in St Ebbe's, Oxford, 1967-1976: Part I', *Oxoniensia* 54, 226

Goodall, A.R., forthcoming — 'Copper alloy objects', in Shepherd Popescu, E., *Norwich Castle: Excavations and Historical Survey 1987–98*, E. Anglian Archaeol.

Goodall, I.H., 1984 — 'Iron objects', in Rogerson, A. and Dallas, C., *Excavations in Thetford 1948–59 and 1973–80*, E. Anglian Archaeol. 22, 77–105

Goodall, I.H., 1987a — 'Medieval iron kitchen equipment', in Moorhouse, S. *et al.*, *The Medieval Kitchen and its Equipment*, synopsis of papers presented to the Finds Research Group 700–1700 and The Medieval Pottery Research Group

Goodall, I.H. 1987b — 'Objects of iron', in Beresford, G., *Goltho: The Development of an Early Medieval Manor c. 850–1150*, English Heritage Archaeol. Rep. 4, 177–87

Goodall, I.H., 1990 — 'Locks and keys', in Biddle, M. (ed.), *Object and Economy in Medieval Winchester,* Winchester Studies vol. 7.ii (Oxford), 1001–36

Goodall, I.H., 1993 — 'Iron textile manufacturing tools', in Margeson, S., *Norwich Households: Medieval and Post-Medieval Finds from Norwich Survey Excavations 1971–78*, E. Anglian Archaeol. 58, 182–83

Grand, R. and Delatouch, R., 1950 — *L'agriculture au moyen age, de la fin de l'empire romain au XVIe Siècle* (Paris)

Grant, A., 1982 — 'The use of tooth wear as a guide to the age of domestic ungulates', in Wilson, B., Grigson, C. and Payne, S. (eds), *Ageing and Sexing Animal Bones from Archaeological Sites* (Oxford), 91–108

Grant, A., 1988 — 'Animal resources', in Astill, G and Grant, A. (eds.), *The Countryside of Medieval England* (Oxford), 149–261

Grayson, D.K., 1984 — *Quantitative Zooarchaeology* (Orlando)

Green, Z., 1997 — *Oysters: What Can You Do With Them?*, unpublished B.Sc. dissertation, University of Bradford

Greene, J.P., 1989 — *Norton Priory: the Archaeology of a Medieval Religious House* (Cambridge)

Greene, J.P., 1992 — *Medieval Monasteries* (Leicester)

Gregory, A.K. and Metcalf, D.M., 1994 — 'The coins', in Ayers, B.S., *Excavations at Fishergate, Norwich, 1985*, E. Anglian Archaeol. 68, 13–14

Griffiths, N., 1986 — *Horse Harness Pendants*, Finds Research Group Datasheet 5

Guilloré, P., 1985 — *Méthode Fabrication Mécanique et en Série des Lames Minces* (Paris)

Gurney, D., 2001 — 'Archaeological finds in Norfolk 2000', *Norfolk Archaeology* 43(4), 694–707

Hale, R. and Rodgers, M., 1991 — *The Greyfriars of Norwich* (Norwich)

Harcourt, R.A., 1974 — 'The dog in prehistoric and early historic Britain', *J. Archaeol. Sci.* 1, 151–76

Harden, D.B., Painter, K.S., Pinder-Wilson, R.H. and Tait, H., 1968 — *Masterpieces of Glass* (London)

Harman, M., Baker, J. and Bramwell, D., 1985 — 'The bird bones', in Atkin, M.W., Carter, A. and Evans, D.H., *Excavations in Norwich 1971–1978, Part II*, E. Anglian Archaeol. 26, 222–3

Harrod, H., 1859 — 'Queen Elizabeth Woodville's visit to Norwich in 1469', *Norfolk Archaeol.* 5, 32–7

Harvey, J.H. (ed.), 1969 — *William Worcestre. Itineraries* (Oxford)

Hawes, T. (ed.), 1989 — *An Index to Norwich City Officers, 1453–1835*, Norfolk Record Society 52

Higham, C.F.W., 1969 — 'The metrical data attributes of two samples of bovine limb bones', *J. Zoology* 157, 63–74

Hinton, D.A., 1974 — *Catalogue of the Anglo-Saxon Ornamental Metalwork 700–1100 in the Department of Antiquities, Ashmolean Museum* (Oxford)

Hinton, D.A., 1990a — 'Hooked tags', in Biddle, M. (ed.), *Object and Economy in Medieval Winchester,* Winchester Studies vol. 7.ii (Oxford), 548–52

Hinton, D.A., 1990b — 'Pendants', in Biddle, M. (ed.), *Object and Economy in Medieval Winchester*, Winchester Studies vol. 7, ii, 643–6

Hluvko, S., 1991 — *Red Pigments in English Medieval Wall Painting,* unpublished dissertation, Conservation of Wall Painting Department, Courtauld Institute of Art

Hobley, B., 1988 — 'Lundenwic and Lundenburh: two cities rediscovered', in Hodges, R. and Hobley, B. (eds), *The Rebirth of Towns in the West AD 700–1050*, CBA Res. Rep. 68, 69–82

Hockey, S.F., 1975 — *The Account Book of Beaulieu Abbey* (London)

Hodge, C.A.H., Burton, R., Corbett, W., Evans, R., George, H., Heaven, F., Robson, J. and Seale, R., 1983 — *Soils of England and Wales, Sheet 4, Eastern England* (Southampton)

Holdsworth, P., 1976 — 'Saxon Southampton: a new review', *Medieval Archaeol.* 20, 26–61

Holmes, J.M., 1981 — 'Report on the animal bones from the resonance chambers of the Whitefriars Church, Coventry', in Woodfield, C., 'Finds from the Free Grammar School at the Whitefriars, Coventry (*c.* 1545–1557/8)', *Post-Medieval Archaeol.* 15, 126–53

Horsman, V., Milne, G. and Milne, C., 1988 — *Aspects of Saxo-Norman London: 1. building and street development*, London Middlesex Archaeol. Soc. Spec. Pap. 11

Hörter, F., Michels, F.X. and Röder, J., 1951 — 'Die Geschichte der Basalt Lava Industrie von Mayen und Nidermendig', *Jahrbuch für Geschichte Kultur des Mittelrheins und seiner Nachbargebiete* 2–3, 1–32

Houben, G.M.M., 1984 — *2000 Years of Nested Cup-Weights* (Netherlands)

Howard, H., 1988 — *Blue Pigments in English Medieval Wall Painting*, unpublished dissertation, Conservation of Wall Painting Department, Courtauld Institute of Art

Howard, H., 1997 — *Scientific Examination of an Oyster-Shell Palette from the Carmelite Friary, Coventry*, unpublished report, Conservation of Wall Painting Department, Courtauld Institute of Art

Howard, H., forthcoming — 'Medieval and post-Reformation shell palettes', in Nadolny, J., Kollandsrud, K., Sauerberg, M.L. and Frysaker, T. (eds), *Medieval Painting in Northern Europe: Techniques, Analysis, Art History. Studies in Commemoration of the 70th birthday of Unn Plahter* (London).

Huddle, J., 2005 — 'Antler, ivory and bone worked objects', in Shelley, A., *Dragon Hall, King Street, Norwich: Excavation and Survey of a Late Medieval Merchant's Trading Complex*, E. Anglian Archaeol. 112, 154–7

Huddle, J., forthcoming — 'Bone, antler and ivory objects', in Shepherd Popescu, E., *Norwich Castle: Excavations and Historical Survey 1987–98*, E. Anglian Archaeol.

Hudson, W., 1884/7 — 'The stone bridge by the horse fair in St Faith's Lane, Norwich', *Norfolk Archaeol.* 10, 117–41

Hudson, W. (ed.), 1892 — *Leet Jurisdiction in the City of Norwich during the 13th and 14th Centuries with a Short Notice of its Later History and Decline*, Selden Society 5

Hudson, W., 1910 — 'The Norwich taxation of 1254', *Norfolk Archaeol.* 17, 46–158

Hudson, W. and Tingey, J.C. (eds), 1906/10 — *The Records of the City of Norwich*

Hughes, H. and Lewis, P., 1988 — 'Paint palettes', in James, T.B. and Robinson, A.M., *Clarendon Palace: The History and Archaeology of a Medieval Palace and Hunting Lodge near Salisbury, Wiltshire* (London), 258–60

Hughes, H. and Strong, S., 1990 — *Examination of a shell containing pigment from Acton Court, Avon*, Ancient Monuments Laboratory Report 82/90 (London), unpublished

Hull, M., 1963 — 'The Roman potters' kiln of Colchester', *Rep. Res. Comm. Soc. Antiq. London* 21

Hurst, J., Neal, D., and van Beuningen, H., 1986 — *Pottery Produced and Traded in North-West Europe 1350–1650* (Rotterdam)

Hutton, E., 1926 — *The Franciscans in England, 1224–1538* (London)

James, T., 1997 — 'Excavations at Carmarthen Greyfriars, 1983–1990', *Medieval Archaeol.* 41, 100–94

Jankuhn, H., 1943 — *Die Ausgrabungen in Haithabu 1937–1939* (Berlin)

Jarrolds, 1885–1922 — *Jarrolds Norwich Directories* (Norwich)

Jennings, S., 1981 — *Eighteen Centuries of Pottery from Norwich*, E. Anglian Archaeol. 13

Jennings, S., 1983 — 'The pottery', in Atkin, M., Ayers, B. and Jennings, S., *Waterfront Excavation and Thetford Ware Production, Norwich*. E. Anglian Archaeol. 17, 74–91

Jennings, T.S., 2006 — *Temporary Site Bellfounding Technology and the Itinerant Bellfounder's Technique: the archaeological and archival evidence in Great Britain and Europe before 1850* (Loughborough)

Jervoise, E., 1932 — *Ancient Bridges of Mid and Eastern England* (London)

Jones, A.K.G. and Scott, S., 1985 — 'The fish bones', in Atkin, M.W., Carter, A. and Evans, D.H., *Excavations in Norwich 1971–1978, part II*, E. Anglian Archaeol. 26, 223–8

Kellys, 1935, 1952 — *Norwich Directory*

Kelly, T., 1969 — 'Norwich, pioneer of public libraries', *Norfolk Archaeology* 34, 215–22

Kelso, W.M., 1995 — *Jamestown Rediscovery 1: Search for 1607 James Fort*, Association for the Preservation of Virginia Antiquities, Jamestown (USA)

Kenyon, G.H., 1967 — *The Glass Industry of the Weald* (Leicester)

Kerridge, E., 1985 — *Textile Manufactures in Early Modern England* (Manchester)

Kershaw, I., 1973 — *Bolton Priory. The Economy of a Northern Monastery* (Oxford)

Kilmurry, K., 1980 — *The Pottery Industry of Stamford, Lincs AD 850–1250*, Brit. Archaeol. Rep. Brit. Ser. 84

King, D., 1974 — *Stained Glass Tours around Norfolk Churches* (Woodbridge)

King, D., 1987 — 'The window glass and lead', in Rogerson, A. *et al.*, *Three Norman Churches in Norfolk*, E. Anglian Archaeol. 32, 34-40

King, D., forthcoming. — *The Medieval Glass-Painting in the Church of St Peter Mancroft, Norwich*, Corpus Vitrearum: Great Britain

Kingsford, C.L., 1915 — *The Greyfriars of London* (Aberdeen)

Kirkpatrick, J., 1845 — *History of the Religious Orders and Communities ... of Norwich* (London and Norwich)

Kitchin, G.W., 1892 — 'Compotus rolls of the Obedientiares of St. Swithun's Priory, Winchester', *Hampshire Record Soc.* vol. 7

Knight, B., 1988 — 'Oyster shell containing pigment', in Sherlock, D. and Woods, H., *St. Augustine's Abbey: Report on Excavations, 1960–78* (Maidstone)

Knowles, D., 1948 — *The Religious Orders in England* (Cambridge)

Knowles, D. and Hadcock, R.N., 1953 *Medieval Religious Houses: England and Wales* (London)

Knowles, D., and Hadcock, R.N., 1971 *Religious Houses of England and Wales* (London)

Kyriacou, C., Mee, F. and Rogers, N., 2004 *Treasures of York* (Landmark)

Larsen, S.C., 1997 *Bioarchaeology. Interpreting behaviour from the human skeleton* (Cambridge)

Lawrence, C.H., 1994 *The Friars: the impact of the early mendicant movement on western society* (London)

Lawson, A.J., 1976 'Shale and jet objects from Silchester', *Archaeologia* 105, 241–75

Lawson, G., 1978 'Medieval tuning-pegs from Whitby, North Yorkshire', *Medieval Archaeol.* 22, 139–41

Lawson, G., 1990 'Musical instruments', in Biddle, M. (ed.), *Objects and Economy in Medieval Winchester* (Oxford), 710–18

Leach, H., 1987 'Stamford ware fabrics', *Medieval Ceramics* 11, 69–74

Leah, M., 1994 *Grimston, Norfolk: The Late Saxon and Medieval Pottery Industry, Excavations 1962–92,* E. Anglian Archaeol. 64

Lentowicz, I., 1996 'Pottery', in Percival, S., *Busseys Garage, Palace Street, Norwich: Report on an Archaeological Evaluation*, Norfolk Archaeological Unit report 142 (unpublished)

Lentowicz, I., forthcoming a 'Pottery', in Shepherd Popescu, E., *Norwich Castle: Excavations and Historical Survey 1987–98*, E. Anglian Archaeol.

Lentowicz, I., forthcoming b 'The pottery', in Bown, J., *Excavations at Calvert Street, Norwich*

Lentowicz, I., and Kemp, R. forthcoming 'Ceramic building material', in Shepherd Popescu, E., *Norwich Castle: Excavations and Historical Survey 1987–98*, E. Anglian Archaeol.

Levitan, B., 1989 'Bone analysis and urban economy, examples of selectivity and a case for comparison', in Serjeantson, D. and Waldron, T. (eds), *Diet and Crafts in Towns. The Evidence of Animal Remains from the Roman to the Post-Medieval Periods*, Brit. Archaeol. Rep. Brit. Ser. 199, 161–188

Lewis, M., 2000 'Non-adult palaeopathology: current status and future potential', in Cox, M. and Mays, S., *Human Osteology in Archaeology and Forensic Science* (London)

Lindsay, W.J., with a contribution by Howard, H., 1989 'Wall plaster, pigment containers and pigments', in Stones, J.A. (ed.), *Three Scottish Carmelite Friaries: Excavations at Aberdeen, Linlithgow and Perth 1980–1986* (Edinburgh), 153–4

Little, A., 1994 'The pottery', in Leah, M. (ed.), *Grimston, Norfolk: The Late Saxon and Medieval Pottery Industry. Excavations 1962–92*, E. Anglian Archaeol. 64, 109

Little, A., 1995a 'Non-ferrous metal objects', in Andrews, P., *Excavations at Redcastle Furze, Thetford, 1988–9*, E. Anglian Archaeol. 72, 90–2

Little, A., 1995b 'The pottery', in Andrews P., *Excavations at Redcastle Furze, Thetford 1988–9*, E. Anglian Archaeol 72, 101–16

Little, A.G., 1892 *The Greyfriars in Oxford*, Oxford Hist. Soc. 20 (vol. for 1891)

Little, A.G., 1940 'Theological schools in medieval England', *English Historical Review* 55, 624–30

Little, A.G., 1943 *Franciscan Papers, Lists and Documents* (Manchester)

Lloyd, R., Holmes, M., and Soden, I., 2002 *Excavations at King Street, Norwich (831N and 26577N): Assessment and Updated Project Design*, Northamptonshire Archaeology, unpublished

Locker, A., 1987 'Fish remains', in Ayers, B., *Excavations at St. Martin-at-Palace Plain Norwich, 1981*, E. Anglian Archaeol. 37, 114–17

Locker, A., 1994 'Fish bones', in Ayers, B.S., *Excavations at Fishergate, Norwich, 1985*, E. Anglian Archaeol. 68, 42–4

Locker, A., 1996a *The Saxon, Medieval and Post-Medieval Fish Bones from Castle Mall, Norwich*, report submitted to the Norfolk Archaeological Unit

Locker, A., 1996b *The Fish Bones from the Late 15th to Early 16th Century Deposits from the Flint Shaft (Barbican Well) Castle Mall, Norwich*, report submitted to the Norfolk Archaeological Unit

Locker, A., 2001 *The Role of Stored Fish in England 900–1750 AD: the Evidence from Historical and Archaeological Data* (Sofia)

Luff, R.M. and Moreno García, M., 1995 'Killing cats in the medieval period. An unusual episode in the history of Cambridge', *Archaeofauna* 4, 93–114

Lyman, R.L., 1994 *Vertebrate Taphonomy* (Cambridge)

MacGregor, A., 1976 'Bone skates: a review of the evidence', *Archaeol. J.* 133, 57–74

MacGregor, A.., 1982 *Anglo-Scandinavian Finds from Lloyds Bank, Pavement and Other Sites*, The Archaeology of York: The Small Finds 17/3 (London)

MacGregor, A., 1985 *Bone, Antler, Ivory and Horn. The Technology of Skeletal Materials since the Roman Period* (London)

MacGregor, A., 1991 'Antler, bone and horn', in Blair, J. and Ramsey, N., *English Medieval Industries* (London), 355–78

Mackie, C., 1901 *Norfolk Annals* (Norwich)

Maltby, J.M., 1979 *The Animal Bones from Exeter 1972–1975,* Exeter Archaeological Reports 2 (Sheffield)

Mainman, A., and Rogers, N.S.H., 2000 *Craft, Industry and Everyday Life: Finds from Anglo-Scandinavian York*, The Archaeology of York 17/14 (London)

Mann, J., 1982 *Early Medieval Finds from Flaxengate, I: objects of antler, bone, stone, horn, ivory, amber and jet*, The Archaeology of Lincoln vol. 16/1

Margeson, S. and Williams V., 1985 'The artefacts', in Ayers, B.S., *et al.*, *Excavations within the North-East Bailey of Norwich Castle, 1979*, E. Anglian Archaeol. 28, 27–48

Margeson, S., 1982 'Worked bone', in Coad, J.G. and Streeten, A.D.F., 'Excavations at Castle Acre Castle, Norfolk, 1972–77', *Archaeol. J.* 139, 241–55

Margeson, S., 1993 *Norwich Households: Medieval and Post-Medieval Finds from Norwich Survey Excavations 1971–78*, E. Anglian Archaeol. 58

Margeson, S., 1995 'The non-ferrous metal objects', in Rogerson, A., *A Late Neolithic, Saxon and Medieval Site at Middle Harling, Norfolk*, E. Anglian Archaeol. 74, 53–68

Margeson, S., 1997 *The Vikings in Norfolk* (Norwich)

Marks, R., 1993 *Stained Glass in England during the Middle Ages* (London)

Martin, A.R., 1933 'The Greyfriars of Walsingham', *Norfolk Archaeology* 25, 227–71

Martin, A.R., 1937 *Franciscan Architecture in England* (Manchester)

McCray, W.P., Osborne, Z.A. and Kingery, W.D., 1995 'The technology of Venetian girasole glass', in Vandiver, P.B. (ed.) *Materials Issues in Art and Archaeology* IV, 201–11

Mellor, J.E., and Pearce, T., 1981 *The Austin Friars, Leicester*, Counc. Brit. Archaeol. Res. Rep. 35, 130–44

Mellor, M., 1976 'The pottery', in Rogerson A., *Excavations on Fullers Hill, Great Yarmouth*, E. Anglian Archaeol. 2, 169–96

Merrifield, M., 1849 *Original Treatises on the Arts of Painting*, I (London)

Miller, P. and Saxby, D., forthcoming. *Merton Priory, Surrey*, Museum of London Archaeology Service (London)

Millican, P., (ed.), 1934 *The Register of the Freemen of Norwich, 1548–1713* (Norwich)

Millican, P., (ed.), 1952 *The Freemen of Norwich, 1714–1752*, Norfolk Record Society 23

Mills, J.S. and White, R., 1994 *The Organic Chemistry of Museum Objects*, 2nd edn (Oxford)

Moody, B.E., 1988 'The life of George Ravenscroft', *Glass Technology* 29, 198–210

Moody, B.E., 1989 'The Life of George Ravenscroft: an addendum', *Glass Technology* 30, 191–2

Mook, W.G., 1986 'Business meeting: recommendations/resolutions adopted by the Twelfth International Radiocarbon Conference', *Radiocarbon* 28, 799

Moore, D.T., and Ellis, S.E., 1984 'Hones', in Rogerson, A. and Dallas, C., *Excavations in Thetford 1948–59 and 1973–80*, E. Anglian Archaeol. 22, 107–11

Moorhouse, S., 1971 'Finds from Basing House, Hampshire (*c.* 1540–1645): part two', *Post-Medieval Archaeol.* 5, 35–76

Moorman, J.R.H., 1945 *Church life in England in the 13th-century* (Cambridge)

Moorman, J.R.H., 1952 *The Grey Friars in Cambridge, 1225–1538* (Cambridge)

Moorman, J.R.H., 1968 *A History of the Franciscan Order from its Origins to the Year 1517* (Oxford)

Moorman, J.R.H., 1974 *The Franciscans in England* (London and Oxford)

Moreno-García, M., 1996 *Animal Bones from the Flint Shaft, Castle Mall, Norwich*, report submitted to the Norfolk Archaeological Unit

Moreno-García, M., Orton, C. and Rackham, J., 1996 'A new statistical tool for comparing animal bone assemblages', *J. Archaeol. Sci.* 23, 437–53

Moretti, C. and Toninato, T., 1987 '"Cristallo" e "Vetro di piombo" da riceltari del '500, '600 e '700', *Rivista della staz. sper vettro*, 31–40

Morris, R., 1989 *Churches in the Landscape* (London)

Murphy, C.P., 1986 *Thin Section Preparation of Soils and Sediments* (Berkhamsted)

Murphy, P., 1987 'Molluscs', in Coad, J.G., Streeten, A.D.F. and Warmington, R., 'Excavations at Castle Acre Castle, Norfolk, 1975–92', *Archaeol. J.* 144, 302–3

Murphy, P., 1991 *Ipswich, Suffolk: plant macrofossils from sites IAS 3104 (Buttermarket), IAS 3201 (ABC cinema) and IAS 5203 (Greyfriars Road)*, unpublished Ancient Monuments Laboratory Report Series 33/91 (London)

Murphy, P., 1994 'Mollusca', in Ayers, B., *Excavations at Fishergate, Norwich, 1985*, E. Anglian Archaeol. 68, 48–9

Murphy, P., 1995 'Mollusca', in Wymer, J.J. and Brown, N.R., *North Shoebury: Settlement and Economy in South-East Essex 1500 BC–AD 1500*, E. Anglian Archaeol. 70, 142–5

Nicholson, R.A., 1993 (for 1992) 'Investigation into the effects on fish bone of passage through the human gut: some experiments and comparisons with archaeological material', *Circaea* 10, 1

Noddle, B.A., 1975 'The animal bones', in Platt, C. and Coleman-Smith, R. (eds), *Excavation in Medieval Southampton 1953–1969* 1, 332–9

Noddle, B.A., 1977 'Mammal bone', in Clarke, H. and Carter, A. (eds), *Excavations at King's Lynn, 1963–1970*, Soc. Medieval Archaeol. Monogr. Ser. 7, 378–99

Noel, M. and Batt, C.M., 1990 'A method for correcting geographically separated remanence directions for the purpose of archaeomagnetic dating', *Geophys. J. Roy. Astr. Soc.* 102, 753–6

North, J.J., 1975 *English Hammered Coinage*, 2 vols (London)

North, J.J., 1994 *English Hammered Coinage: vol 1, Early Anglo-Saxon to Henry III, c. 600–1272*, 3rd edn (London)

Oakley, G.E. and Harman, M. 1979 'The worked bone', in Williams, J.H., *St. Peters Street, Northampton Excavations 1973–76* (Northampton), 308–18

Oakley, G.E., 1979 'The worked bone', in Williams, J.H., *St. Peters Street, Northampton Excavations 1973–76* (Northampton), 308–18

O'Connor, T.P., 1982 'Animal bones from Flaxengate, Lincoln, *c.* 870–1500', *The Archaeology of Lincoln* 18/1 (London)

O'Connor, T.P., 1988 *Archaeological Bones Samples Recovered by Sieving: 46–54 Fishergate, York, as a Case Study*, Ancient Monuments Laboratory Report 190/88, unpublished

O'Connor, T.P., 1993 'Bone assemblages from monastic sites: many questions but few data', in Gilchrist, R. and Mytum, H. (eds), *Advances in Monastic Archaeology*, Brit. Archaeol. Rep. Brit. Ser. 227, 107–11

Ortner, D., and Putschar, W.J., 1981 *Identification of Pathological Conditions in Human Skeletal Remains* (Washington DC)

Ottaway, P., 1992 *Anglo-Scandinavian Ironwork from Coppergate*, The Archaeology of York: The Small Finds 17/6 (London)

Ottaway, P., 1993 'Knives' in Rogers, N.S., *Anglian and Other Finds from Fishergate*, The Archaeology of York: The Small Finds 17/9 (London), 1273–7

Öye, I., 1988 *Textile Equipment and its Working Environment, Bryggen in Bergen c. 1150–1500*, The Bryggen Papers, Main Series 2 (Oslo)

Park, D. and Howard, H., 1996 'The medieval polychromy of Norwich Cathedral Priory', in Atherton, I., Fernie, E., Harper-Bill, C. and Smith, H. (eds), *Norwich Cathedral: Church, City and Diocese* (London), 379–409

Park, D. and Stewart, S., 1996 'The painted wall plaster', in Kemp, R.L. and Graves, C.P., *The Church and Gilbertine Priory of St. Andrew, Fishergate* (York), 302–8

Parkhouse, J., 1976 'The Dorestad quernstone', *BROB* 26, 181–8

Parkhouse, J., 1977 *Anglo-Saxon Commercial Connections with the Continent: with Specific Reference to the Distribution and Typology of Rhenish Basalt-Lava Quernstones and their Use as an Indicator of Trade*, unpublished MA thesis, University of Manchester

Parsons, D. (ed.), 1990 *Stone Quarrying and Building in England AD 43–1525* (Chichester)

Payne, S., 1975 'Partial recovery and sample bias', in Clason, A.T. (ed.), *Archaeozoological Studies* (Amsterdam) 7–17

Penn, K., 1999 *Results of an Archaeological Evaluation at the Former Brewery Site, King Street, Norwich*, Norfolk Archaeological Unit Report 342, unpublished

Penn, K., 2000 *Anglo-Scandinavian Norwich: an Archaeological Desk-Top Survey*, Norfolk Archaeological Unit Report 488, unpublished

Peers, C. and Ralegh Radford, C.A., 1943 'The Saxon monastery of Whitby', *Archaeologia* 89, 27–88

Percival, J.W., and Hutcheson, A.R.J., in prep. *Excavations between Theatre Street and Bethel Street, Norwich, 1998–99*, E. Anglian Archaeol.

Perring, D., 1981 *Early Medieval Occupation at Flaxengate, Lincoln*, The Archaeology of Lincoln vol. 9/1 (London)

Philp, B., 1968 *Excavations at Faversham, 1965: The Royal Abbey, Roman Villa and Belgic Farmstead* (Bromley)

Philp, B., 1973 'Lower Warbank, Keston', *Excavations in West Kent, 1960–1970. The Discovery and Excavation of Prehistoric, Roman, Saxon and Medieval Sites, Mainly in the Bromley Area and in the Darent Valley*, second research report in the Kent series

Priestley, U., 1985 'The fabric of stuffs: the Norwich textile industry c. 1650–1750', *Textile History* 16, 183–210

Pritchard, F., 1991 'The small finds', in Vince, A. (ed.) *Aspects of Saxo-Norman London: II Finds and Environmental Evidence* (London), 120–278

Rackham, J., 1986 'Assessing the relative frequencies of species by the application of a stochastic model to a zooarchaeological database', in Wijngaarden-Bakker, L.H.V. (ed.), *Database Management and Zooarchaeology* (Strasbourg), 185–92

Rahtz, P.A., 1979 *The Saxon and Medieval Palaces at Cheddar: Excavations 1960–62*, Brit. Archaeol. Rep. Brit. Ser. 65

Rawcliffe, C., 1999 *Medicine for the Soul: the Life, Death and Resurrection of an English Medieval Hospital, St Giles's, Norwich c. 1249–1550* (Norwich)

Read, B., 1995 *History Beneath Our Feet* (Ipswich)

Redknap, M. and Freestone, I.C., 1995 'Eighteenth-century glass ingots from England: further light in the post-medieval glass trade', in Hook, D.R. *et al.* (eds), *Trade and Discovery*, Brit. Mus. Occas. Pap. 109, 145–58

Redstone, L.J. (ed.), 1944 'The cellarer's accounts for Bromholm Priory, Norfolk, 1415–16', *Norfolk Record Soc.* 17, 47–91

Reuck, de, A., 1991 *Dating Sword Chapes*, unpublished

Riall, N. and Shelton-Bunn, V., 1989 *Excavations at Borelli Yard, Farnham, Surrey 1985–86* (Farnham)

Richardson, D., 1980 'Boyton: the church, the Giffards, and their successors', *The Hatcher Review* 9, 26–33

Richmond, H. *et al.*, 1982 'Nos 28–34 Queen Street, King's Lynn', in Richmond, H., Taylor, R. and Wade-Martins, P. (eds), *Trowse, Horning, Deserted Medieval Villages, King's Lynn*, E. Anglian Archaeol. 14, 108–24

Riddler, I.D., forthcoming a *Objects and Waste of Bone, Antler and Ivory from Excavations in Ipswich, 1974–88*

Riddler, I.D., forthcoming b *Organic Materials and the Textile Industry at Hamwic*

Rigg, J.M. (ed.), 1901 *Select Pleas ... from the Rolls of the Exchequer of the Jews (1220–1284)*, Selden Society 15

Roach Smith, C., 1854 *Catalogue of the Museum of London Antiquities* (London)

Roberts, C. and Manchester, K., 1995 *The Archaeology of Disease* (Stroud)

Roes, A., 1963 *Bone and Antler Objects from the Frisian Terp Mounds* (Haarlem)

Roes, A., 1965 *Vondsten van Dorestad* (Groningen)

Roesdhal, E. and Wilson, D.M., 1992 *From Vikings to Crusader: Scandinavia and Europe 800–1200* (Sweden)

Rogers, N.S.H. 1993 *Anglian and other Finds from Fishergate, York*, The Archaeology of York 17/9: The Small Finds (London)

Rogerson, A. and Adams, N., 1978 *A Saxo-Norman pottery kiln at Bircham*, in E. Anglian Archaeol. 8, 33–44

Rogerson, A. and Dallas, C., 1984 *Excavations in Thetford 1948–59 and 1973–80*, E. Anglian Archaeol. 22

Rogerson, A., 1977 *Excavations at Scole 1973*, E. Anglian Archaeol. 5, 97–224

Rogerson, A., in prep. *Excavations at Greyfriars, Grantham, 1972–3*

Rogerson, A., Ashley, S. and Penn, K., forthcoming *Lavastone in Norfolk Churches*

Rooksby, H.P., 1962 'Opacifiers in opal glasses', *GEC Journal* 29 (1), 20–6

Roy, A. and White, R., 1982 *Wells Cathedral: West Front Polychrome*, unpublished report, Scientific Department, National Gallery

Rulewicz, M., 1994 *Rybołowstwo Gdańska na tle Ośrodków Miejskich Pomorza od IX do XIII Wieku*, Gdańsk Wczesnośredniowieczny 10 (Gdansk)

Ryder, M.L., 1956 'Report on the animal bones', in Owen, D.E., *Kirkstall Abbey Excavations, 7th Report* (Leeds), 41–53

Rye, W. (ed.), 1903 *A Short Calendar of Deeds Relating to Norwich Enrolled in the Court Rolls of that City, 1285–1306* (Norwich)

Rye, W. (ed.), 1905 *Depositions Taken Before the Mayor and Aldermen of Norwich, 1549–1567* (Norwich)

Salway, P., 1996 'Sidney before the College', *Sidney Sussex College, Cambridge: Historical Essays* (Woodbridge)

Salzman, L.F., 1952 *Building in England down to 1540* (Oxford)

Salzman, L.F., 1964 *English Industries of the Middle Ages* (London)

Samuel, M.W., 1992 *The Blackfriars & Whitefriars, Ipswich: Appraisal report of the 'moulded' stone*, unpublished report for Suffolk County Council Planning Department

Sandred, K.I. and Lindström, B., 1989 *The Place-Names of Norfolk*, Part 1 (Nottingham)

Saul, A., 1981 'The herring industry at Great Yarmouth *c.* 1280–*c.* 1400', *Norfolk Archaeol.* 38, 33–43

Scheuer L. and Black, S., 2000 *Developmental Juvenile Osteology* (London)

Schwarz-Mackenson, G. 1976 'Die Knochennadeln von Haithabu', in K. Schietzel (ed.), *Berichte über die Ausgrabungen in Haithabu* 9 (Neumünster), 1–94

Serjeantson, D., 1989 'Animal remains and the tanning trade', in Serjeantson, D., and Waldron, T. (eds.), *Diet and Crafts in Towns. The Evidence of Animal Remains from the Roman to the Post-Medieval Periods*, Brit. Archaeol. Rep. Brit. Ser., 129–46

Shelley, A., 2005 *Dragon Hall, King Street, Norwich: Excavation and Survey of a Late Medieval Merchant's Trading Complex*, E. Anglian Archaeol. 112

Shelley, A., 2003 *A Moated Rectory at Wimbotsham, Norfolk*, E. Anglian Archaeol. Occas. Pap. 12

Shelley, A., in prep. 'The Austin Friary at Norwich: excavations and observations 1968–2000', *Norfolk Archaeol.*

Shepherd E. and Lentowicz, I., 1998 *Norwich: Cemeteries, Radiocarbon Dates and the Ceramic Sequence,* Norfolk Archaeological Unit Project Design, unpublished

Shepherd, J.D., forthcoming. 'The glass', in Parnell, G., *Excavations at Broad Arrow Tower, Tower of London*

Shepherd Popescu, E., forthcoming. *Norwich Castle: Excavations and Historical Survey 1987–98: Parts I and II*, E. Anglian Archaeol.

Sherlock, D., 1976 'Discoveries at Horsham St Faith Priory', *Norfolk Archaeol.* 36(3), 202–23

Silver, I.A., 1969 'The ageing of domestic animals', in Brothwell, D. and Higgs, E.S. (eds), *Science in Archaeology*, 2nd edn (London), 283–302

Smart, V., 1985 'The moneyers of St Edmund', *Hikuin* II, 83–90

Smith, R.A.L., 1943 *Canterbury Cathedral Prior: a Study in Monastic Administration* (Cambridge)

Smith, D., 1993 'Querns', in Margeson, S., *Norwich Households: The Medieval and Post-Medieval Finds from Norwich Survey Excavations 1971–78*, E. Anglian Archaeol. 58, 202

Soden, I., 2001 *Exavations in St Faiths Lane, Norwich 1998–9: Assessment and Updated Research Design*, unpublished report by Northamptonshire Archaeology

Spencer, B., 1985 Catalogue entries in *Santiago de Compostela: 1000 ans de Pèlerinage Européen* (Ghent)

Stallibrass, S., 1990 'Canid damage to animal bones: two current lines of research', in Robinson, D.E. (ed.), *Experimentation and Reconstruction in Environmental Archaeology* (Oxford), 151–65

Stone, E.D. (ed.), 1938 *Norwich Consistory Court depositions, 1499–1530*, Norfolk Record Soc. 10

Stuiver, M. and Kra, R.S., 1986 'Editorial comment', *Radiocarbon* 28(2B), ii

Stuiver, M. and Pearson, G.W., 1986 'High precision calibration of the radiocarbon time scale, AD 1950–500 BC', *Radiocarbon* 28, 805–38

Stuiver, M. and Polach, H.A., 1977 'Reporting of C data', *Radiocarbon* 19, 355–63

Stuiver, M. and Reimer, P.J., 1986 'A computer program for radiocarbon age calculation', *Radiocarbon* 28, 1022–30

Stuiver, M. and Reimer, P.J., 1993 'Extended C data base and revised CALIB 3.0 C age calibration program', *Radiocarbon* 35, 215–30

Taavitsainen, J.P., 1982 'Keskijan Kangaskaupasta ja Esineellisten Lähteiden Valossa', *Eripainos* 23–43 (Helsinki)

Tanner, N.P., 1984 *The Church in Late Medieval Norwich, 1370–1532* (Toronto)

Tatton-Brown, T., 1989 *Great Cathedrals of Britain* (London)

Taylor, R., 1821 *Index Monasticus* (Norwich)

Thawley, C.R., 1981 'The mammal, bird and fish bones', in Mellor, J.E., and Pierce. T., *The Austin Friars, Leicester,* CBA. Res. Rep. 35, 173–5

Theophilus (trans. Hawthorne, J. G. and Smith, C.S., 1979) *On Divers Arts* (New York)

Thorpe, J.F. and Whiteley, M.A., 1937 *Thorpe's Dictionary of Applied Chemistry,* 4th edn (London)

Thorpe, W.A., 1935 *English Glass* (London)

Tillyard, M. 1988 'The documentary evidence', in Ayers, B.S., Smith, R. and Tillyard, M., 'The Cow Tower, Norwich: a detailed survey and partial reinterpretation', *Medieval Archaeol.* 32, 184–207

Tingey, J. and Johnson, F. *Calendar of Norwich Deeds*, Private MS, Norfolk Record Office

Trotter, M., 1970 'Estimation of stature from intact long limb bones', in Iscan, M.Y. and Kennedy, K.A.R., *Reconstruction of Life from the Skeleton* (New York)

Trow-Smith, R., 1951 *English Husbandry. From the Earliest Times to the Present Day* (London)

Turner, W.E.S. and Rooksby, H.P. 1959 'A study of the opalising agents in ancient glasses throughout three thousand four hundred years', *Glastechnische Berichte*, Sonderband: V Internationaler Glaskongress, 32K, VIII, 17–28

Tweddle, D., 1986 *Finds from Parliament Street and Other Sites in the City Centre*, The Archaeology of York 17/4 (London)

Uerpmann, H.P., 1973 'Animal bone finds and economic archaeology: a critical study of 'osteo-archaeological' method', *World Archaeol.* 4, 307–22

Ulbricht, I., 1978 *Die Geweihverarbeitung in Haithabu*, Berichte uber die Ausgrabungen in Haithabu 7 (Neumünster)

Veale, E., 1957 'The rabbit in England', *Agr. Hist. Rev.* 5, 85–90

Venn, J., 1922 *Alumni Cantabrigiensis Part I. Earliest Times to 1751*

Vince, A., 1991 *Aspects of Saxo-Norman London II: Finds and Environmental Evidence*, LAMAS Spec. Pap. 12 (London)

Wade, K., 1976 *Excavations at Langhale, Kirstead*, in East Anglian Archaeol. 2, 101–29

Wallace, M., 1992 *Medieval People of Norwich* (Norwich)

Wallis, H., in prep. a *Excavations at Coslany Street, Norwich, 1996*

Wallis, H., in prep. b *Excavations at Norwich Cathedral Refectory*, E. Anglian Archaeol.

Walton Rogers, P. 1993 'Spindle whorls', in Rogers N.S.H., *Anglian and Other Finds from 46–54 Fishergate*, vol. 17, Fascicule 9, 1266–9

Walton Rogers P., 1997 *Textile Production at 16–22 Coppergate*, The Archaeology of York: The Small Finds 17/11 (London)

Ward Perkins, J.B., 1940 *London Museum Medieval Catalogue* (London)

Wardle, A., 1998 'Musical instruments', in Egan, G., *Medieval Finds from Excavations in London: 6. The Medieval Household Daily Living c. 1150–c. 1450* (London), 283–90

Waterman, D.M., 1959 'Late Saxon, Viking and Early Medieval finds from York', *Archaeologia* 97, 59–105

Watts, D.C., 1974 'How did George Ravenscroft discover lead crystal?', *The Glass Circle* 2, 71–84

Webster, L. and Backhouse, J. (eds), 1991 *The Making of England: Anglo-Saxon Art and Culture AD 600–900* (London)

Webster, L., 1991 'Metalwork', in Webster, L. and Backhouse, J. (eds), *The Making of England: Anglo-Saxon Art and Culture, AD 600–900* (London), 220–39

West, B., 1982 'Spur development: recognising caponised fowl in archaeological material', in Wilson, B., Grigson, C. and Payne, S. (eds), *Ageing and Sexing Animal Bones from Archaeological Sites*, Brit. Archaeol. Rep. Brit. Ser. 109, 255–61

West, I.M., Anderson, F.W. and Faulkner, P.A., 1975 'The stone', in Platt, C. and Coleman-Smith, R., *Excavations in Medieval Southampton* (Leicester), 2122 *etc.*

Wheeler, A. and Jones, A.K.G., 1989 *Fishes* (Cambridge)

Wheeler, A. and Jones, A.K.G., 1976 'Fish remains', in Rogerson, A., *Excavations at Fuller's Hill, Great Yarmouth*, E. Anglian Archaeol. 2, 208–24

Whitmore, D., 2001 *Report on an Archaeological Evaluation at the Former Mann Egerton Site, Rose Lane, Norwich*, Norfolk Archaeological Unit Report No. 564, unpublished

Whitmore, D., 2004 *Former Nestle Factory and Chantry House, Chapelfield Development, Norwich: Assessment Report and Updated Project Design*, Norfolk Archaeological Unit Report No. 823

Williams, J.H., 1979 *St Peter's Street, Northampton: Excavations 1973–76* (Northampton)

Williams, D., 1984 *Excavations at 43 High Street, Reigate, 1981*, Surrey Archaeological Collections 75

Williams, J.H., 1984 'A review of some aspects of late Saxon urban origins and development', in Faull, M.L. (ed.), *Studies in Late Anglo-Saxon Settlement* (Oxford)

Williams, G., 1999 'Anglo-Saxon and Viking coin-weights', *British Numismatic Journal* 69, 19–36

Williams, V., 1987 'The artefacts', in Rogerson, A. and Williams, P., 'The late eleventh century church of St. Peter, Guestwick', *Three Norman Churches in Norfolk*, E. Anglian Archaeol. 32, 72–4

Williams, V., 1988a 'Coins and tokens', in Ayers, B.S., *Excavations at St Martin-at-Palace Plain, Norwich, 1979*, E. Anglian Archaeol. 37, 62–3

Williams, V., 1988b 'Iron objects' in Ayers, B.S., *Excavations at St Martin-at-Palace Plain, Norwich, 1981*, E. Anglian Archaeol. 37, 67–70

Williams, V., 1988c 'The bone, antler and ivory objects', in Ayers, B.S., *Excavations at St Martin-at-Palace Plain, Norwich, 1981*, E. Anglian Archaeol. 37, 100–06

Williams, V., 1994a 'Bone and antler objects', in Ayers, B.S., *et al.*, *Excavations at Fishergate, Norwich, 1985*, E. Anglian Archaeol. 68, 29–31

Williams, V., 1994b 'The coins', in Ayers, B., *et al. Excavations at Fishergate, Norwich, 1985*, E. Anglian Archaeol. 68, 13–14

Williams, V., 1994c 'Glass objects', in Ayers, B.S., *Excavations at Fishergate, Norwich, 1985*, East Anglian Archaeol. 68, 18–19

Williams, V. 1994d 'Non-ferrous metal objects', in Ayers, B.S., *Excavations at Fishergate, Norwich, 1985*, East Anglian Archaeol. 68, 14

Wilson, C.A., 1973 *Food and Drink in Britain From the Stone Age to Recent Times* (London)

Wilson, D.M., 1964 *Anglo-Saxon Ornamental Metalwork, 700–1100* Brit. Mus. Cat. Antiq., Later Saxon Period 1 (London)

Wilson, D.M., 1979 'Copper alloy', in Rahtz, P., *The Saxon and Medieval Palaces at Cheddar: Excavations 1960–62*, Brit. Archaeol. Rep. Brit. Ser. 65 (Oxford), 274–87

Wiltshire and Emery 2000 *Report on an Archaeological Watching Brief at Riverside, Norwich*, Norfolk Archaeological Unit report 354 (unpublished)

Winbolt, E.S., 1933 *Wealden Glass* (Hove)

Winder, J., 1980 'The marine mollusca', in Holdsworth, P., *Excavations at Melbourne Street, Southampton, 1971–76*, Counc. Brit. Archaeol./Southampton Archaeol. Res. Comm., 121–7

Wood, E.S., 1965 'A medieval glasshouse at Blunden's Wood, Hambledon, Surrey', *Surrey Archaeol. Collect.* 62, 54–79

Woodcock, T., Grant, J. and Graham, I., 1996 *Dictionary of British Arms, Medieval Ordinary Vol. 2* (London)

Woodeforde, C., 1937 'Franciscan saints in English mediaeval glass and embroidery', in Little, A.G. (ed.), *Franciscan History and Legend in English Mediaeval Art* (Manchester), 22–31

Woodforde, C., 1950 *The Norwich School of Glass-Painting in the Fifteenth Century* (London)

Woodland, M., 1990 'Spindle-whorls' in Biddle, M. (ed.), *Object and Economy in Medieval Winchester,* Winchester Studies vol. 7.ii (Oxford), 216–25

Woolgar, C.M. (ed.), 1992 *Household Accounts from Medieval England, Part 1*, Records of Social and Economic History, new series, xvii

Index

Page numbers in *italics* denote illustrations. Streets and locations are in Norwich unless otherwise indicated.

East Anglian Archaeology

is a serial publication sponsored by ALGAO EE and English Heritage. It is the main vehicle for publishing final reports on archaeological excavations and surveys in the region. For information about titles in the series, visit **www.eaareports.org.uk**. Reports can be obtained from:

Phil McMichael, Essex County Council Archaeology Section
Fairfield Court, Fairfield Road, Braintree, Essex CM7 3YQ

or directly from the organisation publishing a particular volume.

Reports available so far:

No.1,	1975	Suffolk: various papers
No.2,	1976	Norfolk: various papers
No.3,	1977	Suffolk: various papers
No.4,	1976	Norfolk: Late Saxon town of Thetford
No.5,	1977	Norfolk: various papers on Roman sites
No.6,	1977	Norfolk: Spong Hill Anglo-Saxon cemetery, Part I
No.7,	1978	Norfolk: Bergh Apton Anglo-Saxon cemetery
No.8,	1978	Norfolk: various papers
No.9,	1980	Norfolk: North Elmham Park
No.10,	1980	Norfolk: village sites in Launditch Hundred
No.11,	1981	Norfolk: Spong Hill, Part II: Catalogue of Cremations
No.12,	1981	The barrows of East Anglia
No.13,	1981	Norwich: Eighteen centuries of pottery from Norwich
No.14,	1982	Norfolk: various papers
No.15,	1982	Norwich: Excavations in Norwich 1971–1978; Part I
No.16,	1982	Norfolk: Beaker domestic sites in the Fen-edge and East Anglia
No.17,	1983	Norfolk: Waterfront excavations and Thetford-type Ware production, Norwich
No.18,	1983	Norfolk: The archaeology of Witton
No.19,	1983	Norfolk: Two post-medieval earthenware pottery groups from Fulmodeston
No.20,	1983	Norfolk: Burgh Castle: excavation by Charles Green, 1958–61
No.21,	1984	Norfolk: Spong Hill, Part III: Catalogue of Inhumations
No.22,	1984	Norfolk: Excavations in Thetford, 1948–59 and 1973–80
No.23,	1985	Norfolk: Excavations at Brancaster 1974 and 1977
No.24,	1985	Suffolk: West Stow, the Anglo-Saxon village
No.25,	1985	Essex: Excavations by Mr H.P.Cooper on the Roman site at Hill Farm, Gestingthorpe, Essex
No.26,	1985	Norwich: Excavations in Norwich 1971–78; Part II
No.27,	1985	Cambridgeshire: The Fenland Project No.1: Archaeology and Environment in the Lower Welland Valley
No.28,	1985	Norfolk: Excavations within the north-east bailey of Norwich Castle, 1978
No.29,	1986	Norfolk: Barrow excavations in Norfolk, 1950–82
No.30,	1986	Norfolk: Excavations at Thornham, Warham, Wighton and Caistor St Edmund, Norfolk
No.31,	1986	Norfolk: Settlement, religion and industry on the Fen-edge; three Romano-British sites in Norfolk
No.32,	1987	Norfolk: Three Norman Churches in Norfolk
No.33,	1987	Essex: Excavation of a Cropmark Enclosure Complex at Woodham Walter, Essex, 1976 and An Assessment of Excavated Enclosures in Essex
No.34,	1987	Norfolk: Spong Hill, Part IV: Catalogue of Cremations
No.35,	1987	Cambridgeshire: The Fenland Project No.2: Fenland Landscapes and Settlement, Peterborough–March
No.36,	1987	Norfolk: The Anglo-Saxon Cemetery at Morningthorpe
No.37,	1987	Norfolk: Excavations at St Martin-at-Palace Plain, Norwich, 1981
No.38,	1987	Suffolk: The Anglo-Saxon Cemetery at Westgarth Gardens, Bury St Edmunds
No.39,	1988	Norfolk: Spong Hill, Part VI: Occupation during the 7th–2nd millennia BC
No.40,	1988	Suffolk: Burgh: The Iron Age and Roman Enclosure
No.41,	1988	Essex: Excavations at Great Dunmow, Essex: a Romano-British small town in the Trinovantian Civitas
No.42,	1988	Essex: Archaeology and Environment in South Essex, Rescue Archaeology along the Gray's By-pass 1979–80
No.43,	1988	Essex: Excavation at the North Ring, Mucking, Essex: A Late Bronze Age Enclosure
No.44,	1988	Norfolk: Six Deserted Villages in Norfolk
No.45,	1988	Norfolk: The Fenland Project No. 3: Marshland and the Nar Valley, Norfolk
No.46,	1989	Norfolk: The Deserted Medieval Village of Thuxton
No.47,	1989	Suffolk: West Stow: Early Anglo-Saxon Animal Husbandry
No.48,	1989	Suffolk: West Stow, Suffolk: The Prehistoric and Romano-British Occupations
No.49,	1990	Norfolk: The Evolution of Settlement in Three Parishes in South-East Norfolk
No.50,	1993	Proceedings of the Flatlands and Wetlands Conference
No.51,	1991	Norfolk: The Ruined and Disused Churches of Norfolk
No.52,	1991	Norfolk: The Fenland Project No. 4, The Wissey Embayment and Fen Causeway
No.53,	1992	Norfolk: Excavations in Thetford, 1980–82, Fison Way
No.54,	1992	Norfolk: The Iron Age Forts of Norfolk
No.55,	1992	Lincolnshire: The Fenland Project No.5: Lincolnshire Survey, The South-West Fens
No.56,	1992	Cambridgeshire: The Fenland Project No.6: The South-Western Cambridgeshire Fens
No.57,	1993	Norfolk and Lincolnshire: Excavations at Redgate Hill Hunstanton; and Tattershall Thorpe
No.58,	1993	Norwich: Households: The Medieval and Post-Medieval Finds from Norwich Survey Excavations 1971–1978
No.59,	1993	Fenland: The South-West Fen Dyke Survey Project 1982–86
No.60,	1993	Norfolk: Caister-on-Sea: Excavations by Charles Green, 1951–55
No.61,	1993	Fenland: The Fenland Project No.7: Excavations in Peterborough and the Lower Welland Valley 1960–1969
No.62,	1993	Norfolk: Excavations in Thetford by B.K. Davison, between 1964 and 1970
No.63,	1993	Norfolk: Illington: A Study of a Breckland Parish and its Anglo-Saxon Cemetery
No.64,	1994	Norfolk: The Late Saxon and Medieval Pottery Industry of Grimston: Excavations 1962–92
No.65,	1993	Suffolk: Settlements on Hill-tops: Seven Prehistoric Sites in Suffolk
No.66,	1993	Lincolnshire: The Fenland Project No.8: Lincolnshire Survey, the Northern Fen-Edge
No.67,	1994	Norfolk: Spong Hill, Part V: Catalogue of Cremations
No.68,	1994	Norfolk: Excavations at Fishergate, Norwich 1985
No.69,	1994	Norfolk: Spong Hill, Part VIII: The Cremations
No.70,	1994	Fenland: The Fenland Project No.9: Flandrian Environmental Change in Fenland
No.71,	1995	Essex: The Archaeology of the Essex Coast Vol.I: The Hullbridge Survey Project
No.72,	1995	Norfolk: Excavations at Redcastle Furze, Thetford, 1988–9
No.73,	1995	Norfolk: Spong Hill, Part VII: Iron Age, Roman and Early Saxon Settlement
No.74,	1995	Norfolk: A Late Neolithic, Saxon and Medieval Site at Middle Harling
No.75,	1995	Essex: North Shoebury: Settlement and Economy in South-east Essex 1500–AD1500
No.76,	1996	Nene Valley: Orton Hall Farm: A Roman and Early Anglo-Saxon Farmstead
No.77,	1996	Norfolk: Barrow Excavations in Norfolk, 1984–88
No.78,	1996	Norfolk:The Fenland Project No.11: The Wissey Embayment: Evidence for pre-Iron Age Occupation
No.79,	1996	Cambridgeshire: The Fenland Project No.10: Cambridgeshire Survey, the Isle of Ely and Wisbech
No.80,	1997	Norfolk: Barton Bendish and Caldecote: fieldwork in south-west Norfolk
No.81,	1997	Norfolk: Castle Rising Castle
No.82,	1998	Essex: Archaeology and the Landscape in the Lower Blackwater Valley
No.83,	1998	Essex: Excavations south of Chignall Roman Villa 1977–81
No.84,	1998	Suffolk: A Corpus of Anglo-Saxon Material
No.85,	1998	Suffolk: Towards a Landscape History of Walsham le Willows
No.86,	1998	Essex: Excavations at the Orsett 'Cock' Enclosure
No.87,	1999	Norfolk: Excavations in Thetford, North of the River, 1989–90
No.88,	1999	Essex: Excavations at Ivy Chimneys, Witham 1978–83
No.89,	1999	Lincolnshire: Salterns: Excavations at Helpringham, Holbeach St Johns and Bicker Haven
No.90,	1999	Essex:The Archaeology of Ardleigh, Excavations 1955–80
No.91,	2000	Norfolk: Excavations on the Norwich Southern Bypass, 1989–91 Part I Bixley, Caistor St Edmund, Trowse
No.92,	2000	Norfolk: Excavations on the Norwich Southern Bypass, 1989–91 Part II Harford Farm Anglo-Saxon Cemetery
No.93,	2001	Norfolk: Excavations on the Snettisham Bypass, 1989
No.94,	2001	Lincolnshire: Excavations at Billingborough, 1975–8